To Irene,

I am sure that you will enjoy this book as much as we hoped. It has been in our library for about 50 years.

Safe Travels

Mary and Bill

BOOKS BY WILL DURANT

The Story of Philosophy
Transition
The Pleasures of Philosophy
Adventures in Genius

THE STORY OF CIVILIZATION
BY WILL AND ARIEL DURANT

The Pleasures of
PHILOSOPHY

A Survey of Human Life and Destiny

by

WILL DURANT

A TOUCHSTONE BOOK
PUBLISHED BY SIMON AND SCHUSTER

23   24   25   26

ISBN 0-671-58110-4 PBK.
MANUFACTURED IN THE UNITED STATES OF AMERICA

To

ARIEL AND ETHEL

Confession

THIS BOOK, *despite its gay new title, is a revised edition of* The Mansions of Philosophy, *which was published in 1929. That volume has been out of print for ten years; and the inquiries for it have mounted to the point where a new edition seems forgivable. Some pages betray their composition a quarter of a century ago, and the reader will smile at several bad guesses that they contain; I have since found it safer to write about the past than about the future. Certain pages are heavily sentimental, but they still express me faithfully. Others are cynical or unduly pessimistic, especially in Chapter XVIII; having discovered my own fallibility, I should be more lenient now with my fellow men, and with governments. Despite these sins the book has, I like to believe, some redeeming qualities; and I send it forth again on the seas of ink to find here and there a kindred soul in the Country of the Mind.*

WILL DURANT

Lake Hill, N. Y.
November 15, 1952

Invitation

THIS BOOK is an attempt at a consistent philosophy of life. It u..s to do for the problems of philosophy what *The Story of Philosophy* sought to do for the personalities and systems of the major philosophers—to make them intelligible by transparent speech, and to vitalize them by contemporary application. We shall miss here the anecdotes, and the strokes of quoted genius, that there lightened the burden of our theme; but perhaps we shall be repaid by coming closer to the concerns of our own life in our own day. For the subject here is ourselves.

Human conduct and belief are now undergoing transformations profounder and more disturbing than any since the appearance of wealth and philosophy put an end to the traditional religion of the Greeks. It is the age of Socrates again: our moral life is threatened, and our intellectual life is quickened and enlarged, by the disintegration of ancient customs and beliefs. Everything is new and experimental in our ideas and our actions; nothing is established or certain any more. The rate, complexity, and variety of change in our time are without precedent, even in Periclean days; all forms about us are altered, from the tools that complicate our toil, and the wheels that whirl us restlessly about the earth, to the innovations in our sexual relationships, and the hard disillusionment of our souls. The passage from agriculture to industry, from the village to the town, and from the town to the city, has elevated science, debased art, liberated thought, ended monarchy and aristocracy, generated democracy and socialism, emancipated woman, disrupted marriage, broken down the old moral code, destroyed asceticism with luxuries, replaced Puritanism with epicureanism, exalted excitement above content, made war less frequent and more terrible, taken from us many of our most cherished religious beliefs, and given us in exchange a mechanical and fatalistic philosophy of life. All things flow, and we are at a loss to find some mooring and stability in the flux.

In every developing civilization a period comes when old instincts and habits prove inadequate to altered stimuli, and ancient institutions and moralities crack like hampering shells under the obstinate growth of life. In one sphere after another, now that we have left the farm and the home for the factory, the office and the world, spontaneous and "natural" modes of order and response break down, and intellect chaotically experiments to replace with conscious guidance the ancestral readiness and simplicity of impulse and wonted ways. Everything must be thought out, from the artificial "formula" with which we feed our children, and the "calories" and "vitamins" of our muddled dietitians, to the bewildered efforts of contemporary governments to direct and coördinate all the haphazard processes of trade. We are like a man who cannot walk without thinking of his legs, or like a player who must analyze every move and stroke as he plays. The happy unity of instinct is gone from us, and we flounder in a sea of reasoning and doubt; in the midst of unprecedented knowledge and power we are uncertain of our purposes, our values, and our goals.

From this confusion the one escape worthy of a mature mind is to rise out of the moment and the part, and contemplate the whole. What we have lost above all is total perspective. Life seems too intricate and mobile for us to grasp its unity and significance; we cease to be citizens and become only individuals; we have no purposes that look beyond our death; we are fragments of men, and nothing more. No one dares today to survey life in its entirety; analysis leaps and synthesis lags; we fear the experts in every field, and keep ourselves, for safety's sake, lashed to our narrow specialties. Everyone knows his part, but is ignorant of its meaning in the play. Life itself grows meaningless, and becomes empty just when it seemed most full.

Let us put aside our fear of inevitable error, and survey all the problems of our state, trying to see each part and puzzle in the light of the whole. We shall define philosophy as total perspective, as mind overspreading life and forging chaos into unity. And since philosophy is for us no scholastic game played with dead concepts far from the interests of society and man, it shall here include, with no matter how little precedent, all questions that vitally affect the worth and significance of human life. We shall dally for a while with logic, and try to answer Pilate; we shall merely graze epistemology, and acknowledge the limits of human understanding; these usurping disciplines will find here the modest space which is all they need have in the mansions of philosophy. Then we shall leap into the metaphysical center of things, and make up our minds about materialism; we shall see, if we may, whether thought is a function of matter, and whether choice is the delusion of a transiently animated machine. From that focus we shall adventure into the realm of ethics, and inquire into the nature of the good life; we shall seek the causes and forecast the results of our changing morals, our dissolving marriage, and our loosened love; we shall discuss the modern woman without gallantry, and without revenge; we shall confront Zeno with Epicurus, and search for the haunts of happiness; and we shall bring our findings together for the guidance of education and the reconstruction of character. Esthetics will claim us for an hour, and we shall consider the meaning of beauty and the prospects of art. We shall look at history, and seek for its lessons and laws; we shall question the quality of progress, and weigh the destiny of our civilization. Then political philosophy will lure us, and we shall find ourselves debating, as in our passionate youth, the problems of anarchism, communism, socialism, conservatism, democracy, aristocracy, and dictatorship. The philosophy of religion will put to us the old queries about immortality and God; and we shall try to see the past and future of Christianity in the perspective of the general history of religion. Finally we shall bring the pessimist and the optimist together, appraising the boons and pains of human existence; and looking over the whole we shall try to state in conclusion the value and meaning of our life. It will be a tour of the infinite [1]

---

[1] Unfortunately, the logical order of the material places the most difficult subjects first. Readers newly won to philosophy will do well to begin with Chapter V, leaving Chapters I–IV to the last.

The busy reader will ask, is all this philosophy useful? It is a shameful question: we do not ask it of poetry, which is also an imaginative construction of a world incompletely known. If poetry reveals to us the beauty our untaught eyes have missed, and philosophy gives us the wisdom to understand and forgive, it is enough, and more than the world's wealth. Philosophy will not fatten our purses, nor lift us to dizzy dignities in a democratic state; it may even make us a little careless of these things. For what if we should fatten our purses, or rise to high office, and yet all the while remain ignorantly naïve, coarsely unfurnished in the mind, brutal in behavior, unstable in character, chaotic in desire, and blindly miserable?

Ripeness is all. Perhaps philosophy will give us, if we are faithful to it, a healing unity of soul. We are so slovenly and self-contradictory in our thinking; it may be that we shall clarify ourselves, and pull ourselves together into consistency, and be ashamed to harbor contradictory desires or beliefs. And through this unity of mind may come that unity of purpose and character which makes a personality, and lends some order and dignity to our existence. Philosophy is harmonized knowledge making a harmonious life; it is the self-discipline which lifts us to serenity and freedom. Knowledge is power, but only wisdom is liberty.

Our culture is superficial today, and our knowledge dangerous, because we are rich in mechanisms and poor in purposes. The balance of mind which once came of a warm religious faith is gone; science has taken from us the supernatural bases of our morality, and all the world seems consumed in a disorderly individualism that reflects the chaotic fragmentation of our character. We face again the problem that harassed Socrates: how shall we find a natural ethic to replace the supernatural sanctions that have ceased to influence the behavior of men? Without philosophy, without that total vision which unifies purposes and establishes the hierarchy of desires, we fritter away our social heritage in cynical corruption on the one hand, and in revolutionary madness on the other; we abandon in a moment our pacific idealism and plunge into the coöperative suicide of war; we have a hundred thousand politicians, and not a single statesman. We move about the earth with unprecedented speed, but we do not know, and have not thought, where we are going, or whether we shall find any happiness there for our harassed souls. We are being destroyed by our knowledge, which has made us drunk with our power. And we shall not be saved without wisdom.

WILL DURANT

Table of Contents

* Chapters marked with a star are technical.

PART THREE

METAPHYSICS

PART FOUR

PROBLEMS OF MORALITY

PART FIVE

ESTHETICS

PART SIX

PHILOSOPHY OF HISTORY

PART SEVEN

POLITICAL PHILOSOPHY

PART EIGHT

RELIGION: A DIALOGUE

PART NINE

ENVOI

The Pleasures of

PHILOSOPHY

PART ONE

INTRODUCTION

CHAPTER I

The Lure of Philosophy

I. PRELUDE

WHY IS PHILOSOPHY no longer loved to-day? Why have her children, the sciences, divided her inheritance, and turned her out of doors, like another Lear, with ingratitude unkinder than the winter's wind?

Once the strongest men were willing to die for her: Socrates chose to be her martyr rather than live in flight before her enemies; Plato risked himself twice to win a kingdom for her; Marcus Aurelius loved her more passionately than his throne; and Bruno burned at the stake for loyalty to her. Once thrones and papacies feared philosophy and imprisoned her votaries lest dynasties should fall. Athens exiled Protagoras, and Alexandria trembled before Hypatia; a great pope courted timidly the friendship of Erasmus; regents and kings hounded Voltaire from their lands, and fretted in jealousy when at last all the civilized world bowed before the sceptre of his pen. Dionysius and Dionysius' son offered Plato the mastery of Syracuse; Alexander's royal aid made Aristotle the most learned man in history; a scholar-king lifted Francis Bacon almost to the leadership of England, and protected him from his enemies; and the great Frederick, at midnight when all his pompous generals had gone to sleep, held high revelry with poets and philosophers, envious of their boundless realms and their timeless sway.

Those were great days for philosophy when bravely she took all knowledge for her province, and threw herself at every turn into the forefront of the mind's advance. Men honored her then; nothing was held nobler than the love of truth. Alexander rated Diogenes second only to Alexander, and

Diogenes bade Alexander stand aside lest his royal carcass should hide the sun. Statesmen and thinkers and artists listened gladly to Aspasia, and ten thousand students made long pilgrimages to Paris to learn from Abélard. Philosophy was not then a timid spinster hiding in locked towers from the rough usage of the world; her bright eyes did not fear the day; she lived dangerously, and made distant voyages into unknown seas. Could she ever, in those years when she held court before monarchs, have contented herself with the narrow boundaries within which to-day she has been imprisoned? Once she was a many-colored light that filled with warmth and radiance the profoundest souls; now she is the ignominious satellite of fragmentary sciences and scholastic disciplines. Once she was proud mistress of all the intellectual globe, and counted the loftiest among her happy servitors; now, despoiled of her beauty and her power, she stands by the wayside desolate, and none so poor to do her reverence.[1]

Philosophy is not loved to-day because she has lost the spirit of adventure. The sudden uprising of the sciences has stolen from her, one by one, her ancient spacious realms. "Cosmology" has become astronomy and geology; "natural philosophy" has become biology and physics; and in our own day the "philosophy of mind" has budded into psychology. All the real and crucial problems have escaped from her: no longer does she concern herself with the nature of matter and the secret of vitality and growth; the "will" whose "freedom" she debated in a hundred wars of thought has been crushed in the mechanism of modern life; the state, whose problems were once her own, is the happy hunting ground of petty souls, and less than ever honors the counsels of philosophy. Nothing remains to her except the cold peaks of metaphysics, the childish puzzles of epistemology, and the academic disputes of an ethics that has lost all influence on mankind. Even these wastes will be taken from her; new sciences will rise and enter these territories with compass and microscope and rule; and perhaps the world will forget that philosophy ever existed, or ever moved the hearts and guided the minds of men.

II. EPISTEMOLOGS

And as philosophy has been written these last two hundred years, it may well deserve this dishonor and oblivion. What has philosophy been since Bacon and Spinoza died? For the most part it has been epistemology, the scholastic theology of knowledge, the technical and esoteric, the mystic and incomprehensible dispute about the existence of the external world. The intelligence that might have made philosopher-kings has gone to erudite analyses of the reasons for and against the possibility that stars and oceans

---

[1] Certain exceptions should be noted: Bergson has fascinated great audiences with his eloquence, and Bertrand Russell has had the honor of frightening a government.

and bacteria and neighbors exist when they are not perceived. And for two hundred and fifty years this battle of the frogs and mice has been going on, with no appreciable result for philosophy or life, and with no profit for any man but the printer.

Something of the blame for all this belongs to that simple, almost naïve remark of Descartes,—*Je pense, donc je suis.* Descartes had hoped to begin his philosophy with a minimum of assumptions; he would call into question, by "methodic doubt," all the beliefs and even the axioms of men, and would try to build a consistent system of knowledge from the single premise, —"I think, therefore I am." It was a highly dangerous thing to make being depend so much upon thought; wits would be sure to conclude that on this basis existence was an aristocratic privilege, and cynics might with its authority deprive an entire sex not only of a soul (as Weininger was to do) but of reality.

The chief damage, however, was done to philosophy. For to erect an exposition of the world upon the fact that one man thinks is to create such a mess of difficulties that the arachnid subtlety of ten generations of epistemologs has been spent, almost in vain, on the task of disentanglement. First of all, this "I" or "ego" of Descartes was conceived as a spiritual, nonmaterial "soul." Now a body, presumably, can be moved only by contact with other bodies; how then could this incorporeal spirit act upon the molecular substances of the brain? From this pretty *impasse* came the marvels of materialism, idealism, and "psychophysical parallelism." The parallelist argued that if mind and brain are so different, neither can act upon the other, and the two series of events, material and mental, cerebral and intellectual, must be separate and distinct, without influence upon each other, but miraculously parallel. The materialist argued that since the "mind" undeniably acts upon the body, it must be of like substance with the body, as corporeal and material as the bile. The idealist argued that since the sole reality we could be sure of was the one with which Descartes had begun— the reality of thought—all other existences were real to us only as perceived by our senses and constructed by our minds; the body was a perception, and matter was merely a bundle of ideas.

So the merry war began; and now there is war only, but no merriment. Occasionally an epistemolog is found who is capable of smiling, like Bradley or William James; occasionally one is found who understands that his 'ology is only a game, and, therefore, plays it with a worldly twinkle in his eye, like David Hume. But never was there, for the rest, so deadly solemn a tribe; from John Locke to Rudolf Eucken they have kept their faces straight and made them longer with every generation, as if to be in keeping with their dismal discipline. Bishop Berkeley announced that nothing exists unless it is perceived—by man or God; so far as we know, the Bishop did not smile, though we may have our suspicions of so clever an Irishman.

Now no doubt it is truistically, tautologically, platitudinously true that nothing exists *for any mind* but that which *that* mind perceives. But what a world away this is from the proposition so often confused with it, that nothing exists unless it is perceived! That confusion was necessary and valuable to philosophers who trembled at the coarse materialism of Holbach and Moleschott and Büchner; it was brilliant of Berkeley to get rid of all materialism with one strategic blow simply by proving that matter does not exist; it was a towering masterpiece of logical prestidigitation, and gives us fair warning that persons studying philosophy should keep both eyes on the philosopher. But it was a trifle dishonest; even a bishop might have hesitated at such a pious fraud. "That which distinguishes man from animals," says Anatole France, "is lying and literature." [1] Now how much of this idealistic epistemology comes under literature?

This does not mean that there is no problem in epistemology. God knows that there are problems a-plenty there, as perhaps we shall have a chance to see. But these puzzles of the relation between subject and object, of the mode in which the knower knows the known, of the objective and the subjective elements in knowledge, of the objectivity of space and time, and the degree in which the qualities which we ascribe to objects belong to objects or to the minds that perceive them—these, in their details, are puzzles for the science of psychology, fields for repeated and accurate observation and experiment; they are no more specifically problems for philosophy than the analogous mysteries of metabolism, or the chemistry of roast beef. Every problem belongs to philosophy as much as this one, and this one belongs to it only in its relation to all the rest; it is a villainous accident that one actor in the great drama of ideas should have usurped nearly all the roles, and mouthed nearly all the lines, in the play of modern philosophic thought.

III. THEOLOGIANS

Almost as bad is the presumption that the function of philosophy is to serve as a critique of scientific method. Here too the wish surreptitiously fathers the thought: unable to show the unreality of matter, apologetic professors decided to show the unreliability of science. The admissions of Mach, Pearson and Poincaré, that the conclusions of science were merely "shorthand" formulations of the "habits" of a nature never completely observed, and that these conclusions might at any time be violated and overthrown by wider observation, were seized upon as the Achilles' heel of the murderer who had killed the cock robins of theology; here was a noble chance to show that reason is fallible, that science gives us not certainty but only probability, and that *ergo* all the dear dogmas of our childhood might be taken out of the museum, reclothed in carefully unintelligible

[1] Brousson, J. J. *Anatole France en Pantoufles*, p. 134.

phraseology, and sold to the next generation as only slightly damaged goods. Gentlemen arose on every side who sedulously examined the axioms of mathematics, the concepts of space and time, of number and measurement, of quantity and quality, and who concluded, from learned abracadabra, that there was a Santa Claus after all.

Is it any wonder, after this indecent sleight-o'-hand, that honest men have grown chary of philosophers? Of what use is all this logic, if its syllogisms are but the dishonest disguise of our secret hopes? "Metaphysics," said Bradley, "is the finding of bad reasons for what we believe upon instinct; but to find those reasons is no less an instinct." [1] Sometimes it is the finding of bad reasons for what we want others to believe. Voltaire was honest enough to say that he wished his maid and his cook to accept the orthodox beliefs of their place and time; it slightly lessened the chances, he thought, of their pilfering his jewelry or poisoning his food. A philosophical theory, said Lotze, is an attempt to justify "a fundamental view of things which has been adopted in early life." [2] Philosophers "all pose as though their real opinions had been discovered through the self-evolving of a cold, pure, divinely indifferent dialectic; . . . whereas in fact a prejudicial proposition, idea, or suggestion, which is generally their heart's desire abstracted and refined, is defended by them with arguments sought out after the event." [3] So wrote the honest Nietzsche.

Perhaps we have here the *caput Nili* of the faults that disfigure philosophy: it dishonors truth in the very search for it. It becomes the apologist of a transient dogma, and falls tragically short of that intellectual conscience, that patient respect for the evidence, that uphill attention to negative instances, which distinguishes a scientist like Humboldt or Darwin, or an unprofessional "literary" philosopher like Leonardo or Goethe. The Scholastics, who are wrongly rated as philosophers, having been primarily theologians, set the fashion of subordinating the search for truth to the promulgation of the Faith; their gigantic *Summas* were official Yellow Books issued by the Propaganda Office of the Vatican in the war on heresy. *Philosophia ancilla theologiæ*, they frankly said; philosophy is the chambermaid of theology. And though the great fathers of modern philosophy—Bacon, Descartes and Spinoza—protested against this philosophic harlotry, their grandchildren of our day have largely surrendered to the old tradition.

Out of this theological taint the other faults of philosophy grow like the mysteriously multiplying illnesses of a diseased heredity. To what is the obscurity of philosophy due if not to its imperfect honesty? No doubt some measure of the darkness which encompasses modern thought is due to the elusiveness of truth, and the abstruseness of cosmic considerations; but ob-

---

[1] *Appearance and Reality*, p. xiv. All references are to editions named in the Appendix.
[2] In Muirhead, *Contemporary British Philosophy*, p. 15.
[3] *Beyond Good and Evil*, § 5.

scurity of that sort alone would not keep human interest away. Shelley is obscure, but who does not honor him, at least with the lips? Woman is obscure, but what man this side of decay is not lured into the everlasting enterprise of penetrating that obscurity and solving that mystery? No, there is another and quite different obscurity in modern philosophy. When a man romances he is harder to understand than when he tells the truth; for every fact there are many possible imaginings; and only an expert can make his mendacity as consistent as the truth. But experts in mendacity do not become philosophers; they are too urgently needed in the service of diplomacy; and divine philosophy is left with inferior novelists, whose plots fall apart at the first touch of this living world.

In the end it is this initial dishonesty that breeds the sterile intellectualism of contemporary speculation. A man who is not certain of his mental integrity shuns the vital problems of human existence; at any moment the great laboratory of life may explode his little lie and leave him naked and shivering in the face of truth. So he builds himself an ivory tower of esoteric tomes and professionally philosophical periodicals; he is comfortable only in their company, and dreads even the irritating realism of his home. He wanders farther and farther away from his time and place, and from the problems that absorb his people and his century. The vast concerns that properly belong to philosophy do not interest him, they frighten him; he does not feel any passion for pulling things together, for bringing some order and unity into the fertile chaos of his age. He retreats fearfully into a little corner, and insulates himself from the world under layer after layer of technical terminology. He ceases to be a philosopher, and becomes an epistemologist.

It was not so in Greece, where philosophers professed less, and undertook more. Parmenides pondered nebulously over the mystery of knowledge; but the pre-Socratics kept their eyes with fair consistency upon the firm earth, and sought to ferret out its secrets by observation and experience, rather than to create it by exuding dialectic; there were not many introverts among the Greeks. Picture Democritus, the Laughing Philosopher; would he not be perilous company for the dessicated scholastics who have made the disputes about the reality of the external world take the place of medieval discourses on the number of angels that could sit on the point of a pin? Picture Thales, who met the challenge that philosophers were numskulls by "cornering the market" and making a fortune in a year. Picture Anaxagoras, who did the work of Darwin for the Greeks, and turned Pericles from a wire-pulling politician into a thinker and a statesman. Picture old Socrates, unafraid of the sun or the stars, gayly corrupting young mèn and overturning governments; what would he have done to these bespectacled seedless philosophasters who now litter the court of the once great Queen? To Plato, as to these virile predecessors, epistemology was but the vestibule of philosophy, akin to the preliminaries of love; it was pleasant enough for a while, but it was far from the creative consummation that drew wisdom's lover on. Here and there, in the shorter dialogues, the Master dallied amorously with the problems of perception, thought, and knowledge; but in his more spacious moments he spread his vision over larger fields, built himself ideal states, and brooded over the nature and destiny of man. And finally in Aristotle philosophy was honored in all her boundless scope and majesty; all her mansions were explored and made beautiful with order; here every problem found a place and every science brought its toll to wisdom. These men knew that the function of philosophy was not to bury herself in the obscure retreats of epistemology, but to come forth bravely into every realm of inquiry, and gather up all knowledge for the coördination and illumination of human character and human life. They understood that the field of philosophy is not some petty puzzle hiding in the clouds and destitute of interest or influence in the affairs of mankind, but the vast and total problem of the meaning and value and possibilities of man in this boundless and fluent world.

IV. SCIENTISTS

All this being what philosophy is not, or should not be, it remains to say what philosophy is, or ideally might become. Can we restore the Queen of the Sciences to her ancient scope and power? Can we again conceive philosophy as unified knowledge unifying life? Can we outline a kind of philosophy that might make its lovers capable of ruling first themselves and then a state, men worthy to be philosopher-kings?

Technically, as we defined it long ago, philosophy is "a study of experience as a whole, or of a portion of experience in relation to the whole." [1] At once it becomes clear that any problem can be the material of philosophy, if only it is studied in total perspective, in the light of all human experience and desire. The mark of the philosophic mind is not so much subtlety of speculation as breadth of vision and unity of thought. For Spinoza's *sub specie eternitatis* let us substitute *sub specie totius*. The two outlooks focus on the same result, as the eyes meet on the object seen; but whereas man can gather his own experience into a relatively ordered whole, to see things from the standpoint of eternity is the prerogative of the immortal gods, who perhaps do not exist.

The relation of science to philosophy needs no further clarification: the sciences are the windows through which philosophy sees the world, they are the senses of which it is the soul; without it their knowledge is as chaotically helpless as sensations that come to a disordered mind, making an idiot's lore. Spencer was right: philosophy is the most generalized knowledge. But he

[1] *Philosophy and the Social Problem*, p. 1.

was wrong: it is not merely knowledge; it implies that difficult and elevated vision in which mere knowledge is lifted up into a total view that orders and clarifies the confusion of desire; it involves that strangely different quality called wisdom.

Without science philosophy is impotent; for how can wisdom grow except on knowledge fairly won, with honest observation and research, and recorded and charted by impartial minds? Without science philosophy becomes decadent and dishonest, isolated from the flow of human growth, and falling more and more into the dreary futility of scholasticism. But without philosophy science is not merely helpless, it is destructive and devastating. Science is descriptive: it looks out with eye or telescope, with microscope or spectroscope, and tells us what it sees; its function is to observe carefully the fact at hand, and to describe it objectively and accurately, regardless of the result to man. Here is nitroglycerine, or chlorine gas; it is the business of science to analyze them calmly, to tell us just what these compounds or elements are, and what they can do. If they can kill whole cities, if they can destroy the fairest shrines of human art, if they can lay waste and bring to nothing an entire civilization, with all its treasured loveliness and wisdom,—science will tell us how it can be done scientifically, expeditiously, and with the least expense to the tax-payers, should they survive. But whether civilizations ought to be destroyed,—what science tells us that? Whether life is sweetest when engrossed in acquisition and possessed with possessions, or when it is absorbed in creation and construction; whether it is better to seek knowledge and disillusionment, or the passing ecstasy of beauty; whether we should try to forego all supernatural sanctions in our moral life; whether we should view matter from the standpoint of mind, or mind from the standpoint of matter—what science shall answer us here? How shall these ultimate choices of our lives be clarified except by the light of our whole experience, by that wisdom to which knowledge is mere raw material, and in whose total vision all the wealth of all sciences finds place and order and a guiding significance?

Science is the analytical description of parts, philosophy is the synthetic interpretation of the whole, or the interpretation of a part in terms of its place and value for the whole. Science is a committee of ways and means, philosophy is a committee on resolutions and program; facts and instrumentalities have worth and meaning only in relation to desire. That the desires themselves should be consistent, that they should become ordered parts of a harmonious personality, an integrated life,—that too is the task of philosophy, and one of its highest goals.

Of necessity philosophy is more hypothetical than science. Science itself must use hypothesis, but only as its starting-point; it must, if it be science, issue in verifiable knowledge, objectively independent of individual utility or whim. Philosophy, on the contrary, uses science and fact and veri-

fied knowledge as its starting-point (if it does not it is high time it should);
and it proceeds to make vaster hypotheses about ultimate problems on which
no conclusive data are at hand. It is a perilous and imaginative completion
of understanding; it fills out with experimentally unprovable assumptions
the gaps in our scientific knowledge of the world. In this sense every man
is a philosopher, even *malgré lui:* the most cautious sceptic, the most modest
agnostic, or the most matter-of-fact "behaviorist" philosophizes, at the
very time that he protests to all the world that philosophy is impossible. If
an agnostic could live with such perfect neutrality as neither to believe nor
to disbelieve in God, if he could divide his thoughts and actions impartially
between acceptance and denial, he might achieve a breathless and motionless
moratorium on philosophy, a state of philosophic coma, a cosmic unconsciousness. But this is too difficult and inhuman; we find that we actually
take sides; we live denial or we live acceptance; we behave as if we had
chosen one or the other horn of those terrible dilemmas which constitute
philosophy. *Fingimus hypotheses:* we make hypotheses, even as Newton
did. The lure of the absolute draws us ever on.

Shall we admit that philosophy perpetually contradicts itself in the historical succession of systems, that philosophers are all a-rage with fratricidal
mania, and are never content until they have destroyed every rival claimant
to the realms and throne of truth? How can a man occupied with life spare
time to unravel these learned contradictions, or to pacify this war? Do not
these philosophies cancel one another out? Consider Omar's experience:

> Myself when young did eagerly frequent
> Doctor and saint, and heard great argument
>   About it and about; but evermore
> Came out by the same door wherein I went.

Well, perhaps Omar was romancing; perhaps he did not really come out
by the same door wherein he went, unless, like a good Mohammedan, he
had left his wits with his shoes at the temple gate. No man can frequent
the company of the great philosophers without changing his mind and widening his views on a thousand vital points. Indeed what was it that altered
Omar's childhood faith into a sceptical worship of beauty and the grape?
What is it that lends majesty to Omar's verse if it be not philosophy?

Let a man study the history of science and he will discover there such ka-
leidoscopic changes as make the vacillations of philosophy melt away in the
scope and depth of its agreements and fundamental unanimity. To what
distant star has our famous Nebular Hypothesis flown?—does contemporary astronomy countenance it, or smile in its clouded face? Where are
the laws of the great Newton now, when Einstein and Minkowski and other
distinguished gentlemen have upset the universe with their unintelligible
relativity? Where are the indestructibility of matter and the conservation

of energy in the chaos and dispute of contemporary physics? Where is poor Euclid, greatest of text-book makers, now that mathematicians forge new dimensions for us at their own sweet will, and juggle infinities of which one can contain another as its part, and prove that in physics, as in politics, a straight line is the longest distance between two points? Where is eugenics now that infantile environment replaces heredity as the passing deity of science? Where is Gregor Mendel now that "unit characters" are in bad odor with geneticists? Where is the kindly destructive Darwin himself, now that evolution by fortuitous and continuous variations is displaced by the speedier method of mutations?—and are these mutations the illegitimate offspring of mating hybrids?—and are we to be forced back, for our explanation of evolution, to the transmission of acquired characters?—shall we find ourselves returning over a century to embrace again the neck of Lamarck's giraffe? What shall we do with the laborious laboratories of Professor Wundt, and the questionable questionnaires of Stanley Hall, now that no "behaviorist" can write a page of the latest and most scientific psychology without scattering the entrails of his predecessors to all the constellations of the zodiac? Where is the new "science" of history now that every Egyptologist makes his own ladder of dynasties and dates, differing from the others by only a few thousand years; and every good anthropologist laughs at Tylor and Westermarck and Spencer, and the poor be-knighted Frazer knows nothing about primitive religion now that he is dead? What have our sciences come to? Have they suddenly lost their infallibility, and their eternal truths? Can it be, even, that the "laws of Nature" are only the hypotheses of man? Is there no certainty or stability in science any more?

Perhaps if we desire stability of mind and soul we shall have to seek it less in science than in philosophy. The differences among philosophers are due rather to the changing terminology of their times than to the hostility of their ideas; indeed, in great measure they are due to the inconstancy of science itself, with its passionate devotion to some hypothesis for a while, and then its satiety, and apathy, and flight to the novel face of some younger theory. What marvelous agreement there is, after all, in the judgment of the greatest thinkers on the vital problems of human life, when the varied fashions of their speech are resolved into their essential thought! Santayana modestly announces that he has nothing to add to Aristotle, but will offer merely an application of that older philosophy to our time; could a modern physicist, or a modern biologist, or a modern mathematician speak likewise of any scientist among the Greeks? Aristotle's science is contradicted at almost every point by the science of today; but his philosophy will remain illuminating and profound when the science of today will be a thing of scorn and ridicule, deposed and cast out by the passing infallibilities of another age.

V. THE QUEEN OF THE SCIENCES

We may feel, then, that philosophy is still *Regina Scientiarum,* and would be everywhere recognized as such if she clothed herself in her ancient majesty, brought all the sciences into her service, and took all knowledge as her instrument. The world is her subject-matter, and the universe is her specialty. But as a wise queen assigns the various provinces of her kingdom to skilled governors, and these apportion among subordinates the tasks of accumulating data and dealing with details while they and the ruler confine themselves to the organization of intelligence and enterprise; so philosophy divides her empire into many realms, and in her paradise there are many mansions.

The first realm of her kingdom, and the vestibule of her home, is called by the unalluring name of *Logic;* as if philosophy deliberately hid her beauty from strangers' eyes, and bade all suitors pass through this ordeal first, and prove their worthiness to share her "dear delight." For the pleasures of philosophy are like the heights of love, to which no mean soul can come. How shall we know Truth when we behold her, if we have not learned to picture at least her semblance, and have not pondered the tests and trials by which we shall assure ourselves of her "real presence"? How shall we answer Pilate's tantalizing question? Shall we follow our frail, adventurous reason, our profound and obscure intuition, or the brute verdict of our eyes and ears and groping hands? How shall we cleanse our senses and our thoughts of all distorting prejudices and all deceiving "idols," keeping all the lamps of our intelligence alight, that every passing truth may come to us and find welcome, and an ordered place? How shall we train ourselves, like athletes, for the pursuit and love of wisdom?

And then, still distant from the throne and center of the kingdom, lies another realm of trial, home of the great dragon *Epistemology.* If our feet lagged in the weary paths of Logic, here our eyes shall be almost useless in the dark; we shall stumble into many a marsh, and perhaps we shall wander too near the mouth of the dragon, and be charmed by his majestic language, and suddenly be swallowed up in his cavernous vacuity, becoming epistemologs forever. But we must face this test too, and answer in some forgivable way the riddle of knowledge, the problem of the reality and honesty of the world that we perceive. And then perhaps we shall pass on and stand humbly in the court of the Great Queen.

A lordly realm is *Metaphysics,* dark also, and illumined only by the light we bring, but full of treasures for the soul. Here Nature hides her secret essence, and puzzles us with a hundred clues. Here philosophy reveals something of that "highest music" which she sang to Pythagoras; for through her, now, nature is made conscious, criticizes her own purposes, and becomes a meaningful thing. Here we may ponder the problems of matter and life, of brain and mind, of materialism and spiritualism, of mechanism and vitalism, of determinism and freedom. What is man?—a thing of coils and springs and tangled wheels, moved from without by the blind forces of earth and sky?—or, in his small and ridiculous way, a creative god?

Another realm is called *History,* where a hundred thousand menials, and some geniuses, bring their lore from distant times and lands, that we may look upon it all in unity and learn its lessons. Is there any meaning in the past? Are there any laws of growth and decay, marking and perhaps determining the rise and fall of nations, of races, and of civilizations? Here we shall come upon Montesquieu and Buckle discoursing of the influence of geography on the fate of peoples; here Condorcet, about to die, will console himself with the thought of progress, and the indefinite perfectibility of man; here Hegel will show us his dialectical sleight-o'-hand, and Carlyle will tell us of his heroes; here the great chauvinists will sing the strength of their races' seed, and will curse the coming of the barbarians; here Marx will frighten us with a mountain of figures and arguments for the economic determination of history; and here perhaps we shall find one or two seekers who will explain to these splendid monomaniacs that their truths are but facets of the fact, and that history and nature are more varied than they have dreamed of in their philosophies. And off in a corner we shall find the gloomy Nietzsche singing his song of Eternal Recurrence, and Spengler passionately proving the downfall of the western world.

And then if we pass on to still another realm we shall hear discourse on *Politics;* for a moment we shall be dismayed, fearing that we have discovered America. But it cannot be, for these men discuss democracy without reverence, and anarchism without fear; they love socialism though they know its defects, and they honor aristocracy while despising its injustice to unpedigreed ability. And sometimes they speak with the enthusiasm of youth of a fair land called Utopia, in which only wise men rule, and every city is rich and beautiful.

With that last word still making music in our souls we enter into the heart of the realm, and gaze upon Philosophy herself, as she reveals to her lovers the beautiful, the immortal, and the good. For Philosophy has a secret jealousy of Art, and envies her creative passion for beauty; here, and not in science, is her great rival for the possession and loyalty of the noblest men. Wisdom might gracefully yield, admitting that it is wiser to worship Beauty than to seek Truth; for eternal Truth is so proudly elusive that perhaps we shall never be allowed even to touch the hem of her garments, while Beauty, knowing that she must die, welcomes and rewards our adoration. So Philosophy modestly studies Beauty, while Art reveres and re-creates her; Art knows her in the ardent intimacy of love, in the fair strength of architectured temples, and the voluptuous splendor of sculptured forms, and the warmth of color, and the music of words, and the concourse of sweet sounds; but Philosophy, alas, knows only the problems of beauty: whence beauty comes, and what it means, and whether it lies in the form itself or only in the hunger of our hearts. And this is the realm of *Æsthetics,* made dreary for centuries by scholastic minds, but still full of wonder and delight.

Here, also in the center of the kingdom, is the realm of Morals or *Ethics;* again a region arid with academic abstractions, but in some ways the richest of the mansions of philosophy. For even higher than the life of art is the art of life; and Ethics is the lore of the art of life. Here Philosophy lifts her varied knowledge into living wisdom, and from her many mansions gathers guidance for mankind. What is the best life after all? Of what good is good- ness, and what right is there in power? Does the highest virtue lie in the wisdom of Socrates, or Nietzsche's bravery, or the gentleness of Christ? Shall we be Stoics with Zeno and Spinoza, or Epicureans with Epicurus and Renan? Is pleasure the aim of life? Is love immoral except within the law? What is justice, and what does justice say of our industrial world?—Here if anywhere are vital questions, in which entire civilizations may find their fate involved; here are dilemmas that touch every state and every heart; problems by the side of which science, with its bookkeeping and its short- hand, its liquids and solids and gases, seems something remote and inhu- manly cold, something not so much allied to life as unwittingly in league with death.

But then death too belongs to philosophy; and when all other debates are stilled, thought turns fearfully to consider the Great Enemy, and philosophy enters the portals of *Religion.* Theology is the study of supernatural beings, and their relationship with man; of these beings philosophy has nothing to say. But of man's relationship with the sum of life and the totality of things, of his origin on this earth and his final destiny, philosophy would speak, though with a modesty commensurate with human ignorance. It is concerned with the question of immortality as it is concerned with every vital issue; perhaps we might define philosophy as a matter of life and death. And finally it is concerned with God. Not with the God of theology, con- ceived presumably as outside the realm of Nature; but with the God of philosophers, the law and the structure, the vitality and the will of the world. If there is any intelligence guiding this universe, philosophy wishes to know and understand it and reverently work with it; if there is none, philosophy wishes to know that also, and face it without fear. If the stars are but transient coagulations of haphazard nebulæ, if life is a colloidal accident, impersonally permanent and individually fleeting, if man is only a com- pound of chemicals, destined to disintegrate and utterly disappear, if the creative ecstasy of art, and the gentle wisdom of the sage, and the willing martyrdom of saints are but bright incidents in the protoplasmic pullulation of the earth, and death is the answer to every problem and the destiny of every soul—then philosophy will face that too, and try to find within that narrowed circle some significance and nobility for man.

Shall we begin?

PART TWO

LOGIC AND EPISTEMOLOGY

CHAPTER II

What Is Truth?[1]

I. SENSATION VS. REASON

"IN THE WHOLE New Testament," says the gentle and saintly Nietzsche, as offensively as possible, "there appears but a solitary figure worthy of honor: Pilate, the Roman Viceroy. . . . The noble scorn of a Roman, before whom the word 'truth' was shamelessly mishandled, enriched the New Testament with the only saying in it that has any value—'What is truth?' " [2] Anatole France considered it the profoundest question ever asked.[3] For what other question does not depend upon it?

Logic is a poor *hors d'œuvre* for the feast of philosophy; it dulls a thousand appetites for every one it whets. We suspect logic because we have learned that most reasoning is desire dressed in a little rationality; we pretend to be constructing edifices of impartial thought, when actually we are selecting only such facts and agreements as will give dignity to some personal or patriotic wish. We suspect logic because middle age has taught us that life is larger, surer, profounder than our syllogisms; logic is static, puffed up with "invariable truths," while life is fluent and changeful, and surprises all formulas. "The number of things that reason at first refused to recognize, and yet had in the end to admit, is considerable." [4] Perhaps in our youth we memorized all the rules of perfect thinking, only to find that the pursuit of knowledge, the recognition of truth, and the wisdom of life, fell incalculably

---

[1] See footnote to Table of Contents.
[2] *Antichrist*, sect. 46; referring to John, xviii, 38.
[3] *On Life and Letters*, First Series, p. 8.
[4] Le Bon, G., *The Evolution of Matter*, p. 72.

15

outside this elegantly ordered realm. How gladly we would leave to the end this logic that can make even philosophy dry and spiritless, rather than set it here as a barrier to problems less basic, possibly, but so much more directly vital to our lives! And yet we must not; we cannot ride forth on our quest of truth without determining in advance what we are looking for, by what road we propose to seek it, and how we shall know it if we come upon it. Any other order would not be logical!

At the very outset we find the main problem of logic clearly caught and clearly answered by those unappreciated free lances of the ancient world—the Sophists. Knowledge, they said (Locke, two thousand years later, was thought to have discovered this), comes from the senses only; therefore the test of truth, the answer to Pilate's question, is Sensation: truth is what you taste, touch, smell, hear, see. What could be simpler? But Plato was not satisfied: if this is truth, he said, there is no truth, for we all taste, smell, hear, touch, and see things differently; the baboon, then, is the measure of truth equally with the sage—and who shall decide between them? Plato was sure that reason was the rest of truth; the ideas of reason were to the reports of the senses what statesmen were to the populace—unifying centers of order for a chaotic mass.

Aristotle agreed with him, and made logic for the first time a separate study by seeking to formulate the laws of reason. Nothing should be judged true unless it might be made the conclusion of a perfect syllogism: so man is a rational animal (this credulous proposition is still found in the books of logicians); but Socrates is a man; therefore Socrates is a rational animal. Not at all, said Pyrrho; [1] every syllogism is a *petitio principii*—a begging of the question. For your major cannot be true unless your conclusion is true in advance—which you have no right to assume; and unless you presume that Socrates is rational you must not start with the proposition that man (who includes Socrates) is a rational animal; perhaps he is merely a rationalizing animal. Reason, therefore, is always uncertain. Very well, said Epicurus; let us go back to the Sophists, and trust to our senses. But again, asked the Sceptics, how can this be? To our sense the sun is as small as a pumpkin, and the stars might be "a rash on the sky"; shall we believe our senses here? Nothing is certain, concluded Pyrrho; and when he died his students, though they loved him, did not mourn him, for they could not be sure that he was dead.

So the game of sense vs. reason filled many a philosophic day, until Greece and Rome melted from the scene, and left Europe to Christianity and the Church. And then, because divine dogmas compelled the faith of men, and it was holy to believe what the senses denied, the Sophists and Epicurus were forgotten; and, though the Scholastics defined truth as the adequate

[1] 360–270 B. C.

correspondence of thought to things, they followed Plato and Aristotle in exalting reason. Best of all was deductive reason, that would derive, from a creed defined and sure, a coherent system of the world. Ideas were greater realities than sounds and sights; for these things of the flesh had their beginning and ceased to be, but "universals," or class-ideas, were deathless, existing before, and in, and after, the passing things wherein they took particular form; man was more real than any man, beauty more real than any rose. Even Descartes, still slave to that from which he made men free, demanded of every philosopher that he reject the evidence of sense, and hold nothing certain but clear thought.

Modernity began with the reënthronement of sensation—in science with Galileo, in philosophy with Bacon. The astronomer multiplied the senses with instruments; the philosopher chastened reason with observation, and subpœnaed the most sacred deductions to the bar of inductive test. If one must read logic, let it be through Bacon's *Novum Organum* first of all: here logic is as brilliant as a duel, reasoning becomes an adventure and a conquest, and philosophy is a detective story in which the villain is the hunted truth. What epigrams, and what wisdom! Consider the very beginning of the book: "Man, as the minister and interpreter of nature, does and understands as much as his observations on the order of nature . . . permit him; and neither knows nor is capable of more." Was there ever a completer declaration of war on all mysticism, obscurantism, and pedantry? This was "the bell that called the wits together," and sounded the tocsin of the Renaissance.

And then a heavy debate ensued between England and the Continent. Leibnitz, Kant and Hegel riddled the senses with doubts, and upheld the claims of reason as the arbiter of all sense reports; Hobbes and Locke and Mill scorned as senseless a reason that dared to seek truths beyond the reach of sight and touch and taste and smell and sound. But surely, said Kant, mathematics was independent of sensation, true *a priori*, before experience; the square of 5 would be 25 no matter what the senses might say. No, answered Mill; we believe that $2 \times 2 = 4$ only because we have again and again, in the experience of the individual or in the socially transmitted experience of the race, felt or seen 4 as the result of 2 and 2. All knowledge, said Locke, is derived from sense, and even the loftiest deductions of higher mathematics are precariously uncertain until the experience of the senses stamps them with approval.

No debate has ever had a stranger termination: apriorism—the defense of truths independent of experience—died on the Continent, and transmigrated to England; empiricism—the reference of all knowledge to sensation as its source and test—died in England, and found resurrection in America. England had had for centuries a practical bent, and the matter-of-fact conclusions of her logic had reflected the rule of her life by the middle class; but now, even as that middle class was consolidating its victory over the country gentleman, English thinkers, grown suddenly subtle and incomprehensible, imported all the remains of Kant and Hegel, reduced the senses to nonsense, and constructed from deductive reasoning new laws of thought that would hold not only for logic but for the world. Bradley called experience the Absolute, and then analyzed it all away; Bosanquet reduced logic to the psychology of inference, and then defined inference, with Teutonic magnificence, as "the indirect reference to reality of differences within a universal, by means of the exhibition of this universal in differences directly referred to reality." [1] Bertrand Russell abandoned logic as the science of reasoning, and made it "the science of the most complete abstractions"; with Professor Whitehead he reared a mathematical structure of deductive certainties, as completely divorced as possible from all experience, and then added his definition of truth:

> A form of words is true when it has a certain relation to a certain fact. What relation to what fact? I think the fundamental relation is this: a form of words is true if a person who knows the language is led to that form of words when he finds himself in an environment which contains features that are the meanings of those words, and these features produce reactions in him sufficiently strong for him to use words which mean them. [2]

Alas, are Britons learning their English in Germany? And are we in for another age of scholasticism—the pursuit of ideas without correlation in experience or fruitfulness in life? How much of contemporary thought consists in putting what everybody knows into knowledge that nobody can understand!

It seemed to William James, against the background of an America too active to be patient with abstractions, that obscurity was not a prerequisite of philosophy, and that the meaning of truth was simple enough to be stated in terms that even a business man would understand. Truth was efficacy. Instead of judging an idea by its origins, or by deduction from inviolate first principles, James called it to the test of action, asked for its practical consequences when applied, and turned the face of thought again to things. To John Dewey thought seemed to be an instrument, like stomach and legs, and its test was therefore the proper fulfilment of its function—the comprehension and control of life. Here was the inductive, empirical tradition of England restored to youth; pragmatism was "a new name for an old way of thinking"; it was only the elaboration of Bacon's view, that "that rule which is most effective in practice is also most true in theory," and of Bentham's manufacturing philosophy, that utility is the test of all.

[1] *Encyclopedia Britannica,* art. *Logic.*
[2] *Philosophy,* p. 262. It should be added that this obscurity is unusual in one who is the clearest and most straightforward of contemporary philosophers.

There are many faults in pragmatism, because its genial creator allowed simple souls to suppose that all their fondest beliefs were true if these had any efficacy to aid and comfort them against the brutal impartiality of the world. But of course personal and temporary utility did not confer upon a belief the brevet of truth; only permanent and universal utility would make an idea true; and since this was a condition that was "ever not quite" fulfilled, truth was never more than probability. When some pragmatists spoke of a belief having "once" been true because once useful, they talked learned nonsense; it had been a useful error, not a truth; and we shall never be certain that our dearest truth may not be, in Nietzsche's phrase, merely "the most useful form of error" that we have known. The world was not made for reason.

So we are driven back to the Sophists, and our conclusion is only theirs: the senses are the test of truth. But *all* the senses; one alone may well deceive us, as light deceives us about color, or distance about size; and only another sense can correct the error which one sense has made. *Truth is consistent sensation.* But again, "sensation" must include all that we learn from the instruments with which we enlarge and sharpen sense; the spectroscope, the telescope, the microscope, the sensitized plate, the X-ray, are proliferations of our eyes; the telephone, the stethoscope, even the radio, are prolongations of our curious ears. And finally, sensation must include the internal sense; our inward "feel" of our own life and mind is as immediate and trustworthy as any report, to that life and mind, from the sense-organs that variously touch the external world. After all, despite our skill in self-deception, there is nothing that we know so well as our own selves.

It is true that sensation misses certainty; so does life. Hume was right: the senses reveal no mystical "causality," but only sequence; we cannot be quite sure that because *B* has always followed *A,* it will follow *A* forever. Sensation can never completely guarantee one moment of the future; we must risk our necks upon the probability that regularities observed in the past will continue in the future. And this is all we need; only a logician requires more. The world is so varied and fluent that our "truths" must always be one-sided and precarious. There are no absolutes, there are only relatives; and we must learn to get along with relatives.

There are other persons than ourselves in this world, and their senses— and therefore their "truths"—will not always agree with ours. When Signora Cini, in Pirandello's play, says that she will believe what she sees with her eyes and feels with her fingers, Laudisi tells her: "You should show some respect for what other people see with their eyes and feel with their fingers, even though it be the exact opposite of what you see and feel." [1] Yes; where more than one of us is concerned, truth must be socially consistent sensa-

[1] *Right You Are If You Think You Are,* p. 161.

tion; and when more than one moment of time is concerned, it must be permanently consistent sensation. Reality is a dome of many-colored glass, and from his little corner each of us sees a different combination of colors in the kaleidoscope. Perhaps truth is only the common denominator of our delusions, and certainty is an error in which all men agree. We must be content with that.

Where, then, shall be the place of reason in this ridiculously plebeian logic of ours, that confirms the prejudices of the commonest man in the street? Its function here, as elsewhere, is to coördinate—sensations into ideas, ideas into knowledge, knowledge into wisdom, purposes into personality, individuals into society, societies into peace. The role of reason in the conquest of truth is secondary but vital: it must weave the chaos and contradictions of many senses into unified and harmonious conclusions, which it shall hold subject to verification or rejection by subsequent sensation. It is not half so certain as sensation; for "in transcending what is given by actual perception, we without doubt make use of an inference"; [1] and every inferential step away from immediate sensation lowers the probability of our truth. But this, too, is a gamble that life must make; we must attempt the reconciliation of discordant senses and partial views, if we are to extend our understanding and our mastery. Just as Köhler's chimpanzees reasoned best when they took in the entire situation, so for ourselves reasoned truth, like philosophy and wisdom, like morality and beauty, is total perspective, the harmonious union of the part with the whole. Through sensation we stand firmly with our feet on the earth; through reason we lift the mind's eye beyond the present scope of sense, and conceive new truths which some day the senses may verify. Sensation is the test of truth, but reason is its discoverer.

II. THE MYSTERY OF KNOWLEDGE

Here we stand, but not without danger on every side. For the idealist scorns and denies the veracity of sensation, and the mystic questions the reliability of reason. What shall we say to them?

"By use there is good and bad, by use there are sweet and sour; but in reality there are only atoms and the void." So Democritus, the materialist, founded epistemology, and laid the bases of idealism, twenty-three hundred years ago. For in that strange fragment it is obvious that the Laughing Philosopher had in mind the "subjectivity of sense qualities," the existence of color, sound, weight, heat, shape, taste, smell and pain, not in the objects felt, but in the organism feeling them. "All qualities called sensible," said Hobbes twenty centuries after his Greek prototype, "are in the object so

[1] Bradley, F. H., *The Principles of Logic*, p. 225.

many several motions of the matter by which it presseth against our organs diversely." Sound is a motion of the air, light is a movement of the ether or a corpuscular bombardment of the eye; heat is merely accelerated molecular motion, and color depends upon the rate and amplitude of the waves of light, and the portion of the retina affected; "objective reality" itself is neither hot nor cold, neither foul nor fair, but dark and colorless and silent. How could there be light if there were no eyes or sensitive tissue in the world, how could there be sounds if there were no ears? The loveliest rainbow is in our vision rather than in the sky.

Let the idealist speak—he who believes that nothing is known to us except ideas. "This external world, which you suppose exists independently by yourself, is first of all a world of colors. But colors are subjective—they are in you, not in the thing you see. Some people are blind to certain colors and find, for example, no red in nature; if we were all like these would the rose be red? Color changes as you pass from dawn to noon to twilight to artificial light; which of these colors is 'real'? Is the color of a cloth that which you see when you buy it in the store, or that which it has in the sunlit air? The eyes of the lower animals—the crustacea, for example—are quite different in structure from our own, and presumably report shapes and colors otherwise than ours; which shape or color is 'real'? Our eyes are insensitive to large areas of the spectrum; animals with better eyes see more completely the forms and hues of the world than we; which of us—animal or man—sees the world 'as it is'? And this table that you call round; does it really seem round to you, when you look at it with unprejudiced eye, or does it seem elliptical? Are all shapes, as well as all colors, dependent upon the perceiver?

"Consider odors and tastes. One man's meat is another man's poison; thousands like caviar, millions pretend to like it; poor Chinese like the taste of rotting fish, and rich Europeans like the taste of rotting cheese. So with hot and cold; put one hand into hot water, the other into cold water, then both into lukewarm water; the lukewarm water will seem cool to one hand and warm to the other; which is it 'in reality'? So with pleasure and pain: when the nerves from the palate to the brain are severed, or affected by a cold, we find no savor in our food; is the taste, then, in the food, or the palate, or the brain? Your tooth aches?—but anesthetize the nerve between it and the brain, and the tooth aches no more; was it the tooth that ached, or only the brain? So with beauty and ugliness: this woman is beautiful, you say; but is she as beautiful to her brother, or to her rival, as she is to you? Is her beauty in herself, or in your desire? Take away from the 'objective' world all those qualities which you put into it by your presence and perceptions, and what remains? 'Atoms and the void?'—matter and space and time?

"But this matter—how do you know it except as sensations brought together into ideas in your mind? What is space but behind and in front, alongside, under, on top, here, there, near, far, large, small?—and what are these but the attitudes of a perceiving mind? Are objects in themselves in front rather than behind, here rather than there, large and not small; or are they such only with reference to ourselves? *A* appears as *a* to the eye, *b* to the microscope, *c* to the telescope; which is it 'in reality'? 'My master,' said M. Bergeret's dog, 'becomes larger as he approaches, and smaller as he recedes; I am the only being that keeps the same size no matter where I go.' Which is the real size of the orange—what the circumnavigating fly feels it to be or what it seems to me as I hold it in my hand, or what it seems to the man across the street? You cannot escape by measuring the object with a rule, and calling this measure real; for the inch on your rule or your tape is like the orange itself—smaller to you than to the fly, and larger to you than it might be to some gigantic visitor from Mars. Verily 'Man is the measure of all things,' and creates most of the world which he perceives.

"Einstein announces, as the essential result of his theory of relativity, that by it 'the last remainder of physical objectivity is taken from space and time.' [1] What is time but your feeling of before and after some dividing point in your own experience?—and would there be before and after if there were no minds? Perhaps the sense of time is more minute in the moth you crush against the wall, than in your slower-moving life; which time is 'real'? The man from Saturn, in Voltaire's tale, complained that the length of life, on that hurried planet, was but fifteen thousand years; and what could one learn or accomplish in that brief span? A year in which we have had many experiences seems longer than one in which reminiscence finds no stopping-place; and time is always doubled in a dental chair. Flammarion tells of the man who saw the events of the French Revolution unfolding themselves in reverse time-order because he was receding from the earth at a rate greater than the velocity of light. Space alters time, as it does on an ocean voyage, or as it did on M. Passepartout's 'Tour of the World in Eighty Days.' Time alters space: the star which we see in the northern sky is not there; it has moved since emitting the light which comes to us now. Space-time is an inextricable complex of location and judgment; it is a mode of perception, not an external thing. Your mind is a jail; it can never know how much of the object it knows is in the object, or in the mind that 'knows.' Such are the sensations whose verdict gives you 'truth.'

"No, sensation cannot be the test of truth. All that we know is our ideas; and we can never test these by an external world which our own sensations have so largely made. How can we ever discover what the 'object' would look like had it not been forced to disguise itself into those visual, auditory,

[1] Cassirer, E., *Substance and Function*, p. 356.

tactual, olfactory and gustatory sensations through which alone we know it? These 'things' which you suppose are the judge of thought are constructs of thought itself; they are the ideas we form after combining into an arbitrary and perhaps confused mosaic, the multiple sensations that have come to us so diversely through our nerves; we put together sights, sounds, noises, pressures and tastes, and name the resulting construct this or that; we create the 'thing' by perceiving it. The only world that certainly exists is the world of mind, of ideas; everything else is a supposition."

Is it so? Perhaps. Philosophy does not deal in certainties; and in epistemology, as in art, we can only say that about tastes there is no disputing. To one prejudiced in favor of clarity, this idealistic devastation of the external world remains an unconvincing feat of logical legerdemain, a relic of primitive magic and medieval mysteries. Experience cannot be everything, for beyond it must be its source; and this source is what we mean by matter, though we can say no more of it than Stuart Mill said—that it is the "permanent possibility of sensation."

The secret of the idealist's trick is the confusion of meaning with existence. Objects unperceived by any organism have no meaning; but they may have, none the less, a brute existence. "To be real, or even barely to exist," says Bradley, "must be to fall within sentience." [1] But did not the distant stars exist before they were revealed by our telescopes?—and must we say that no stars now exist that are not within reach of our present instruments? Doubtless they did not, and do not, exist precisely as we see them. This point of light that we call Sirius may be merely a mass of dark matter emitting particles at such white-hot speed that they become luminous on the way. But the source of the particles is *there;* the telescope does not create it. A mathematician, by careful calculation, predicted that if observatories would point their telescopes at a certain moment to a given spot in the sky, they would discover a planet hitherto unknown. The telescopes looked, and caught their prey; did they therefore create Neptune? [2]

We must grant that the existence of the stars while unperceived is but an inference, and that no inference is sure. But an inference verified by direct sensation night after night for a thousand years is a very reasonable inference, sufficient for human life, and for any philosophy that hopes to affect life rather than play solitaire forever. When we leave our study, and no life (presumably) is left there to perceive it, does the room cease to exist? Probably not; for by a strange fatality it is always there when we return. It is a comfort to find that Miss May Sinclair, who amuses herself between novels by writing books in defense of idealism, admits that she does not give

[1] *Appearance and Reality,* p. 144.
[2] Cf. *Encyclopedia Britannica,* vol. x, p. 386.

birth to her room when she enters it.[1] Theology deceives women well; but men can also be fooled with epistemology.

What do the words "objective" and "subjective" mean? Perhaps the game depends upon not defining them? We shall take the idealist at his word, and divide the world of ideas, which alone he calls real, from those other realities that exist for us, and not for him; the subjective realm will then be composed exclusively of ideas, and everything else will be "objective." But there a difficulty lies; for included in this objective world is the perceiver's body, with all its paraphernalia of eyes and nose and tongue and ears and finger-tips; his senses are as surely part of the "external" world as his legs; and his legs are as surely part of it as the ground on which he stands so hypothetically. And once this is seen, it becomes obvious that sense-qualities are determined for the most part by objective conditions. Let us see.

What determines color? Three things. First, the physical and chemical constitution of the external cause of our sensation. (We assume the existence of this external cause, for reasons given above; and we shall hereafter call it the "object.") Second, the amount, the nature, and the incidence of light, including the chemical composition of its source, and the rate and amplitude of its waves. Third, the eyes, the optic nerves, and the optic centers in the brain, of the individual who perceives. None of these conditions is "subjective"; conceivably, through instruments not much subtler than those that exist in other fields, a man might see his own retina, his own optic nerves, and even the optic centers in his brain; all these are part of the "external world," not part of consciousness or the perceiving idea.

These three determining conditions of light constitute what we may call the *objective situation*, made up of cause, intermediary, and sense. The color varies with, and may be changed by, each of them; we can make candy red with chemicals, we can make blue clothing black with artificial light, and we can make the retina convey sensations of tiny purple stars by pressing the ball of the eye. Color is a varying function of a varying objective situation; it is not the unchangeable quality of the object, nor is it the creation of the perceiving mind. The idealist rightly believes that no tree would be green if no eye were there to see it; he wrongly supposes that his perception makes the greenness of the tree. If that were so, his perception would make all things green—trees and clouds, roses and golden hair. It is as always: where contraries are debatable, the truth is in their union.

So much for color; obviously it would not be very different with shape. Likewise with sound: it is determined by an objective situation composed of external cause (two objects, say, have suddenly come together), intermediary air-waves, and the auditory nerve. So, too, with the lukewarm water that is hot and cold; the temperature felt is a complex of sensory receptors

[1] *The New Idealism*, p. 5.

and physical conditions; and since one hand is, by hypothesis, warmer than the other, the resultant sensations will differ for each hand. But the conditions—the water and the hands—are both of them objective; neither is made by the perceiving mind. What is the real color, the real shape, the real temperature, and the real note? No one can dogmatically say; each man's senses enter into the situation, and senses vary. For the purposes of life it is enough to consider as "real" those phenomena which are reported similarly by many different persons; we may believe that those elements in which the observations of divers individuals agree, are objective elements, independent of their separate selves. Truth is socially consistent sensation.

We have left for the last the problems of space and time, for here confusion is so desperate that even scientists like Steinmetz and Einstein have surrendered to Kant. Space as the sense or measurement of distance is partly subjective, since location and distance are relative to ourselves; but space as the sum of all possible lines of motion is lamentably independent of mankind. One would imagine that idealism here had been sufficiently refuted by William James, who indicated, with the casualness of common sense, that relations are perceived as directly as anything else; and if this were not enough, the experiments of Köhler with chimpanzees should have settled the matter once for all. We perceive juxtaposition, inequality, motion, rest; and when we see an insect moving across a still background we directly perceive both time and space.

For time is the child of motion; if there were no movement there would be no change; and if there were no change there would be no time. Time as a sense of before and after, a feeling of the flow, is subjective, and only minds could give it to the world; time as change is objective, and would doubtless go on if every mind were dead. Though no mind perceived it the tree would still bud and blossom, flourish and shed its leaves, through many springs and autumns, and then die; though no mind felt or measured it, the ebb tide would still follow the flow, and continents would still melt into the sea. The ocean rolled before Byron commanded it, and after he had lived the last line of his poetry. The world, even of time and space, is a brute fact, which a wise man will accept as not less valid than any metaphysic. Its existence is our condition, our limitation, and our source. What mind gives to the world is not existence, but significance; the world of things has no meaning but that which we pour into it. Perhaps that is why it is so unintelligible.

Let us hope that the epistemological fantasia in the movement of philosophy is over, and that the clear themes of the problems of life and death will soon be heard again. Idealism, beneficent though it was in tracing the contributions of the senses to the world which man perceived, had something disingenuous about it. If idealists had lived up to their theory, if they had behaved as though they really thought the external world unreal, we might have honored them as we honor saints who practice stoically their noble delusions; but strange to say, these deniers of the world lived and lusted like any realist, and yearned unreasonably for non-existent gold. Even Fichte, as Madame de Staël suggested, must have doubted, in his humbler moments, that he had created his wife by perceiving her.

It was from Germany, the land of fairy-tales, that this greatest fairy-story came, of the mind that made the world. And it was out of the Romantic Movement that this legend arose, as a reaction of sentiment and imagination against the realism, the materialism, and the scepticism of classical Voltairean days. It was a protest against the Copernican humiliation of mankind; in the face of Darwinism it grows fainter from day to day, and perhaps it will soon be still. One hears comparatively little of idealism in the philosophy of France; men there are more wont to desire without hypocrisy, and they do not think that in order to be immortal they must destroy the world. For the world was here before our coming, and will survive our going hence; it laughs when it hears that man is the measure of all things; it knows that man is only a line in Nature's Odyssey. Philosophy is an attempt to see the part in the light of the whole; let us be modest.

III. REASON VS. INSTINCT

We have dealt with the idealistic attack on the senses from above; now, before logic will let us come to grips with life, we must face the mystic attack on reason from below. Hume remarked that when reason is against a man the man will soon be against reason; if thought cannot rationalize desire into the semblance of logic, desire may, as a last resort, deny the authority of thought altogether. In a life based on hopes that far outdistance reason, it was to be expected that men would invent a logic, not of reason, that would justify their dreams.

And just as the materialist Democritus laid the bases of idealism, so the sceptic Zeno of Elea helped to make a case for mysticism. Zeno, a century before Socrates, poked fun at reason with "paradoxes" that reduced it to absurdity. Achilles pursues the tortoise; but the tortoise has a start, and therefore Achilles can never overtake it. For while Achilles traverses the distance from his starting point to where the tortoise began, the animal advances a certain distance, however small; and while Achilles covers this distance, the tortoise moves on again,—and so indefinitely, until you see that reason can prove anything, and consequently nothing at all.[1] Likewise, a moving arrow does not move. For so long as anything is in one and the same place

---

[1] The difficulty rests upon the supposition that the motion of Achilles and the tortoise can be divided endlessly into "moments." Cf. next note.

it is at rest; but a moving arrow is, at each moment, in one place alone; therefore it is at rest at that moment; therefore at every moment in its flight. "Anything can be proved by reasoning," Anatole France concludes. "Zeno of Elea has demonstrated that the flying arrow is motionless. One might also prove the contrary, although, to confess the truth, it would be more difficult." [1]

The Greeks and the Romans were Stoics, even when they were Epicureans; if they found that reason contradicted desire they accepted the limitation calmly, and sought to follow reason though they smiled at its pretensions. But out of the East the forces of mysticism, perpetually renewed in human hope, poured into Greece, and overwhelmed the frail and feebly-rooted Life of Reason that had flowered there. Divine inspiration and revelation came to comfort the oppressed; and when Greece was ruined and every Greek was poor, reason died, and faith (which never dies) put an end to the classic world. It mattered little now what logic proved; God had spoken wondrous things; and if they seemed impossible, so much the more glory would one win for believing them; *credo quia impossibile* became the motto of a million slaves. For fifteen centuries truth was defined not by sensation or reason, but by searching the Scriptures and convening the cardinals.

It was a great mistake when the Church permitted the Scholastic game of proving revelation with reason; how could she tell that the game would run smoothly, or that some unforeseen cleavage would not find the most brilliant minds seduced to the side of rationality? So it chanced. Descartes fell in love with reason, Spinoza starved for it, Bruno burned at the stake for it; and men honored the new mistress all the more for being sadistically cruel to her lovers. The worship of reason became itself a religion and a faith: the Enlightenment based upon it its noble belief in "the indefinite perfectibility of mankind"; and the Revolution raised altars to a beautiful Goddess of Reason. There was no boon which the intellect would not bring to men.

Rousseau was unhappy in this rarefied air; he suffered much, and needed much belief; when reason laughed at him, he called it a disease. "I venture to declare," he said, "that a state of reflection is contrary to nature, and

---

[1] *On Life and Letters,* London, 1924, vol. iv, p. vi. Bertrand Russell thinks Zeno correct in saying that the arrow is at rest in every moment of its flight, but he denies the inference that the arrow remains at the same point—though the inference seems logical. (Art. *Zeno, Encyclopedia Britannica,* and *Principles of Mathematics,* pp. 346 f.) It would be better, perhaps (if one wishes to play this game), to deny the premise, that an arrow which is at any moment in one and the same place must be at rest; this is a static interpretation of motion, which leaves motion out. There is no such thing as a "moment" in the sense of a station in time; time stops at no stations; it has movement, but no moments; the moments are our own intellectual parcelings of time's unbreakable continuity.

that a thinking man is a depraved animal." The story of Greece and the
Orient was played again; men wearied with life, and harassed with Revolution, Terror, and Glory, flocked back to faith, and covered their retreat with
an appeal to instinct and feeling. *Il faut déraisonner*, said De Musset; "we
must unreason." Hume, the sceptic, offered unwitting aid to the enemy, by
reducing causality, induction and science to the level of assumption and
probability; Kant, the subtlest reasoner of them all, repeated Zeno, and
told Europe that it might believe whatever it liked about God, free will and
immortality, since reason was an imperfect thing, unworthy of receiving
from man the sacrifice of Heaven and Utopia. Schopenhauer bared the
menial servitude of intellect to will, and Freud proved with a thousand instances the superficiality of a reason that merely clothed with respectable
argument the selfish purposes of the flesh. Nietzsche called instinct "the
most intelligent of all forms of intelligence." Bergson denounced the intellect
as a constitutional materialist, a cinema that missed, in its static fragments,
the continuity of life and the spirituality of the soul. All that long age from
Émile to *Creative Evolution*, from Rousseau and Kant through Schopenhauer and Nietzsche to Bergson and William James, was a Romantic reaction against the Age of Reason. Today the battle of Confucius against
Lao-tse, of Socrates against Zeno, of Voltaire against Rousseau, must be
fought anew; the ways of reason must be justified once more against instinct, intuition, mysticism, and unintelligible faith.

What is instinct? If we were to believe the latest fashions in psychology
we should reject it as a name for a non-existent thing; but when we find that
those who have thrown instinct out of the door are dragging it back through
the window as "unlearned response," we may be content to retain the old
bottles for the old wine, and call with the plain name of instinct our inherited tendencies to walk and run, to eat and play, to fight or seek escape,
to woo and wed, and love our children when they come.

These are useful economies of behavior, developed to meet, without the
delays of deliberation, recurrent exigencies in the career of the race. But
they adapt us only to these ancient and stereotyped situations; they were
built up against the needs and background of our animal and hunting life;
and though they serve us well when there is no time for thought, they adapt
us rather to yesterday than to today. A child will run from a snake, and
play with a loaded gun; a man may be a profound philosopher, and bind
himself for life to some decerebrated doll—so Socrates married Xanthippe,
and Goethe took Christiane. By instinct "we fear not the carriers of malaria
and yellow fever, but thunder and the dark; we pity not the gifted debarred
from education, but the beggar's bloody sore; we are less excited by a great
injustice than by a little blood; we suffer more from such scorn as untipped

waiters show than from our own idleness, ignorance and folly." [1] Instinct sufficed, perhaps, for the primitive life of the chase; it is to this, and not to tillage, that our natural impulses fit us, and for this that we long in our periodical and youthful desire to "return to nature." But ever since civilization began, instinct has been inadequate and life has called for reason.

When did the career of reason begin? Perhaps when the great surges of ice came down relentlessly from the Pole, chilling the air, destroying vegetation almost everywhere, eliminating countless species of helpless and unadaptable animals, and pushing a few survivors down into a narrow tropical belt, where for generations they clung to the equator, waiting for the wrath of the North to melt. Probably it was in those critical days, when all ancient and wonted ways of life were nullified by the invading cold, and inherited or traditional patterns of behavior found no success in an environment where everything was altered, that the animals with comparatively complete, but inflexible, instinctive equipment were weeded out because they could not change within to meet the change outside; while the animal we call man, dowered with a precarious plasticity, learned the arts of fire, of cooking, and of clothing, weathered the storm, and rose to an unquestioned supremacy over all the species of the forest and the field.

It was in some such life-and-death emergency as this, presumably, that human reasoning began. That same incompleteness and adaptability of native reactions which we see today in the infant, and which, though making it inferior to a new-born animal, leaves to it in recompense the possibility of learning—that same plasticity saved man and the higher mammals, while vast and powerful organisms like the mammoth and the mastodon, that had prowled about hitherto supreme, succumbed to the icy change, and became mere sport for paleontological curiosity. They shivered and passed away, while man, puny man, remained. Thought and invention began; the bewilderment of baffled instinct begot the first timid hypotheses, the first tentative putting together of two and two, the first generalizations, the first painful studies in similarities of quality and regularities of sequence, the first adaptation of things *learned* to situations so novel that reactions instinctive and immediate broke down in utter failure. It was then that certain patterns of action evolved into modes of thought and instruments of intelligence: what had been watchful waiting, or stalking a prey, became attention; fear and flight became caution and deliberation; pugnacity and assault became curiosity and analysis; manipulation became experiment. The animal stood up erect and became man, slave still to a thousand circumstances, timidly brave before countless perils, but in his precarious way destined henceforth to be master of the earth.

Out of such beginnings reason grew till now, as Graham Wallas thinks,

[1] Thorndike, E. L., *The Original Nature of Man,* p. 281.

it, too, is partly instinctive. Given a new situation, it is by instinct that we hesitate; and thereby at last the varied aspects of the problem arouse each its own incipient reaction in us, until our response is a complex and relatively complete reaction to a situation almost completely perceived. Reflex action is a local response to a local stimulus, as when we scratch a sore; instinct is a general response to one element in a situation, as when we pursue a pretty face; reason is total response to the total situation; therefore, it ruins love, and might destroy the race. Just as sensations weave themselves, under the bludgeoning of desire, into the order of ideas and thought, so instincts and habits, in delayed response, fall after a thousand trials and errors into the semblance of reason. Between instinct and reason there is a difference not of kind but only of degree; one provides the elements of the other. Deliberation is the alternation of conflicting impulses; discernment or discretion is the separation of a situation into its elements, as a prelude to complete reaction. Reason is the analysis of stimulus and the synthesis of response.

Its weakness lies in the delay that gives it birth. Many a blossoming philosopher has been destroyed by a situation before he could analyze it to his satisfaction. "If we reflect too long," said the syndicalist Griffuehles, "we shall never accomplish anything." Hence the syndicalists of France liked the intuitionism of Bergson; he proposed a cloture on thought, and suggested conclusions and explosions first, and reasoning afterward—in the leisure that would ensue. Moreover, reason, when it forgets its loyalty to sensation, may put the premium not on evidence but on subtlety; then it becomes like written history, a meretricious advocate of any powerful desire. Reason, as every school-girl now informs us, may be only the technique of rationalizing desire; for the most part we do not do things because we have reasons for them, but we find reasons for them because we want to do them. It is the simplest thing in the world to construct a philosophy out of our wishes and our interests. We must be on our guard against being communists because we are poor, or conservatives because our ship is in. Whatever philosophy delights us best must be most suspected. "What we need," as Bertrand Russell says so well, "is not the will to believe, but the wish to find out, which is the exact opposite." [1]

Or again, thinking may lead to scepticism, dilettantism, and futility: each reason begets an equal and opposite reason with almost the fatality of the second law of motion. "That is undoubtedly true," says Anatole France to Brousson; "but the contrary is also true." [2] And he quotes from the mystic Barrès: "That which distinguishes an argument from a play upon words is that the latter cannot be translated." [3]

[1] *Sceptical Essays*, p. 157.
[2] *Anatole France en Pantoufles*, p. 45.
[3] *On Life and Letters*, Fourth Series, p. vi.

Yes, reason is an imperfect instrument, like medical science, or the human eye; we do the best we can with it within the limits which fate and nature set. We do not doubt that some things are better done by instinct than by thought: perhaps it is wiser, in the presence of Cleopatra, to thirst like Antony rather than to think like Cæsar; it is better to have loved and lost than to have reasoned well. But why is it better? Is it because instinct is sounder, or because a mystic intuition has revealed this wisdom to us? No, but because experience—yes, in the long run, sensation—has taught us that a moment of rapture is worth a year of reasoning.

If we reason it is not because we like to, but because we must; our modern world is too slippery and fluent to let itself be met with stereotyped response. There may yet be ancient avenues of life in which instinct will serve—motherhood, or tillage, or the home; but even here reason has to enter as contraception limits instinctive motherhood, and woman is drawn out of the simple home into complicated industry, and the once isolated farm is caught up into a mesh of relationships with middlemen and distant markets and crafty financiers. As for us in the city, immediate and instinctive response becomes every day more perilous. For each instinct has an egoism and a selfishness of its own, and seeks its particular satisfaction at whatever cost to the total personality; each is a part of us that pretends to the throne. Only by weaving these parts together can we achieve clarity, wholeness, sanity and reason.

Consider the sexual instinct: it drives us on to copulation, perhaps to promiscuity; its vision is narrowed by its own intensity, and it does not stop to think of the results. We marry by instinct, and with reason we are divorced. Instinct would throw every girl into the arms of the first soldier that came her way; it would make every husband an adulterer, and every mother only a mother, marking each weaning with another pregnancy; it would multiply mouths as fast as intellect and invention could multiply goods, and the last condition of man would be as bad as the first. By instinct the starving man, finding food, gorges himself, and dies; by instinct the child, learning to walk, marches blithely over the top of the stairs or the edge of the porch; by instinct we tremble with useless fear when the caged lions roar at the zoo; by instinct the timid recruit becomes, in battle, a beast red in tooth and claw, blind with hatred and despair, and doomed to a dirty death; while the instructed and deliberate general stands safely in the rear, writes the story of *his* victory, and coming home inherits the earth.

Therefore we leave to our patient brothers in the monastery their unverifiable intuitions and their consoling but precarious faith, as we leave to our cousins in the jungle and the forest the superior precision and directness of their instincts. "Man," said Confucius, "differs from the animal only by a little; most men throw that little away." For our part we cast in our lot with sensation and reason, content to accept life as the test of our thinking, and resolved, if we can, to add thinking to our life. We shall fall into many errors, and there is no surety that we shall find happiness in the end; the joy of understanding is a joy shot through with pain, even like the lovers' ecstasy. We shall shed many certainties as our thought gropes on, and delusions that gave us courage will fall away. But "a life without reasoning is unworthy of man"; it is better to be Socrates in prison than Caliban on the throne. Let us reason together.

PART THREE

METAPHYSICS

CHAPTER III

Matter, Life, and Mind[1]

I. AGNOSTIC PRELUDE

WHAT IS THE NATURE of the world? What are its matter and form, its constituents and structure, its ultimate substances and laws? What is matter in its innermost quality, in the secret essence of its being? What is mind?— and is it forever distinct from matter, and master of it, or a derivative of matter, and its slave? Are both the external world which we see in perception, and the internal world which we feel in consciousness, subject to mechanical or deterministic laws, so that

> The First Morning of Creation wrote
> What the Last Dawn of Reckoning shall read—

or is there in matter, or in mind, or in both, an element of chance, spontaneity, and freedom? These are questions which few men ask, and which all men answer; they are the final sources of our philosophies, on which everything else, in a coherent system of thought, must at last depend. We would rather know the answers to these questions than possess all the goods of the earth.

Let us resign ourselves at once to inevitable failure. And not merely because this one realm of philosophy would require, for its mastery, a completely known and completely adequate mathematics, astronomy, physics, chemistry, mechanics, biology, and psychology; but because it is not reasonable to expect that the part should ever understand the whole. That total

[1] See footnote to Table of Contents.

perspective which is our lure in these airy adventures will here elude all the snares and magnets of our thought. A little modesty and a little honesty are enough to assure us that life and the world are too complex and subtle for our imprisoned minds. Very probably our most honored theories would form a subject of irony and pity among omniscient gods; and all that we can do is to pride ourselves on having discovered the abysses of our ignorance. The more we learn, the less we know; every advance reveals new mysteries and new uncertainties; the molecule discloses the atom, the atom discloses the electron, the electron discloses the quantum, and the quantum defies and overleaps all our categories and all our laws. Education is a moulting of dogmas, a progress in the art of doubt. Our instruments, we perceive, are bound up with matter, and our senses are bound up with mind; it is through these mists that we "flakes on the water" would comprehend the sea.

Therefore we approach these problems like a priest mounting the altar to perform for the first time the mystery of the Mass. We shall not solve those problems; at best we shall merely bare to one another the secret preferences of our hearts. If religion has offended us by too great belief, we may react in protest to a bold materialism, as the reckless Shelley, believer in God and immortality, called himself "atheist" to fling his challenge into the face of a smug and reactionary Church. If we are tender-minded we shall cling to faith, and look upon a mechanical and Godless world as too hard to be borne. Or perhaps we are mellowing into age, and the rebellions of our youth seem now unnecessary and extreme; truth shines out again from old ideas that once seemed treacherous and false; and we accept with grateful welcome any news from the world of science or history that may restore to us some glimmer of our ancient creeds. All our physics and chemistry, all our astronomy and biology, will be but hunting grounds in which we shall seek dignity for our assumptions, or comfort for our hopes.

Nevertheless. . . .

II. MATERIALISM

As materialism is the first philosophy to be adopted by a mind that has thrown off supernatural belief, so it is the first conception of the world that appears in a nation whose official theology has begun to die. The pre-Socratic thinkers, whom Bacon and Nietzsche rated above their famous successors, were nearly all materialists. Thales, Anaximander and Anaximenes interpreted the universe as a derivative of water, fire, or air; and Leucippus and Democritus gave to materialism that atomic form which satisfied all orthodox heretics until the atom burst into pieces under the impact of modern physics and chemistry.

For many generations this simplest of philosophies maintained itself against the scepticism of Zeno and the dualism of Anaxagoras. Then Socrates "turned round" from the external world, and discovered a self so different from matter that he thought it might be immune to death. Plato called matter "nothing," and reverenced mind above all things; he saw the outer world as subject to mind in perception, and to Ideas in structure and operation; all the world seemed to him a middling copy of a perfect model conceived by some creative spirit. Aristotle, the biologist, found the world a changing and striving thing, and could not quite reduce it to "atoms and the void"; its essence was *entelechy*—in every substance some potency was hidden that left no rest until it was realized; every "form" was the "matter" of a higher form, and all reality was pregnant with development; materialism could not adequately describe this burgeoning vitality. For a century Democritus was forgotten.

He had his avatar and revenge in Epicurus, who almost anticipated Planck and Bohr and the Curies by finding in the atom a principle of liberty and uncertainty, and yet a symbol of exhaustion and decay; all things were free, and all things would die. Lucretius, sickened with life, was glad to hear of this certain and endless death; it seemed to him a beautiful, though sombre, thing that even poets were made of atoms, and that every organism, and every atom, would disintegrate and pass away, safe from suffering forevermore.

Then Christianity came, and for fifteen hundred years matter was a pariah in philosophy. Some of the early heterodox sects conceived the soul as a fine gas, and God himself as a yet finer gas,—approaching Haeckel's youthful definition of the deity as a "gaseous vertebrate"; but for the most part matter was a fallen angel, the Lucifer of philosophy, a tribulation and a dungeon for the spirit. Strange to say, matter found high place in the philosophy of Aquinas; it was made potentially as old as time, and it became the "principle of individuation": through its forms and limitations the One became Many, and the ocean of spirit was divided into little pools called immortal souls.

However, it was not until Descartes that matter began to come into its own. True enough, the cautious Gaul did not exalt it into the one reality; and in beginning his philosophy with the self and thought ("I think, therefore I am"), he opened the door to that very idealism which was to become matter's subtlest foe. But he conceived the external world as a mechanism, and the proudest animals as somnolent machines; everything but the soul of man obeyed the principles of physics; and even the intricate phenomena of digestion, respiration, secretion and reproduction declared the glory of mechanics. It was in this hard cosmology of Descartes that materialism found its second youth.

There are two large movements in modern thought, the thesis and antithesis, as Hegel would say, of a synthesis which our own generation must begin to make. The first starts with the external world—with matter, physics, mechanics, and mathematics; it represents, as in the rebellion of the disillusioned individual, the first and extreme reaction against a supernatural reading of the universe; it formulates the laws of reality from the observation of matter, and then interprets mind in terms of these objective laws; inevitably its conclusions are materialism, mechanism, determinism, and a behaviorism that prides itself on its natural inability to pass from matter to consciousness; its heroes are Galileo, Descartes, Hobbes, Newton, Diderot, Holbach, La Mettrie, Haeckel, Spencer, Russell and Watson. The equal and opposite movement begins with consciousness, and finds itself unable to pass from it to matter; it takes its stand within the internal world—with mind, psychology, epistemology and ethics; it represents an extreme reaction against a materialistic conception of the universe; it sees all things as sensations and ideas, and therefore reduces matter to a state of mind; inevitably its conclusions are spiritualism, idealism, vitalism, and free will; and its heroes are Descartes (*vide supra*), Leibnitz, Berkeley, Kant, Fichte, Hegel, Schopenhauer, Nietzsche, Bergson, and William James. So hostile philosophies war with one another, like male and female, and become fruitful only when they merge.

The first movement dominated the philosophic thought of Europe in the seventeenth and eighteenth centuries. Spinoza stood aside from this development, faced the problem for himself in his solitary attic, and offered the world panpsychism as a solution: matter and mind are the outside and inside of one complex reality, and "all things, in however different degree, are filled with life." Europe did not believe it. On the contrary, Hobbes reduced reality to matter, and denounced as scholastic verbiage any term or phrase that did not indicate material conditions. Gassendi politely submitted to Descartes various objections to his dualistic conception of the independence of matter and mind, and suggested that philosophy had not yet improved on the theorems of Democritus. Newton, while sincerely professing the most orthodox piety, and writing weird commentaries on the Apocalypse, analyzed the external world into laws of motion so simple and orderly that when they were imported into France its logic-loving philosophers could not resist the conclusion that these laws applied to everything from the fall of an apple to a maiden's prayer. La Mettrie came forward bravely with his book on *Man the Machine,* and showed how various corporeal states, like enthusiasm or disease, correspondingly affect the mind, and betray its physical constitution; Holbach brought man and matter alike into his rigid and logical *System of Nature;* and Helvétius reduced morality and virtue to physical laws. Diderot was not certain that epistemology could explain consciousness; he felt himself obliged to conclude, with Spinoza, that matter is instinct with mind; but he was resolved for spite to call himself a materialist "until the last king had been strangled with the entrails of the last priest."

Materialism is brother to socialism: it is a flag of protest waved in the face of reaction and tyranny by rebellious and unplaced youth; it is a flag which middle age quietly furls and takes in when thought, growing in maturity and modesty, perceives the irrational complexity of the living world.

III. IDEALISM

Meanwhile the second movement had found its prophet in Bishop Berkeley. After all, said the Bishop, this matter of yours is known to you only through sensation and perception; its *esse est percipi*—if it could not be perceived by some mind, it would not (so far as we could ever tell) exist at all. Not only that, added Kant; these sensations are in themselves a jumble without meaning; it is the "transcendental unity of apperception" that weaves the chaotic reports of many senses into the world of ordered thought; the order and the unity, it may be, are contributed by the mind, and the "thing" is half created by our perceiving it. How could such a constitutive mind be a passive product of the matter whose very form it has produced?

You are right, said the clearest head of them all, Arthur Schopenhauer; the sole reality that we can directly and intimately observe is our own introspected selves. It is ridiculous to reduce that which we know so immediately, to a "matter" which is known to us only as an idea in our thought, and solely through the distorting intermediary of our imperfect senses. Perhaps if we could know matter from within as well as from without, as we can know ourselves, we should find, in the heart of matter, an energy of will far more akin to the subtle power of our minds than to the external and menial mechanism of our flesh. Under these circumstances, materialism is, in strict logic, impossible. Büchner, Moleschott and Feuerbach are simpletons:

> The crude materialism which even now, in the middle of the nineteenth century, has been served up again under the ignorant delusion that it is original, . . . stupidly denies vital force, and first of all tries to explain the phenomena of life from physical and chemical forces, and those again from the mechanical effects of matter. . . . But I will never believe that even the simplest chemical combinations will ever admit of mechanical explanation; much less the properties of light, heat, and electricity. These will always require a dynamical explanation.[1]

Nietzsche inherited this view of matter along with that "will-to-power" which was his pirated edition of Schopenhauer's "will." No pietist could be more hostile to materialism than this scorner of priests and theologies. "Absolute exclusion of mechanism and matter" is his uncompromising pro-

[1] *The World as Will and Idea,* vol. i, p. 159; vol. iii, p. 43.

gram; "both only forms of expression for the lower stages, the least spiritual shape that the will to power takes." He swallows the idealistic position whole, like a good German; matter, he thinks, is a delusion, a mental construct which we make to explain our sensations. "As regards materialistic atomism it is one of the best-refuted theories that have ever been advanced; and in Europe there is now perhaps no one in the learned world so unscholarly as to attach serious signification to it." And he concludes like Schopenhauer: "The hypothesis must be hazarded whether all mechanical action, inasmuch as a power operates therein, is not just the power of will, the effect of will." An atom is merely a quantum of the Will to Power.[1]

It is astonishing what influence idealism has had upon rebels inclined to materialism as a weapon against religious belief. "Were we compelled to choose," said Herbert Spencer, "between the alternatives of translating mental phenomena into physical phenomena, or translating physical phenomena into mental phenomena, the latter alternative would seem the more acceptable of the two." [2] And Bertrand Russell, that charming apostle of despair, writes, in our own day:

> The belief that matter alone is real will not survive the sceptical arguments derived from the physiological mechanism of sensation. . . . Historically we may regard materialism as a system of dogma set up to combat orthodox dogma. . . . Accordingly we find that as ancient orthodoxies disintegrate, materialism more and more gives way to scepticism. At the present day the chief protagonists of materialism are certain men of science in America and certain politicians in Russia, because it is in those two countries that traditional theology is still powerful.[3]

IV. WHAT IS MATTER?

Passing over these epistemological doubts, as having been sufficiently considered in preceding pages, and taking it for granted that the external world, which is forever giving us the most irritating and indisputable reminders of its existence, is "objectively real," let us push forward, and inquire into its constitution.

Our first discovery is that the old inert matter of nineteenth-century physics is gone. The "matter" of Tyndall and Huxley was indestructible; it rested and slept, like the fat boy in *Pickwick Papers,* wherever it was put; and it resisted, with all the dignity of its volume and weight, every effort to set it moving, or to change the direction of its motion once it had

---

[1] *Will to Power,* §§ 712 and 634; *Joyful Wisdom,* § 109; *Beyond Good and Evil,* §§ 12 and 36.

[2] *Principles of Psychology,* vol. i, p. 159.

[3] Introduction to Lange's *History of Materialism,* pp. xi, xii.

condescended to move. With the greatest ease Bergson showed that so inert a substance could never explain motion, much less produce life and mind. But even as Bergson wrote, physicists were abandoning the conception of matter as inert, and were discovering in it an unsuspected vitality. Here, for example, was electricity—utterly inexplicable in terms of inertia and atoms; what was this mystical force which, added to mass, increased its energy, but added nothing to its dimensions and its weight? How did an electric charge travel along a wire, or through the wireless air? Was it something that moved through the atoms of the wire—and then there were atoms smaller than the atoms? And in those electric waves, almost as fleet as light itself, what was it that moved?—atoms, or "ether," or nothing? Or when, in the X-ray, an electric spark passed through a vacuum, emitting rays that penetrated the walls of the tube and changed a chemically sensitive plate,— what was it that passed through the vacuum or the walls? And when, as in radium, matter seemed inexhaustibly active, and atoms (the "uncuttable") seemed indefinitely divisible, and every atom became a planetary system of electric charges moving about nothing more substantial than another electric charge—to what a pass had matter come to have lost its mass and weight and length and breadth and depth and impenetrability, and almost all those sturdy properties that had once won it the reverence of every tough and matter-of-fact mind! Was inertia, then, a myth? Could it be that matter was alive?

There had been signs of this energy in matter before: cohesion, affinity, and repulsion had suggested it. Now it seemed probable that these, as well as electricity and magnetism, were forms of "atomic energy," phenomena due to the restless motion of electrons in the atom. But what is the electron? Is it a bit of "matter" manifesting energy, or is it a measure of energy quite dissociated from any material subtance? The latter is inconceivable to us. "It would no doubt be possible," says Le Bon, "for a higher intelligence to conceive energy without substance; . . . but such a conception cannot be achieved by us. We can only understand things by fitting them into the common frame of our thoughts. The essence of energy being unknown, we are compelled to materialize it in order to reason about it." [1] We are, as Bergson put it, constitutional materialists; we are accustomed to dealing with matter and mechanisms; and unless we turn away from them to look into ourselves, we shall picture everything as a material machine. And yet Ostwald describes matter as merely a form of energy; Rutherford reduces the atom to units of positive and negative electricity; Lodge believes that the electron does not contain a material nucleus in addition to its charge; and Le Bon says simply: "Matter is a variety of energy." [2] "Some of the ablest men in the world at present," says J. B. S. Haldane, "regard matter

[1] *Op. cit.,* p. 13.
[2] *The Evolution of Matter,* p. 10.

as merely a special type of undulatory disturbance." [1] Matter, says Eddington, is composed of protons and electrons—i. e., positive and negative charges of electricity; a plank "is really empty space containing sparsely scattered electric charges." [2] "The notion of mass," says Whitehead, "is losing its unique preëminence as being the one final permanent quantity. . . . Mass now becomes the name for a quantity of energy considered in relation to some of its dynamical effects." [3] To such low state have the mighty fallen. We come back to the old Jesuit, Boscovich, to the incomprehensible proposition that matter, which occupies "space," is composed of points which do not. "Boscovich and Copernicus," said Nietzsche, "have hitherto been the greatest and most successful opponents of ocular evidence." [4] No wonder Dewey concludes that "the notion of matter actually found in the practice of science has nothing in common with the matter of materialists." [5]

Could anything be more mystical and anomalous than this announcement, by physicists, that "matter," in the sense of spatial substance, has ceased to exist? The electrons, we are told, have none of the properties of matter: they are not solid, nor liquid, nor gaseous; they have neither mass nor form; and their dissociation in radio-activity casts doubt upon the dearest dogma of modern science—the "indestructibility of matter." Hear a physicist again:

> The elements of atoms which are dissociated . . . are irrevocably destroyed. They lose every quality of matter—including the most fundamental of them all, weight. The balance no longer detects them. Nothing can recall them to the state of matter. They have vanished in the immensity of the ether. . . . Heat, electricity, light, etc., . . . represent the last stages of matter before its disappearance into the ether. . . . Matter which dissociates *dematerializes* itself by passing through successive phases which gradually deprive it of its material qualities, until it finally returns to the imponderable ether whence it seems to have issued.[6]

Ether?—but what is this ether? Nobody knows. The ether, said Lord Salisbury, is only a noun for the verb to undulate; [7] it is a fiction created to conceal the learned ignorance of modern science; it is as mystical as a ghost or a soul. Einstein, by reinterpreting gravitation, deposed the ether; latterly he has decided to restore it for a while, with a limited sovereignty; whenever a physicist is puzzled he answers, "Ether." The ether, says the latest authority, Professor Eddington, "is not a kind of matter"; it is "non-

[1] *Possible Worlds*, p. 296.
[2] *The Nature of the Physical World*, p. 3. Really?
[3] *Science and the Modern World*, p. 149.
[4] *Beyond Good and Evil*, § 12.
[5] *Experience and Nature*, p. 74.
[6] Le Bon, *op. cit.*, pp. 7, 12, 14.
[7] In William James, *The Meaning of Truth*, p. 59.

material." [1] That is to say, a non-material something, by certain mysterious contortions (vortices, as Lord Kelvin called them), transforms itself into matter; that which is without dimension or weight becomes, by adding bits of it together, spatial and ponderable matter. Is this theology restored, or a new Christian Science, or a form of psychical research? At the very moment when psychology is attempting by every prestidigitation to get rid of consciousness in order to reduce mind to matter, physics regrets to report that matter does not exist. "O physics!" Newton exclaimed, "preserve me from metaphysics!" [2] Alas, it cannot any more.

"Physical science," says Bertrand Russell, "is approaching the stage when it will be complete." [3] The evidence is all to the contrary. According to Henri Poincaré, modern physics is in a state of chaos, reconstructing all its bases, and meanwhile hardly knowing where it stands. The fundamental ideas of physics have completely changed in the last twenty years, in regard to both matter and motion; the work of the Curies, of Rutherford and Soddy, of Einstein and Minkowski, has not allowed any of the classical conceptions of the Newtonian physics to survive. Laplace envied Newton for having found "the" system of the world, and mourned that there were no other systems to discover. But the Newtonian world is all awry now; gravitation is no longer a matter of "attraction," and the "laws" of motion have been wrenched in every direction by the theory of relativity. Once philosophy dealt with "shadows" and abstractions, and science dealt with substance, the "concrete," and "matter-of-fact" realities; now physics is an esoteric mass of abstract formulas, and "in the scientific world the concept of substance is wholly lacking." [4] Philosophy was to be set aside (some people still predict its death "within fifty years") while science was to solve our problems; now, just at a time when the man in the street is transferring to science and scientists all the notions of inspiration and infallibility that were once attached to the Bible and the Church, we are modestly informed that "scientific investigation does not lead to knowledge of the intrinsic nature of things." [5] Instead, we are told that a clock goes faster according to the speed with which it is carried through space, and that a ruler can be lengthened by the simple process of changing its position from a right angle to a straight line with the direction of the earth's motion. We must be humble in the face of the unintelligible formulas which have replaced the ancient clarity of physics; who knows but they may be correct? However, one suspects a science that grows more erudite from day to day, and every day refutes its yesterday; that offers us atoms, and then electrons, and then quanta, and at last a holy picture of a material world mi-

[1] *Op. cit.*, p. 32.
[2] In Brousson, *Anatole France en Pantoufles*, p. 218.
[3] *What I Believe*, p. 2.
[4] Eddington, p. 274.
[5] *Ibid.*, p. 303.

raculously built out of electric charges having no material nuclei. Spengler alone has the courage to call this what it is: "every atomic theory is a myth, and not an experience." [1]

Let us be on our guard against theology wherever we find it, even when we come upon it in the "exact" sciences. Probably matter continues to exist despite our shifty omniscience; and the stone that encountered Dr. Johnson's toe was at least as real as his pain. It is true that the stone, for the Doctor, was but a "bundle of perceptions," as Hume was to describe it; but then that sort of a bundle—that obstreperous resistance to our muscles and our senses,—is just what we mean by matter. We may indulge ourselves in the new scholasticism of science, but in actual life we shall expect to find all energy associated with matter, with something spatial and ponderable, "something, not ourselves, that makes for" sensations.

What that matter is, we do not yet know; and let us say so unmistakably. But one thing is certain—that this attenuated matter is not the old inert matter of nineteenth-century science; it is the form and vehicle of incalculable energies. It is alive with cohesions, affinities, repulsions, electrolytic and osmotic processes, heat and electricity and leaping light, and the restless dance of electrons. Movement, energy, vitality are everywhere; we no longer dare call anything lifeless. "A body as rigid in appearance as a block of steel represents simply a state of equilibrium between its own internal energy and the external energies—heat, pressure, etc.—which surround it. . . . When we place our hand near a block of metal, the movement of its molecules is modified." [2] The old simile of Lucretius becomes additionally significant:

> When mighty legions, waging the mimicry of war, fill with their movements all the plain, the glitter of it lifts itself to the sky, and the whole earth gleams with brass, and from below rises the noise of the tramping of men, and the mountains, stricken by the shouting, re-echo the voices to the stars of heaven. . . . And yet there is some spot on the high hills from which all these moving men seem to stand still and merely to shine as a spot of brightness on the plains. [3]

The more we study matter the less we see it as fundamental, the more we perceive it as merely the externality of energy, as our flesh is the outward

---

[1] *The Decline of the West,* vol. i, p. 387. In this most erudite and chaotic of contemporary thinkers the word *scientific* has lost its aroma of perfection, and becomes playfully derogatory. All science, to Spengler, is a *fable convenue,* a mythology in which "electricity," "positional energy," "forces" and "laws" take the places of demons and gods, and the schematizing intellect cramps the actualities of life into the forms of mathematics and mechanics. "It will be the characteristic task of the twentieth century to get rid of this system of superficial causality." Vol. ii, pp. 180, 30, 56, 144, 31.

[2] Le Bon, *op. cit.,* pp. 248–9.

[3] *On the Nature of Things,* tr. Munro, Book ii, lines 323 f.

sign of life and mind. "In respect to 'action,' " says Eddington, "physics has taken the bit in her teeth, and has insisted on recognizing this as the most fundamental thing of all." [1] A Hindu physicist, Sir Jagadis Chandra Bose, has shown "fatigue" in metals—their inability to continue their normal reactions to certain agents beyond a certain time—and the disappearance of this fatigue after rest; and he has demonstrated the sensitivity of metals to excitants, depressants, and poisons. These experiments have been repeated and verified on three continents. [2] The expression, "the life of matter," meaningless twenty-five years ago, has come into common use. "We now see physicists and chemists groping after biological ideas; the extension of biological concepts to the whole of nature may be much nearer than seemed conceivable even a few years ago." [3] We hear of the "evolution of matter"; the atom, it seems, is born, develops, loses its vitality, and dies.

This modern physics of energy invites us to reformulate the old problem of materialism vs. spiritualism. Which aspect of the external world is more fundamental—the spatial, extended aspect, which physics once described as "matter," or the activating, moving aspect which we name energy? The answer must be energy; this is the "Unknowable," the "Thing-in-Itself," the "Absolute." Is this energy itself a spatial and extended thing, a material substance? We cannot conceive it so, any more than we can conceive thought to be spatial and material. In the heart of matter, giving it form and power, is something not material, possessed of its own spontaneity and life; and this subtle, hidden and yet always revealed vitality is the final essence of everything that we know.

But these words, "heart" and "in," are metaphors, beckoning us into a blind alley; we must not let ourselves think of energy as something distinct from matter, and dwelling in it as the mercury lurked in the statues of Dædalus to give them stability and apparent life. This vital element, this activating energy, is not, as most vitalists think, a separate entity, divorcible from matter; it is inextricably bound up with it, as mind is with body, and forms with matter the inward and outward aspects of one indivisible whole. In a large sense the materialist is right: what he meant to do, by exalting matter, was to express his faith that there is no break in the continuity of development, that philosophers have descended from apes, and apes from protozoa, and these from supposedly inorganic substances, and these from the simplest atoms. But we cannot believe this unless we also believe that within the apparently inert body of matter (the spatial metaphor steals in again) there is a principle of life, a power compelling evolution. We bridge the gap between matter and mind not by reducing mind but by raising matter. The world is as the materialist thought, one world, every particle of it

---

[1] P. 240.

[2] Le Bon, pp. 250-1.

[3] Haldane, J. S., *Mechanism, Life and Personality*, p. 101.

materially formed; but throughout every particle of that material world there works a spontaneous energy which is the analogue and promise of life and mind. We may say of the dullest clod what Heraclitus said when he received distinguished visitors into his prosaic and primitive kitchen. "Come," he told them, "enter; for here, too, there are gods."

V. LIFE

We have tried to reconcile spiritualism and materialism by combining the basic position of one—that the core of all things is more akin to mind than to matter—with two of the most fundamental positions of the other— that life and mind are irrevocably bound up with matter, and that all higher (i. e., more complex) structures have evolved from lower structures of less complexity. We have defended the first position out of the mouths of physicists themselves; but we have still to face the difficulties involved in the other proposition. Let us take the last problem first, and inquire into the continuity between the highest and the lowest forms of reality.

If this continuity involves abiogenesis—the development of life from non-living things—then the evidence of biology is against it. There is no known case of such a development. The experiments of Pasteur, carried on over a period of seven years (1862–9), seem to disprove the notion that protozoa could arise from inorganic matter; and the opinion of contemporary science repeats in various forms the motto of Sir William Harvey— *omne ovum ex ovo, omnis cellula e cellula, omne vivum e vivo:* every egg comes from an egg, every cell from a cell, every life from a living thing. "There is not the remotest possibility," says J. S. Haldane, "of deriving the organic from the inorganic." [1] "To create living matter?" exclaims Gustave Bonnier—"How can it be hoped for for an instant in the present state of science, when we think of how many accumulated characteristics, how much heredity, how much complicated future, there are in a fragment of living protoplasm?" [2]

But despite the form of this doubt, one suspects that these sceptics, half unconsciously, are comparing "dead" matter with complex organisms; the difficulty diminishes when we restrict it to the gap between the simplest organism and the most complex colloid. Synthetic chemistry today produces 130,000 organic carbon-compounds; only a dogmatist who has not yet learned the practicability of the "impossible" can be sure that chemistry will never produce life. What nature does, is possible, and may some day be learned by man; but whenever a plant changes the rays of the sun and the chemicals of the soil into its own sap and tissue we have the transforma-

[1] *Mechanism, Life and Personality*, p. 100.
[2] In Le Bon, *The Evolution of Forces*, p. 369.

tion of inorganic into organic substances. True, the agency of a living being is here involved; but the transformation is none the less real, and is the natural counterpart and balance of that equally mysterious, but evidently not impossible, process whereby the organic is changed into the inorganic in corruption and death. Organic and inorganic are perhaps two aspects or polarities in one process of evolution and dissolution. Who knows but that matter, as Fechner suggested, may have degenerated from living substance, and that the inorganic and the "mechanical" are the relic and waste of departed life?

Presumably the earth was once unfit for organisms, and presumably life appeared upon it only when a suitable environment had come. It will not help us to follow Arrhenius to distant stars as the source of life; to postpone a problem is not to meet it. Let us suppose that a catastrophe kills all plant and animal life on the earth; and let us suppose the re-appearance, after a long interval, of a climate as mild and moist as that which prevails on our planet today, with all other related physico-chemical conditions. Is it not probable that the soil would again produce bacteria, protozoa, vegetation, and a million forms of life? Once we accept evolution we cannot limit it; there is no place in the line, from Shakespeare down to Paramecium, at which we may stop and abandon continuity for a miraculous interposition. As Huxley argued that the gap between man and the chimpanzee is not so great as that between the lowest monkeys and the highest apes, so we may say that the gap between synthetic proteins and the *Amœba* is a smaller distance than the unbroken line that separates and connects the *Amœba* and the saint.

The new conception of matter as "alive" softens the contrast between organic and inorganic, and reduces the difficulty of conceiving continuous evolution. Life is a product not of that outward aspect of reality which gives us weight, solidity, and extension, but of that inner aspect which gives us the energy of the atom, the electric restlessness of the "ether," and the groping vitality of the cell. The simple conceptions of nineteenth-century physics and chemistry made the gap between living and non-living things impassable; and even Spencer, though eager to make evolution complete, was compelled to shirk the problem, and to write: "We are obliged to confess that Life in its essence cannot be conceived in physico-chemical terms." [1] When physics and chemistry learn to accept the concept of life as coterminous with the concept of matter, the division of reality and development into irreconcilable halves disappears; and a matter whose core is vitality combines with a life whose form is matter, to give to the world that complete unity and complete harmony without which neither science nor philosophy will ever rest.

[1] *Principles of Biology*, vol. i, p. 120.

VI. THE MATERIALIST SPEAKS

But if there is some difficulty in accepting the development of life from inorganic substance, how much more difficult it will seem to accept the natural evolution of what we mystically call the "mind"! "The development of matter" (old style) "into a thinking subject," said Nietzsche, "is impossible." [1] We shall find here, as before, that the conception of matter as inert leads to an *impasse* of difficulties which can only be overcome at the cost of sacrificing the continuity of evolution. Spiritualism and materialism again offer us their irrefutable arguments, and leave us torn between two halves of the truth that are not content to be parts of a whole. Let us follow these half-truths for a while.

The materialist begins by "establishing continuity." Bose's experiments indicate a certain sensitivity in matter: so a thin rod of platinum in the bolometer [2] responds to a rise of one one-hundred-millionth degree in temperature.[3] Doubtless this sensitivity is of a different kind than that which we find in organisms; it does not lead to an adaptive reaction increasing the power of the subject over its environment; but it offers us some suggestion of the way in which nature bridged the chasm between "matter" and "mind."

The next stage in the evolution of mind is visible in the sensitive reaction of plants to position, contact, temperature, moisture, and light. Yerkes believes that the chief power and characteristic of mind—the ability to learn, to respond differently as the result of experience—is a mark of even the lowest protoplasm. It was Bose again who thrilled the British Association for the Advancement of Science by demonstrating before them [4] the detailed resemblance between the circulatory systems in plant and man, and the susceptibility of the flowing sap to stimulants, depressants, and poisons. Edward Tangl discovered delicate threads of protoplasm, passing from cell to cell of the plant, which most botanists consider analogous to the nerve fibrils in animals.[5] Certain plants are so sensitive to light that they have been turned into "floral clocks." There are five hundred species of insectivorous plants, some of which, as Darwin showed, have sensitive papillae capable of detecting one seventy-eight-thousandth of a gramme.[6] In this primitive adaptation of reaction to ends beneficial to the organism we have the first definite beginnings of mind.

Sensitiveness increased with mobility. Plants, having the power to turn

---

[1] In Salter, *Nietzsche the Thinker,* p. 481.
[2] A delicate instrument for measuring radiant heat.
[3] McCabe, *The Evolution of Mind,* p. 33.
[4] Session of August 6, 1928.
[5] Holt, E. B., *The Concept of Consciousness,* p. 172.
[6] McCabe, *op. cit.,* p. 21.

inorganic material into food, did not have to move, except as they thrust their roots into the soil, or their stalks into the sky; but they paid for this simple life by sacrificing many of their powers of directive response. Plants that moved became animals, and developed that magnificent and painful organ of adventure and control—the nervous system. And yet in the lowest animals there is no nervous system; sensitivity—or irritability, as some nervous biologist christened it—is generalized, and appears impartially in all the tissues of the organism. But even in those lowly realms a certain specialization begins: in *Volvox* and other colony-forming protozoa the external cells show an especial irritability, while the internal or reproductive cells remain comparatively indifferent to outward stimuli. Another stage upward in the scale, and the specialization of sensibility increases: in the jelly-fish certain nerve cells projecting from the periphery of the organism are connected by a "nerve-net" ring of conductive cells running around the edge of the "umbrella"; here specialization has differentiated the nerve-cells into two classes—sensitive "end-organs," and conductive neural tissue. This is the first appearance of a nervous *system,* the potential instrument of mind.

In the flatworm two of the nerve-cells are of unusual size, and serve as "central ganglia" or brain for the other cells of the system. The localization of these ganglia near the mouth created the head; the head developed to protect the mouth, as the body grew around the stomach to protect and aid the processes of digestion. In the earthworm the nerve-line knots itself into ganglia in every segment of the body; and from this stage to man the nervous system is "segmented"—i. e., it is divided into ganglia corresponding, in the chordates, to the vertebræ of the spine. In the earthworm these ganglia, while connected, are almost independent of one another, so that any severed part may wriggle at its own sweet will. But with the mounting complexity of structure and function in the higher species, the necessity for connection and coördination grew; and though the spinal ganglia continued to serve as centers for local reflexes, the number of fibres passing from these centers to the cerebral ganglia in the head increased; and a "central nervous system" appeared, able to feel and govern the body as a whole. The integration is not complete even in man; many functions remain outside of cerebral control, subject only to that "sympathetic nervous system" which is our relic from the nerve-net stage. But what we call the "mind" operates apparently through the central or "cerebro-spinal" system above all; and the prime and primitive function of the mind is the integration of behavior, the subjection of motor responses to central guidance and control. It is obviously through the nervous system that thought became a reality.

If we may judge from embryology, the brain grew out of the enlargement of the olfactory nerve; it was a modest adjunct to the nose, and intelligence for some æons operated through the sense of smell. Then other nerves bound themselves up with the cerebral ganglia: nerves from the eyes, the face, the ears, the throat, the tongue, the neck, and the viscera. Bit by bit the spinal nerves were brought into the cerebral system, the head ruled the body more and more, and coördination, adaptation and control grew in action and reaction with the growing brain. In fishes the brain weighs $\frac{1}{5668}$ of the body; in reptiles, $\frac{1}{1321}$; in birds, $\frac{1}{212}$; in mammals, $\frac{1}{186}$; in a two-year-old chimpanzee, $\frac{1}{25}$; in a two-year-old child, $\frac{1}{18}$. This is the ladder by which we climbed.

One thing is clear, then: the most complex mind is a natural development from the unspecialized irritability of the simplest protoplasm in the lowest line; it represents merely one more specialization of living matter, one more organ for mastering the environment. Further, its complexity grows step by step, in the embryo and the phylum, in the individual and the race, with the developing complexity of structure in the nervous system; the growth from generalized sensitivity to local ganglia to cerebrum is accompanied by the advance from tropism to reflex to learned response. Extirpation of the cerebrum need not be fatal to animals, as Goltz showed with his dog; it is always fatal to man, because man cannot live if he forgets all that he has learned since birth. This individual experience seems stored up in the association-fibres of the cortex, which show so large a development from child to adult and from animal to man.

No one has ever answered the question how body and mind could act upon one another if they were so utterly distinct as mindless matter and immaterial mind. "For when the soul," said Lucretius, "is seen to move the limbs, or rouse the body from sleep, or alter the countenance, or guide and turn about the whole man; and when we see that none of these effects can take place without touch, nor touch without body, must we not admit that the mind and the soul are of the same nature as the body?" [1] Or pass over two thousand years and find Mark Twain playing philosopher:

> *Old Man* (sarcastically). Being spiritual, the mind cannot be affected by physical influences?
> *Young Man.* No.
> *Old Man.* Does the mind remain sober when the body is drunk? [2]

Insanity may come from injuries to the brain, sleep may come from fatigue, unconsciousness may come from drugs, disease, or lack of oxygen or blood. Consciousness depends upon sensations; Strümpell's boy, who had no other sense than sight, always fell asleep when he closed his eyes. In the sense of awareness, consciousness arises out of a conflict of impulses or reflexes; where there is no conflict the action is better performed without

[1] Book iii, lines 161 f.
[2] *What is Man?* p. 97.

attending to it. Perhaps consciousness is a transitory nuisance; an animal perfectly adapted to its needs by its impulses and senses would not be conscious. Nietzsche thought consciousness would lessen and disappear as man developed into secondary automatism the habits required by his environment.

As for the self or soul, it is merely the sum-total of the hereditary character and the acquired experience of the organism. If experience changes, the self changes. A man looks with alien externality upon the boy he was. Given certain disturbances, and we get double personality: some center of experience, some node of fibres in the brain, is detached from the rest, and sets up a secession government of its own. Obviously the self is a precarious unity of heredity, memory and purpose, more fragile than immortal.

Thought is incipient action. Attention is a tension, aversion an averting, appetite a seeking, emotion a motion. An idea is the first stage of a response; we call it an idea because some other action-tendency has intercepted it before its external fulfilment. Deliberation is the alternate possession of the body by rival incipient actions, emotions, or desires. Emotions, as Cannon showed, are conditions of the blood, produced by glandular secretions; without adrenals we could not be angry; without proper thyroids we become idiots. All action and all thought are determined by desire, which is a condition of the body: hunger is an emptiness of certain cells, love is the repletion of others; erotic imagery is aroused by physiological maturity; and half the poetry of the world is due to the interstitial cells. The mind in all its functions is a part of the body; it grows with its growth and dies with its decay; it is no more outside of corporeal nature than digestion, respiration, and excretion. It is merely the highest function of the flesh.

VII. THE IDEALIST REPLIES

This is shameful, says the idealist; nothing could be more ridiculous than this naïve materialism. Is it conceivable that matter should, by whatever transformations, become capable of turning around to perceive and know and dominate itself? Even the lowest forms of mind are unintelligible in material terms; how, for example, could matter feel pain? One might imagine matter remembering; but matter foreseeing, or matter recognizing? If mind is brain, then we should find lesions in the brain for every gap in the memory; but we do not.[1] The whole effort to correlate mind and brain, except as director and instrument, master and mechanism, has broken down; is there any greater intellectual debâcle in our time than the failure of physiological psychology?

But these are simple considerations: turn around and look at thought. It is true that William James, introspecting, reported that he found no

[1] Bergson, *Matter and Memory*, London, 1911, p. 316.

other consciousness but "I breathe." But the "I" is the important thing here, not the "breathe." We see nothing in introspection, because we look for something spatial and material; we find it hard to report what we "see," because we strive for concrete images, and even "see" is a materialistic assumption. But no one has even begun to bridge the gap between the spatial relations that constitute the external world, and the spaceless operations of the mind. We can think of large spaces as easily as of small ones; our conception of a mile takes no more room or effort than our conception of an inch. We can think of great stretches of time, or concentrate on a moment's memory. We can at will magnify, reduce, or combine images, regardless of how they have been combined in our experience. And the image is not the thought; many observers find, on occasion, no imagery in their thinking. What images we have are not fundamental, but instrumental; a triangular hat, or a hand on a fat belly, serves to carry the idea of Napoleon in a hundred aspects and connotations. The more often we think of a thing, the less imagery we need to use; the image is important only when it is the rehearsal of an action, the brain picture of an intended motion. Where there is no action, thought goes on with a minimum of imagery, and becomes obviously a process beyond any material category or metaphor.

Consciousness in general is too hard a nut for the materialist to crack; with more courage than candor he solves the problem by pretending that consciousness does not exist; he is on a par, mentally, and morally, with the extreme idealist who denies altogether the reality of an external world. Philosophers will always be the last to discover the truth. It took them three hundred years to find out that the external world existed; and when the New Realists, with blowing bugles and beating drums, announced that the thing was now almost certain, the empyrean of philosophy was filled with surprise and doubt—perhaps there was an external world after all? Three hundred years hence, it may be, behaviorists and materialists will discover the internal world, and the reality and efficacy of consciousness; then at last they will know as much as the man in the street.

Huxley admitted with characteristic honesty that materialism could not explain consciousness, that it was compelled by its own logic and premises to take the position that consciousness is an "epiphenomenon,"—a useless addition to the brain and nerves, like the heat in a lamp, or the light in a fire. It is true that many useless structures survive in evolution, but presumably because they were harmless, or are the relics of once useful things. The materialist, however, is forbidden to believe that consciousness was ever useful, or even that it is ever injurious; though if, as is likely, he is a shy intellectual, he will admit that self-consciousness can be a handicap and a nuisance. Which of us can walk properly while thinking of his legs? And how can the materialist forgive the evidence that consciousness has developed side by side with the power and flexibility of life, and that those animals that have the highest degree of consciousness dominate creation?

VIII. SYNTHESIS

It is time that we draw these threads together, and weave these half-truths into amity. Leibnitz blithely proposed to effect the merger by the theory of "preëstablished harmony": mind and body were parallel but independent; they ran side by side and neck to neck, but never touched or influenced each other; their apparent accord at every moment was only another proof of divine Providence. The sole advantage that this theory has is that it is not more foolish than most. There is not much to choose between it and the "neutral stuff" of the latest fashion in philosophy. To our "neutral monists," of whom Bertrand Russell is the least unconvincing, physics has reduced matter to a system of relationships and events; psychology has reduced mind to a system of relationships and events; and perception is the transient crossing of these kindred worlds. This too must be a God-sent reconciliation of ancient opposites: out of this ocean of "neutral stuff"—this filmy tissue of relations and events—come both matter and mind! To such gossamer thinness have souls and bodies shrunk.

As for ourselves, we shall continue to believe that the "events" which constitute our knowledge of the external world reveal a tangible and impressive reality quite worthy to be called matter, and regrettably independent of our wishes and our feelings. Matter being not inert but alive, the problem of matter and mind fades off into a fallacy of mistaken premises. Certainly it would be difficult for the inert matter of materialists to evolve into mind; but one who has followed the adventures of contemporary physics will not be sure that the dynamic matter of latter-day science is not as vital and mysterious as mind itself; from such a matter it would be no miracle that mind should have evolved. But it is not a question of one of these evolving from the other; the problem, rephrased, is, could the lowest forms of mind-matter develop into the highest forms?

For mind is not matter, and matter is not mind; there is mind-matter. Mind is not a distinct entity within matter, any more than life is a thing that resides in the body like a man in a house; *mind* is an abstract noun, a collective name which we give to the operations of living substance when it thinks, as sight is the name we give to the operations of substance when it sees, or as love is the name we give to the operations of substance when it hungers to possess or serve. There is "interaction of mind and body," not in the sense that two distinct entities influence one another, but only in the sense that one organ and function of the body (nerves—thought) influences, and is influenced by, other organs and functions of the body (lungs—respiration, stomach—digestion, limbs—locomotion, gonads—reproduction, glands —secretion) ; a more highly evolved portion of living substance, through the "integrative action of the nervous system," unifies and directs the remainder of the organism. The highest form of "mind" is kin in nature, and continuous in development, with the lowest form of life and the primitive vitality of the atom. Even consciousness, though we cannot explain (make material and mechanistic diagrams of) it, falls intelligibly within the evolving plan, because we derive it not from the important inertia of the materialist's "matter," but from that abounding energy which is matter's life.

If, then, we speak of thought as one function of the body, let it be understood that this body is conceived not as "matter," but as life; in even the simplest cell the vitality is central, and the material shape, to fall into deceptive metaphor once more, is but a shell. The life is not a function of the form, the form is a product of the life; the weight and solidity of matter are the result and expression of intra-atomic energy,[1] and every muscle or nerve in the body is the moulded instrument of desire. It is incorrect to suppose that life and mind begin with sensations that build themselves up automatically into thought; on the contrary, desire, or remoulding energy, is the very essence of specifically organic things. Except for external interference, it is desire that determines purpose, interests and motion, and thereby selects sensation and experience. Experience is not the Absolute, as Bradley thought, for it is a created instrument of desire; the Absolute, if we must have one, is energy, rising from the disintegrative vitality of the atom to the integrative activity of the mature mind that makes its purposes one, and sees all things in the light of the whole. It was the energy of living substance that specialized and moulded organs and nerves and brains. Now we can think because we have brains; but once life made the brain by trying to think; even now that is how the brain grows, through the trial and error of desirous thought. Life is first, and within; matter, coëval with it in time and inextricable from it in space, is second to it in essence, in logic, and in significance; matter is the form and visibility of life.

This is vitalism, but monistic vitalism; it accepts life as the fundamental reality of which matter (i. e., extension) is the outward dress; but it does not admit, with Bergson, that matter and life can ever be apart; everywhere the two are one. And let no one charge us with mysticism here: the omnipresent unity of mind and matter is no more mystical, and no more difficult of comprehension, than the union of will-full thought and restless flesh in a living man. How could there be mysticism in accepting life as fundamental, when we know life more directly and intimately than anything else, and know all other things only through this life?

[1] Le Bon. *The Evolution of Matter.* pp. 10, 309.

Materialist mechanism was an attack against religion, and subjective idealism was an attack against irreligion; if we are not afraid of our thoughts, or our time, we may reject them both. And yet in this psycho-physical monism, materialism, idealism and spiritualism are not rejected, they meet and fuse: materialism in so far as it conceives all reality as bound together in one unbroken evolution and unity; idealism in so far as it confines all knowable reality to experience; and spiritualism because it conceives the essence of reality to lie not in extension, solidity and weight, but in an activating power which is at once the life of the atom, and the energy and secret of genius—"a motion and a spirit that impels all thinking things, *and all objects of all thoughts,* and rolls through all things." Science has verified this poetry.

We have attempted a synthesis that tries in some measure to catch the total perspective and multitudinous complexity of the world. Doubtless we have failed, and only made more obscure that which we perceive and feel; again how can the drop of water understand the sea?

> Logic and sermons never convince;
> The damp of the night drives deeper into my soul. . . .
> Now I reëxamine philosophies and religions.
> They may prove well in lecture-rooms, yet not prove at all under the spacious
>   clouds and along the landscape and flowing currents.

But that is only because the flowing currents and the landscape, and even the spacious clouds, teem with incalculable life.

CHAPTER IV

Is Man a Machine?

I. PERSPECTIVE

WE PASS NOW from the outer world to the inner, and inquire not into the nature of mind, but into the mode of its operation. We would not divorce the two worlds, for we have seen that they are separable only in thought, and are in actuality a unit both in space and in time: every atom has a living nucleus, and every mind has a material form; the highest mind is bound up in continuous development with the lowest atom, and the laws of one must be the laws of the other. If the atom is mechanical, then man is a machine.

Determinism is the oldest of philosophies, as animism is the oldest of religions. The simplest faith sees whimsical will in everything; and the earliest speculation reacts against that vivid creed by asserting the helplessness of the individual in the face of omnipresent law. From these diverse beginnings religion and philosophy may reach one goal: the universal will may be shorn of its whims and identical with the inviolable order of the world. In the ancient Orient, where the feverish fertility of man has outrun the patient bounty of the soil, and the soul is broken with hardship and dwarfed by the engulfing crowd, the primitive belief in will tends to disappear from religion as well as from philosophy; happiness is conceived as the cessation of desire and the bliss of surrendered personality; and a sombre fatalism envelops priest and sage. In those seething cauldrons of humanity the individual can have no fundamental value or significance; against this background of an endless and tragic past he sees himself a futile atom projected unasked out of nothing, struggling pretentiously for a while, and then drawn down irresistibly, as by some unreasoning enemy, into the dark. Even the Tent-maker saw it so, and wrote it in lines that every rebellious youth has learned by heart.

But in active and progressive civilizations—where the mysterious flame of thought, burning brightly in the face of fate, achieves some passing mastery of the environment, and rears fair temples to divinity and proud structures of philosophy—the individual finds better reason for believing in his own creative personality; he feels in himself a spark of spontaneity, and fashions on his own model even the Olympian deities. So the Greeks saw growth and evolution in the universe; everywhere there were gods, and in the midst of contraries harmonies appeared; it seemed to Plato and Aristotle that all the world moved towards some perfect purpose, as if drawn by a lover's eyes. Yet that exuberant culture was only a happy interlude, born of wealth and victory. When Spartan arms destroyed the Athens of Pericles, and Alexander leveled Thebes, men seemed no longer akin to the immortals; and philosophy, in the Oriental Zeno, reached the conclusion announced by Sophocles many generations before, that *Moira,* dark fate, holds power over gods and men.

Tired civilizations, like senile souls, are apt to be deterministic; unable to overcome the forces of death, they dignify their fatigue as fatality, and their defeat as destiny. It was in the black soil of this despair that Christianity grew, a slender flower of hope in a disintegrating world. And always in the heart of the new religion (where it was not richly overgrown with pagan rites and joys) lay the pessimism out of which it came; the other side of faith in heaven was distrust and fear of life. That gloomy faithlessness reached its nadir in the predestination of the melancholy Calvin; God had foreseen all things, and therefore also the final lot of every man; the eternal selection or damnation of each soul has been determined before its birth, for the future would not dare to violate the infinite prescience of God. Christianity, which had sought to comfort the bereaved and to solace the oppressed, fell apart for a while into creeds more cruel and bitter than any earthly fortune.

It remained for modern minds to glorify this merciless theology with the new infallibility of science. Galileo, enamored of the patient regularity which he discovered in the stars, laid it down as the goal of every science that it should reduce its field of knowledge to mathematical and quantitative law. The high repute of Newton, and the transient perfection of his work in mechanics, cast a spell upon every student; physiologists and psychologists hungered for mechanical explanations and mathematical formulas for the growth of the cell and the perturbations of desire. Then philosophy became intoxicated with mathematics: Descartes suggested, with a cautious obscurity, that all the world was a machine, a geometry in motion; and Spinoza emulated the rigor of the universe in the Euclidean structure of his thought. It pleased the rebels of the Enlightenment to learn that man was made not in the image and likeness of God, but rather on the model of the machines that had in their age begun to replace the work of human hands and wills.

It was the Industrial Revolution that destroyed the old philosophy of freedom. For first, it accustomed the mind to dealing with machines, and induced it more and more to think of causes as mechanical. The worker immured within factory walls, seeing all the throbbing life about him slip by on pulleys and revolve on wheels, forgot the older agricultural existence in which life had seemed a matter of seeds miraculously sprouting from the soil, responding actively to every encouragement, and multiplying with a spontaneous fertility. The world, which had once been a field of growing plants and wilful children, of fond mothers and ambitious men, became for the modern mind a vast array of mechanisms, from the planets that mechanically circled round the sun, to the microscopic life that mechanically congregated about a ray of light. Science was sure that it had at last been permitted behind the curtain of the cosmic drama; it marveled at the un-suspected machinery that had created delusions and shifted a thousand scenes; it concluded, in modest admiration, that the property man was the real dramatist, and that the wires were the play.

But again, the Industrial Revolution made cities, and cities made crowds, and crowds unmade men. Once more in the modern metropolis those condi-tions appeared which in the Orient had shorn the individual of personality and meaning, and had led to a similar philosophy of fatalism and despair. In this teeming welter of population one became a number or a "hand"; the mind became an instrument for measuring and counting, and man be-came part of the machines he fed. Democracy, which had proposed to liberate the individual, became itself a mechanism, a chain of "machines," automatically leading mindless masses to the ballot-box. It was as useless for the individual to protest against this system of wires, pushes and pulls, as it had been for him to indulge in self-assertion against the crushing crowds and conformities of the distant East. Even the "leaders" became half-inanimate portions of the new contraption, as dull and will-less as the de-luded herds whose noses were counted (or not counted) at the polls.

If the slaves rebelled against this mechanism it was with a philosophy that acknowledged the supremacy and divinity of machines. Socialism un-hesitatingly allied itself with determinism and mechanistic science; it fed its recruits on Büchner and Haeckel, Spencer and Marx. Not only was the world a machine, but history was a machine, in which every move was caused by the price of bread, and a good economist sufficiently cognizant of present and past could predict with fatal certainty every turn and destiny of the future. Man was now a creature composed of heredity and environ-ment; whatever he did was the result of ancestral or physical causes over which he had had no control; he was merely a marvelous, superfluously-animated automaton. Therefore he was "not guilty": if he committed crimes, society was to blame; if he was a fool, it was the fault of the machine, which had slipped a cog in generating him; he should not be deprived for that reason of his right to vote or to be president. What the world needed was a bigger and better machine, a nationalized machine; one hundred million mechanisms managed by one executive machine, pressing a presidential button mechanically.

In an aristocratic age the leaders might have allowed to the oppressed masses a monopoly of this narcotic philosophy. But in a democratic century the loftiest thinkers felt themselves called upon to share patriotically in the metaphysics of the mob. It became unfashionable and antediluvian to doubt the omnipresent and omnipotent machine. Great writers hastened to announce that they too were machines, whose thoughts had been put into them, with a time-attachment, a million millennia before. Taine acknowledged the new god, and created a theory of criticism in his honor; Zola wrote interminable tragedies to show that one must pay a price for having ancestors; Thomas Hardy presented man as helpless in the fell clutch of circumstance; Anatole France mourned with immaculate elegance the slavery of the soul and the futility of life; and D'Annunzio saw everywhere the triumph and mockery of death.

Perhaps this abdication of personality is one cause of the secret sadness that lurks behind the glitter and wit of the modern mind. To one who had read *What Is Man?* the pessimism of Mark Twain is no longer mysterious or strange. For this unhappy humorist was a determinist of the most determined sort; he believed that all his joyous quips had been pre-ordained by the gaseous composition of the primeval nebula (for what sins has not this poor gas been blamed?), and he saw in the bubbling vitality of Tom Sawyer only the effervescence of a carbon compound. A little philosophy is a dangerous thing, and inclineth a man's mind to pessimism. It is said that the hilarious machine that created Huckleberry Finn had some difficulties with his spouse; but what woman could peaceably share her bed and board with an ebullient mechanism that looked upon her as a set of wheels wound up in the infancy of time and now unwinding itself, with superfluous sound and fury, to eternal impotence and silence?

Doubtless the loss of our childhood faith has saddened us; and the double bereavement of every mature soul, which must lose the theological ideals of its childhood and then the social ideals of its youth, leaves the young heart a little heavier with the weight of all this unintelligible world. But something of the sombre undertone that runs beneath our superficial gayety is the result of the jejune precipitancy of our thought. It was not demanded of us that we should fly from a theology that scorned the natural basis of existence to a philosophy that ignored the creativeness of life and the initiative of mind. It was not asked of us that having abandoned our puerile pretense at being the center and summit of universal history, we should humble ourselves before the machines in our factories, and accept them as the Platonic Ideas on whose august models fortuitous variation had fashioned our souls. We were not called upon to give up our share in the vitality of the world, in the restless expansiveness of life, or the persistent constructiveness of thought. But defeated on one part of the battlefront, we fled from the field in absolute surrender.

Was it necessary to yield so completely? Is human behavior of the same order as the erosion of the hills, or the flight of the wind, or the tides of the sea? Is the inexhaustible solicitude of motherhood, or the eager lust of youth, or the quiet considerateness of love, merely a mechanical redistribution of chemical elements and physical force? Is the resourceful pertinacity of life an appearance only, the striving for perfection but a blind compulsion, the efficacy of thought a delusion, and the reality of will no more than a dream?

Is man a machine?

II. MECHANISM

Consider locomotion. Let us take some simple machine, say a toy automobile that will run resolutely enough when its spring has been wound up and released. At its head we attach a square of rubber as a sensitive proboscis. We set the toy down upon a smooth floor, directly facing a slightly distant wall. We wind the spring, and then release it. We shall suppose that the alignment of wall and floor and toy are as perfect as in mathematical and mechanical theory. Under such conditions the car will rebound from the wall in the same line by which it came, and will approach the wall in that same line again. In theory it will do this repeatedly, always in a straight line against the wall, until its artificial energy is completely spent. It behaves mechanically.

Now fill a rectangular glass bowl with water. Across the center place a transparent glass partition, as much shorter than the width of the bowl as will leave a narrow passage at each side. Into one side of the bowl drop a bit of food; drop into the other side some lowly organism, as simple as possible,—say *Paramecium.* Observe it under the microscope. It moves directly towards the food; it strikes the glass partition; it retreats in a straight line; apparently it is a machine. But suddenly it veers slightly about; then it sets out again, at an angle, and once more strikes the glass. It rebounds, and veers, and strikes again. . . . It rebounds, and veers, and passes through the opening to the food. There is nothing in the make-up of any machine, nothing in the principles of mechanics, that will explain this judicious veering about, this appearance of directive *purpose* in the lowest animals known to man.

Or consider the behavior of a similar animalcule, *Stentor raselii,* a delicate infusorian of trumpet-like form, attached to plants or débris in marshy pools. Let a thin stream of water fall upon the peristome or disc at the organism's mouth, and at once it shrinks and curls up into its stalk. A minute later it expands to its normal size, and is apparently as it was. Now let the stream of water strike it again, precisely as before. *Stentor* pays no attention to it. Disturb slightly the object to which it is rooted, and it shrinks once more into its tube; repeat the same stimulus a minute later, and no response ensues. Why this quickly-acquired adaptation? Is it due to fatigue—to exhaustion from the violence of the first response? No; for while *Stentor* remains indifferent to the stream of water falling upon its disc, it reacts with vigorous withdrawal to harmful stimuli. But let any *harmless* stimulus be several times repeated, and the organism adjusts itself philosophically to the new environment, and puts up quietly with what it cannot help.¹ Let the mechanist sharpen his teeth against these selective and adaptive reactions in the lowest phylum of the animal world. He will comfort himself theologically: "Some day, somehow," he will assure us, like a pietist, "we shall find a mechanical explanation for these things." *Les savants,* said Anatole France, *ne sont pas curieux:* scientists have lost the art of doubt.

Consider digestion. Some sensitive plants, like the *Dionœa* or the *Drosera,* close upon and absorb particles of food placed on their surfaces; but to inedible substances similarly placed they make no response at all. The *Amœba* normally rejects what cannot serve for its nourishment. The little swan-animalcule, *Dileptus anser,* thrusts out a neck swollen with trichocysts (coiled stinging threads), which it discharges only upon fitting prey. The cells of the human intestine are selective in their action; each class of cells acts upon certain foods and no others. Every cell in the human body chooses from the blood-stream the specific substances which it needs; it ignores the rest; and pours into the blood the products of its own metabolic waste. It breaks down into parts the materials which it chooses, and reunites their elements into the compounds required for its support and its activity. It breathes, and eats, and excretes, and grows, and reproduces, and dies, as if it were an organism with an individuality of its own. "That which these cells accomplish in every instant of our existence soars far above all that the most advanced science can realize. The scholar capable of solving by his intelligence the problems solved every moment by the cells of the lowest creature would be so much higher than other men that he might be considered by them as a god."²

Consider growth. How could a machine grow? Why should it care to grow? Was there ever a mechanism so marvelous that it might offer analogy to the astounding expansiveness of life? Consider the lilies of the field: what enchanting power is it that draws them from their prison in the soil, and lifts them slowly and patiently towards the sun? Behold the swal-

---

¹ Jennings, H. S., *Behavior of the Lower Organisms,* pp. 170–3.
² Le Bon, *The Evolution of Forces,* p. 363.

lows of the air: there are no cogs in them, no pulleys, and no wheels; and

> Yet if we could scorn
>   Hate, and pride, and fear;
> If we were things born
>   Not to shed a tear,
> I know not how thy joy we ever should come near.

Here is a child; why does it hunger and thirst for nourishment, and reach out with its soft fingers to possess the world? See it grow: it needs but one food to make from it chubby cheeks, rich curls and laughing eyes. See it raising itself for the first time, fearfully and bravely, to a vertical dignity; why should it long so to stand and walk? Why should it tremble with perpetual curiosity, with perilous and insatiable ambition, touching and tasting, watching and listening, manipulating and experimenting, observing and pondering, *growing*—till it weighs the earth and charts and measures the stars? What mysterious transfiguration of puberty is this, that takes the boy and quiets and broadens him into a man, that takes the girl and fashions her into a living beauty fairer than any art?

Consider regeneration. Cut off any ray of a starfish, and the ray will be regrown; cut them all away, and the center will regenerate them; cut away the center, and the rays will grow it again. A machine out of order does not repair its parts; it stands senselessly still, and waits for the touch of a living hand to reorder its parts into meaning and efficacy. But these larger phenomena, which Bergson has described, are not the most significant; the simplest healing of the slightest wound is unmechanical and marvelous enough. With what artistry the new cells are laid over the injured flesh, as if some cellular intelligence were guiding the beneficent work: we offer mechanical or chemical aids to these vital processes, but we know that they have the same relation to nature's healing power as marble or clay to the artist's hand. We know that in some way which mechanism will never illuminate, the energy and impetus of life will bear us on through a thousand battles and a thousand injuries, till that resilient vitality is spent, and finds for itself a rejuvenating form.

Consider consciousness. What is this mysterious faculty that we have of being aware of what we are doing, or have done, or intend to do; of seeing the conflict among our own ideas and desires, and criticizing each by means of the rest; of imagining possible reactions and foreseeing through memory probable results; and at last of meeting a patiently analyzed situation with all the resources of thought and desire coördinated into a remoulding and creative response? The experiments of Köhler, indicating the role of total insight, as against the conditioned reflex, in learning, have discredited the mechanistic conception of mental processes.[1] What unwitting dishonesty has come upon us, that today, if we wish to be in the vogue, we must deny the existence of consciousness in order to save a mechanistic philosophy that could not possibly explain it?

We begin with things that we know only externally, in their outward and superficial form (as matter is, in modern physics, the superficial form of energy); and then, naturally enough, we find ourselves baffled in passing from these surface mechanisms to that inward consciousness which is the most palpable and immediate datum in all our knowledge. But the behaviorist does not hesitate to sacrifice an obvious fact to a questionable theory; he announces, bravely, that this nuisance of a consciousness, which mechanism can not explain, is a superfluous thing, and does not really exist. Like a good theologian, he takes his dogmas from without (i. e., from dead physicists), and sees to it that no facts shall be admitted which might inconvenience his generalization. The behaviorist is a good psychologist, but he is only a poor philosopher; though in his divine simplicity he also believes that philosophy is worthless, and will die out within a generation. It is an index of the vulgarized superficiality of contemporary thought that this inverted theology is gaining adherents as rapidly as its counterpart and complement, Christian Science. What a pass we have come to, when half of us deny matter, and the other half deny consciousness! We may imagine the sad smile with which a Goethe or a Voltaire would look upon the intellectual bedlam of our age.

Last of all, consider reproduction. Here is a tiny ovum, invisible to the eye; and here is a restless sperm, moving about in worlds unrealized. Each of these microscopic cells is infinitely rich with hereditary characters bearing the memory of a thousand generations; each carries within it unique and subtle qualities of body and mind, impulses and dispositions and aptitudes, hunger and eagerness and love; perhaps in their plasm already lie the passion and patience of genius. Well, let sperm and egg unite; suddenly those possibilities become realities, and the miracle of a new life begins. By some internal urgency, nourished with placental blood, the fertile cell divides into two cells, into four cells, into eight, into a hundred million cells that seem to grow in unity even as their number mounts. A heart forms and begins to beat; a brain forms and begins to feel; hands and feet bud forth and stir in the womb. And then the little marvel enters the world; air and cold and sound and light impinge upon it; its eyes and lips and ears open, and all its nerves tingle with sensation. Life has broken through death again, and pours itself lavishly into its new mould, joyful and strong and young once more.

[1] Cf. Everett Dean Martin's splendid book on *The Meaning of a Liberal Education*, pp. 36–39.

Is it mechanical? Jacques Loeb discovered that he could fertilize the egg of a sea-urchin with a salt solution or the prick of a pin; he concluded, in haste, that he had proved the mechanical nature of reproduction. In truth he had merely shown that in certain cases the female organism can of herself generate offspring without even that casual assistance to which nature limits the male; he had rediscovered that peculiar parthenogenesis which biologists had known for a thousand years. That the female herself was hardly as mechanical as the pin, or as chemically simple as the salt, might go without saying; indeed the performance of the unaided female seems a little more marvelous than that of her more fortunate sisters. It is also more ominous, and indicates that the emancipation of the once weaker sex may in our century proceed to unpleasant extremes.

Far more revealing than these experiments of Loeb were the allied discoveries of Hans Driesch.[1] Driesch had been brought up in the laboratory of Ernst Haeckel at Jena; he had every inducement to be a mechanist of the purest dye. But he found phenomena undreamed of by his master. He cut a fertilized egg in half, and nevertheless it developed normally. He haphazardly disarranged the cells after the second division, and nevertheless the organism developed normally. He disarranged the cells after the third division, with the same result.—Now try to imagine, first, the cohabitation of two machines for the generation of a third machine. Imagine that each part of either machine is also endowed with the power and habit of reproduction, and continually divides and grows. Imagine, further, that certain parts of the parent machines coalesce to form the model of the new machine; that the model produces the complete machine by spontaneously dividing into two, into four, into eight . . . ; and that the more it divides, the more it becomes one. Imagine that some Brobdingnagian Driesch appears, who cuts the coalesced machine into halves, or disturbs its parts into a deliberate chaos. And to cap it all, imagine that the machine proceeds normally and successfully with its work, as if nothing had happened. Was there ever a jollier hoax in science or philosophy? Is there any miracle in any religion, ancient, medieval or American, that could compare with this magnificent and monstrous myth?

III. DETERMINISM

But the mechanist will tell us that we are unfair, that we have taken his term in too literal a way, and have attacked a position which he has not proposed to defend. We may imagine his reply.

"What we mean is not so much the machine-like character of human behavior, as the inviolable sequence of cause and effect in the mental as in the physical world. Man is a part of nature, and is presumably subject to

[1] *Science and Philosophy of the Organism.*

its laws. It is inconceivable that there should be a break in the causal chain; such a break would involve the destruction or the creation of energy. But the cortinuity and conservation of energy stand out visibly everywhere. Cease to feed a man, and soon his reactions stop. Feed him properly, and he becomes virtuous and patriotic; feed him wrongly, and you can make him an invalid, a criminal, a pessimist, an idiot, a believer in free will. Measure a man's activity from birth to death; it will correspond almost precisely with the energy in the nourishment he has received. Obviously mental energy in man is a product of the energy contained in the organic substances which he uses as his food. But these substances are ultimately derived, through plant metabolism, from inorganic materials in the soil and in the air. To admit a rigid causal chain in the inorganic world is therefore to accept it for even the subtlest processes of human life or human thought.

"Again, it appears that the more we know of human behavior the more successfully we can predict it. Presumably, if we knew all the conditions affecting the actions of our friends, we could foretell their responses with the same accuracy with which we predict the phases and eclipses of the moon. But if determinism were untrue, if human actions did not follow invariable laws, it would be impossible to develop the prediction and control of human behavior by increasing our knowledge of man.

"Above all, a man's conduct is clearly the result of his character and the circumstances that surround his action. His character is the product of his past environment (back to his conception) and his heredity. 'We are the tail-end of a tape-worm of ancestry.'[1] We originate nothing, and we decide nothing; we are moved, directed, and compelled by forces ultimately external to us, and over which, in the last analysis, we have no control. Choice is a delusion; it is only a composition of determining forces. 'Men think themselves free because they are conscious of their volitions and desires, but are ignorant of the causes by which they are led to wish and desire.'[2] In truth our behavior is as rigidly determined by the forces that produce and encompass us, as the fall of a stone is fixed in time and space by its mass, its velocity, and its direction. It is in this sense that man is a machine."

Let the determinist honestly envisage the implications of his philosophy. If every action is necessarily the result of pre-existing and ultimately physical conditions, we must conclude that determinism and mechanism are identical, and that Michelangelo's piety and Shakespeare's passion, Socrates' nose and Cleopatra's smile, were due to the mechanical and chemical structure of the primeval nebula. It is a large order; one wonders at the readiness of professional sceptics like Taine, Renan and Anatole

[1] Mark Twain, *What Is Man?* p. 5.
[2] Spinoza, *Ethics,* Bk. i, Appendix.

France to swallow this deterministic camel. But even doubters are believers, in this "new age of faith"; their proudly scientific rejection of one creed is soon followed by their blindly human acceptance of another. Mechanists never suspect how much naïve credulity lies behind their unmethodic doubt.

Historians will consider it a marvel that this tremendous nebula never choked the gullet of belief. What hypnotism was it that made us for a generation accept the transient categories of physics as the laws and symbols of our lives? Which of us really believed that he was a machine, and acted honestly on that humorous hypothesis? Or did we secretly know, beneath this Byronic pretense, that sense and mind are active as well as passive things, and that we are in our little ways initiative centers in the flux of force? How could we honestly conceive in terms of mechanism and determinism the vast variety and fertility of life, its endless experiments and forms, its inexhaustible ingenuity, its resolute transformation and conquest of the earth?

Our determinism came of Locke's conception of the mind as a clean slate on which sensations wrote, a passive wax shaped and reshaped helplessly by external things. But we are being taught today a different psychology. At the bottom of our souls we find desire, desire which is "the very essence of man"; we can trace in a thousand ways the selective and formative action of desire on our sensations, perceptions, memories and ideas. Life has divided its great hunger into specialized impulses and capacities; it is these that determine our actions, our attitudes, and the orientation of our senses; we are unconscious of innumerable stimuli that vainly try to send their messages to us; we ignore vast realms of sensible reality because we select through our purposes the sensations that we need. We hear certain sounds that interest us, and are deaf to a thousand others; we look at some temporarily meaningless object and see straight through it to some goal that fills our minds and therefore guides our eyes. It is our purposes that interpret sensations into perceptions and ideas. We are told to add given pairs of numbers; soon the "mental set" of addition "determines" without effort the association of stimulus and response; and hearing "7 and 7" we answer "14." But if we had been told to multiply, we should have reacted with "49" to that *identical* sensation. It is purpose, then, and not recency or frequency or vividness, that explains the association of ideas; we are not the helpless recipients and victims of whatever stimuli may chance to impinge upon our flesh; we are agents of selection. That same initiative inventiveness which has filled our factories with machines is the best refutation of the theory that likens the mind of the inventor to the passive product of his brain.

In this process of active adaptation we perform mental prodigies which it is difficult to conceive as mechanical: we analyze wholes into parts, and recombine parts into new wholes; we dissociate ideas in perception, and reassociate them in reasoning; we consider purposes, measure values, imagine results, and devise ways and means for our innermost desires. We recall the issue of past responses, vision their like again in these surroundings, and judge them in the light of our purposes. Knowledge is the memory of the results of various modes of action; the more our knowledge, the greater our foresight can be; the greater our foresight the wider is our freedom. Consciousness provides a stage for the rehearsal of imagined responses; through memory, imagination and reason we eliminate unwise reactions, and express with some success our final aim. Freedom, like reason, is delayed response leading to total response; our freedom grows as by delay we permit a complex situation to arouse in us all relevant impulses, and as by imagination we combine these partial impulses into a total reaction that expresses our complete and maturest self.

Mechanism is secondary; what we see as primary, fundamental, and immediate, what we take for granted in the actual and genuine philosophy of our lives, is that every organism, in proportion to the flexibility of its structure, is a center of redirected force, and, in some measure, of spontaneous initiation. Life is creative, not because it makes new force from nothing, but because it adds its own remoulding energy to the powers that enter from without. Will is free only in so far as the life of which it is a form actively reshapes the world. To reshape the world, life *invents* and *constructs* mathematics and mechanics to deal with external things; it only laughs and passes on when these creatures of its mind and will turn insolently around and try to understand it in those terms which life itself has made.

Can this conception of freedom withstand the assaults of the determinist? He will remind us, if he is clever, that "will" is an abstract term; he will take care to forget that "force" is not less so. To which we should reply that by will we mean no abstract entity, but the propulsive and expansive behavior of life itself. What life is, another page has tried to tell; but let us not turn a fact into a mystery.

Or the determinist will recall the conservation of energy: the organism cannot emit more energy than it has received. Which is to forget that life itself is energy, visibly transforming the forces and materials brought to it into combinations that aim at the mastery of environment by thought, and occasionally succeed. What issues from action may be no more in quantity than what entered in sensation; but how different in quality! This transforming power of life is the highest energy we know; it is known to us more directly and surely than any other energy in the world; and it is the source and promise of our modest freedom.

The determinist supposes that freedom is illusory because the "stronger" motive always wins. Of course this is a vain tautology; the motive that is strong enough to win is stronger than those that fail. But what made it stronger if not its harmony with the will, with the desire and essence of the soul?—"Yet there cannot be any uncaused actions." Verily; but the will is part of the cause; the circumstances of an action must include the forward urgency of life. Each "state" of mind follows naturally from the total preceding state of all reality; but that state and this include the transforming energy of life and will.—"The same effect always follows the same cause." But the cause is never the same, for the self involved is always in flux, and circumstances are forever changing.—"If I knew all your past and present I could infallibly predict your response." You could if you knew also the nature and power of the life-force within me; you could, perhaps, if you abandoned mechanistic principles and asked yourself, for your guidance, what you—i. e., life—would do in this complex of circumstance. Probably you could not predict successfully even then; probably there is in life an element of incalculability and spontaneity which does not accord with our categories and our "laws," and which gives peculiar zest and character to organic evolution and human affairs. Let us pray that we shall never have to live in a totally predictable world. Does not the picture of such a world seem ridiculously incongruous with life—mechanism in life being, as Bergson said, a passing jest?

"But all action is the result of heredity and environment." Not quite; the determinist modestly fails to take account of himself. He supposes once more that life is the passive product of external forces; he neglects (if we may use a pleonasm) the very vitality and liveliness of life. We are not merely our ancestors and our circumstances; we are also wells of transforming energy, we are parts of that stream of directive force, of capacity for adaptive choice and thought, in which our forefathers also moved and had their being. These ancestors are in truth living and acting within us; but the will and the life that were once in them is in each of us now, creating the "spontaneous me." Freedom is narrower and wider than as imagined of old; it is subject, no doubt, to ancestral and environing limitations of a thousand kinds; nevertheless it is as deep as life, and as broad as consciousness; it grows in scope and power with the variety of experience, the breadth of perspective, and the clarity of thought.[1] Will is free in so far as life is creative, in so far as it enters, with its remoulding energy, as *one* of the determining conditions of choice and action. There is no violation of "natural law" in such a freedom, because life itself is a natural factor and process, not a force outside the varied realm of nature. Nature itself, as its fine name implies, is that living power through which all things are begotten; probably throughout the world this spontaneity and

---

[1] Cf. Goethe: "One has merely to declare oneself free, and one feels the moment to be conditioned. But if one has the courage to declare oneself conditioned, then one has the feeling of being free." In Spengler, *Decline of the West*, vol. ii, p. 267.

urgency lurk which we have claimed for life; how else could life have acquired it? [1]

To say that our characters determine our actions is true. But we *are* our characters; it is we, then, that choose. To say with Huxley that we may be free to act out our desire, but are never free to choose what our desire shall be, is also true, and also tautological; for we are our desires; desire is life itself; and in realizing our desires we realize ourselves. It is not enough to say that external and hereditary forces compel and conquer us; the other half of the truth is that life itself is a force of its own, with its own direction and power, cruelly limited and constrained, but effecting its will in an amazing degree, rising from the lowliest organisms to the lonely heights of genius, and covering the world with its forms and its victories. If life were not an active and remoulding force, prejudiced in favor of development, there would never have been any evolution.

This realization of our directive vitality restores to us our responsibility and our personality, and the integrity of our theory with our lives. For even while we talked determinism we knew that it was false; we never

---

[1] Certain technical considerations suggesting this view may be added here. Students of the methodology of science need not be told that Mach, Pearson and Poincaré have changed our conception of "natural law" from an external force regulating phenomena, to our subjective formulation of certain sequences in human experience; all scientific terms and formulas are "shorthand" expressions for our hypothetical theory of the world. Determinists assume that all that we know indicates determinism; but this is because they mean by "all," our knowledge of the physical and chemical world. It would be ridiculous to say that all that we know of the mental or organic world indicates determinism; on the contrary our direct experience, which is the last test of truth, shows us a whimsical spontaneity everywhere. Our "laws" are taken from the world of "matter," and are then artificially applied to "mind." "The mind has by its selective power fitted the processes of Nature into a frame of law, a pattern largely of its own choosing; and in the discovery of this system of law the mind may be regarded as regaining from Nature that which the mind has put into Nature." (Eddington, *The Nature of the Physical World*, p. 244.) Even the indestructibility of matter and the conservation of energy are weakening before the phenomena of radio-activity; and the atom itself has revealed, in the "quantum," a degree of indeterminateness and irresolution almost human.

The quantum theory, now accepted by practically all physicists, describes the motion of the electrons as discontinuous and irregular: there is no predictable order in their behavior; and though they may change their place or speed, they move from one place or speed to another apparently without passing through the intermediate positions or velocities. "It is as though," says Professor Whitehead, "an automobile moving at the average rate of thirty miles an hour did not traverse the road continuously, but appeared successively at the successive milestones, remaining for two minutes at each." (*Science and the Modern World*, p. 52.)

"It is a consequence of the quantum theory that physics is no longer pledged to a scheme of deterministic law," says Eddington. "Determinism has dropped out altogether in the latest formulations of theoretical physics, and it is at least open to doubt whether

treated ourselves or our children, as machines.[1] If there is an almost eternal recurrence of philosophies of freedom, it is because direct perception can never be beaten down with formulas, or sensation with reasoning. After all, there was something cowardly in mechanism, with its shifting of guilt to heredity and society—those poor abstract scapegoats of our vice and sloth; it may be that the weakness and instability of contemporary character are bound up, both as effect and as cause, with the domination of the individual by the machine in philosophy and life. Machinery wins triumph after triumph, and extends immeasurably our power to realize ancient and contradictory ends: we move over the clouds and through the depths of the sea; we produce millions of standardized articles once

---

it will ever be brought back. . . . The great laws hitherto accepted as causal appear in minute examination to be of statistical character," and all predictability is due to the statistical regularity of indeterminate particulars. (Eddington, pp. 294, 298.) I. e., the predictability of a lunar eclipse is due to the average behavior of the constituent atoms of the sun, the earth, and the moon; in a large mass the incalculability of atomic action may be ignored, precisely as postal officials can calculate with great accuracy the number of unaddressed envelopes which will be mailed within the year. But what if mental processes differ from those *mass* phenomena from which our "laws" are derived?

Bertrand Russell, though still a determinist, makes a characteristically candid statement of the situation. "We have seen that on the basis of physics itself, there may be limits to physical determinism. We know of no laws as to when a quantum transaction will take place, or a radio-active atom will break down. We know fairly well what will happen *if* anything happens, and we know statistical averages, which suffice to determine macroscopic" (large-scale) "phenomena. But if mind and brain are causally interconnected, very small cerebral differences must be correlated with noticeable mental differences. Thus we are perhaps forced to descend into the region of quantum transactions, and to desert the macroscopic level where statistical averages obtain. Perhaps the electron jumps when it likes; perhaps the minute phenomena in the brain which make all the difference to mental phenomena belong to the region where physical laws no longer determine definitely what must happen. This, of course, is merely a speculative possibility; but it interposes a veto upon materialistic dogmatism." (*Philosophy*, p. 393.) "So far as quantum theory can say at present, atoms might as well be possessed of free will, limited, however, to one of several possible choices." (*The Analysis of Matter*, p. 38.)

One would not care to rest a philosophy of action upon so precarious a basis in transient physical theory; the best foundation for a belief in the reality of choice is our direct and intimate perception of the unmechanical nature of our own vitality and thought. If the concept of cause makes this inescapable consciousness of choice seem a delusion, we shall have to transcend physics with biology, and redefine cause in terms not of matter but of life. Perhaps the conception of causality as a living process will be the next step in philosophy.

[1] Cf. C. D. Broad: "If a man referred to his brother or to his cat as 'an ingenious mechanism,' we should know that he was either a fool or a physiologist. No one in practice treats himself or his fellow-man or his pet animals as machines; but scientists who have never made a study of Speculative Philosophy seem often to think it their duty to hold in theory what no one outside a lunatic asylum would accept in practice." (In Muirhead, *Contemporary British Philosophy*, p. 98.)

cheap in price, and always cheap in artistry; step by step skill disappears before mechanism, quality before quantity, art before industry, and character before wealth; soon man himself will disappear, and only buttons and switches will remain. Is it any wonder that a generation content with talking movies instead of drama, with tenements instead of homes, with telegraph poles instead of trees, and with politicians instead of statesmen, has at last surrendered all personality and initiative, and permitted itself to be described as a procession of machines?

Mechanism reflected also the overshadowing of personality by the ever-growing city and the rapacious democratic state; in a mob or an election it is difficult to retain initiative and individuality. Above all, determinism was a result of the intoxication of physics with its own external glory, so that it thought to include the universe of mind and art and love in its precarious and partial formulas. Slowly, as we pass out of the age of machinery into an age of creative culture, we shall learn to see, behind the surface mechanisms of the earth, the pulsing life beneath. After many errors and many doubts, we shall come to understand that in our little measure we too participate in the activity of the world, and that if we wish we may, with imagination and knowledge, write some modest lines in the mysterious drama that we play.

IV. THE AGE OF BIOLOGY

Let us take note, in closing, that the naïve mechanical approach is breaking down in philosophy, in biology, in psychology, in physiology, even in physics itself. "Today," says Lucien Poincaré, "the idea that all phenomena are capable of mechanical explanations is generally abandoned."[1] "In modern physics," says Cassirer, "the mechanical view of the world has been more and more superseded and replaced by the electro-dynamic view."[2] "In spite of the efforts of thousands of workers," says Le Bon, "physiology has been able to tell us nothing of the nature of the forces" that produce the phenomena of life. "They have no analogy with those that are studied in physics."[3] As chemistry needs the concept of quality in addition to that concept of quantity with which physics tries to be content, so physiology needs, in addition to quantity and quality, the concepts of organism and totality. Physics and chemistry are the study of parts which determine the behavior of their wholes; biology is the study of wholes which determine the behavior of their parts. Even science must some day learn to see things whole.

Among the biologists themselves the rejection of mechanism has be-

[1] Le Bon, *Evolution of Forces,* p. 8.
[2] *Substance and Function,* p. 355.
[3] Le Bon, p. 367.

come a common thing: Driesch and Pavlov and Haldane are names that might make any mechanist take thought. The *Gestalt* movement in psychology is a reaction from the mechanistic to the organic point of view. "The mechanistic theory," says J. S. Haldane,

> has on the whole fared very badly. Schwann's simple mechanical theory of growth . . . has long been abandoned. We now know that all cells are formed by division of pre-existing cells, and that the problem of the process of cell growth and cell-nutrition is not one which we have at present any prospect of solving in a mechanical direction. Nor is it any different with the problems of secretion and absorption. The simple chemical theories of the respiratory and other metabolic processes . . . have likewise disappeared. . . . It has become evident that no simple physio-chemical theory of muscular or other physiological movements will suffice. . . . With every year of physiological advance we seem to get further and further away from any prospect of such a solution. . . . The work of Sherrington and others [is making it] quite clear that the old idea of simple and definite reflex mechanisms in the central nervous system must be abandoned. . . . As a physiologist, I can see no use for the hypothesis that life, as a whole, is a mechanical process. This theory does not help me in my work; and indeed I think it now hinders very seriously the progress of physiology. I should as soon go back to the mythology of our Saxon forefathers as to the mechanistic physiology.[1]

It is significant that Schopenhauer and Nietzsche, with all their hostility to traditional theology, rejected mechanism scornfully. Said Nietzsche, sarcastically, to the mechanistic physicist:

> That a world-interpretation is alone right by which *you* maintain your position, by which investigation and work can go on scientifically in *your* sense (do you really mean *mechanically?*), an interpretation which acknowledges numbering, calculating, weighing, seeing and handling, and nothing more— such an idea is a piece of grossness and naïveté, provided it is not lunacy and idiocy. . . . I say this in confidence to my friends the Mechanicians, who to-day like to hobnob with philosophers, and absolutely believe that mechanics is the teaching of the first and last laws upon which . . . all existence must be built. . . . Would the reverse not be quite probable, that the most superficial and external characters of existence . . . should let themselves be apprehended first? [2]

[1] *Mechanism, Life and Personality*, p. 61.

[2] *Joyful Wisdom*, Engl. tr., p. 339. German philosophy seems now to have definitely turned against mechanism. "To attempt to get an 'exact' science out of the ever mysterious soul is futile," says Spengler (*Decline of the West*, vol. i, p. 301); and Keyserling writes: "If men of education have already passed through the materialistic stage, the masses are only just entering it." (*The World in the Making*, p. 265.)

Biology is at a standstill to-day because it has been dealing with death rather than with life; with specimens preserved in alcohol, with butterflies not on the wing but on the pin, with carcasses left by the gallows for *post-mortem* study, with "preparations" of tissue on microscopic slides. Goethe foresaw it all a hundred years ago, and made his brilliant devil say:

> He that would study and portray
> A living creature, thinks it fit
> To start with finding out the way
> To drive the spirit out of it.
> This done, he holds within his hand
> The pieces to be named and stated,
> But ah! the spirit-tie, that spanned
> And knit them, has evaporated.
> This process, chemic science pleases
> To call *Naturæ Encheiresis,*
> And in the very doing so, it
> Makes of itself a mock, and does not know it.[1]

Perhaps biology will rebel soon against its domination by the methods and concepts of physics; it will discover that the life which it is privileged to study reaches nearer to the bases of reality than the "matter" of physics and chemistry. And when biology is at last freed from this dead hand of the mechanistic method, it will come out of the laboratory into the world; it will begin to transform human purposes as physics changed the face of the earth; and it will bring to an end the brutal tyranny of machinery over mankind. It will reveal even to philosophers, who for two hundred years have been the slaves of mathematicians and physicists, the directive unity, the creative resourcefulness, and the magnificent spontaneity of life.

[1] *Faust,* tr. Martin, p. 87. This is an example of what happens to Goethe when he is translated.

PART FOUR

PROBLEMS OF MORALITY

CHAPTER V

Our Changing Morals

I. THE RELATIVITY OF MORALS

MORALS, WHICH CHANGE so slowly, are changing today like clouds before the wind. Customs and institutions older than human memory melt under our eyes as if they were superficial habits, recently acquired and easily forgotten. Chivalry, which agreed with Nietzsche that "one cannot be too gentle with women," and gallantry, which graced the gravitation of bodies with the courtesies of the mind, have not survived the emancipation of women; men have accepted the challenge of equality, and find it hard to worship a sex which so unwarrantably flatters them with imitation. Chastity and modesty, which lured the lover to heroic enterprise, giving to every power a double power, have fallen into low repute, and young women woo their foes with charms so generously shown that curiosity no longer lends its aid to matrimony. City life has aggregated millions of esurient males for convenient exploitation by the purveyors of titillation; the stage rivals the candor of Restoration days, and modern literature becomes as phallic as ancient piety. Marriage, which used to be the way of all flesh, and which at an early age provided some stability for human life and conduct, is losing its popularity; its uses, men come to think, can be gotten without its pains; at either end it narrows and is consumed—by postponement to unnatural years, and by the noisy encroachments of divorce. The family, once nurse of morals and cherished basis of social order, yields to the individualism of urban industry, and is broken to pieces in a generation; homes built with sacrificial toil to shelter sons and daughters are silent and desolate, the children scattered in loyalty to wandering tasks, the father

73

and mother left alone in their bleak houses, every other chair vacant, and
every room echoing with the absence of familiar sounds.

Let us consider how the great transition through which we are passing
has caught and changed our morals.

It is a delicate question in psychology today whether our young people
find more pleasure in their strutting sins than their elders find in denouncing
them. Life, from the point of view of morals, seems to be divided into two
periods; in the first, we indulge, in the second we preach; passion yields to
caution, and the great currents of desire become the winds of speech; the
tempo of life slackens, the mood changes, and senility finds it hard to forgive youth. "Truth" in these matters is a function of age, and "immorality"
is other people's morals.

Those of us who have simmered down from youth, and not yet (perhaps)
congealed into old age, may make with some chance of success an attempt to understand our heirs. The proper orientation is historical; we
must contemplate the variability of the Good, the fluid relativity of morals;
we must see the earthly and fallible source of moral ideas, and their dependence upon the changing bases of human life.

Morals, in etymology and history, derive from customs (*mores*); morality,
in origin, is adherence to those customs which are considered essential to
the health and preservation of the group. Some customs are mere conventions, like the ritual of knife and fork at table, and have no moral aspect;
to cut one's salad with a knife is not a sin, though it is more severely
punished than adultery. But certain customs, like monogamy or polygamy,
endogamy or exogamy, abstention from murder within the tribe, and willingness to kill outside it, come to be looked upon as vital to the common
good; they develop into "categorical imperatives"—commands not to be
questioned—and are defended by passionate prohibitions, exhortations and
excommunications. Conventions are customs which are more practised than
preached; morals are customs which are more preached than practised. They
are duties which we require of our neighbors.

It is astonishing how the moral code has varied from time to time and
from place to place. St. Augustine was disturbed by the polygamy of
Abraham, but rightly pointed out that it was not "immoral" for the ancient Jews to pay the expenses of several wives, since it was the custom of
the time, and was not considered injurious to the group. Indeed, in an age
of war, polygamy may become a virtue, for it is blessed with many children. Before social order replaced the recurrent conflicts of tribe with
tribe, the death rate of men far exceeded that of women, and polygamy
was the natural result of the numerical superiority of the once weaker sex;
a woman would rather have a bit of a man than none at all. Monogamy is
one of the penalties of tribal peace.

Let us recall some instances of the relativity of morals. Orientals cover the head to show respect; Occidentals bare it. A Japanese woman (though this, like so many truths, may be no longer true) pays no attention to the nudity of a workman, and yet she can be as modest as Priscilla Dean. It was "obscene" (literally, "on the stage,"—referring to the Aristophanic looseness of ancient comedy) for an Arab woman to show her face, or a Chinese woman her foot; either concealment aroused imagination and desire, and served the good of the race! The Melanesians buried alive their sick and their old, and thought it a kindly way of disposing of their waste.[1] In China, says Lubbock, a coffin is (was?) regarded as an appropriate present for an aged relative, especially if he were in poor health.[2] On the Island of New Britain, says Sumner, "human flesh is sold in shops, as butcher's meat is among us. In at least some of the Solomon Islands, human natives (preferably women) are fattened for a feast like pigs."[3] It would be a simple matter to gather a hundred further instances in which the "immoral" of our time and place is the "moral" of other ages or other lands. If, said an old Greek thinker, you make a heap of all customs somewhere considered sacred and moral, and then take from it all customs somewhere considered impious and immoral, nothing will remain.[4]

II. THE AGRICULTURAL CODE

Apparently moral codes may change; what is it that changes them? Why is it that actions considered good at one time, or in one place, can come to be considered bad in another?

Probably it is an alteration in the economic basis of life that determines the moral change. There have been two profound transformations of this sort in history; one was the passage from hunting to agriculture, the other was the passage from agriculture to industry. These are the two pivotal events in human development, on which all other fundamental incidents and processes have turned. And in each case the moral code which had served group welfare in the older mode of life, was found maladapted, and was slowly and chaotically transformed under the new regime.

Nearly all the races of men once lived by pursuing beasts, killing them, cutting them up—usually on the spot—and eating them, often in the raw, and always to the cubic capacity of the hunter's stomach. For civilization, in the sense of economic provision and security, did not yet exist, and greed was a virtue necessary to self-preservation. Primitive man ate like the modern dog, because he did not know when his next meal would come;

---

[1] Sumner, W. G., *Folkways*, pp. 324, 431, 440.
[2] *The Origin of Civilization*, p. 24.
[3] *Op. cit.*, p. 324.
[4] The *Dialexeis*, in Gomperz, T., *Greek Thinkers*, vol. i, p. 404.

insecurity is the mother of greed, as cruelty is the child of fear. How much of our contemporary cruelty and greed, our surviving violence and occasional relish for war, goes back to the hunting stage! Hear this man in the restaurant whispering to the waiter, "Bring it to me rare"; he is still in the hunting stage.

Every vice was once a virtue, and may become respectable again, as hatred becomes respectable in war. Brutality and greed were once necessary in the struggle for existence, and are now ridiculous atavisms; man's sins are not the result of his fall; they are the relics of his rise. To select our impulses according to current demands, parents, neighbors and preachers pour out praise or blame upon us as we give sugar or whippings to the dogs that we are training; certain qualities of character with which nature has endowed us too moderately are thus encouraged, and certain others in which we excel beyond contemporary social need are trimmed down with such forms of dissuasion as being kept after school, or being cauterized in the electric chair. Let a mode of behavior, which is now censured or praised, diminish or develop to excess—i. e., to the point of imperiling the group— and censure or praise will gradually change to encouragement or blame. So America fostered the acquisitive impulses, and deprecated military virtues, as long as her resources needed exploitation from within and little protection from without; now something less of exploitation seems demanded, and (so they say) something more of protection; the mere millionaire is too common to be honored, while our admirals take the air with unaccustomed grandeur. There is a supply and demand in morals as well as in goods; and if the demand creates the supply more slowly in one field than in the other, it is because the soul is subtler and less tractable than the soil. But it too will receive varied seed, and produce wholesome or bitter fruit.

We do not know just when or how men passed from hunting to tillage; but we may be sure that the great transition created a demand for new virtues, and that many old virtues became vices in the settled and quiet routine of the farm. Industriousness was now more vital than bravery, thrift more desirable than violence, peace more profitable than war. Above all, the status of woman changed; she was more valuable on the land than in the hunt, for now she earned her keep ten-fold by doing the hundred chores of the home. To engage a woman for these varied tasks would have been expensive; it was cheaper to marry. More than that: every child the wife bore was soon a help far beyond the cost of its simple food and raiment. Children would work for their parents, on the farm, till adolescence was complete; no money had to be spent on their education; and even girls were moderately useful. Therefore motherhood was sacred, birth control was immoral, and large families were pleasing unto God.

It was in that rural *milieu* that our inherited moral code took form. For on the farm a man matured at an early age—matured both in mind and in self-support. At twenty he understood the tasks of life as well as he would at forty; all that he needed was a plough and a willing arm, and an eye for the weather's whims. So he married early, almost as soon as nature desired; he did not fret long in the restraints which the moral code placed upon pre-marital relations; the requirement of continence seemed reasonable even when he violated it. As for women, chastity was indispensable, because its loss might bring unprotected motherhood.

And when the precepts of Christianity enforced strict monogamy and indissoluble marriage, these seemed reasonable too. For the peasant's wife gave him many children, and it was right that father and mother should remain loyal to each other till these children were established in the world. By the time the last of them had grown up, the lust for variety had faded away in the weariness of the flesh and the assimilation and merger of two souls. On the farm the code of the Puritans, though hard, was practicable, and produced a sturdy race capable of conquering a continent in a century. Morality has always demanded more than. it expected, in order to get what it needed.

For fifteen hundred years this agricultural moral system of chastity, early marriage, divorceless monogamy, and multiple maternity maintained itself in Europe and European colonies. It could do so with the greater ease, since on the farm the family was the unit of production, tilling the soil together, and sharing the fruits. Even when industry began to appear, it was domestic industry, carried on not in factories but in homes, filling the household with new noise and busyness, new functions and new significance. And when the work of the day was done, the little sovereign group gathered about one table in the evening, or before one fire on the hearth, and played games, or read books about the wonders of the distant world. Everything conspired to strengthen the ties that held brother to brother, child to parent, and man to wife. It had its virtues, that Puritan civilization.

III. THE INDUSTRIAL CODE

Then suddenly factories appeared; men and women and children began to leave home and family, authority and unity, to work as individuals, individually paid, in dismal structures raised to shelter not human beings but machines. Cities grew; and instead of sowing seed and reaping harvests in the fields, men fought a life-and-death struggle, in dark and filthy shops, with belts and pulleys, great knives and saws, ten thousand wheels and presses, iron arms and teeth. Inventions bred like the *prolétaires* who worked them; every year a new progeny of mechanisms made life more difficult to handle and understand. Mental maturity came now much later than on the farm. At twenty, in a modern city, a man was still a boy in the face of a changing and intricate world; it took him another decade to shed his major delusions about men and women and states; at forty, perhaps, he approached maturity of mind. Adolescence lengthened, and a vast extension of education became a necessity to adjust the brain to the new tasks of modern life.

At once the passage from tillage to industry began to affect the moral behavior of mankind. Economic maturity came almost as late as mental maturity; only in the manual working class was a lad self-supporting, and ready to marry, at the age of twenty-one. Above those ranks the age of self-sufficiency mounted higher with every rise in luxury and place; in the professions above all was economic maturity delayed. In commerce and industry a thousand new factors, too distant or too complete for individual control, affected a man's work and might at any moment snatch it from his hands.

And man, burdened as never before by the demands and subtleties of life, saw woman shorn of her old functions by the development of factories and machines; if he married he would be compelled, by traditions coming down from the agricultural code, to keep his wife in the home—in a home now denuded of significance and work; she would be a beautiful parasite, an animated piece of interior decoration, and nothing more; all the work which she would have done in the house of olden days was now done in the factories, and would have to be paid for out of the products of the man's toil. And if, to avoid this functionlessness, the woman became a mother, the difficulties, in the city, would be increased: motherhood was now an expensive affair of doctors, nurses, hospitals, and instruments; and the modern woman could not bear children as easily and simply as her grandmother had done. But if she bore many, so much the worse. Every one of them would be a liability rather than an asset; they would have to be educated until sixteen, and perhaps until twenty-six; they would add to the rent and the cost of travel; they would interfere with a proper attendance at theatres and cabarets; they would have to be clothed in the latest style, to keep up with other children trying to keep up with them. By the time they earned an income they would have fled from parental authority to the freedom of the irresponsible individual life; and even if they did not go off of their own accord, the call of the job and the wage, the migration of markets and factories and trades, would tear them from the home, and scatter them like fragments from an exploding shell. Therefore, in the towns, motherhood seemed a form of slavery, an absurd sacrifice to the species, which a clever woman would accept as late as possible, and better never than late. Birth control achieved rapid respectability, and contraceptives became one of the problems of philosophy.

The invention and spread of contraceptives is the proximate cause of our changing morals. The old moral code restricted sexual experience to marriage, because copulation could not be effectively separated from parentage, and parentage could be made responsible only through marriage. But to-day the dissociation of sex from reproduction has created a situation unforeseen by our fathers. All the relations of men and women are being changed by this one factor; and the moral code of the future will have to take account of these new facilities which invention has placed at the service of ancient desires.

Out of all these conditions has come the wider and more general cause of our moral change—the deferment of marriage. In Paris, in 1912, the average age of marriage for men was thirty; in England it was twenty-six.[1] Very probably it has risen in England in the last seventeen years, and visibly the rest of the "civilized" (industrialized) world is moving in the same direction; for morals, like fashions, tend to come from Paris. This deferment of wedlock is greatest in the more capable ranks of urban society, which are best able to rear children in mental and physical health. Many never marry at all. Of 36,000,000 population in England and Wales in 1911, i. e. of 20,000,000 adults, 7,000,000 adults had successfully evaded the bonds of matrimony.[2] As the countryside is abandoned and the cities fill, the age of marriage mounts, and the tutelage of the courtesan has a longer period in which to graduate the male into incapacity for love.

More and more, the man of the middle class tends to consider marriage as a disadvantage for the male. A thousand women wait for him to provide satisfaction for his flesh, and what else than this does marriage offer, now that children are a burden and homes have been replaced by tenements? The bachelor observes the pace at which his married friends must toil to maintain their wives in that luxurious and mischievous idleness which is considered fitting to their station, and he wonders what could have driven these masculine men to such unprecedented slavery. Or he perceives the high standard of life and respectability—the entourage of furs and motors and maids—with which the middle-class parent surrounds his daughters in the effort to marry them away and raise the price they will bring; he wonders how he could rival, with his adolescent income, these comforts of a long-established home. He consults his banker, and decides to cherish felicity awhile.

So the city offers every discouragement to marriage, while it provides every stimulus and facility for sex. Erotic development comes as early as before, economic development later. That restraint of desire which was feasible and reasonable under the agricultural régime, seems now a difficult and unnatural thing in an industrial civilization that has postponed marriage, for men, even to the thirtieth year. Inevitably the flesh begins to rebel, the old self-control begins to weaken; chastity, which was a virtue, becomes a jest; modesty, which made loveliness more lovely, disappears; men

[1] Gallichan, W. M., *The Great Unmarried*, p. 47.
[2] *Ibid.*

plume themselves upon the variety of their sins, and women call for a single standard in which all shall be equally entitled to limitless adventures. Pre-marital experience becomes an ordinary thing; professional promiscuity is driven from the streets, not by the police, but by amateur competition. The old agricultural moral code has fallen to pieces, and the urban world ceases to judge by it any more.

Leibnitz was of the opinion that whether a man should marry is a question requiring a lifetime of consideration; [1] and our young men apparently agree with him. Some of them reflect too long, and become bachelors, wedded to *ennui:* one sees them in the parks, trying to catch life at second hand from sec nd-hand newspapers, shifting meanwhile from one sore bone to another; or at the cabaret, listless, tired of their kaleidoscope of legs, discovering that all chorus girls are alike, and bored at last even by vice. Contrasted with the emptiness of the average celibate's life, the difficulties of marriage are as nothing; better a hundred times those enlargening responsibilities, those hounding problems, than the growing sense of incompleteness, the lonely rotting of a limb that has borne no fruit.

We do not know how much of the "social evil" may be laid to the door of the deferment of marriage. Some of it, doubtless, is to be accounted for by our incorrigible love of variety; nature does not build us for monogamy. Some of it rests on the patronage of married men, who prefer a venal and venereal novelty to the boredom of laying siege to a surrendered citadel. But presumably most of it is due, in our time, to the unnatural postponement of connubial bliss; and even post-marital promiscuity must be in large part a product of pre-marital habituation. We may try to understand the biological and social causes of this flourishing industry, and may condone it as an unavoidable thing in a man-made world: this is the fashionable attitude of the most advanced minds. But it is a little shameful to accept complacently the picture of half a million American girls offering themselves as living victims to the Moloch of promiscuity, while our theatre and our literature are befouled by their eagerness to turn into gold the sexual irritability of men and women shut out by our industrial chaos from the health and wholesomeness of marriage.

The other side of the picture is almost as desolate. For every man who, deferring marriage, patronizes the ladies of the avenue, some woman waits in desiccating chastity. The man finds for the gratification of his own impulses, in this period of postponement, an international institution equipped with the latest improvements and organized with the most scientific management; the world seems to have devised every conceivable method for the stimulation and satisfaction of his desires. But the girl whom he will marry after ten years of experimentation must apparently maintain herself untouched and innocent until he deigns to receive her into his practised

[1] Williams, H. S., *The Science of Happiness*, p. 218.

arms. (Balzac compared the average bridegroom to an orang-utang trying to play the violin.) It is a somewhat irrational arrangement. No doubt it owes something to the high price which the chastity of their daughters used to bring to fond fathers in the days of marriage by (open) purchase; and no doubt it is bound up with that double standard, sanctified by time, which demands a one-sided fidelity of the mother in order that property may know its heirs. But in "pure reason" it seems an abominable injustice; and its days will not be long in the land.

There can be no honest questioning of the fact that continence is unnatural after maturity, that it leads to countless neuroses and perversions, and that it is an unwarrantable strain put upon mind and body in precisely that critical period of transition when mind and body need unstinted health. It is ridiculous for a moralist to inveigh against pre-marital relations unless he offers active resistance to the forces that lead to the deferment of marriage; we shall not long be able to make these demands unless the conditions under which they once were reasonable can be restored. It is time we faced our dilemma honorably; we must widen pre-marital liberty, or we must persuade marriage to return to the natural age.

IV. OUR IMMORAL ELDERS

It is the custom to associate our sexual riot with youth, but it runs through all ranks not yet exhausted by the pace. The deferment of marriage has flooded our cities with men and women who struggle to replace the engrossing tasks of parentage and the home with the external stimulations of variety; it is mainly this type (and the rural elder on his moral holidays in the metropolis) that feeds those night-clubs wherein lonely gullibles allow themselves to be stupefied with liquor in order to be fleeced by fair beasts of prey in whom they thought to find some substitute for love. Rapidly the habits of this class are pervading every class; it becomes fashionable to be promiscuous, and no man dares admit that he is faithful to his wife, or prefers consciousness to intoxication. It is promiscuous middle age, rather than romantic youth, that sets the tone of the day.

The source of our moral flux, as we have seen, is the deferment of marriage in modern communities; and here too, so far as personal causes enter, it is the parents, rather than the "younger generation," at whose door we must lay the change. The instincts of youth are sound, and would lead a lad to the halter soon enough; it is the cautious father and the jealous mother who ask the boy, indignantly, how much he is earning to let himself in for this madness of love? The wisdom of the pocket-book seems to form the essential philosophy of parental middle age; it forgets its own dead ecstasies, and never suspects that the youthful heart may have reasons which the old head cannot understand. It is the older generation, then, that is the more fundamentally immoral; they who, careless of the good of the community or the race, frustrate the wise imperatives of nature, and in effect counsel years of promiscuity as preparation for a happy marriage and vigorous children. Parents with a larger perspective would see how secondary a thing finances are, by the side of individual and social happiness and health; they would coöperate with nature and make some sacrifice to render the early marriage of their offspring possible. Until that parental perspective comes we shall be warranted in tracing the "immorality" of the young to the commercialism of middle age.

And who shall say that the looseness of youth is worse than the marital instability of middle age? The progressive conquest of marriage by divorce must startle even those who are sated with statistics. In Denver, in 1921, the number of separations granted equalled the number of marriages. In the preceding four years the proportion of divorces to marriages had risen from 25 to 50 per cent.[1] In Chicago, in 1922, there were 39,000 marriages, and 13,000 divorces. In 1924, in the state of New York, marriages decreased 4.6 per cent as compared with 1923; divorces increased 8.2 per cent.[2][3]

The "causes" assigned by the courts for this guillotining of marriage are ingeniously superficial: desertion, cruelty, neglect, intoxication, and what not,—as if these were unknown when divorce was rare. Beneath such surface factors lies the new distaste for parentage, and that passion for variety which, though it is as old as man, is enhanced ten-fold today by the individualism of modern life, the urban multiplicity of sexual stimuli, and the commercial supply of sexual gratification.

Woman's attractiveness as a mate is largely a matter of beauty; man selects for beauty because beauty was once the silent pledge of robust maternity. But marriage is long and beauty is fleeting; a thing of beauty is not a joy forever to one who marries it. Man's attractiveness as a mate is largely a matter of personality and vigor; but even the most brilliant personality, and the most virile ardor, must fade after years of compulsory companionship and devotion. The man saves himself for a time by daily absences; the woman seeks to preserve her beauty by postponing motherhood, and cultivating her skin with such an assortment of chemicals as makes scientific agriculture seem primitive and incompetent. But the heart of the matter soon appears. Woman's sexual attractiveness must, for the preservation of the marriage, be replaced by her attractiveness as a mother: thereby splendors flourish in her which were not dreamt of in the male's philosophy; now she changes and grows and is a revelation again, and the ancient wonder of the child wraps her about in a novel and irresistible

---

[1] *Literary Digest*, Feb. 17, 1923.

[2] New York *Times*, Nov. 15, 1925.

[3] In 1949 one marriage out of four, in the United States, ended in divorce. Los Angeles *Times*, Apr. 14, 1949.

charm. That missing, home becomes a house—dead walls around the corpse of love; and soon there are only fragments where there might have been a family.

V. THE FAMILY

Yet the family is the most natural and spontaneous of social institutions, resting directly on native dispositions not merely to mate but to rear children; so that one would not normally consider it necessary to make it the object of moral disquisitions. What we call the "reproductive instinct" is a labyrinthine complex of impulses, aptitudes, and preferences; and perhaps the mating motive should be distinguished strictly from such reproductive dispositions as the desire for offspring, and the tendency to care sedulously for children once they have arrived. For though some women and many men believe themselves exempt from the desire for offspring, there are few men and fewer women who do not soon find even the unwelcome and infinitely troublesome infant an admirable and lovable phenomenon. The coldest philosopher is prejudiced in favor of his child. If the child is sickly, love for it grows with the care it requires, as the artist loves with rising passion the picture that forms under his hand. If the child is ugly, kind nature blinds the parental eye, and lends imagination power over sense; "God sends the medicine with the disease." It is a kindly fate that has not given us the gift of seeing ourselves as others see us.

Of course children do not exist for parents, but parents for children; and the origin and significance of the family derive from the invaluable helplessness of the child. The family has been the saving vehicle of those customs and arts, those traditions and morals, which make the substance of our human heritage, and constitute the psychological cement of social organization. The child is an anarchist; there are no laws or conventions which he feels bound to respect, and prohibitions are his natural prey. But the family—through the other children as well as through the parents—turns the little individualist by bribes and blows, by candy and commandments, into a social being willing to coöperate—even, for a time, into a communist willing to divide. The family is the first social unit to which the individual learns allegiance; and his moral development would consist in learning loyalty to ever larger units, until at last even the far-flung borders of his fatherland would cramp his soul. But on leaving the *terra firma* of the home, youth plunges into the maelstrom of competition, and loses after a while the coöperative willingness fostered in the family. Middle age, prosperous but unhappy, turns back at times to the old homestead with a sense of comfort and relief, as to a communistic isle in a raging individualistic sea.

Now this function of the family, as the moral and integrating center of society, grew from its position as the producing unit of mankind. All the world knows that this focal position of the family is gone, and that our industrialized populations are in the unstable condition of shifting their moral base from an institution which has lost its economic and political footing. The migration of industry from home and field to factory and the road, the development of the elusive job as the geographically variable center of the individual life, the mobility of labor called everywhither as the flow of capital or the appearance of natural resources may decree, have cut through the bonds that held sons to their fathers in the conserving unity of the home. Large-scale industry and a consequently centralizing state have combined in that disruption of the home for which mere theories have received the blame. Family loyalty and devotion are drying up, and their emotional wealth is being absorbed by patriotism, just as parental power yields year by year to the broadened functions and exalted powers of the state. Everywhere the spontaneous coöperation of natural human association breaks up, and finds precarious replacement by the external and artificial bonds of law and order, of indoctrination and compulsion. At last this economic and political individualism mirrors itself in a moral individualism unsurpassed in the strategy of profit, and typical of those ages in which great civilizations have melted into the undistinguishable past.

VI. CAUSES

Let us recapitulate. The basic cause of these moral changes is the Industrial Revolution, which for good or evil has had a hand in almost every modern flux. The rise of the factory system has put back marriage by rendering the individual insecure; it has multiplied promiscuity by this incontinent postponement, and by throwing millions of people together amid the stimulating contacts and protective anonymity of city life; it has brought the emancipation (industrialization) of women, with pre-marital experiments as an incidental result; it has weakened the moral influence of the family; and it has led to the replacement of Puritan asceticism and restraint by an Epicurean efflorescence of every pleasure and every perversion. The development of contraception has coincided and coöperated with each of these causes in turn.

As it was the wealth of the Renaissance that led to its freedom, its license, and its art, so it is the wealth of our day and place, far more than any literary revolt, that has substituted for the rigid moral code of the Pilgrims the gay laxity of emancipated souls. Our changed Sabbath, day now not of rest and worship but of wanderings and pagan joys unconfined, is a visible sign of our altered morals and our liberated lives. It is easier to be virtuous when one is poor, and a man can sometimes resist temptation if it is expensive. But let our pockets bulge, while the solitude of the crowd conceals us from our neighbors' eyes, and we shall seek forgetfulness in every pretty face, and itch to demonstrate our manhood to our own uncertain hearts. Against our modern luxury of ornament and temperament moralists will sing their jeremiads in vain; for it is based upon impulses that have always existed, and that now find unusual opportunity. Until economic circumstances alter the case, the result will be the same. So long as machinery multiplies leisure, and replaces manual with mental tasks, energies once spent in physical labor will mount in the blood, and make us abnormally sensitive to all the stimuli of sex.

Perhaps this renaissance of joy has coöperated more than we thought with the Darwinian attack upon religious belief. When young men and women, bold with money, discovered that religion was denouncing their pleasures, they found a thousand reasons in science for denouncing religion. Puritan obscuration and deprecation of sex gave place to a reaction in which literature and psychology made sex as large as life. The old theologians disputed whether it was sinful to hold the hand of a girl; [1] today we wonder whether it would not be sinful to leave so pleasant an opportunity unexplored. Men have lost faith, and tend to fly from ancient caution to reckless experiment; it is a meet penalty which our morality pays for having bound itself up with supernatural belief. The old moral code was built upon fear—fear of punishment here, and Hell hereafter; but knowledge is bad for fear, and knowledge grows—the old code could not survive the coming of education. Our untempered lives cry out now for a new ethic, based in the nature of men and the values of this life, to salvage a civilization left to shift for itself by the sudden flight of the gods.

To the decay of agriculture and religion add the decay of the Anglo-Saxon stock. Puritanism has fallen not only because its once reasonable restrictions on human impulse have become unreasonable under the altered conditions of our day, but again because those ethnic stocks in which the old code still found vigorous example and support have in our cities reduced themselves to a helpless minority. Immigration and differences in the birthrate have exalted the humble and taken the mighty from their seats; it is the "non-Nordic" peoples from Ireland, Russia and Southern Europe that now dominate the politics of our larger cities, and give to literature and life the general tone of their lenient moral code. The domestic virtues of the Anglo-Saxon do not appeal to the jolly Irishman, the passionate Italian, or the easy-going Slav. Just as the New-England age in our literature is ended, while the later immigrants slowly and crudely experiment to find some form and style for their realistic and pessimistic philosophy, so the morals of our time flounder in a chaotic interlude while minorities once op-

[1] Ellis, *Studies in the Psychology of Sex,* vol. vi, p. 180.

pressed become the possessors of literature, the stage, the Church, and imminently of the State. Morality in America has shifted its ethnic, as well as its economic, base.

The final factor in the change was the First World War. That War broke down the habits of coöperation and peace which had been formed under the reign of industry and trade; it accustomed men to brutality and promiscuity, and returned thousands of them to their countries as centers of moral infection; it cheapened the value of life by its wholesale killing, and prepared the psychology of gangs and crime; it destroyed the faith of millions in a benevolent Providence, and took from conscience the prop of religious belief. After the idealism and unity of Armageddon a disillusioned generation reacted into cynicism, individualism, and a reckless immorality. States fell apart, classes resumed their war, industries sought profits regardless of community good, men avoided the responsibility of marriage, women were flung into a corroding slavery or a degenerative parasitism, and youth found itself endowed with new liberties, protected by invention from the ancient consequences of amatory adventure, and assailed on all sides by a million erotic stimuli in art and life.

These, then, are the varied causes of our moral change. It is in terms of their transit from farms and houses to factories and city streets, that we must understand the generation which so boisterously replaces us. Their lives and problems are new and different. The Industrial Revolution has them in its grip, and transforms their customs, their garb, their work, their religion, and their conduct; to judge them in terms of the old code is as unfair and unhistorical as to force upon them the corsets and bustles, the beards and boots of our ancient days. The words "morality" and "immorality" are in a flux, between old moorings lost and new ones yet to find; no one knows just what they should mean, and how they may be redefined to help us understand human conduct in an industrial and urban age.

We stand between two worlds—one dead, the other hardly born; and our fate is chaos for a generation. We are like Socrates and Confucius, conscious that the morality of restraint and fear has lost its hold upon men; and we too must look for a natural moral code that shall rest upon intelligence rather than fear, and be able to convince even educated men. Those of us who have children are faced by a thousand questions in morals and psychology for which our old answers will not serve. We are compelled, despite ourselves, to be philosophers, to scrutinize our assumptions and our habits, to build for ourselves a system of life and thought that shall be consistent with itself and with the experience and demands of our time. We stand before the stars almost naked of supernatural creed and transmitted moral code; everything must be rebuilt, even as if we had been cast into the wilderness and forced to begin civilization anew.

Where shall we find a moral code that shall accord with the changed conditions of our lives, and yet lift us up, as the old code lifted men, to gentleness, decency, modesty, nobility, honor, chivalry and love?—or to new virtues as beneficent as these? How shall we re-define the Good? How shall we remake the moral basis of the Great Society?

CHAPTER VI

Morality and Immorality

I. MORALITY AS INTELLIGENCE

LET US LISTEN for a moment to what the philosophers have to say on the subject of morality. They will disturb our judgment further; but only by letting all the factors in the situation play upon us can we find a response that will be adequate to our problem.

At the very outset we are plunged into the thorny center of the moral maze by those ruthless founders of European ethics, the Greek Sophists. For they offer proposals and analyses which make Nietzsche seem second-hand and tame; they steal, two thousand years in advance, half his thunder from the gentle blond beast of German philosophy. Morality, says the Callicles of Plato's *Gorgias,* is an invention of the weak to chain the strong, a way of restraining the Superman within the limits and capabilities of the mediocre average. The wise man will retain a superior impartiality between "virtue" and "vice"; he will have great desires, and will seek, as the noblest qualities, the strength, the courage and the skill to realize them.[1] And the Thrasymachus of the *Republic* proclaims to the world that "might is right, and justice merely the interest of the stronger; the 'unjust' is lord over the truly simple and just, and the 'just' is always loser by comparison." [2] He is careful to add that he is "speaking of injustice on a large scale"; he doubts the advisability of being unjust if one cannot do it wholesale.

It is instructive to see how old this critique of "goodness" is; can it be that Nietzscheanism belongs to the youth rather than to the maturity of thought? The Sophists represent the intoxication of freedom that came to Greek philosophy when it had thrown off the shackles of polytheism and tradition. The old moral code among the Greeks had rested insecurely on a theological basis and sanction, like a man with his feet in the air; the discovery that the basis was unsound inevitably hurt morality; and unmoralism, like atheism, materialism, and determinism, became one of the

[1] Plato, *Gorgias,* sect. 483 f.
[2] *Republic,* Book I.

natural incidents of youth's passing revolt. So with us: when we perceive that the Jehovah of our childhood fears—that Michelangelesque Moses of the sky—is no real deity, but only a bogey man designed to keep us from stealing marbles and hanging our teachers, we come to the conclusion, transiently, that since this barbaric god does not exist, all the things that he forbade are now legitimate, and theft and murder and procrastination are respectable activities if practised on the right scale and with a decent regard for the opinion of the police. As Dostoievski's Ivan put it: "If there is no God" (meaning the aforesaid Nocturnal Terror), "all is permitted"; it is only necessary to be careful. The problem of ethics (which is the rational study of morality) is whether it is desirable to be "good" as well as careful; and if so, how men may be persuaded thereof.

Only in the light of this Sophistical adolescent Nietzscheanism can we understand the high place of Socrates in the development of moral philosophy. For Socrates saw Athens hovering between two dangers: democratic majority compulsion to return to orthodox belief, and that unmoral and unscrupulous individualism which came of disillusionment with the ancient creed, and was to make chaotic Athens a helpless prey to Sparta's sternly nurtured aristocracy. Need we specify the analogies with our contemporary scene? Socrates visioned the greatest problem of philosophy as that of developing a natural ethic to take the place of the supernatural ethic which philosophy had destroyed. If one could build a system of morality absolutely independent of theological creeds, then these might come and go without loosening the moral cement that makes of separate individuals the peaceful citizens of a commonwealth. If, for example, *good* meant *intelligent,* and *virtue* meant *wisdom;* if men could be taught to know their real interests, to see afar the distant results of their deeds, to criticize and coördinate their desires out of a self-canceling chaos into a purposive and creative whole—this, perhaps, would provide, for the educated and sophisticated man, the morality which in the unlettered relies on supernatural sanctions and policemen's clubs. Possibly all sin is ignorance, a failure of total vision? Would not intelligence, spread by unstinted education, be a virtue sufficient to maintain all necessary social order?

A subtle individualism lay hidden in this doctrine, which was conceived as the ethical counterpart of an aristocratic political philosophy. It assumed that the honor of a real nobility could be established by the instruction of a generation; it never faced the question whether intelligence might not make a villain more intelligently villainous. The old dilemma remained: to render intelligence social, or to find for morality some basis outside of intelligence and reason. Plato tried the first solution: intelligence, he argued, is no merely intellectual affair; it is an esthetic or artistic harmony of the elements in a man's character, a symmetry, or order, or proportion, in human conduct; and the highest virtue is not brilliance of mind, or unmoral strength, but the harmony of the parts with the whole, whether in the individual or the state. Here was a sound base from which to make further ethical explorations; but philosophy did not pursue it. Greece fell to pieces despite her moralists; and when Christianity came, all the world was ready for a moral code that should reinforce the weakness of altruism and honesty with the hopes and fears of another life. The old problem of a natural ethic, independent of theologies, was left unsolved.

II. NATURAL MORALITY

Here, as in so many fields, it was Francis Bacon who offered a clue. A remarkable sentence in *The Advancement of Learning* contains in outline an entire theory of secular ethics. "All things," says the great Chancellor, "are endued with an appetite to two kinds of good—the one as this thing is a whole in itself" (this appetite we call the individualistic instincts), "the other as it is part of some greater whole" (this other appetite we call the social instincts); "and this latter is more worthy and more powerful than the other, as it tends to the conservation of a more ample form." [1] That is to say, morality, like immorality, has its basis in human nature; there are social as well as egoistic impulses, instincts for group and race preservation, as well as for self-preservation; and these social instincts, Bacon thinks, are ultimately stronger than the instincts that aim to preserve the individual. Certainly this is interesting, if true; and it is along this line that the search for a natural morality must move.

It was not until Darwin that this new lead of Bacon's found, unwittingly, some scientific basis. At first the ethical implications of Darwinism seemed to favor Nietzscheanism; if evolution is a struggle for existence and a survival of the fittest, then survival is the test of fitness in everything, not excepting morals; the only good man is the man who succeeds, and might becomes right once more. Huxley was horrified to see where the theory of evolution was leading; he agreed with Tennyson that nature (by which he meant the process of natural selection) was "red in tooth and claw," utterly hostile to all the ethical principles that had so ameliorated human life. Evolution meant, to all appearances, the elimination of the weak by the strong (already evolutionists like Karl Pearson were protesting against the dysgenic effects of charity); morality, however, meant the aid of the weak by the strong. Evolution involved a struggle to survive, by whatever means; morality involved the restriction of struggle within the limits of humaneness and honor. The great goal of morality was peace; the great test of survival was war. "The ethical progress of society," Huxley concluded, "depends not on imitating the cosmic process . . . but on combating it." [2]

[1] Book vii, ch. 1.
[2] *Evolution and Ethics*, p. 83.

It was a disastrous position to take; for if morality is contrary to nature, morality is doomed. Huxley himself was clear-eyed enough to see it: "The cosmic nature born with us, and to a large extent necessary to our maintenance, is the outcome of millions of years of severe training, and it would be folly to imagine that a few centuries will suffice to subdue its masterfulness to purely ethical ends." [1] The moral problem—of securing human decency without fables and without force would be utterly insoluble if morality and nature should be found so radically opposed.

It was the modest Darwin who showed the way out. The philosophers had not observed—and would not, till Kropotkin [2] pointed their noses to it—that in the fourth chapter of *The Descent of Man* the great "destroyer" had laid the foundations of a moral code that would rest not on theological creeds but on biological facts. Aristotle and Bacon were right; man was by nature social, because societies had existed long before man, and humanity had inherited social habits—had carried sociability in its blood—along with the individualistic impulses to compete and kill. Even in the lower stages of animal life, social organization has been developed, as in the ants and bees, to a point of coöperation superior to any seen in the human race. As societies evolved, competition within them was restrained by the necessity of preserving internal solidarity in the face of competition without; natural selection played less and less upon the individual, more and more upon groups; weak individuals might be preserved by the growing social habits of their fellows, but weak nations like Spain, weak races like the Tasmanians, weak species like the mastodon or the buffalo, could be destroyed in the war and competition of groups. Evolution ceased to be physical, it became social; survival came not by individual power, but by group coherence and ability. Organization made superfluous the heavy defensive apparatus borne constantly about by solitary creatures relying only on their individual strength and cunning for defense; in ants and bees, where social organization was most complete, the individual burden of armament—tusks and teeth and claws and thick hides—had almost entirely disappeared. The development of external danger and competition unified the members of a group into some measure of fellow-feeling (sym-pathy), group-feeling (kindness), sociability, and mutual aid; those simple virtues which the unsocial Nietzsche had considered feminine were really social necessities for group survival; and the strange paradox appeared that the very violence of competition and strife among societies was the cause of coöperation and peace within; it was war, or the possibility of war, that made morality, as it made morale.

In the light of this biological approach it becomes sufficiently obvious that the natural and inevitable basis and definition of morality is the co-

[1] *Ibid.*, p. 85.
[2] *Mutual Aid as a Factor in Evolution.*

operation of the part with the whole. It is that total perspective in which each desire coöperates with the whole body of desire, each individual with his family, each family with the state, every state with humanity, and humanity itself with the upward movement of life. In youth we try to define morality in terms of the rebellious individual: we canonize intelligence, forgetting the treacherous subservience of intellect to desire, its menial readiness to find reasons for any questionable deed; we laud self-reliance, non-conformity, and bravery; we sing the "simple, separate person," and say like the solitary Ibsen that he is strongest who stands alone, as if either Brand or Peer Gynt found it so. It is a wholesome reaction against the heavy sociability of the family, and only means that the boy is grown up, and wishes to announce himself to the world. Later we discover that the "society" which we scorned, and to which we opposed the magnificent individual, consists of nothing else than individuals too, each as precious as our incomparable selves. After long resistance we admit that morality can never be defined in terms of the individual, and that we must accept the good of the whole as the ultimate criterion by which to judge (when we must judge) the behavior of the part.

The parenthesis is the saving grace of our conclusion. How often must we judge? As the best government is still that which governs least, so the best morality is that which forbids least; freedom of life is so great a boon that those who wish to make morals for their neighbors are rightly considered enemies of the human race. We have seen how precarious every moral judgment is; how the "immoral" may be only a groping transition between one code of morals and another. Above all, this abstemiousness in moral judgment is "indicated" in the treatment of men and women who are afflicted with genius; such persons are set aside by nature, so to speak, to experiment with new ways of action, feeling, and thought; and to subject them to our normal and necessary "herd-morality" is to frustrate the very purpose of their coming. We need not be much more severe with them than Pope Paul III, who, when advised to imprison Cellini for various acts of homicidal enthusiasm, replied: "You should know that men like Benvenuto, unique in their profession, stand above the law." Let us extend to our geniuses something of the leniency which we offer to our millionaires.

We have arrived deviously at a most respectable and ancient conclusion, that the test of morality is community good. But our biological approach must not deceive us into supposing that our instincts here conform with reason. Nature knows no community and no morality except those of the hive, the family, and the hunting-pack. Bacon and Darwin and Kropotkin were optimistic in believing that the social instincts are stronger than the instincts of self; it may be so within the family, where self-sacrifice is natural, and needs no other external stimulus than love or praise; but outside that little realm the individualistic impulses are in the saddle, as he who runs may see, and heroism is heroic precisely because it is so rare. Hence the vast mechanism which society evolves for the reinforcement of the social impulses by religion, education, editorials, and statues in the streets. We are not even the most social of species; we stand midway between the individualism of the jungle and the coöperation of the ants; and the best we can say is that the social instincts—which seem to be more recent in origin than those of competition and acquisition, and have been temporarily weakened by the decay of religion and the family—are being slowly strengthened by the growing survival value of coöperation. Perhaps, in some distant day, those who hunger and thirst for individual possessions and power will be weeded out by those who have learned to work in harmony and justice with their fellow-men. We shall be elsewhere then.

If the conservative is too well pleased with this formulation of the moral principle, let him consider some of its implications. Nothing is immoral unless it injures one's fellows: therefore, under certain circumstances, suicide is sinless. If a man is convinced that death is a boon, if he has fulfilled his obligations to the race, and leaves no living soul dependent or bereaved, his life is his own, to do with what he wills. Again, if instinct or pleasure calls us, we shall not be wrong in following it, provided that no fellow-being is thereby harmed, and we ourselves suffer no hurt, of body or mind, to the detriment of the race. "Sin" ceases to have meaning except where the good of the whole is involved.

Finally, we should realize that the coöperation in which morality consists arises less from the growth of the soul than from the widening necessities of economic life; the flower grows out of the soil. Morality spreads as economic and social units increase; the whole with which the part must coöperate to be saved becomes greater as the world is woven into ever larger units by rails and wires and ships and the invisible bonds of the air. Once trade and common interest merged tribes into nations, and tribal morality degenerated into the last refuge of a scoundrel. Slowly trade and common interest merge nations into vast national groups, and provide the basis for an international morality. Soon all the world will agree that patriotism is not enough.

III. THE CRITERION OF MORALS

There is, then, one criterion of morality which seems to hold good at all places and all times, however various the languages it may speak. But every solution is a problem: no sooner do we reach our definition of morality as the coöperation of the part with the whole, than a hundred new questions appear. With what group shall we coöperate—with the family, or the state, or humanity, or life? And what shall we do if our loyalties conflict?

When a man turns forty his great temptation is to conceive morality as solely devotion to his family. Not that he quite lives up to his conception; if he did, perhaps (as Confucius thought) no other morality would be required. If the state has grown like a leviathan, and has absorbed one parental right and function after another, it is not merely because our economic life has developed complex interrelations and contradictions which demand at the center of the community a coördinating and adjudicating authority; it is also because the individualism of industry has disintegrated paternal authority, and shorn the family of its ancient roles. When nearly every American family was an economic sovereignty, growing its own food, weaving its own clothing, shooting its own Indians, and seldom dealing with other groups, family morality might have sufficed. If the man was a good father, if the woman was a good mother, and if the children accepted the father's authority as final, the family was a sound unit of social order, so self-sufficient that the state was a minor and almost negligible thing: let China serve as illustration. But when the family falls to pieces, or when the relations of its members with other individuals and groups come to play a vital role in its economic and moral life, then the old natural morality breaks down: a man may be generous to his children, and ruthless with unseen employees; a man may sell his country for pieces of silver, and be reputed a model husband and father; a man may secretly steal and cheat to keep financial peace with his wife, and yet be honored in every church which he deigns to attend. Family morality is not enough.

Are we driven, then, into the arms of the omnivorous state? Must our moral code resolve itself into loyalty to politicians?—to the ward boss, the district leader, the "Organization," the Governor, the Senate, and the Commander-in-Chief of the Army and Navy? That is the answer which the politicians give; and, reinforced with every military and provincial voice, it drowns out any reply that overleaps the sovereign state. It is not quite without reason. For until an international order is a reality, and humanity is organized to use and protect the allegiance of the individual, an ideally perfect morality—a coöperation of the part with the completest whole—will be but a counsel of perfection, like the command to resist not evil; what order there is in the world must be supported until a larger community comes. So on a planet whose population, uncontrolled in its multiplication and its movements, would flow from every direction to the highest level of wages, ruining every experiment in the conquest of poverty, it is well that the more highly organized unit should protect itself from the lower, as man, however loyal to life, must protect himself against the beast. In the long run it is good for all mankind that advanced peoples should so protect themselves; for it is indispensable to evolution that there should be somewhere an imitable excellence. Until industry evolves some international control, the whole with which it must coöperate, and whose interests it must not injure, will be the national community.[1]

But even within that lesser group our conscience is still unformed. There is a morality of industry and politics, as well as of love and marriage; and those who complain about the vagaries of modern sex may be just the men who are filching profits or betraying states. We tremble at one lost maiden, but cannot find it in our hearts to put corruptionists in jail; we censor books, but do not mind when munition-makers stir up war. Of all the nonsexual difficulties that confront morality today, the only one that catches our concern is the absorbing problem of getting alcohol. Doubtless there is an ethical issue there, and the lawlessness that stems from a questionable law weakens the moral fibre of the whole community. But it is a sign of our immaturity that our conversation and our campaigns should overflow with arguments about drink, while enterprises of great pith and moment go awry for lack of attention and understanding.

Here is the largest industrial system that history has ever seen: what if it is being managed with no thought of the whole, no consideration of the effect of industrial, commercial and financial policies upon the future of the nation and the race—is this a little thing? When we say that "business is business" we mean, presumably, that there is no morality in business; that the industrial process, through large-scale production, absentee ownership and cut-throat competition, has become inhuman and impersonal, a mechanism for buying cheap and selling dear, a machine that turns schools into apprentice-shops and soldier-factories, that employs women in preference to men, and children in preference to women, that ruins the national physique and character,—but makes profits. And this conception of the economic life is true of the *prolétaire* as well as of the manufacturer; he thinks of his own good or the good of his class, seldom of the good of the whole. Each faction has "ideals"; but an ideal, in industry or politics, is usually the suppressed desire of a class, dressed up in the dignity of reason; and most theories of ethics are merely our notions as to how other people should behave.

"Economics," said Nassau Senior, "is a science of wealth, not of welfare." That is, industry should concern itself with the production of the greatest possible quantity of goods, regardless of the results to producer and consumer. The older science was better, though Carlyle dubbed it dismal; it

---

[1] This is not to say that our present restrictions on immigration are reasonable or just. On the contrary they seem to have no other basis than ethnic prejudice and fear. Statesmanship would limit immigration, perhaps even more than now, till unemployment ends; it would restrict it, however, not by invidious racial discriminations which are quite without warrant in science, but by raising the standards of health and intelligence required of the immigrant.

called itself "political economy," and recognized that economics had something to do with the body politic. It was once permissible to speak of human
"rights"; and though that term is now in disrepute, it held in it this core
of reality and value, that there are some demands which an individual or a
class may make upon society, that would, if met, make for the good of the
whole; such a demand may reasonably be called a "right." If, for example,
agriculture is essential to a nation's safety from blockade and starvation,
then farmers have a "right" to such governmental aid as may be needed to
keep them moderately alive; England is learning this lesson. If chemicalized
industries ruin the health of workers, those workers have a "right" to whatever protection the state can give them, for the health of its citizens is a
proper concern of the community. If women are being made unfit for motherhood by the occupations they pursue, it is right that government should
protect such of them as desire protection. If investors or traders pursue
methods likely to arouse foreign hostility to America, we are again within
our rights in subjecting such investments and such trade to national regulation. At every step the economic process affects the fortunes of the community, and impinges upon morality.

But alas, the only instrument now open to us for the control of industry
within communal good is the state; and the state is not a moral entity, but
a perpetually changing assortment of elected persons. The reformer longs
for an omnipotent government, forgetting that this merely means omnipotent politicians. Better a hundred times that men should build up their
own methods of coöperation and control, than that they should rely upon
aldermen and policemen! Perhaps a new order of society is being born
quietly in the unheralded lower strata of distribution, in the coöperatives
that yearly form (and almost yearly fail) to bridge the widening gap, and
to escape the growing army of intermediaries, between him who makes and
him who buys; here economics touches morality again, and the moralist
warms at the thought that another century of effort and experiment may
replace with coöperation the individualistic competition upon which we
must now rely for the business of the world. A picture of men working together, engaging technicians and managers together, sharing profits together, sharing losses together—it seems as unreal as a modern corporation
would have seemed in the days when industry was being born.

Our instincts are ultimately individualistic, but our institutions and our
social necessities mould us more and more to coöperation. Already industry
is kind compared to the horrors of the factory system a hundred years ago;
welfare becomes a part of every modern establishment; and industry
finances, with a goodly portion of its profits, hospitals, colleges, libraries
and scientific research. Saints are still born among us, helpful men meet us
at every turn, modest girls can be found if we like to find them, patient
mothers hide in a thousand homes, and heroism rivals crime in the daily

press. A flood comes, a thousand people go to help, and a million men contribute financial aid; a nation starves, and her enemies succor her; explorers are lost, and others give their lives to rescue them. No one has yet fathomed man's potentialities for good. Behind our chaos and our crime lies the fundamental kindliness of the human soul. It waits till the riot is over, and another moral order emerges, by trial and error, to lift it to nobility.

IV. THE LARGER MORALITY

Perhaps, while we stand by and scoff, even a world of international order is evolving before our unseeing eyes. Commerce and finance are making it, by cross-investment and the desirability of keeping one's creditors solvent and one's markets prosperous; it is not workingmen but millionaires that are now the great enemies of war. Hear the crowd applaud when the government talks war; but watch the ticker and see how a thousand enterprises are cramped with fear as the news of hostilities resounds. It was not always so; but it is so today.

Now this was just what the world waited for, that the great web of commercial exchange and interdependence, which had made states into a Union, and nations into empires, should at last build an international economic order. For precisely as ideal emotions in the individual are unsound and precarious if they have no natural physiological basis, so moral and political ideas can stand securely only on economic realities. When we have an economic world-order we shall begin to have a political world-order; when we have a political world-order we shall begin to have an international morality. Conscience follows the policeman; it arises in submission to order, and grows with habituation. Visibly today an international order is being born; and now, whenever national interest seems to us contrary to the interests of mankind, nothing should prevent us from being loyal to humanity, and rising in morals and diplomacy to that sense of the whole which is the secret of the good life, as it is the guide to wisdom and the test of truth.

Therefore let every experiment and tentative towards the new world-order be applauded and encouraged. Let science continue to organize itself upon a basis that ignores frontiers; and let labor renew its broken pledges against war. Despite all its weakness, its cowardice, its inconsistent exclusion of Russia, its (intentionally) impossible constitution, let us enter the League of Nations,[1] strengthen it with our coöperation, and put an end to our provincialism, our chauvinism, our armament competition, and the secret dream of a few scoundrels to dominate the world. Here in truth, to apply beyond his intent a phrase of Mirabeau's, *la petite morale est l'ennemi de la grande:* the little morality is the enemy of the large. We cannot expect the state to teach the international conscience to its children in school, so long as dan-

[1] Written in 1927.

ger of war survives; but we free-lances of the spirit, why should we again be suicidally divided here?—What is to prevent *us* from accepting the larger morality, and being loyal to all life?

Back of this perpetual division among liberals is the individualism that lurks as a corrosive in nearly every freedom. The greatest of America's criminal lawyers [1] rejoices in the futility of the League of Nations, on the ground that a supernational political order would be another despotism— that the separation of states and an occasional war are preferable to a gigantic political authority that might stand like an irresponsible despot over the thought and movement of mankind. It is an honest and reasonable doubt; but if it was well to run these risks in uniting the Colonies, it is well to run the same risks in uniting nations today, when one touch of science in one day of war can kill entire armies, destroy whole cities, and reduce all life, all order, all freedom and all thought to the level of savagery again. It is not in strong but in weak governments that the danger to freedom lies; it is when a state is imperiled that it puts an end to liberty. We must choose between a *Pax Romana* and a Balkanized world.

V. SEX AND MORALITY

Nothing will so displease the individualist as this almost physiological definition of morality in terms of coöperation between the parts and the whole. He will protest that the only true morality is intelligence; [2] or he will go the full length and say with Anatole France, *L'hygiène est la seule morale* —hygiene is the sole morality. But a criminal may use all the advertised necessities of cleanliness, and yet make a vast fortune by selling narcotic drugs; a great French premier may be a man of exceptional intelligence and ability, and yet kill a million Frenchmen for the privilege of taxing Alsace-Lorraine; the most antiseptic lechery may replace marriage with promiscuity, children with lap-dogs, and national vigor with national decay. Intelligence would suffice if it were complete, and could be made to graduate into wisdom; but what shall we do while we wait for its completion? Men steal and kill and die before we can mature them into philosophers. No; we must begin with youth and patiently teach coöperation; we must build it into the habits and feelings of the growing individual; we must find some way of giving, even to intelligent men, a restraining sense of the whole. Perhaps in the end this will not be far different from real intelligence: the whole perspective of thought will include the whole perspective of society, and comprehension will bring loyalty.

Even our young neolaters will understand, when they grow up, that since the life of the group depends upon the quality of the race and the careful

---

[1] Clarence Darrow.
[2] As the present author did in *Philosophy and the Social Problem*.

nurture of children, our sexual ambitions must submit to certain moral limitations. We may be tolerant of our inventive immorality, we may wish to study homosexuality, zoöerotism, . . . scatophilia, on the stage, we may smile at these audacious tentatives as guideless gropings towards another moral code. But we cannot satisfy our own hearts with any ethic that ignores the group; we feel, in the very aftermath of an unsocial act, the need of a sounder and cleaner life; we want an existence in which we shall know not only the pleasures of the skin, but the quiet contentment of comradeship and coöperation. We wish to be healthy animals, but we wish also to be citizens.

Can anything be done to transform our moral chaos into order, our license into responsibility? We must not exaggerate the influence of discussion and ideas here; these changes in the relations of the sexes have not come through thinking, and they will not be frightened away by our syllogisms. We face an impersonal process of economic transformation affecting the moral life; and unless our thought falls in with that stream of invention which determines the course of history, we shall be left stranded by the flux, righteous and impotent.

And yet the passion for understanding will not let us rest; we must take this moral change apart, and analyze its causes and results; we do not give up the hope that here, too, knowledge will be power, and clarity will bring control. Let us begin at the beginning, and examine that flame of love which breaks through every moral code, consuming the individual and preserving the race. Let us study the character of the sexes, and see the nature of those two strange organisms—man and woman—whose mutual attraction and hostility generate the problems of sexual morality. Let us observe for a while the emancipated woman, and consider the influence of her sudden liberation upon the morals of our time and the future of mankind. Then we shall be ready to face the breakdown of marriage with some knowledge of its background and causes; and diffidently we shall offer some suggestions for the reconciliation of this difficult institution with human happiness and social health. Finally we shall bring ethics down to earth, and discuss the training of children and the formation of character. So the circle will be complete.

CHAPTER VII

Love

I. WHY DO WE LOVE?

LOVE IS BY ACCLAIM the most interesting of all forms of human experience; and it is astonishing that so few have cared to study its origin and development. What a majestic stream of literature has poured forth about it in every language, and from almost every pen—what epics, what dramas, what fiction, what passionate and endless poetry—and yet how little science, how scarce the efforts to scrutinize the wonder objectively, to find its source in nature, and the causes of its marvelous growth from the simple merging of the protozoa to the devotion of Dante, the ecstasy of Petrarch, and the loyalty of Héloïse to Abélard!

Yes, of course, men desire women, and love, "which moves the sun and the other stars," lifts every soul to some passing nobility before life ends. But why? Poetry has proved its point—that love springs eternally in the human breast; but where is the secret fountain of its youth? Why does a lad thrill at the sight of curls flashing across arched eyes, or at the touch of feminine fingers on his arm? Is it because the lady is beautiful? But does not his love create her beauty as much as her beauty creates his love? Why does he love?

There is nothing in human affairs so strange as the readiness of men, this side senility, to pursue women,—unless it be the readiness of women, this side the grave, to be pursued. There is nothing in human conduct so persistent as the measuring glance of male upon female at every moment of the day. See the wily animal eyeing his prey as he pretends to read his inevitable newspaper. Hear his conversation, how it roams about the everlasting hunt; imagine his imagination, how restlessly it flits about the magnetic flame. Why? How did this come to be? What are the origins of this profound desire, and through what stages did it pass to its present glory and madness?

Let us try, rashly, to find the answers to these questions which lovers never ask. Let us bring together such science as we can, from Stendhal, and Ellis, and Moll, and Bölsche, and De Gourmont, and Freud, and Stanley Hall, and see if we can make a composite picture in which love, finding its perspective, will reveal its function and its significance. Let us retrace, as far as we can, the path by which love came.

II. A BIOLOGICAL APPROACH

As hunger and love alternate in the individual, so life as a whole revolves about nutrition and reproduction as the great foci of its orbit. Nutrition is a means to reproduction, and reproduction is a means to nutrition. We eat that we may live, that we may mature, that we may fulfil ourselves in parentage; and in reproduction we separate from our dying flesh new life that shall have the power to feed and grow again, perhaps to finer stature than before.

In the simplest cell, apparently, it is growth that compels that bursting apart which is the lowliest form of reproduction. The mass of the cell grows faster than the surface through which it feeds; to restore the proportion it divides in two; and the surface, spreading down through the division, is again made adequate to the mass. The explanation is theory, but the division itself is fact enough. Bacteria—the smallest organisms that we know —multiply themselves by tireless division and redivision, until the mind faints numbering them. The central mass or nucleus of the *Amœba* undergoes a strange separation of elements into two nuclei, and then the entire animalcule divides and forms two new *Amœbœ*. Here is parentage, but as yet no differentiation of the sexes, and presumably no love.

Such division of an organism into two is the essence of nature's devices for the continuity of life, even in *Homo sapiens;* and though she develops the formula into a thousand complications, she never quite abandons it. Among the protozoa (or single-celled animals) this generation by division prevails; budding is only a variation on the theme. A baby *Hydra* buds from the stalk of the older one, and grows by feeding on the life-stream of its parent; as it matures it reaches out pugnaciously for food in competition with the very organism from which it buds; at last it tears itself loose, finds new rootage somewhere, and sets up its own establishment.

Sometimes the divided cells of a protozoön, as in the case of *Volvox,* remain embedded in a gelatinous matrix and form a "colony." Then a startling differentiation of function arises: the external cells specialize in nutrition, and the internal cells in reproduction; the colony becomes a social organism, with interdependent and coöperative parts. At the very beginning of its panorama life offers us an example of that "isolation of the germ-plasm" upon which Weismann based the prevailing theory of heredity in man.

But though division is universal, it does not suffice; the time comes, after many generations, when the repeatedly subdivided protozoön seems to lack the energy required to form new organisms. At this point a new phenomenon appears. Two weakened protozoa of the same species coalesce, and each pours out from its nucleus a stream of protoplasm which passes into the substance of the other. Then they separate, and seem strangely strengthened by this "rejuvenating conjugation"; for soon each of the two divides with pristine vigor, and for many generations division serves again the purposes of continuity. It is with the protozoa here as with our human selves and groups: when a man marries he is made stronger; when races mingle they are renewed.

Nevertheless, significant as this simple union is, there is in it no analogue to that mating of dissimilar individuals which is the root of the flower of love. Can we find such an analogue in the lowest organisms? We approach it in *Pandorina,* a protozoan colony of sixteen cells. Each of the cells divides not into two independent cells, but into many infinitesimal bits or "spores," apparently all alike; and a new organism arises only when two spores unite. Pass to another colonial protozoön, *Eudorina,* and what we seek is found: here each cell breaks into dissimilar spores, some large and quiet, some active and small; and not till a small spore merges with a large one is a new organism formed. In *Eudorina* nature began to discover sex.

For a time she hesitated; and in *Volvox* we have the older method of reproduction alternating queerly with the new. In one generation the cells of the colony multiply by the traditional division; but the cells of the second generation, so produced, break up like *Eudorina* into unlike spores; and two dissimilar spores must unite to form the cells of the third generation. New things are seldom established except by insinuating themselves into the old —a lesson which youth learns when youth is gone.

In more complex organisms certain portions of the body, like the stamens and pistils of plants, are specialized for the production of spores. The two kinds of spores themselves are more highly differentiated, and become, in the later stages of life's development, ova and sperms. But these two opposite elements are still, in many species, produced in the same body, by the same parent. The earthworm, for example, produces in one of its segments ova, and in another segment, at another season, sperms. It is the same with the oyster and other molluscs, certain tunicates, the perch, and even the ancient and honorable herring. Nature, having hesitated at differentiating the generative elements, hesitated again before differentiating into male and female the organisms that produced them.

One of the simplest known forms of this differentiation appears in the syngame—an internal parasite of birds. Here we find a large organism which turns out to be female—i. e., producing ova; and a much smaller organism, permanently attached to the side of the female, and giving no forecast, by its diminutive size, of the strutting dominance of the human male. This little sperm-producing creature is like a parasite upon a larger parasite, or like an organ of an organism; one would never suspect that it is the lady's husband.

Consider, also, the sea-worm *Bonellia;* the female of the species is half a foot long, and prosperous in diameter; the male is a sorry speck one-sixteenth of an inch in length—i. e., almost a hundred times smaller than his wife. Each female supports some twenty such modest mates; they enter her digestive tract, pass down into her body, and there meet and fertilize the ova which she holds within her. Among insects the female is almost always larger and stronger than the male. The lady butterfly is fifteen times as long, and ten times as heavy, as her mate. In some insect species the male is so small that "his proportion is that of an ant strolling over a peach." [1] Only among birds and mammals is the male superior; and here he owes his power to the fact that the female, having taken over most of the burdens of reproduction, is physically handicapped in the eternal war of love.

This subordination of the younger sex comes to a point in the actual sacrifice of the male in the act of fertilization. In many species the female eats the male immediately after union. In the Epirus spider the male lives apart from the female for safety's sake, till a certain restlessness comes over him. Then, like some timid Dante approaching Beatrice, he attaches himself to the outer threads of the female's web, builds a careful strand of exit from it as an avenue of retreat, and advances diffidently. Often the female eats him at once, without letting the poor fellow know any of the luxuries of love; perhaps she mistakes him for an assailant, or possibly she is a sophisticated person who prefers a meal to an amour. If she is in a mood for love she goes through the ritual of modesty: she retreats coyly, though she is larger and stronger than the male; she slides down one thread and up another, while the male excitedly pursues her; at last she lets herself be caught, and gives the male the delightful delusion of mastery. Their emotion is at this stage romantic and refined; they pat each other gently with their feelers, and declare their intentions delicately. Scarcely is the mating over, when the female leaps upon the male and consumes him with all the cynicism of completed love. Sometimes she begins to eat him before his task is finished. Occasionally he is alert enough to escape her destructive mandible, and slides down his thread of refuge for dear life. After that he becomes a philosopher, till restlessness returns.

The female mantis, says Fabre, eats her suitors with a like ferocity, and superior appetite. Other insects refuse the male when they have been fecundated; but the lady mantis accommodates from two to seven mates, accepts their ultimate gallantry, and then eats them one after another at her leisure. In many cases, unable to wait for her meal, she turns her head

[1] Gourmont, R. de, *The Natural Philosophy of Love.*

and eats the forward part of the male while he is engrossed in his racial task. Poiret tells of a case in which the female bit off the head of a male as soon as he appeared; but the decapitated gallant went through with his reproductive function as if nothing had happened, and a head was of no use in love. Jacques Loeb cut off the abdomen of *Gammarus,* a male Crustacean, while it was copulating; it continued undisturbed; apparently all its sensory capacities were absorbed in another direction. "In fact, unless my memory deceives me," Loeb reports, "these males without abdomen, when torn away from the female, were ready to hold another as soon as they could find one." [1]

One wonders, looking at the subordinate role of the male in the lowest species, if he represents a late specialization developed by nature from a type of organism like the earthworm, where both sexes are housed in the same frame. All that was necessary for the invention of sex was a variation in which some organisms, though born of a bi-sexual species, were nevertheless uni-sexual,—i. e., capable of producing only one of the generative elements.

But what could have made such a variation favorable? Of what use was this novel separation of life into female and male? It could not be that the new male was quite indispensable to the female; both nature and experiment question this. For there are many instances in which the female, even in species in which the division into two sexes has been completed, can procreate, apparently, without the aid of the male. In the little plant-louse *Aphis,* male and female mate normally in the fall, and the female lays a large "winter egg" which survives till spring, while all the rest of the species die. In spring this super-egg hatches into wingless females, which, though never having seen a male of their species, beget offspring—all female —to the summer's end. Then, suddenly, males appear among the larvæ; some of these males mature, and fertilize the females of their generation, who then produce large winter eggs—*da capo.*

It may be that such cases of "parthenogenesis" (literally, virgin-birth) are due (as Trembley thinks) to the transmission, by the mating females in the fall, of part of their store of fertilized eggs to the subsequent mateless generations: of these things there is as yet no certainty. But the actual possibility of dispensing with the male has been demonstrated in many laboratories. Jacques Loeb persuaded the unfertilized eggs of sea-urchins and starfish to develop into adults merely by subjecting the eggs to alcohol, ether, chloroform, strychnine, sugar, salts, acids, or alkalis: such was the alarming variety of substitutes for the supposedly indispensable male.

Evidently the male does not owe his appearance in nature to the needs of fertilization. To what, then? Very probably to the necessity for *cross-*

[1] *Comparative Physiology of the Brain,* p. 231.

fertilization. The separation of the sexes made it possible to unite in the offspring the hereditary qualities and capacities of two distinct lines of ancestry. The advantages of such double heredity are so obvious that we might expect some arrangement to develop whereby self-fertilization would be avoided. And it is so. Flowers (which are the reproductive organs of plants) are so constructed that it is seldom possible for the pollen of a plant to enter the pistil of that plant. Even in the snail, where both sexes exist in the same body, the parts are so arranged that self-fertilization is impossible. And so nature works, till in our own species social and psychological factors conspire to prevent the mating of brother and sister, and powerful taboos forbid even the marriage of members of the same tribe. The prohibition of incest, and the laws of exogamy, are merely the highest form of that same drive towards cross-fertilization which is responsible for the differentiation of the sexes.

Having divided organisms into two sexes, the next problem was to ensure their coöperation, through the meeting of the generative elements. Here the wastefulness of nature is astounding. It is most lavish among the flowering plants: thousands of species rely upon the wind to carry the fertilizing seed from one plant to another; the very air reeks with pollen, whose particles constitute the fragrance of the flower; and billions of such particles are used to bridge a distance of five yards between two nettles. The sturgeon female carries in her body 3,000,000 eggs (900 pounds); enough for 6,000 caviar sandwiches. In the herring the process is yet more extravagant: the males and females gather by the hundred thousands in such proximity that they make a kind of herring jelly; the eggs and the milt are thrown into the water so abundantly that the sea is whitened with their waste. Then the fishermen come, catch the reckless lovers in mass formation, and snare them by myriads in great nets. But meanwhile some eggs are being fertilized by the milt, and careless nature, scorning the individual life, consoles herself with the preservation of the species.

The same profusion of material survives, concealed, in our own race: out of 72,000 ova produced by one normal female, and billions of sperms produced by one normal male, only a few (in these days only one or two) will be used in reproduction. Bölsche believes that this abundance is not mere waste; that it provides the material out of which natural selection weeds the weaker ova and sperms, and chooses the stronger. Perhaps; but the professor, one suspects, does nature too much honor; she is not so intelligent as he thinks. It is from our great mother nature, doubtless, that we inherit our resourceful stupidity.

This wastefulness is corrected in the higher animals partly by the provision of structures for the guidance and union of ovum and sperm, and partly by the development of parental care. The star-fish keeps her arms over her fertilized eggs and her hatched young. The male stickleback brings the female into his pit to lay her eggs; then she goes away and he takes care of the offspring himself, like a modern husband. In the sea-horse *Hippocampus hudsonius* the female lays her eggs into a pouch on the body of the male, who cares for them until they hatch. In the thousands of fish that merely lay eggs and depart, the yearly average is over a million to each couple; in the 200 species that show some parental care the average is only 56 eggs per couple per year. Birds that make no nests give twelve eggs per year; those that make rude nests, eight; those that make careful nests, five.[1] So, bit by bit, parental love replaces and atones for nature's waste. In mammals, named for maternal care, the average couple produce three young per year; and this decreases with the higher species. Slowly the family develops as an external womb to care for offspring through an ever longer time. And as adolescence lengthens, civilization, which depends so largely on the period of education, rises to loftier levels than before.

And now how does the problem of love stand from the viewpoint of this rapid biological approach? Plato's Aristophanes answers humorously in the *Symposium* (189–192): "There was a time when the two (sexes) were one, but because of the wickedness of men God . . . cut men in two, like a sorb-apple which is halved for pickling, or as you might divide an egg with a hair. . . . Each of us when separated is but the indenture of a man . . . and he is always looking for his other half. . . . The *desire and pursuit of the whole* is called love." It is a noble definition, and tempts us to a learned interpretation of the great dramatist's myth. There was a time, we might say, when both sexes were in one body, as in the earthworm still. Then nature separated them into two organisms; and now each part, when separate, feels itself only a half, and longs for union and completion.

But that would be a mystical answer to the question, What is love? It would assume a highly philosophical consciousness in the lowliest protozoan spore. Presumably, when the male function was first specialized in a separate organism, very few of those aboriginal males sought or found union with their "better halves"; and only those who sought and found became the parents of the next generation. And so in each generation it was the lovers—the individuals that achieved completeness by merging themselves with their complements—who transmitted into the stream of life their passion for unity. Those that felt no such strange urge, or felt it slightly, died without offspring or with few, and their nonchalance was weeded out. Therefore the great hunger grew with every generation; no wonder it became the ruling passion, stronger than death—death which it cheats so patiently with vicarious continuance. Perhaps—*perhaps*—that is the road by which love came.

[1] Sutherland, A., *Origin and Development of the Moral Instincts,* vol. i, pp. 4–5.

III. THE PHYSIOLOGICAL FOUNDATION

So much for love in its evolution through the chain of life; let us watch it grow now in the individual. If you would understand anything, said Aristotle, observe its beginnings and its development.

Is there anything in children that corresponds to the later passion of love? Freud answered the question confidently in the affirmative, and built astonishing castles of psychiatry out of the erotic possibilities of thumb-sucking and nursing at the breast. But when the facts here are separated from theory they become microscopically small. Watson and his assistants kept several hundred infants under observation for a considerable time, and found no sexual behavior of any kind.[1]

Very soon, however, the child shows consciousness of the other sex. A certain anatomical curiosity appears, which is encouraged by concealment and evasion. Each sex becomes a mystery to the other, and evokes a reaction of mingled shyness and attraction. There is hardly more than that; and if love comes before puberty it is likely to be in the form of the "Œdipus complex": the boy forms an attachment for his mother, and the girl for her father. But this is not the terrible thing that Freud made it out to be; it is not a complex, because it is neither unconscious nor abnormal; it is nature's way of preparing the child for wholesome love. When the relationship is otherwise—when the son forms an emotional attachment for his father, or the daughter for her mother—then the psychiatrists may be reasonably alarmed.

It is at puberty that love sings its first clear song. Literally puberty means the age of hair—the sprouting of vegetation on the male; particularly hair on the chest, of which he is barbarically proud, and hair on the face and chin, which he removes with the patience of Sisyphus. The quality and abundance of the hair seem to rise and fall (other things equal) with the cycle of reproductive power, and are at their best at the acme of vitality. This sudden foliage, along with the deepening of the voice, is among the "secondary sexual characters" that come to the male at puberty; while to the blossoming girl nature brings the softened contours that will lure the eye, the widened pelvis that will facilitate maternity, and the filled-out breast that used to nurse the child.

What causes these secondary characters? No one knows; but Professor Starling has found favor for his theory that when puberty comes, the reproductive cells begin to produce not merely ova and sperms, but certain "hormones" which pass into the blood and cause a physical and psychical transformation. It is not only the body that is now endowed with new powers; the mind and character are affected in a thousand ways. "There are in life,"

---

[1] Watson, J. B., *Behavior*, p. 262.

said Romain Rolland, "certain ages during which there takes place a silently working organic change in a man"—or in a woman. This is the most important of them all.

New feelings flood the body and the soul; curiosity drives the mind forward, and modesty holds it back; the young man becomes awkward in the presence of the other sex, and the girl learns how to blush. Children stupid before may suddenly become bright; those obedient before may show now an unreasoning recalcitrance. Spells of introspection come, strange Russian moods of brooding and reverie. Imagination flowers, and poetry has its day; at this age all the literate world is an author, and dreams of deathless renown. Every power of the mind quickens, and reason makes a fresh assault of questions upon the universe. If the reasoning continues long, the individual becomes a scientist or a philosopher; if it is soon abandoned, he becomes a successful man, and may rise to the highest office.

It is at this time that the overflow of love waters the roots of art and social devotion. Love imagines beauty, seeks beauty, and may create beauty; love imagines goodness, seeks goodness, and goes out resolute to make it. If religion presents itself now as theological dogma it may rouse the youthful passion for debate, and suffer dismemberment; if it presents itself as the pursuit of the good it touches the idealism of the changing soul, and becomes an ineradicable part of the personality.

All in all this period of puberty is our marvelous age. It is the Age of Reason, and yet the epoch of emotion; new riches of mind and heart scatter on all sides a shower of ideas and a wealth of love. Never does the world seem so strange and yet so beautiful, so inaccessible and yet so conquerable, as in these moulting years; every later age looks back to them with longing. It is the springtime of every power, the seed-time of every growth; in it all noble passions find their nourishment. It is life's Renaissance.

Meanwhile what subtle force is this that drives the lad fearfully to the girl, and draws the girl yearningly away? What mystery is working in the secret recesses of the flesh, to create this fairest flower of all our lives—the love of a man for a maid?

The germinal cells of the body are swelling and burgeoning with vitality, as if they would overcome every effort to contain their new opulence. As the biological source of love is the natural selection and development of the instinct for union, so the physiological basis of it in the individual is the accumulation of germinal material. The entire organism feels the irritation of impeded growth, of the restless expansiveness of life; and the heart is filled with a sweet but heavy sadness, as if it knew itself incomplete, and thirsted to be made whole.

In this condition of irritability youth finds itself sensitive to a thousand stimuli which it passed unfeelingly before. Certain sounds appeal to it: song and music charm it beyond wont; and the voice (which perhaps began in the mate-calls of lowly animals) takes on new tenderness, and becomes a delight to the lover. Certain odors appeal: the sweetness of the growing flesh, the fragrance of cleanliness, the aphrodisiac potency of perfume,—all these are intoxicants to love. Certain movements appeal: the rhythm and pressure of the dance, the swing and confidence of athletes, the graceful buoyancy of girls. More than all else, certain sights appeal: colors swarm in the season of love, and red is a challenge to possession; youth spruces up in mating time, as birds and beasts develop crests and combs and nuptial plumage riotously; savages paint and mutilate themselves to catch the eye and rouse the sense; clothing becomes not a utility but an ornament, a suggestion, and a stimulant; bravery and strength make gentle hearts flutter, and every soft contour lures desire. These new experiences—of odor and sound and touch and sight, of perfume and song and dance and varied display—fill the days and the introspective thoughts of youth, and become the irresistible provocatives of love.

Suddenly all the stimuli unite, all the conditions appear together; the needs of the race speak through the hunger of body and soul; and love is born, love mounts in the heart like light in the morning sky, and fills all with its warmth and radiance. And great Lucretius sings:

> Thou, O Venus, art sole mistress of the nature of things, and without thee nothing rises up into the divine realms of life, nothing grows to be lovely or glad. Through all the mountains and the seas, and the rushing rivers, and the leafy nests of the birds, and the plains of bending grass, thou strikest all breasts with fond affection, and drivest each after its kind to continue its race with hot desire. For so soon as the spring shines upon the day, the wild herd bound over the happy pastures, and swim the rapid streams, each imprisoned by thy charms, and following thee with love.[1]

IV. THE SPIRITUAL DEVELOPMENT

From this sound and natural basis rises the love that is spirit and poetry. From this passion of life for perpetuation comes the loyalty of mate to mate; from this hunger of the flesh comes the fairest devotion of soul to soul; from the lust of the savage in the cave comes at last the poet's adoration. This is the gamut of man.

Primitive peoples seem to have known very little of love; they hardly had a word for it; when they married they were actuated by nothing more akin to romance than a desire for children and regular meals. "In Yoruba," says Lubbock (the anthropologists are enamored of outlandish places), "marriage is celebrated by the natives as unconcernedly as possible; a man

---

[1] *On the Nature of Things,* tr. Munro, Book ii, lines 991 f.

thinks as little of taking a wife as of cutting an ear of corn—affection is altogether out of the question." [1] Nietzsche thought that "romantic love" was an invention of the Provençal troubadours; but doubtless a "spiritual" element developed in the reproductive impulse wherever civilization arose. The Greeks knew romance, though in their own inverted way; and the *Arabian Nights* bears witness that love did not wait for medieval song. But the Church's exaltation of purity, lending to woman the charm of the inaccessible, helped to mature the poetry of love. Such "love is to the soul of him who loves," says even the great cynic La Rochefoucauld, "what the soul is to the body which it animates." "All men," says De Musset, "are liars, traitors, babblers, hypocrites, strutters; all women are vain, artificial, and perfidious; . . . but there is in the world one thing holy and sublime, and that is the union of these two imperfect beings." And Nietzsche pauses from his idol-breaking to do it reverence: "The chastest utterance I ever heard: *Dans le veritable amour c'est l'âme qui enveloppe le corps*—in true love it is the soul that embraces the body."

How shall we explain this transformation of physical desire into romantic love? What brought it about that hunger should flower so into gentleness, that the agitation of the body should become the tenderness of the soul? Was it because civilization, as it grew, postponed the age of mating, and left the flesh with an unfulfilled longing, a longing that turned inward to imagery, and clothed the beloved object in the ideal colors of unrealized desire? That which we seek and do not find becomes more precious through our not finding it; the beauty of the object, as we shall see, is in the strength of the desire; and desire, which is weakened by fulfilment, is made richer by denial. Therefore love is most spiritual in the youth of the individual and in the maturity of a civilization; for it is then that repression is at its height, and restraint tempers the flesh into poetry.

However it comes, consider the psychological development of love. It begins, most often, with a special tenderness of the girl towards her father, and of the boy towards his mother. Then it changes to a more passionate devotion to some person slightly nearer to the lover's age. Every class-room has children who are in love with a teacher of the opposite sex. Goethe has made a classic story of his flame for a woman who broke his heart by calling him her child. Romantic embellishment is already at its height in these transient loves; imagination is stirred by the growing body, and conceives fair images which it would so willingly make real that it enshrines any propitious object in the colors of its fancy. The physical element does not here enter consciously at all. "The first propensities to love in an uncorrupted youth," says Goethe, "take altogether a spiritual direction." [2]

Soon afterward comes that ethereal experience which we ignobly name

[1] *Origin of Civilization*, p. 51.
[2] *Truth and Fiction*, p. 178.

after the calf—though one would not detract for a moment from the placid beauty of that graceful animal. Such love is usually secret and unconfessed; even the little gifts it sends are nameless. Girls are bolder at this stage than boys; and though they lose (externally) some of this audacity in their more conscious years, they retain to the end a superior technique in the arts of love. The boy looks sheepish, but the girl is self-possessed, and remains master of the situation. The boy sometimes goes out of his way to avoid the girl he longs to have; he spends lonely hours in the dark of night, or wanders desolate by day, in bitter meditation on the awkward things he has done or said in the beloved presence; in some youths, maternally protected and attached, this sensitivity may so fetter them as to keep them celibate to the end. In other lads the spirit of display is fed; and when the girl of his dreams stands by, the boy will risk his life in games to lay some laurel at her feet. Youth reproduces on the athletic field the bloody combats of male animals for possession of the female, and anticipates the economic contests which maturity will wage to capture the fair lady and keep her approving smiles. So love makes the world go round.

From these early manifestations, coming soon after the fulness of puberty, love passes on through various stages, normal if temporary, abnormal if permanent. A perversion is an atavism—some ancient form of behavior originally normal and useful, then improved upon and surpassed. The healthy organism moves through these dubious conditions like Dante through Inferno; he experiences them, and is deepened by them, and then passes on to adult and normal love.

Now come courtship days, the fairest part of human destiny. Not that courtship waited till maturity; half the games our childhood played were love games; and even a girl of five can flirt with skill. Courtship serves vital purposes: it stimulates love to greater fulness, and gives time for that selection of the best which slowly raises the quality of life. In adults the ritual of courtship is acquisitive advance by the male, and seductive retreat by the female. There are exceptions here and there; in New Guinea the girls court the men, and lavish presents on them; but this admirable custom has not yet developed in our land. And occasionally some Anne deliberately pursues and snares a Tanner,—at least in Bernard Shaw. Usually the male takes the positive and aggressive role, because he is by nature the fighter and the beast of prey; the woman is to him a prize which he must conquer and possess. All courtship is combat, and all mating is mastery.

"Some male grasshoppers fight so hard," says Stanley Hall, "that they can be matched like young cocks. Many male fish fight to the death during the breeding season and on the spawning grounds, and the teeth of the male adult salmon become sharp, and differ radically from those of the female. Male lizards can hardly meet during the spring without fighting. Most male birds are pugnacious in the spring, and use beak, claws, and spurs on both

wings and legs. With them the season of war is also the season of love." [1]
In men the war becomes one of commercial competition and display; we
fight with bank-books rather than with teeth, and all our claws are hidden
behind the courtesies of trade.

Women, if they are wise, fight with flight and modesty. Modesty is a
strategic retreat, born of fear and cleanliness, and developed by gentleness
and subtlety. It is not peculiar to the human species; for it has an obvious
analogue and source in the reluctance of the female animal to make love
out of season or out of bounds. Man, said Beaumarchais, differs from the
animals in that he drinks without being thirsty, and makes love at all seasons.
In civiliz d peoples modesty is one of the fairest psychical developments
of love; it grows to a unique splendor, and sometimes overcomes the deepest
impulses of the soul. In ancient Milesia wise legislators ended an epidemic
of female suicides by decreeing that the corpses of women who had killed
themselves should be carried naked through the streets. [2]

William James believed that modesty was not instinctive but acquired:
women had found that generosity breeds contempt, and they had transmitted the finding to their daughters. Diderot went further back, and traced
it to the jealousy of husbands, whose sense of ownership led them to enforce
modesty upon their wives. In many tribes only the married women are
clothed, their husbands (wiser than the creator of *Penguin Isle*) believing
this to be an aid in the maintenance of property rights. When purchase replaced capture as the fashionable mode of marriage, and parents found that
chaste daughters brought the highest price, they virtuously encouraged
modesty.

From these varied sources, modesty grew into one of the subtlest charms
of woman. Immodest women are not attractive, except passingly, to male
men; reserve in display and economy in gifts are better weapons in the hunt.
When esoteric anatomy is taught us in the streets our attention is aroused,
but our "intentions" are seldom moved. The young man is drawn to lowered
eyes; he feels, without thinking of it, that this delicate reserve promises a
tenderness which is an excellent thing in woman. Modesty, by sparing its
rewards, incites the capacity and courage of the male, stirs him to enterprises
of some consequence, and calls out the reserve energies that lie beneath the
comfortable level of our mediocrity. Who knows how far the constructive
achievements of men may be due, like the colored glory of the bird, to sex
rivalry and display?

Let the lure have its way, and love completes itself in parentage, closing
the circuit of desire with a child. Probably there is no specific instinct of
reproduction, but only the instincts of mating and parental care. Nature

---

[1] *Adolescence,* vol. ii, p. 368.
[2] Ellis, H., *Studies in the Psychology of Sex,* vol. i, p. 24.

deviously secures her ends, and mankind is a by-product of its greatest pleasure. Nothing could be more ridiculous than nature's mode of propagating the forked radish: hear those shrieking women and those squealing babies in the hospital. But what impish skill she shows in soothing the mother with anesthetic ecstasy, and the father with a blinding pride that smilingly pays the gigantic costs now assessed against those who dare to continue our perhaps unnecessary race!

When the infant comes, love in the parents is renewed, but it is strangely different from the flame that burned before. Indeed, that flame, in these hectic days, is wont to have flickered to an unsteady minimum by the time a child arrives; and the child itself is likely to take from both parental hearts some of the affection which made them transiently one. The mother tends to forget the father in her new devotion; and the father, if the little marvel is a girl, is tempted to pass on to her the adoration with which he wooed his wife. But in the end these distractions lose their charm, and fresh bonds are forged to weld the mates again.

It is time that makes at last the complete marriage of two souls. For in those years of parentage how many trials must come; and how many vicissitudes of fortune, how many tortures of the body and terrors of the heart! Sickness brings to the fickle fancy a certain depth and soberness, and love takes on new life in the imminence of death. Plans made and tried together, victories won hand in hand, and desolation shared, mortise congenial minds into a spiritual partnership that almost rises to a merger of personalities; even the two faces may become alike. To watch together over the cradles of children, to see them grow, and to give them at last, reluctantly, to some younger love, is to be made one.

When the home that has echoed with the laughter of children is haunted with their still memory, love, as if in consolation, brings all its wealth again to the comrades of many years. Its great gamut is not full till it has soothed with its warmest presence the loneliness of age and the nearness of the Great Enemy. Those who knew it as desire knew only the root and flesh of it; the soul of it remains now, with every physical element burned away. In this re-mating of old hearts the spiritual flowering of the body's hunger is complete.

Such is the cycle of love. See it again at a glance—in the merging cells of minute protozoa, in the violent passion of the beast, in the savage's crude lust, in the brooding and melting eyes of youth, in the sonnets of Elizabeth Browning or in Francesca's tale, and in the old couple who tremble with happiness as their children and their children's children gather to honor half a century of love. What could be more wonderful than that transformation, that slow rise from the magnetism of the elements to the poetry of adoration and the loyalty of all life's span? Once more one recalls Santayana's profound words: "Everything ideal has a natural basis, and everything natural has an ideal development." Let love be unashamed of its origins, and let desire be mortified if it does not mount to devotion.

It was love's philosopher, Plato, who said: "He whom love touches not, walks in darkness." [1] Laplace, dying, rebuked the friends who tried to console him with the fame of his discoveries and his books; these, he told them sadly, were not the important things in life. "What then?" they asked. And the old scientist, fighting for one more breath, answered, "Love."

All things must die, but love alone eludes mortality. It overleaps the tombs, and bridges the chasm of death with generation. How brief it seems in the bitterness of disillusion; and yet how perennial it is in the perspective of mankind—how in the end it saves a bit of us from decay, and enshrines our life anew in the youth and vigor of the child! Our wealth is a weariness, and our wisdom is a little light that chills; but love warms the heart with unspeakable solace, even more when it is given than when it is received.

[1] *Symposium,* 197.

CHAPTER VIII

Men and Women

GORKI AND TCHEKOV were walking in the Crimea. They came upon Tolstoi as he sat on the beach, his great head bent in meditation, his beard sweeping the sand. They squatted down beside him, and began to talk about women. For a long time Tolstoi listened in silence. Then suddenly he said: "And I will tell the truth about women only when I have one foot in the grave. I shall tell it, jump into my coffin, pull the lid over me, and say, 'Do what you like with me now.' "[1] Bernard Shaw, invited by Count Keyserling to contribute an essay to *The Book of Marriage,* refused, saying, "No man dare write the truth about marriage while his wife lives." Nevertheless we proceed, *limiting ourselves here to an analysis of average and traditional types,* and reserving for the next chapter an examination of the modern emancipated minority.

The literature of this subject is the most interesting and unreliable in the world. It is interesting because it directly concerns ourselves, except where it deals with the faults and vices of mankind. It is unreliable because it is autobiographical; and all autobiography is fiction. It is frequently the voice of revenge; only defeated warriors contribute to it; and when a man writes a book about women it is his wounds that speak. (This does not apply to mere chapters.) When a man wins with a woman it is usually (if he is a gentleman) with the Pyrrhic victory of marriage; after which he preserves a judicious silence—two cannot speak at once. When he loses, he writes books. More interesting than the essays which Schopenhauer, Nietzsche, Weininger, and other jilted men have written about the foreign sex would be a candid analysis of men by women, who understand and manipulate human nature so much more intelligently than the hesitantly intellectual male. But women are too clever to reveal themselves in literature; they are content to have realized Job's wish, that their enemy might write a book.

[1] Gorki, M., *Reminiscences of Tolstoi,* p. 65.

Any normal person must be one-sided on our present subject; he knows only half of it from within, perhaps but a fraction of that half intimately, and not even that fraction honestly or well. It is difficult to be impartial in war-time. Hence the weakness of science in this field; the slight and incidental observations of Professor Thorndike, and the laborious records of intelligence tests, are the tentative pseudopodia of a branch of research that has hardly the courage to grow. The last study of mankind will be man; the last science will be psychology; and its last subject will be women.

Let us, however, be as careful as we can. Conveniently but artificially we shall divide human nature into the basic instincts that so largely make it up, and we shall ask in each case how the mind and character of women differ from the mind and character of men. We shall assume (with a bow to the behaviorists) that man is born with certain fundamental predispositions and tendencies of response and feeling, which philosophers and psychologists since Schopenhauer have called instincts; and we shall adapt Prof. Marshall's classification of these hereditary propensities, according as they subserve the purposes of the individual, the group, or the race.[1] For there are certain instincts—like food-getting, fighting, flight, and play—which tend to preserve the individual; and other instincts—like gregariousness and love of approval—which tend to preserve the group; and other instincts still—like mating and parental care—which tend to preserve the race. There are some questionable statements here; but we must not enter into technical controversies that do not vitally affect our problem.[2] We need only ask whether men and women are differently endowed with these instincts, in kind or in degree. And we shall begin with the racial or reproductive instincts, since for our present purpose they are the most important of all, and from their different operation nearly all those diversities flow which distinguish the sexes in body, character, and mind.

II. DIFFERENCES OF CHARACTER

1. Racial Instincts

Even the male is struck with the predominance of the female in the animal world—not merely in size (which we have seen), but in her biological priority as the direct carrier of the body of the race. In the lower orders of life reproduction goes on chiefly by division, and there are no sexes; in the

---

[1] Marshall, H. R., *Instinct and Reason*.

[2] The usual mode of proving that a given instinct does not exist is to show that it is not observed in infancy. But most instincts, of course, are set to go off, so to speak, at a certain time in life, dependent chiefly on the development of the physiological capacities required. Walking, fighting, and love are obvious examples.

human race the actual process of generation takes place in the female, who reproduces by division as literally as the *Amœba*. Man's function is incidental, superficial, and not indispensable; nature and the laboratory have corroborated each other in demonstrating the ultimate superfluity of the male. It becomes bitterly obvious that the female is primary and basic, the male secondary and tributary, in the species; the male is a late specialization and embodiment of functions which were once performed without him. In the great drama of reproduction, around which all life revolves, he plays a minor and almost a supernumerary role; in the crisis of birth he stands sheepishly and helplessly aside, understanding at last how trivial and subordinate an instrument he is in the development of the race. At that moment he knows that woman is far closer to the species than he, that the great current of life flows turbulently through her, that creation is the work of her flesh and blood; and he begins to understand why primitive peoples and great religions worshiped motherhood.

The superior modesty of woman obviously subserves the purposes of reproduction. Her coy retreat is an aid to sexual selection; it enables her to choose with greater discrimination the lover who shall be privileged to be the father of her children. The interests of the race and the group speak through her, as the interests of the individual find their strident voice in man. Once her purpose is achieved, and she has fulfilled herself in motherhood, her modesty declines; there is a delightful simplicity in the pride with which a peasant mother, so lately shy, will publicly nurse her babe. And she is right: of all the sights and pictures in the world of life and art, that one is loveliest.

Woman is cleverer than man in love because, normally, her desire is less intense, and does not so obscure her judgment; this is the secret of her ancient wisdom. Darwin considered the female of most species to be comparatively indifferent to love; Lombroso, Kisch, Krafft-Ebing and other scholars who rushed in where angels fear to tread will have us believe, our cities to the contrary notwithstanding, that forty per cent of our own weaker sex enjoy a similar apathy. It is not (we are told) physical delight that woman seeks, so much as an indiscriminate admiration and a lavish attention to her wants; and in many cases the sheer pleasure of being desired contents her. "Sometimes," says Thomas Hardy, "a woman's love of being loved gets the better of her conscience." [1]

What we have vaguely called the spiritual element in love—that part of love which has no thought of the flesh—finds more welcome in woman than in man. Some students of her impenetrable heart believe that her love is maternal rather than sexual. "Love in woman," says Lombroso, "is in its fundamental nature no more than a secondary character of motherhood, and all the feelings of affection that bind woman to man arise not from sexual

[1] *Jude the Obscure*, p. 286.

impulses, but from the instincts—acquired by adaptation—of subordination and self-surrender." [1] Alfred de Vigny thought that man's love is the memory and desire of the mother's breast; and who knows but that every lover is to woman only another child to be comforted—and fed?

Less intense than in man, love has in woman a greater extent, and overflows into every nook and cranny of her life. She lives only when she is loved; attention is her vital medium. A woman, reproached by a French magistrate for staying with a thief, replied: "But when I am not in love I am nothing." Perhaps it was this psychological need that Weininger had in mind when he argued that woman has no "soul"—that her existence tends (or tended?) to be focused upon a man. In many cases she seems to take her character from him. But this is delusive: it is only his opinions that she imitates; within herself she remains individual and resolute; she knows that man, in his infinite egotism, would be repelled if she showed too much personality of her own.

If the woman surpasses man in the art of love, he surpasses her in friendship. Men may be friends, but women can only be acquaintances. When women speak well of other women the stars are disturbed in their courses. They find it difficult to entertain themselves; they are bored to desperation in one another's presence, and can bear it only by talking of men. And it is all very natural; as La Rochefoucauld long since noted, "The cause why the majority of women are so little given to friendship is that it is insipid after they have felt love." [2] Love, as the poet said, is for man a thing apart, but it is woman's whole existence. We are what we must be.

Man's jealousy, like his love, is more intense and less extended or prolonged. The sense of possession is stronger in the male, and constitutes half his love; love is not merely self-abandonment, it is also, by the contradictoriness of things, an enlargement and victory of the self. Jealousy is the instinct of acquisition harassed with competition; it is prosecution for infringement of copyright. "I am the Lord thy God; thou shalt not have strange gods before me." Woman is not so anxious as the male is to have a mate who has never been possessed before. But she makes up in extent for what her jealousy lacks in intensity and depth: she can be jealous not only of her husband's lovers, but of his friends, his pipe, his newspaper, and his books. Gradually she divorces him from his friends; and if there is no other way to do this, she flirts with them, flavoring policy with sin. When in his turn the man shows jealousy of her own admirers, she is not ruffled; she enjoys and encourages his feeling, for she knows that she is desirable to him only when his possession of her seems insecure; she understands, with prenatal sagacity, that there is no medicine like jealousy for a dying love. And again these pretty faults are to be forgiven her; she is at a disadvantage, and needs these

[1] In Kisch, *The Sexual Life of Woman*, p. 133.
[2] *Reflections*, no. 440.

arts to balance the physical superiority of the male. She must at all costs protect herself, for it is upon her that the race relies for its perpetuation and its strength. She pays too great a price for her own brief share in love to warrant us in complaining of her subtlety. "One cannot be too gentle with women." [1]

2. Individualistic Instincts

The function of the woman is to serve the species, and the function of the man is to serve the woman and the child. They may have other functions also, but wisely subordinate to these; it is in these fundamental and half-unconscious purposes that nature has placed our significance and our happiness.

Hence the natural industry of the male is protective, acquisitive, and adventurous. His task is to leave the nest or the home in search of food; he is life's agent of nutrition as woman is life's instrument of reproduction. Food is his great aim; if he becomes acquisitive of other things, or of everything, it is because (though he may not think of them so) these other things represent wealth, which in a crisis would offer some assurance of food. Metrodorus said that all good things have reference to the belly; and though it is impolite to say so, it is largely true of the human male. He loves food with a surpassing love, and can be easily subjugated with it; he is fonder than woman of eating and drinking; and ever since Eve offered Adam an apple woman has ruled man through his stomach, ruining at once his digestion and his morals.

Venturing about for food, the male becomes a fighter; among the animals he fights with tusks and claws, among men with financial rivalry, among nations with armies, navies, and newspapers. Kipling thought the female more deadly than the male; but perhaps he had suffered some wound (east of Suez) that discolored his view. The woman's nature is to seek shelter rather than war; and in some species the female seems quite without the instinct of pugnacity. When she fights directly it is for her children; if she has in her a potential fierceness it is for these racial emergencies. But visibly she is less given to violence, and her infrequent crimes are often associated with her periods of physiological disturbance. She is more patient than man; and though he has more courage in the larger issues and crises of life, she abounds in diurnal and perennial fortitude for facing the smaller and endless irritations of existence. She bears illness more quietly, as if she found in it some secret pleasure, some rest from her endless toil; whereas the male, unused to a stationary life, bears illness restlessly, and informs the universe of his pains.

But woman is pugnacious vicariously. She goes for a soldier and delights in a masterful man; some strange masochistic element in her thrills at the

[1] Nietzsche.

sight of strength, even when its victim is herself. In every generation she selects the pugnacious male, unconsciously mindful of the protection her home and her brood will need. Occasionally this ancient joy in virility overrides her more recent economic sense, and she will marry a fool if he is brave. She submits gladly to a man who can command; if she seems less submissive in our days it is because men have less force of character than before. Perhaps the stupefying routine of industry and the enervating artificiality of the intellectual life have habituated men to slavery, and worn their courage away.

Woman wins her victories not through fighting, nor through bravery, but through persistence and tenacity. The male's pugnacity is more intense and open, but less sustained; he is readier to make up, or to surrender for the sake of peace. He may growl, and even beat his woman; but in the end she will triumph by repetition, like an advertisement. If she repeats it is because she cannot strike; weak species, peoples, sexes, and individuals are rich in patience and subtlety. Napoleon, who could master a continent, could not rule his wife; his strength found nothing to aim at in Josephine's physical weakness and timidity; and for the weapons which she used he had no armor. "My force of character," he tells us, "has often been praised; yet to my own family I was nothing but a weakling, and they knew it. The first storm over, their perseverance, their obstinacy, always carried the day; and from sheer fatigue they did what they liked with me." [1] This sounds the characteristic note of every domestic symphony. In these luxurious days, when the middle-class wife expands and blossoms idly in her workless and childless home, conditions hardly favor the male; he returns to his apartment cell exhausted by the day's irritation and toil, to find his ancient enemy waiting for him with fresh and accumulated energy; he is defeated before the battle begins. And if by some chance he should win, the woman need only cry, and he is lost. Maria Louisa boasted that she always received what she wanted if she wept for it twice. The wise wife will put it down as a fundamental rule of war: "If at first you don't succeed, cry again."

In what might be called the instincts of action—crawling, walking, throwing, leaping, climbing, running, play—the female of the species seems less positive than the male. He is inclined to useless movement, and she to superfluous stability. She is lazier, and therefore she is the more dangerous sex; for idleness is the mother of adultery. To be virtuous, as to be happy or graceful, one must be busy.

3. Social Instincts

In the group of instincts which we have just surveyed—the instincts that preserve the individual—man's superiority is manifest and natural. But in

[1] Johnson, R. M., *The Corsican,* p. 485.

the instincts that preserve the group, woman is as superior as in the instincts that preserve the race. She is more social and more sociable; she likes company and multitudes, and surrenders herself with delight to the anonymity of crowds. She does not ask which are the best plays, concerts, or resorts, but which are the best attended; though the difference here between herself and her mate is microscopic. (At least she tries to like the best, whereas the normal male is dragooned into attendance upon concerts, art exhibitions, and problem plays only by fear of his wife.) She is less capable of solitude than man, and does not produce hermits. She feels more incomplete without him than he without her,—doubtless because she needs his protection and, usually, his leadership. She is a gregarious animal.

Therefore she is more talkative. Rumor has it that she is a sieve for secrets. Franklin thought that "three can keep a secret if two of them are dead"; but to make this true of both sexes one would have to raise the rate of mortality. Yet women can suffer silently longer than men, "after the way of women" (says Meredith), "whose bosoms can be tombs." [1] Woman is more expressive because she is more frequently possessed with feeling and emotion. Her greater susceptibility to neuroses—to chorea, convulsions, hysteria, obsessions, phobias, automatisms, mediumistic inspirations, etc.—is rooted here, and in the sterner suppressions which society enforces upon her erotic impulses. Her face is almost as mobile as her speech; she has not learned, like the stoic *prolétaire* or the cautious business man, to maintain a countenance unchanged in the flux of profit and loss, of pleasure and pain. With this fluid immediacy of facial expression goes a greater ability to detect the signs of feeling and thought in others; hence it is harder to deceive a woman than a man—as everyone discovers, having tried both.

Gregariousness, as Galton showed, varies with timidity and imitation. Woman usually leaves initiative to the man, even (despite Shaw) in love; here above all his mastery lies; and if the first fresh wine of desire does not intoxicate him he may cruelly keep her waiting for years while he calculates, accumulates, and experiments venereally. The woman is uncertain of herself; always her physical weakness and her economic dependence weigh upon her, dulling the edge of her courage, withdrawing her from rebellion and enterprise. She clings to the customary and the conventional, piously imitative of the past, and nervously imitative of every present wind of fashion in dress, or manners, or ideas. She offers slightly readier material than man for the fads and crazes which in America tend to replace the orderly advance of thought; the psychoanalyst delves pruriently into her harassed soul, the spiritualistic medium comforts her with apparitions, and M. Coué finds bread and butter in her trustful fantasy.

She dares not vary from the norm and average so recklessly as man. She gives the world fewer idiots, and fewer geniuses. She is more like the others

[1] *Ordeal of Richard Feverel,* p. 32.

of her sex than the man is like other men; the compulsion of a changing environment, and of diverse occupations, professions and trades, has differentiated man into a thousand varieties; but the traditional industry of the home, and the ancestral tasks of finding a mate and rearing a child, have operated on almost all women, forming them in one mould, wherein the face is always different, and the soul always the same. Perhaps this is part cause of the male's complacent passage from one love or mistress to another; he need only learn a new name, but no new artistry; even the old letters will sometimes serve. But a woman who has loved and lost may find her loss irreparable; she has bound her spirit to a specific image; and wherever she may go her heart will linger with her memories.

The last corollary of this greater gregariousness in woman is her passion for social approval. The opinion of her neighbors weighs more with her than with the man, for social relationships tend to absorb such hours in her life as are unfilled with love and motherhood. She surpasses man in vanity; she is more conscious of her virtues and her beauty, and will spend half an hour in powdering her nose; though there is not much to choose between woman's vanity and man's conceit. Her expressiveness lends itself to gossip, and her imitativeness to conformity. Even more than her mate she is anxious to rise in the world; and her hunger for position forms half the wind in his sails. Therefore she is very inferior to her superiors, and very superior to her inferiors. But for the same reason she is more polite; and, her social sensitivity merging with her motherhood, she is kinder and more sympathetic than the male. Her charming vanity is amply balanced by her considerateness and her gentleness, her readier disposition to nurse or help the ill or the weak, her richer endowment in the qualities that make for altruism and morality.

Finally these characteristics of mind and heart make her more religious. Her emotional tension renders her quickly sensitive to the profound appeal which religion makes to the senses and the feelings. The severer repression in her of the erotic dispositions leaves her charged with a vague devotion which fastens gratefully upon every object of adoration. She feels more keenly the bereavements that sadden life; and her longing for reunion with loved ones whom she has lost convinces her of immortality. Nature remains a sublime mystery to her; and who knows but in this humble inability to understand she may be closer to nature's secret than our mechanistic science? Instinctively she worships where the man might seek control. Physically dependent, she yearns for omnipotent protection; mentally bewildered by the world, she prays for heavenly guidance; fearing solitude and loving society, she thirsts for the divine presence, and peoples the air with spirits that will befriend her in her loneliness and her need. She is the first to welcome new forms of belief, and the last to relinquish the old. Man, in despair, may kill himself; but woman, when every other hope is lost, throws herself upon the mercy of heaven, and finds strength and solace in a loving God.

III. INTELLECTUAL DIFFERENCES

These, then, are the instincts of man and woman; but it must not be supposed that such elemental dispositions remain unchanged by experience and education. There is in both sexes a development of habit and intellect upon the basis of these propensities. How does this intellectual superstructure differ in men and women?

It is wider and higher in men. Through many generations men have been drawn out of the traditional home into the varied world; they have had to meet new situations and new stimuli, to which the old instinctive reactions proved inadequate; of necessity they have developed (some of them) that flexible capacity for successful novel response which constitutes the intelligence of the instinct. For instinct too can be intelligent; let the stimulus or situation be of a traditional kind, such as humanity has faced for many centuries, and instinct is likely to suffice, likely even to prove more intelligent—i. e., better adapted and more successful—than the precarious processes of thought. Until recently the central tasks in the life of woman were to find a mate and to rear a child; and this still holds true for all but the women of large cities, and in the cities for all but the women of the middle class. These central tasks were very ancient problems; every woman had faced them as far back as memory could record; and for these situations nature had built up instinctive responses occasionally disastrous, but normally beneficent and intelligent.

Hence woman (always barring metropolitan exceptions) excels man in the unity, thoroughness, and precision of her instincts. Man is more critical and sceptical, more sicklied o'er with the pale cast of thought; his instincts have been broken up for flexibility, and have lost immediacy and assurance; in the presence of woman he is always at a loss. She is the more self-possessed and practical, the cleverer to plan and the quicker to execute, wherever the problem in hand has to do with snaring a mate, keeping a lover, or making a home. No man under thirty is a match for a woman of twenty in the gentle war of love: watch any man, however old, in love with any woman, however young, and see which will twist the other around her finger. There are some things that woman knows before she is born, by the divine right of the accessory chromosomes; but man can learn them only by hard experience and disillusionment. Woman sees more than she can formulate, man formulates more than he can see. Woman thinks without thought, and lies without premeditation; she far outdistances man in inventive mendacity; in any crisis of detection it is she who imperturbably explains.

Being better equipped at birth for the normal tasks of life, woman matures more rapidly, and has a shorter adolescence. Some men have therefore classed her as a lower species; but this is to be precipitate—on such a basis the turtle would be the noblest work of God. It would be as reasonable to conclude to woman's mental superiority, from the greater proportion which her brain, as compared with man's, bears to the weight of the body. Perhaps her accelerated adolescence is acquired, put upon woman by some imme- morial compulsion to premature maternity. The male too could be a father at an age hardly half the average age of marriage for the modern man, but economic circumstance has not willed it so. Adolescence is of the mind as well as of the body, and admits of many variations; some men mature early, some late, some never. Visibly our human adolescence lengthens, our help- lessness grows against a world that becomes daily more involved and more uncongenial to our native aptitudes and arts; few men in our time achieve mental maturity before they have reached the middle point of life. By com- parison woman, whose life has the simplicity of profound and natural things, ripens in body and mind at an early age; she learns more readily the ameni- ties of social behavior; she is cleverer in school than the boy of equal years; at Radcliffe College recently she showed herself superior, in intellectual tests, to the learned lads of Harvard. But this rapid development tends to com- plete itself sooner than in the man; the woman does not grow so far from what she is at birth as the harassed and experimental male; she clings to heredity as he ventures into variation; she is the organ and seat of racial stability, as he is the agent and herald of change. She is the base and trunk of the human tree, tenaciously clinging to the soil in which it grows, and widening its roots securely as its branches aspire into the sky.

The other side of this stability is a certain conservatism of feeling and an inadequacy of thought. Woman's interests are familial, and normally her environment is the home; she is as deep as nature and as narrow as four walls. Instinct adapts her to the traditional, and she loves the traditional as any expert loves the sphere which reveals his excellence. She is less experi- mental in mind and morals (barring again certain metropolitan exceptions); if she resorts to "free love" it is not because she finds freedom in it, but be- cause she despairs of achieving normal marriage with a responsible male. How gladly she would draw the man closer to her and absorb him into the home! Even if, in younger years, she thrilled to the shibboleths of political reform, and spread her affection thin over all humanity, she withdraws these tentatives when she finds an honest mate; rapidly she weans him and her- self from this universal devotion and teaches him an intense and limited loyalty to the family. "I would give the world for you," the youth says in courtship's ecstasy; and when he marries he does.

It is just as well. The woman knows, without needing to think of it, that the only sound reforms begins at home; she serves as agent for the race when she transforms the wandering idealist into her children's devotee. Nature cares little about laws and states; her passion is for the family and the child;

if she can preserve these she is indifferent to governments and dynasties, and smiles at those who busy themselves with transforming constitutions. If nature seems now to fail in this task of protecting the family and the child it is because woman has for the while forgotten nature. But nature will not be long defeated; she can at any time fall back upon a hundred reserve expedients; there are other races and other peoples, greater in number and extent than ourselves, through whom she can maintain her resolute and indiscriminate continuity.

IV. WOMAN AND GENIUS

Women are born with intelligence, some men achieve it, most men have it thrust upon them. Under the chaotic changes of the Industrial Revolution life has been for the male a kaleidoscope of enlarging responsibilities unelected and unforeseen. Many men have broken under the strain; many others have developed a range and brilliance of mind which uses all the reserve energies of the nervous system; they produce geniuses and madmen as never before. As industry sucks them in, women are being subjected in like manner to this forcing process of intellectual development; but rapidly as they change, they still retain some mental differences from the male. Woman seems to be less at home with abstract thought; she has a sharp eye for facts, and a good memory for them, but she is not adept at generalization or original interpretation; and she may lose herself and her purpose in details. She is interested in persons rather than in processes or things; she discusses not problems but men, for men are her problem. It is her lot to be occupied with persons—with husband and child; it is man's fate to be flung into the maelstrom of commerce and industry, and to deal with causes, processes and effects as well as with women and men. It is easier for a man to interest himself in a book which propounds an idea; a woman's book must tell a story, of a man. She is still an animist, and sees divine personalities and heroic wills where perhaps there is only an impersonal process of cosmic, social, and economic change.

It has always comforted male students of the mental differences between the sexes to observe how little genius woman has given to the world. Even in art, which might be supposed to have some relation to beauty, and in music, which thrives on emotional sensitivity, woman has produced less than her efforts and opportunities would appear to warrant. More women play music than men, and more men compose viable music than women. Where men acknowledge intellectual or artistic genius in women it is only to recapture it for the male by pronouncing these geniuses masculine. Schopenhauer assures us that there is a war between genius and motherhood; if we believe him we shall conclude that no woman can be mentally superior without being as dangerously abnormal as Schopenhauer. George Sand smoked a very masculine cigar, and Spencer found George Eliot too male to thaw his glacial soul. Mme. Girardin thought that in each of George Sand's novels one could trace the influence and manner of her latest lover; "it is," she said, "when we are criticizing the works of women writers that we are most often obliged to exclaim with Buffon, 'The style is the man.' " [1]

The causes of this infrequency of genius in women are multiple and elusive. Perhaps we define the term with prejudice, and forget that there may be as much genius in motherhood as in politics, literature, or war. Equality in genius should be judged (quite as happiness in life is achieved) not by ability to do all things with equal skill, but by the ability to perform with excellence the tasks and functions natural to each age and sex. We are here subject to the same error which sees less genius in our age than in some time to which distance lends enchantment; we tend to look for genius today in those same fields in which it flowered in the past; whereas it may well be that some of the mental force that once made literature and art is now absorbed into the widened realm of science and industry. We are consumed at present in our effort to remake the physical world with our new knowledge and our new power; we have great inventors and scientists, executives of international business, and world-compelling financiers; we must not also expect, in the same age, Platos and Shakespeares, Leonardos and Beethovens.

Perhaps men have surpassed women in genius because geniuses usually appear among the educated minority of each sex; so that comparisons will be odious until the proportion of persons receiving higher education is equal in both sexes. Male geniuses are successes out of millions of educated men; female geniuses are successes out of mere hundreds of educated women; when opportunity and training are given them, women produce great poets like Sappho, great novelists like George Eliot, great physicists like Mme. Curie, great mathematicians like Hypatia and Sonia Kovalevsky, great thinkers like Aspasia and Mme. de Staël, even, so to speak, forceful statesmen like Queen Elizabeth and Catherine de' Medici. Under the circumstances it is remarkable how many geniuses woman has furnished to the race. Probably, however, women lack the sheer physical vitality which artistic work involves; and perhaps they are less gifted than men with that sense of beauty which lures the soul to spiritual reproduction. One might here refer again to a certain sexual anesthesia—or rather a delayed sensitivity—in women, of which many (male) psychopathologists assure us, but of which there is inadequate evidence in contemporary morals. In general, woman seeks, in her mate, not beauty but ability and strength, as a promise of protection; it is the male who selects for beauty, less because (as in Stendhal's phrase) it is a promise of pleasure, than because, normally, it is the flag of vigor and health. Woman forfeits something of the esthetic

[1] Brandes, G., *Main Currents of Nineteenth Century Literature*, vol. iii, p. 71, note.

frenzy because she desires not to possess but to be possessed. Hence she inspires art more than she produces it; perhaps she does not find in man, proud ridiculous man, the beauty that stimulates creation. And why should she seek beauty when she embodies it? Living beauty is better than the fairest plastic art, and nobler even than intelligence; for it is the source of one and the purpose of the other. If life were beautiful it would not need to be intelligent; but if it were intelligent it would strive to become beautiful.

V. ARE THESE DIFFERENCES INNATE?

There is but one thing further to ask: are these mental differences hereditary or acquired? It is hard to say; for this is a field where science rivals philosophy in uncertainty of knowledge and fertility of hypothesis. One might hazard the presumption that though these differences are readily and intimately associated with native differences of structure and function, they are for the most part socially transmitted and individually acquired. They depend over a large area upon the ideals which men, for their own utility and satisfaction, have formed of women, and imposed upon them through a thousand environmental influences. As a lady professor protests: "Boys are encouraged to individuality. They are trained to be independent in thought and action. . . . They are encouraged to experiment and make things for themselves. Girls are taught obedience, dependence, and deference. They are made to feel that too much independence of opinion or action is a drawback to them—not becoming or womanly. A boy is made to feel that his success in life . . . will depend upon his ability to accomplish something new. . . . No such social spur is applied to girls." [1]

In a sense we are enabled, as the result of a vast experiment, to give a scientific answer to the question whether the mental and moral differences of men and women are innate. Economic circumstance has conducted the experiment, and life itself has been the laboratory. It is as if nature had put to herself the problem which puzzles us, and had decided to solve it by an almost cosmic test. Men were intellectually superior to women: was it by birth or by environment? To settle the question it was necessary to submit a large number of women to the varied and changing industrial life which was forming men, and to observe how quickly and fundamentally these wider occupations transformed the mind and character of the women who were involved. All England and half of America became the scene of the great trial. Factories and offices and professions were opened to either sex; economic exigency drew millions upon millions of women out of the ancient home and flung them with brutal precipitancy into industrial and commercial rivalry with men. What was the result of the experiment?

The result was so rapid a transformation of the "emancipated" women

[1] Thompson, H. B., *Mental Traits of Sex*, p. 178.

that all the world stood agape. Within three generations these new servitors of industry made their way into every field where physical strength was not indispensable; and in all these fields they acquired enough of the intellectual and moral qualities of the male to make every moralist in Christendom deplore the masculinization of the once gentler and weaker sex. Lady lawyers, lady physicians, lady governors, lady bandits demonstrated the ability of women, within a measure amply proportioned to their still narrow opportunities, to rival the arts of the preëstablished male. Colleges graduated women whom no man would marry, because their intellectual superiority excluded certain masculine pretensions to leadership which are among the prerequisites and casualties of marriage. The mental and moral gap between the sexes decreased as rapidly as shops and factories replaced farms and homes.

We shall later study this change in greater detail; we consider it now only as indicating that if women should choose to live in utter completeness the occupational life of the male, they would rival him and be assimilated indistinguishably with him in mental and moral traits. But probably women will show better taste. Their present period of imitation will pass; they will discover that men do not deserve this flattery; they will perceive that intellect is not intelligence, and that happiness, like beauty and perfection, lies in the fulfilment of our natural selves. Those women who carry emancipation onward will seek not to be imperfect men, but to become perfect women; they will make motherhood an art involving as much preparation and intelligence as the manipulation of levers and pulleys and throttles and wheels; perhaps they will discover that it is the greatest art of all.

Their new freedom has brought them problems as complex and crucial as those that lay in their old slavery. Men cannot help them here, for the intellect of man is too mechanical and crude to permit him to understand with delicacy and sympathy the critical changes that are disordering the life and mind of woman. Only her own new knowledge can cope with this new situation. Very probably she will succeed; the energy which achieved her liberty will meet the issues which her liberty has raised. She will find a way to unite the tenderness that flowers out in love and motherhood, with the varied ability, the alert intelligence, and the ageless beauty that distinguish her today.

CHAPTER IX

The Modern Woman

I. THE GREAT CHANGE

THE FOREGOING ANALYSIS has left aside, for separate discussion, the industrialized women of our modern cities; for these constitute a unique type, difficult to classify, and almost without precedent in history. If in imagination we place ourselves at the year 2000, and ask what was the outstanding feature of human events in the first quarter of the twentieth century, we shall perceive that it was not the Great War, nor the Russian Revolution, but the change in the status of woman. History has seldom seen so startling a transformation in so short a time. The "sacred home" that was the basis of our social order, the marriage system that was our barrier against human passion and instability, the complex moral code that lifted us from brutality to civilization and courtesy, are visibly caught in that turbulent transition which has come upon all our institutions, all our modes of life and thought, since factories outwooed the fields, and cities absorbed the natural and human resources of the countryside. It is not without excuse that our minds are a little unbalanced in this unmoored age.

That woman should be anything but a household slave, a social ornament, or a sexual convenience, was a phenomenon known to other centuries than ours, but only as a phenomenon, as an immoral exception worthy of universal notice and surprise. Plato pled quixotically for the opening of all careers, and the equality of all opportunity, without regard to sex; but Aristotle, more congenial to the prejudices of his time, classed woman as an arrested development, and explained her as nature's failure to make a man. She belonged with slaves as naturally subordinate, and quite unworthy of participation in public affairs.

This was also the view of Jehovah, who grouped wives and mothers with cattle and real estate in the last of the commandments which, it is rumored, he handed down to Moses. Jehovah had been made in the image of the Jews, who, like any warlike people, looked upon woman as a misfortune, a necessary evil to be tolerated as the only available source of soldiery for the time being. No candles were lit when a daughter was born among the ancient Jews; the mother who gave birth to a girl had to undergo a double purification; and the boy, proud of the abbreviation which was his covenant with Jehovah, repeated regularly the prayer: "I thank thee, God, that thou hast not made me a Gentile nor a woman." [1] But the Jews were not exceptional; indeed they were in many ways ahead of the moral code of their day. Everywhere in the East women were despised until they became the mothers of sons, and were never fully honored till their sons lay slain on some battlefield. Even the feminist Plato thanked God that he had been born a man.

From that day to ours there have been, no doubt, a thousand variations and fluctuations in the status and treatment of women; we must not retail them here. The *hetairai* who lent so picturesque an aspect to the life of ancient Athens, and the courtesans who took their name from the courts of modern kings, sought emancipation from male mastery through the expert development and manipulation of their sexual charms: Aspasia and Phryne mingled with philosophers and artists, and the salons of Du Barry and Pompadour became the intellectual centers of the maturest culture that the world has known. For a time the Revolution promised universal liberty; Condorcet presented to the National Assembly a petition for woman suffrage, and Mary Wollstonecraft added the *Rights of Woman* to the *Rights of Man*. But when the bloodshed was over, and women had given half a million sons to make France free, they found that *Liberté* and *Egalité* had never been thought of as applying to the home, and that the Sansculottes who took the Tuileries could be as stern rulers of their wives as the Romans whose names they loved to wear. Freedom was for men only, and was only grammatically feminine.

These views held to our own century. Which of us on the dark side of forty does not recall the truculent treatise in which Otto Weininger proved that women had no souls? Which of us males missed the joy of reading Schopenhauer's "Essay on Women"—"that under-sized, narrow-shouldered, broad-hipped, and short-legged race"? Did we not thrill with superiority as Nietzsche counselled us—"When thou goest to woman, remember thy whip"? We did not care that these books which so delighted us were but part of the eternal war of the sexes, military manuals for the besieged, voicing the wisdom of beaten men. We neglected to observe, as pertinent to the question of the partiality of these witnesses, that Schopenhauer was jilted by a pretty Venetian lass who preferred Byron's title and good looks; that Nietzsche was jilted by his Dark Lady, Lou Salomé, after he had pursued her over half a continent, wooing her with philology and apothegms; that Weininger, the proud genius, was jilted by a Viennese waitress, and in dramatic despair shot himself dead in the house of the great Beethoven. We

[1] Royden, A. M.. *Woman and the Sovereign State,* p. 45.

read those books gratefully because they vicariously and safely expressed our secret hostility to the sex which we shall always love.

Until 1900 or so a woman had hardly any rights which a man was legally bound to respect. In the nineteenth century the women of Africa were still bought and sold as slaves, as so much agricultural machinery; in Tahiti and New Britain they suckled the pigs.[1] In Merrie England the husband might beat his wife and be well within the law if he left her moderately alive; he might commit adultery every evening, and unless he also deserted her she had no redress except to imitate him. If she earned money it belonged to him; if she brought him property in marriage it was his to spend. That she would ever have the privilege of working in a factory, or the sacred honor of marching to the polls, never occurred to any man.

And then came the Great Change. These once pretty slaves began to talk about freedom and other fetiches, about equality and other impossibilities; they smashed windows, ruined letter-boxes, made interminable parades and ferocious perorations. To vary another *Comedy of Errors:*

> In bed we slept not for their urging it;
> At board we fed not for their urging it;
> In company they often glanced at it.

They made up their minds, and had their way. Now we cannot beat them any more, they will not cook for us any more, they will not even stay at home with us of an evening. Instead of worrying about our sins they are busy with their own; they have acquired souls and votes at the very time when men seem to have lost the one and forgotten the other; they smoke and swear and drink and think, while the proud males who once monopolized those arts are at home superintending the nursery.

II. CAUSES

How shall we explain this precipitate overturn of stable and respectable customs and institutions older than the Christian era? The pervading cause of the change was the multiplication of machinery. The "emancipation" of woman was an incident of the Industrial Revolution.

For, first, it brought the industrialization of women on a scale unknown and undreamed of before. They were cheaper labor than men; the employer preferred them as employees to their more costly and rebellious males. A century ago, in England, men found it hard to get work, but placards invited them to send their wives and children to the factory gate.[2] Employers must think in terms of profits and dividends, and must not be distracted by

---

[1] Thomas, W. I., *Sex and Society,* p. 138.
[2] Hammond, J. L. and B.: *The Town Labourer,* 1760–1832.

the consideration of morals, institutions, or states. The men who unwittingly conspired to "destroy the home" were the patriotic manufacturers of nineteenth-century England.

The first legal step in the emancipation of our grandmothers was the legislation of 1882, by which it was decreed that thereafter the women of Great Britain should enjoy the unprecedented privilege of keeping the money they earned. It was a highly moral and Christian enactment, put through by the factory-owners in the House of Commons to lure the ladies of England into attendance upon their machines. From that year to this the irresistible suction of the profits motive has drawn women out of the drudgery of the home into the serfdom of the shop. In England today one woman out of every two works in an office or a factory; the proportion of women in industry is multiplying four times as fast as the proportion of men. In the cities of the future, presumably, every woman will work outside the home, except in her rare intervals of motherhood. It is to some of us a vision unpleasant to contemplate, but we shall become accustomed to it in a decade or two; habit makes everything seem reasonable.

The industrialization of women naturally involved the decay of domestic life. As machinery bred new machines in a perpetually rising flood, and large-scale production with new modes of power cheapened costs, the factory outdid and outbid the home in a hundred occupations which had once varied woman's life. Bit by bit her old work was stolen from her; one by one the tasks that had made her drudgery slipped away, leaving the house empty of interest, and herself functionless and discontent.

It is to woman's credit that she went out of the home into the factory; she sought the work that had gone from her hands; she knew that without it she would become a meaningless parasite, an impossible luxury for any but economically established or physiologically decadent men. She received her first pay envelope with the pride and happiness of the boy who, to escape from school, has accomplished manhood through industrial employment and a Sunday cigar. The exhilaration with which woman accepted her new slavery was the joy of having found something to do; it was the happiness of functioning, somehow, again.

So the home being empty, no longer a place where things were done or life was lived, men and women abandoned it, and began to live in boxes, honeycombs called apartment-houses, dormitories for people whose lives, day and evening, were spent outside, in the roar and babble of the street. An institution which had lasted ten thousand years was destroyed in a generation. Scientific sociologists and social psychologists had taught that institutions, customs and morals could not be altered except by slow and imperceptible gradations; but here was one of the greatest changes in the history of civilization, and it had come almost overnight, between the boyhood and the maturity of one man. Our editors and preachers and statesmen had warned against permitting socialists to destroy the home; and meanwhile, under their eyes, in the very midst of their lives, the impersonal processes of economic change accomplished the tragedy before the moralists could realize where the causes lay.

The home might have survived had children filled it with trouble and babble; but the Industrial Revolution had taken them too away. Children, who had been such helps and joys on the spacious farm, were expensive hindrances in the crowded city and the narrow apartment. The world had too many workers; the old-fashioned fertility had to stop, lest men should be always poor, and always ignorant. The coming of machinery had made factories, and factories had made cities, and cities had made democracy, socialism, and birth-control. No one had willed it; the brilliant expositions of the rights of women to some surcease from multiple motherhood had had very little to do with it; and the exhortations of clergymen and presidents could not stop its course. The whole history of Europe and America in the last one hundred years would have had to be transformed to forestall these results. But history, like energy, is irreversible. It carries within itself a certain fatality; it must run its course.

Not only were children a luxury in cities where they could not be put to work at five, and where every addition to the family added to the burden of rent; but motherhoood itself had become no longer a normal incident but a perilous operation. Through work in the factory, or lack of work at home, the modern woman had become physiologically weaker than her ancestors. The decadent esthetic sense of the modern male had made matters worse by idolizing the slenderest and frailest figure; such women as Rubens knew, or such mothers as Bonaparte's Lætitia, were not to the taste of our artists or men about town, who judged beauty in terms of transient sexual lure rather than as a promise of robust maternity. So women became more and more incapable of bearing children; they avoided motherhood as long as they could, and reduced it to a vanishing minimum. Their husbands for the most part agreed with them, not knowing, in their innocence, that children cost less than cabarets.

And then those new machines, called contraceptives, completed the circle, and coöperated silently in emancipating women. Freed from the care of offspring, freed therefore from the last task which might have made the home a tolerable and meaningful environment for her, she went into the office, the factory and the world. Proudly she took her place beside man in the shop; she did the same work, thought the same thoughts, spoke the same words, as the man. Emancipation, for the most part, proceeded *via* imitation. One by one the new woman took over the habits, good or bad, of the traditional and old-fashioned male; she imitated his cigarettes, his profanity, his agnosticism, his hairdress, and his trousers. The new diurnal propinquity made men effeminate and women masculine; like occupations, like surroundings, and like stimuli fashioned the two sexes almost into one. Within a generation it will be necessary to label them with distinguishing badges to prevent regrettable complications. Already one cannot be quite sure.

How profound a change the childless woman, or the mother of one child, represents as compared with the woman of the past, stands out impressively if we recall the horror with which both men and women once viewed sterility. Until our century the respect in which a woman was held varied in close correlation with the number of children she had borne. The function of a woman was to be either a mother or a harlot, and in either case as often as possible. Daily from Christian Europe and the heathen world a million prayers ascended to a hundred gods to grant the gift of children. Rosaries were recited, shrines were visited, holy stones suffered pious abrasion. Among the Mayas disappointed couples fasted and prayed, and brought dainty offerings to propitiate the deity of many births. An African king, asked how many were his children, answered sadly that he had only a few, hardly more than seventy.

Why is it that pictures of motherhood touch us to the heart and bring tears to the eyes? Because, before cities came, children were needed in great number; and our feelings were the reflex of that need. Now the city need not reproduce; it can draw to it with its bright lights and long nights the offspring of unweakened rural loins; the new Moloch holds out its arms, illuminated with a million vari-colored bulbs, and the children come; by hundreds of thousands every year they come, and in their turn grow wise and barren. The city does not believe that children are necessary; therefore it trains women to be courtesans, and does not soil them with maternity. The tenderness for motherhood which thaws, occasionally, even our sceptically chilly souls is the product of a rural adolescence in which women still bore children now and then; and our feelings survive after the conditions under which they rose are changed and gone. We who were born before the nineties, and grew near the open fields, will believe to the end that (as the Slavonic proverb warns us) "those who have no children have no happiness"; and that to raise a family of virile sons and kindly daughters is an achievement that calls for more character, and has perhaps a more substantial result, than painting neoimpressionist pictures, or composing modern music, or writing essays on the modern woman.

III. OUR DAUGHTERS

The emancipated woman, then, is the product of economic developments not willed by herself; and nothing is so absurd as the moral tirades which denounce her for being what she is. We should be able, with this orientation, to look upon her with some degree of objectivity and impartiality. Let us consider her.

In industry she is adapting herself with an astounding versatility, with an unsuspected flexibility of mind. Most of the tricks and habits of intelligence which a fairly recent psychology pronounced innately male, turn out to be superficial acquisitions which women can take on as readily as rouge. Observe these office girls everywhere; they may be slightly lacking in initiative (outside of *erotica*), but their quiet competence, their patient courtesy, their unassuming assumption of most of the real work of the office—while the superincumbent male smokes his cigar, leans back in his chair, and looks pontifically about—is a source of perpetual surprise and humble admiration. Within a generation or two the weaker sex has made such progress in conquering a position in industry, in pervading almost every field of it except the brutally physical occupations, that even honest John Stuart Mill would be amazed today to see how needlessly modest his hopes were for the sex which he made his protégé. (One pictures him standing in bewilderment at the sight of women policemen directing traffic in the busiest section of—Constantinople.) [1] There is no telling how far this feminine permeation of industry will go; the time may come when the superior tact of women, and their skill in the manipulation of details, will all but balance the greater strength and bolder initiative of men. When electric power takes the dirt and muscular strain out of industry, even man will have to become intelligent to keep his place in the economic world.

In politics our daughters will not be so fortunate. No doubt the industrialized woman had to enter this sorry game to protect herself against man-made decrees and contemporary discrimination. Had not the villainous male surrounded his hoary privileges with a thousand legislative barriers, and fortified his force at a hundred points with venerable laws? These had to be undone, every road had to be opened for the unspent energy of a sex suddenly shorn of domestic labor and freed from the burdens of biennial motherhood. What passionate ability they poured into this struggle for enfranchisement! Never was half a world of resistance so rapidly and so valiantly beaten down. During the same time, with forces as vocal and numerous, and against the same hostility and abuse, the rebellious *prolétaires* of England and America achieved, through political agitation, nothing. The bravery of embattled men drunk with the sound and fury of war could not outmatch the courage of these women marching to the polls, knocking at the gates of power, knocking till the doors were opened and democracy was forced to take them in. Fifty years from now they will realize how completely they have been taken in.

Some of them understand it now, and perceive that nose-counting is not emancipation, and that freedom is not political, but of the mind. A million alert and happy girls are filling with color and charm the class-rooms and dormitories and campuses that once harbored only the strutting heirs of creation. In a thousand colleges everywhere we come upon them, their

[1] Montreal *Gazette,* April 2, 1928.

faces newly serious with the literature and science of the world, their bright eyes shining with the lust for knowledge, their athletic bodies leaping with the sense of a fuller life. Perhaps their beauty blinds us, and we judge too favorably their bubbling gayety and their profound frivolity. But have you heard them interrogate their teachers? Have you watched them as they tore a theory to tatters, and remade the world nearer to their hearts' desire?

What will come of all this education? Will it coöperate with the widened life of the modern woman, with the thousand new experiences which are remoulding her, to give her an intelligence capable of coping with this changing world? Will this new diversity of mind and interest disrupt that unity and wisdom of instinct which once served woman so well in her endless war with the hesitating and intellectual male? Will this new intelligence in woman disturb and frighten off the possible suitor, and make it difficult for the educated woman to find a mate? The Roman citizen, we are told, was filled with horror at the prospect of a learned wife. And so is every man; he is unhappy in the company of a woman whose mind is the equal of his own; he can love only what is weaker than himself, as the woman can love only what is stronger. Hence the girl whose culture is of knowledge and ideas rather than of natural charm and half-unconscious skill, is at a disadvantage in the pursuit of a mate; she is trespassing upon fields which men have for centuries reserved for them. Sixty per cent of women college graduates remain unmarried.[1] Sonia Kovalevsky, a distinguished scientist, complained that no one would marry her. "Why can no one love me? I could give more than most women, and yet the most insignificant women are loved and I am not." [2] A clever lass will conceal her mental superiority until it is too late.

In some fifty years, then, women have proved that the mental differences between the sexes are due far more to environment and occupation than to unalterable nature. This need not mean that women will at any early date overcome the intellectual handicaps with which time and custom have encompassed them. Their cultural development has but begun; they have no age-long tradition and impetus behind them, no great exemplars to inspire them with confidence or serve as models for their growth. Only in our time has the average woman enjoyed educational opportunities on any scale remotely approaching equality with the male; for many generations yet the proportion of women to men in our colleges will be far less than the proportion of women to men in our population. Perhaps, also, motherhood, even at its present fashionable minimum, will still absorb a large share of women's energies; she may again come to look upon it as her greatest achievement, and be content to surrender such incidental occupations as art and literature to unsexed men. She may discover that there are greater things than writ-

[1] Siegfried, A., *America Comes of Age*, p. 111.
[2] In Ellis, H.. *Studies in the Psychology of Sex*, vol. vi, p. 141.

ten words in this world, and that there is some difference between the intellectual and the intelligent.

Meanwhile, what has happened to the modern woman's body? Has her expulsion from the home and her welcome into the factory led to any physical deterioration? Very probably. She does not look so robust and healthy as her agricultural or domestic grandma; she has less color of her own, and she cannot bear children without such prolonged helplessness and pain as would fill a primitive lady with scorn. But that is true of all of us; men too have lost vigor since they left the fields. The modern mind is more alert; it handles complex tools and vehicles with steady confidence and comparative security; but the modern body is incapable of the strains and burdens which once it bore as part of the day's routine.

Yet with all her ailments the woman of our time remains sufficiently beautiful to make philosophers grow dizzy as she passes by. We cannot be too grateful to her for the sly arts by which she preserves her seductive charms to an age which brought the ladies of past centuries to the first stages of senility. Once a woman of forty was old, decrepit, and trustworthy; today there is nothing so dangerous. Even lipstick and rouge are from this viewpoint forgivable adjuncts to art and civilization; though a natural color is an admirable substitute for cosmetics.

Perhaps this pretty frailty, this physical enfeeblement of the contemporary woman, is a passing and superficial condition. In a world operated by electric power, factories will be as clean as homes once were; cities will spread out, and human beings will begin to breathe fresh air again. What with "hikes" and tennis and basketball, the modern girl may recapture the roses which urban industry has snatched from her cheeks. The impediment of constrictive dress is being overcome; the body of the modern girl is boldly emancipated from the dignified accoutrements which were once among the impediments of matrimony. Short skirts are a boon to all the world except the tailors. The sole harm they do is in contributing to the atrophy of the male imagination—and perhaps women would have no beauty if men had no imagination. All in all, the new woman has added considerably to the color and variety of modern life; she has become livelier and happier under the stimulus of her freedom. It is difficult for some of us to accustom ourselves to bobbed hair (ancient as that is), and to feminine cigarettes; but the coming generation will not mind these surface alterations. Anything at all, if done by pretty women consistently, will seem attractive to the normal man; custom makes morals, and has a hand in beauty too. In former days old women smoked malodorous pipes, and the world rolled on mindlessly; it will roll on as nonchalantly now that old women are flirts and young women blow rings of smoke into their lovers' eyes. Smoking may be injurious as well as pleasant; but if men and women prefer a short life and a merry one, shall they not have their choice? How can we be certain that gayety is not wiser than wisdom?

But what shall we say of the *delirium tremens* called the modern dance? Was it women who invented it, or some neurotic male? And can it be that our forefathers raged as morally as we do now, when the voluptuous waltz replaced the pirouetting of aristocratic days? [1] What again shall be said of the growing proficiency of ladies in the gentle arts of robbery, murder, and politics? In 1926, as a respectable Baltimore periodical [2] informs us, "an unidentified man was brought to a hospital here in a critical condition, suffering from painful injuries said to have been inflicted by three girls in a wood near Hurlock. The man was walking . . . when the girls, in an auto, offered him a 'lift.' He accepted. After riding a short distance, he said, the girls stopped the car on a lonely road. During a petting party which followed, . . . one of the girls became enraged at his lack of ardour. A scuffle ensued. While two held him, the third stabbed him with a hatpin. The girls fled, leaving him helpless on the ground." After this can we any longer doubt the emancipation of women?

It would seem that Huxley was right: "Women's virtue was man's most poetic fiction." They have always had these passions; but once they concealed them more sedulously, because they thought that gentlemen preferred modesty. Now men seem to respond more quickly to immodesty; and the modern girl tends to an anatomical and psychological candor which transiently allures the senses, but hardly draws the soul. A mature man revels in resistance, and loves a delicate reticence in woman. No doubt when men remain immature, stranded in promiscuity, insensitive to the joys of comradeship and loyalty, and unaware of any charms but those of the flesh, extraordinary measures must be taken to rouse their interest and lure them into matrimony. But when a legal union issues from this fitful temperature of the blood, it goes to wreck as soon as the flame of passion has been extinguished by the use and wont of marriage. Shaw was wrong: matrimony is not a maximum of temptation combined with a maximum of opportunity. The opportunity endures; but the temptation is soon reduced to a minimum.

IV. OUR MATRIARCHATE

The picture of the modern working-class girl busy with the work of the world, and resplendent with vitality and freedom, is more pleasing to contemplate than the picture of the modern middle-class woman married, successfully attached to an income, and devoted to a career of bridge, shopping, and social reform.

Let us look at ourselves through foreign eyes. "In America," says Count

---

[1] Cf. De Musset, *Confessions of a Child of the Century*, p. 112.
[2] Quoted in the *American Mercury*, March, 1926.

Keyserling, "the husband has come to be just as oppressed as the wife used to be in the old Orient, with corresponding psychological recessions which are becoming more and more evident." He adds that American women are becoming breastless Amazons, and produce "an effect of coldness, hardness and soullessness,"—though what did the Count expect on first acquaintance? [1] We must allow some discount here for views derived from a background of Brandenburg aristocracy; but what remains may suffice to reveal to us the coming subjection of men, and their imperative need for a Susan B. Anthony. Soon, doubtless, we shall have polyandry, and masterful women will collect harems of industrious males, guarded by lady eunuchs who will stand for no nonsense. Perhaps in the future we shall have three sexes, as among the ants and bees; some women will procreate the race, and others will give themselves so completely to economic activity as to lose first the desire, and then the capacity, for motherhood. Evolution gives us no reason for expecting that the future will confine itself to the past.

How did this inversion of roles come about? Presumably through the passage of prestige from physical superiority.[2] The subjection of woman was based essentially on the muscular prowess of the male; he was the master because in the last resort (which he did not too long postpone) he could knock her down. Now men can still knock women down; and it becomes a delicate question in philosophy why they have abandoned this ancient custom. Probably the growing moral sense of man made him ashamed of the last resort; and the greater freedom of woman from sexual desire placed her in the strategic position of one who gives to one who asks. But behind that secondary phenomenon was the primary economic fact that the complexity of modern affairs, calling more and more for intelligence, less and less for strength, destroyed the reputation of mere brawn, and took from the man of the middle class his sole superiority to his wife; after which her superior subtlety and tenacity gave her the advantage over his shyness, his sensitiveness, and his fatigue. Where the reputation of muscle still survives, as in the proletariat, the male is still master of the home, and the woman earns her keep with a vengeance.

Behold, in consequence, the parasitic woman. Freed from domestic toil by the withdrawal of industry from the home, and freed from the burden of motherhood by contraceptives or nurses and maids, she is left with hands, head and heart restlessly idle, a rich soil for alien seed. And by a natural development, the less she has to do the lazier she becomes, and the less willing she is to perform what remains of the work which once made her a helpmeet instead of a doll.

No insult is offered here to the woman who works, at home or in the shop, as producer of human life or of humanly valuable goods. The insult

[1] *Europe*, pp. 66–67.
[2] Mill, J. S., *The Subjection of Women*, p. 4.

is offered, for what it may be worth, to the woman who commercializes her beauty, in marriage or without; who drives hard bargains in luxury and finery for her love; who spends her days in resting, primping, powdering, curling, and (at last) dressing, and her nights in amusement and flirtation. In all the varied panorama of modern life there is nothing so offensive as the expensive idleness of these women. They have few children or none, but they need many servants; they have no function, but they have endless needs; they specialize in the art of doing nothing in a thousand fancy ways. The effect is to force the man to a nerve-racking pace of toil, and to a bitter consciousness that his significance is merely that of a commissary clerk.

If women wait today, as never before, to have marriage offered them, it is in large measure the fault of this parasitic class. For such a woman offers to her husband very little that he might not just as well secure by short-term investments properly diversified. Under these circumstances marriage, to a critical bachelor, appears not as the fulfilling goal of a mature man, but as a civilized and long-drawn-out rendition of a theme dear to nature in the insect world, where, as we have seen, the female eats the male, as likely as not, while he is absorbed in the entanglements of love. No wonder that men, seeing the utter unproductiveness of these ladies of the afternoon, take to their heels at the thought of the golden bonds of matrimony. A million women waste away in loneliness because a million wives, having caught their prey, devour it so publicly that all hunted souls retreat into a baccalaureate solitude. Here, and not in the bobbed hair or shortened skirts of active youth, lies the immoral monstrosity of our time.

Let us hope that these are but difficulties of transition, that our chaos of mind and morals, of politics and art, is an illucid interval between a system of order that is dying, and one that emerges slowly, not from our jeremiads and our arguments, but from the trial and error adjustment of human impulses to the novel and artificial conditions of our industrial, urban and secular age. That very lengthening of adolescence which has so delayed marriage and transformed morality may be a subtle sign of loftier levels soon to be reached by men; for in human history the lengthening of adolescence—and therefore of education and training—has been one of the great levers in the elevation of the race. Probably we are not witnessing the end of a civilization, as our moralists suppose; we exceptional and unmoral people are a small minority, perhaps neurotic and diseased, and doomed to extinction by sterility. Around us on every side the great mass of the simple people will go on marrying and reproducing, and their children will inherit the earth. There is every reason to believe that they will carry the world on until a new order, a new stability of conduct and thought, has established mankind on the higher plane to which our blind experiments may lead.

CHAPTER X

The Breakdown of Marriage

AND SO WE COME to marriage.

It was Bernard Shaw, presumably, who said that more nonsense had been uttered on the subject of marriage than on any other topic in the world. It is as simple to be foolish about love as in it, and with less excuse. Approaching the problem, even the most disembodied intellectual perceives that ideas have only a modest (though this is hardly the word) influence upon the relations of the sexes; that economic changes override philosophies and morals; and that the best that thought can do is to analyze the changes, foresee their development and result, and find some intelligent adjustment of behavior that may protect the individual and the race. In these affairs it is useless to preach, and helpful to understand.

In the midst of our wars and our machines, we have lost sight of the fact that the basic reality in life is not politics, nor industry, but human relationships—the associations of a man with a woman, and of parents with a child. About these two foci of love—mate-love and mother-love—all life revolves. Recall the story of the rebel lass who, when her lover (killed in the Moscow uprising of December, 1917) was buried at the "Red Funeral," leaped into the grave, flung herself prostrate upon the coffin that held him and cried out: "Bury me, too; what do I care about the Revolution now that *he* is dead?" She may have been deluded in thinking him irreplaceably unique—we are so similar that broken hearts and broken vows are alike unreasonable; but she knew, with a wisdom born in the blood of woman, that this tremendous Revolution was a transitory trifle compared with that Mississippi of mating, parentage, and death which is the central stream of human life. She understood, though she might never have found a phrase for it, that the family is greater than the State, that devotion and despair sink deeper into the heart than economic strife, and that in the end our happiness lies not in possessions, place, or power, but in the gift and return of love.

141

I. THE EVOLUTION OF MARRIAGE

What is the meaning of marriage? Perhaps if we can uncover its origin, we shall better realize its significance.

Picture a starfish, among the lowliest of animals, stretching out her rays or arms over her fertilized eggs and her hatched young. It is the beginning of one of the central phenomena in nature—parental care. In the plant and animal world generally, the species is preserved not by maternal solicitude but by lavish and wasteful procreation. A flower must fill the air with pollen and allure some insect that will serve as messenger to the mate it will never see. The little blood-red *Hæmatococcus* has been known to turn an arctic landscape from snow white into scarlet by its reproductive energies in a single night. The oyster, with Mayflower-like fertility, deposits millions of eggs, and then with characteristic nonchalance, leaves them to their fate; a few of them develop, but most of them serve as food or are lost as just plain waste.

Slowly nature, as we have seen, discovered and developed parental care as a substitute for this reckless extravagance. From the lowest vertebræ to the highest tribe of men the size of the litter, the brood, or the family decreases, and parental care increases, with every stage of development in the genus, the species, the variety, the race, the nation, the class, and the individual. Marriage came, not to license love, but to improve the quality of life by binding mates in permanence to care for the offspring they produce.

It is not an exclusively human phenomenon. Some species of birds are more monogamous than man. De Crespigny writes of the orang-utangs of Borneo: "They live in families. They build commodious nests in the trees; and so far as I could observe, the nests are occupied only by the female and the young,—the male passing the night in the fork of the same or a neighboring tree." Westermarck describes the gorilla as "living in families, the male parent building the nest and protecting the family; and the same is the case with the chimpanzee." "It is not unusual," says Savage, "to see the 'old folks' in a gorilla family sitting under a tree regaling themselves with fruit and friendly chat, while their children are leaping around them and swinging from branch to branch in boisterous merriment." [1]

Gradually selection weeds out those species that take little care of their offspring, and develops in the survivors that instinct of parental care which slowly raises the individual and the race. Ape mothers have been known to die of grief upon the death of their young. In one species of ape the mother carries her babe clasped in one arm uninterruptedly for several

[1] Westermarck, E., *History of Human Marriage*, p. 14.

months.[1] In man the impulse becomes almost the ruling passion, stronger even than love; what woman loves her husband as she loves her child? Savage mothers nurse their children sometimes for twelve years; and among some tribes, as in the New Hebrides, it is no rarity that a mother should kill herself to take care of her dead child beyond the grave.[2] There are few things more marvelous in human history than the almost complete (though passing) transference of a woman's egotism to her child.

Along with this powerful impulse of parental care rose a central and dominating institution—the family. The origin of the family lay in the invaluable helplessness of the child, in its increasing susceptibility to development and training after birth. Evolution in animals is biological chiefly—it concerns the growth of new organs; but evolution in man is social—it concerns the increasing transmission of an accumulating heritage of technology and culture from generation to generation. The family was invented by nature to bind the male in service to the female whom nature had bound in service to the child. Men are by nature slaves to women, and women are by nature slaves to children and the race; in that natural slavery is the secret of their deepest and most durable content.

Let us understand, then, that marriage is not a relation between a man and a woman, designed to legalize desire; it is a relation between parents and children, designed to preserve and strengthen the race. If it had been a personal instead of a racial matter, it would not have been made the first concern of human custom and laws. Why have states legislated so carefully and spent so lavishly to regulate the love of a man for a maid? Why all this paraphernalia of license bureaus, marriage ceremonies, divorce courts, moral exhortations and taboos, if not for the reason that marriage is the most fundamental of all institutions, the one which guards and replenishes the stream of human life? It is clear enough, God knows, that marriage was never intended for the happiness of the mates, but for the mating and rearing of children.[3] The average tenure of human existence in primitive days was so pitifully brief that no one seems to have bothered about the individual. Only with the modern lengthening of life, the superabundance of humanity (the one commodity that violates the law of supply and demand), and the reduction of parentage to a phase rather than the sole content of marriage, has the individual raised the query whether his own happiness in mating is not to be considered along with the continuance and elevation of the race. It is in the Age of the Individual that the revolt against marriage has risen to its present irresistible tide.

The evolution of marriage has followed the broadening lines of racial

[1] McDougall, Wm., *Social Psychology*, p. 70.

[2] Kropotkin, Prince, *Mutual Aid*, pp. 89, 101.

[3] Cf. Shelley: "A system could not well have been devised more studiously hostile to human happiness than marriage."—Notes to *Queen Mab*.

interest. As far back as the eye of history can see, the freedom of the individual in choosing a mate was strictly limited by social need. The first sexual taboos seem to have aimed at preventing the mating of parents and children, then of brothers and sisters; gradually the prohibitions spread to "exogamy," which forbade the marriage of a man with a woman of his own tribe. Early sociologists like Lewis Morgan were inclined to attribute these restrictions to the primitive mind's perception of the disadvantages of inbreeding; later students, like Westermarck and Ellis, rather cynically ascribed it to the contempt which comes of familiarity. But it will not do to exaggerate the inability of our savage forebears to put two and two together a..d make their own systems of sociology; probably they also had the race in mind when they limited the individual.

Marriage evolved as economic relations changed. In the nomad stage, the male, a mighty hunter before the Lord, took his club and perhaps a friend, stole into another tribe, snatched some fair maiden from her tent, and carried her away after the manner of the Sabine rape. Then, through the growth of wealth and peace, morals improved, and the man took not a club, but a valuable present or an offer of long service, to the father of the woman he desired; marriage by purchase replaced marriage by capture. Today the institution is a strange mixture of capture and purchase.

In those early days war was frequent and perils were many; death came upon the male with less procrastination than upon the female; and polygamy was a crude attempt of the surviving men to take care of the women who so outnumbered them. As women nursed their children for many years, and abstained from marital relations until the child was weaned, the male found it convenient to have a variety of partners to meet his perennial demands. Besides, polygamy produced more children than monogamy; and abundant offspring came as a blessing to a people forever harassed with accident, disease, and war.

But as war decreased in frequency, and life and health became more secure, the numerical superiority of women was reduced, and monogamy began. It was an advantage to the children, who had now a united care, a concentrated love, and more food to eat since there were fewer mouths to feed. It was an advantage to the man, for it enabled him to center his bequests, to found a family instead of scattering his wealth, like his seed, among a horde of progeny. He found himself still free to satisfy his variegated appetites in secret, while he could surround his wife's fidelity with all the guards of custom and power, and so secure the transmission of his property to children probably his own. Above all, and despite this double standard (so rooted in the institution of bequest), monogamy was an advantage to the woman. It solved some part of that problem of jealousy which must have made polygamy a bedlam; it gave woman at least a biological equality with man; and it made it possible for her, from that modest leverage, to move and raise the world.

The rest of the history of marriage has been a struggle between woman and property, between wealth and love. One might have supposed that as riches grew they would dominate unchallenged the choice and rule of mates, and that the subordination of woman as a mechanism for producing heirs, and an economical substitute for a slave, would become ineradicably established among the customs of the race. But it was the other way. Wealth brought education, education soothed the savage breast of the male, and after centuries of evolution the simple lust of body for body was replaced, over widening areas, by romantic love.

The marriage of convenience remained, and in many countries the girl was still mated by her parents to some potential millionaire; but in England and America, and here and there in every nation, the proprietary marriage yielded, and the Troubadours triumphed. Slowly woman, who had been made gentle by the brutality of the male, softened his brutality by her gentleness; slowly by her tenderness and her maternal sacrifice she lifted him from his proximity to the brute, and taught him to see and to seek in her some qualities less tangible and corporeal than those which had lured him to her lair. Gradually upon the physical basis of desire civilization built the frail and precious superstructure of poetic love.

We have studied elsewhere the remarkable and picturesque development of spiritual love from the roundelays of the medieval singers, through the monumental sentiment of *Clarissa Harlowe* and *La Nouvelle Héloïse,* to the novels that struggled to meet the nineteenth century appetite for romance. Who can say how far this ocean of fiction cleansed away something of the coarser aspects of modern love, making incipiently real that hunger of soul for soul which had been at first, perhaps, the consolatory fancy of aging virgins and imaginative males? Certainly romantic love became real: youth burst forth at puberty into sonnets and madrigals dripping with sincerity; men knelt to women, bowed to kiss their hands, and loved them for something more than the cosy softness of their flesh. They killed themselves in jousts to win a smile; they created literatures in the ecstasy of their devotion; and gradually they brought all their proud wealth to lay at the feet of frail creatures who had no power over them except through their beauty and their subtlety. When, in many hearts, desire became devotion rather than possession, and a man, wooing a maid with limitless loyalty, pledged his faith to her through every trial until death, marriage reached the climax of its long development, the zenith of its slow ascent from brutality to love. Perhaps we shall never know it in all its fulness again.

II. THE DISSOLUTION OF MARRIAGE

For now is the day of the machine, and everything must change. Individual security has lessened even as social security has grown; physical life is safer than it was, but economic life is harassed with a thousand intricacies that make every day a peril. Youth, which is braver and more conceited than before, is materially helpless and economically ignorant beyond anything in the past. Love comes, and youth, finding its pockets empty, dares not marry: love comes again, more weakly (years have passed) and yet the pockets do not bulge enough for marriage; love comes once more, with half of its early freshness and power (years have passed), and now the pockets are full, and marriage celebrates the death of love.

Tired of waiting so long, the urban girl, as like as not, plunges into maturity, a frail, adventurous thing. The terrific compulsion is on her, she feels, of getting attention, entertainment, stockings, and champagne—everything except a wedding-ring—through sexual favors or display. Sometimes her freedom of behavior is the outcome and reflex of her economic freedom; she is no longer dependent on the male and may therefore risk the male's decreasing distaste for marrying a lady as learned as himself in the arts of love. Her very capacity to earn a good income makes the possible suitor hesitate; how can his modest wage suffice to keep both at their present standard?

At last she finds a mate who offers her his hand in marriage. They marry. Not in a church, for they are sophisticated people; they have no more religion, and the moral code which rested so largely on their abandoned faith has lost its hold upon their hearts. They marry in the basement of some City Hall (perfumed with the aroma of politicians), to the melody of an alderman's incantations; they are making not a vow of honor but a business contract, which they shall feel free at any time to end. There is no solemnity of ritual, no majesty of speech, no glory of music, no depth or ecstasy of emotion to burn the words of their promise into their memories. They kiss with a laugh, and frolic home.

Not home. There is no cottage waiting to greet them, bowered amid fragrant grass and shady trees, no garden that shall grow for them flowers and food made fairer and sweeter because they have planted them. They must hide themselves timidly as if in prison cells; in narrow rooms which can not hold them long, and which they will not care to improve and ornament into an expression of their personalities. This dwelling is no spiritual entity, like the home that has taken form and soul under the care of a score of years; rather it is a merely material thing, as hard and cold as an asylum. It stands amid noise and stone and steel, where spring will have no entrance, and will give them not growing things, but only rain; where autumn will bring no rainbows in the skies nor any colors on the leaves, but only lassitude and sombre memories.

The woman is disappointed; she finds nothing here that can make these walls bearable night and day; soon she runs from them at every chance, and creeps into them only towards the dawn. The man is disappointed; he can not putter about here, solacing his hammered thumbs with the sense of building or rebuilding his own home; slowly it comes to him that these rooms are precisely like those in which he had brooded as a lonely bachelor, that his relations with his wife are prosaically like those which he has had for years with women of undiscriminating receptivity. There is nothing new here, and nothing grows; no infant's voice disturbs the night, no merriness of children brightens the day, no chubby arms sanction toil with a prattling welcome home. For where could the child play?—and how could they afford another room, and the long years of care and education required of children in the city? Discretion, they think, is the better part of love; they resolve to have no children until—until they are divorced.

Their marriage being no marriage—being a sexual instead of a parental association—it decays for lack of root and sustenance; it dies because it is detached from the life of the race. They shrink into themselves, single and separate fragments; the altruism of love sinks into an individualism irritated by the compulsion of masquerade. The natural varietism of the man reappears; familiarity has bred contempt; through her very generosity the woman has nothing new to give.

Childless, they find a thousand reasons for discord. The word "dear," that had thrilled them in hearing and in utterance, becomes the cheapest syllable in the language, facile and meaningless. The wife mourns the departed tenderness of early days; and therefore, in the home, she neglects that care of body, dress, action and speech, which had drawn the man to her as to something brighter and higher than himself. If there is any sexual incompatibility between them it becomes an insuperable barrier, because they conceive of marriage as a purely sexual relation. If they are poor, the man regrets the burdens he has assumed, and the woman dotes on the Prince of Wales. If they are rich, the pretended communism of love and marriage conflicts with the individualism of greed and fear; quarrels about money begin as soon as the delirium of love subsides. If they are modern, they play at equality; and a tug of war ensues till one or the other has established an irritating mastery. If the woman works, she resents her continued slavery; if she is idle, time hangs heavy on her hands until Satan finds something for them to do. They thought they could not afford a child; but they discover, like Balzac, that "a vice costs less than a family." If either has friends, the other is jealous of them; if neither has friends, the two are forced back upon themselves, into an inescapable intimacy too monotonous to be borne. The freedom indispensable to personality disappears before the passions of ownership and curiosity; the soul finds no sanctuary in which it can heal itself with peace and solitude. Love, which had always been a combat and a chase, becomes a war, in which the night's embrace is but a passing armistice.

For meanwhile anatomical disillusionment sets in. Man and woman alike discover that love's fitful fever burned not primarily for their joy, but for the continuance of the race. The woman finds herself changed from a goddess into a cook—unless, perchance, she has found one of those gentle husbands who change a cook into a goddess. She senses the polygamous propensities of the male, and watches him jealously because she knows that she cannot trust him far. She observes that his attentions become less frequent and thoughtful, that he makes love, if at all, with absent-minded punctuality. He lacks the imagination to see his wife as a stranger sees her, or to see a stranger's wife as she will appear at nine o'clock the next morning; in all his thinking (and in hers) distance lends enchantment to the view, and the new is mistaken for the beautiful. Add childlessness or idleness on the part of the woman, and she too begins to hunger for some unfamiliar face or scene that may restore the charming flatteries of desire. Neither premeditates adultery; they only long for "life." Suddenly the senses conquer sense, loyalty slips away, suspicion comes on feline feet, and the final fury of detection is welcomed as simplifying a situation too complex for successful pretense and mastery.

And so they are divorced. See them, first, in the domestic relations court; waiting sadly while other tragedies are aired; exaggerating each other's cruelties, and flinging hot names into faces once idealized by desires; reconciled, perhaps, but only for a while; hating each other now as only those can hate who remember the promises of love. Soon they are free, as the desert is free; they are divorced, and can experiment again. But the conditions are as before; how can the end be different?

Year by year marriage comes later, separation earlier; and fidelity finds few so simple as to do it honor. Soon no man will go down the hill of life with a woman who has climbed it with him, and a divorceless marriage will be as rare as a maiden bride. And the divorced are but a fraction of those who are unhappy in marriage. Let us not inquire how many long to be separated, but dare not ask; how many have asked and were denied. Do not look into the hearts of these others—there is no telling what we might find there: instead of separation, fear of shame; instead of love, indifference; instead of faithfulness, deceit. Perhaps it were as well that they too were torn apart, and that the breakdown of marriage should stand out naked and startling before our eyes, challenging every statesman who thinks in generations, and every lover who honors love enough to wish that it might not die so young.

III. THE RECONSTRUCTION OF MARRIAGE

To describe is easy; to prescribe is hard. What can we say that has not been said a thousand times before? What nostrum can we recommend that has not been tried and found wanting? What counsel can we give that will not be an insult to the wounds that we would heal?

Perhaps we should abandon the problem and say, with the oldest of the Christian religions: Close every door of escape, and the prisoners will forget that they are in jail. If marriage is for children and the race, and not for individuals and mates, then for the children's sake let marriage be irrevocable, and what God has joined together let no man part. There is, after all, so little difference between one of us and the next, that if we can not get along with the mate we have, we shall soon find like difficulties with another. Man was not made for happiness; he is born for suffering; let him marry then, and hold his peace.

But shall we call indissoluble the vows that immature youth has made? Shall we shackle two souls for life though their love has fallen over into hate? Here is no tempting choice; the devil and the deep sea invite us. But now that children are fewer, and the career of the parents does not end as soon after the birth or maturing of the offspring as reckless nature arranged in the lower realms of life, we can afford to consider the mates a little more; it would be ridiculous to sacrifice a career of three score years and ten to considerations that arose when women had children wholesale, and were worn out at forty-five. The very growth of the race in quality depends upon reducing the sacrifice which it requires of its members; the race is greater than the individual only because it may produce greater individuals. Beyond that, it is a name and an abstraction; and the medieval theory of marriage belongs to pre-nominalist days.

Out of our individualistic age comes an opposite theory, more interesting and as extreme; and how attractively it is named!—"Free Love." Since vows are made to be broken, why make any vows at all? Since marriages are now made to be dissolved, why bother a thousand courts with a million matings and separations? If love is the best motive for marriage, its death is sufficient reason for divorce; how can love be real if it is not free? Let us then release these pompous judges who pretend to solder our souls; let lovers wed with only their mutual pledge of honesty and honor; and when love is gone let them without hindrance seek other mates, and recreate their love and their youth.

This solution of the marriage problem is gathering new popularity every year. Judge Lindsay, reporting that marriage licenses fell 25 per cent from 1921 to 1922, explains the decrease as due to the spread of unlicensed *ménages*. These free unions would offer an admirable exit from the difficulties of our current code were it not for the continued economic dependence of woman upon man, and her psychological dependence upon him before marriage binds him to her whims. Periodic disabilities, and the possibility of pregnancy, reduce the woman's earning power; unless she can secure a home and some fairly permanent protection in return for the risks she runs, the advantage of "freedom" is all on the side of the male. At present—though this feeling too is in flux, and tends to grow weaker day by day—a woman is lowered in the eyes of a man by her surrender; the male is a fighter, or likes to conceive himself so, and relishes at least a pretense of resistance to dignify his victory; when he has quite won he seeks new fields of glory. At present, but again subject to change without notice, the male likes to think that the woman whom he chooses as his permanent mate has never belonged to any other man; he will readily agree to a temporary union with an experienced woman, but he seldom desires her for his legal wife. It is as if he accepted Weininger's brutal statement, that every woman is by temperament either a mother or a rake; and as if he suspected that a woman who has loved her neighbors as herself will revert to that promiscuity as soon as the novelty of marriage, or the burden of motherhood, disappears. The male never dreams of applying the same scrutiny or judgment to himself; he assumes his ability to pass from variety to monotony without any likelihood of deviation from uxorious fidelity. What actuates him is not reason, but the proprietary sense; his feelings go back to the ancient and almost universal custom of marriage by purchase; he is buying something on the market, and does not want to pay a good price for second-hand material. He thinks of woman as the author of the tenth commandment thought of her.

All that will change; and perhaps when woman's economic independence is complete, and contraceptives have quite differentiated mating from parentage, men will apply to women the same lenient standard by which they judge themselves, and our ancient moral code will come definitely to an end. But during the long transition woman will suffer through the reckless egoism and irresponsibility of man. Free love is love free for the male; it is a trap into which the emancipated woman falls with a very emancipated man. Some day woman may be master of her own life, and motherhood may not leave her at the mercy of a naturally promiscuous male; some day, far distant, we may find a way of caring for children without binding the man to the woman who has borne them by him. Then free love will be a boon to all, and the ideal state of a finally liberated race. Till then we had better obey the law.

Confused with Free Love in the popular mind is companionate marriage. Hysteria conceives this in various shocking ways; but when we discover that its doughty protagonist defines it as "legal marriage, with legalized birth control, and with the right to divorce by mutual consent for childless couples, usually without payment of alimony," it does not seem so very terrible; there is nothing in it (except for that bitter line about alimony) which does not already exist in the practice of presumably respectable families; and divorce by mutual consent, where there are no children, is preferable to divorce by collusion or "desertion." What people fear in the plan is the thoroughness with which it establishes the equality of the sexes.

Very rapidly the luxurious ladies of the bourgeoisie are bringing down upon all their sex the revenge of the tired male; marriage is changing to a form that will not tolerate the unproductive women who are the ornament and horror of so many expensive homes; the men are inviting their modern wives to earn for themselves the money which they are to spend. For companionate marriage provides that until maternity is in the offing, the wife shall go to work. Here hides the joker by which the liberation of woman shall be made complete: she shall be privileged henceforth to pay her fare from A to Z. The Industrial Revolution is to be carried out to its logical and merciless conclusion; woman is to join her husband in the factory; instead of remaining idle in her bower, compelling the man to produce doubly as a balance to her economic sterility, she shall become his honored equal in toil as in reward, in obligations as in rights. Such is emancipation.

Much credit is due the man who has dared all the devils of orthodoxy to propose a specific cure for the sickness of modern marriage. But there is something hard and ruthless in the plan, which a lingering gallantry will consider unfair so long as woman's economic and moral equality with man is incomplete. For man, as we have said, is secretly and ravenously polygamous. Give him a form of marriage in which he shall be free to leave his mate as soon as she has lost for him the lure of novelty and the pleasure of resistance, and he will itch for alien charms and uncaptured citadels; and sooner or later he will say adieu. It does not help to answer that the consent of both parties would be required for divorce; the modern woman will grant consent when it is asked. And then? Then she will find herself "free and independent" again, flung back upon the thorns and spikes of industry, immeasurably more depreciated than the male.

These are minor difficulties, and presumably the plan is offered as subject to amendment by experience. What is most constructive in it is the encouragement which it offers to early marriage. For here, after all, is the heart of our moral problem: If we could find a way to restore marriage to its natural age we should at one stroke reduce by half the prostitution, the venereal disease, the fruitless celibacy, the morbid chastity, and the experimental perversions that stigmatize our contemporary life.

Consider again how few are the men or the women who marry the one whom they love best. The bright passion of youth comes too soon for our finances; we shrink from the great adventure, and let love die away. And yet the earlier the love, the fresher and deeper it must be; no man can love after thirty with the ardor and self-abandonment of youth.[1] The devotion which first love evokes in the soul is too profound to be worn away with a year of intimacy and trial; this new tenderness of the boy, this clear-eyed

[1] This is the harmless remark which, abbreviated in caption by a hurried editor, was broadcast throughout the country as "No man can love after thirty." Publicity makes us and breaks us.

trust of the girl, must carry them on happily through years whose memories will be like a fragrance in their lives.

Picture a marriage of first love. See the newlyweds, in ideal, choosing not
a cell in a box, but a separate little home where nature has not yet been
utterly dispossessed; furnishing it to the tune of a hundred merry debates
as to what should be bought and where it should stand; planting flowers
and growing with their growth; filling the home with color and music and
books and friends; making it more lovable than the glare and blare of the
street; and completing it at last with the turbulence and jollity of a child.
Many times we have revenged ourselves with wit upon the hard restraints
of marriage; and yet, in our secret hearts we shall always look back with
longing to those sentimental days when love was young.[1]

There are many objections to early marriage. First it is useless to offer
counsels of perfection; we cannot conquer the economic caution of youth
with moral exhortations and real-estate poetry.—But it is the parents, not
the children, that advise, and financially enforce, delayed marriage; there
is nothing further to be asked of the recklessness of youth. Let us persuade
the mistaken parents that by compelling the deferment of marriage they
are inviting an endless chain of coarsening substitutes and demoralizing
perversions; that wisdom would lie not in making impediments to the marriage of true minds, but in providing for sons, as well as daughters, a substantial dowry that would balance their economic immaturity and strengthen
their courage to face the world. It would be a debt of honor, which the
children would repay to the next generation; no one would lose, everyone
would gain. There was a time when fathers were generous enough for that.

With such assistance even a cautious lad might surrender to the call of
love. And any lad, marrying, will find a grain of truth in the old proverb,—
"God will take care of you"; pride will stiffen his vertebræ, add power to
his arm, and persistence to his courage; the compulsion of responsibility
will deepen him; marriage will make him a man. If nothing else will serve,
let the little goddess go forth to her daily labors as before, until she en-
visages motherhood. It is better that she should have something for her
hands to do than pose as a bit of fragile ornament; and better that they
should delay parentage, than fret in the irritability of mating unnaturally
postponed: we must permit the separation of marriage from reproduction
in order to diminish the separation of sex from marriage. Should the man
relax under this aid, the only remedy for him is fatherhood; the child will
stir him on to manhood, or there is no man in him at all.

The second difficulty adduces the ignorance of youth. "At a time when
a man is in love," said Nietzsche, "he should not be allowed to come to a
decision about his life and to determine once for all the character of his

---

[1] For a strong endorsement of early marriage from the biological standpoint, cf.
Holmes, S. J., *Studies in Evolution and Genetics*, pp. 177–8.

society on account of a whim. We ought publicly to declare invalid the vows of lovers, and to refuse them permission to marry." [1] It is true that youth is blind, and cannot judge; but age is old, and cannot love. Perhaps at no time should we be permitted or required to make irrevocable decisions. It is not shown that men choose more wisely at thirty than at twenty in the matter of taking wives; and as all wives and all husbands are substantially alike, it does not make all the difference in the world. If a man cannot find some mode of concord with his wife it is, in a great majority of cases, because of some defect in his own behavior and philosophy, which would operate to the same result if he could exchange his neighbor's wife for his own. Divorce is like travel: it is useless if we cannot change ourselves.

Nevertheless the ignorance of youth is real; indeed, when, in these matters, do we cease to be ignorant? Which of us men yet understands women, and how many of us can manage them? To reduce the area of the unknown let us restore the old custom of requiring a public betrothal six months before marriage. During that pleasant half year the lovers would discover each other mentally; perhaps they would even begin to quarrel like man and wife; and there would be an opportunity for separation before the bonds of matrimony had made them one. Those six months would add to our marriage institutions a moral fibre and beauty which they sadly need; they would provide a lyric interlude amid the prose of economic life.

The last and greatest difficulty is the absurdity of encouraging youth, before experience has sobered sense, to enter a house which at any moment may become a prison, incarcerating one for life. If early marriage is to be a reasonable arrangement, matrimony must have an exit as well as an entrance, and divorce must be obtainable by mutual consent. It may appear ridiculous, having argued that divorce is a regrettable thing, and that marriage exists for the care of children rather than for the happiness of mates, to urge the extension of divorce at the apparent cost of the family and the child. But who knows that the acceptance of mutual consent as a sufficient reason would multiply divorce? Or that the compulsory association of distrustful and alienated mates is any better for their children than the allotment or alternation of the children between two households separate and at peace? If we refuse divorce to a man and a woman merely because they unite in asking for it, we invite them to some form of collusion which will satisfy our irrational demands. Doubtless some delay is salutary; it would serve wisdom and order to require a trial separation for some considerable time before granting a definite decree; for in that interval the constant warriors might discover that solitude is worse than strife, and distance might reveal virtues which nearness had concealed.

In a Middle Western city recently a congressman and his wife joined in asking for a divorce; it was refused them on the ground that they had not

[1] *Dawn of Day*, sect. 151.

violated a sufficient number of divine commandments and human laws. The fact that they agreed in desiring liberty was considered irrelevant, and they were "handcuffed for life." Such conditions are a provocation to adultery; there is nothing for a gentleman to do, under these circumstances, except to supply the law with its pound of flesh. For many years now Japan has given divorce for mutual consent, and yet its divorce rate is lower than our own. Russia has had such a law since the respectable days of 1907. Rome had it. Bonaparte put it into the Napoleonic Code; but the Bourbons, having learned nothing, struck it out. It is highly probable than an amendment of this kind would add little if at all to the number of separations; it would merely add to the honorableness of our conduct and the decency of our courts.

What the conclusion of our experiments will be let others tell who know. Probably it will be nothing that we shall wish or will; we are caught in a current of change, and shall doubtless be borne along to fated and unchosen ends. In this rushing flux of customs, habits and institutions, anything at all may come. Now that the home, in our large cities, is disappearing, monogamy has lost its chief attraction. Without doubt, companionate marriage will be more and more condoned where there is no intent to reproduce. Free unions, sanctioned or not, will multiply; and though their freedom will be chiefly for the male, women will take them as a lesser evil than the sterile loneliness of uncourted days. The "double standard" will be broken down, and woman, having imitated man in all things else, will emulate his premarital experience. Divorce will grow, and every city will be crowded with the derelicts of shipwrecked unions. The entire institution of marriage will be recast into newer and looser forms. When the industrialization of woman is complete, and birth-control is the secret of every class, motherhood will be an incident in woman's life, and state institutions for the care of children will replace the home. *Panta rhei.*

IV. ON HAVING BABIES

The last word, however, must be for monogamy. The life-long union remains the loftiest conception of human marriage; and it is still the goal which the complete lover will set himself when he pledges his troth. There is something cowardly in divorce, like flight from the field of war; and something unstable and superficial in one who flits from mate to mate. Men and women of character will solve these difficulties as they arise, knowing that difficulties as great would meet them on any other battleground. Their reward comes when the hard years of mutual readjustment are over, and a steady affection tenoned and mortised in the care of children and the sharing of a thousand vicissitudes has supplanted the transitory ardor of physical desire, and made two minds and two hearts one. Only when that test of the soul has been passed will they know the fulness of love.

That fulness cannot come without children. It is, again, for children that marriage was invented; it was designed not to unite mate with mate so much as to perpetuate the species by uniting parents with children in loyalty and care. Emancipate as we will, free ourselves as much as we can from the prejudices of our past, the voluntarily childless woman still fills us with a sense of something abnormal and disagreeable. Objective beauty, like subjective happiness, lies in the easy fulfilment of natural purposes and functions, so that those women who remain to the end without children seem a little ridiculous, and never quite convince us that they know content. If a woman has found another function than motherhood to absorb her energy and fill her life, it is passing well, and nature will bear with her; but if she wanders about aimless and dissatisfied, moving from one place, one man, or one amusement to another, and finding no interest anywhere, it is because she has turned her back on the natural purpose of love. A woman, as Nietzsche said, is a riddle, whose solution is a child.

The modern girl will laugh at this old-fashioned suggestion, and will remind the world that the day is gone when she can be used as a maternity machine. So we refute one another's extremes, and life moves roughshod over our arguments. No one with a sense of history, or a perception of irreversible economic developments, could think of asking a woman for the large family which was her lot on the farm; everyone understands (except the rural assemblymen who still rule our state legislatures) that the multiplication of machines and the reduction of the death rate have put an end to the need for the mass-production of children. If community good seems to require a large population it is because we delude ourselves by thinking in terms of quantity, or aspire to imperial and militaristic expansion, or vision a fertile China overflowing upon the West. But quantity never won a battle; it is brains and tools that win. And by the time the Chinese equal us in tools they will also have taken over from us those methods of controlling population which are the modern substitute for infanticide and abortion. There is no communal need, no moral claim, for large families any more; and if one suggests that women should still retain, in moderate measure, the function of motherhood, it is rather with a view to their own self-fulfilment and happiness than for the sake of the group.

It is remarkable how marriage withers when children stay away, and how it blossoms when they come. Before, marriage was a business contract for the mutual provision of physiological conveniences; now it recovers its natural meaning, it lifts little egos into a larger whole, and the union sprouts and flowers like a watered plant. The woman finds, in the midst of turmoil, trouble, worry and pain, a strange content that is like a quiet ecstasy; never in her idleness and luxury was she as happy as in these tasks and obligations that develop and complete her even while seeming to sacrifice her to the race. And the man, looking at her, falls in love with her anew; this is another woman than before, with new resources and abilities, with a patience and tenderness never felt in the violence of love; and though her face may be pale now, and her form for a time disfigured for corrupt and abnormal eyes, to him it seems as if she had come back out of the jaws of death with a gift absurdly precious; a gift for which he can never sufficiently repay her. Work that was bitter toil becomes now as natural and cheerful as the honey-seeking of the bee; and the house, that was but walls and a bed, becomes a home, filled with the laughter of rejuvenated life. For the first time in his career the man feels himself complete.

For through parentage (unless he is a genius, whose passion and complete-ness lie in intellectual maternity) he does not merely fulfil his function as a member of society, and as an individual in a species; he fulfils *himself*—he accepts the responsibilities that mature and widen him, he enjoys the satis-faction of an unsuspectedly profound instinct of parental love, he lays up the comradeship of children as a solace for his age, and in some measure eludes the searching scythe of Death. That ruthless scavenger takes of us only the decaying flesh and bones; he must clear them away to make room for youth; but in the youth which he protects is our own blood, our own life, and our own souls. We but surrender a part of ourselves to the grave that another part, generated from our substance, fed by our hands, and reared with our care, may survive as our reincarnation in the flow of life. Our chil-dren will bring us daily tribulation, and bitter pain, and perhaps in the end heart-breaking disillusionment; but they will bring us, just as surely, a fathomless delight that will surpass even the ecstasies of love. Let a man be complete. Not as a fragment, not as a ruthlessly competitive and narrowly separate individual, can he fulfil himself and be made whole; but as a sharer in a larger self, as a lover giving more than he receives, as a father gladly caught in the toils of the species, willingly consumed in the continuity and immortality of life. For in that coöperation of the part with the whole he shall find the essence of all morals, the secret of all living things, and a quiet lane of happiness for many years.

CHAPTER XI

About Children: A Confession

I. PERSONAL

AND NOW, HAVING SUNG a pæan to parentage, let us consider very frankly and intimately that most ancient and arduous task, the bringing up of children—the transformation of baby animals and savages into ladies and gentlemen. I ask permission to be personal in this chapter, and to use the favorite pronoun freely, because the methods and conclusions which I would suggest are the result of a very limited experience, and I should like to present them for just what they are—the adventure of two parents with one child. I admit at the outset that I am intensely interested in these three persons, far beyond anything which a total perspective would allow. Nature inoculates us with egotism that we may consent to live; who could bear to see himself in the light of eternity?

I am absurdly enthusiastic about a certain youngster, and find it difficult to conceive of any child surpassing her in health or intelligence, in rosy cheeks or abounding hair. When I walk her to school, and after the last crossing bid her good-bye, and see with what heavenly *élan* she dances off to join her class, I consider the worries and troubles of this world as trivial; this leaping girl explains all mysteries and heals all grief. As I march back to my study a ridiculous parental ecstasy envelops me, and all things seem forgivable— pain and sorrow and death—in a nature whose impartial cruelty and tender· ness bring out of the most unreasonable suffering a lovable child.

It is clear, then, how prejudiced I am, and how unlikely it is that I shall be able to discuss the problems of parentage with objective calm or universal validity. This will be not a treatise but a confession; not a text-book of pedagogy but an admission of conduct conceivably reprehensible. I am as uncertain about these matters as about the most abstruse problems of metaphysics. Nevertheless, deep down in my heart, I believe these ideas of mine to be very philosophical and profound, an *open sesame* to resplendent generations; and I dream, as I look over the top of my page, that others may find in these confessions some little light for their own homes and their own parental love.

II. PHYSICAL

I think that from the beginning we looked upon Ethel, in the words of the catechism, as a creature composed of body and soul. The body was born first, and the soul was born when Ethel smiled. From that moment we realized that all this pink flesh, these fat arms and legs, these blue eyes, red lips and yellow curls, were but the machinery and instrument, however luscious in themselves, of an intangible Life that would soon begin to love and hate, to desire and dream, to wonder and grow, becoming another self and center around which all the world would seem to revolve. Somehow that Life would be dependent upon this body; it would be a brighter flame, we thought, if the body that expressed it should be made sound and strong. We resolved that till Ethel reached ten we would hold her flesh and blood as our supreme care, relying on nature to bring forth from the perfect body the first flowers of kindliness and intelligence. We suspected that behind most misconduct or slow wits some physical ailment lay; and instead of psychoanalyzing Ethel, or preaching morals to her, we offered her fresh air and wholesome food.

In the first three months we were guilty of a grave blunder, for we allowed our child to be used as a laboratory for a new-fangled form of desiccated milk. It is a crime which many years of parental solicitude cannot quite clear from our memories. We believe now, with Ben Franklin, that the human race should beware of young doctors and old barbers. Undeserved luck covered up our mistake. Despite wrong food Ethel bloomed and expanded marvelously; and when we discovered the error of our ways we could only attribute this good fortune to the air which Ethel had enjoyed in that first quarter of a year—the air of a quiet village in the hills, where just to breathe was to be made whole. Ever since, it has been Rule No. 1 with us that air comes first, even before that astounding miracle, omnipotent milk. Every night, whatever the season may be, open windows call in the wind to turn the cheeks of Ethel Benvenuta (we called her Welcome) into roses and flame.

Many a bribe of tender words, and dimpled arms about the neck, has been offered us for permission to "stay up" beyond the year's decreed retiring time. But here we have been quietly and inconspicuously resolute; we will not condescend even to discuss so absurd a proposal; we turn it aside as a criminal idea, and send Ethel up to Morpheus every evening at her usual early hour. Now, though she is a great lady of almost ten years, she still disappears regularly at eight-fifteen, wishes us from the staircase "tight sleep and pleasant dreams," and is all tucked in and set by half-past eight. The law has been broken now and then, as when some genius of the piano was honoring our home; but for the most part it has been with us a sacred monastic rule, a trifle of surpassing moment in our philosophy.

After air, food. We found that Ethel flourished on a vegetarian diet helped out with plenty of milk and whole wheat bread; she grew tall and strong, athletic and alert; and it seemed to us that she was getting every element needed for full development. But the vegetarians will be scandalized to hear that very soon in Ethel's history we added chicken to her menu once or twice a week. We call her a "chicken vegetarian"; and on that queer unprincipled diet this little household has been prospering physically for a decade. Ethel's health-record is not perfect: she encountered German measles in her infancy, but outlaughed it in a week; at four she caught whooping-cough from a playmate, and beat it down with the help of the new serum; at eight she developed swollen tonsils, whereupon they were removed. These are the blots on her 'scutcheon; otherwise she is a stranger to doctors and disease. "How does it feel to have a stomach-ache?" she wants to know.

Play comes next, and taking all these growing muscles, senses and limbs, teaches them coördination, precision, unity. The perfect parent would have, as an element in his artistry, a knowledge of just what toys to buy to encourage the development of every organ and every power. Surely the first principle here is that the toys should be such as to require accurate perception, agile manipulation, and above all, movement in the open air. Roller-skates, "scooters," archery sets, quoits, jumping ropes, baseball and tennis equipment, bicycles (if you live in the country and away from the gasoline lanes): these are first aids to a nature that wisely counsels play in order that every capacity may be practised to perfection. Best of all are swimming and skating. Summer and winter were invented for them; every muscle is called into harmonious use, the breath comes fast and deep, the blood surges rapidly, and the heart leaps with joy. Let me confess with shame that I cannot skate. But I swear that this winter, when Ethel learns, I too shall take my falls and try. I can see them sweeping by—lads and lasses—arm in arm or locked about the waist, laughing eyes and glowing cheeks, singing the song of perfect motion under the winter sky. And we shall go tobogganing together!—even an aging scribe can hug a sled and dig a steering toe into the snow. What times we three shall have when the snowflakes fly!

III. MORAL

The body comes first, and the fresh beauty of its growth is a perpetual delight. But once that firm basis has been laid, once digestion has found a healthy regularity and has allowed itself to be forgotten, then the problems of character, of "bringing-up," stand before us in pell-mell multitude. The child is greedy at table, stingy with toys, quarrelsome in play, conceited in bearing, loudly loquacious, dishonest, moody, secretive, and unattracted by water and soap. What shall we do about it?

First, don't *don't*. If a child misbehaves, apologize to it; for you have mis-fed or maltreated it. *Don'ts* are necessary, but every parent should be re-stricted to a limited number of them, like a doctor with alcoholic prescrip-tions; and perhaps, like the doctor, he should exhaust his annual allotment on January first, and leave himself a clean slate for the rest of the year. Surely we should say Yes whenever it is possible. Many parents, having been crossed in lucre or love, revenge themselves on life by forever setting up prohibitions and objections in the way of the child: parental authority is the last refuge of a scoundrel. Weak people love to dominate, and the right to nag is one of the consolations of matrimony. Let the child be happy, and let us not deceive ourselves with too much sacrifice of the present to the future. For our part we are resolved to keep Ethel smiling till she marries; God knows what will happen to her after that.

To command a child is to arouse pugnacity and resistance; this rule is almost as certain as Newton's laws of motion, and likelier to survive Ein-stein. All the sleeping dogs of pride are aroused against us when we give orders; at every imperative we stir up armies of defense. Ask and it shall be given unto you, command and you shall be refused. Be fair to the child, earn its love and trust, and your requests and suggestions will be more effective than commands. It is shameful how many things Ethel's mother and father get by suggestion. We walk to school with Ethel, and express our envy of her happy school-days; we wonder does it not help her to absorb the joy of these childhood years when she sees that others value them. At luncheon we ply her with questions as to her luck in class; she is glad we are concerned, and catches by contagion our interest in history, geography, spelling, even arithmetic; the suggestion seeps into her that these things need not be dull, that they may be as exciting as a battle, a voyage, a love-letter, or an income-tax report.

So with the piano. This is a problem that agitates every home—"Go and do your practice!" It is a silly phrase, for it suggests, most unmistakably,—"Piano is a bore, practising is torture; go and suffer; you deserve it." We tried another plan with Ethel; we merely offered her the opportunity to learn the piano if she wished; we left it to her choice. But for weeks before putting the question we spoke of the glory of music, and of the high privilege of per-forming or composing it. Then we looked about for a teacher who would begin not with sleepy scales and terrifying finger-exercises, but with simple, ear-catching melodies that would set the whole household humming them. We found the teacher, and soon our home rang with tunes played by a chubby finger laboriously. We older ones went about our work singing the melodies that Ethel evoked; she was pleased to note our delight, and felt herself already an artist; at the very outset the piano meant music to her, not noise and pain.

Later a plateau in her progress came: she did not want to practise any more; and we had to gird our loins and fight the demons of passion and custom that bade us command and compel. Instead, I sat down at the piano and practised the lesson myself; it was within the measure of my ability. Then I invited Ethel to join me and make it a program for four hands. She came, and for a week I practised with her; when she did not care to come I played her pieces alone. The teacher provided us with simple duets, and we learned them together. (At this very moment she has called up to me, "Daddy, come down and practise with me!") Rapidly her pleasure in the piano returned. Soon she was playing simplified selections from Beethoven, Mozart, Schumann, Schubert, Händel, Haydn and Bach; we sang these famous strains with gusto, and made her know how grateful we were that she was filling our hearts with song. She came to feel that music was a great boon, worth all the trouble that it involved. "Now," she says, after playing the *Adieu to the Piano*, "I understand why you're so crazy about Beethoven."

I pass for further illustration from the piano to the swimming pool, though there is little dignity in the transition. Have you watched mothers or fathers teaching a child how to love the water? They coax it for a while, then scold it, then take it up forcibly and baptize it with total immersion. Half the time the plan works, half the time it frightens the child into such horror of the water as may prevent it from ever learning to swim at all. Here an ounce of example is worth a ton of compulsion. Ethel was no more anxious to go into the water than any other child; her fear was a natural and wholesome thing, rooted in generations of perilous history. We merely put her into a bathing suit and let her play in the sand, while we splashed about and swam and gave every suggestion that the water was fine. She grew envious, and soon of her own accord took to wading. We bought her a life-belt, bound it about her with disarming laughter, and showed her that with its help she could paddle about in deep water without so much as wetting her hair. She watched the boys and girls, imitated their motions, and was soon able to navigate in any desired direction. At the end of her first season in the water she had learned, without compulsion of any kind, and even without coaxing, enough of the breast stroke to swim some ten yards. We took off the belt, and she was amazed to find that she knew how to swim. In the next season, without compulsion, but helped with the skilled instructions of a friend, she learned the crawl and the dive. Now she teaches her father, and puts him to shame with the vigor and variety of her strokes.

Example is so powerful that if it is good, nothing else is necessary. The best home and the best school, other things equal, are those that govern least. It is remarkable how well-behaved a child can be without punishments and without commands. When the libertarian method fails it is most often because we parents ourselves violate the rules we would have our children obey. We counsel temperance, and eat and drink to excess; we teach amiability, and quarrel publicly; we inveigh against the dangers of candy and violent moving pictures, but surreptitiously we indulge in them until the child finds us out. We ask for gentleness loudly, and rudely command courtesy; we advise modesty, and pose as infallible gods. But children learn by what they see us do, not by what we tell them; when they are most troublesome it is very likely that they are imitating our past performances. Show me your children and I will tell you what you are.

If you want your child to be polite, be polite. If you want your child to be neat, be neat; nothing else is required. To use strong or excited language to the child, even under great provocation, is to set up in it, for imitation, the memory of violent speech. Good manners can be taught only by patiently persistent example. It is difficult, and involves almost the reëducation of ourselves; in this way our children bring us up. More than once the present moralist has slipped from these high principles into vulgar shouting, has lost his temper with his wits, and has descended to commands and force. I set up these counsels of perfection for my own encouragement, and trust that I may some day practise what I preach.

We have tried to direct every instinct in Ethel to some beneficent end. She has been as acquisitive as any young animal, and has not been any more disposed to share her toys than most children are. But she has been impressed by our way of dividing things with her and helping her whenever we can; and the sense of security that has come from this friendly aid has made her more considerate and generous. For a time she hankered after pennies and nickels. We steered around this by arranging a monthly "salary" for her, dependent upon her keeping her room tidy, making her own bed getting up promptly, arriving at school on time, and doing her lessons well My friends have taken me to task for "corrupting" Ethel with this monthly wage; and I have often doubted the wisdom of the plan. It is too early to say whether my friends are right or wrong, but I think the signs are against them; the money has made Ethel less acquisitive, not more. With it she buys her own toys, and every now and then comes tripping in with a gift for us. She has tremendous plans for my birthday. "Why do you think I'm saving if not to buy you something nice?" she asks. This minute, as I write, she has prevailed upon us to buy her a baby collie; having won her victory she tells me, "Of course I'll pay for it out of my bank." I am afraid that this time the bank will break.

As with acquisition, so with pride; it can be a nuisance and an absurdity, or it can be a source of character and development. I would not want a child to be humble or submissive; and when Ethel is wilful I console myself with the thought that she will make things hot for anyone who may try to exploit her when she is grown. Character has to have some pugnacity in its make-up, some willingness, occasionally, to resist. As to pride, it is the mother of honor and the verteber of courage; it can be used to good purpose endlessly. We suggest to Ethel that she is too proud to let any one see her untidy or unclean;

that she is too proud to take more than her equal share of anything; too proud to run forward for gifts or favors or preferment; too proud to let any one surpass her considerably in her work. (I hope she will not see this revelation of our secrets.) Pride is an admirable substitute for punishment; it is a positive stimulant, not a negative deterrent; it begets backbone and bravery, and beats down timidity and cowardice. "What is good?" asks Nietzsche—and answers: "To be brave." But how could one be brave without pride?

Perhaps, too, we can substitute praise for blame in forming the character of the child. Censure cramps the soul, and makes the imperfect task forever hateful; praise expands every cell, energizes every organ, and makes even the most difficult undertaking an adventure and a victory. Egotism is the lever by which we can move the world. Instead of pouncing upon work ill done and heaping up reproaches for it, we keep an eye alert for things done well, and mark it with praise that shall linger sweet in the memory as a call to further accomplishment. If Ethel has to report that she has fallen short in arithmetic (which is her *bête noire*), we show regret, but we have not the heart to reprove her; may she never learn how much better her marks are than those which we received at her age! But when she comes home with news of perfect marks we dance and celebrate, and exhaust our ingenuity to show new joy at each victory. When she has done something that especially delights us we have slipped a dollar into her bank, to the disgust of the aforesaid friends. What if this method of praise and fondness should work less well than the method of invectives and penalties?—We would rather lose by one way than win by the other. We shall vote for any plan that makes for Ethel's happiness. If we must choose, we prefer to spoil her with affection, rather than make her hard with suffering. In a crisis it is affection, not sternness and stoicism, that will help us all.

I do not know whether it has been a problem or a blessing that through fate's decree we have had but one child. I confess that we have spent more time on Ethel than we could possibly have given her if the stork had been more generous. I have seen households with two or more children, and found them a little too noisy for my taste. I do my work at home, and see a great deal of Ethel; but if she had had brothers or sisters I must have sought an office or an attic at least a mile away. As it is, Ethel's nearness is no disturbance, but an inexpressible delight; the sound of her voice in the other rooms, even her occasional invasion of mine, stimulates and refreshes me; and I consider myself fortunate that I am permitted to do my work not in the chaos of the city, but to the quiet accompaniment of such happy growth.

Nevertheless, this single-child-blessedness presents difficulties. We try to solve them by welcoming playmates from the school, by encouraging the return of these visits, by having a splendid young nephew live with us in vacation and holiday time, by occasional week-ends in other homes, and above all by playing children ourselves, joining Ethel in her studies and games. She is having French lessons; well, we shall learn her week's vocabulary with her, and make a jolly competition of the task, digging each word into the memory with quips and puns. Or she has difficult home-work in arithmetic; we sit together around the dining-room table, and the whole family adds, subtracts, divides and multiplies together for an hour. Is it a waste of time for the parents? Well, how do you waste *your* time? How could we spend our leisure hours better than in these rejuvenating ways?

The secret of parentage is the ability to be young again, to throw off all dignity and degrees and play on an honest equality with the child. Perhaps by such unassuming intimacy we may win that complete trust and love which is the cornerstone of education. How shall we ever succeed in the development of character if we cannot, by honesty, draw honesty and honor out of the native moral resources of the child? [1] We tell Ethel that every thought imperceptibly moulds her face, and that in the long run all elements of character are written on the countenance for every eye to read; but we are not content with frail intellectualities of that sort. We know that if we wish her to be honest we must be honest ourselves, even when it hurts; and that we must never frighten her with the fear of any worse punishment than to let her see how her defection from honor has darkened the day for all. We are confident that example and affection will make her honest with us. Lying is sometimes permissible with adults (as few moralists will admit), for adults resent the truth; but it is hardly ever wise with children, who hunger for knowledge,—though moralists are especially apt to fight shy of the truth when children seek it. Ethel has fallen short of the ideal here as in other things; but I suspect that it is because her father has not been honest with her to the hilt. We shall try again.

IV. EROTIC

The severest test of honesty is in the sexual education of the child. Why do we resist that passionate curiosity which is the root of science and the nurse of education? Proximately, I suppose, because the Puritan heritage in America has left in us a certain horror of the physical side of love; distantly, because of the secrecy that has always surrounded mating, even in the animal kingdom, as an offset to the danger of attack which it involved; essentially, because the increasing postponement of marriage from puberty to a later age has left a dangerous interval in which every unnecessary stimulation to a latent and powerful instinct must be avoided. It is a difficult question, with more than one side to it; but even here we are resolved to take our chances with the truth. We shall do what we can to keep these questions out of mind till the last possible moment; in the overheated atmosphere of

---

[1] I cannot add anything to the perfect chapter on "Truthfulness" in Bertrand Russell's *Education and the Good Life.*

modern life they will in any case come soon enough. But we want to answer those questions before uninstructed or prurient children answer them. Nor shall we deal with them in any other way, or in any other tone, than with other questions; "reverence" here is the wrong cue, an invitation to mystery and mischief; a man should speak of sex as he would speak of digestion or respiration, with the quiet impartiality of the scientist. Truth is wholesome enough, in the long run, without being wrapped in awe.

Knowledge and health are the best psychoanalysts; where the body is strong and the mind is clear, "complexes" will not grow. Diderot said that anatomy is the first thing he would teach his daughter, though I should be in no hurry about it. The usual disturbances of youth in this regard will not worry us; we shall let nature take her course, without sermons and without lies; but we shall provide the child with all the sporting goods in the catalogue, and lure it out into the sun. When a boy plays baseball with gusto his morals are good enough for me.

Sterilized with truth, the love life of the child can be, like everything else around it, a thing of beauty and delight. Here, for example, Ethel comes from school, sits on the arm of my chair, "takes me 'round," as she puts it, and whispers coyly, "Daddy, I'm in love." What am I to do?—berate her for this terrible romance? I can't; instead I laugh, and invite full details. Why should we darken that bright soul with morality?

But what shall we do when puberty comes? At the first sign of it we shall flood the situation with knowledge; we shall leave no pebble unturned to avoid the sensibility, the self-consciousness, and the brooding introversion that so often discolor life at this critical turn in its tide. Let that first year of adolescence be no year of fretting and tragedy, but the spring-time of the soul, *Frühlingserwachen:* seed-time of devotions and ideals, season of adventure and poetry, May-time of health and growth in body and brain. Now intelligence sprouts with doubled pace; from this moment the body recedes into the background, character stands as already formed, and the task of the educator centers at last on the problems of the mind.

V. MENTAL

I do not know when Ethel's "mind" began; but we did not bother much about it till she could say, with Milne, "Now we are six." She would not want me to imply that she had no mind to speak of before that; had she not taken lessons every hour or so in the abominable irregularities of the English language? Here too the choice was between commands and example; and so we had to admit that if Ethel was to talk English correctly we must learn to speak it pardonably ourselves; that if Ethel was to keep rough-neck phrases from her vocabulary they must find no entrance to ours. Not that the juicier metaphors of slang were excluded; these might be the very life-color of a sentence, and say in a word what would have taken a paragraph from Dr. Johnson. But we suggested a preference for accurate as against slovenly speech; and we put into Ethel's way, as soon as she could read, the best-written literature for her age.

Meanwhile we had to face the question of private schools. Should we send Ethel to the neighborhood public school, or to a private institution of high repute but inconvenient location? We visited both, and were astonished to see what progress the public schools had made since the days when I taught in them for ten dollars a week. Bright class-rooms, smaller classes, individual desks, competent and cheerful teachers, every material and scholastic facility: we could hardly believe our eyes. I had heard so much against the schools, I had even written against them as hard disciplinary prisons to which children came as gods in embryo and from which they were graduated as gods in ruins. Could it be that I had only mouthed clever phrases?

We tried the public school, and everything went well. Perhaps there was a little too much of patriotification; but all in all we had no objection to having Ethel learn to love her country, if she might be permitted to value the greatness of other nations as well; and we shall see to that. The four public schools to which Ethel has gone were models of efficiency and humanity. Some were better than the others, but not so much because of the schools as because of the associations involved; we could see our little girl changing in manners and interests as she passed from one school to another. Now she is in the best of them all, and we are grateful and happy.

I must not generalize from this experience; and I confess that in some localities we would not use the public school if we could help it. Associations are half the game in life, and we must be forgiven for selecting them. "Send your son to college," said Emerson, "and the boys will educate him." In one case such a consideration drove us to experiment with a private school— among the finest in New York. We soon discovered that Ethel disliked it; she complained of the noise and disorder which the principal called freedom; and though she learned some interesting little crafts, and had much out-door play well supervised, she asked us, time and again, "When are they going to teach me something?" At the end of the private-school year we entered her in a public school (which had still a month to run), and found that despite an intelligence-quotient several years beyond her age, she was behind in many branches necessary for her promotion. We had to spoil her summer with lessons.

Having found a school, the next thing is to coöperate with it. To permit no absence or lateness except for the most vital reasons, to keep an eye on daily progress and monthly reports, to watch the home-work and show keen interest in the class-lessons of every day; all this is part of the parental job. It not only helps the school but it helps the child; any worth-while regularity or order is a boon to character. And when we take walks through the fields or the woods we turn the talk, if we can, to history, or geography, or literature; and the exciting tales of great men's lives serve us better than fairies and fiction.

Geography is dull? How is it then that a ship at anchor in the harbor, or setting out under full sail or steam, is an irresistible suggestion of romance? Every child longs to see foreign lands; therefore the way to teach geography is by real or imagined travel. The teacher lands her class at Shanghai or Singapore, and all the mystery of Asia welcomes them; or they go up the Nile from Alexandria to Abyssinia, and through a thousand strange tribes to Johannesburg and Cape Town, and Africa becomes a reality rather than a name. Why should not every school be equipped with "movie-tone" travelogues such as those that Holmes and Newman give, with views and moving-pictures a hundred times more fascinating than the vulgar imaginations of the screen? And history—surely for children it should be what Carlyle called it, "the Biography of Great Men." To accustom the child to honor genius is to offer it a devotion that age will not wither though every other love depart.

To enter that Country of the Mind, where all remembered geniuses still live and teach, it is only necessary to read and see. To see, without haste, those pictures and statues in which artists have written their philosophies of life into a figure or a face; to drink in leisurely the nobility of the Parthenon or the grace and tenderness of Chartres; and to read without haste those books which time has winnowed for us, out of the dross of every age, to carry down the intellectual heritage of mankind. How pleasant it is to have Ethel tell stories, heard in school, of Raphael and Rembrandt, of Leonardo and Michelangelo, of Reynolds and Gainsborough, of Rubens and Van Dyke!—at her age I had not dreamed of the existence of these men. And still sweeter to entice her into the realm of letters, to regale her with the lives of Shakespeare and Shelley, Milton and Byron, Goethe and Hugo, Whitman and Poe!

She is just graduating from the literature that is specifically written down to her age. The older items in this literature—such things as *Alice in Wonderland* and the *Nonsense Book* of Lear—are admirable enough; but most of the later volumes written for children are spoiled by underestimating and insulting the intelligence of the child. There is no stimulation in this material, it does not produce active reading, or make for growth; it is intellectual coddling, and alert children may lose all their taste for reading if they are fed on this skimmed milk. There are many supposedly adult classics that can be enjoyed at nine or ten—say *The Three Musketeers, The Talisman,* even *Les Misérables;* and the child will relish the book all the more if told that it was not meant for children. Nowhere in the world are there better books for the child than *Robinson Crusoe* and *Gulliver's Travels;* and yet neither of them was written for children, and one of them is not yet understood by adults.

In every home that cherishes books it should be pleasant to have an hour of reading aloud together one evening or more in the week. Children and adults can take turns at the book; corrections may be postponed till the entire reading is over, and then made privately. I remember how Ethel and her black-eyed cousin Louis, with three of us oldsters, read *Enoch Arden* in this way; how every line was received with intense interest by the children; and how at the end we were all silent, until Ethel went and hid herself in her mother's arms, and wept. Now we are planning to get several copies of *The Merchant of Venice,* apportion the characters among us, and read the play with every flourish of eloquence before our burning logs.

I believe that it is through reading, rather than through high school and college, that we at last acquire a "liberal education." Mr. Everett Dean Martin has admirably described the meaning of this term, and I warmly recommend his book to those who wish to know what it is to be mature. Today we think a man is educated if he can read the newspaper morning, noon and night; but though our colleges turn out graduates like so many standardized Fords every year, there is a visible dearth of real culture in our life; we are a nation with a hundred thousand schools, and hardly a dozen educated men.

No wonder that Mr. Wells and others have questioned the use of a college education. This is pessimism exaggerated to make a point; but it is well that some one should check us up in our notion that the multiplication of schools and graduates can make us an intelligent people. Our schools and colleges have suffered severely from Spencer's conception of education as the adjustment of the individual to his environment; it was a dead, mechanical definition, drawn from a mechanistic philosophy, and distasteful to every creative spirit. The result has been the conquest of our schools by mechanical and theoretical science, to the comparative exclusion of such "useless" subjects as literature, history, philosophy and art. So we make good office-boys, good clerks, and good technicians, who, when their workday is over, devour the pictorial press and crowd into theatres that show them forever the same love-scenes on the screen and the same anatomy on the stage.

This mechanical and "practical" education produces partial, not total, men; it subordinates civilization to industry, biology to physics, taste and manners to wealth. But education should make a man complete; it should develop every creative power in him, and open his mind to all the enjoyable and instructive aspects of the world. A man who is heavy with millions, but to whom Beethoven or Corot or Hardy, or the glow of the autumn woods in the setting sun, is only sound and color signifying nothing, is merely the raw material of a man; half the world is closed to the blurred windows of his spirit. An education that is purely scientific makes a mere tool of its product; it leaves him a stranger to beauty, and gives him powers that are divorced from wisdom. It would have been better for the world if Spencer had never written on education.

It is well that Latin and Greek are passing from our colleges, for they consumed a hundred times more effort than they were worth. As Heine said, "The Romans could not have had much time left to conquer the world if they had first had to learn Latin." [1] But though the languages of Greece and Rome are necessary only to philologists, the literature of these nations is almost indispensable to education. A man may conceivably ignore Virgil and Horace, Lucretius and Cicero, Tacitus and Marcus Aurelius, and still become mature; but of all possible instruments of education that I know, none is so fine and sure as a study of Greek life in all the varied scope of its democracy and imperialism, its oratory and drama, its poetry and history, its architecture and sculpture, its science and philosophy. Let a student absorb the life and letters of the Periclean age, the Renaissance, and the Enlightenment, and he will have a better education than any college can give him. Education does not mean that we have become certified experts in business, or mining, or botany, or journalism, or epistemology; it means that through the absorption of the moral, intellectual and esthetic inheritance of our race we have come to understand and control ourselves as well as the external world; that we have chosen the best as our associates both in spirit and in the flesh; that we have learned to add courtesy to culture, wisdom to knowledge, and forgiveness to understanding. When will our colleges produce such men?

VI. ECSTATIC

How good it is to see Ethel seated near the fireplace of an evening, her sturdy brown legs thrown over the side of the chair, her chubby arms exposed, her red ribbon flashing across her blouse, her hair falling down upon her book, her face lighted up with interest and feeling, her soul snatched away for a while to distant places and times, traveling and broadening its borders, and making itself fitter, day by day, for the company of great women and great men. One by one she shall court them and listen to them, from Sappho to Duse, from Empedocles to Nietzsche, from Buddha to Dostoievski, from Lao-tse to Anatole France. We see her growing with them year by year, learning wisdom from Socrates, devotion from Leonardo, and gentleness from Christ. We dream of all that she may be.

We hope she will not become too learned to love life, and that she will never think of books as better than friendships, or nature, or motherhood. We will not hold her complete, whatever her career, if she does not some day

[1] *Memoirs,* vol. i, p. 12.

lift up another child beyond her height as we try to lift her beyond ours. But she shall be free, even to disappoint us; no one can say what is right for another; she shall choose her own path, and define her own good. It is enough for us that she has come, and that into this life so questionable in origin and so obscure in destiny, her laughter and her guilelessness have brought sparkling fountains of delight.

CHAPTER XII

The Reconstruction of Character

I. THE ELEMENTS OF CHARACTER

SO MUCH FOR THE MORAL and intellectual training of the child. But as for us grown-ups,—is there any likelihood that we may be able to mould ourselves into something better than we are?

One of the many privileges which an observant mind enjoys in this vigorous and complex age is to sit in at the birth of a science. It is clear, from the commotion in the laboratories, that Philosophy, Alma Mater of ungrateful sciences, is being delivered of another child, and that the study of the "mind" is passing slowly and painfully out of the dark womb of metaphysics into the light of controlled observation and experiment. The delivery is not yet complete; even in Freud the infant science is still bound to its mother, and is almost suffocated with theory and myth.

Psychology stands today where physics stood when Francis Bacon wrote his *Advancement of Learning*, three hundred years ago. With an audacity that startled even the brave Renaissance, Bacon laid down a program for the sciences, pointed to the vital problems that craved solution, and predicted, on page after page, the conquests that would come with the new knowledge. Today these physical triumphs are real, universal, and profound, far beyond even Bacon's royal imagining; and everywhere physics and chemistry, mathematics and mechanics, have remade the face of the earth nearer to the will of man. Only man himself, his will and his character, seem to have remained unchanged.

What if psychology is moving to similar accomplishments? If another Bacon should plot its problems and foretell its victories, who would believe him? We are on the shore of a great strange sea, still darkened with mythology and superstition; we do not know its lanes and distances, nor what happy isles may lie beyond; but the new science will venture forth, tacking its way about with trial and error against the winds and clouds of prejudice and ignorance. Three hundred years hence psychology will be where physics is today, still incomplete like some groping figure of Rodin's, but masterful none the less, with the hand of science laid at last upon "mind" and "heart" and "soul," and the raw material of our chaotic wills slowly forged by knowledge into the strength and kindliness of a higher race.

What interests us is ourselves; and so far as psychology deals with us, and not with abstractions, it is as absorbing as a drama of which we can be the heroes. What are we, after all? Apes?—or gods?—or apes on the way to being gods? What is that "human nature" which appears to determine so many histories with irrevocable tragedy? What are the foundations and elements of character and conduct?—and are they so universal and profound that character can never be changed? Or can we, like Baron Münchausen, lift ourselves by our own bootstraps out of the stream and flow of our heritage? Let us forget everything else for a moment, and inquire into the nature of character, taking it to pieces for observation and understanding. Later we shall put the pieces together again,—if we can.

The older psychology, when it condescended to deal with so earthly a thing as human conduct, divided characters into sanguine, melancholic, choleric, and phlegmatic. These have the sound of bloody and unnatural things; but they merely mean that men are cheerful, or gloomy, or passionate, or Anglo-Saxon. It may be so; but these words are adjectives, not explanations. One suspects their inventor of having an interesting physiological view of character, as determined by blood, or bile, or—but one hesitates at cholera and phlegm. Bain suggested the classification of characters into intellectual, emotional, and volitional, according as thought, feeling or will was dominant; but since the volitional type may be also emotional (as in Alexander or Elizabeth), or also intellectual (as in Cæsar and Napoleon), and even the intellectual may be emotional (as in Plato, Abélard, Voltaire, or Nietzsche), we come out by the same door wherein we went.

There are as we have seen,[1] two ways of studying man. One begins outside with the environment, and considers man as a mechanism of adjustment; it reduces thought to things and "mind" to "matter," and issues in the disguised materialism of Spencer and the behaviorism of Watson. It is a point of view that has lordly names among its representatives: Democritus, Epicurus, Lucretius, Hobbes, and even the gentle Spinoza. In biology it gave us Darwin and the theory of natural selection—by the environment—as the determinant of evolution; in sociology it gave us Buckle, Spencer, and Marx, and the explanation of history in terms of economic influences, impersonal masses, and unwilled events.

The other way begins within: it looks upon man as a system of needs, impulses, and desires impelling him to study, to use, and to master his environment; it would love to reduce things to thought, and matter to mind; it starts

[1] Ch. III.

with the "entelechy" of Aristotle (who held that an inner purpose determines every form), and issues in the vitalism of Bergson and the pragmatism of William James. Here, in addition to these three, belong Plato, Descartes, Leibnitz, Kant, and Schopenhauer. In biology this attitude gave us Lamarck and the theory of evolution through repeated efforts issuing from insatiable desire; in sociology it gave us Goethe, Carlyle, and Nietzsche, and the explanation of history in terms of psychological influences, inventive genius, and dominating wills.

The analysis of character to be given here adopts this second way, though aware of the pitfalls that lurk in the path; it looks upon man as transforming his environment far more than his environment transforms him; every garden on the road, and every airplane in the sky is a sign and symbol of initiative life. Character is in this view a sum of inherent dispositions and desires; it is a mosaic of instincts colored and rearranged by environment, occupation, and experience. We may list the basic impulses of human character in a rough classification that will distinguish the fundamental elements from those that are derived.

TABLE OF CHARACTER ELEMENTS

Instincts		*Habits*		*Feelings*	
Positive	*Negative*	*Positive*	*Negative*	*Positive*	*Negative*
I. Food-getting	Avoidance	Hunting Tearing Hoarding Acquisition	Cleanliness	Hunger Cruelty Greed	Disgust
II. Fighting	Flight	Approach Curiosity Manipulation Mastery	Retreat Hesitation Thought Submission	Anger Wonder Pride	Fear Doubt Humility
III. Action	Sleep	Play	Rest	Buoyancy	Fatigue
IV. Association	Privacy	Speech Suggestibility Imitation Love of approval	Secretiveness	Pleasure in society Vanity	Shyness Shame
V. Reproduction Parental care	Refusal	Courtship	Blushing	Sex desire Parental love	Modesty

These instincts, habits and feelings are the universal elements of human character. Every man and woman has them all; we differ in character and temperament only because these elements never appear in any two of us in the same degree. Our species and our race determine what instincts we shall have; environment determines what objects they will seek, and what habits they will generate. An environment without danger may turn pugnacity into the domineering of the bully; let danger be plentiful, and the same pugnacity subsides into cunning; the instinct is the same, the expression is different. Slight injuries tend to develop flight into prudence; a severe injury may intensify it into cowardice. All experience is in this way a process of elicitation and repression; every day some tendency is nourished by success, another is weakened by inaction or defeat. Each of us has several potential characters (habit-mosaics), one of which is gradually selected and strengthened by environment, like the iron filings drawn by the magnet from the midst of unresponsive wood. Hence the first principle in changing one's character is to seek another environment, to let new· forces play upon our unused chords, and draw from us a better music.

We shall find more illumination for our purpose in the list of elements which we have made, if we add to it certain incidental observations. Note that each instinct is the psychological expression of a physiological system; food-getting is the result of empty, restless cells; fighting and flight seem made for arms and legs ("If the Almighty has given a man a pair of cowardly legs," said Lincoln in forgiving deserters, "how can he help running away with them?"); action instincts (creeping, walking, running, climbing, throwing, etc.) are the poetry of all bodily parts in harmonious operation; reproduction is the result of congested elements; and association, which begins as the family, is the result of reproduction. Each instinct is rooted in our structure, and any change of character that mutilates an instinct does injury to the body as well as to the soul.

Note again that every instinct has an emotional accompaniment, a mode of feeling as original and profound as the impulse to which it corresponds. So hunger goes with the seeking of food, and disgust with avoidance; anger with fighting and fear with flight; wonder with curiosity and doubt with hesitation; pride with mastery and humility with submission; buoyancy with action and fatigue with rest; social satisfaction with association, and a certain nameless relief with occasional privacy; desire with mating, shame with retreat, and parental love with parental care. As each instinct is bound up with our flesh and bone, so it is burned into our natures with the heat of feeling.

Finally, observe that nearly every instinct has an opposite in the same person; that there is a positive and negative here as Empedocles thought there must be in all things. We are equipped, so to speak, with impulses to seek food and to avoid unwholesome things; to fight and to take to our heels; to overcome and to submit; to move forward with curiosity, and to stand still with doubt; to move and manipulate, to sit and rest and sleep; to court and to resist, to make display and blush with shame; to lead and to follow, to initiate and to imitate, to seek society and to retire into solitude. In general we are prepared by nature (i. e., by native character) both to approach and to avoid a stimulus, a problem, or a situation.

Here, in this dichotomy of elements, lies the clue to the fundamental distinction among human characters. We shall not be helped in understanding history, or in dealing with our neighbors, if we divide men and women into sanguine or melancholy, good or bad; the only distinction which nature and history accept is that between positive and negative characters, strong and weak. We build a thousand ideal schemes in terms of goodness, and reality shatters them in terms of strength. Obviously there are persons in whom the positive impulses predominate; in whom the tendency is to approach, to seek, to overcome and to possess; let us call them positive characters. And there are others in whom the negative impulses predominate; persons in whom the general tendency is to hesitate, to retreat, to find shelter and safety, to submit; we shall call them negative characters. No man or woman is entirely one or entirely the other; the distinction is like masculine and feminine, and allows of every gradation and every mixture. But if we try to visualize these hostile types in their ideal completeness, we shall know the poles between which human character oscillates, and the ultimate constituents of every personality.

II. THE NEGATIVE CHARACTER

Here is the negative character. He tends to be undersized; and though he admires intensely every redeeming quality of his face, his form, his mind he is always awkwardly conscious of his physical inferiority, and looks enviously out of the corner of his eye at the tall and vigorous workman, or the man of affairs, who passes by erect in the pride of stature and health. What the negative person lacks above all is body, energy, horsepower; he has not blood enough to be strong.

Watch him at table; he has no appetite; he is finicky with food, and easily disgusted; he cannot eat meat without thinking of slaughter-houses, and he looks upon fishing as brutality. There is no relish in his eating; he nibbles and samples like a bird that has never known a worm. He cleans his fingers carefully, and wonders if he has left a sufficient tip. He walks from the room as if he hoped that no one would see him, and felt that everyone did.

If he meets a man he observes him unobserved, looking at everything but the eyes, and measuring the other's power and intentions. If insult or danger comes, he trembles with surprise and fear; he does not feel active anger, but is consumed with a fretful resentment; his violence is the mask of one who knows that he will submit. He shrinks from responsibility and trial, and longs for the quiet security and retreat of his home. He likes to read, especially novels of peril and adventure, and philosophies of will and power; he admires the cowboy and the Superman, and believes that the world would entrust him with leadership if it had intelligence. If he succeeds in anything, he credits himself; if he fails, he is "not guilty"; it is the environment (i. e., other people) that is at fault, or the government, or the arrangement of the stars. He is a pessimist about the world, and an optimist about himself.

Nevertheless he may be great by the very force of that unrestrained imagination which flourishes in him because of his physical limitations. Unchecked by action or objective observation, his fancy is free to wander in the airy realms of metaphysics and poesy; and out of these unseen lands, if he can control himself for an hour's patient labor now and then, he may draw ideal beauties, or idealist philosophies, or novel forms and figures in literature and art. At his height here he may become a poetic genius; at his lowest he is an intellectual—not a thinker, but a man who only thinks. As civilization develops, and life becomes fatiguingly complex, and physical ability becomes less vital to survival, every city is crowded with these shifting, self-gnawing souls, Don Quixotes of imagination and Hamlets of achievement.

In such a man the instincts of action are few and weak; he is not given to play or sport, except of thought and speech; he puns, but he does not swim. If he goes to games it is only to see, not to partake; seeing is easier than doing. The impulse to rest is here supreme; he never walks when he can ride, he never stands when he can sit, he never remains awake when he can sleep. Hence he cannot sleep well; he has not been sufficiently awake to bring on sleep; his nerves are tired, but his flesh is not. And since action does not absorb his energies, and emotion forever arouses him without finding the physical outlet which it craves, he is forever on edge, and never knows repose.

Retreat and inaction being his essence, he shuns the sharper realities and tasks of life, and shrinks into a world of reverie, in which he wins many victories. His shyness now becomes a secretive privacy, his privacy becomes a subtle dissimulation frequent in those whom nature has made weak. He is social in the sense that he reacts from solitude to a passionate gregariousness with some small and sympathetic circle; if he finds an ear that will listen to him he is in paradise. The tea-rooms throng with him. And he is social in his hunger for popular approval; he conforms timidly to the conventions, and though he lacks the aristocratic sense of honor, he has in some measure the democratic conscience that echoes faithfully the morals of the group. Withal he is kindly and affectionate, grateful and loyal and reverent; there is no cruelty in him, and little coarseness; he is inclined to erotic abnormalities, but he may be trusted to commit only the smallest crimes.

These being his impulses, he is weak above all because they are not coördinated by some purpose that dominates and unifies his life. He is restless though always seeking rest; he passes discontent from project to project and from place to place; he is a ship that never makes a port, while all its cargo rots. He is incapable of regularity or industry; and though he seems at times nervously busy, he finds himself unable to persist in a definite purpose despite the monotony, distastefulness, or difficulty of the means. He is intense in intention and lax in application; he is given to bursts of passion that simulate strength, but they end in quick exhaustion and accepted chaos. He has a thousand wishes, but no will.

Finally, in love he is the courted rather than the wooer; even if he appears to approach, to besiege and overcome, it is the lady who arranges it for him with the smooth invisibility of a statesman. Indeed he is a little ashamed of his victory, and blushes to think of it; he questions would he not have enjoyed an imaginative riot more keenly, and with less expense. But he yields to destiny, becomes a faithful and industrious husband, reproduces his like as often as chance dictates, and wears himself out fretfully for his children. He dies prematurely, darkened with a sense of futility, and wondering if it would not have been better had he never been born.

III. THE POSITIVE CHARACTER

This man is positive. He has health and vigor, a sufficiency of flesh and blood to warrant him in looking straight into the eye of the world, and wearing his hat as he likes. If he looks at you it is face to face; but he does not look at you; he is absorbed in his enterprise, intent on his goal. He is less interested in persons than in purposes.

All the impulses of approach are strong in him. He eats with gusto and without formality; many hecatombs are sacrificed to appease him. This natural propensity to surround and engulf the fauna and flora of his country develops into a general passion for acquisition and possession; his motto is *To have and to hold.* And because he is more self-assertive and successful than the negative man, he makes every modern nation into a replica of himself,—rapaciously acquisitive. (Or perhaps he has an extravagant wife.)

In older days he would have been a feudal baron or a soldier, instead of an executive, a merchant, a trade union leader, or an engineer; and much of that old pugnacity remains in him, mitigated and disguised, but as positive as when it brandished a javelin. It is this pugnacity that gives power to his purposes; in him desires are not timid aspirations, they are unavoidable impulses; for their sake he will accept responsibilities, dangers, and wearing toil. He has more courage than virtue, and less conscience than pride. He has powerful ambitions; he despises limits, and suspects humility. If he meets a man stronger or firmer than himself, his impulse is not to bow down before him in propitiation, but to honor him with emulation and rivalry. When he is defeated it is after a struggle to exhaustion.

He is curious; all processes lure him, and his mind plays actively about strange and novel things. But he has no taste for theories; his thinking is directed with strait immediacy to action and his goal; he cannot understand why a man should bother with higher mathematics, or poetry, or painting, or philosophy. If he is a philosopher he engages in affairs as well as in thought; he is a Seneca rather than an Aristotle, a Bacon rather than a Berkeley, a Voltaire rather than a Kant.

He believes in action rather than in thought, and like Cæsar he thinks nothing finished if anything remains undone. He likes a tumultuous life, and is not tempted by rural simplicity and peace; peace, he thinks, was made for old age, and does not become a man. He is domineering, and likes to feel that men are bricks to his trowel, to build with them what he likes; and they find a secret zest in being led by him, he is so certain, so confident, and so cheerful. His activity makes him healthy, and leaves him no time for thought or gloom. He enjoys life, bad as it is, and does not ponder much on the future or the past. He is sceptical of Utopias, and had as leave that all radicals should be shot at sunrise. He abhors ideologists,—people who make speeches, or write articles, and settle international affairs from their garret eminence.

Nevertheless, in some of his avatars he is a man of ideas: not a poet, nor a painter, nor a theoretical philosopher, nor a scientist who buries himself in test-tubes or ancient tomes; but an inventor, an architect capable of original designs, an engineer brave enough to span great rivers with poems of woven steel, a sculptor commanding marble into life, a scientist willing to face all the world in defense of his new truth. Even so, he has a hundred lives of action for one life of thought.

Normally he is social; he gets along well with all whom he meets, unless their ideas are sharply unconventional. He likes privacy of an evening, but it is the privacy of his family rather than a brooding retreat into solitude and himself. He seldom stops to introspect; he has few "complexes," and he never talks of psychology. When his wife irritates him he goes to his club; and when his club bores him he forgets himself in his work. The routine of his active life defends him against nerves.

What he has above all is will. Not wills, but will; not a medley of ambitions and desires canceling one another in unreconciled hostility, but a unity of aim, an order and perspective and hierarchy of purposes, moulded in his character by some persistent and dominating design. His will is disciplined; he draws a circle defining possibility, and then within it he wills the means as resolutely as the end He produces work, not fragments or "impressions"; and he is so absorbed in his effort that he never thinks what comments it will evoke. He is quiet; he does not talk much; he does not waste himself in violence of action or speech. He has passions, great ones, but they form one passion moving to one end, not tattered fragments blown in chaos. He knows the pleasure of self-control; he can resist immediate desires and stimuli, and slowly organize himself into a whole. Health and intelligence made him.

He takes the initiative in love, and wins his way through with a directness and despatch that endear him to all women. He marries early, because he makes up his mind quickly, and prefers curious approach to cautious retreat; it is better, he thinks, to be burdened with wife and childen than with solitude and chorus-girls; and the compulsions which parentage place upon him help to make him strong. But he knows how to mix gentleness and tenderness with his strength; his children not only love him, they respect him. In middle age he learns something of the art of leisure; and in old age he rejuvenates himself with his children's children. He dies never doubting that life was a boon, and only sorry that he must leave the game to younger players.

IV. REMAKING CHARACTER

We have drawn two ideal portraits, and have made an almost Manichæan division of humanity into weak and strong. Left so, these pictures would be extreme and useless; but placed side by side they make it easier for us to analyze, and perhaps to reorganize, ourselves. Can we in a modest measure rid ourselves of negativity and weakness, and take on some of that positive firmness which is the secret idol of our hearts? Can we, by taking thought, add a cubit to our statures?

It is usual to answer this question with a pessimistic No; a man's character, we are told, is his fate; and what he is at birth he must remain to the end of his story. Human nature, it is said, never changes. And very often the qualities of character are rooted in the condition of the body, in matters of health and strength and organic structure and function; how can characteristics so based be altered?

There are facts that cast grave doubt upon this ancient dogma of the unchangeability of human character. The history of our own time has given us a profound and startling example of the wholesale transformation of negative into positive characters. Fifty years ago one might have described women as normally negative in comparison with men, and one might have labeled them with most of the adjectives which we have used to describe the weaker type. Their physical handicap was the basis of a sense of inferiority which revealed itself in the secret regret, lurking almost universally in the hearts of women, that they had not been born men; and out of that "complex" came a burning resentment, like some subterranean fire, which periodically erupted in the hot lava of their speech. It was their nature to be gentle in action; and if at times they were violent in words it was in compensation and "over-correction" of that physical subjection which met them like a nemesis at every turn in the road of life. They were the "weaker sex."

It was on that bodily basis that the diffidence and submissiveness of woman rested. She did not thrill so much as the male with the lust for achievement; indeed, her lot seemed to be the same from generation unto generation—always and only the adventure of motherhood. She bowed to her master, took his blows affectionately, surrendered her name and property to him with her flesh, and sought her happiness in accomplishing his will. Life was hard and dull for her, but she made up for it by reveling, as often as she could, in romantic fiction and poetry that raised her for a while into a brighter world.

And then industry caught her in its toils. Variety entered her life like a flood; individual responsibility and economic independence came; she received her own money and moulded her own morals. She had already doubted the superiority of the male; she had always found him, in elementals, gullible and tamable and manageable. But now she discovered, as he himself (timid worshiper of pugilists and athletes) was so long in discovering, that in the modern world the race is not to the swift, nor the battle to the strong; that selection was now more than ever by cunning and intelligence, ever less by human horsepower and simple brawn. She found, to her delight, that physical inferiority was no impassable obstacle to success and mastery; that the greatest geniuses had sometimes the smallest frames; and that even a woman, though suffocated with corsets, harassed with skirts, and cramped by traditions and pins, might rise to leadership and power, and be master of her soul.

Therefore, as the Great Change advanced, she outgrew her negativity and took on positive traits. She became a personality, capable of initiative, of executive management, of realistic thinking. She imbibed the lust for acquisition, and became a mighty digger of gold. She neglected the quiet tidiness of the home for the noisy noisomeness of the streets, and took to powder as a substitute for water. She loosened her stays, and shortened her skirts, and bared her neck to the sun; she prayed a little less, and played a little more; she drank deep draughts of the bracing air of her new freedom, and became stronger and braver in soul. Almost in a generation she blossomed and sprouted into an unprecedented positivity.

The male was startled and shocked, and complained moralistically about the "new woman." But the change had come without his connivance, and persisted without his permission. He found himself faced with woman in industry, woman in commerce, woman in the professions, woman in education, woman in all those fields which had from time immemorial been exclusively his by the divine right of possession. He was displeased with this independence of work and will; he longed for the ancient days of modest maidens and clinging vines, for the old domestic bliss (as it seemed to idealizing memory) of babies and apple pie. He fought the invasion manfully and querulously.

He lost. In America at least, woman has almost completed her dizzy transition from negative submission to positive domination. The old qualities of virginal docility and marital obedience disappear; of the two sexes it is man that now lowers his eyes in modesty, and discovers with bashful awe the ankles and calves and knees and other attractions of the modern lass. The words "love, cherish and obey" have been withdrawn from the marriage service; shortly they will be restored, among the questions asked of the male. But they will be superfluous.

Judge, from so rapid a change, the possibility of altering character. Obviously those qualities which we have called positive and negative are not irrevocably rooted in the flesh; they have their basis in the strength and weakness of the body, but they can be transformed indefinitely by opportunity and environment. The same woman has, in a hundred thousand cases, developed from timidity to audacity, from submission to mastery. It is obvious that character can be changed—if we will.

But here we encounter subtle difficulties. Some of us do not wish to change our characters; we seem so sweetly perfect to ourselves, and our very faults are so lovable, that the notion of making a few repairs in our foundations hardly appeals to us. And again there is a moral problem involved: positivity of character does not coincide with morality; and a nation exclusively constituted of such resolutes as we have pictured might become a madhouse of ruthless rivalry and war. Let us acknowledge that we are not engaged here in teaching goodness, and that there will be something unmoral in our prescriptions. If we seem intent, for the moment, on developing strength rather than virtue, it is because strength of character is itself a noble virtue; and perhaps we can rely upon the fell clutch of circumstance to produce a sufficient supply of bowed heads and broken wills.

If we are to make ourselves stronger we must understand, first, what will is: not some mystical entity standing among the elements of character like the conductor of an orchestra, bending now to one side and now to that; but merely the sum and substance of all functioning impulses and dispositions. These motive forces that constitute character have no leader whom they may obey, outside of themselves; it is from their own number that some powerful impulse must come to dominate and unify the rest. This is "strength of will"—that one supreme desire stands out so high above the others that they may be drawn to it and harnessed by it to move in one direction to one goal. If we cannot find a coördinating goal, some master purpose to which we will readily sacrifice every other desire of our heart, unity is beyond us, and we must be in the end a stone in another man's building.

Hence it will not help us to read books that offer royal roads to character. Here, for example, is a volume by one Leland (London, 1912), entitled, *Have You a Strong Will? or How to Develop . . . Any Faculty of the Mind by the Easy Process of Self-Hypnotism.* There are a hundred such masterpieces, which simpletons can buy in any city. But the way is harder than that, and longer.

It is the way of life. Will, which is unified desire, is (as Schopenhauer showed) the characteristic form of growing life; and its strength and stature increase only as life finds for it new labors and new victories. If we wish to be strong, we must first choose our goal and plot our road; then we must cleave to it whate'er betide. The way of caution here is to undertake at first only that which we may rely upon ourselves to carry through; for every failure will weaken us, and every success will make us stronger. It is achievement that makes achievement; by little conquests we gain strength and confidence for larger ones; practice makes will.

But then one can be too cautious, and by turning away from the beckoning of great deeds, remain forever small. Make sure that modest victories shall not content you; on the morning after your triumph, having feasted for a day, look about you for the next and larger task. Face danger, and seek responsibility, it is true that they may defeat you, may even destroy you; but the date of the one death which you must die is too slight a chronological detail to disturb philosophy. If they do not kill you they will strengthen you, and lift you nearer to greatness and your goal. Make or break.

One of the less unreliable and fantastic phases of psychoanalysis offers us here another illustration of the flexibility of human character and destiny. In the illuminating theory of Adler the basis of both genius and neurosis lies in some organic defect—some weakness or malformation of a portion of the body—whose inescapable presence stings the soul into a struggle to conquer the imperfection. As Francis Bacon said: "Whoever hath anything fixed in his person that doth induce contempt, hath also a perpetual spur in himself to rescue and deliver himself from scorn." So the club-foot Byron learned to dance perfectly, and to sin sufficiently to make himself a social lion; the stuttering Demosthenes became a perfect orator; and Beethoven, losing his hearing, fought his way to incomparable music. So woman, burning with her "masculine protest" against physical weakness and subjection, broke her way bravely through all traditions and impediments. "This feeling which the individual has of his own inferiority," says Adler, "furnishes the inner impulse to advance." It is those who were behind that forge to the front and lead the race; it is out of the working class that great inventors come; time and again diseased bodies have given shelter and stimulus to lordly souls.

V. RECIPES

But all that is general, and as vague as any counsel of perfection. Let us come to closer quarters with our quarry. What *specifically* must one do to win mental and moral strength?

Seek health first, and all things else will be added unto you, or their absence will count with you as but a little thing. As Nietzsche put it, "the first requisite of a gentleman is to be a perfect animal." It would be necessary, for this, to choose proper ancestors; this being difficult, we can at least choose proper diet and habits. *Der Mensch ist was er isst,* said Moleschott; man is considerably what he eats. There is no universal nostrum here; each man must discover his own poisons, and avoid them. Whatever disturbs you, put it on a blacklist, and let it never come near your innards again; until, by a process of ruthless elimination, you have found a diet that gives you digestive peace. And if your waste will not eliminate itself without a druggist's aid, ask yourself what evil substance is it that weakens you so shamefully: is it your beautiful white flour, or feminine cakes and sweets, or a green-less and fruit-less meal? Keep your bowels open and your mouth shut; this is the gamut of wisdom.

If we would remake ourselves, then, we must begin with the stomach; and then every other part of the body must be permitted and encouraged to prosper. Nature did not make us for intellectuals, for clerks and journalists and philosophers; she made us to move about, to lift weights, and run and climb; she fashioned us for a life of arms and legs. The ideal career would combine physical with mental activity in unity or alternation; there must be some wisdom in a Kaiser who daily chops wood. But this is a luxury which few of us can afford; life is so complex and competitive that we must, apparently, give all our time and all our energy to one subject and one purpose, in order to conquer eminence. But let us at least mow our lawns, clip our hedges, and prune our trees; and let us make any sacrifice to have a lawn, and hedges, and trees. Some day, perhaps, we shall have time for a garden. After all, it is better to be healthy than to be famous; for genius is miserable while it lives, and famous only when it is dead.

To seek health and strength we may need a new environment; and it is always a consolation to reflect that though we cannot change our heredity we can alter our situation. The old determinist philosophy of Mid-Victorian science conceived man, in its new catechism, as a creature composed of environment and heredity; it is not quite true, since man is composed of environment, heredity, and that strange progressive and remoulding force which we call life; but it is so true that we may put it down in our tablets that we shall not change ourselves substantially unless we change the stimuli that beat upon our flesh from hour to hour, and form us at last in their image. Are we living amongst unclean people, or illiterates concerned only with material and edible things?—let us go off, whatever it may cost us, and seek better company. Is there, within however distant reach, a finer soul than ours, a better furnished mind, a firmer character?—let us ferret him out, and hitch our wagon to him for a while until we can of our own selves rival his gait and equal his stroke; and then let us look for greater men still. Better to listen to greatness than to dictate to fools. Cæsar was wrong; it is nobler to be second in Rome than to be first among barbarians.

If (as you are likely to think) there is no greater one than you in the circle to which life narrows you, then make friends of genius in the past; for a penny you can buy their counsel, and listen familiarly to their speech, and mould yourself in the clear air which runs about them. It is an error to suppose that books have no influence; it is a slow influence, like flowing water carving out a canyon, but it tells more and more with every year; and no one can pass an hour a day in the society of sages and heroes without being lifted up a notch or two by the company he has kept. There is no excuse for being small when we can sit at table with Napoleon, or walk with Whitman, or have midnight suppers with Frederick and Voltaire.

So much for the things outside us. Within, the problem is more difficult; for what a wilderness we are, what an unweeded garden of desires! How shall we know which plants to nourish here, and which to discourage and let die?

The first great rule of character is unity—in Goethe's words, "to be a whole or join a whole." And the second is: Approach, do not retreat. That is the line of growth, from which the wise man will permit some deviations, but not enough to let the exceptions cloud the rule. In the first group of instincts, for example, we may leave room for cleanliness, even though it roots in the negative impulse of disgust. "In the child," says Nietzsche, "the sense of cleanliness should be fanned into a passion; and then later on he will raise himself, in ever new phases, to almost every virtue." Cleanliness is next to godliness; and what if there are no gods? But we do not wish to become ascetics of the perennial cold shower, or Apollos of the plastered hair, or victims of the manicure girl; and we shall always feel a secret envy of a late theological statesman who did not let his orthodoxy interfere with his appetite.

We may take the same attitude to pugnacity and its advance agent, pride; these are virtues, not vices; and though we shall prune them, it is only to make them grow. Not quarrelsomeness, and not conceit: conceit is the imagination of victories to come, pride is the remembrance of victories achieved, and quarrelsomeness is the pugnacity of the weak. To fight does not mean of necessity to shout and strike; it may mean to persist quietly and politely to one's goal. To be ambitious need not mean to be cruel and greedy; the strong man gives as readily as he earns, and finds his joy in building rather than in owning; he makes houses for others to live in, and money for others to spend. Character does not come from conspicuous consumption, it comes from construction and creation.

And from action. Avoid professions in which you will have to think and think and think, with never a chance to do. Better be a carpenter cutting sweet-smelling lumber under the sun, and watching things grow with every stroke of the hammer, than to add debits and credits from day to day, or ponder, in some lonely flat, new arguments for the reality of the external world. Better play one piece of music than listen to a hundred; better strike out on the corner lots than see a world-series game. Let us play and laugh; and if, now and then (as on a stormy day at sea), life seems a bitter jest, let us remember the jest, and forgive the bitterness.

Marry. It is better than burning, as Holy Writ has it, and enables one to think of something else. For an abnormal man like Nietzsche, a sister may be better than a wife; but a normal man will find a sister inadequate. Once that elementary problem is solved, we can move about in the world without being distracted at every turn by the flutter of a skirt; we realize that however different the garments may be, women are substantially identical; that under the varying phenomena (as a metaphysician would say) there is always the same underlying reality. And so we become moderately content, and even learn to love our mates after a while. It may be true that a married man will do anything for money; but only a married man could develop such versatility.

Have friends. If you cannot make them, remake yourself until you can. Solitude is a medicine, a healing fast; but it is not a food; character, as Goethe put it once for all, grows only in the stream of the world. If we become introspective we are lost, even (we are told) if our business is psychology; to look persistently within is to invite the disaster that would come to a tennis-player who consciously measured distance, speed, angle, and stroke, or to a pianist who thought of his fingers. Friends are helpful not only because they will listen to us, but because they will laugh at us; through them we learn a little objectivity, a little modesty, a little courtesy; we learn the rules of life, and become better players of the game. If you wish to be loved, be modest; if you wish to be admired, be proud; if you wish both, combine external modesty with internal pride. But pride itself may be made modest; it should seldom be seen, and never heard. Do not be too clever: epigrams are odious when they pierce the skin; and our motto should be, *De vivis nil nisi bonum.* Never put a man in the wrong; he will hold it against you forever. Nothing is the most useful thing in the world: it is often a good thing to do, and always a good thing to say; do not be too anxious to tell the truth. You must accept the conventions which society exacts of you, in order that you may take a little liberty with its laws; it will allow you to do anything, if you do it gracefully, and do not talk about it. Meanwhile try to move forward quietly, and without arousing unnecessary hostility; always approaching, always welcoming experience, always tempting life to give you as much as you can bear of it before you pass out from the sanctuary, leaving your children to guard the flame.

But in all this where is intelligence? Is character a matter of impulse only, finding no use for reason and imagination? Would that it were; how simple character would be! The strongest passions, then, would make the strongest man.

Of course it is not so; and in the complete soul imagination and intellect are like light in the fire. We may lose ourselves in imagery, but we may win great victories through foresight. "Before he fought a battle," says Emerson, "Bonaparte thought little about what he should do in case of success, but a great deal about what he should do in case of a reverse of fortune. 'When I plan a battle no man is more pusillanimous than I am. I magnify to myself all the dangers and all the evils that are possible under the circumstances.' " Imagination may destroy us, as it destroyed Napoleon in 1812; or, by letting us rehearse a variety of responses before we slip into action, it may save us from a thousand disasters.

Reason's healthy function is to serve as an aid to action; when it becomes an industry in itself it makes Hamlets and logicians; the tug of war remains undecided, and muscle and character rot. But when it becomes the play of desire upon desire, the criticism of impulse by impulse, the checking of passion by passion, then it is that highest state of man, in which the elements that are mingled in him move hither and thither until they melt into unity, and issue in total perspective and complete response.

Our impulses are the wind in our sails, but each of them, if unhindered, would drag us after it as its slave. Who has not seen the man that is only greed, or only sex, or only pugnacity, or only chatter, or only play? Perfect freedom for every impulse would dissolve character, as it did with the sons of Cyrus, who, brought up by women that flattered every wish, became weakling degenerates. Hence in the play of knowledge upon desire, which is the very essence of reason, we have the source and armory of self-discipline, that power of inhibition which is the last necessity of character and will. The world disciplines us, or we discipline ourselves; we have our choice. In the end character is what Mill called it long since: "a completely fashioned will."

Synthesis is always more difficult than analysis; psychology has not yet put together the human nature which it has taken apart; and it is still easier to describe man than to say what he should be, and how he may be changed. We have touched one aspect of a great subject which in our century will draw many initiative minds. We have the knowledge, now we seek the art, to remake ourselves as we have remade continents and seas. But knowledge is power, and every science becomes an art at last, bringing forth fruits to enlarge the empire of man. Before our children pass away, men will be building minds and hearts as today they build ships and planes. Human impulses, which have remained becalmed and almost changeless while all the world without has been transformed, will be consciously reshaped to the subtle and accelerated life which restless invention makes. Already the mental capacity of man has been increased and multiplied, so that the highest modern mind seems to belong to another species than the slow reactions of the peasant. Some day our brains will catch up with our instruments, our wisdom with our knowledge, our purposes with our powers. Then at last we shall behave like human beings.

PART FIVE

ESTHETICS

CHAPTER XIII

What Is Beauty?

I. THE SENSE OF BEAUTY AMONG PHILOSOPHERS

"I BELIEVE," SAID ANATOLE FRANCE, "that we shall never know exactly why a thing is beautiful." [1] This judgment of a great artist and a great scholar might counsel us to turn our backs upon the problem we have set ourselves. If we go forward it must be with the understanding that in philosophy there are many "Absolutes," but no certainties.

It is strange enough that this question has not found a larger place in philosophy and psychology. Every heart hears the call of the beautiful, but few minds wonder why. The savage sees beauty in thick lips and livid scars; the Greek found it in youth, or in sculptured symmetry and calm; the Roman found it in order, sublimity, and power; the Renaissance found it in color; and the modern soul finds it in music and the dance: everywhere, and at all times, people have been moved by beauty of some sort, and have spent many lives in seeking it. But only philosophers have been anxious to understand its nature and to discover the secret of its power.

The question belongs to psychology, but the psychologists have left it to philosophy, as every science leaves to philosophy the problems it cannot solve. (Hence most important problems belong to philosophy, and it has small excuse for being dull.) The physical emphasis of modern science, its passion for laboratories and experiments, its tendency to seek mathematical and quantitative formulas for all phenomena, have left it helpless in dealing with such elusive (if not always intangible) realities as beauty; not till the biological approach finds further acceptance in psychology will the

[1] *On Life and Letters,* vol. ii, p. 176.

esthetic problem fall into its proper place. Meanwhile philosophy is privileged to rush in where science fears to tread; and even the dry bones of metaphysics tremble and thrill a bit as beauty for a while replaces truth, and seeks a niche in wisdom.

Nevertheless the philosophers have not taken readily to the alluring subject, and have left it for the most part in a primitive obscurity. There was something pagan in it which repelled religious men, and something irrational in it which left the sceptical intellectualist unmoved. Baumgarten, the first thinker to recognize the nature of beauty as a distinct realm of inquiry, and the first to give it the terrible name of *esthetics*, apologized for including so undignified a subject-matter among the mansions of philosophy; doubtless he feared that even under the repellent label which he had put upon it the problem would make his readers think of statues and fair women; and he blushed at the possibility.

Even where beauty was most honored and most produced—in ancient Greece—philosophers were helpless to pierce the secret of its lure. Pythagoras began the game of esthetics by reducing music to a mathematical relation, and ascribing a subtle harmony to the spheres. The pre-Socratic Greeks, being, like pre-Darwinian scientists, under the domination of physics and mathematics, sought to define beauty in spatial and quantitative terms: music was a regularity of sounds, and plastic beauty was a regularity of proportions.

Plato, who was nothing if not a moralist (anxious to halt the decadence of his people), went to another extreme, and merged the beautiful in a sublime identity with the good. Art was to be a part of ethics; and except for the pedagogical uses of music (even then, it seems, they coddled with verse man's memory of dates and kings), there was to be a minimum of art in the Master's paradise. In Aristotle we find the typical Greek answer to our question; beauty is symmetry, proportion, and an organic order of parts in a united whole. It is a conception that pleasantly accords with that "co-operation of the part with the whole" which has echoed through these chapters; and the temptation to systematize and formulize is here almost irresistible. But why symmetry and proportion, order and unity, should delight the soul—here is a question that lures us beyond our formulas.

Winckelmann and Lessing added little to these answers, and took their lead too readily from the oppressive Greeks. Beauty remained an affair of structure and form, of carved and painted marble, and temples rising serenely on the hills; it was a quality almost indigenous to the Parthenon and its frieze. That a statue imitated some warm and living loveliness, and that the secret of beauty might better be sought in the original than in the copy, found little welcome in these stern and academic minds, more classic than the Greeks.

In Kant and Schopenhauer a new note sounds: beauty becomes that quality whereby an object pleases us regardless of its use, stirring in us a will-less contemplation, a disinterested happiness. In this objective and impartial perception, Schopenhauer would have it, esthetic appreciation and artistic genius lie; the intellect is for a moment emancipated from desire, and realizes those eternal forms, or Platonic Ideas, which constitute the outward aspects of the universal Will. But in Hegel we are back once more with the Greeks: beauty is again unity in variety, the conquest of matter by form, the sensuous manifestation of some metaphysical ideal. No wonder the dullest books in the world are those which men have written about beauty.

II. THE SENSE OF BEAUTY IN ANIMALS

What if all this was a wrong approach? Perhaps beauty is a function of life, and not of matter and form? Perhaps biology can help us here, where physics and mathematics cannot?

Let us go to the animal and try to track the sense of beauty to its source. We are wrong if we suppose that man alone is gifted with esthetic feeling. Many animals are more beautiful than the featherless biped that transiently rules the earth; and for all we know they may realize it more clearly than ourselves, and may look upon us, as sometimes they seem to do, with a calm and leisurely contempt. We think that we alone are conscious of beauty, because we associate beauty in our species with sight and visible form; in animals, if we may venture to speak so intimately of them, the esthetic tremor comes humbly through the nose. "The smell of a dog," says M. Bergeret's poodle, "is a delicious smell." Doubtless to Riquet men were diverse offensive odors.

Nevertheless the sense of hearing may also have esthetic value for the beasts. Certain of our quadruped ancestors are notoriously susceptible to music. "Experiments among a variety of animals in the Zoölogical Gardens with performances on various instruments," says Ellis, "showed that with the exception of some seals none were indifferent, and all felt a discord as offensive. . . . A tiger, who was obviously soothed by the violin, was infuriated by the piccolo; the violin and the flute were preferred by most animals." [1] Ellis's dog whined and howled at a nocturne by Chopin, but went to sleep indifferent when a cheerful piece was played. And Dean Swift adds, delicately: "Does not Ælian tell how the Libyan mares were excited to horsing by music? (Which ought to be a caution to modest women against frequenting operas.)" [2]

Nor are the eyes of animals insensitive to beauty. Certain birds, says Darwin, adorn their nests with gaily colored leaves and shells, with stones

[1] *Studies in the Psychology of Sex*, vol. iv, p. 122.
[2] *Ibid.*, p. 131.

and feathers and bits of cloth or ribbon found in the haunts of men.[1] The bower-bird builds a special nest for his mate, covered with brush-wood and carpeted with gathered grass; he brings white pebbles from the nearest brook and places them artist-wise on either side; he adorns the walls with bright feathers, red berries, and any pretty object he may find; at last he dignifies the entrance and the exit with mussel shells and gleaming stones: this is the palace the bower-bird builds for his love. "You have only to take one look at this nuptial bower," says Bölsche, "to become convinced that a direct esthetic joy in the 'beautiful' resides in this bird's little brain." [2]

Some birds have been seen gazing at themselves in mirrors. The lark can be caught in large numbers by a small mirror made to glitter in the sun; despite decimating shots the birds come toward it with all the fatality of blind desire. The magpie, the raven and other birds steal and secrete bright objects, silver, jewels, etc.; whether through vanity, or curiosity, or greed, or esthetic taste, who shall tell? [3] But these cases of beauty found by animals in inanimate things are exceptional; and the esthetic appreciation which they reveal is thin and secondary compared with the sensitive anxiety of the male displaying himself before the female in mating time. "With the great majority of animals," says Darwin, "the taste for the beautiful is confined, as far as we can judge, to the attractions of the opposite sex." [4]

Nothing could be more fruitful for our quest than this simple proposition of the most modest and illuminating of scientists. If Darwin is right, it becomes evident that the sense of beauty (as so often affirmed and forever denied) arises as an offshoot and overflow of sexual attraction. The beautiful is primarily that which is sexually desired; and if other things seem beautiful to us it is derivatively, and by ultimate relationship with this original fount of the esthetic sense. When Schopenhauer, in "The Metaphysics of the Beautiful," puts the problem of beauty in his characteristic terms—"How are satisfaction and pleasure in an esthetic object possible without any reference of the same to our will?" [5]—the answer is: It is not possible; the object secretly accords with our will; and on Schopenhauer's own premises, the fundamental and ultimate will, in the individual, is the will to mate. Let us see.

III. PRIMARY BEAUTY: PERSONS

A thing is beautiful, first of all, because it is desired. As (in Spinoza's words) we desire nothing because it is good, but call it good because we

---

[1] Darwin, C., *The Descent of Man*, pp. 112, 469.

[2] Bölsche, W., *Love-Life in Nature*, vol. ii, p. 285; Gourmont, R. de, *The Natural Philosophy of Love*, pp. 132 f

[3] *Descent of Man*, p. 469.

[4] *Ibid.*, p. 104.

[5] Essay on "The Metaphysics of the Beautiful."

desire it; so we desire nothing originally because it is beautiful, but we consider it beautiful because we desire it.

Anything that meets a fundamental need of our natures has in it certain esthetic possibilities. A plateful of food must be as beautiful to a starving man as *une femme de trente ans* to a well-fed sophomore. Let the sophomore be starved, and his esthetic sense will be dulled even to the loveliest nymph; he will consider her only as something good to eat. (Something of that primordial appetite remains in all our love.) To the author who has struggled for years to find his way into print, his first published page will seem to him a thing of compelling beauty, which no intelligent nation will surrender to decay; but to a farmer or an artisan who has healthier ambitions than to write books, that same page may be only a bit of waste to wipe his razor on. The beautiful, then, is in its lowest stages the sensory aspect of that which satisfies a strong desire. At bottom it differs from the useful only in the intensity of our need.

The beautiful and the ugly, says Nietzsche, are biological; whatever has proved racially harmful seems ugly. We do not eat sugar because it is sweet, but we consider it sweet because we are accustomed to find in it one main source of energy. All useful things become, after a time, pleasing; Eastern Asiatics like putrid fish, because it is the only nitrogenous food they can secure.[1] "The sky," says Sutherland, "never became blue to please our eyes, but our eyes have grown adapted to find pleasure in the blue of the skies. All forms and colors give a natural delight in proportion to their frequency in the experience of the race." Green grass and the blue sky are beautiful, but habit could as well have made us take pleasure in a green sky and blue grass.

Obviously beauty, as distinguished from use, is bound up with a certain keenness of satisfaction that reflects the intensity of desire. So money is rather beautiful than useful to the miser. Anything takes on beauty if it stimulates and invigorates the organism. Hence the beauty of light, and rhythm, and a gentle touch. Ugliness lowers our vitality, and disturbs our digestion and our nerves; it may produce nausea, or set the teeth on edge,[2] or make poets call for a revolution. Beauty, says Santayana, is pleasure objectified.[3] Or, as Stendhal phrased it, unknowingly following Hobbes,[4] "beauty is a promise of pleasure."

As art usually appears in a nation only after the accumulation of an economic surplus and the growth of a leisure class, so in the individual, when hunger is no longer worried or intense, erotic sensitivity increases and over-

---

[1] Sutherland, A., *Origin and Growth of the Moral Instincts,* vol. ii, pp. 85–91; Fuller, Sir B., *Man as He Is,* p. 68.

[2] Ellis, H., *The Dance of Life,* p. 328.

[3] *The Sense of Beauty,* p. 52.

[4] Cf *Encyclopaedia Britannica,* eleventh edition, vol. ix, p. 827.

194   *The Pleasures of Philosophy*

flows into the sense of beauty. Our susceptibility to the beautiful tends to rise and fall with the curve of generative potency. Love creates beauty at least as much as beauty creates love; every Quixote believes his Dulcinea to be the sweetest of the fair. "Ask a toad what is beauty," says De Gourmont, "and he will answer that it is his female, with two great round eyes coming out of her little head, her large flat mouth, her yellow belly and brown back."

So clearly is beauty bound up with love that it depends, in the human species, on those parts of the organism that are secondary sexual characters, formed at puberty by the hormones of the interstitial cells: breasts, hair, hips, rounded contours, and a softened voice. To make themselves more beautiful in the eyes of their men, the women of lower races artificially enlarge the reproductive structures, while their descendants in higher tribes adopt (for a while) the opposite but similar policy of concealment; for concealment attracts as successfully as exaggeration. Clothing (like modesty) enhances beauty because it is a form of resistance, and resistance increases desire. "Goddesses," says Santayana, "cannot disrobe, because their attributes are their substance." [1] Perhaps this was his careful way of suggesting that clothing is, in sophisticated and imaginative days, essential to beauty.

For our race the loveliness of woman is the highest form of beauty, the source and standard of all other forms. "I am the beauty of woman," says Paphnuce's vision in *Thaïs;* "whither do you think to fly from me, senseless fool? You will find my likeness in the radiancy of flowers, and in the grace of the palm trees; in the flight of pigeons, in the bound of the gazelle, in the rippling of brooks, in the soft light of the moon; and if you close your eyes you will find me within yourself."

Man's beauty might have ruled our esthetic sense if Hellenic standards and propensities had prevailed. Greek friendship dominated Greek love; at Sparta and Athens the ideal of beauty was the virile youth, beautiful and brave in one. So Greek art became an exaltation of the perfect male, and reflected the athletic field, while our sense of beauty reflects the boudoir and the dominance of woman in our hearts and lives. If, occasionally, man's beauty moves us still, it is again because of that element in love which may be channeled over to give passion and devotion to friendship, as it did among the Greeks.

Woman becomes the fount and norm of beauty because man's love for her is stronger, though briefer, than her love for him; and the intensity of his desire creates her surpassing loveliness. Woman accepts man's judgment in considering herself more beautiful than man; for since she loves to be desired rather than to possess, she learns to value in herself those charms which intensify desire. For the rest, woman does not look for beauty in the

[1] *Reason in Society*, p. 241.

male, and need not imagine it in the man she loves; it is strength which she craves in him, ability to protect her and her children, and to bring to her feet as much as possible of the treasures of the world.

It is an illuminating sign of beauty's generation by desire, that when the desired object is securely won, the sense of its beauty languishes; few men are philosophers enough to desire what they have, and fewer still can find beauty in what no longer stirs desire. Thereby hang most tales. However, let death snatch our mates from us, or some gay corsair of hearts cast alienating glances upon our property, and desire will flame again and brighten the embers of departing beauty. How remarkable it is that the same face which to us has become mere prose may be, for eyes untired by repetition, the very embodiment of poetry and romance! Would the gods the gift might give us to see our mates as others see them!

IV. SECONDARY BEAUTY: NATURE

Love, then, is the mother of beauty, and not its child; it is the sole origin of that primary beauty which is of persons and not of things. But how shall we account for the myriad objects which seem beautiful to us and yet have no apparent connection with love? How shall we explain the endless beauty of the external world?

As so many words in our lexicons have secondary and acquired, as well as primary and original, meanings, so every instinct has primary as well as secondary objectives and satisfactions. The instinct to get food becomes the general instinct of acquisition, eager for anything of value. The instinct to fight for food or mates spreads into a general instinct of pugnacity, in which fighting is its own reward. So the esthetic emotion (part of that "tender emotion" which accompanies the instinct of love) may overflow from the person desired to the objects attached to her, to her attitudes and forms, to her manners of action and speech, and to anything that is hers by possession or resemblance. All the world comes to partake of the fair one's splendor.

Consider the things that seem beautiful to our touch: round things, smooth things, curved things; why do they delight us? Is it just because they are round, or smooth, or curved? And yet a square might have beauty for certain types of mind, as for Aristotle it could symbolize justice. Or do we prefer the round and curved and smooth because our memories associate them with the soft contours of the desired sex?

Consider olfactory beauty: why do we take pleasure in the wholesomeness of clean bodies, the fragrance of flowers, or the intoxication of perfume? Is it because sexual selection acted originally through smell? Flowers enshrine the generative portions of plants, and our favorite perfumes, till synthetic chemistry came, were made of the reproductive elements of various sacrificial animals. What every woman knows includes the artistry of aphrodisiac perfumes.

Consider auditory beauty. Our notion of what is beautiful in sound comes originally from the song or speech of the desired mate. "A gentle voice is an excellent thing in woman," and may delight and draw us even more than the charms that come to the eye; while a harsh voice may cancel half the beauty of the divinest form. "Some women's voices," says Mantegazza, "cannot be heard (*sic*) with impunity." Woman, on the other hand, likes what Ellis calls "a bearded male voice," because in general she prefers strength to beauty, and those sonorous tones in the male which have been developed, presumably, through the sexual selection of vigor as a promise of protection and abundance.

It may be that the voice itself arose as a sex call; the imaginative ear can catch all the many-sounding billows of Homer's verse and the Niagara of Shakespeare's imagery in the chorus of the frogs and the chirping of the birds. Out of the voice grew song, which is almost inseparably bound up with love (though religion and war have stolen some of it away); out of the song came the dance, which is a portion of love's ritual; and out of the song and the dance came music.

Music has spread afar on all sides from this amorous origin; but it is still bound to its mother, and no lass can love without it. The girl who woos with music seldom goes to the piano after a few years of marriage; why should one seek to charm an animal that has been captured and tamed? The male who roared and mewed behind his fiancée loses his musical propensities when matrimony lays its dire compulsions upon him; and only under protest does he submit to the social necessity of bearing with Stravinsky, Schönberg, and Richard Strauss.

But love alone does not explain enough in these derivative fields of auditory beauty; the pleasure of rhythm enters as an independent element. Inspiration and expiration, the systole and diastole of the heart, and even the bilateral symmetry of the body, dispose us to the rhythmic rise and fall of sounds; and not love only but all the soul is pleased. We make a rhythm from the impartial ticking of the clock and the even stamp of marching feet; we like rocking, dancing, verse, antistrophes, antitheses and extremes.

Music soothes us with its rhythm and lifts us on its lullaby to worlds less brutal than the earth. It may relieve pain, improve digestion, stimulate love, and help to capture escaped lunatics. It enabled the Jesuits of Paraguay to bring some alleviation, and yet some increase, to the work of their Indian slaves. It may enable the soldier to march into the jaws of death with some rhythmic satisfaction. Haydn did greater service to the Hapsburgs than any general, and no one knows how much of the Imperial Russian army's unquestioning courage came from their powerful national hymn. Thoreau thought there was nothing so revolutionary as music, and marveled that our institutions could withstand it. But that was because Thoreau was a revolutionist; music may lull us into passivity as well as arouse and stimulate us to action. "Where you want to have slaves," said Tolstoi to Gorki, "there you should have as much music as possible. Music dulls the mind." The old Russian Puritan would have agreed with Plato, in whose Utopia no man would have followed music after he had reached sixteen.

Last of all, consider visual beauty. When erect stature came, smell lost its potency and leadership, and sight soon grew to dominate the esthetic sense. The beauty of things seen is, like that of things heard, far removed from the beauty of a woman loved; and we are flung again upon the crux of the esthetic problem: are curved lines, symmetrical proportions and organic unity the cause or the effect of personal beauty? Are they primary, or derived? Do we love woman because she embodies symmetry, unity, and every luring contour; or do these forms attract us, in whatever realm we find them, because they recall, or once recalled, the perfection of woman? We say, "She has a neck like a swan," and so make the swan the norm of grace; but perhaps, originally, one felt, "The swan has a neck like a beautiful woman." The lovely is primarily that which is loved.

Art seems to have its origin in the deliberate imitation, by animal or man, of the colors which nature develops on bird and beast in the mating season, and flaunts before the eyes of the selecting mate. The bird ornaments its nest with bright objects, as we have seen; and man adorns his body with vivid colors that fan desire. When clothing came, the colors passed from the body to the raiment, but with the same purpose of attracting the eye; and red was kept as the color that most stirred the blood. So song and dance, music and poetry and many forms of sculpture flower out of love. Architecture alone seems to be independent; but only because the secret of its power lies not in the beautiful but in the sublime.

Sublimity is related to beauty as male to female; its delight comes not from the desired loveliness of woman, but from the admired strength of man. Woman is probably more susceptible to the sublime than man, and man is more susceptible to beauty—keener to use it, more passionate in desiring it, more persistent in creating it. The sublime, as Burke showed, is the powerful and dangerous to one who is secure. Hannibal and Cæsar made no comments (at least for posterity) on the sublimity of the Alps; to them they were a terror rather than a scene. Contrast with their male indifference the feminine sensitivity of Rousseau, who discovered the Alps for the modern soul. But Rousseau was safe; he did not have to lead armies across those desolate heights. Perhaps (as Sergi argues) the Greeks failed to produce landscape painting because nature was still too uncontrolled a danger in their lives to let them stand aside and see its grandeur.

It is in the appreciation of landscape that beauty wanders farthest from its source in love. Much of the joy which natural scenery gives us is due to masculine sublimity; but much of it comes from a restful beauty akin to the warm repose which every fair bosom promises. Here is a Corot: green waving fields, shade-giving oaks, and brooks that ramble leisurely beneath overhanging boughs: where does woman's beauty lurk in this natural delight? *Cherchez la femme.*

We need not be too anxious to stretch a formula to embrace the world; nature resents generalizations that ignore her infinite variety, and will fling a thousand exceptions into the face of our universal principles. Let us be content to say that a feeling originally sexual may overflow to objects unconnected with love at all: the ever-growing strength of sex may spend its surplus in scenic admiration, just as it may water the roots of religion, friendship, social idealism and art.

Yet even here there are subtle bonds. A child is for the most part insensitive to the beauty of the earth and sky; only by imitation and instruction does it thrill to them. But let love lay its warmth and passion on the soul, and suddenly every natural thing seems beautiful; the lover pours out upon trees and streams and bright cool dawns the overflow of his affection and his happiness. Flowers are fair above everything else that nature gives us; and yet those flowers too are symbols and means of generation, and the tokens, among men, of tenderness and devotion. When the years dull us with repetition, and love's passion dies away, the appreciation of nature ebbs; and the very old, like the very young, are not moved by the charm and fragrance of the woods, or the gay splendor of the stars, or the undiscourageable fingers of the rising sea. Across all the glory of earth and sky Eros has left his trail.

V. TERTIARY BEAUTY: ART

This overflow of love, which spreads from persons to things, and beautifies the very soil we tread on, reaches at last to the creative fury of art; having once known beauty, man carries its picture in his memory, and weaves from many fair things seen an ideal beauty that binds into one vision the partial perfections of them all.

Biologically, art arises in the song and dance of mating animals, and in their efforts to enhance with artifice that efflorescence of color and form with which nature marks the season of love. When the bower-bird built the first bower for his pleased and fluttering mate art was born. Historically, art arises in the decorative painting, clothing, or mutilation of the body among savage tribes. The Australian native, according to Groos, always carries in his sack a provision of white, red and yellow paint. On ordinary days he is content with a few spots of color in his cheeks; but in time of war he daubs his flesh with bizarre designs calculated to discourage the enemy; and on festive and amorous occasions he illuminates his entire body with paint to catch the eyes of the girls. For both of these games—war and love—red is the favorite color; some tribes so value it that they undertake great expeditions, lasting several weeks, to renew their supply. The men paint more than the women; and in some localities unmarried women are sternly forbidden to color their necks.

But paint gets washed away; and the savage, like the Greek (who scorned painting for its quick decay) seeks some more lasting art. He takes to tattooing, piercing himself at a thousand points with a needle that deposits the pigment underneath the skin. Very frequently he resorts to scarification: skin and flesh are cut, and the scar enlarged by filling the wound with earth for a while. Along the Torres Straits the men bear such scars on their shoulders like commanding epaulets. Worst of these primitive arts is incision. The Botocudo gets his name from the *botoque,* or plug, which is inserted into the lower lip and into the ears in early youth, and repeatedly replaced by a larger plug until the openings are as much as four inches in diameter. Civilized ladies, reading of such barbarism, shake their ear-rings in horror.

The first use of clothing, apparently, was artistic rather than utilitarian. When Darwin, in pity for a freezing Fuegian, gave him a red cloth to wrap about his body, the native joyfully tore the bright garment into strips, and distributed these among his fellows, who bound them round their limbs as ornaments. From this delightful sacrifice of utility to beauty how small a step there is to the modern girl who wears furs in summer and bares her neck fearlessly to the winter wind!

Having sufficiently decorated his body, primitive man passed to the decoration of objects. Weapons were painted to blind or frighten the foe, much after the fashion of Achilles' shield; tools of flint and stone were painted, and survive to this day from prehistoric times. Paleolithic man adorned the walls of his caves with admirable representations of the animals which he hoped to capture in the hunt, or which he worshipped as totems of his tribe.

Religion, though not the source of beauty, has contributed only less than love to the development of the arts. Sculpture arose, as far as we can tell, from rude pillars placed to mark a grave; as artistry improved, the top of the pillar was carved into some semblance of a head; later the whole pillar was cut roughly into the shape of a man (the Hermes of primitive Greek art); then, care and patience increasing, the sculptor sought to give some refinement to his work, and make it perpetuate the features of the god or the ancestor whom he strove to commemorate. Only in the higher forms does sculpture take cognizance of love; Pheidias always comes before Praxiteles, Giotto before Correggio.

Architecture began with tombs that housed the dead; the most ancient architectural monuments in the world—the Pyramids—are tombs. Churches began as shrines to the dead, and places for worshipping them. Gradually the burial-place was taken out into the neighboring ground; but still, in Westminster Abbey, the graves of great ancestors are within the church. From these beginnings came the proud temples raised by the Greeks to Pallas Athene and the other gods; and from similar beginnings came those fairest works ever reared by man, the Gothic cathedrals, whose altars, like those early tombs, harbor the relics of the holy dead.

Drama seems to have come from religious ritual and festal processions. To the days of the sceptical Euripides it remained a sacred thing at Athens; and modern drama, the most secular of contemporary arts, began in the Mass and in the pious parades which pictured for the medieval mind the life and death of Christ. Sculpture found a new splendor in the adornment of the cathedrals; and painting reached its zenith under the inspiration of Christianity.

But even in the service of religion art showed its secret bondage to love. A pagan element of splendid flesh intruded into the holiest pictures of the Renaissance. The Madonnas became plump Venuses, the St. Johns were tender Adonises, and the St. Sebastians were candid studies in the nude. When the Renaissance passed from Rome to Venice the pagan element triumphed, and sacred yielded to profane love.

As even religious art drinks at the fount of Eros to sustain itself, so with every other element that enters into the creation of beauty. Rhythm enters, but at once associates itself with love to generate the song, the dance, and poetry. Imitation enters, and helps to beget sculpture and painting; but very soon it is love, filial or sexual, that determines the object which imitation makes. Combine rhythm and imitation with the love-motif and you have nine-tenths of literature; even the divine song of Dante, though designed as an allegory of human life, becomes in the end a lyric of love.

It is this subterranean river of erotic energy that feeds the creative passion of the artist. In some the relationship takes the form of a rapid development of sex and art at once; and from this union the romantic type of genius comes. Sappho, Alexander and Lucretius; Byron, Shelley, Keats and Swinburne; Hugo, Rousseau and Verlaine; Petrarch, Bruno and Giorgione; Schiller, Heine and Poe; Schumann, Schubert and Chopin; Strindberg, Artzybasheff and Tchaikovsky: these are of the type in which imagination dominates intellect, and in which sex and art, drawing riotously from the same source, consume the artist and leave him physically or spiritually dead before his youth is ended. Because desire is a torment in them they are sensitive, emotional, forever suffering, and imaginative beyond restraint; the extreme, the exotic and the strange lure them everywhere. It is they who create the poetry, the painting, the music and the philosophy of love; and every lover cherishes them.

But in other artists the flood of sex is damned, and channeled almost wholly into creation. Love loses its power, emotion is controlled, reason flourishes, and intellect dominates everything. Out of this immense sublimation comes the classic genius: Socrates, Sophocles, Aristotle; Archimedes, Cæsar, Galileo; Giotto, Leonardo, Titian; Bacon, Milton, Newton, Hobbes; Bach, Kant, Goethe, Hegel; Turgenev, Flaubert, Renan, Anatole France. These are calm men, who have mastered desire and lifted their chaos into a dancing star. They work slowly with resolution and patience, rather than with "inspiration" and passion; they speak and act with measure and restraint; they develop slowly, create better after thirty than before, achieve a tardy fame, and live for the most part to a great old age. They do not excel the romantic type in that fund of superior energy which is the common dominator and source of all genius; but from that fund they draw little for sex and nearly all for art. Michelangelo, Beethoven and Napoleon were supreme because in them both types of genius were fused into an almost superhuman unity.

"A man's genius," said Nietzsche, "is a vampire": it burns him up in its flame. But so does love; and if both consume a man at once he will speak passionately and brilliantly, but his voice will soon be stilled. All genius, like all beauty and all art, derives its power ultimately from that same reservoir of creative energy which renews the race perpetually, and achieves the immortality of life.

VI. OBJECTIVE BEAUTY

And now, among the many questions left unanswered, one in particular makes demands upon us. Is beauty an objective thing, or only a personal and subjective prejudice?

Ellis, whose judgment compels respect because it is based upon the most ecumenical learning of our time, believes that beauty is independent of the observer; and rests his case upon what seems to him the substantial similarity of esthetic preferences in most of the races of the world. One would not judge so from Chinese music or Zulu mutilations. Beauty, like morals, tends to vary with geography. The natives of Tahiti, according to Darwin, admired flat noses, and compressed the nostrils and foreheads of their children, as they said, for beauty's sake.[1] The Mayas pierced nose and ears with ornaments, chipped and inlaid their teeth, flattened their infants' heads to a sugar-loaf profile with a board, and made them squint because they regarded that as beautiful.[2] Mungo Park was astonished to hear the colored gentlemen of Africa ridicule his white skin. When Negro boys on the East African coast saw Richard Burton they cried out: "See the white man; doesn't he look like a white ape?" And we are as likely to

---

[1] *Descent of Man,* p. 665.

[2] Thorndike, L., *Short History of Civilization,* p. 395.

think that the Zulu looks like a black gorilla. Perhaps, as Voltaire would say, we are both correct.

Or consider what we shall obscurely call the steatopygy of certain African belles. "It is well known," says Darwin, "that with many Hottentot women the posterior part of the body projects in a wonderful manner . . . ; and Sir Andrew Smith is certain that this peculiarity is greatly admired by the men. He once saw a woman who was considered a beauty, and she was so immensely developed behind that when seated on level ground she could not rise, and had to push herself along until she came to a slope. Some of the women in various negro tribes have the same peculiarity; and according to Burton, the Somal men are said to choose their wives by ranging them in a line and by picking her out who projects farthest *a tergo*. Nothing can be more hateful to a negro than the opposite form." [1] *De gustibus non disputandum.*

Even among Europeans the ideal of beauty varies from people to people and from time to time. It was once fashionable to be stout; observe the overflowing ladies of Rubens, and the buxom lasses of Rembrandt; even Raphael's Madonnas are physically prosperous. But the belles of Reynolds, Gainsborough and Romney are more modestly designed; and the women of Whistler are slender and cushionless. Within our own lifetime, feminine architecture has changed from a Doric rotundity to a Corinthian delicacy; and fashions in bodies take on some of the variability, and inviolability, of fashions in dress.

Apparently, then, there is a large subjective element, racial and personal, in the esthetic judgment. One objective element remains; and that is the almost universal preference of normal men for women whose form gives promise of robust maternity. Primarily it is the perfection of natural function that pleases the healthy taste; first in woman, then in anything; any task well done, any life well lived, any family well reared, any tool well made for its work, compels us to say, "It is beautiful." If we were quite sane, we should consider the healthy woman nursing her healthy babe as the summit of beauty in this world. Here the Middle Ages and Renaissance, with their Madonnas and the Child, were finer and sounder in their taste than we; misled by a degenerate art we hanker destructively for thin and wasp-like women who cannot reproduce half so well as they can sting.

If our instincts were not deceived by cosmetics or perverted by finance, our sense of beauty would be biologically right, and love would be the best eugenics. Beauty would be again, as nature wished it to be, the flower and herald of health, and the guarantor of perfect children; it would make once more for the good of the race and not for its enfeeblement; ethics and esthetics would coincide, and we should arrive at Plato's con-

[1] *Descent of Man*, p. 660.

clusion, that "the principle of goodness reduces itself to the law of beauty." [1]

The Master hesitated in this matter and did not know just where to bend the knee—to stern Athene's wisdom, or Aphrodite's smiling loveliness. Perhaps he was wise to hesitate; and beauty as we have it now could hardly be made the prop and basis of a perfect state. But of what use is wisdom if it does not make us love the beautiful and create new beauty fairer than nature gives? Wisdom is a means; beauty, of body and soul, is an end. Art without science is poverty, but science without art is barbarism. Even divine philosophy is a means, unless we broaden its flight to cover all the coördinated significance, instrumentalities and values of the fullest life. And a philosophy that is not stirred by loveliness is unworthy of a man.

Everything is gone of Egypt but the colossal grandeur which it lifted from the sand; everything is gone of Greece but its wisdom and its art. Living beauty is greatest, but age withers it and time decays; only the artist can seize the passing form and stamp it in a mould that resists mortality. Let Gautier speak:

> All things pass; strong art alone
>   Can know eternity;
> The marble bust
>   Outlives the state:
>
> And the austere medallion
>   Which some toiler finds
> Under the earth
>   Preserves the emperor.
>
> Even the gods must die;
>   But sovereign poetry
> Remains,
>   Stronger than death.

[1] *Philebus*, § 64; in Bosanquet, *History of Æsthetic*, p. **33**.

PART SIX

PHILOSOPHY OF HISTORY

CHAPTER XIV

The Meaning of History: A Symposium

CHARACTERS OF THE DIALOGUE

ANATOLE FRANCE

FRANÇOIS MARIE AROUET DE
 VOLTAIRE

JACQUES BÉNIGNE BOSSUET

HENRY THOMAS BUCKLE

THOMAS CARLYLE

FRIEDRICH RATZEL

WILLIAM JAMES

GABRIEL TARDE

CHARLES LOUIS DE SECONDAT,
 BARON DE MONTESQUIEU

FRIEDRICH NIETZSCHE

GEORG WILHELM FRIEDRICH
 HEGEL

LESTER WARD

KARL MARX

JOSEPH ARTHUR, COMTE DE
 GOBINEAU

MADISON GRANT

PHILIP

ARIEL

THE NARRATOR

SCENE: *A Garden in the Country of the Mind.*

I. PROLOGUE IN PAUMANOK

As WE WALKED through a valley in Paumanok, we talked with enthusiasm of Croce's belief that history should be written only by philosophers, and philosophy only by historians. While our senses took in gratefully the freshness of the earth, the cool shade of the crowded trees, the bright waters of the lake, and the ridged gold of the sunset sky, our thoughts were with the books we had been reading that summer afternoon.

"I'm so glad," said Ariel, "that we're studying history now. I was getting tired of your logic, your epistemology, and your metaphysics; instead of teaching me new truths they have only taken from me those that I had before."

"It is not good," said Philip, "to have too many truths."

"Perhaps," I said, "those duller studies are worth while even if they do no more than give us the philosophical habit of mind—I mean the habit of dealing with large wholes, and applying total perspective to our little concerns."

"You're in love with that phrase *total perspective,* aren't you?" said Ariel, with a forgiving smile.

"Yes, I'm a devotee of perspective, an addict of integration. I want to see things whole."

"Good," said Philip, heartily. "But that's just what the historians don't care to do. They have some theological dogma they want to prove, or some party program to exalt, or some patriotic delusion to inculcate; they don't dare see their country, their party, or their creed, in perspective. Eighty per cent of all written history is like Egyptian hieroglyphics; it exists to glorify the noble exploits of priests and kings."

"Even our beloved Gibbon talks too much of kings, don't you think?" asked Ariel.

"Yes," I said, "and yet he paints canvases as big as Michelangelo's, and writes music like Bach's. I won't hear a word against him. But think of Woodrow Wilson, who defined history as 'past politics'—that's a blunder for you. As if there's anything in politics that mankind would care to remember."

"The Chinese government was more honest," said Ariel. "Until a few years ago, and for the last twenty-six hundred years, it hired historians to record the imperial virtues and victories, and to kalsomine imperial vices and defeats."

"The ideal history for patriotic school-boards," said Philip. "But things were not much worse in ancient China than in modern Europe. The Middle Ages, the Renaissance, and the Enlightenment gave us histories of the world; but the nineteenth century discovered nationalism, and corrupted nearly all the historians. Treitschke and von Sybel, Michelet and Martin, Macaulay and Green, Bancroft and Fiske, were patriots first and historians afterward; their country was God's country, and all the world outside it was filled with villains or barbarians. There's not much difference between such writers and the bar-room statesmen who speak of Goethe's people as Huns, of Chopin's people as Polacks, of Spinoza's people as Sheenies, and of Leonardo's people as Guineas, Dagos and Wops. Those historians are just press-agents for the politicians, recruiting officers for the army and navy."

"Who was it," asked Ariel, "that suggested that the royal road to international peace would not be through treaty, nor through trade, but through the abolition of history?" [1]

"But the twentieth century," I ventured, "is not much better than the nineteenth. I don't quite relish the contemporary style of proving that all great men are small, and that the most important thing about them is that they swore, lied, drank, and loved too widely. I can't forgive Wells for bringing Napoleon and Cæsar down to his own level. I cling to my last religion—the worship of great men."

"I don't agree with you," said Philip. "These biographers who show us the seamy side of genius, or find all the Freudian complexes in *The Raven* and *Huckleberry Finn*, are just as partial, it may be, as the white-wash style of biographer; but it takes both kinds to give us something of the truth between them. Far more offensive are the university historians who devote whole lifetimes to proving that small things are great, and write monographs as pedantic and useless as doctorate theses in philosophy. Watch them prowling about the libraries: they bury themselves in specialist minutiæ, and apply themselves with the patience of ants to piling up facts for the sake of facts. They lose themselves in documents and statistics, and demonstrate laboriously and tediously the indisputable truth of unimportant things; they see the trees, and never dream of the forest. It never enters their heads that the past is dead except as it lives and works in the character and purposes of men today, and that history has value for us only in so far as it can illumine the present and help us direct the future. They are the scholastics of history, fit brothers to the epistemologs you hate so much. They are like the biologists who kill an insect, preserve it in alcohol, slit it open at leisure, dissect its digestive tract, and think they are studying life. Or they're like those patient beavers who burrow away, in the laboratories of experimental psychology, to demonstrate by exhausting measurement, by graphs and charts and coefficients of correlation, what every man has known of human conduct for thousands of years."

Ariel smiled at his passion.

"Down with them!" she cried.

"What they need," I suggested, "is a breath of philosophy that will give them some sense of the whole."

"Yes," said Ariel, "I'd like to see history integrated, as you call it. I'd like to know if there are laws in it, or at least lessons; whether progress is real, or only a sweet delusion of our time; whether the past can guide us as we plunge into the future. I shall never forget a sentence of Napoleon's, one of the last he spoke. 'May my son study history,' he said, 'for it is the only true philosophy.' I'm sure we'd learn more about the real nature of man

[1] The "Drifter," in *The Nation*, New York, Sept. 13, 1922.

from history, if it were properly written, than from all the text-books of psychology and philosophy in the world. I'd like to know men as great statesmen knew them—without delusion and without reproach."

"A lovely phrase, Ariel," I said.

"Well," said Philip, "why not do as Croce says, and combine philosophy with history? There's a certain intellectual stricture and meagreness in our time which makes us scorn what used to be called 'philosophy of history.' Just as large, long-term designs disappear from a statesmanship that is only politics, so the old philosophic grasp of Gibbon and Voltaire disappears from written history. Synthesis is out of style."

"In a sense," I objected, "this is the result of a wise caution. Philosophical history suffers from the diseases of all speculation: it generalizes too readily, it exaggerates an idea, and it cramps all the past into a formula or a phrase."

Philip would not be denied.

"But without philosophy," he said, "history is mere fact-grubbing, Grad-grinding, losing its nose in the past for the past's sake. And without history philosophy is epistemology, or some cobweb castle in the air, irrelevant to creative men." He lifted a hand towards the twilight sky. "History is the ground on which philosophy must stand while it weaves all knowledge together for the enlightenment and betterment of human life."

"Bravo, Philip," said Ariel.

As she spoke, the evening star appeared, and the moon cut the sky like a shining scimitar. We had climbed a little hill, and stood for a while entranced; never had we seen the moon so white, or the heavens so blue. Then it seemed to us that we heard quiet voices almost at our feet. Peering through the twilight we saw a pleasant garden, spacious and modestly adorned, and traversed with a brook that made perpetual music. On the grass, or on rustic seats placed about a marble-basined pool, sat a strange and motley company of great men. They were dressed in the fashions of many epochs gone, but some faces were as familiar to us as if we had known them since our minds' awakening.

"Surely," whispered Ariel, "that is our beloved Voltaire."

"As I live," said Philip, all excitement, "it is the divine monkey of Ferney."

"And that," I said, "is his great-great grandson, Anatole France. He is shorter than I thought, but what a face!—half the wisdom and all the kindliness of the ages are in his eyes."

We scrutinized one after another, recognizing many. I thought a portly bishop, dressed in the flowing robes of his station, and sitting as if in meditation, with his hands crossed in his lap, was Bossuet, brave court preacher to Louis XIV, and tutor of Louis once the Well-Beloved. Near Voltaire was a French noble, wearing the costume, as I thought, of the feudal ages; I mistook him for Montaigne. A man of forty, nervous and frail and absorbed in thought, looked like pictures I had seen of Buckle, the historian of civilization.

"Great Scott!" whispered Philip, "that's my old teacher, Lester Ward."

An ugly and very serious German reminded me of Hegel. Near him, with fierce moustache and gentle eyes, was Nietzsche, champing silent apothegms. In a modest corner, gloomy and alone and unmistakable, sat Thomas Carlyle, a mountain-crag of a man, with brows like cliffs and the eyes of a warrior caught and subdued at last. Standing by the fountain was a tall and graceful figure whom I recognized as William James, as energetic as an American and as vivacious as a Frenchman. Face to face with him, their beards almost touching in lively argument, was Karl Marx, short, dark and serious. A tall and scholarly German, a lawyerly-looking American, a French magistrate, and a French aristocrat, all unknown to me, rounded out the little group.

Anatole France was speaking, with the voice of a priest and the humor of M. Bergeret. Unseen in the darkness that had fallen so rapidly, we found seats within hearing distance on the grass, and listened in silence, lest we should break some mystic charm.

II. THE THEOLOGICAL INTERPRETATION OF HISTORY

ANATOLE FRANCE. Your greatest book, dear Arouet, is your *Essai sur les mœurs et l'esprit des nations, et des principaux faits de l'histoire, depuis Charlemagne jusqu' à Louis XIII.*[1] The title was worthy of your immense masterpiece. You effected a great revolution in the writing of history.

VOLTAIRE. I was not the first. Bishop Bossuet had prepared the way by writing his *Histoire Universelle.*[2] Before that there were merely chronicles. Perhaps the Bishop will do us the great honor of imagining that we are the court of Louis XIV, and will preach us a little sermon on the subject of history.

BOSSUET. Gentlemen, you are an academy of sceptics, and I am afraid you will laugh at an old man who believes in God the Father, and in history as the manifestation of Divine Providence. I wished to teach the Dauphin the meaning of history; and I wrote for him a book which sought to do for all nations and epochs what a map of the world does for continents and seas and states; I wished to show every part in its relation to the whole.

A. F. It was an admirable purpose. Accomplished, it would have been a complete philosophy.

---

[1] *Essay on the Morals and Character of the Nations, and on the Principal Facts of History, from Charlemagne to Louis XIII,* 1756.

[2] *Universal History,* 1681.

Bossuet. History was to me the drama of God's Holy Will, and every event was a lesson taught from heaven to man. I warned Louis XV that revolutions were ordained by God to teach humility to princes.

A. F. My dear Bishop, if you will forgive me for saying so, you remind me of the good Bernardin de St. Pierre, who said of the melon: "It is externally divided into sections, because nature intended it for family eating." I assure you that your royal pupil turned out to be a good-for-nothing rascal, that he had many mistresses, ground the faces of the poor, and lived to a ripe old age. His successor, Louis XVI, was a man of modesty, temperance, and virtue; he did his best to serve his country and to prevent violence and misery; and he was guillotined in 1792.

Bossuet. The ways of God pass our understanding, but we must trust Him.

A. F. And yet what I admired most in your book was its confident explanation of many mysteries, such as the creation of Eve, and the terrible misfortunes of God's Chosen People. I regret to see how much knowledge and certainty have gone out of the world, and how obscure many things have become which were once so clear. We shall never know so much again.

Buckle. I was impressed by the Bishop's knowledge of chronology. I discovered in him the exact dates of the murder of Abel, the Deluge, and the mission of Abraham.[1] In all my library I could not find any assurance on these points.

Bossuet. It is very simple, my son. I believe in the inspiration of the Scriptures. Without faith there can be no knowledge.

Carlyle. 'Tis likely, sir, 'tis very likely.

A. F. Nevertheless, your Reverence, we owe you a great debt. You reduced history to the Will of God, but you taught your unworthy pupil that the Divine Will works for the most part through secondary and natural causes, and you suggested that the historian should seek those secondary causes which determined the succession of civilizations and states. It was much to put the question of philosophical history so clearly. Hardly a step remained from this to your brilliant enemy, M. de Voltaire.

Voltaire. But again you do me too great honor. We are forgetting the services of Giovanni Battista Vico. I regret that I could not visit Italy in my youth and talk to this learned Italian. M. Buckle will perhaps tell us something of him.

Buckle. He stands midway, in time and theory, between the Bishop and yourself. He acknowledged an omnipotent and benevolent Providence; but having made that obeisance to the Holy Office of the Propaganda, he proceeded to construct his *Scienza Nuova* [2] on a purely terrestrial basis. He asked why there was no science of history as of other matters, and he

[1] Buckle, H. T., *Introduction to the History of Civilization,* vol. i, p. 570.
[2] *Principles of a New Science,* 1725.

suggested that there might be laws as true for the apparently lawless vicissitudes of societies as Newton's laws were true for the wildest vagaries of motion.

A. F. Alas, poor Newton, I must tell him about Einstein. But proceed, Monsieur.

BUCKLE. Certain regularities appeared to Vico to stand out in history. All cultures, he thought, passed through three stages.

HEGEL. Three stages? It was clever of him to anticipate me so.

BUCKLE. The first stage was savagery, in which there was no thought, but only feeling. The second stage was barbarism, in which imaginative knowledge created Homers and Dantes, and made the age of heroes. The third stage is civilization, in which conceptual knowledge produces science, law, and the state. The Roman Empire, Vico believed, had built the loftiest of all civilizations. As the barbarians overthrew it by pitting brute strength and endless numbers against a debilitating refinement and a diminishing population, so every culture in the future would rise to philosophy and poetry only to be laid low by primitive peoples unspoiled with sensitivity and thought. In politics he saw a similar sequence: barbarism generates chieftains who become an aristocracy; aristocratic tyranny and exclusiveness lead to revolution and democracy; and the leaderless disorder of democracy brings barbarism back again. The motto of history is *da capo*.

A. F. All philosophers are sad. I have always said that thinking is a great misfortune. The ancients considered the power of piercing the future as the most fatal gift that could be bestowed upon man.[1] You yourself, M. Arouet, were not very cheerful in the conclusions you drew at the end of your great history.

VOLTAIRE. I was dealing with a brutal period. I had gone through the immense scene of revolutions that the world had experienced since the days of Charlemagne. To what had they all tended? To desolation and the loss of millions of lives. Every great event had been a capital misfortune. Perhaps it was the fault of my sources; the chroniclers had kept no account of times of peace and tranquillity, they had related only ravages and disasters. So history seemed to me nothing more than a picture of crimes and misfortunes. Absurd superstitions, irrational habits, sudden irruptions of brute force—these were the moving powers of history. Seldom could I find human reason playing any part in events; on the contrary, the smallest and most undignified causes seemed to have had the most magnificent and tragic effects. And the only Providence I found was Chance.[2]

BUCKLE. Your disciple Turgot was not so pessimistic. You will recall that in the famous Discourses which he delivered at the Sorbonne in 1750

[1] *M. Bergeret in Paris*, p. 174.
[2] *Works of Voltaire*, St. Hubert Guild, ed., vol. xvi, p. 133.

he sketched a history of civilization, and announced his faith in the progress of the human mind.

VOLTAIRE. Sir, it delights me to hear you speak well of him. I loved the man, and my heart broke when the King dismissed him from the Ministry of Finance; from that moment it seemed to me that all was lost. As for the idea of progress, it was very popular in my time; it particularly excited my young friend the Marquis de Condorcet while French civilization was being destroyed. But Turgot was right; history can be borne with only when it is the record of civilization. Only philosophers should write history. They will know how to distinguish the little from the great in the material they work on; they will avoid details that lead to nothing and are to history what baggage is to an army—*impedimenta;* and they will look at things in the large. The progress of intellectual enlightenment, material prosperity, and moral elevation is not only a feature in the history of a nation, it constitutes that history; while all records of other transactions have no true historical value except for the light they shed upon this economic, intellectual and moral progress. Therefore my object, in writing the *Essai sur les mœurs,* was to discover the history of the human mind. I wanted to know the steps by which men passed from barbarism to civilization.[1]

A. F. Master, you have justly described the ideal history. I marvel at a generation that could produce your *Essai sur les mœurs,* and *L'esprit des lois* of M. de Montesquieu, and the eloquent volumes of M. Gibbon. Together you emancipated history from theology, and gave it to philosophy and science. When I reflect that our race of metaphysical monkeys has climbed four times to wisdom and urbanity,—when I think of the age of Socrates, the age of Horace, the age of Rabelais, and your own age, Monsieur, which should always be named from you,—I am partly consoled for the wars and crimes, the miseries and injustices, of history. Mankind is justified only in its great men.

III. THE GEOGRAPHICAL INTERPRETATION OF HISTORY

BUCKLE. I am glad, Sir, that you have mentioned M. de Montesquieu. For thus far we have spoken only of the method of writing history; we have not considered the causes to which we should attribute the grandeur and decadence of nations. After moving the center of history from heaven to earth, from kings to humanity, and from war to civilization, it remained to ask what were the deciding factors in history; was it, as your last remark seemed to suggest, the genius of great men?—or the power of accumulated knowledge?—or the inventions of scientists and technicians?—or the blood

---

[1] Pellissier, G., *Voltaire Philosophe,* p. 213; Morley, J., *Voltaire,* pp. 215, 223; Buckle, *op. cit.,* vol. i, p. 580.

of superior races?—or the conditions of economic production and distribution?—or the peculiarities of climate, soil, and geographical condition? M. de Montesquieu deserves the credit of being the first to seek the specific causes of national greatness and decay.

MONTESQUIEU. It is very kind of you to mention me. I am afraid that your countrymen, M. Buckle, remember me better than my own. Even M. de Voltaire, who could be very generous, did not care much for my books.

VOLTAIRE. To this day, Seigneur, it is hard for me to forgive you the brilliance of the *Lettres Persanes*, and the erudition of *L'esprit des lois*.

MONTESQUIEU. I know. Great men always behave like little men to one another. My contemporaries referred to my first and second publications—the *Persian Letters* and the *Considerations on the Causes of the Grandeur and Decadence of the Romans* as "the grandeur and decadence of Montesquieu"; they liked persiflage better than philosophy. I invited Fontenelle, Helvétius, and other learned friends to come to La Brède, where I lived, and listen to some chapters of *The Spirit of Laws*, to which I had devoted twenty years of labor. They were unanimous in advising me not to publish the book. In short I have been very popular in England.

BUCKLE. I consider *The Spirit of Laws* as the greatest production of French literature in the eighteenth century. You were the first to show that personalities count for nothing in history, and that single events—even great battles like Philippi or Actium—are not the causes of a nation's rise or fall. You taught us that great individuals, and great events, are but symbols and results of vast and lasting processes, some of them as impersonal as the configuration of the land, or the temperature of the air.

MONTESQUIEU. Hippocrates, in the fourth century before our era, wrote a volume called *Airs, Waters and Places*, in which he spoke briefly of the influence which the geographical environment can have on the physical constitution of peoples and the legal constitution of states. Aristotle attributed the success of the Greeks, and even their mental superiority, to their "intermediate" climate—though I do not think that we should use that word to describe the temperature of Athens.

A. F. Another of your forerunners in this field, Monsieur, was Bodin, who in the sixteenth century wrote on the relations between geography and courage, intelligence, manners, and morals; even virgins varied with latitude.

MONTESQUIEU. Of course it is an error to suppose that I would reduce history to geography. Various causes have proved decisive in various nations: in some, laws; in others, religion; in others, customs and morals; in still others, nature and climate. These last rule only over savages; customs governed the Chinese, laws the Japanese, and morals the Spartans;

while maxims of government, and the ancient simplicity of manners, determined for many generations the character of the Romans.[1]

BUCKLE. But what most interested me in your book, Monsieur, was its discussion of climate and history.

MONTESQUIEU. I confess that the subject interested me too. I believe that differences of character and temperament, which so largely affect the destiny of nations, are due in great part to the influence of climate. In the colder zones, for example, people tend to be vigorous, while in the tropics they tend to be lazy. This is a platitude, and yet how fertile it is in consequences! The Hindus believe that repose and non-existence are the foundations of all things, and the ideal end in which they terminate; hence they consider inaction as the most perfect of all states, and the object of their hopes. Idleness is with them the highest good, and constitutes, in their thought, the very essence of heaven; heat, on the contrary, is the vital element in their conception of hell. Everywhere, as the result of this early view, idleness has become a mark of high estate, and those who do not work regard themselves as the sovereigns of those who do. In many places people let their nails grow, so that all may see that they do not work.[2]

A. F. French heels once served the same purpose amongst us, until the patience of vanity made them universal.

MONTESQUIEU. Why is it that southern nations seem fated, one after another, to be conquered by northern tribes, unless because the north invigorates and the south enervates? Slaves come from the south, masters from the north; eleven times Asia has been subjected by northern barbarians.

VOLTAIRE. You probably know, Monsieur, that the word *slave* comes from *Slav*. It goes back to the time when our Holy Mother the Church forbade the enslavement of Christians. The Slavs were not yet converted, and could be captured and sold with a good conscience; in this way a word which once meant glory came to mean servitude. These northern slaves would be an exception to your rule, but not a vital exception.

MONTESQUIEU. It is very good of you to correct me. But I understand, M. Buckle, that you yourself have studied extensively the relation of climate to history.

BUCKLE. I could not do much, Monsieur. I was already half dead when I was born. I was frail all through childhood, and could not join the other boys in play. In my forty years of life I never knew a day without illness and pain. I was afflicted with poor eyesight, so that my mother, careless of the wits of my time, taught me knitting instead of reading. At eight I did not know the alphabet.

CARLYLE. Tut, tut, man; everybody knows that at forty you were the

[1] *Spirit of Laws*, vol. i, p. 294.
[2] *Ibid.*, pp. 225, 296.

most learned mannikin in England. Huxley told me you could not carry your head straight, it held so much. You had French, German, Danish, Italian, Spanish, Portuguese, Dutch, Walloon, Flemish, Swedish, Icelandic, Frisiac, Maorian, Russian, Hebrew, Latin and Greek, and you could write English; I heard Mr. Darwin say, at one of his monkey parties, that your style was the best he'd ever read. I don't know; but I liked your footnotes.

BUCKLE. I dreamed of writing a complete history of civilization in England; but after twenty years of work on it I had written only the introduction, which took up four volumes. Then my mother died, and I couldn't write any more. If I had been a strong man I might have accomplished something.

MONTESQUIEU. Will you not tell us your conclusions?

BUCKLE. You must know, Sir, that the Belgian economist Quetelet showed a remarkable statistical regularity in such apparently voluntary actions as marriage, and in such accidental trifles as dropping unaddressed letters into the mails. From these and similar data I infer that though human behavior seems free when considered in detail, it reveals itself, when seen in the mass, as clearly determined by forces outside the individual will. In the great march of human affairs individual peculiarities count for nothing, and the historian has no business with them. Progress is due not to great individuals, but to the accumulation and transmission of knowledge. I observe no progress in morals, no improvement from one age to the next in human impulses and feelings; only natural science grows, and slowly transforms the earth.[1]

MONTESQUIEU. It is a very reasonable conclusion; I once heard old Fontenelle say very much the same thing.[2]

BUCKLE. Like you, Sir, I am interested in the influence of geography upon history. Climate, food, soil, and the general aspect of nature have affected the life-story of every race. The majestic natural scenery of India overwhelmed the Hindu mind and courage and inclined it to superstition and worship; the simpler scenery of Europe left man uncowed, and permitted the growth of a disposition to control nature instead of worshiping it.[3]

A. F. It is clear that you never crossed the Atlantic, M. Buckle. Among the barbarians who now inhabit North America an unprecedented advance in natural and applied science goes along with a ferocious addiction to piety. You would have been interested in the Americans, M. Buckle.

BUCKLE. I could not spare the time, nor was I much encouraged by the reports of Mr. Dickens. But I studied the history of America with care. I discovered in the Western Hemisphere a peculiar combination of geo-

[1] Buckle, vol. i, p. 593.
[2] Nordau, M., *Interpretation of History,* p. 286.
[3] Buckle, vol. i, pp. 29, 47.

graphical conditions. North of Mexico the west coast has heat without moisture, and the east coast has moisture without heat. The Hence American civilization before Columbus was confined chiefly to Mexico and Central America, because only in this narrowing strip of land did the Western Hemisphere offer that union of moisture and heat which is necessary to plants, animals, and men. Later the arrival of Europeans, and the introduction and multiplication of inventions, lessened the dependence of men upon natural conditions.[1]

MONTESQUIEU. You limit the geographical interpretation, then, to the early stages in the history of nations?

BUCKLE. As man's mastery of the environment increases, objective and physical conditions lose more and more of their power in determining events.[2]

WILLIAM JAMES. I'm glad to hear you say that, old man, for I was a little worried lest you should reduce us all to latitude and longitude. But you will be interested to learn that the geographical interpretation of history has been applied even to advanced states by Herr Friedrich Ratzel, who has been listening modestly to this discussion.

BUCKLE. I am eager to know the most recent developments.

RATZEL. The great American philosopher exaggerates my importance. My work was only a small part of the geographical study of my time; Ritter, Kohl, Peschel and Réclus were masters in this field; and in your own country, Dr. James, Professor Huntingdon has carried on the most illuminating researches.

BUCKLE. Tell us what you have found, Mr. Ratzel.

RATZEL. We would modify a little the conclusions to which M. de Montesquieu and yourself were led with regard to climate. The difficulty of life in the tropics is not so much the heat, but the dangers: earthquakes, pestilence, storms, beasts, and bugs. In semi-tropical countries the modified heat is beneficent: it leads to outdoor life, sociability, high sexuality, and a consequent disposition to art and culture. In the colder north the industrious industry and the busy business, if I may so speak, of the dominant classes, the lust for activity, achievement, and acquisition, lead to the development of science rather than of art, to wealth rather than to leisure. The indoor life makes for an unsociable reserve, and the restless competition produces a hard individualism.

MARX. I shall show you later that all these effects which you attribute to climate are due to economic changes.

BUCKLE. But go on, Professor, even if you do not love England well.

RATZEL. The climate may even determine stature or physiognomy; many observers report that the Americans are acquiring a copper-like

[1] *Ibid.*, pp. 69, 71.
[2] *Ibid.*, p. 33.

complexion, like that of the Indians whom they replaced; and Professor Boas has shown that the American climate tends, regardless of inter-marriage, to reduce the stature in the descendants of tall immigrants, and to raise the stature in the descendants of short immigrants; while (again without intermarriage) the variety of immigrant head-types drops towards uniformity as immigration subsides. And Professor Huntingdon, following up the findings of Prince Kropotkin—

A. F. The anarchist saint. I knew him well.

RATZEL. Professor Huntingdon has shown that the quantity of rainfall may decide a nation's fate; dried-up lake-beds reveal the secrets of vast migrations; and periodically the pulse of Asia passes from rain to drought, and civilizations wither and die.

W. J. It would be a nice how-d'ye-do if the great migrations, conquests, and empires of history were to be traced at last to a certain periodicity in the spots on the sun.

RATZEL. Everything is possible. Consider the influence of rivers. The Nile and the Ganges, the Hoang-ho and the Yang-tse, the Tigris and the Euphrates, the Tiber and the Po, the Danube and the Elbe, the Seine and the Thames, the Hudson and the St. Lawrence, the Ohio and the Missis-sippi—on their fruitful shores nearly all civilizations have had their base. And the Danube—ah, gentlemen, if the blue Danube could speak, how many tales it might tell of a thousand varied peoples following its waters from dying Asia to the once sparsely settled fields of Europe! If the rivers of Russia had run north instead of south do you think she would have longed so for Constantinople, fighting war after war for it? It was because Russia's rivers flowed into the Black Sea and the Caspian Sea that the Dnieper made her Byzantine, and the Volga made her Asiatic; not till Peter built St. Petersburg and opened the Neva did Russia look west and begin to be part of Europe.[1]

BUCKLE. It is extremely interesting, Professor. Go on.

RATZEL. Consider the part played in history by coast-lines. The Medi-terranean bound a dozen civilizations together with her waters, until the Atlantic led Europe to America and changed all the currents of trade.

HEGEL. In my *Philosophy of History*, which no one has mentioned yet, I remarked that the history of antiquity could not be conceived without the Mediterranean—it would be like ancient Rome or Athens without the forum, where all the life of the city came together.[2]

RATZEL. I remember the passage well, Herr Doctor. A superior coast-line, and a thousand neighborly islands, gave Greece access to a water-route to Persia and the East, and made her the pivot of commerce in the Mediterranean. A low ratio of coast-line to area retarded the growth of

[1] Semple, E. C., *Influence of Geographic Environment,* p. 348.
[2] Hegel, G. F. W., *Philosophy of History,* p. 87.

wealth in Asia by hindering exchange; and a similar condition exists in Africa today. Even the United States, with their great spread from ocean to ocean, might have remained a backward country if railroads had not brought every inland region nearer to the sea.

A. F. During the Great War, Doctor, Russia fought for a port on the Baltic, Germany for the mouth of the Rhine, France for all the Rhine, Austria for Trieste and Fiume; England for the world, and America for democracy. Still I am inclined to think that you exaggerate the role of geography. What you have done, honored Sir, is to gather together certain aspects of the past that admit of being classified under geography. But there are many other aspects, not less important, and I fear that the life and destiny of peoples has slipped through your formula. Great nations have appeared almost everywhere on the face of the earth, and in their unlike climates have had like parabolas of exaltation and decay.

RATZEL. Do not mistake me, gentlemen; I do not propose to explain everything in history by geography. I explain something, that is all.

W. J. You are very modest, Doctor. A great American teacher once said that there is "a certain diminuendo movement in history so far as the relative influence of physical environment is concerned." [1]

BUCKLE. That is quite right, I should say. Geography provides limiting conditions, but seldom decisive forces; it is the charmed circle within which other forces lift a nation to leadership or drag it down to extinction. A change in the Gulf Stream might ruin England, but it was not the Gulf Stream that made England great. In all higher civilizations the determining factors are economic or mental.

VOLTAIRE. A very reasonable conclusion. I have always said that the English were a sensible people. It is the one point on which M. de Montesquieu and I agree.

NIETZSCHE. Perhaps you are both mistaken.

IV. THE RACIAL INTERPRETATION OF HISTORY

A. F. You might have said, M. Buckle, that the determining factors are economic, or mental, or racial. For in my time it was race to which a great many students were attributing the rise and fall of nations. In this way it was possible for professors to be scientists and patriots at the same time. Count Gobineau, here, is an exception: he was neither a professor nor a patriot.

GOBINEAU. When you were but ten years old, Monsieur, I published a book on *The Inequality of the Races of Man,* in which I expressed the conviction that everything in the way of human creation, science, art, civilization—all that was great and noble and fruitful on the earth—pointed

[1] Sumner, W. G., *Folkways*, p. 53.

to a single source, and was sprung from one and the same root: the Teutonic race. This great branch of the human family probably had an entirely different origin from that of the yellow and black races. It formed a special breed of men, whose various branches have dominated every civilized region of the world.[1] It is race that explains history; as my young friend Herr Nietzsche puts it, leadership requires not intellect, but blood.

NIETZSCHE. I admire you a great deal, Count Gobineau; but I will have nothing to do with the race-swindle. I found good blood in every race, and perhaps better in a Venetian gondolier than in a Berlin Geheimrath.[2]

A. F. The English and the Germans, my dear Count, have not been displeased with your theory. Professor Freeman embraced it with indecent haste. Professor Treitschke adopted it gladly, and Dr. Bernhardi admitted that the Germans are the greatest civilized people known to history. M. Chamberlain, who had abandoned England only to become a German, wrote a tremendous book called *The Foundations of the Nineteenth Century,* in which he proved that "true history begins from the moment when the German with mighty hand seizes the inheritance of antiquity." I presume that the creators of that inheritance did not make history. M. Chamberlain believed that if a man showed genius it was a proof of Teutonic blood: Dante's face struck him as characteristically German; he thought he heard unmistakable German accents in St. Paul's *Epistle to the Galatians;* and though he was not quite certain that Christ was a German, he was confident that "whoever maintains that Christ was a Jew is either ignorant or dishonest." [3] Richard Wagner put the theory to music. After suffering poverty for fifty years, this great barbarian discovered that by adopting the Teutonic interpretation of history, and recalling the piety of his childhood, he might persuade the aristocracy of his country to pay the bills at Bayreuth.

NIETZSCHE. I loved him a great deal. But you are right, he was a charlatan.

A. F. Every genius is. Without a little quackery he would starve to death. It is especially necessary in democratic countries.

W. J. The *Zeitgeist* was in favor of the race theory in our day. Galton was reducing genius to inheritance, eugenics was beginning its campaign for aristocratic babies, Max Müller was vivifying philology with his theory of an "Aryan" race that had come from India and mastered Europe, and Weismann was "proving" (they prove many things in science—for a day) that the germ-plasm is hermetically sealed somewhere in our disreputable regions, and is immune to all influences from the environment. The biologists were betting on heredity, and so the historians bet on race.

---

[1] Todd, A. J., *Theories of Social Progress,* p. 275.
[2] Salter, W., *Nietzsche the Thinker,* p. 469.
[3] In Todd, p. 276.

A. F. Perhaps you do not know, gentlemen, that M. Madison Grant, who has just come to us from New York, is an authority on this subject. In my old age I saw a copy of his book, *The Passing of the Great Race*. I took it up presuming that he meant the French; when I saw that he meant the Germans and the English I concluded that it was not necessary for me to read any further to know that he was mistaken.

VOLTAIRE. Tell us your views, M. Grant. And do not be disturbed if M. France does not agree with them. There is always a slight possibility that we Frenchmen are wrong, and the rest of the world right.

GRANT. My theory differs from Chamberlain's, or M. Gobineau's. I reject the "Teutonic" race as a mixture of various stocks not yet fused into unity. I limit my argument to what I call the Nordic race, which in our day is most distinctively seen in those Germans who are of Baltic origin, and those Englishmen and Americans who are of Anglo-Saxon descent. But these are modern variants; the race is as old as history. The Nordics first appear as the Sacæ introducing Sanskrit into India; they were white invaders from the north, and invented the caste system to prevent inter-marriage and the depreciation of their stock. "Caste" means color, and its function is not economic but biological; it aims not to monopolize opportunity but to protect blood.

We next find the Nordics as Cimmerians pouring down through the Caucasus into Persia; as Achæans, Phrygians and Dorians conquering Asia Minor and Greece; as Umbrians and Oscans overrunning Italy. Wherever they go they are warriors, adventurers, sea-explorers, Vikings, rulers, disciplinarians, organizers, in sharp contrast to the other European races—the quiet and acquiescent "Alpines," and the passionate, temperamental, unstable and indolent "Mediterraneans." [1] The contrast is clearest in Italy. The southern Italians, who are of the Mediterranean type, are largely descendants of nondescript slaves of all races, chiefly from southern and eastern lands, who were imported by the Romans under the Empire to work their vast estates. The northern Italians are of finer stock, because for the most part they are descendants of the German invaders from the time of Cæsar to that of Charlemagne; it was these men who made the Renaissance in Florence, and then took it with them to Rome; Dante, Raphael, Titian, Michelangelo, Leonardo da Vinci, were all of the Nordic type. [2] In Greece the Achæan Nordics intermarried with the peoples they had conquered, and produced the brilliant and subtle Athenians of Pericles' day.

A. F. It was very careless of the Achæans to intermarry that way, don't you think?

VOLTAIRE. Don't mind him; go on; your theories are fascinating.

[1] Grant, M., *The Passing of the Great Race,* pp. 155, 158.
[2] *Ibid.*, pp. 65, 191.

GRANT. The Dorians intermarried least, and became the Spartans, a military Nordic race ruling over "Mediterranean" Helots. The upper-class Greeks were blond, the lower classes dark. The gods of Olympus are almost all described as blond; it would be difficult to imagine a Greek artist painting a brunet Venus. In Church pictures today all angels are shown as blond, while the denizens of the lower regions revel in deep brunetness. Most ancient tapestries show a blond earl on horseback, and a dark-haired churl holding the bridle. In depicting the Crucifixion no artist hesitates to make the two thieves brunet in contrast with the blond Saviour. This is something more than a convention; for such quasi-authentic traditions as we have of Our Lord indicate His Nordic, possibly Greek, physical and moral attributes.[1]

A. F. It is very unfortunate to be a great man. You starve all your life, and after your death you are made into every form but your own. But proceed; let the Nordics have Christ, since the Jews do not want Him.

GRANT. Greece fell before Macedon when the Greek stock had been diluted by too much intermarriage. The Macedonians were pure Nordics; and they conquered Persia too when the Persians weakened themselves by mingling their blood with non-Nordic Asiatic types. We do not see the Nordics in triumph again until the age of the great invasions. They had found their way to the Baltic, had peopled Scandinavia, and from that region they had spread in a hundred directions and exploits as Goths, Ostrogoths, Visigoths, Cymri, Cimbri, Gauls, Teutons, Suevi, Vandals, Saxons, Angles, Jutes, Frisians, Danes, Lombards, Franks, Normans, and Varangians. There is hardly a country in Europe which these marauders did not overrun, and where they do not yet rule. Rome was conquered first; and the great dukes of the Renaissance were Nordic types. Gaul was conquered again and again; the Franks were Nordic Teutons, and gave France its German name; Charlemagne was a German emperor, had his capital at Aachen, and used German as the official language of his court. Till the Thirty Years' War, Europe was dominated by Germany. Chivalry, knighthood, feudalism, class distinctions, racial pride, personal and family honor, the duel, were Nordic habits and traits. It was this same domineering type that made the Norman conquest of France, Sicily, and England; the same that as Varangians subjected Russia and ruled it till 1917; the same that colonized America, Australia, and New Zealand; the same that opened up India and China to European trade, and set their sentinels in every major Asiatic port. It is these men who scale the highest mountains, use the Alps as a playground, and make useless trips to the Poles.[2]

I regret that this masterful race is passing away. It lost its footing in France in 1789; as Camille Desmoulins told his audiences at the cafés,

[1] *Ibid.*, p. 199.
[2] *Ibid.*, pp. 146, 165.

the Revolution was the revolt of the original French stock (of the "Alpine" French, as we should say) against the Teuton chieftains who had conquered them under Clovis and Charlemagne and had maintained their feudal sway over France for a thousand years. The suicidal militarism of the Nordics in the Crusades, the Thirty Years' War, the Napoleonic Wars, and the World War depleted the Nordic stock everywhere. In England and Germany the Nordics seem doomed by their low birth-rate; in Russia they have fallen before barbarians led by a Mongol and a Jew; in America they are rapidly losing power and influence through immigration from southern Europe, the high birth-rate of their competitors, and the democratic empowerment of numbers and manipulation of masses.[1]

A. F. A good phrase, Monsieur, a good phrase.

GRANT. The result is a deterioration of culture, a debasement of standards and taste, in both England and America. The songs, the music, the dances, the plays, the politicians, that dominate, now come from the dregs of the people. A few years ago I thought that strict control of immigration, and the severest condemnation of intermarriage between Nordic and non-Nordic types, would save the great race in America. But already it is too late. Differences in the birth-rate will complete the work begun by immigration and intermarriage. By the year 2000 the Nordics will have fallen from power everywhere. And with them the civilization of Europe and America will disappear in a new barbarism welling up from below.

A. F. It is a terrible prospect. But the Alpine French, the Italians, the Austrians, and the Russians will be left. Let us console ourselves. It is clear that the Russians do not intend to be destroyed by democracy. What villainy it was of those Nordics, the English, to invent the sovereignty of numbers! But tell me, Monsieur, do you really think these Nordics are such wonderful fellows? They were great warriors, pirates, marauders, tax-gatherers; but is this civilization?

GRANT. They organized the states of modern Europe and made our civilization possible.

NIETZSCHE. If they organized the states of modern Europe the case against them is very strong. It would have been better if these modern states had never been born. Then the popes would have ruled a united Europe; and in its security the Church, as in Renaissance Italy, would have mellowed into art and freedom, and the educated classes would have been as free as at Paris and Vienna today, or as at Rome under Leo X; while the people would have received the consolations of the sacraments.

GRANT. You are a pagan, Sir.

NIETZSCHE. Certainly. How could I be otherwise, having learned Greek?

A. F. The other day some of our company held a kind of caucus, and

[1] *Ibid.,* p. 173.

voted, as the Americans vote on biology, to determine who were the greatest among us in this realm where our lives are for a time prolonged. I think I can remember the successful candidates. There was Shakespeare, of course; no one yet dares to leave him out; though I trust M. Shaw will one day enlighten you about that jolly Bombasto Furioso. There was the mad Beethoven, and Michelangelo's Moses. And Jesus, a really lovable young man when you get to know him. Plato represented the philosophers, and Leonardo the artists. I wouldn't let them omit M. de Voltaire. Herr Nietzsche insisted on including Napoleon, and Brandes persuaded us to admit Cæsar. I wanted Rabelais for number ten, but the electors, with the stupidity characteristic of assemblies, chose Darwin instead. How does the list strike you, M. Grant?

GRANT. Fairly well.

A. F. You should not have answered before considering how unfair that list is to your Nordics. You get three names out of ten; the rest are Jewish, Greek, and Latin. I am driven to conclude that in art and letters, in philosophy and religion, in the things of the mind and the heart, the Nordics have not been as preëminent as in the science of butchering one another, pillaging their neighbors, and levying taxes.

GRANT. You make me very uncomfortable, Monsieur. I shall have my revenge when Brousson arrives.

A. F. I shall buy him a return ticket.

GRANT. But after all, you may be partly right. The Mediterranean race, while inferior in bodily stamina to both the Nordics and the Alpines, is probably the superior of both in intellectual attainments. In the field of art its preëminence is unquestioned. So far as modern Europe is concerned, culture came from the south and not from the north. The ancient Mediterranean world was of this race; the long-sustained civilization of Egypt, the brilliant Minoan empire of Crete, the mysterious empire of Etruria (the predecessor and teacher of Rome), the Hellenic states and colonies throughout the Mediterranean and the Black Sea, the maritime and mercantile power of Phœnicia and its mighty colony, imperial Carthage—all were creations of this Mediterranean race. To it belongs the chief credit for the classic civilization in Europe.[1]

A. F. Your admissions are very generous. I will not press you about the superiority, in everything but war, of the Athenians, who were a product of Nordic and "Mediterranean" intermarriage, to the Spartans, who were, you say, pure Nordics. I will merely ask you to look at Scandinavia, which has produced the terrible Ibsen and the Nobel prize (yes, they were very good to me); compare the contributions to civilization of these "pure" Nordics with the art, the literature, the science and the philosophy of those Renaissance Italians who, if I may believe you, were the result of inter-

[1] *Ibid.*, pp. 147–8. 198

marriage. Would you not have to say, then, that the intermarriage of Nordics with non-Nordics produces good results?

GRANT. Sometimes.

NIETZSCHE. What is a race?

GRANT. It is as indefinable as anything else that is immediately evident. Approximately it is a group of people of similar origin, having, in the great majority of its members, a characteristic color of the skin, texture of the hair, shape of the head, and stature of the body.

A. F. When I was in England M. Hilaire Belloc told me of a man who had found that he was Nordic by descent and Alpine by head-form, stature, color, and hair. A certain woman, he assured me, had five children, of whom two were Mediterranean, one Alpine, one Nordic, and one a mixture of all three. All these types may be found in England, but M. Belloc suggested that perhaps the lady had traveled.[1]

GRANT. I will agree that no race is pure, that every individual has in him the blood of many stocks; but surely the English aristocracy are a purer breed than the Americans who are to come of the present "blood-chaos" in the United States.

BUCKLE. I understand that the English are the product of the mingling of Celts, Romans, Angles, Saxons, Jutes, Danes, Normans . . .

GRANT. But most of these were varieties of the Nordic type. Ultimately they were all of one race.

RATZEL. Gentlemen, may I invade the argument? I have studied the question carefully, and have come to the conclusion that all three of the so-called races of Europe are branches of one original group which, coming from the east, was primitively like the "Alpines," but which, spreading to north and south, was moulded into different types, "Nordic" and "Mediterranean," by different geographical and economic condition.[2] Differences of race are produced by differences in the environment, so that the racial factor can hardly be called the decisive element in history. Northern peoples rapidly take on the characteristics of the southern peoples when they live for many generations in the tropics. Mountaineers all over the world tend to be tall, regardless of their race. I have observed that those Germans who have long lived in southern Brazil have lost their "Nordic" vigor; like the English in South Africa they sit under a tree and hire a colored man to work for them.[3] Racial characteristics are in the long run a result of geographical environment.[4]

[1] Langdon-Davies, J., *The New Age of Faith*, p. 244.

[2] Cf. Ripley, W. Z., *The Races of Europe*.

[3] Inge, Dean R. W., *Outspoken Essays*, Second Series, p. 225.

[4] Dr. C. B. Davenport, in a paper read at the November 21, 1928, session of the National Academy of Sciences, claimed to have proved native differences of mental capacity between whites and blacks; but his report does not give us sufficient assurance that the results were not affected by differences in mental training and opportunity.

V. THE ECONOMIC INTERPRETATION OF HISTORY

MARX. Not so fast, Herr Ratzel. Why merely "geographical environment"? Why shouldn't stature be determined by diet as well as by climate or race? I am shocked that this discussion has gone so far without a mention of the economic interpretation of history.

VOLTAIRE (*to* ANATOLE FRANCE). Who is this dark grim beard of a god?

A. F. (*to* VOLTAIRE). He is the Socrates of the Barricades, Karl Marx. He has written a terrible book proving that the strong exploit the weak.

VOLTAIRE. It is a very novel discovery. Does he tell us how to stop it?

A. F. The weak are to rise in their might and overthrow the strong.

VOLTAIRE (*to* MARX). What is your theory, Monsieur?

MARX. Nothing could be simpler. The basic factor in history is at all times the economic factor: the mode of production and distribution, the division and consumption of wealth, the relationship of employer to employee, the class-war between the rich and the poor, these determine, in the long run, every other aspect of life—religious, moral, philosophical, scientific, literary and artistic. The sum of the relations of production constitutes the economic structure of society, the real foundation on which rise legal and political superstructures, and to which correspond the definite forms of social consciousness.[1]

VOLTAIRE. This is very abstract, and gives me a slight headache. Perhaps Monsieur will give us a few illustrations.

MARX. Very well: I will retrace the whole history of humanity from the viewpoint of my theory.

A. F. I trust you will remember my tale of the king and the historians.

MARX. First, I do not divide history into ancient, medieval and modern; that in itself is a medieval division. I divide human history into the hunting and pastoral stage, the agricultural and handicraft stage, the industrial and machine stage. The great events are not political but economic; they are not the battle of Marathon, or the assassination of Cæsar, or the French Revolution, but the Agricultural Revolution—the passage from hunting to tillage—and the Industrial Revolution—the passage from domestic industry to the factory system.

VOLTAIRE. That is to say, the forms of poverty and wealth change from time to time.

MARX. Not only that. Economic conditions determine the rise and fall of empires; political, moral and social conditions have little to do with it; immorality, luxury, refinement—these are not causes but effects. At the bottom of everything is the nature of the soil: is it fit for tillage, or only for hunting and pasturage? Does it contain useful minerals? Egypt became

---

[1] Marx, K., *Critique of Political Economy*, preface.

powerful because of its iron, ancient Britain because of its tin, modern Britain because of its iron and coal. The failing silver mines of Athens weakened her, the gold of Macedon strengthened Philip and Alexander. Rome fought Carthage for the silver mines of Spain, and decayed when her soil lost its fruitfulness.

A. F. I know nothing of history but the useless frills of literature and philosophy; but I can support you, Monsieur, from the wars of my own day; they were all fought for the natural resources, or trade opportunities, of some foreign land.

MARX. Thank you. You speak of trade opportunities; these, too, play a great role in history. Why did the Greeks fight the Trojan War? For the beauty of a loose woman? Hardly; if Helen ever existed she served only as a legend to cover economic considerations; the Greeks were anxious to oust their rivals, the Phœnicians and their allies, from a city that controlled the water route to Asia. Even Agamemnon knew how to make catch-words.

W. J. So her face never launched a thousand ships?

MARX. Not to my knowledge. And you know, of course, that the naval fleet built by Themistocles against Xerxes was the basis of Athenian commercial power in the fifth century before Christ, and that the money of the Delian Confederacy made Athens rich enough to adorn the Acropolis with temples; it was stolen gold that made this perfect art. Most great periods of art have come after the amassing of national wealth. But Athens had made the mistake of depending upon imported food; all that Sparta had to do was to blockade it. Athens starved, surrendered, and never recovered.

Note, incidentally, how the enslavement of the workers in Greece prevented industrial invention and development; how the enslavement of women prevented the growth of normal love; how this resulted in homosexualism, and how this affected Greek sculpture. The mode of production in material things determines the general character of the social, political, and spiritual processes of life. It is not the consciousness of men that determines their existence, but on the contrary their social existence determines their consciousness. The individual thinks that he has evolved his ideas, his systems of philosophy, his moral notions, his religious beliefs, his party prejudices, and his artistic preferences by logical and impartial reasoning, never knowing how profoundly the underlying economic conditions of his life mould his every thought.

MONTESQUIEU. How would you apply your theory to Rome?

MARX. Rome was essentially a slave-driving corporation; never were masters so ruthless or so corrupt. But what was the end of it all? The farmers were gradually forced into bankruptcy, rich men bought up the land, and imported slaves to till it. The slaves did their work listlessly and carelessly, the soil was ruined, and Rome had to depend upon foreign food. Great slave-revolts tore the country to pieces. At the same time, the trade between Europe and Asia began to pass less and less through Rome, more and more across the Bosphorus; Constantinople grew, and Rome declined.

BOSSUET. You cannot deny that during the Middle Ages it was religion, not economic affairs, that ruled men's lives.

MARX. This is only a superficial view. The power of the Church began in the poverty of ruined or enslaved peoples hungry for supernatural comfort and hope; it flourished on the ignorance and superstition that go with poverty, and with relapse from urban to rural life; and it established itself firmly through gifts and bequests, appropriations like the "donation of Constantine," tithes and levies and Peter's Pence, which together brought two-thirds of the arable land of Europe into the possession of the Church; this was the economic basis of her power. So with other aspects of the Middle Ages; they all had their economic causes. The Crusades were an attempt to recapture a trade route from the "infidels"; the Renaissance was the efflorescence of gold that had come to northern Italy as the result of renewed trade between Europe and the East through north-Italian ports; and the Reformation came when the princes of Germany made up their minds to keep for themselves the money that was pouring from the pockets of their people into the coffers of the Vatican.

BOSSUET. You are profoundly mistaken, Monsieur.

MARX. The French Revolution came not because the Bourbons were corrupt, nor because you, Voltaire, wrote brilliant satires; it came because through three hundred years a new economic class, the commercial bourgeoisie, had been rising towards equality with the land-owning aristocracy; and because at last they had acquired more wealth, and more economic power, than those gilded futilities who fluttered about the court of Louis XVI. Political power sooner or later follows economic power; successful revolutions are merely the political signatures to preceding economic victories. As Harrington expressed it many years ago, the form of government depends upon the distribution of the land: if most of it is owned by one man, you have monarchy; if it is owned by a few, you have aristocracy; if it is owned by the people, you get democracy.

GRANT. There is a great deal in that. Perhaps the fall in the proportion of land-owners to landless city-dwellers is one source of the break-down of democracy in America.

MARX. Why was America discovered? For Christianity's sake? No; for gold. Why did the English win it from the Spanish, the Dutch and the French? Because they had the money to build better fleets. Why did the Colonies revolt against England? Because they did not wish to pay unreasonable taxes, because they wanted to end the tyranny of English aristocrats holding power over them by royal grants of land; because they desired to trade without hindrance, both in rum and in slaves; and because they wished to pay their debts in a depreciated currency.

W. J. What's that?

MARX. Surely, Sir, you are aware of the researches by which your countryman, Professor Beard, has revealed the economic causes of the American Constitution, and of Jeffersonian Democracy? Or did you ever read Daniel Webster? "Our New England ancestors," said your great orator, "were on a general level in respect of property. Their situation demanded a parceling out and division of the lands, and it may be fairly said that this necessary act fixed the future frame and form of their government. The character of their political institutions was determined by the fundamental laws respecting property. . . . The freest government would not be long acceptable, if the tendency of the laws were to create a rapid accumulation of property in a few hands, and to render the great mass of the population dependent and penniless. In such a case the popular power must break in upon the rights of property, or else the influence of property must limit and control the exercise of popular power. Universal suffrage, for example, could not long exist in a community where there was great inequality of property." [1]

VOLTAIRE. That is an excellent speech, by both of you.

A. F. There is only one flaw in it from M. Marx's point of view, and that is the careless assumption of the original orator that the laws can create changes in the distribution of property. If that is so, your theory, Monsieur, is in a bad way. You believe that political institutions are determined by economic conditions, and that revolutions can succeed only when they are backed by a group already possessed of the balance of economic power. Does not the Russian Revolution refute you?

MARX. Not at all; I will refute the Revolution. Slowly the political form must bend or break before the economic reality: a proletarian revolution in a country of peasants must bring, sooner or later, a government that will keep a proletarian show-window, perhaps, but will be essentially the instrument of those who control the land.

A. F. I am afraid that these brave Bolsheviks are not good Marxians.

MARX. I have always said that I was not a Marxian.

VOLTAIRE. Does it not seem to you, M. Marx, that a military dictatorship can sometimes maintain itself devilishly well though it represents no great economic power—as in the days of the Prætorian Guard?

MARX. Only for a time, Sir.

A. F. I do not know if you are acquainted, Monsieur, with what we moderns call birth-control; I believe you did not practise it. In effect it gives a great advantage to the Catholic Church, which in its ancient wisdom prohibits family-limitation among the faithful, and sits back patiently while the lower birth-rate among Protestants and philosophers slowly renders first Germany, then America, Catholic again. If the policy of the Church should succeed (and her silent foresight has won many battles), if

[1] Beard, C., *The Economic Basis of Politics*, p. 38.

the Reformation, and perhaps even the Enlightenment, should be undone by the birth-rate, would you not consider this a very important event? And yet it would hardly fall under an economic interpretation of history. Perhaps we need a biological interpretation of history?

MARX. You are mistaken, Sir. What are the causes of birth-control? They are economic causes: a higher standard of living, urban congestion, and land laws like those of your country, which compel parents to bequeath their property in equal shares to their sons.

GRANT. But surely you will admit that racial factors often outweigh economic factors?

MARX. Never.

GRANT. How else can you explain the conquest of Asia by the European Nordics?

MARX. By the accident of their priority in the Industrial Revolution. Watch your Nordics get out of Asia when China becomes an industrial country.

GRANT. But I have often seen great masses of people, such as American workmen on strike, or the whole American people in a presidential election, divide on racial rather than on economic lines.

MARX. Individuals and groups are often moved by noneconomic motives—racial, religious, patriotic, sexual; but these individuals and groups, where their action enters into the determination of history, are manipulated by persons quite conscious of economic interest. Are the politicians who send soldiers to battle, with martial speech and music, altogether innocent of economic motive? They say that Columbus sought the Indies to present new Christians to the Pope; it is quite possible, though improbable, that the old man had such ideas in his head; but do you suppose that Ferdinand and Isabella helped him for such reasons? Individuals may act for other than economic motives; they may sacrifice themselves to their children, their fellow-men, or their gods; but these stray deeds of heroism or insanity have no importance in determining the rise and fall of nations. I do not apply economic determinism to individuals.

W. J. I am glad to hear it. I used to think that moral forces, like the revulsion against slavery under Wilberforce and Garrison, had something to do with history; but I have no doubt you will correct me on that point.

MARX. There are no moral forces in history. Economic factors lurk behind every great event. Garrison made no headway against slavery by moral appeals; and when Lincoln freed the slaves it was as a war measure, intended to weaken the South; he said frankly that he would have left them slaves if that would have made for peace. The South wanted to separate from the North because it was being injured by the tariff, and had lost all hope of ever again controlling Congress; the North wanted to keep the South as a market for manufactures and a source of food and raw materials.

The "ideals" on either side were fig-leaves. In every case an ideal is a material need phraseologically disguised as a moral aspiration.

A. F. Would you say that also of socialist ideals?

MARX. Yes.

A. F. Alas!

VI. THE PSYCHOLOGICAL INTERPRETATION OF HISTORY

HEGEL. Sir, I think your views are an outrage. Taking all these theories together, I find every factor included except the human mind. To hear you one would suppose that intelligence and courage are worthless in this world; and that since the same geographical, economic, and racial conditions affect individuals, and sometimes nations, alike, it will make no difference whether the individual is a genius or a fool, or whether the citizens are intelligent or ignorant. Your play has left out the hero.

MARX. There are no heroes. Thought is the instrument of desire, and in groups and nations desires are always economic; as Bismarck said, there is no morality between nations. And the great man too is merely an instrument, the mouthpiece and agent of mass movements or impersonal forces; if he is not this he is an ineffectual crank, and history passes him by without noticing him. Ideas are to history as thought is to individual action; in either case the real cause of the result is not the idea, but some desire of which the individual need not be conscious at all. Indeed, the whole culture of an age bears the same relation to its economic life as thought does to the body; it is an interpretation and expression of underlying processes and powers.

HEGEL. I am astounded that a German should speak so. Apparently, since the great days of Kant, Lessing, Herder, Goethe, Schiller, Beethoven and myself, Germany has lost its soul in industry; it produces chemists and mechanics now, but not philosophers and artists; and so it interprets all the world and all history in terms of machinery. I should like to hear Goethe tell you what he thinks of your theory. Or Herder, who far back in 1787 stirred us all with his *Ideas for a Philosophy of the History of Mankind;* Herder, who saw all history as the education of the human race.

A. F. Tell us your own view of history, Herr Professor. When I was a boy my country was full of your name, and Cousin swore by you. To tell the truth, none of us could make head or tail of what you were driving at. Here in these Elysian Fields, face to face, we have at last a chance to understand Hegel.

HEGEL. Sir, I had to be obscure, lest fools should understand me. It was no easy task to reveal to my generation that intelligence exists in this universe only in so far as we put it there, and that God is not so much the First Cause as the Final Cause. I had to speak in such a way that I could put a good face on matters if I saw the hangman coming down the street.

VOLTAIRE. I can understand, Monsieur. After the death of Frederick, thinking was illegal in Germany.

HEGEL. But in fact, my philosophy was very simple. God is the Absolute, and the Absolute is the sum total of all things in their development. God is Reason, and Reason is that web and structure of natural law within which Life or Spirit moves and grows. God is Spirit, and Spirit is Life. History is the Development of Spirit, that is (without capitals), it is the growth of life. At the beginning life is an obscure force unconscious of itself; the process of history is the coming of Spirit or Life to self-consciousness and freedom. Freedom is the essence of life, as gravity is the essence of water. History is the growth of freedom; its goal is that the Spirit may be completely and consciously free.[1]

VOLTAIRE. This, M. Hegel, is really the language of revolution.

HEGEL. Certainly; I meant it so. I saw three stages in history: first, the Oriental stage, in which only one is free; second, the Greco-Roman stage, in which a few are free; and third, the modern stage, in which the Spirit becomes conscious of its freedom, organizes it in the state, and so makes all men free.

MARX. We members of Young Germany could not forgive you for your exaltation of Prussia—the most reactionary of European states; but we saw the secret meaning of your metaphysics, and we valued your dialectic. How my ears still ring with the memory of "thesis, antithesis, synthesis!" Krause told us that "the old world is the thesis, the new world is the antithesis, and Polynesia is the synthesis." We students had a better formula: "Thirst is the thesis, beer the antithesis, and the synthesis is under the table."[2]

HEGEL. Laugh if you will, you brood of my Left Wing; but see how all history, like all metaphysics, lights up under the flash of my dialectic! Every age contains in itself some subtle contradiction, just as your capitalism does; development makes the contradiction evident and acute; at last there is a division, war, revolution, break-up; the opposed elements, like those chromosomes which Bateson showed us the other day, reunite in fresh formations, and a new age begins. The formula helps you to predict the future: out of one stage you do not get its opposite, but a synthesis of it with its opposite. So capitalism, in conflict with socialism, leads not to socialism, but to state capitalism: the revolutionists become capitalists, call themselves the state, and though many people suffer, the matter is advanced, and a higher stage is reached.

MARX. But why, then, didn't you welcome the young rebels of your time as the heralds of the future? Why did you pretend that there was more liberty in Prussia than in ancient Greece? You thought that Prussia repre-

[1] Hegel, *Philosophy of History*, pp. 18–21.
[2] Nordau, *op. cit.*, p. 71.

sented the highest civilization ever known; and as Prussia had a monarchy, whose professor you were, you shuffled history to show that in the lowest stage, where only one is free, we have despotism; in the second stage, where some are free, we have aristocracy or democracy; and in the highest stage, where all are free, we have monarchy! God in heaven!—monarchy! You assorted and labeled the nations like a boy arranging postage stamps. You evolved the formula that the process of development forces civilization farther and farther west, and that the more western a civilization is, the higher it is. As a result you put Assyria above China, and you should have put America above Germany; but you preferred to be a patriot.

HEGEL. When you are in Rome you must do as the Romans do.

MARX. No, Sir; whether you are in Rome or elsewhere, there is only one truth.

A. F. You speak, Monsieur, as if you had it, this truth. Do not be so sure. Perhaps it does not even exist.

CARLYLE. If you will let an old man put in a word—you have still left genius out of history, and so, with all your palaver, we're not much better off than before. As I take it, Universal History, the history of what man has accomplished in this world, is at bottom the History of the Great Men who have worked here. They were the leaders of men, these great ones; the modellers, patterns, and in a wide sense creators, of whatsoever the general mass of men contrived to do or to attain; all things that we see standing accomplished in the world are properly the outer material result, the practical realization and embodiment, of Thoughts that dwelt in the Great Men sent into the world; the soul of the whole world's history, it may justly be considered, were the history of these. Could we see *them* well, we should get some glimpses into the very marrow of the world's history.[1]

W. J. Hear! Hear! This is rare good sense, Carlyle; it's high time we should be getting at the source of the *ideas* that move the world.

HEGEL. Be calm, gentlemen. The ideas are what I called the *Zeitgeist.* All the thinking and feeling in an epoch constitute the Spirit of the Age; and everything in history is the result of this. (I am told that Herr Lamprecht is saying the same thing over again today, but that he covers up his theft by a new phrase, the "social psyche.") Great men have efficacy only when they are the unconscious instruments of the *Zeitgeist.* If an exceptional man is not in harmony with the Spirit of the Age, he is wasted—he might just as well never have been. The genius whom posterity acclaims may not have been greater than his predecessors; they too had placed their stones upon the pile; but somehow he has the good fortune to come last, and when he places his stone the arch stands self-supported. Such individuals had no consciousness of the general Idea they were unfolding; but they had an insight into the requirements of the time; they knew what was ripe for

[1] Carlyle, T., *Heroes and Hero-Worship,* p. 1.

development.[1] Great men, therefore, are not so much creators as midwives; they help the time to bring forth that which is already in the womb.

CARLYLE. I do not know about your midwives, Herr Hegel; but I know that without Cromwell history would have been different; that without Frederick it would have been different; that without Napoleon mankind could never have forgiven the French Revolution. Disbelief in heroes is the ultimate atheism.

NIETZSCHE (*as if to himself*). Hero-worship is the relic of the worship of gods. And yet—and yet nobody knoweth any longer how to revere. Dead are all gods; now we will that Superman live!

VOLTAIRE. Is he mad?

A. F. He is inspired, Master.

W. J. But I am interested in this Great Man theory of history. What are the causes that make communities change from generation to generation— that make the England of Queen Anne, for example, so different from the England of Elizabeth? Herr Marx says, the changes are irrespective of persons, and independent of individual control. I don't believe it. The difference is due to the accumulated influence of individuals, of their examples, their initiatives, and their decisions. No, Mr. Marx, the masses do not accomplish much in history; they follow the lead of exceptional men. In a generation Bismarck turned metaphysical Germany into militaristic and imperial Germany; in a generation Napoleon took France, pacific through exhaustion and disgust, and by the hypnotism of his example and his genius filled it with his own fever for glory. Theodore Roosevelt came near doing the same thing with America. I hold with Emerson, who said, "I accept the saying of the Chinese Mencius: 'A sage is the instructor of a hundred ages. When the manners of Loo are heard of, the stupid become intelligent, and the wavering determined.'" And I believe my friend M. Tarde will agree with me; for my own notion of history would be incomplete if I could not add to it his doctrine of imitation.[2]

TARDE. Yes, dear colleague, I surely agree with you. There are little men and big men in the world, and it is only the big men who change things. Given all the geographical, racial and economic conditions you like, some one must take the initiative in every event and in every change. The small man never takes the initiative; he is afraid; and probably he never dreams that any need exists for aught but the most traditional responses; custom and habit suffice him. But the great man feels the need, the great man *thinks*, and everything is changed. Perhaps he fails. If he succeeds, a few lesser men, still exceptional, will imitate him. If they succeed, a wave of imitation runs like a flood through the community. One Japanese merchant

[1] *Op. cit.*, p. 30.
[2] Barnes, H. E., *The New History and the Social Sciences*, p. 87; Emerson, *Representative Men*, p. 17.

imitated Western methods and ideas; ten imitated him; now a hundred thousand have followed suit, and all Japan is transformed. Why was I a Catholic? Through imitation. Why was I a Frenchman?—that is, not a man different from you, Herr Hegel, in blood or race, but different in mannerisms and speech, in fashions and modes of feeling and thought. Because of imitation. The career of imitations is on the whole the only thing that is of interest to history. Back of economic and geographical factors lies the fundamental process of biology, the natural selection of favorable variations. The genius is the variant, his idea is the variation, the *Zeitgeist* and the physical conditions are the environment that permits the variation to succeed. History is the war between mediocrity and genius.[1]

CARLYLE. I thank ye, Sir; it is well said, God knows.

LESTER WARD. Gentlemen, there is only one thing to add, and that is that history is the history of great inventions. Behind economic changes are mechanical changes, behind these is the progress of natural science, and behind this is the solitary thinking of the exceptional man. Great men may not be the causes of the events usually featured in history—wars, elections, migrations, etc.; but they are the causes of the inventions and discoveries that remake the world, and change every generation from the last. The growth of knowledge is the essence of history.

BUCKLE. You are right. The political history of every country is to be explained by the history of its intellectual progress.[2]

WARD. You wished to know, M. Voltaire, by what steps man had passed from barbarism to civilization. By inventions. The important men in American history are not the politicians, not the presidents, but the inventors— Fulton, Whitney, Morse, McCormick, the Wright brothers, Edison; the effects of the work of these men will continue for centuries after the names of the presidents are forgotten. It was the steam-engine that made the nineteenth century; it is electricity, chemistry and the airplane that will make the twentieth.[3]

MARX. I admit that behind economic changes lie new inventions. But technical advances, and even scientific research, are due to economic needs and demands; a technical want gives more impetus to science than ten universities. And every invention is a last step in a lengthy search; it comes by small, sometimes imperceptible, increments; and it is due in the long run to economic necessities and wants.[4]

A. F. It is due to the needs of our life, Monsieur, of which economics is but a part. Some inventions, and much history, have been due to the need for love, which has no economic base; indeed when love touches economics

[1] *Laws of Imitation,* p. 139.
[2] Buckle, *op. cit.,* vol. i, p. 422.
[3] Barnes, *op. cit.,* p. 18.
[4] Friedrich Engels, in Barnes, p. 393n.

it begins to die. And why, on your theory, should men have written music?

MARX. It is an excrescence, an accident, a by-product, like coal-tar and soap.

NIETZSCHE. Life without music would be a mistake.

A. F. Let us not argue any longer. Yes, M. de Montesquieu, M. Buckle, M. Ratzel: we live on the earth, and we shall always be limited by it, though we shall get around its barriers, and even fly over the Himalayas now and then. And it may be, M. Grant, that some races, through the long good fortune of a beneficent environment, are superior in physique, in blood, even in mental capacity, to some others; but let these best races change places with the lowest for a little thousand years, and see what happens. As for M. Marx, I do not expect to persuade him that you are all in the right as well as he; I know that that will not satisfy him. But you, Professor Hegel, will be content to accept the Great Man if MM. James, Tarde and Carlyle will accept your *Zeitgeist* as the mental environment that selects. All in all I see that we shall agree well enough if we can doubt ourselves a little.

For my part I shall continue to care only for great men, whether they are the causes of history or not. I would rather have France's ten greatest heroes of the mind than all the rest of France without them. And remember, when you write history, that great events, whatever their causes, speak through great men. Do not take all genius from your pages; I assure you that your charts and your statistics will not enable me to feel the past as when I am made to see it through the eyes of genius. It is as if, in great men, all the threads that wove the past together are brought to unity for our enlightenment. How could we understand and forgive Germany without Goethe, or England without Shakespeare, or France without M. de Voltaire?

VOLTAIRE. Come, it is late. Even the immortals must sleep.

VII. COMPOSITE HISTORY

"The old man is correct," said Philip, as we picked our way up the hill to the road that would lead us home; "all these theories of history are foolish fragments when taken separately, and have sense only when put together. I'm tired of analysis; I'm hungry for synthesis."

"The wisest thing said to-night," I suggested, "was Voltaire's remark, apparently stolen from Croce, that history should be written only by philosophers, because 'they will look at things in the large.' There's the whole thing in a word."

"But you forget how big a thing history is," Ariel protested. "No man can live long enough to get it in full perspective—not even on a vegetarian diet."

"That's true," said I. "We need specialists to supply the philosophers with data—in history just as in science; but in both cases the matter leads to destructive nonsense if no unity pulls these special parts together. Philosophy ought to be to history what it ought to be to science—total correlation."

We walked in silence for a while, drunk with gods and stars. Then Philip—

"Do you know, this discussion suggests an entirely new way of writing history. Usually, when a man writes, say, a 'History of Greece,' he means a history of the political—or at most the economic and political—life of Greece. Then another man comes along and writes a history of Greek industry and commerce, an economic survey like Zimmern's. Another gives us a history of Greek religion, another of Greek philosophy, another of Greek literature, another of Greek social life, another of Greek art. And we students are expected to put all these fragments together and form a picture of the whole complex life of Greece; we're supposed to do what is considered too big a job for even the most learned historian to attempt. The life of a people is torn into pieces, each part is artificially isolated from the rest, and we study it in longitudinal sections, getting only the relationships of sequence and time, and losing all the correlations of mutual influence, of illuminating conflict, of coöperation. What a way of describing the past!

"Shredded history," said Ariel.

"Philosophers have no courage today," I complained. "They choose little jobs—they will discuss, for example, the question whether Plato means A or means B; whether the sun is in the sky, or just in our heads; whether an orange is yellow in the dark, etc. I think they're afraid of the universe since the Church stopped telling them what to think."

"Well, I have an idea," said Philip. "History as she is writ has been longitudinal-section history; you take one topic, like politics, or philosophy, or science, and trace its transformation, growth, etc., over a long lapse of time. We'll call that shredded history, as Ariel has named it. Now why shouldn't we have, in addition to this (and admitting the need of these special studies), a sort of cross-section history, in which a man takes one period, like the age of Pericles, or the age of Voltaire, limits himself to one century, if necessary to one generation, in order to make his job possible, and then undertakes to write the history of all phases of the nation's life in that period—economic, political, military, scientific, philosophical, religious, moral, literary, dramatic and artistic? Our trouble is that we're too much under the influence of the idea of evolution; we think of everything as in a stream of lineal sequence and causation; we think of Plato's philosophy, for instance, as caused by Socrates', of Aristotle's as caused by Plato's, of Spinoza's as caused by Descartes's. But there's a collateral causation, too; events are the result not only of preceding conditions in their own field, but of conditions around them in other fields; Plato's philosophy might have been influenced less by Socrates than by the general political and cultural development of his time—say by the speeches he heard in the agora, or the plays he attended at the theatre, or the statues he saw in the temples and the squares; and Aristotle may have taken more of the color of his thought from his friends in Macedon than from his teacher in the Academy."

"Very good, Philip," said Ariel; "you're doing excellently."

"Don't laugh at me, Ariel. I'm serious. I want to see history written as a whole, I want to see all these activities of men and women in one age woven into unity, shown up in their correlations, their interdependence, their mutual influences; I want the past presented as it was—all together! Take the age of Napoleon: see how the political conditions depended largely upon economic conditions, how the fate of the Napoleonic Wars was decided by English gold, how behind Wellington lurked Rothschild; see how the literature reflected the political and religious issues of the time, as in Shelley and Byron and Chateaubriand; how the arts aped the revolutionary imitation of Rome, how Talma strutted the stage after the manner of Roscius; how the music took on an heroic and romantic tone, how Beethoven mirrors, sometimes consciously, the passions of the Revolution and the grandeur of Napoleon. The whole age was one; and not only in France, but in all Europe west of Russia. I want a history of that age which will show me the past united in all its phases, as it was when it was living."

"You ask too much," said Ariel; "it is impossible."

"Perhaps," I proposed, "it would be as possible to study all subjects in one period as it is to study all periods in one subject. It should be as practicable to write the history of the age of Voltaire as it was to write *The Decline and Fall of the Roman Empire,* or the *Essai sur les mœurs,* or Grote's *History of Greece.* In a sense, Philip, Symonds did what you are asking for when he wrote his seven volumes on the Renaissance."

"Yes it was magnificent. But I want every age done in that way. Think how much better our conception of history and human life would be if we had such works! Better yet, think what completer men we'd be if we studied history in that composite, rounded-out way! Oh, for Goethes, Leonardos, Aristotles!—gods of the total view!"

"Why shouldn't you write such a history yourself, Philip?" asked Ariel. "Example is everything. If it can be done, do it."

"I'd love to write the history of the nineteenth century in that way, limiting it, for human possibility, to Europe. Even then it would be too much for one lifetime. Perhaps the three of us together could do it. Would you join in? Think what a drama that century is! *Act I: The Napoleonic Age:* Revolution, Directory, *Coup d'état,* Chateaubriand, Mme. de Staël,

David, Ingres, Goethe, Fichte, Hegel, Beethoven, Wordsworth, Coleridge, Scott, Shelley, Keats, Byron, Pope Pius VII, De Maistre, Fulton, Austerlitz, Nelson, Trafalgar, Humboldt, Lavoisier, Laplace, Lamarck, Alexander I, Pushkin, Wellington, Waterloo, St. Helena, Curtain. *Act II: The Romantic Age:* Fichte, Schelling, Novalis, Schlegel, Dorothea Mendelssohn, Jean Paul, Hugo and *Hernani,* Gautier and his waistcoat, Balzac and Stendhal, De Musset and George Sand, Cuvier and St. Hilaire, Herschel and Lyell, Schopenhauer and Comte, Newman and the Oxford Movement, Stephenson and the steam engine, Carlyle and Macaulay, Turner and Delacroix, Weber and Mendelssohn, Schubert and Schumann, Heine and Chopin, Robert Owen and the Chartists, the Utopian Socialists and the machine-wreckers, Rothschild and Louis Philippe, Louis Blanc and Louis Napoleon, 1848 and revolution everywhere—what a climax! *Act III: The Realistic Age:* Napoleon III, Gladstone, Disraeli, Bismarck, Cavour; railroads and ocean liners, Dickens and Thackeray, Tennyson and Browning, George Eliot and the Brontës; above all, Darwin and Spencer; Huxley and Tyndall and the war with the bishops; Renan, Flaubert, Zola, De Maupassant, Sainte-Beuve and Taine, Corot and Millet, Lenbach and Constable, Liszt and Wagner, Gogol and Herzen, Bakunin and Lassalle, Marx and Engels, the International, Mazzini, Garibaldi, the liberation of Italy, the Franco-German War, Sedan and *débâcle,* the Third Republic and the Commune— 10,000 workers shot down in the streets of Paris. *Act IV: The Imperial Age:* inventions—electricity, telephone, telegraph, cables, wireless, steel, X-rays, Pasteur, Lister, Mendel, big industry, corporations, cartels, the European conquest of Asia, imperialism, naval competition, standing armies, Gambetta, Cézanne, Van Gogh, Anatole France, Debussy, Maeterlinck, Rossetti, Holman Hunt, Burne-Jones, Swinburne, Arnold, Wilde, Hardy, Shaw, Dostoievski, Turgeniev, Tolstoi, Gorki, Kropotkin, Moussorgsky, Tchaikovsky, Rimski-Korsakov, Grieg, Björnson, Ibsen, Verdi, Brahms, Nietzsche, Brandes, Loisy and the Modernists, Leo XIII and Sarah Bernhardt, Hauptmann and D'Annunzio, Grey and the Kaiser, Poincaré and Isvolski, the Archduke, Serajevo, 1914, madness and conflagration. Oh, to bring it all together in one narrative, in one picture—the great chaotic, intricate, marvelous life of Europe in the nineteenth century!"

"Let's do it," said Ariel. "I'll do the ladies. When shall we begin?"

"To-morrow," said Philip.

"But there's one thing," said Ariel, "that leaves me discontent with our vision of the immortals to-night. They never told us whether there is progress in history, or whether we can predict the future."

"Well," said Philip, "perhaps we shall meet them again."

CHAPTER XV

Is Progress a Delusion?

I. THE YOUTH OF PROGRESS

THE GREEKS, WHO SEEM, in the enchantment of distance, to have progressed more rapidly than any other people in history, have left us hardly any discussion of progress in all their varied literature. There is a fine passage in Æschylus (*Prometheus,* 451–515), where Prometheus tells how his discovery of fire brought civilization to mankind, and gives in fifty lines such a summary of the stages in cultural development as would be considered immorally modern in certain American states. And there is a fleeting reference to progress in Euripides (*Supplices,* 201–18). But there is no mention of the idea in Xenophon's Socrates, nor in Plato; and Aristotle's cold conservatism puts the notion implicitly out of court. The Greeks conceived history, for the most part, as a vicious circle; and the conclusion of the Stagyrite, that all arts and sciences had been invented and lost "an infinite number of times," strikes the note of classical opinion on the subject from Thales to Marcus Aurelius. The Stoics counseled men to expect nothing of the future. Even the Epicureans took their pleasures sadly, and seem to have felt, like Mr. Bradley, that this is "the best of all possible worlds, and everything in it is a necessary evil." [1] Hegesias the Cyrenaic pronounced life worthless, and advocated suicide; doubtless he lived as long as Schopenhauer.

Pessimism was to be expected in an Athens that had lost its freedom; but the same despair sounds in Latin letters at every stage of Roman history. Lucretius speaks of men *pedetentim progredientes*—progressing step by step; and yet he gives a brutally brief answer to the question of our chapter when he says, *Eadem omnia semper*—all things are always the same. Would the great poet and philosopher, if he could return to us, use the same word to describe our contemporary civilization? Surely he would be impressed by our immense multiplication of mechanisms and instru-

[1] *Appearance and Reality,* p. xiv.

mentalities for the achievement of every desire; but probably he would ask, in his unhappy way, whether the men and women who use these magnificent machines are finer human beings, mentally, physically or morally, than those unfortunate ancestors who had to use their legs. He would be interested to know that a young wife had killed her husband with a sashweight, and he would be driven to concede that mankind had taken many centuries to discover the admirable utility of sashweights in this regard. Inevitably, however, he would suggest that this was a difference of means and not of ends—that the business of killing husbands was a very ancient industry. *Plus ça change, plus c'est la même chose.* What if all our progress is an improvement in methods, but not in purposes?

The other Romans are worse than Lucretius; they not only doubt the future, but they praise the past. Horace is a *laudator temporis acti;* Tacitus and Juvenal deplore the degeneracy of their age; and Virgil turns from pleasant fancies of a new Saturnian glory to phrase with his melodious felicity the gloomy vision of an Eternal Recurrence, a perpetual cycle and aimless repetition of identical events.

> Alter erit tyum Tiphys, et altera quæ vehat Argo
> Delectos heroas; erunt etiam altera bella,
> Atque iterum ad Trojam magnus mittetur Achilles—

"there will be another Tiphys" (an ancient prophet) "and another Argo to carry beloved heroes; there will be also other wars, and great Achilles will again be sent to Troy." [1] The hour-glass of æons will turn over and pour out the unaltered past into an empty and delusively novel present. There is nothing new under the sun; all is vanity and a chasing after the wind. And Marcus Aurelius, after achieving almost the highest form of human existence—the union of statesman and philosopher in one man, writes:

> The rational soul wanders around the whole world and through the encompassing void, and gazes into infinity, and considers the periodic destructions and rebirths of the universe, and reflects that our posterity will see nothing new, and that our ancestors saw nothing greater than we have seen. A man of forty years, possessing the most moderate intelligence, may be said to have seen all that is past and all that is to come; so uniform is the world. [2]

What were the causes of the hostility or apathy of the Greeks to the idea of progress? Was it due, as Professor Bury thinks, to the brevity of their historical experience, the very rapidity with which their civilization

---

[1] Fourth Eclogue, quoted by Bury, J. B., *The Idea of Progress*, p. 12.
[2] Bury, p. 13.

reached its apex and sank again? Or was it due to their comparative poverty in written records of the past, and a consequent absence of the perspective that might have made them realize the measure of their own advance? They too had had a medieval era, and had climbed for a thousand years from barbarism to philosophy; but only towards the end of that ascent had writing graduated from bills of lading to the forms of literature. Parchment was too costly to be wasted on mere history. Or again, was this unconcern with progress due to the arrested development of Greek industry, the failure of the Greeks to move appreciably beyond the technology of Crete, or to produce in quantity those physical comforts that are at the basis of the modern belief in progress?

In the Middle Ages it was a like dearth of luxuries that kept the notion of progress in abeyance, while the hope of heaven became the center of existence. Belief in another world seems to vary directly with poverty in this one, often in the individual, always in the group. When wealth grows, heaven falls out of focus, and becomes thin and meaningless. But for a thousand years the thought of it dominated the minds of men.

Wealth came to Western Europe with the Renaissance and the Industrial Revolution; and as it multiplied, it displaced the hope of heaven with the lure of progress. That greatest single event in modern history—the Copernican revelation of the astronomic unimportance of the earth—made many tender souls unhappy; but its reduction of heaven to mere sky and space compelled the resilient spirit of man to form for itself a compensatory faith in an earthly paradise. Campanella, More and Bacon wrote Utopias, and announced the imminence of universal happiness. Europe, *nouveau riche,* imported luxuries, and exported ascetics and saints. Trade made cities, cities made universities, universities made science, science made industry, and industry made progress. Gargantua writes to Pantagruel: "All the world is full of savants, learned teachers, vast libraries." "In one century," says Pierre de la Ramée,[1] meaning 1450–1550, "we have seen a greater progress in men and works of learning than our ancestors had seen in the whole course of the previous fourteen centuries." This has an ironically contemporary sound; what century has not crowned itself with some spacious estimate of this kind? But such self-confidence was the key-note of the Renaissance: we hear it as an organ-point in every line of Francis Bacon, striking the dominant chord of the European as against the Asiatic soul; obviously the conception of progress is for industrial and secular civilization what the hope of heaven was for medieval Christendom. The dearest dogmas of the modern mind, the *crura cerebri* of all our social philosophy, are the beliefs in progress and democracy. If both of these ideas must be abandoned we shall be left intellectually naked and ridiculous beyond any generation in history.

[1] 1515–72.

II. PROGRESS *IN EXCELSIS*

The notion of progress found its first definite expression in the exuberant optimism of the eighteenth century. Rousseau was out of key, and preferred American savages, whom he had not seen, to the cruel Parisians who had rasped his nerves; he thought thinking a form of degeneracy, and preached a Golden Age of the past that echoed the Garden of Eden and the Fall of Man. But when we come to the irrepressible and undiscourageable Voltaire we catch at first breath the exhilarating air of the Enlightenment. This *"Grand Seigneur* of the mind" had no delusions about Indians; he knew that man was better off under civilization than under savagery. He was grateful for the slow and imperfect taming of the human brute, and he preferred Paris to the Garden of Eden.

It was his disciple Turgot and Condorcet who made the idea of progress the moving spirit of modern times. In the year 1793 a French aristocrat by the name of Condorcet (or, to do him full justice, Marie Jean Antoine Nicolas Caritat, Marquis de Condorcet) was hiding from the gullotine in a little *pension* on the outskirts of Paris. The incorruptible Robespierre, that consistently savage Rousseauian, had invited him to come and be abbreviated because, like Tom Paine, he had voted against the execution of the King. There in a lonely room, far from any friend, without a book to help him, and in a situation that might have warranted a pæan to pessimism and despair, Condorcet wrote the most optimistic book that has ever come from the hand of man, the great classic in the literature of progress— *Esquisse d'un tableau des progrès de l'esprit humain.* Having finished this magnanimous prophecy of the coming glory of mankind, Condorcet fled from Paris to a distant village inn; and there, thinking himself secure, he flung his tired body upon a bed, and fell asleep. When he awoke he was surrounded by *gendarmes,* who arrested him in the name of the Law. The next morning he was found dead on the floor of his cell in the village jail. He had always carried about with him a phial of poison to cheat the guillotine.

To read his book is to realize to what a bitterly disillusioned and sceptical generation we belong. Here was a man who had lost apparently everything, who had sacrificed privilege, position and wealth for the Revolution, who was now hunted to death by empowered barbarians, and who had to bear the culminating bitterness of seeing the Revolution, hope of the world, issue in chaos and terror; and yet his book represents the very zenith of man's hopefulness for man. Never before had men so believed in mankind—and perhaps never again since. What eloquence Condorcet pours forth, for example, on the subject of print! He is sure that it will redeem and liberate men; he has no premonition of the sensational press.

"Nature," he writes, "has indissolubly united the advancement of knowledge with the progress of liberty, virtue, and respect for the natural rights
of man." [1] Prosperity will "dispose men to humanity, to benevolence, and to
justice." And then he formulates one of the most famous and characteristic
doctrines of the Enlightenment: "No bounds have been fixed to the improvement of the human faculties; the perfectibility of man is absolutely
indefinite; the progress of this perfection, henceforth above the control of
every power that would impede it, has no other limit than the duration
of the globe upon which nature has placed us." [2]

And in conclusion he draws a tempting picture of the future—by which
he means our time. As knowledge spreads, slavery will decrease, both
among classes and among nations; "then will come the moment in which
the sun will observe free nations only, acknowledging no other master than
their reason; in which tyrants and slaves, priests and their stupid or hypocritical instruments, will no longer exist but in history and upon the stage." [3]
Science will double and treble the span of human life; woman will be
emancipated from man, the worker from the employer, the subject from
the king; perhaps, even, mankind will unlearn war. And he ends, passionately:

> How admirably calculated is this view of the human race to console the
> philosopher lamenting the errors, the flagrant acts of injustice, the crimes
> with which the earth is still polluted! It is the contemplation of this prospect
> that rewards him for all the efforts to assist the progress of reason and the
> establishment of liberty. He dares to regard these efforts as part of the eternal
> chain of the destiny of mankind; and in this persuasion he finds the true de-
> light of virtue, the pleasure of having performed a durable service which no
> vicissitude will ever destroy. . . . This sentiment is the asylum into which
> he retires, and to which the memory of his persecutors cannot follow him; he
> unites himself in imagination with man restored to his rights, delivered from
> oppression, and proceeding with rapid strides in the path of happiness; he
> forgets his own misfortunes; . . . he lives no longer to adversity, calumny
> and malice, but becomes the associate of these wiser and more fortunate
> beings whose enviable condition he so earnestly contributed to produce. [4]

What generous optimism! What courageous idealism, and what passion
for humanity! Shall we scorn more the naïve enthusiasm of Condorcet, or
the intellectual cowardice of our time, which, having realized so many of
his dreams, no longer dares to entertain the rest?

[1] *A Sketch of a Tableau of the Progress of the Human Spirit,* English translation,
p. 15.
[2] *Ibid.,* p. 9.
[3] P. 216.
[4] P. 244.

Behind this bright philosophy lay the Commercial and Industrial Revolutions. Here were new marvels, called machines; they could produce the necessaries, and some of the luxuries, of life at unprecedented speed and in undreamed-of quantity; it was only a matter of time when all vital needs would be met, and poverty would disappear. Bentham and the elder Mill thought, about 1830, that England could now afford universal education for its people; and that with universal education all serious social problems would be solved by the end of the century. Comte saw all history as a progress in three stages, from theology through metaphysics to science. Buckle's *History of Civilization* (1857) stimulated the hope that the spread of knowledge would mitigate all human ills. Two years later Darwin spoke: the secularization of the modern mind was enormously advanced, and the idea of a coming Utopia replaced not merely Dante's filmy heaven but Rousseau's golden past. Spencer identified progress with evolution, and looked upon it as an inevitable thing. Meanwhile inventions poured from a thousand alert minds; riches visibly grew; nothing seemed hard or impossible to a science at last free from theological chains; the stars were weighed, and men accepted bravely the age-long challenge of the bird. What could not man do? What could we not believe of him in those undoubting days before the War?

III. THE CASE AGAINST PROGRESS

Nevertheless, even in the midst of that mounting wealth and power, and that ever accelerated speed, which have characterized the civilization of the West, voices were raised to question the reality or the worth of progress. "At all times," said Machiavelli, at the height of the exuberant Renaissance, "the world of human beings has been the same, varying indeed from land to land, but always presenting the same aspect of some societies advancing towards prosperity, and others declining." [1] Fontenelle, in his *Dialogues of the Dead* (1683), pictured Socrates and Montaigne discussing the problem of progress, apparently in Hell, where all philosophers go. Socrates is anxious to hear of the advances that mankind has made since his fatal drinking bout; and he is chagrined to learn that men are still for the most part brutes. Montaigne assures him that the world has degenerated; there are no longer such powerful types as Pericles, Aristides, or Socrates himself. The old philosopher shrugs his shoulders. "In our days," he says, "we esteemed our ancestors more than they deserved; and now our posterity esteem us more than we deserve. There is really no difference between our ancestors, ourselves, and our posterity."

[1] Bury, *op. cit.*, p. 31.

And Fontenelle sums the matter up pithily: "The heart always the same, the intellect perfecting itself; passions, virtues, vices unaltered; knowledge increasing." [1]

"The development of humanity," said Eckermann, "seems to be a matter of thousands of years." "Who knows?" replied Goethe, "perhaps of millions. But let humanity last as long as it will, there will always be hindrances in its way, and all kinds of distress, to make it develop its powers. Men will become cleverer and more intelligent, but not better, nor happier, nor more effective in action, at least except for a limited period. I see the time coming when God will take no pleasure in the race, and must again proceed to a rejuvenated creation." [2] "The motto of history," said Schopenhauer, "should run, *Eadem, sed aliter*"—the same theme, with variations. Mankind does not progress, said Nietzsche, it does not even exist; or it is a vast physiological laboratory where a ruthless nature forever makes experiments; where some things in every age succeed, but most things fail. So concludes Romantic Germany.

Disraeli was one of the first to sense the difference between physical and moral progress, between increase in power and improvement in purposes. "The European talks of progress because by the aid of a few scientific discoveries he has established a society which has mistaken comfort for civilization." [3] "Enlightened Europe is not happy. Its existence is a fever which it calls progress. Progress to what?" [4] Ruskin, a rich man, questioned the identity of progress and wealth: were these wealthy shopkeepers and shippers better specimens of humanity than the Englishmen of Johnson's or Shakespeare's or Chaucer's days? Carlyle and Tolstoi acknowledged the enormous advance in man's means for achieving his ends; but of what use were these unprecedented powers if they had merely multiplied the ability of men to realize purposes as contradictory, as stupid, and as suicidal as ever before?

About 1890 Sir Arthur Balfour suggested, in his genial and devastating way, that human behavior and social organization are founded not on thought, which progresses, but on feeling and instinct, which hardly change from thousand years to thousand years; this, he believed, was the secret of our failure to transmute our growing knowledge into greater happiness or more lasting peace. Even the increase of knowledge may be part cause of the pessimism of our time. "He that increaseth knowledge increaseth sorrow," said Ecclesiastes. And his modern avatar confirms him: "In all the world," says Anatole France (if we may believe secretaries), "the un-

---

[1] Nordau, *Interpretation of History,* p. 286; Bury, p. 99.
[2] Bury, p. 259.
[3] In Dean Inge, p. 179.
[4] *Tancred,* Book iii, ch. vii.

happiest creature is man. It is said, 'Man is the lord of creation.' Man is the lord of suffering, my friend." [1]

The socialist critique of modern industry did some damage to our faith in progress. The endeavor to make people vividly realize the injustices of the present took the form of idealizing the contentedness and tranquillity of the past. Ruskin, Carlyle, Morris and Kropotkin painted such pictures of the Middle Ages as made one long to be a serf bound to the soil and owing to some lord an aliquot portion of his produce and his wife. Meanwhile the liberal critique of modern politics, exposing corruption and incapacity in almost every office, made us doubt the divinity of democracy, which had been for a century our most sacred cow. The development of printing and the Hoe press resulted, apparently, in the debasement of the better minds rather than in the elevation of the worse; mediocrity triumphed in politics, in religion, in letters, even in science; Nordic anthropology and will-to-believe philosophy competed with barn-yard eugenics and Viennese psychology. Journalism took the place of literature; the "art" of the moving picture replaced the drama: photography drove painting from realism to cubism, futurism, *pointillisme* and other fatal convulsions; in Rodin sculpture ceased to carve, and began to paint; in the twentieth century music began to rival the delicacy of Chinese pots and pans.

It was the passing of art and the coming of war that shook the faith of our century in progress. The spread of industry and the decay of aristocracy coöperated in the deterioration of artistic form. When the artisan was superseded by the machine he took his skill with him; and when the machine, compelled to seek vast markets for its goods, adjusted its products to the needs and tastes of vast majorities, design and beauty gave place to standardization, quantity, and vulgarity. Had an aristocracy survived as a source of esthetic judgment trickling down among the people, it is conceivable that industry and art might have found some way of living in peace. But democracy had to pay the price of popular sovereignty in art as well as in politics; the taste of innumerable average men became the guide of the manufacturer, the dramatist, the scenario-writer, the novelist, at last of the painter, the sculptor, and the architect: cost and size became the norm of value, and a bizarre novelty replaced beauty and workmanship as the goal of art. Artists, lacking the stimulation of an aristocratic taste formed through centuries of privileged culture, no longer sought perfection of conception and execution, but aimed at astonishing effects that might without doubt be called original. Painting became pathological,[2] architecture halted its splendid development before the compulsion to build for a decade and not for centuries, music went down into the slums and the factories to find harmonies adapted to the nervous organization of elevated

[1] Brousson, p. 61.
[2] Mr. Coolidge's apt word, applied to an exhibition of modern painting.

butchers and emancipated chambermaids. Sculpture decayed despite the growing unpopularity of clothing, and a million lessons in anatomy from every stage. But for automobiles and cosmetics, the twentieth century seemed to promise the total extinction of art.

Then the Great Madness came, and men discovered how precariously thin their coat of civilization was, how insecure their security, and how frail their freedom. War had decreased in frequency, and had increased in extent. Science, which was to be the midwife of progress, became the angel of death, killing with a precision and a rapidity that reduced the battles of the Middle Ages to the level of college athletics. Brave aviators dropped bombs upon women and children, and learned chemists explained the virtues of poison-gas. All the international amity built up by a century of translated literatures, coöperating scientists, commercial relationships, and financial interdependence, melted away, and Europe fell apart into a hundred hostile nationalities. When it was all over it appeared that the victors as well as the fallen had lost the things for which they had fought; that a greedy imperialism had merely passed from Potsdam to Paris; that violent dictatorships were replacing orderly and constitutional rule; that democracy was spreading and dead. Hope faded away; the generation that had lived through the War could no longer believe in anything; a wave of apathy and cynicism engulfed all but the least or the most experienced souls. The idea of progress seemed now to be one of the shallowest delusions that had ever mocked man's misery, or lifted him up to a vain idealism and a colossal futility.

IV. MINOR CONSIDERATIONS

"If you wish to converse with me," said Voltaire, "define your terms." What shall we mean by "progress"? Subjective definitions will not do; we must not conceive progress in terms of one nation, or one religion, or one code of morals; an increase of kindness, for example, would alarm our young Nietzscheans. Nor may we define progress in terms of happiness; for idiots are happier than geniuses, and those whom we most respect seek not happiness but greatness. Is it possible to find an objective definition for our term?—one that will hold for any individual, any group, even for any species? Let us provisionally define progress as increasing control of the environment by life; and let us mean by environment all the circumstances that condition the coördination and realization of desire. Progress is the domination of chaos by mind and purpose, of matter by form and will.

It need not be continuous in order to be real. There may be "plateaus" in it, Dark Ages and disheartening retrogressions; but if the last stage is the highest of all we shall say that man makes progress. And in assessing epochs and nations we must guard against loose thinking. We must not compare nations in their youth with nations in the mellowness of their cultural maturity; and we must not compare the worst or the best of one age with the selected best or worst of all the collected past. If we find that the type of genius prevalent in young countries like America and Australia tends to the executive, explorative, and scientific kind rather than to the painter of pictures or poems, the carver of statues or words, we shall understand that each age and place calls for and needs certain brands of genius rather than others, and that the cultural sort can only come when its practical predecessors have cleared the forest and prepared the way. If we find that civilizations come and go, and mortality is upon all the works of man, we shall confess the irrefutability of death, and be consoled if, during the day of our lives and our nations, we move slowly upward, and become a little better than we were. If we find that philosophers are of slighter stature now than in the days of broad-backed Plato and the substantial Socrates, that our sculptors are lesser men than Donatello or Angelo, our painters inferior to Velasquez, our poets and composers unnameable with Shelley and Bach, we shall not despair; these stars did not all shine on the same night. Our problem is whether the total and average level of human ability has increased, and stands at its peak today.

When we take a total view, and compare our modern existence, precarious and chaotic as it is, with the ignorance, superstition, brutality, cannibalism and diseases of primitive people, we are a little comforted: the lowest strata of our race may still differ only slightly from such men, but above those strata thousands and millions have reached to mental and moral heights inconceivable, presumably, to the early mind. Under the complex strain of city life we sometimes take imaginative refuge in the quiet simplicity of savage days; but in our less romantic moments we know that this is a flight-reaction from our actual tasks, that this idolatry of barbarism, like so many of our young opinions, is merely an impatient expression of adolescent maladaptation, part of the suffering involved in the contemporary retardation of individual maturity. A study of such savage tribes as survive shows their high rate of infantile mortality, their short tenure of life, their inferior speed, their inferior stamina, their inferior will, and their superior plagues.[1] The friendly and flowing savage is like Nature—delightful but for the insects and the dirt.

The savage, however, might turn the argument around, and inquire how we enjoy our politics and our wars, and whether we think ourselves happier than the tribes whose weird names resound in the text-books of anthropology. The believer in progress will have to admit that we have made too many advances in the art of war, and that our politicians, with startling exceptions, would have adorned the Roman Forum in the days

[1] Cf. Todd, p. 135.

of Milo and Clodius,—though Mr. Coolidge was an appreciable improvement upon Nero. As to happiness, no man can say; it is an elusive angel, destroyed by detection and seldom amenable to measurement. Presumably it depends first upon health, secondly upon love, and thirdly upon wealth. As to wealth, we make such progress that it lies on the conscience of our intellectuals; as to love, we try to atone for our lack of depth by unprecedented inventiveness and variety. Our thousand fads of diet and drugs predispose us to the belief that we must be ridden with disease as compared with simpler men in simpler days; but this is a delusion. We think that where there are so many doctors there must be more sickness than before. But in truth we have not more ailments than in the past, but only more money; our wealth allows us to treat and cherish and master illnesses from which primitive men died without even knowing their Greek names.

There is one test of health—and therefore in part of happiness—which is objective and reliable: we find it in the mortality statistics of insurance companies, where inaccuracy is more expensive than in philosophy. In some cases these figures extend over three centuries. In Geneva, for example, they show an average length of life of twenty years in 1600, and of forty years in 1900. In the United States in 1920 the tenure of life of white people averaged fifty-three; and in 1926 it was fifty-six.[1] This is incredible if true. Nevertheless, similar reports come to us from Germany: the Federal Statistical Bureau of Berlin tabulates the average length of life in Germany as twenty in 1520, thirty in 1750, forty in 1870, fifty in 1910, and sixty in 1920.[2] Taking the figures for granted, we may conclude, with the permission of the pessimist, that if life is a boon at all, we are making great strides in the quantity of it which we manage to maintain. Recently the morticians (*nés* undertakers) discussed in annual convention the dangers that threatened their profession from the increasing tardiness of men in keeping their appointments with death.[3] But if undertakers are miserable, progress is real.

V. THE OUTLINE OF HISTORY

Having made these admissions and modifications, let us try to see the problem of progress in a total view. It is unnecessary to refute the pessimist; it is only necessary to enclose his truth, if we can, in ours. When we look at history in the large we see it as a graph of rising and falling states—

[1] Fisher, I., *National Vitality*, p. 624.

[2] New York *Times*, Sept. 7, 1928.

[3] Siegfried, *America Comes of Age*, p. 176. For detailed evidence of progress towards health cf. a masterly essay by C.-E. A. Winslow in Prof. Beard's splendid symposium, *Whither Mankind?* New York, 1928.

nations and cultures disappearing as on some gigantic film. But in that irregular movement of countries and that chaos of men, certain great moments stand out as the peaks and essence of human history, certain advances which, once made, were never lost. Step by step man has climbed from the savage to the scientist; and these are the stages of his growth.

First, *speech.* Think of it not as a sudden achievement, nor as a gift from the gods, but as the slow development of articulate expression, through centuries of effort, from the mate-calls of animals to the lyric flights of poetry. Without words, or common nouns, that might give to particular images the ability to represent a class, generalization would have stopped in its beginnings, and reason would have stayed where we find it in the brute. Without words, philosophy and poetry, history and prose, would have been impossible, and thought could never have reached the subtlety of Einstein or Anatole France. Without words man could not have become man, nor woman woman.

Second, *fire.* For fire made man independent of climate, gave him a greater compass on the earth, tempered his tools to hardness and durability, and offered him as food a thousand things inedible before. Not least of all it made him master of the night, and shed an animating brilliance over the hours of evening and dawn. Picture the dark before man conquered it; even now the terrors of that primitive abyss survive in our traditions and perhaps in our blood. Once every twilight was a tragedy, and man crept into his cave at sunset trembling with fear. Now we do not creep into our caves until sunrise; and though it is folly to miss the sun, how good it is to be liberated from our ancient fears! This overspreading of the night with a billion man-made stars has brightened the human spirit, and made for a vivacious jollity in modern life. We shall never be grateful enough for light.

Third, *the conquest of the animals.* Our memories are too forgetful, and our imagination too unimaginative, to let us realize the boon we have in our security from the larger and sub-human beasts of prey. Animals are now our playthings and our helpless food; but there was a time when man was hunted as well as hunter, when every step from cave or hut was an adventure, and the possession of the earth was still at stake. This war to make the planet human was surely the most vital in human history; by its side all other wars were but family quarrels, achieving nothing. That struggle between strength of body and power of mind was waged through long and unrecorded years; and when at last it was won, the fruit of man's triumph—his safety on the earth—was transmitted across a thousand generations, with a hundred other gifts from the past, to be part of our heritage at birth.

What are all our temporary retrogressions against the background of such a conflict and such a victory?

Fourth, *agriculture*. Civilization was impossible in the hunting stage; it called for a permanent habitat, a settled way of life. It came with the home and the school; and these could not be till the products of the field replaced the animals of the forest or the herd as the food of man. The hunter found his quarry with increasing difficulty, while the woman whom he left at home tended an ever more fruitful soil. This patient husbandry by the wife threatened to make her independent of the male; and for his own lordship's sake he forced himself at last to the prose of tillage. No doubt it took centuries to make this greatest of all transitions in human history; but when at last it was made, civilization began. Meredith said that woman will be the last creature to be civilized by man. He was as wrong as it is possible to be in the limits of one sentence. For civilization came through two things chiefly: the home, which developed those social dispositions that form the psychological cement of society; and agriculture, which took man from his wandering life as hunter, herder and killer, and settled him long enough in one place to let him build homes, schools, churches, colleges, universities, civilization. But it was woman who gave man agriculture and the home; she domesticated man as she domesticated the sheep and the pig. Man is woman's last domestic animal; and perhaps he is the last creature that will be civilized by woman. The task is just begun: one look at our menus reveals us as still in the hunting stage.

Fifth, *social organization*. Here are two men disputing: one knocks the other down, kills him, and then concludes that he who is alive must have been right, and that he who is dead must have been wrong—a mode of demonstration still accepted in international disputes. Here are two other men disputing: one says to the other, "Let us not fight—we may both be killed; let us take our difference to some elder of the tribe, and submit to his decision." It was a crucial moment in human history! For if the answer was No, barbarism continued; if it was Yes, civilization planted another root in the memory of man: the replacement of chaos with order, of brutality with judgment, of violence with law. Here, too, is a gift unfelt, because we are born within the charmed circle of its protection, and never know its value till we wander into the disordered or solitary regions of the earth. God knows that our congresses and our parliaments are dubious inventions, the distilled mediocrity of the land; but despite them we manage to enjoy a security of life and property which we shall appreciate more warmly when civil war or revolution reduces us to primitive conditions. Compare the safety of travel today with the robber-infested highways of medieval Europe. Never before in history was there such order and liberty as exist in England today,—and may some day exist in America, when a way is found of opening municipal office to capable and honorable men. However, we must not excite ourselves too much about political corruption or democratic mismanagement; politics is not life, but only a graft upon life; under its vulgar melodrama the traditional order of society quietly persists, in the family, in the school, in the thousand devious influences that change our native lawlessness into some measure of co-operation and goodwill. Without consciousness of it, we partake in a luxurious patrimony of social order built up for us by a hundred generations of trial and error, accumulated knowledge, and transmitted wealth.

Sixth, *morality*. Here we touch the very heart of our problem—are men morally better than they were? So far as intelligence is an element in morals, we have improved: the average of intelligence is higher, and there has been a great increase in the number of what we may vaguely call developed minds. So far as character is concerned, we have probably retro-gressed; subtlety of thought has grown at the expense of stability of soul; in the presence of our fathers we intellectuals feel uncomfortably that though we surpass them in the number of ideas that we have crowded into our heads, and though we have liberated ourselves from delightful supersti-tions which still bring them aid and comfort, we are inferior to them in uncomplaining courage, fidelity to our tasks and purposes, and simple strength of personality.

But if morality implies the virtues exalted in the code of Christ, we have made some halting progress despite our mines and slums, our democratic corruption, and our urban addiction to lechery. We are a slightly gentler species than we were: capable of greater kindness, and of generosity even to alien or recently hostile peoples whom we have never seen. In one year (1928) the contributions of our country to private charity and philanthropy exceeded two billions of dollars—one half of all the money circulating in America. We still kill murderers if, as occasionally happens, we catch them and convict them; but we are a little uneasy about this ancient retributive justice of a life for a life, and the number of crimes for which we mete out the ultimate punishment has rapidly decreased. Two hundred years ago, in Merrie England, men might be hanged by law for stealing a shilling; and people are still severely punished if they do not steal a great deal. One hundred and forty years ago miners were hereditary serfs in Scotland, criminals were legally and publicly tortured to death in France, debtors were imprisoned for life in England, and respectable people raided the African coast for slaves.[1] Fifty years ago our jails were dens of filth and

[1] Haldane, J. B. S., *Possible Worlds*, p. 302. Cf. Spengler, *Decline of the West*, pp. 110–11: "The number of executions for cult-impiety in Athens alone, and during the few decades of the Peloponnesian War, ran into hundreds." Let the reader who still

horror, colleges for the graduation of minor criminals into major criminals; now our prisons are vacation resorts for tired murderers. We still exploit the lower strata of our working classes, but we soothe our consciences with "welfare work." Eugenics struggles to balance with artificial selection the interference of human kindliness and benevolence with that merciless elimination of the weak and the infirm which was once the mainspring of natural selection.

We think there is more violence in the world than before, but in truth there are only more newspapers; vast and powerful organizations scour the planet for crimes and scandals that will console their readers for stenography and monogamy; and all the villainy and politics of five continents are gathered upon one page for the encouragement of our breakfasts. We conclude that half the world is killing the other half, and that a large proportion of the remainder are committing suicide. But in the streets, in our homes, in public assemblies, in a thousand vehicles of transportation, we are astonished to find no murderers and no suicides, but rather a blunt democratic courtesy, and an unpretentious chivalry a hundred times more real than when men mouthed chivalric phrases, enslaved their women, and ensured the fidelity of their wives with irons while they fought for Christ in the Holy Land.

Our prevailing mode of marriage, chaotic and deliquescent as it is, represents a pleasant refinement on marriage by capture or purchase, and *le droit de seigneur*. There is less brutality between men and women, between parents and children, between teachers and pupils, than in any recorded generation of the past. The emancipation of woman, and her ascendancy over man, indicate an unprecedented gentility in the once murderous male. Love, which was unknown to primitive men, or was only a hunger of the flesh, has flowered into a magnificent garden of song and sentiment, in which the passion of a man for a maid, though vigorously rooted in physical need, rises like incense into the realm of living poetry. And youth, whose sins so disturb its tired elders, atones for its little vices with such intellectual eagerness and moral courage as may be invaluable when education resolves at last to come out into the open and cleanse our public life.

Seventh, *tools*. In the face of the romantics, the machine-wreckers of the intelligentsia, the pleaders for a return to the primitive (dirt, chores, snakes, cobwebs, bugs), we sing the song of the tools, the engines, the machines, that have enslaved and are liberating man. We need not be ashamed of our prosperity: it is good that comforts and opportunities once confined to barons and earls have been made by enterprise the prerogatives

doubts our moral progress read Lea on the Spanish Inquisition, or Taine on the persecutions under Queen Mary (*History of English Literature,* pp. 255–6). We may in some communities make intelligence illegal, but we do not burn it at the stake.

of all; it was necessary to spread leisure—even though at first misused—before a wide culture could come. These multiplying inventions are the new organs with which we control our environment; we do not need to grow them on our bodies, as animals must; we make them and use them, and lay them aside till we need them again.[1] We grow gigantic arms that build in a month the pyramids that once consumed a million men; we make for ourselves great eyes that search out the invisible stars of the sky, and little eyes that peer into the invisible cells of life; we speak, if we wish, with quiet voices that reach across continents and seas; we move over the land and the air with the freedom of timeless gods. Granted that mere speed is worthless: it is as a symbol of human courage and persistent will that the airplane has its highest meaning for us; long chained, like Prometheus, to the earth, we have freed ourselves at last, and now we may look the eagle in the face.

No, these tools will not conquer us. Our present defeat by the machinery around us is a transient thing, a halt in our visible progress to a slaveless world. The menial labor that degraded both master and man is lifted from human shoulders and harnessed to the tireless muscles of iron and steel; soon every waterfall and every wind will pour its beneficent energy into factories and homes, and man will be freed for the tasks of the mind. It is not revolution but invention that will liberate the slave.[2]

Eighth, *science*. In a large degree Buckle was right: we progress only in knowledge, and these other gifts are rooted in the slow enlightenment of the mind. Here in the untitled nobility of research, and the silent battles of the laboratory, is a story fit to balance the chicanery of politics and the futile barbarism of war. Here man is at his best, and through darkness and persecution mounts steadily towards the light. Behold him standing on a little planet, measuring, weighing, analyzing constellations that he cannot see; predicting the vicissitudes of earth and sun and moon; and witnessing the birth and death of worlds. Or here is a seemingly unpractical mathematician tracking new formulas through laborious labyrinths, clearing the way for an endless chain of inventions that will multiply the power of his race. Here is a bridge: a hundred thousand tons of iron suspended from four ropes of steel flung bravely from shore to shore, and bearing the passage of countless men; this is poetry as eloquent as Shakespeare ever wrote. Or consider this city-like building that mounts boldly into the sky, guarded against every strain by the courage of our calculations, and shining like diamond-studded granite in the night. Here in physics are new dimensions,

[1] Bergson.

[2] "By perfecting the organization of labor and by the use of machinery, industry" (in America) "has ceased to rely upon brawn to an extent of which we in Europe have no conception."—Siegfried, *America Comes of Age*, p. 149.

new elements, new atoms, and new powers. Here in the rocks is the auto-biography of life. Here in the laboratories biology prepares to transform the organic world as physics transformed matter. Everywhere you come upon them studying, these unpretentious, unrewarded men; you hardly understand where their devotion finds its source and nourishment; they will die before the trees they plant will bear fruit for mankind. But they go on.

Yes, it is true that this victory of man over matter has not yet been matched with any kindred victory of man over himself. The argument for progress falters here again. Psychology has hardly begun to comprehend, much less to control, human conduct and desire; it is mingled with mysticism and metaphysics, with psychoanalysis, behavorism,[1] glandular mythology, and other diseases of adolescence. Careful and modified statements are made only by psychologists of whom no one ever hears; in our country the democratic passion for extreme statements turns every science into a fad. But psychology will outlive these ills and storms; it will be matured, like older sciences, by the responsibilities which it undertakes. If another Bacon should come to map out its territory, clarify the proper methods and objectives of its attack, and point out the "fruits and powers" to be won,—which of us, knowing the surprises of history and the pertinacity of men, would dare set limits to the achievements that may come from our growing knowledge of the mind? Already in our day man is turning round from his remade environment, and beginning to remake himself.

Ninth, *education*. More and more completely we pass on to the next generation the gathered experience of the past. It is almost a contemporary innovation, this tremendous expenditure of wealth and labor in the equipment of schools and the provision of instruction for all; perhaps it is the most significant feature of our time. Once colleges were luxuries, designed for the male half of the leisure class; today universities are so numerous that he who runs may become a Ph.D. We have not excelled the selected geniuses of antiquity, but we have raised the level and average of human knowledge far beyond any age in history. Think now not of Plato and Aristotle, but of the stupid, bigoted and brutal Athenian Assembly, of the unfranchised mob and its Orphic rites, of the secluded and enslaved women who could acquire education only by becoming courtesans.

None but a child would complain that the world has not yet been totally

[1] Behaviorism is popular not because it is a method in psychology, but because it is a mechanistic philosophy—a series of bold and attractive hypotheses about consciousness and thought. So far as it is itself aware, however, it is a rigidly objective science; and its brilliant founder—*le philosophe malgré lui*—announces that philosophy is dead. This is slightly inconsistent, and seems to prove Dr. Watson's contention, that in behaviorism there is no consciousness.

remade by these spreading schools, these teeming bisexual universities; in the perspective of history the great experiment of education is just begun. It has not had time to prove itself; it cannot in a generation undo the ignorance and superstition of ten thousand years; indeed, there is no telling but the high birth rate of ignorance, and the determination of dogma by plebiscite, may triumph over education in the end; this step in progress is not one of which we may yet say that it is a permanent achievement of mankind. But already beneficent results appear. Why is it that tolerance and freedom of the mind flourish more easily in the northern states than in the South, if not because the South has not yet won wealth enough to build sufficient schools? [1] Who knows how much of our preference for mediocrity in office, and narrowness in leadership, is the result of a generation recruited from regions too oppressed with economic need and political exploitation to spare time for the ploughing and sowing of the mind? What will the full fruitage of education be when every one of us is schooled till twenty, and finds equal access to the intellectual treasures of the race? Consider again the instinct of parental love, the profound impulse of every normal parent to raise his children beyond himself: here is the biological leverage of human progress, a force more to be trusted than any legislation or any moral exhortation, because it is rooted in the very nature of man. Adolescence lengthens: we begin more helplessly, and we grow more completely towards that higher man who struggles to be born out of our darkened souls. We are the raw material of civilization.

We dislike education, because it was not presented to us in our youth for what it is. Consider it not as the painful accumulation of facts and dates, but as an ennobling intimacy with great men. Consider it not as the preparation of the individual to "make a living," but as the development of every potential capacity in him for the comprehension, control, and *appreciation* of his world. Above all, consider it, in its fullest definition, as the technique of transmitting as completely as possible, to as many as possible, that technological, intellectual, moral, and artistic heritage through which the race forms the growing individual and makes him human. Education is the reason why we behave like human beings. We are hardly born human; we are born ridiculous and malodorous animals; we *become* human, we have humanity thrust upon us through the hundred channels whereby the past pours down into the present that mental and cultural inheritance whose preservation, accumulation and transmission place mankind today, with all its defectives and illiterates, on a higher plane than any generation has ever reached before.

[1] Illiteracy is higher in the states and counties that pass or propose anti-evolution laws, than elsewhere; e. g. it is 26.6% in Macon Co., Tennessee, home of the author of the "Scopes" law; but it is only 9% in Tennessee as a whole. (*Scientific American,* Sept., 1927, p. 254.)

Tenth and last, *writing and print*. Again our imagination is too weak-winged to lift us to a full perspective; we cannot vision or recall the long ages of ignorance, impotence and fear that preceded the coming of letters. Through those unrecorded centuries men could transmit their hard-won lore only by word of mouth from parent to child; if one generation forgot or misunderstood, the weary ladder of knowledge had to be climbed anew. Writing gave a new permanence to the achievements of the mind; it preserved for thousands of years, and through a millennium of poverty and superstition, the wisdom found by philosophy and the beauty carved out in drama and poetry. It bound the generations together with a common heritage; it created that Country of the Mind in which, because of writing, genius need not die.

And now, as writing united the generations, print, despite the thousand prostitutions of it, can bind the civilizations. It is not necessary any more that civilization should disappear before our planet passes away. It will change its habitat; doubtless the land in every nation will refuse at last to yield its fruit to improvident tillage and careless tenancy; inevitably new regions will lure with virgin soil the lustier strains of every race. But a civilization is not a material thing, inseparably bound, like an ancient serf, to a given spot of the earth; it is an accumulation of technical knowledge and cultural creation; if these can be passed on to the new seat of economic power the civilization does not die, it merely makes for itself another home. Nothing but beauty and wisdom deserve immortality. To a philosopher it is not indispensable that his native city should endure forever; he will be content if its achievements are handed down, to form some part of the possessions of mankind.

We need not fret then, about the future. We are weary with too much war, and in our lassitude of mind we listen readily to a Spengler announcing the downfall of the Western world. But this learned arrangement of the birth and death of civilizations in even cycles is a trifle too precise; we may be sure that the future will play wild pranks with this mathematical despair. There have been wars before, and wars far worse than our "Great" one. Man and civilization survived them; within fifteen years after Waterloo, as we shall see, defeated France was producing so many geniuses that every attic in Paris was occupied. Never was our heritage of civilization and culture so secure, and never was it half so rich. We may do our little share to augment it and transmit it, confident that time will wear away chiefly the dross of it, and that what is finally fair and worthy in it will be preserved, to illuminate many generations.

CHAPTER XVI

The Destiny of Civilization

I. *POST BELLUM* NEUROSIS

IN THE YEAR 1818 Schopenhauer wrote *The World as Will and Idea*, the most powerful and comprehensive attack ever made upon man's faith in progress and civilization. In the year 1821 Keats died of consumption and despair, after writing perfect poetry scented with the death of autumn leaves and weighted with the tragedy of lost illusions. In 1822 Shelley was drowned, perhaps without an effort to save himself; he had "lived long enough," as Cæsar said, and did not care to survive the universal defeat of liberalism in Europe. In 1824 Byron died of epilepsy, content to disappear from a world which he had described with such acid irony in *Don Juan*. In 1835 De Musset published *Confessions of a Child of the Century*, describing "a ruined world" and a people without hope. In 1837 Pushkin died in Russia, and Leopardi in Italy, after phrasing pessimism in such poetry as neither nation has ever equalled since. It was a despondent generation.

But already by 1850 the vitality of Europe had reasserted itself, and the upward movement of life and letters had been resumed. Invention was laying the basis of the technological triumphs of the century, machinery was beginning to liberate man for leisure, railroads and steamboats were beginning to unite nations and cultures, exchanging goods and ideas everywhere; the same decade which saw the revolutionary triumph of the modern drama in 1830 with Hugo's *Hernani* saw the birth of Ibsen in 1828, Balzac and Stendhal were perfecting the novel, Heine and Hugo were perfecting the lyric, Sainte-Beuve and Taine were perfecting criticism, Tennyson and Browning were publishing their first volumes, Dickens and Thackeray were opening their rivalry, Turgeniev, Dostoievski and Tolstoi were growing up in Russia; Delacroix was fighting the first battle against brown sauce in painting, and Turner was flooding even England with sunshine; Darwin was gathering material for the most vital achievement in modern science, Spencer was preparing a new philosophy, and Renan was writing *The Future of Science* as the flaming herald of a brighter world. Rebirth was everywhere.

It is against this background of death and life, of destruction and renewal, that we must understand and forgive the after-war pessimism of our time. Perspective is everything.

Not that the Great War is the sole or essential cause of our philosophic gloom; the War selected and emphasized ideas and feelings that had been accumulating since the turn of the century. Cassandra Spengler conceived and outlined his masterpiece, *The Decline of the West,* in 1914, before the outbreak of hostilities; but not till Germany had tasted defeat did it acclaim the book as the most significant contribution made to philosophy since Nietzsche (a Frenchman would say, since Bergson). Mr. Mencken has never had much fondness for his time, nor any great expectations of the future; but it was not until the brutality of the War—and worse, perhaps, the cynicism of the Peace—that thousands of young people in America accepted him as the most forceful exponent of their *Weltschmerz,* their disgust with a dying civilization. Only in the world-weariness of the morning after battle could Europe have listened so readily to Keyserling's spiritual translation of Buddha and Confucius, or heard with such faint rebellion his quiet assurance that "the old civilization is in the throes of decline." [1] Dean Inge and Hilaire Belloc agree only in the belief that civilization is doomed.[2]

Various factors had been preparing the Occident for this mood of untraditional humility. Henry Adams had preached a profound pessimism based on the irreversibility and "degradation" of energy. Madison Grant had argued plausibly that the "Nordic" stock was being depleted by war, weakened by intermarriage, outbred by the Mediterranean race, and deposed from its long leadership by revolt in Asia and democracy at home. Lothrop Stoddard popularized these views with great ability and less cau tion; and Professor McDougall added his voice to the general lament. Mean while a great Egyptologist, Professor Flinders Petrie, without consulting these Lord High Executioners, announced that a mixture of stocks was the indispensable prelude to a new civilization. But he too saw in the current mingling of peoples a dissolution of European civilization; that culture, he thought, had reached its zenith about 1800, and had begun to die with the French Revolution; four or five centuries would intervene before the new ethnical *pot-pourri* would produce a stable stock, and another cycle of civilization.[3]

Spengler too looks back with romantic regret to the days before Dr. Guillotin, not having felt, like Rousseau, the whips and scorns of the feudal system on his back. "For Western existence," he says,

[1] Keyserling, Count H., *The World in the Making,* p. 118; *Europe,* pp. 371, 378.

[2] *Outspoken Essays,* pp. 265, 269.

[3] *The Revolutions of Civilization,* p. 128.

the distinction lies about the year 1800—on one side of that frontier, life
in fulness and sureness of itself, formed by growth from within, in one great
uninterrupted evolution from Gothic childhood to Goethe and Napoleon;
and on the other the autumnal, artificial, rootless life of our great cities,
under forms fashioned by the intellect . . . Our tasks today are those of preserving, rounding off, refining, selection—in place of big dynamic creation, the
same clever detail work which characterized the Alexandrian mathematic of
late Hellenism. . . . He who does not understand that this outcome is
obligatory and insusceptible of modification must forego all desire to comprehend history.[1]

We are finished; as this incorrigible German would put it, we are finished
by metaphysical necessity. For Spengler is no pragmatist; he does not know
that life may have reasons which logic cannot understand.

II. THE MORTALITY OF NATIONS

Nevertheless the case for Spengler is strong enough; it rests at last not
on metaphysics, which can always be refuted with a shrug of the shoulders,
but on history, which, when it does not lie, is irrefutable. History, on whose
face mortality is writ; history, whose highest law seems to be the schoolboy's rule that everything that goes up must come down: this obituary of
men and nations, this funeral procession of races and states, is a picture
revealed to us in merciless detail by the researches of the nineteenth century. Never before did men delve so thoroughly or so persistently into the
past as during the last one hundred years—unearthing dead civilizations,
exhuming forgotten geniuses, and playing Hamlet's "Alas, poor Yorick!"
to a billion honorable skulls. The century of progress and historians left a
taste of disillusionment and an odor of decay as a legacy to the century of
airplanes, radios, and poison gas.

What a panorama of fatality history unveils! Here is proud Egypt, building on shifting sands an empire more lasting than any later realm, raising
temples more magnificent than those of Europe, ruling all Mediterranean
peoples, lashing the backs of millions of slaves, and embalming its priests
and princes in "houses of eternity." Poor phrase!—nothing remains of all
that eternity but white hair growing on rotting bones; and even the pyramids convey a sense of death. The sands swirl up out of the desert around
those playhouses of superstition in stone; government gold must yearly be
spent to cart it away. And as the tourist turns back, wiping away the hostile
grains that have crept into the pores of his face, he wonders what would
happen if government gold should cease to flow there for a century or two;
he visions the sands covering stratum after stratum of those monuments,

[1] *Decline of the West*, pp. 38, 90, 353.

until the topmost stone of the tallest pyramid is hidden, and not one sign remains of the glory and the brutality that were Egypt. Perhaps he recalls Shelley's perfect and terrible poem—"Ozymandias":

> I met a traveller from an antique land
> Who said: Two vast and trunkless legs of stone
> Stand in the desert. Near them, on the sand,
> Half sunk, a shattered visage lies, whose frown,
> And wrinkled lip, and sneer of cold command,
> Tell that its sculptor well those passions read
> Which yet survive, stamped on these lifeless things,
> The hand that mocked them and the heart that fed.
> And on the pedestal these words appear:
> "My name is Ozymandias, king of kings;
> Look on my works, ye mighty, and despair!"
> Nothing beside remains. Round the decay
> Of that colossal wreck, boundless and bare,
> The lone and level sands stretch far away.

Or pass to Greece, and climb the hill that leads to the Parthenon. Recall how for nine years Ictinus and Mnesicles guided the erection of that modest and perfect temple, so self-restrained in proportions and style, every line so subtly modulated into a curve that the stone takes on almost the warmth and pliancy of human flesh. Recall how for nine years Pheidias and his pupils carved hard marble into figures for the frieze—figures of men so fair that no one looking at them could help but grow a little in mind and character; figures of gods so majestic and serene that no one looking at them could believe in the old deities of rape and rapine any more. For many centuries that temple crowned the Acropolis, its colors brilliant in the sun; many generations were lifted up by the sight of it, feeling that here, if only for a moment, men had been like gods.

But in 1687 war came; the Turks, holding Athens, used the Parthenon as a magazine for their powder; the Venetians sent gunboats into the harbor at the Piraeus, and the gunners destroyed the Parthenon. When you reach the top of that shrine-like hill, to lay your own little tribute on that ancient altar of beauty and of reason, you do not quite see the Parthenon; parts of the great colonnades remain, waiting for some earthquake to level them; but most of the Parthenon lies beneath your feet, in a hundred million fragments of shining white Pentelic stone. And as you come away you wonder: is this, then, the lesson of history—that man must build for thousands of years with the toil of his hands and the sweat of his brow, in order that time, insensate, relentless time, shall destroy everything that he builds? For time is long, and art is fleeting, and the fairest things die soonest.

The Parthenon is gone. Greece is gone. Rome came, and bestrode the earth like a colossus, so great that none thought it could ever be laid low; intangibles like the birth-rate and the exhaustion of the soil destroyed it; nothing remains of it but memories for dictators to imitate. Crete is gone, Judea, Phœnicia, Carthage, Assyria, Babylon, Persia—they are like gods that have lost their worshippers, temples visited by tourists, but never hearing prayer. Death is on them all.

Europe came—Italy, Spain, France, England, Germany—and reared a civilization as mighty as any that history had known, making cathedrals to rival the Parthenon, making science greater than the Greeks', making music such an antiquity had never dreamed of, accumulating and transmitting knowledge and power beyond any remembered precedent. But Spengler rises, and announces to war-befouled Europe: "You are dead. I see in you all the typical stigmata of decay. Your institutions, your democracy, your corruption, your gigantic cities, your science, your art, your socialism, your atheism, your philosophy, even your mathematics, are precisely those that characterized the dying stages of ancient states. Another century, and civilization will have found her seat far from you. This is your Alexandrian age."

America comes, and builds a civilization broader-based than any that the world has ever seen before, destined perhaps to reach greater heights than any that the world has ever reached before. But if there is any validity in history, if the past has any light to shed upon the future, then this civilization too, which we raise with such feverish toil and care, will pass away; and where we labor today, thousands of years hence savages will roam once more.

Such is the picture which the historian sees in the future as in the past. He concludes that there is only one thing certain in history, and that is decadence; just as there is only one thing certain in life, and that is death.

III. ECONOMICS AND CIVILIZATION

It is a gloomy picture; let us see if it is true.

What is civilization? It is a complex of security and culture, of order and liberty: political security through morals and law, economic security through the continuity of production and exchange; culture through facilities for the growth and transmission of knowledge, manners, and arts. It is an intricate and precarious thing, dependent upon a score of factors, of which any one may determine greatness or decay. We shall try to take the complexity to pieces, and study the factors one by one.

The economic factors are fundamental; the earth comes before man, and though man moulds his environment as much as it moulds him, the environment must first be there. Climatic conditions are an obvious limitation on the availability of the earth; decreased rainfall may by imperceptible stages put an end to a civilization, as it did with Assyria and Babylon, or with the primitive culture that Andrews has excavated in Mongolia. After a tolerable climate comes a fertile soil. It is not indispensable, for Greece and Rome were for the most part built on rocks and marshes and sand; but it was the Roman yeomanry that conquered Greece, and it was the exhaustion of the soil that conquered Rome. The exploitation of farmers by middlemen, the consequent replacement of owners by tenants on the land, and the consequent carelessness of tillage vitally injured Rome, and is beginning to injure America. Conversely the apparent inexhaustibility of China's soil—due, perhaps, to her excellent but ill-mannered method of renitrogenation—explains the repeated return of civilization and culture to that ancient and yet adolescent land. The course of civilization wends its way not necessarily westward, but in the direction of fresh fields; as man starts from the tropics, the path of empire is mostly north and south; and today it may laugh at all formulas and turn backward to the east. But everywhere the culture of the soil precedes and conditions the culture of the soul.

The earth produces metals as well as food; and in some cases gold and silver, iron and coal, may be of more import to national destiny than corn and wheat; let England exemplify again. Greece was weakened by the depletion of the silver mines of Laurium, Rome by the petering out of her silver mines in Spain. England will begin to die when coal is brought to Newcastle; and China may again lead the world in civilization when she develops the mineral wealth that lies buried in her soil. Brooks Adams has noted the passage of industrial leadership from England to Germany after the capture of Alsace-Lorraine (with its coal and iron) in 1871, and the rise of American industrial supremacy after the opening of the coal-fields of Pennsylvania in 1897; it was then that Europe pounced upon China to divide her coal, and America seized the Philippines to enforce the "open door." Coal is king, oil is heir-apparent, and electric power is pretender to the throne.

As vital as any of these economic factors in civilization is commercial position and power: a nation must be traversed by some important trade route, it must provide strategic ganglia for the commercial nerves of the world, if it is to enjoy facilities for that exchange of commodities and culture which stimulates and fertilizes a people. So Greece rose through the capture of Troy and the domination of the Ægean; Rome rose through the defeat of Carthage and the control of the Mediterranean; Spain had its Cervantes and Velasquez because it lay on the line to the New World; Italy had her Renaissance because she was the port of exile and entry for the trade between Europe and the East; Russia developed slowly because land-routes were replaced by sea-routes after the Middle Ages, and no amount of diplomacy or war availed her to win control over the great in-land seas into which her rivers pour. Rome began to die when Constantine made Constantinople his capital, and the ancient Byzantium became the half-way house on the great routes from Russia, Germany and Austria to the Levant; Italy began to die when Columbus discovered America—it was above all a change of trade routes that transferred the hegemony of civiliza-tion from the Mediterranean to the North Atlantic states. The eventual replacement of maritime by air transport may set the high seats of culture inland, along the shortest air-lines between trade terminals; "Berlin to Bagdad" may be no longer a dream; and the wastes of Russia may bloom under a busy sky when China becomes the greatest rival and customer of the West.

Last of the economic factors is industry; and its history is too brief to let us chart reliably the direction of its influence. Industry gives wealth, gathers vast taxable populations into a little space, finances imperialistic aggression, and makes for political mastery; but does it make for civiliza-tion? Industry exalts quantity, and neglects quality, artistry, difference; once every industry was an art, now every art is an industry; once men employed in *manu*factures were handicraftsmen, artisans, now they are "hands." Will machinery mechanize man, and coarsen the soul beyond all possibility of spiritual delicacy and growth? Industrial England has never equalled the literature of Elizabeth, or the pure science of Newton's days, or the painting of the bright dynasty that began with Reynolds and ended with Turner. Germany's great age came with Frederick, Kant, Goethe and Beethoven; it ended with Bismarck and Von Moltke, blood and iron—and coal. France has had less industry than either England or Germany, and more civilization; and though French manners have declined since the vivacious grace of Voltaire's day, French genius has bloomed in every decade since Molière. Now that France has the coal and iron of Alsace-Lorraine she too may abandon art for industry.

No, it is commerce rather than industry that has stimulated life and thought and produced the supreme epochs of European culture. Neverthe-less, industry is young, and the past (*pace* Spengler) does not reveal its future. Who knows that the wealth which it lays up so rapidly may not at last give us leisure to think, and time to learn again the redeeming art of life?

IV. BIOLOGY AND CIVILIZATION

Given the environment, there must come to it, for the purposes of civiliza-tion, a population gifted with that initiative and vigor which life requires to win over a wilderness and mould a *milieu* to growing purposes. In Profes-sor Petrie's theory, as we have seen, a new civilization has its origin in the slow blending of many peoples joined in the conquest of one environment. The mixture has the same rejuvenating effect as in the conjugation of protozoa, where two exhausted organisms, incapable of perpetuating themselves, are strengthened and made fertile by a mutual exchange of nuclear material. "The period of greatest ability," says Petrie, "begins about eight centuries after the mixture, and lasts for four or five centuries." [1] So the mingling of Gauls, Franks and other tribes in the days of Clovis and Charlemagne, preceded by eight centuries the first fine flush of French civilization under Rabelais and Montaigne; and in like manner the re-shuffling of Angles, Saxons, Jutes, etc., to make Englishmen came eight hundred years before Shakespeare and Bacon.

Other nations might not show such genial correlations with the theory; but we may proceed on the assumption that an ethnic blend is temporarily bad, and ultimately good, for the purposes of civilization. The crossing of types probably eliminates subtleties of character for a time, but it strengthens ancient and fundamental qualities of body and mind; and this process of re-invigoration goes on all the more rapidly in new environments because immigration tends to select individuals basically rich and superficially poor, individuals possessing little culture and much vitality. The moral for America is obvious: our "blood-chaos" is the prelude to a new people, a new stability of soul, and a new civilization.

But what shall we say of the contrary theory of Gobineau, Nietzsche, Chamberlain and Grant,—that the intermarriage of distinct peoples leads to deterioration of character and disintegration of culture? Simply that these brilliant thinkers have put the tail before the head; it was the deterioration that led to intermarriage. The decay of Rome came long before the barbarian inundation; it had its root first in emasculating luxury, and secondly in the exhaustion of the ancient Roman stock. Intermarriage with the Germans was an effect of racial depletion, not a cause.

The unpleasant side of Petrie's theory is that a race, like an individual, has a limit of physiological vitality, and must pass inevitably through the stages of childhood, maturity, and decay. The Professor, with that schematism which thrills every scholar's heart, suggests that this cycle of racial life and death has periods of equal length in practically all cases. But life slips through all majestic generalizations; races that till the earth may clearly spin out their epochs over a greater length than those that take on the enervating speed of industrial urban civilization.

Perhaps this is the secret of the exhaustion that came upon the native stock in Rome; it lost its health when it tore its roots from the soil and made, out of a virile yeomanry, a city of corrupt plutocrats and functionless proletaires. Cities are necessary to civilization, even to the word *civilization;* but they contain many seeds of racial decline. Sedentary occupations, stuffy

[1] *Op. cit.,* p. 128.

houses and congested streets, fine clothing and rich food, facilities for infection and degeneracy, work together to weaken health even while public
sanitation and preventive medicine reduce infantile mortality and lengthen
life. Epidemics wiped out half the population of the Roman Empire under
the Antonines, and left Rome helpless before the teeming Germans; the
Black Death so decimated England that it put an end to feudalism. Who
knows but the bacteria that so patiently assail us may conquer us yet?
Man's greatest enemy can be seen only under the microscope.

But there is another factor, more vital than these, in the influence of
urban life upon the destiny of a race; and that is the voluntary control of
parentage. Families grow smaller as cities grow larger; the city recruits its
new citizens less and less through propagation, more and more through immigration from the countryside and foreign nations; older stocks die, and
younger peoples take their place. So the Romans underbred themselves out
of existence; they were conquered not by German soldiers but by German
mothers. It is humorous to find the mighty Cæsar struggling to stop this
drying up of the racial fount by offering rewards to Romans who had many
children, and attacking barrenness through vanity by forbidding childless
women to wear jewelry. Augustus imposed new penalties upon bachelors,
and raised the endowment of motherhood to 1,000 sesterces per child; and
Constantine went so far as to offer state care for all children whose parents
could not afford to rear them.[1] The results were the same as the effects of
Theodore Roosevelt's crusade against "race suicide"—i. e., nothing. The
birth-rate will continue to fall wherever families with few children find an
economic advantage over families with many; these things are not subject
to philosophy.[2]

Will this fall in the birth-rate bring the decay of our civilization? Every
one has heard eugenic Cassandras point with trembling hand and voice to
the comparative childlessness of the educated classes in America, and every
intellectual knows the quip about Harvard graduates who have, by statistical
average, some three-quarters of a daughter, and Vassar graduates who have
a certain percentage of a son. Biologists are familiar with the complaint that
medicine and charity "have pretty well achieved the abolition of natural
selection."[3] The current conclusion is that the stock is breeding from the
bottom, that the most unfit half produces nearly all of the next generation,
and that education is hopelessly frustrated by the sterility of the intelligent.

There is some truth here, though it is not biological. It is clear that the

---

[1] Simkhovitch, V.: *Toward the Understanding of Jesus*, pp. 126–9; Montesquieu, *The
Spirit of Laws*, vol. ii, p. 13.

[2] Perhaps the sterility of the city is a blessing, now that the multiplication of machinery reduces the demand for muscle, and throws a million workmen out of work
every year.

[3] McCollum, E. V., *The Newer Knowledge of Nutrition,* p. 149.

task of the educator is doubled by the fact that most of tomorrow's children are brought up by the simpletons of today; bigotry and superstition, provincialism and reaction continually take on new life through the fertility of the uninformed. But from the biological standpoint this is not so terrible a calamity as it seems to the educator; intellectual acquirements are not transmitted with the chromosomes; even the children of Ph.D.'s must be educated, and go through their measles of dogmas and isms; nor can any man say how much potential ability and genius lurk among the harassed and handicapped children of the poor. Biologically, physical vitality is of more value than intellectual pedigree; socially, strength of character is of more value than knowledge or wealth; philosophers are seldom the best material from which to perpetuate the race. Nietzsche thought that the best blood in Germany ran in peasant veins. So with ourselves: it may be a disguised good that the human material presented to the educator comes from homes where a vigor that may last a lifetime rivals the ignorance that may be dissipated by instruction. Even a Cyclops might see that the solution lies not in accelerating the birth-rate among the rich, but in retarding it among the poor. We must legalize the medical provision of contraceptive information; we must circumvent the fertility of defectives, and we must spread a eugenic conscience to mitigate the myopia of love. Meanwhile we may reconcile ourselves to the sterility of the intelligentsia, and trust to environment and education, rather than to pedigree, for the transmission and extension of civilization. Heredity is but a minor factor in the elevation of the race; evolution is now not biological, but social; give us a healthy stock, and better schools will do the rest.

V. SOCIOLOGY AND CIVILIZATION

Progress, then, depends less upon methods of selection than upon the character of our institutions; it rests upon education and government rather than upon the elimination of the weak by the strong. And our greatest doubt for the future turns not upon the genealogies of the Edwardses and the Jukes, but upon the present status of social institutions that have for centuries organized and supported the development of mankind. The church, the family, the school, the state: how does it fare with them as the carriers of civilization?

The church, as every one knows, has lost a great part of the influence which once made it master of Europe, and which kept it, even after its repeated divisions, a vital factor in education and morals, rivalling the strongest state. We have no more Hildebrands, no more Calvins, no more Wesleys, not even a Brigham Young; no man who, by making himself the voice of a nation's conscience, can wield authority equal to that of presidents and kings. Ever since Luther effected the Reformation by the help of German princes, the state has step by step taken over the property and the power of the church; and the moral leadership of the clergy has suffered visible decay.

To the student of history this melting of creeds and this rapid break-down of the theological sanctions of morality are phenomena of major importance in understanding the present and foreseeing the future. Never since Cæsar smiled as he played Pontifex Maximus has religious belief sunk so low; and seldom has the moral code of a people undergone such strains and changes as affect the ancient Christian code today. Can the state maintain social order without the coöperation of the church? Can morality survive when it is based only on education and is divorced from supernatural belief? Is the modern school a sufficient substitute for the church and the home? Does it spread science without wisdom, knowledge without intelligence, cleverness without conscience? Does it teach a negative and mechanical adaptation to environment rather than esthetic sensibility and creative purpose?

Religion we shall study later; as to the family we have already seen it face to face with decay. The family has been the ultimate foundation of every civilization known to history. It was the economic and productive unit of society, tilling the land together; it was the political unit of society, with parental authority as the supporting microcosm of the state; it was the cultural unit, transmitting letters and arts, rearing and teaching the young; and it was the moral unit, inculcating through coöperative work and discipline those social dispositions which are the psychological basis and cement of civilized society. In many ways it was more essential than the state: governments might break up and order yet survive, if the family remained; whereas it seemed to sociologists that if the family should dissolve, civilization itself would disappear.

But today the state grows stronger and stronger, while the family undergoes a precarious transformation from homes to houses and from children to dogs. Men and women still mate, and occasionally have offspring; but the mating is not always marriage, the marriage is not always parentage, and the parentage is not often education. Free love and divorce abbreviate marriage, invention decimates parentage, the school takes the child from the mother and the state takes his authority from the father; the teacher and the policeman struggle to supply the ancient discipline of the home. Above all, industry replaces agriculture, and the individual job replaces the united tillage of the fields; the individual voter supplants the village community, the town meeting, the *mir*, and the other forms of political organization based on the representation of families by their heads; nothing remains of the old institution but a dormitory, and the unreliable sentiment that attaches a man to a woman, and sons and daughters to the hearth of their youth. The whole onus of social order is centralized, and falls upon the state.

But the state—is it so strong, so well founded in economic and moral fact, that it can bear alone all the responsibility for maintaining, increasing, and transmitting that racial heritage of knowledge, morality and art which constitutes the sap and fibre of civilization? Or does it, by its present political machinery, automatically fall into the hands of second-rate and third-rate men to whom knowledge is anathema and art an alien mystery? Why is it that the largest cities in America are ruled by their smallest men?—why is it that the road to office lies through "organizations" without statesmanship, without patriotism, and without scruple? Why is it that corruption, ballot-frauds, and the embezzlement of public funds, are so widespread that no amount of publicity can stir the people to resentment and action? Why it is that the chief function of government today is the repression or the protection of crime, and the preparation for war between treaties of peace? Is this the institution to which the church and the family must yield the guardianship of civilization?

Let us say it again: great wealth is a danger as well as an aid to a community. For abilities being different, fortunes become more and more unequal as inventions and mechanisms multiply the power of directive and enterprising minds; the gap between classes grows, and strains the body politic like the division of a cell. And as wealth increases, luxury threatens the physical and moral vitality of the race; men find their self-fulfilment less and less in the work of their hands, more and more in the titillation of their flesh; the pleasure of amusement replaces the happiness of creation. Virility decays, sexes multiply, neuroses flourish, psychoanalysts breed. Character sags, and when crisis comes, who knows but the nation may fail? Or, as a young writer put it, far too neatly, in a mood of sedentary pessimism many years ago:

> History is a process of rebarbarization. A people made vigorous by arduous physical conditions of life, and driven by increasing exigencies of survival, leaves its native habitat, moves down upon a less vigorous people, conquers, displaces, or absorbs it. Habits of resolution and activity developed in a less merciful environment now rapidly produce an economic surplus. The surplus generates a leisure class, scornful of physical activity and adept in the arts of luxury. Leisure begets speculation; speculation dissolves dogma and corrodes custom, develops sensitivity of perception and destroys decision of action. Thought, adventuring in a labyrinth of analysis, discovers behind society the individual; divested of its normal function it turns inward and discovers the self. The sense of common interest, of commonwealth, fades; there are no citizens now, there are only individuals.

From afar another people, struggling against the forces of an obdurate environment, sees here the cleared forests, the liberating roads, the harvest of plenty, the luxury of leisure. It dreams, aspires, dares, unites, invades. The rest is as before.[1]

VI. THE PERPETUITY OF CIVILIZATION

These are the factors in the problem, and these are the doubts in our destiny. What shall we say now, in facing the ultimate question of history?

Let us narrow the terms of our query: we are not asking if the earth must pass away—presumably it will; we are not asking if a nation, a race, or a species will last forever—presumably it will not; we are asking if civilization can be indefinitely preserved, or is doomed to be repeatedly destroyed. A civilization is not a material thing, necessarily bound to a certain spot on the earth; it is an intangible complex of technical accomplishments and cultural creations. If these can be carried on to the new home of material power, the civilization is in large measure preserved, and lives on in a disseminated efficacy and reality long after the state, the armies, the politicians and the policemen that thrived on it have passed away.

In this limited sense it is not true that civilizations die; it is nations and peoples that die. Greek civilization is not dead; it is only that the land which once nourished Homer and Alexander is not fertile of genius any more; Greek civilization is not there today. But in another country, in that most spiritual of realms which is the memory of the race, Greek civilization survives: Homer still sings Achilles' wrath, and Alexander marches to the Ganges; Hesiod intones his rural homilies, and Pindar crowns with lyric laurels athletic brows; Solon legislates and learns, and Cleisthenes moulds democracy; Pericles listens to Anaxagoras, and sits with Socrates at Aspasia's feet; Æschylus flings the eternal challenge of Prometheus to the skies, and Euripides makes the victors weep with the Trojans they have slain; Plato walks quietly among the pupils of his infinite Academy, where now a hundred thousand students hear him hourly, in the flesh made word; Diogenes carries his lantern patiently, and Aristotle classifies the universe; Zeno speaks across centuries to Aurelius, and Epicurus walks with Lucretius; Sappho from Lesbos makes verses with Anacreon, and Euclid of Alexandria watches Archimedes making diagrams at the siege of Syracuse. This is not death, it is the very life and soul of the race.

Memory overrides such death, and the memory of mankind is surer and fuller than ever before. Writing transmitted the racial memory poorly; print transmits it better; schools harvest and garner it for all; every day some new and subtle mechanism aids it, rescuing a voice from the grave to sing for centuries, snatching scenes or words from the moment which bore them

[1] *Philosophy and the Social Problem*, p. 7.

and thought to take them away, and carry across a continent some vital utterance to enrich the remembrance of many men.

Yes, nations die. Old regions grow arid or sterile, and man picks up his tools and his arts, and passing on, takes his memories with him. If education has deepened and broadened his memories, civilization migrates with him, and merely changes its home. In the new land he need not begin entirely anew, nor grow without friendly help; communication and transport bind him as in a nourishing placenta with the land that gave him birth; and a vast parental aid of "mother country" to colonies does for the young nation what parental aid did for youth in the infancy of man—protecting, training and teaching, passing ●n the secrets of morals, wisdom and art. Civilizations are the generations of the racial soul. Even as we write and read, print and commerce, wires and waves and the invisible Mercuries of the air are binding nations and cultures together, making the whole world one, and preserving for all whatever each can give.

Civilization need no longer die. Perhaps it will outlive even man, and pass on and upward to a higher race.

VII. THE FUTURE IN AMERICA

Any further and more specific discussion must separate Europe, Asia and America, and consider their prospects individually. Even within Europe there are distinctions: fate looks with dissimilar features upon England and the Continent, Russia and the West, Turkey in its second youth and Italy in its new and stimulating pride. Probably the rushing streams of the Apennines, harnessed to give electric power, will supply Italy with the wealth to finance a lesser Renaissance. In all likelihood Russia will succeed in transforming enough peasants into miners, technicians, railway men and industrial executives, to exhume the rich minerals from her soil, establish a stable system of industry, and take her place among the "powers" of the world. The individual and social health of Germany should enable her, despite indemnities, to recapture the commercial leadership which she was attaining at the outbreak of the War. Unless her unmatched statesmen cheat economic laws, England will lose more and more of her foreign trade, face more and more unemployment and poverty, spend her vitality in factional disruption, and find herself tolerated but ignored in a rejuvenated East.

No, it is impossible to settle fortunes in the lump; the future will have many faces for many states. But if one must deal out destinies to continents, it is easy to say that the English and the French are losing, the Germans and the Russians gaining; that Europe is losing and Asia gaining; and that America is coming of age. The changes are slow; this century will end before China will have established herself as an industrial power equal to any in Europe, and before America will have graduated from commercialism to culture, from riches to art, and from politics to statesmanship.

For commercialism is not, as Spengler thinks, a herald of decay, except for the agricultural aristocracy which commercialism may displace; it is a transition from the static traditions of a rural age to the active culture of a Periclean Athens, an Augustan Rome, and a Medicean Florence—cities ruled by commerce and industry, and long liberated from the power of a landed aristocracy. Pioneering, commercialism, culture: these are the stages in a ripening civilization; and seen in perspective each is forgivable because each is necessary. First the woods must be cleared, the seed must be sown, metals and fuel must be mined, houses and roads must be built, a million wheels must turn; surplus must come, and leisure, before men can pause to write poems, or carve statues, or make music or philosophy. *Primum est vivere:* life comes first. It is good that we should be ashamed of a prosperity as yet unredeemed with art; our shame is the sharp stimulus that may make us graduate from riches to civilization. But we must not develop this sense of cultural inferiority till it becomes a debilitating disease. It is good occasionally to contemplate not only the cathedrals and salons of Europe, but her pogroms, her religious and racial discriminations, her militarism and her conscription; and to see in America not only that wealth which all Europeans envy, and all intellectuals long to share, but the unprecedented generosity of our rich men to education, the unequalled appetite of our people for knowledge and literature, and their eager flocking into every avenue that opens up to them the cultural inheritance of our race.

Spengler has never visited America; he writes against the background of a continent feverish, and perhaps mortally wounded, with war; he can not see that in America the signs and faults of youth far outnumber the tokens of decay. Every valedictorian knows that by all historical analogies we are still in our national adolescence: it is but three hundred years since the Pilgrims came, but one hundred and fifty years since our government was established. It is as ridiculous to expect art or taste from an undeveloped country as it would be to expect metaphysical or political sanity from youth; growth must have its measles and flaunt its sins.

Never before has civilization found prepared for it so vast an economic base. A stimulating climate, knowing every wholesome variation; a fertile soil, still destined to yield many times its present harvests when irrigation and scientific tillage husband it; strata rich in almost every metal, and flowing with fuel oil; railways setting the pace for the world, and improving every day; waterways kept idle by jealous railroads, but needing only a liberating hand to make them unsurpassed; factories well equipped, and sprucing up with belated decency; inventors better organized and more enterprising than anywhere abroad; explorers and aviators writing epics and lyrics in the air; investors holding out their gold and begging industry to use it; a government at last wedded to science and rising to statesmanship: what shall we do with all this good fortune?

Perhaps we shall be ruined by it. A third time let us say it to ourselves, for the good of our souls, that wealth alone does not make a nation great. It can destroy the family instead of building homes; it can corrupt government instead of patronizing art; it can pursue power instead of wisdom, coarseness instead of courtesy, luxury instead of taste; it can give us a rotting Rome as well as a creative Greece. Which of the two is America to be?

What will become of our "polyglot boarding-house"? Is it true, as Madison Grant claimed, that "European governments took the opportunity to unload upon careless, wealthy and hospitable America the sweepings of their jails and asylums"? This is one of those magnificent assertions which constitute the secret of a vigorous style; we get rid of such pronouncements by admitting their half-truth. Some of our immigrants were aristocrats, and some were criminals; the two groups were not quite distinct, and possibly by this time they have been reversed. Environment and circumstance play many pranks with heredity: there is no telling whether the thieves or the baronets who came to us have left us the finer stock, or contributed more to our development.

The Anglo-Saxon is losing his grip here; in municipal politics, in urban morals, and in literary fashions he has forfeited his ancient sway. He did not care to breed as abundantly as his rivals; he thought his quality would suffice to maintain his power and prestige; but time has defeated him, and left him the losing end. The homogeneity of stock that produced the New England era in our cultural history is gone; it will be many decades before the later immigrants will equal the style and substance of Emerson, or the grace and dignity of a New England home. A rough interlude of barbaric modes and dialects must intervene while the rising stocks find their voice and poise; but in the end a new race will emerge, perhaps a new language, certainly a new literature. The passionate and artistic Mediterranean types that now mingle with the staid and prosaic Puritans will bring to our future just those elements of character and feeling that we need; a hundred other peoples will pour their vitality into the stream; and we shall have a race as rich in its resources as the continent given it to rule, a race possessed of that complexity in unity which a nation must have if it is to inherit and perpetuate the civilization of the world.

We have been rebarbarized by immigration and democracy, as Europe has been rebarbarized by war and revolution; but in our case the upward movement towards a new race and a new culture has visibly begun. Our destiny lies not, as the Marxians would have it, in economic environment and circumstance alone, but in the hands of our leaders in industry, government and thought. They must choose.

Wise legislation can give us that freedom of mind and speech—that Athenian *parrhesia,* or liberty to discuss all things—which is our sole guarantee against repeating the barbaric supremacy of Rome. Wise leadership can redeem the abuses of the factory system by shortening hours, replacing coal and dirt with clean electric power, moving industry out to the countryside, and adding the graces of architecture and landscape to buildings made cheerful with light and coöperation within. Wise enterprise in city planning —perhaps with the aid of airplane communication—can spread our urban millions along suburban fields and waters, restoring the moral influence of homes, and saving the health of bodies and minds racked with city noises and speed. Wise philanthropy can give us new facilities for transmitting and augmenting the cultural values of the race. Let our schools and universities be supplied with all their needs; let our teachers be better paid, from the country school-house to the highest chair of instruction in the land; let experiments in education be promoted without hindrance or fear; let a thousand contests and prizes, and a hundred thousand scholarships, stimulate rivalry, study, and creation. Let science be lavishly supported in research, and strictly controlled in its industrial and military uses; let corporations and trustees give a free hand to the artists who design those cathedrals of commerce and those temples of education through which must come the characteristic architecture of our age; and let great benefactors lift up the people with intelligible teaching and civilizing music sent forth every evening on the wings of the air.

Even as these words are written, waves of perfect music rise from the room below. Open the door and let those strains come in; they are the second movement of the Seventh Symphony; and heaven could sing no gentler harmonies. What miracle is this, that brings the profound speech of a great heart long dead, over the barriers of space and time, to a million souls waiting for the touch of genius to heal and quicken them? It is majestic music; all the suffering of a millennium is in it, all the longing, and all the tenderness.

It ends. A telephone rings: a friend wishes to speak of this same mystic beauty that has swept down out of the skies to fill his distant home, this mysterious passage of a dead man through the night, grasping countless hands. And still the room vibrates with the sound of applause; one sees the Stadium—twenty thousand people in the stands, dimly black and white like some gigantic fluttering flower; girls sitting precariously and happily on lofty railings; fine young men, clean, handsome, alert, ready to take over whatever civilization we can give them; musicians exhausted with tension and yet glad with the contact of Beethoven; and above, the stars that shone on the Theatre of Dionysus, and on the streets that Leonardo trod.

Sursum corda! Let us raise our hearts in gratitude and praise.

PART SEVEN

POLITICAL PHILOSOPHY

CHAPTER XVII

In Praise of Freedom

I. LIQUOR AND LIBERTY

IT IS A MARVEL inadequately noted that the contemporary victory of conservatism in the politics and economics of the world has been accompanied by the triumph of liberalism in religion and morals, in science and philosophy, in literature and art. We have selected for our rulers gentlemen who reverently represent the established gods of industry; and we have put behind us, for the while, all thought of experiment in the relations of master and man. We have conferred a mystic popularity upon officials whose only virtue is their timidity; while our scorn of rebels and reformers is so great that we have ceased to persecute them. The capitals and governments of the world are in the hands of caution; and change comes over them only in the night, unseen.[1]

Yet, bewilderingly simultaneous with this virtuous avoidance of the new in the official world, we have in our cities such a riot of moral and literary innovation, such an exuberant rejection of ancient faith and discipline, as makes every gray head shake with sociological tremors, and every aged finger point to corrupt Imperial Rome. Science thinks it has won its battle with the antediluvians; and in the exhilaration of its victory it marches gayly into a mechanical dogmatism that does justice to everything but life. Youth is in the saddle because it is dowered with wealth and opportunity, and because it plies the pens that fill the press. Literature violates every rule and every precedent; the boldest experiment is applauded by the most respectable critics; no one dares admire the classics any more; and

---

[1] These pages were written in 1927.

to be a revolutionist in poetry and painting is as fashionable as to vote for mediocrity and reaction. The stage has suddenly discovered the mysterious beauty of the female form divine; the cabaret is devoting itself esthetically to "artistic nudity"; and alcohol, which was once in bad repute, is now the hero of every conversation, and the *sine qua non* of every well-furnished home. It is a remarkable synthesis of the omnipotent state and the liberated individual.

How shall we explain this humorous anomaly? Partly it is a corollary of our wealth: the same riches that make us timidly conservative in politics make us bravely liberal in morals; when the pockets are full it is as difficult to be an ascetic as it is to be a revolutionist. Puritanism did not die from bromide of *Mercury*, it was poisoned with silver and gold.

Partly the situation issues from a contradiction in our hearts: it is the same soul that hungers for the license of liberty and the security of order; the same mind that hovers, in its fluctuating strength and fear, between pride in its freedom and trust in the police. There are moments when we are anarchists, and moments when we are Prussians. In America above all—in this land of the brave and this home of the free—we are a little fearful of liberty. Our forefathers were free in politics, and Stoically stern in morals; they respected the Decalogue, and defied the State. But we deify the State, and riddle the Decalogue; we are Epicureans in morals, but we submit to all but one of a hundred thousand laws; we are slaves in politics, and free only in our cups.

It is revealing that when an American speaks of liberty's decay he has reference to his stomach rather than to his mind. A convention of the American Federation of Labor threatened a revolution some years ago: not because of the open shop but because of the closed saloon. All the liberalism of the megalopolitan American today confines itself to making alcohol the first necessity of a gentleman, and broad-mindedness the first requisite of a lady. What does it matter that a Polish immigrant is nearly hanged by a Massachusetts court for expressing his scepticism of an ancient faith?—or that troops forbid peaceable assemblage in Pennsylvania?—or that the aged saints of orthodoxy, alleviating the terrors of senility with the theology of infancy, are everywhere introducing bills for the outlawing of biology, and the refutation of Darwin by legislation? What does it matter that freedom to think is lost, if freedom to drink remains? *Primum est bibere, deinde philosophari.*

It is not law that takes our freedom from us, it is the innocuous desuetude of our minds. Standardized education, and the increasing power of mass suggestion in an increasing mass, rob us of personality and character and independent thought; as crowds grow, individuals disappear. Ease of communication facilitates imitation and assimilation; rapidly we all become alike; visibly we joy in becoming as much as possible alike—in our dress, our manners, and our morals, in the interior decoration of our homes, our hotels, and our minds. God knows—perhaps even our moral freedom is a form of imitation; and whiskey, like venery, is popular because without it one cannot be a man.

Yet some rebellion is better than none; and possibly our little draught of liberty will go to the head, and dare to include thought. It is good that men should resist wholesale moralization by the law; to forbid the use of stimulating and consoling liquors because some men abuse them shows the amateurish weakness of a government that does not know how to control the fools without making fools of all. Civilization without wine is impossible. Civilization without restraint is impossible; and there can be no restraint where there is no liberty. "Those things which honor forbids," said Montesquieu, "are more rigorously forbidden when the laws do not concur in the prohibition." [1] If we had spent one-half as much in the propaganda of moderation as we have spent in the "enforcement" of desiccation, we should now be a temperate people.

Let us listen for a moment to those who believed in every freedom. Perhaps it will refresh and strengthen us to forget for a while our countless laws, and walk a little way with the idolators of liberty.

II. THE RELIGION OF LIBERTY

Great part of that order which reigns among mankind is not the effect of government. It had its origin in the principles of society and the natural constitution of men. It existed prior to government, and would exist if the formality of government were abolished. The mutual dependence and reciprocal interest which man has upon man, and all parts of a civilized community upon one another, create that great chain of connection which holds it together . . . In fine, society performs for itself almost everything which is ascribed to government. [2]

Who is it that writes with such unfashionable courage and simplicity? Brave Tom Paine, protagonist of two revolutions, remaker of two continents; the American Voltaire, the English voice of that audacious century which won for itself the name of the Enlightenment. For in that Age of Reason, when the passage of economic power from the idling aristocracy to the thriving middle class had disturbed every tradition, broken the cake of custom, and loosened the hold of ancient superstitions upon mankind, the individual found himself unprecedentedly free, as if for a little while the grip of the past upon the present had been released. The senile dynasty of the Bourbons reigned but it did not rule; the Church, in a society

---

[1] *Spirit of Laws,* Book iv, ch. 2.
[2] Paine, T., *The Rights of Man,* p. 152.

where scepticism was *de rigeur* and even bishops flirted with rationality, was powerful only in the village, powerless in the capitals; every law was relaxed, every canon criticized, every norm of art or conduct violated without fear and without reproach. It was the age in which Rousseau denounced the State as an evil, and Jefferson proclaimed that government best which governed least. It was the epoch of the individual.

From the beginning of human history, presumably, man had fretted under social restraints, and the natural barbarism of the will had seen an enemy in every law. "Laws," said Rousseau,

> are always useful to those who own, and injurious to those who do not . . . Laws gave the weak new burdens, and the strong new powers; they irretrievably destroyed natural freedom, established in perpetuity the law of property and inequality, turned a clever usurpation into an irrevocable right, and brought the whole future race under the yoke of labor, slavery, and misery. . . . All men were created free, and now they are everywhere in chains.[1]

It is remarkable how far the ideology of the rising bourgeoisie, in the century of revolution, partook of that hunger and thirst for liberty which generates in anarchism the simplest and most alluring of political philosophies. Adam Smith, though as respectable as an Englishman, argued that the wealth of nations depended upon the freedom of the individual. Mirabeau *père* and the Physiocrats wished to let nature alone in her management of commerce and industry; and Herbert Spencer, inheriting the liberal tradition from Bentham and Stuart Mill, reduced the state to a vanishing point, retaining it only as a "night-watchman" for his property.

The theorists of politics developed with blind logic this cry of the middle class for freedom from feudal tolls, dynastic government, and aristocratic snobbery. If liberty was good in commerce and industry, it must be good in morals and politics. Godwin was sure that human nature, of its own inherent virtue, would maintain sufficient order without law; let all laws be abolished, and mankind would progress in intellect and character as it had never progressed before. Shelley versified these ideas when their author had ceased to believe in them, and he practised the new liberty with Godwin's daughter without consideration for the right of a philosopher to change his errors with his years. The patriotic Fichte made the individual will the base and apex of the universe, and saw all reality as the creation of a mind walled and moated in from external things and other souls. Stirner, condemned to teach in a young ladies' seminary, solaced himself by conceiving a superman liberated from the despotism of the state: "The state has never any object but to limit the individual, to tame him, to subject him to some-

[1] *Discourse on the Origin of Inequality* (1755), p. 95; *Social Contract*, p. 1.

thing general; it lasts only so long as the individual is not all in all; . . . just straighten yourself up and the state will leave you alone." [1] Nietzsche, protesting that he had never read Stirner, carried on the doctrine of *The Ego and His Own.*

> Somewhere [says Zarathustra] there are still peoples . . . but with us there are states. . . . The state is called the coldest of all cold monsters. And coldly it lieth; and this lie creepeth out of its mouth: 'I, the state, am the people.' It is a lie! Creators they were who created the peoples, and hung one belief and one love over them; thus they served life. Destroyers they are who lay traps for many, calling them the state. . . . But the state is a liar in all tongues of good and evil; whatever it saith it lieth, whatever it hath it hath stolen. . . . Where the state ceaseth, there beginneth the man who is not superfluous. . . . Where the state *ceaseth*—look there, I pray, my brethren! Do you not see it, the rainbow and the bridge of the Superman? [2]

This aspiration to absolute liberty shows an arresting universality and a strange persistency. Among the pupils of Socrates there were Cynics who preferred the life of nature to the rule of law, and aimed, like Aristippus, "to be neither the slave nor the master of any man." Among the Stoics, who had no goods and many bonds, there were some who hoped for an earthly paradise in which all goods would be shared and all bonds would be loosed. Among the primitive Christians the use of force, for any purpose at all, was self-denied, and little saintly groups lived in peace and brotherhood, till wealth increased. The Anabaptists of the Reformation preached anew the gospel of freedom, and anticipated heaven by abolishing marriage. In the French Revolution Marat and Babœuf proclaimed the dawn of liberty and the twilight of the state. During the rebellious forties Proudhon wrote that "the government of man by man in every form is slavery. The highest perfection of a society is found in the union of order and anarchy. . . . In any society the authority of man over man is in inverse ratio to the intellectual development which that society has attained." [3] In revolutionary Russia Tolstoi defined government as "the association of property-owners for the protection of their property from those who need it" (or want it, as the owners would amend). Bakunin, abandoning his wealth and aristocratic position to join the Nihilists, predicted that education would spread so rapidly that by 1900 the state would be unnecessary, and men would obey only the laws of nature. Kropotkin, prince, gentleman, and anarchist, labored to show how, in the Utopia of liberty, men and women would need to work only an hour a day; and

---

[1] *The Ego and His Own.*

[2] *Thus Spake Zarathustra,* I, xi, pp. 62–5.

[3] In Eltzbacher, P., *Anarchism,* p. 73.

almost succeeded in proving that the spontaneous coöperation of man with man has been the basis of all sound social organization, far more powerful and salutary than the artificial compulsions of the state. In England William Morris indicated his respect for government by describing a happy Nowhere in which the Houses of Parliament were used to store Utopian manure. In *laissez-faire* America Emerson preached the frontiersman's self-reliance—"no law can be sacred to me but that of my own nature," and "the only right is what is after my own constitution"; Whitman conceived the function of government as a preparation for the time when men would rule themselves; and Thoreau, while he made his perfect pencils, gayly announced: "I heartily accept the motto, 'That government is best which governs least.' . . . Carried out it finally amounts to this, which I also believe: 'That government is best which governs not at all.' And when men are prepared for it, that is the kind of government which they will have."

III. ANARCHISM

What shall we say of this brave religion of liberty? How far is social order natural, and how long can it maintain itself without the prop of law? How far is freedom possible to man?

In human affairs (to spoil a perfect phrase of Santayana's) everything artificial has a natural origin, and everything natural has an artificial development. Expression is natural, language is artificial; religion is natural, the Church is artificial; society is natural, the state is artificial. Like language and theology, obedience to law comes through social transmission and individual learning rather than through impulses native to mankind. Hence the perpetual conflict, within the self, between the desires of one's heart and fear of the policeman; and hence the joy which triumphant rebels find in violating, with social approval and comparative impunity, an artificial and irksome prohibition. We are anarchists by nature, and citizens by suggestion.

But though in the sanctuaries of our souls we are lawless savages, we are not indisposed by nature to a moderate measure of spontaneous order and decency. Society is older than man, and older than the vertebrates. The protozoa have their colonies, with a division of labor between reproductive and nutritive cells; and the ants and bees bring this specialization of function to the point of physiologically differentiating the organism for its social task. Even the carnivores, whose tusks and hides and claws are individualistic substitutes for the strength and security of social order, include those gentle-eyed dogs who can be more sociable than a salesman and more loyal than a rural editor. "The Hamadryas baboons," says Darwin, "turn over stones to find insects; and when they come to a large one,

as many as can stand round it turn it over together and share the booty.
. . . Bull bisons, when there is danger, drive the cows and calves into the
middle of the herd, while they defend the outside." [1] Imperiled horses gather
head to head, heels outward, forming a *cordon sanitaire*, as the Gauls put
their women at the center when they engaged the foe. (No doubt Napoleon
had this same protection of the helpless in mind when, at the Battle of
the Pyramids, he issued the order: "Asses and professors in the middle.")
It was in such unions for defense, presumably, that animal society had its
origin, and through them that it established a heritage of social impulse
for humanity.

Add to this spontaneous sociability the formative coöperation of the
family, and the case for a purely natural order takes on some plausibility.
"The social instinct," says Darwin, "seems to be developed by the young
remaining a long time with their parents." [2] The brotherhood of man is in
this sense as old as history; it vitalizes a thousand secret societies and forms
of fellowship; there hardly lives the brute with soul so dead that he has
not thrilled at times with a sense of his almost physical solidarity with mankind. Along with natural fraternity a beneficent spread of parental tenderness helps us to mutual aid; and altruism, which the Enlightenment reduced to virtue furnished with a spy-glass,[3] is as natural as love and as
universal as parentage. Kant marveled that there was so much kindness
in the world, and so little justice; perhaps it is because kindness is spontaneous sympathy, while justice is bound up with judgment and reasoning.
Women, in consequence, are a little less than just, and sometimes more
than kind.

Finally, society itself, supported on these instinctive and economic
props, develops in the individual certain social habits which become as
powerful as any second nature, and constitute a pledge of order far more
reliable than law. The longer we live, the more gregarious we become;
the more susceptible to the opinion of our neighbors; the more imitative
and respectable; the more attached to custom and convention; the more
reconciled to those restraints on desire which make civilization depend upon
habit rather than upon force.

Every organized psychological power strives to complete this taming
and socialization of the individual. The church sets up, almost at his birth,
a bombardment of moral exhortations from which some gentle influence
remains even when their theological basis has passed away. As parental
and ecclesiastical authority wane, the school replaces them more and more;
it pretends to prepare the individual for economic and artistic victories;
but quietly and subtly it moulds him, as Aristotle advised, "to suit the

[1] *The Descent of Man,* p. 114.
[2] *Ibid.,* p. 119.
[3] Taine's phrase.

form of government under which he lives." It pours into his receptive
constitution the peculiar habits and morals of his group; and it modestly
covers the naked truth of history with such a glorification of the nation's
past that the patriotic citizen is ready to spur his neighbors to any sacrifice
for the enhancement of his country's power. If the school fails in this
socializing strategy, or the individual eludes it by immigrating when
adult, the press will carry on the work; mechanical invention coöperates
with urban aggregation to bring every mind within reach of that hack-
neyed thing called "news," and that delicate indoctrination which lurks
between the lines.

When these moulding forces are viewed in summary, the drive to good
behavior seems so irresistible that one might reasonably question the necessity of laws that would regulate morality. In a large measure it is society
that exists, and not the individual; as the scornful Gumplowicz has put
it, "what thinks in man is not he, but the social community of which he
is a part"; even his conscience is only his master's voice. "Man," said that
supreme psychologist, Napoleon, "is a product of the moral as well as of
the physical atmosphere." By biological heredity we are bound to our animal past; by social heredity—through our imitative and educational
absorption of the traditions and morals of our group—we are bound to
our human past; and the forces of stability so rooted in our impulses and
our habits leave precious little in us that requires the unnatural morality
of the state.

Since these forming influences act upon us in our tenderest and most
suggestible years, we hardly overcome them except at the cost of a struggle
that involves our very sanity. A miserable nostalgia visits us when we depart from the *mores* of our country and our time; and when we settle
down in life it is most often into one or another of the grooves that the
past has dug. Contented people are usually those who adopt without question the manners, customs, morals, vocabulary and grammar of their group,
becoming indistinguishable molecules in the social mass, and sinking into
a restful peace of self-surrender that rivals the lassitude of love. The greater
the society, the stronger will be the pressure upon the individual to divest
himself of individuality even in those fashionable novelties which delight
the modest soul because they are felt to be not really innovations, but
respectful variations on an ancestral theme. In the final result a large population becomes an almost immovable body; the natural conservatism of
society outruns the chauvinism of the state. The individual, made in the
image of the whole, becomes so docile and well-behaved that the compulsions and punishments of law appear as a gratuitous extravagance; and
we are for a moment tempted to sign our names defiantly to the doctrine
of those fearful anarchists whom we exclude, or deport, or vilify, or imprison,
or hang.

IV. THE DIFFICULTIES OF FREEDOM

Let us reassure ourselves: there are defects in this philosophy of freedom. For first, it underestimates the violence of the strong: the same ruthless domination that makes the state would rule with more visible and direct force, and with more suffering and chaos, if there were no state at all. Civilization is in part the establishment of order and custom limiting the use of the weak by the strong. The precariousness of international law reveals the imminence of violence among the mighty; only little states are virtuous. "If, while living among mankind," said Socrates to Aristippus, "you shall think it proper 'neither to rule nor to be ruled,' I think you will soon see that the stronger know how to treat the weaker as slaves." [1] Every invention strengthens the strong and the unscrupulously clever in their manipulation of the unintelligent, the scrupulous, and the weak; every development in the complexity of life widens the gap and makes resistance harder. It is a bitter thing to realize; but society is founded not on the ideals but on the nature of man. His ideals are as like as not an attempt to conceal his nature from himself or from the world.

Again, the social dispositions upon which a natural order rests are far less deeply rooted in us than those individualistic impulses of acquisition and accumulation, of pugnacity and mastery, which underlie our economic life. Even the cry for liberty comes from a heart that secretly hungers for power; it is because of that hunger in the human beast of prey that liberty is limited and bound. In some measure it is the weak who by pressure of majority ideas curtail the freedom of the individual, lest unshackled strength should so widen the gap between itself and the unfortunate that the social organism would burst into revolution. The first condition of freedom is its limitation; life is a balance of interferences, like the suspension of the earth in space. Men are so diverse in capacity and courage that without restraints their natural differences would breed and multiply through a thousand artificial inequalities into a stagnant and hopeless stratification of mankind. The French loved Napoleon because, with all his despotism, he kept career open to all talents wherever born, and gave men in unprecedented abundance that equality which timid souls love a little more than freedom.

Ages of liberty, therefore, are transitions, brave interludes between eras of custom and order. They last while rival systems of order struggle for ascendency; when either system wins, freedom melts away. Nothing is so disastrous to liberty as a successful revolution; the greatest tragedy that can befall an ideal is its fulfilment.

Why is it that wherever there has appeared in history the spontaneous

---

[1] Xenophon, *Memorabilia,* Book ii, ch. i, § 12.

order that rests solely on the natural sociability of mankind, as in primitive societies, or in the California of 'forty-nine, or in the Alaska of the nineties, it has passed eventually into the artificial and compulsory order of the state? It is a large question, for which a single answer will not suffice. Doubtless part of the cause lies in the passage from the family to the individual as the unit of production and society. Visibly the family loses its functions, even to the care of the child; filial respect and fraternal loyalty give way to a patriotism that becomes the only piety of the modern soul. Divested of its functions the family rots away; nothing remains but centrifugal individuals, magnificently independent in a common slavery. For slavery looks much like freedom when the master is never seen.

Meanwhile the aggregation of people in cities breaks down neighborhood morality as a source of spontaneous order; every egoistic impulse is free in the protecting anonymity of the crowd. Where natural order is still powerful, as in simple rural communities, little law is necessary; where natural order is weak, as in our sprawling cities, legislation grows. The state replaces spontaneous society as the corporation replaces the small dealer, or as the great railroad system replaces the stage-coach of picturesque frontier days. The developing complexity of life has bound us into a highly integrated whole, and has taken from us that independence of parts which once was possible when each family was economically a self-sufficient sovereignty. Political and industrial liberty decays for the same reason again that moral laxity increases: because the family and the church have ceased to function adequately as sources of social order, and legal compulsion insinuates itself into the growing gaps in natural restraint. Freedom has left industry and the state, and survives only in the gonads.

If the implements of production had remained as in days of barbaric simplicity—a spade and a plot of land—the state would not have swollen into the monster that now dwarfs our petty lives. For then each man might have owned his tools and controlled the conditions of his earthly life; his freedom would have kept its necessary economic support, and political liberty would not have become, like political equality, a baseless sham. But invention made tools more complex and more costly; it differentiated and evaluated men according to their capacity to use or direct or acquire the subtler or larger mechanisms; and in the end, by the most natural process in the world, the ownership of tools was centered in a few, self-sufficiency disappeared, and freedom became a politician's phrase, an honored relic commemorated annually like the rest of our noble dead.

On every side, then, we are caught in a current of development in which ancient and natural liberties are swept away. Our industrial relations are too vital to community health to be left entirely to individual control; certain functions—e. g., transport, finance, and communication—are so strategically powerful that without legal limitation they would bestride all industry like some colossal beast of prey. All in all it is well that these processes should fall under regulation by the state, incompetent and partial and corrupt though every state must, in our generations, be. Perhaps all the main *channels* of the economic life should be under such national control, and every vital artery between producer and consumer should be withdrawn from the strangling dominance of entrenched and irresponsible individuals. Production itself should remain free.[1]

When all the avenues of distribution welcome every user on equal terms, production and consumption will be as free as human lust will tolerate. Cured of economic arteriosclerosis—freed from the multiplying intermediaries that narrow and harden the arteries of exchange, and threaten our security in the very heyday of our wealth—industry would sprout and flourish like an unbound plant or a swelling seed. The initiative and enterprise of individual ownership would be liberated rather than enchained; coöperatives would find some protection from the hostile lords of our distributive machinery; and freedom, so pruned and trained, might in the outcome be deeper and richer than ever before.

V. THE JEFFERSONIAN STATE

All this is a grudging concession; for the Jeffersonian ideal of government that governs least still grips the heart with its simple lure, and every added law desecrates the sovereignty of the soul. Order is a means of liberty, and not an end; liberty is priceless, for it is the vital medium of growth. "In the end," as old Goethe said, "only personality counts." The state was made for man, and not man for the state. Heredity was invented to preserve variations; and every custom began as a broken precedent. Evolution feeds on difference and change; social development demands innovation and experiment as well as order and law; history moves through genius and invention as well as through impersonal forces and unthinking crowds.

If we let our economic lives be limited we ought to guard a hundred times more jealously the freedom of the mind. Mental liberty should be at least as dear to us as liberty of body to an animal; caught and caged, it never reconciles itself to captivity, and paces about forever on the watch for a way to freedom. Perhaps it is because we can bear to see such pitiful prisoners, and can look without remorse into eyes deepened and softened with the longing for liberty, that we are unworthy of the freedom our fathers had when they met the animal on equal terms, and killed it in fair fight instead of jailing it as a pleasant sight for a Sunday afternoon. But

[1] Nietzsche, the anti-socialist, goes much further: "We should take all the branches of transport and trade which favor the accumulation of large fortunes—especially therefore the money market—out of the hands of private persons and private companies and look upon those who own too much, just as upon those who own nothing, as types fraught with danger to the community." (*Human All Too Human*, vol. ii, p. 340.)

we ourselves are caged, and do not complain; how can we understand the hunger of these fettered beasts?

There is a Chinese proverb to the effect that when a nation begins to have many laws it is slipping into senility. The ancient Thurians provided a halter for every unsuccessful proponent of new laws, suggesting his fit punishment for mutilating liberty. Our legislatures in America, one hears, pass some sixteen thousand laws per year; [1] if this is so, we are a nation of thieves, and we need not laws but education. Sessions of Congress are a source of national apprehension, to rich and poor alike; and perhaps the quiet esteem in which the last president [2] was widely held was due to the fact that he was a *roi fainéant,* who might be relied upon, like an English king, to do nothing but draw his salary. Even his vetoes were gratefully received; what if the laws they contracepted might by some chance have been good?—even a good law is a law, and no one mourns at its funeral.

If this appears to imply that our current moral lawlessness is not so unmixed an evil as those of us suppose who soothe our consciences by making other people virtuous, the presumption is correct. Much of our immorality takes the form of honesty; we oldsters were as lax as we could afford in our guarded and impecunious youth; when we sinned we sinned in silence, and carried pious faces into meeting. The growing generation is not so skilled in secrecy, and likes to boast of greater crimes than it commits. Its sins are superficial and will be washed away in the confessional of time; experience will make men mature enough to love moderation and modesty again. How shall we dissuade youth from making *vade mecums* of whiskey flasks, except by ceasing to forbid it? What does it matter that nudity can be seen more readily and less furtively than in our hooped and petticoated days, and undue stimulation replaces morbid brooding? Habit will correct the evil gently by dulling sensitivity, and clothing will have to be restored to generate again the illusions of desire.

Against this magnificent uprising of the young the old can only think of laws. Every timid and jealous voice calls upon the immaculate assemblymen of America to come to the rescue of morality. Because some sleek panders have made filthy lucre by exposing God's supreme handiwork upon the stage, tired people demand that policemen be empowered to revise all pictures and dramas before their public unveiling. But one supposed the police had full power to stop indecency by preëxisting legislation. There is no need to resort again to indiscriminate prohibition; public opinion, unweakened by hasty laws, would suffice to control excess, and might prove (as it does in the case of drink) more effective than any law. We should be stamped indelibly as a provincial and infantile nation if we relapsed into the straitjackets of Puritanism at the very time when America begins

[1] Pringle, H. F., *Alfred E. Smith,* p. 132.
[2] Calvin Coolidge.

to create its own literature, its own drama, and its own art. Better a Charles II than a Cromwell.

Luckily for us, life is on the side of youth in these matters, and youth is on the side of life. Our heirs may commit suicide, and prefer baseball to epistemology, and forget to say grace before drinking, but these diversions must not obscure for us the buoyant health and bright good-nature of contemporary adolescence. Let the young be happy; soon enough they will be old; and the lassitude of the flesh will make them virtuous. If morals are transiently too lax, they will correct themselves as knowledge and wisdom grow; in the end, as Socrates suggested, we must instruct rather than forbid. If we wish to improve other people's morals let us improve our own; example speaks so loud that precept is unheard. The best thing we can do for the community is not to fetter it with laws, but to straighten our own lives with tolerance and honor. A gentleman will have no morals but his own.

The time must come when men will understand that the highest function of government is not to legislate but to educate, to make not laws but schools. The greatest statesman, like the subtlest teacher, will guide and suggest through information, rather than invite pugnacity with prohibitions and commands; [1] his motto will be, Millions for education, not one cent for compulsion. The state, which began as the conquest and taxation of peaceful peasants by marauding herdsmen, will become again, as it was for a moment under the Antonines, the leadership of a great nation by great men. We need not so despair of our race as to believe that government will be in the hands of politicians forever. Day by day a hoard of knowledge rises; generation after generation the heritage of culture grows, and finds transmission to a larger minority of mankind; soon men will not tolerate the charlatans that we have suffered so patiently and so long. Our children's children, lifted up by our care, will choose their rulers more wisely than we chose. They will ask not for lawmakers but for creative teachers; they will submit not to regimentation but to knowledge; they will achieve peace and order not through violence and compulsion, but through the advance and spread and organization of intelligence.

---

[1] The practise of Mr. Hoover as Secretary of Commerce was ideal. Into a region of chaos and waste his department brought economy and order; not through legislation or compulsion, not even through regulation, but through information, conference, and agreement. This was statesmanship.

CHAPTER XVIII

Is Democracy a Failure?

I. THE ORIGINS OF DEMOCRACY

DEMOCRACY—WHOSE PRINCIPLE, said Montesquieu, is virtue—was born of money and gunpowder. Cannon and musketry battered down the feudal castle, made proud knights, conspicuous on their steeds, the easy prey of infantry, equalized villein and lord on the field of battle, and gave for the first time since Pythagoras some dignity to number. The invention of coinage and credit eased the ways of trade and the accumulation of wealth; it built at the cross-roads of commerce thriving towns, and at the ports of trade free cities, strong enough to throw off the yoke of feudal fees; it generated in the face of a functionless landed aristocracy an energetic moneyed bourgeoisie, a *tièr état* that clamored for a political position commensurate with its growing economic power.

Voltaire and Rousseau were the heralds of this change; they popularized those invaluable shibboleths, *liberté* and *égalité,* to the music of which the middle class marched to political supremacy. Originally liberty meant freedom from feudal tyranny and tolls; originally equality meant the admission of the middle classes, along with the aristocracy and the clergy, to the honors and spoils of government; originally, one suspects, fraternity meant the open access of bankers and merchants, butchers and bakers and candlestickmakers, to aristocratic and episcopal *salons.* It was not supposed that these splendid words would be so misunderstood as to embrace all male adults, much less all women; mere wives and workingmen would understand that no reference to them was intended. Rousseau, father of democratic theory, wished to exclude all women, and all propertyless persons, from political power, and did not include them in the term "people." [1] Under the Constitution adopted by the French Revolutionary Assembly, three-fifths of all adult males were excused from participating in the franchise. Under the laws of various states in our own republic a property qualification was at-

[1] Beard, *Economic Basis of Politics,* p. 78.

tached to the franchise until the days of Andrew Jackson.- -By its origin, then, and still in its current development, democracy means the rule of the middle class, government by the second best.

Contributory factors coöperated with this fundamental economic cause. The Protestant Reformation had cleared the way for that rebellious individualism which underlies the democratic brotherhood of man. The reverberation, through print, of the blows struck at superstition by scientists and philosophers from Copernicus to Darwin, had the effect of replacing an inactive and insincere belief in Heaven with a naïve but active trust in an Earthly Paradise, wherein all men, geniuses and fools alike, would share in happiness and power. The Industrial Revolution taught men to judge one another in terms of productive ability—which might appear in any rank—rather than through fortuitous pedigree. The cost of government compelled kings to turn ever more politely to wealthy business men, and gave to the lower chamber of legislative bodies an increasing power and prestige. And the rivalry of privileged groups led each minority in turn to extend the franchise in the hope of securing in this way a continuance of its supremacy. When the masters fell out the people fell in. When the men fell out the women fell in. Now we are all in the morass together; and it becomes a problem worthy of Baron Münchausen, how we can find some one to drag us out, when every one is in.

While these general causes were operating in Europe, producing in England, France and Germany the revolutions of 1688, 1789 and 1918, and in Russia the first phase of the revolution of 1917, they were reinforced with certain special factors in the development of American democracy. Our Revolution of 1776, now distant enough to be admirable, was not only a revolt of Colonials against England; it was, perhaps more fundamentally, a revolt of the middle classes against an imported aristocracy; it was part and parcel of that long series of political earthquakes which cracked and dislocated the social surface of the Western world, broke up and submerged the land-owning aristocracies, and reared an erratic formation of popular governments everywhere.

And as in Europe the triumph of the bankers over the barons was facilitated by peasant *jacqueries,* by the lust of the harassed serf for a soil liberated from feudal rights and tithes, so in our country the rise of the middle class was eased and quickened by the abundance of free land. Democracy came naturally to America, because America began with equality and freedom; like communism, real democracy tends to appear rather at the simple beginnings of a civilization than in its later stages of complexity, luxury, and differentiation. De Tocqueville marvelled at the economic equality which he saw here in 1830. Land might be obtained from Congress for the asking—a privilege now reserved for corporations. Democracy was actual because political equality rested upon an approximate equality

of possessions, upon a widespread ownership of the soil; men who stood
upon their own ground and controlled (within the limits of nature) the
conditions under which they lived, had personality and character, and
could be called democrats beyond the narrow meaning of a quadrennial
admission to polling-booths. It was such men who made Jefferson president—Jefferson, who was as orthodox as Thomas Paine, and as conservative as a man might be who favored a revolution every nineteen years. It
was such men who provided the basis for Emerson's self-reliant individualism, and Whitman's glorification of the common man. It was such men
who gave to the Yankee his European reputation for shrewdness, individuality, and independent judgment,—a legend now as curious to an observer
of contemporary politics as the election of another Jefferson is inconceivable.

Again secondary factors crowd upon the scene. Doubtless the freedom
of competition in the early days of our republic provided another prop of
independence and personality. Perhaps the proportion of skilled workers
was greater then than it is now, when the untrained peasantry of con-
tinental Europe pours in to form the helpless proletariat of our towns.
Men were not merely "hands" in those early days; the pride of skill in a
specific trade gave some vertebræ to character, some leverage against that
wholesale denudation of individuality which we achieve through standardized education and the press. In some measure, too, the rural isolation
of the early citizen enhanced his liberty and vitalized his democracy,
much as our national isolation gave us freedom and security within our
protecting seas. These and a hundred other conditions came together to
make American democracy real.

II. THE DECAY OF DEMOCRACY

All those conditions are gone. National isolation is gone through trade,
communication, and the invention of destructive mechanisms that facilitate
invasion. Personal isolation is gone through the growing interdependence
of producer, distributor and consumer. Skilled labor is the exception now
that machines are made to operate machines, and scientific management
reduces skill to the inhuman stupidity of routine. Free land is gone, and
tenancy increases. Free competition decays; it may survive for a time
in new fields like the automobile industry, but everywhere it gravitates
towards monopoly. The once independent shopkeeper is in the toils of the
big distributor: he yields to chain drug-stores, chain cigar-stores, chain
groceries, chain candy-stores, chain restaurants, chain theatres—everything
is in chains. Even the editor who owns his individual paper and moulds
his own mendacity is a vestigial remnant now, when a thousand sheets
across the country tell the same lie in the same way every day better and

better. An ever decreasing proportion of business executives (and among them an ever decreasing number of bankers and directors) controls the lives and labors of an ever increasing proportion of men. A new aristocracy is forming out of the once rebellious bourgeoisie; equality and liberty and brotherhood are no longer the darlings of the financiers. Economic freedom, even in the middle classes, becomes rarer and narrower every year. In a world from which freedom of competition, equality of opportunity, and social fraternity begin to disappear, political equality is illusory, and democracy becomes a dream.

All this has come about not (as we thought in hot youth) through the perversity of men, but through the impersonal fatality of economic development. Men can be free only when they are approximately equal in capacity and power; and nevertheless their equality is destroyed by their freedom. Inevitable hereditary differences in vigor or ability breed social and artificial differences; strength is made stronger, and weakness weaker, by every invention and discovery. Equality is an unstable relation, as of scales poised in equilibrium; it decreases as organization and complexity grow; the very nature of social evolution involves increasing inequality because it specializes functions, differentiates abilities, and makes men unequally valuable to society. "Equality is only a transition between two hierarchies, just as liberty is only a passage between two disciplines." [1] See how the original equality in colonial America has been overgrown and overwhelmed by a thousand forms of economic and political differentiation, so that today the gap between the most fortunate and the least fortunate in America is greater than at any time since the days of plutocratic Rome. Of what use can equality in ballots be when power is so unevenly distributed, and political decisions must obey the majority of dollars rather than the majority of men?

This disappearance of economic equality and freedom is the deepest root of our political hypocrisy and decay. But once again there are contributory causes; and our understanding of the problem will be precariously partial if we ignore them. Let us state them as briefly as may go with clarity.

There is, first, the growing size of the political unit—the imperial expansion of America. The larger the state, the more difficult it is to preserve personality and democracy. "Democracy dies five miles from the parish pump"; [2] it was meant for city-states, where men could come and "vote in the first person." [3] Large populations are more easily ruled than small ones, because their inertia is greater, and it is more difficult for them to agree in their grievances or to unite in their action. Pericles and Cleon,

[1] Tarde.
[2] H. G. Wells.
[3] Tom Paine.

though they differed in everything else, concurred in the opinion that democracy is inconvenient in empires.

Consider, next, the growing complexity of government—a natural result of the enlargement of the political unit and the increasing intricacy of national economic relations. Once a government consisted of a king, his courtiers, and his courtesans; today it is a vast and lumbering mechanism for the adjustment of a thousand conflicting groups. It requires the full time of those who play in it any but the most subordinate roles; it would be impossible to rule a modern state on that plan of popular rotation in judicial office, or that hasty decision of issues by vast uninformed assemblies, which gave Athens its liberties and brought it to an early grave. In the most natural way in the world, "machines" develop in every party, every union, every convention and every parliament; democracy is the matrix in which oligarchies grow. The sovereign voter is absorbed in bread and butter; how can he keep himself abreast of the thousand problems that arise and change and melt away in his party, or his union, or his church? He cannot answer intelligently the questions placed before him; he does not know. Democracy is government by those who do not know.

Consequently it is the first casualty of war. De Tocqueville predicted that America would have to abandon democracy the moment it became entangled in the politics and wars of Europe. "Many an army has prospered under a bad commander," said Macaulay, "but no army has ever prospered under a debating society." Labor unions tend to oligarchy for the same reason: they are military organizations designed for offense and defense. "Democracy is a luxury; it can be maintained only in a moderately secure and pacific world." [1] Reactionaries know it, and may be relied upon to produce an occasional war as a substitute for birth-control, or as a unifying discipline of the national will. Democracy is not a cure for war, but war is a cure for democracy. Perhaps the cure will be made permanent when our political internes stage the next international operation.

The last contributory cause of our democratic failure is the popularity of ignorance. "The imbecility of men," said Emerson, "is always inviting the impudence of power." [2] The intelligence tests confirmed the opinion of those who had watched the elections of the preceding twenty years. The theory of democracy had presumed that man was a rational animal; no doubt some one had seen this in a book of logic. But man is an emotional animal, occasionally rational; and through his feelings he can be deceived to his heart's content. It may be true, as Lincoln pretended to believe, that "you can't fool all the people all the time"; but you can fool enough of them to rule a large country. It has been computed that the supply of

[1] Weyl, W., *The End of the War*, p. 83.
[2] *Representative Men*, p. 21.

fools, on this planet, is replenished at the rate of two hundred every minute; which is a bad omen for democracy.

Apparently it is not democracy alone that is a failure; it is ourselves. We forgot to make ourselves intelligent when we made ourselves sovereign. We thought there was power in numbers, and we found only mediocrity. The larger the number of voters, the more ordinary must be the man or the qualities that will appeal to them. We do not demand greatness or fore-sight in our elected officials, but only bare-toothed oratory and something this side of starvation. According to Bacon, "the ancient politicians said of democracies that 'the people were like the sea, and the orators like the wind.' " [1] Indeed, we do not much care who governs us; we hardly realize that we are being governed, just as formerly we thought we paid no taxes because we paid them through the landlord or the tariff.

Voltaire preferred monarchy to democracy, on the ground that in a monarchy it was only necessary to educate one man; in a democracy you must educate millions, and the grave-digger gets them all before you can educate ten per cent of them. We hardly realize what pranks the birth-rate plays with our theories and our arguments. The minority acquire education, and have small families; the majority have no time for educa-tion, and have large families; nearly all of each generation are brought up in homes where the income is too small to provide for the luxury of knowl-edge. Hence the perennial futility of political liberalism; the propa-ganda of intelligence cannot keep pace with the propagation of the ignorant. And hence the weakness of Protestantism; a religion, like a na-tion, is saved not by the wars it wins, but by the children it breeds.

Hence also the conservatism of democracies. Anatole France bemoaned the neophobia of the crowd. Bismarck looked to universal suffrage to support monarchical policies. "Direct election and universal suffrage," said the old cynic, "I consider to be greater guarantees of conservative action than any artificial electoral law." [2] Woman suffrage won a comparatively easy victory because party leaders believed it would make for conservatism. The liberals of Switzerland passed certain reforms, including the popular referendum; the conservatives put these reforms to a referendum; the re-forms, including the referendum, were defeated.[3] The extension of the suf-frage in England in 1918 brought in the most reactionary government in half a century. The new compulsory-voting law in Australia raised the proportion of actual to possible voters from sixty per cent in 1912 to ninety per cent in 1925, and resulted in an overwhelming conservative victory. The extension of the suffrage in America. . . .

[1] *Advancement of Learning*, p. 227.
[2] Headlam, J. W., *Bismarck*, p. 255.
[3] Maine, Sir H., *Popular Government*, p. 40.

"It is one of the strangest of vulgar ideas," Sir Henry Maine predicted, "that a very wide suffrage could or would promote progress, new ideas, new discoveries, new inventions, new arts of life. The chances are that it will produce a mischievous form of conservatism." [1] We shall have to admit to the prejudiced Englishman that democracy seems hostile to genius and apathetic to art. It values most those things which come within the comprehension of the average mind; it builds motion-picture palaces and thinks they are Parthenons; if the Athenian assembly had had its way there would have been no Parthenon at all.[2] The intellectual tyranny of the majority may be as harassing as the political tyranny of monarchs; already, in some American states, more than a little knowledge is a dangerous thing. This democratic suspicion of individuality is a result of the theory of equality; since all men are equal a count of noses must establish any truth, and sanctify any custom. Not only is democracy a result of the machine age, and not only does it rule through "machines"; it holds in itself the potentiality of the most terrible machine of all, a vast weight of ignorant compulsion ostracizing difference, crushing the exceptional mind, and discouraging untraditional excellence. Nowhere is education so lavishly financed and equipped as in the United States; nowhere is it so little honored or so little used. We have devoted ourselves magnanimously to the provision, on an unprecedented scale, of schools, high schools, colleges, and universities; and now that they are all built and full, we have made education a disqualification for public office.

III. THE MECHANISMS OF DEMOCRACY

In a nation where the few who really rule must get some show of popular consent, a special class arises whose function it is, not to govern, but to secure the approval of the people for whatever policy may have been decided upon by that inevitable oligarchy which hides in the heart of every democratic state. We call this class of men politicians. Let us not talk about them.

The politicians divide into parties, and align the people into hostile camps. The natural party-spirit of mankind makes such organizations easy; they are a survival of warlike tribal loyalties. Australian savages will travel across their vast continent to take, in a fight, the side of those who wear the same totem as themselves.[3] The totem still helps us to organize; and the parties that use an elephant or an ass as their sacred emblems seem to get along better than those that naïvely choose the torch.

Now party organization is expensive, and requires angels—realistic idealists who pay the costs of pool-rooms, club-rooms, excursions and cam-

---

[1] In Sellars, R., *The Next Step in Democracy*, p. 216.
[2] Plutarch, *Life of Pericles*.
[3] Maine, *op. cit.*, p. 31.

paigns, and are satisfied, as their reward, to select the candidates, secure certain contracts and appointments, obtain protection from the enforcement of absurd and irksome laws, and play a quiet role in the arduous tasks of legislation. "They who nominate, govern." [1] The people cannot nominate any one, even at primaries. For they are unorganized and uninformed; they may be trusted to divide their favors with approximate equality; and a small but well-organized minority, by casting its votes entirely on one side, can usually decide a convention, a primary, or an election. The "machine" triumphs because it is a united minority acting against a divided majority. Perhaps this is what Carlyle meant when he said, "Democracy is by the nature of it a self-cancelling business, and gives in the long run a net result of zero." [2] "A true democracy," said that passionate democrat, Jean Jacques, "has never existed, and never will exist; for it is against the natural order of things that the majority should govern the minority." All politics is the rivalry of organized minorities; the voters are bleacher athletes who cheer the victors and jeer the defeated, but do not otherwise contribute to the result.

Under such circumstances voting is superfluous, and is carried on largely to grease the grooves of social control by establishing in the minds of the people the notion that the laws are made by themselves. In democracies, said Montesquieu, taxes may be greater than elsewhere without arousing resistance, because every citizen looks upon them as a tribute which he pays to himself.[3] *L'état c'est lui*—he is the state, and the president is the chief of his servants. Tickle a man's pride and you may do anything with him. The Romans ruled the people through *panem et circenses;* our masters need only give us a quadrennial circus—we will provide the bread for ourselves, and pay for the circus.

About the only advantage which an election has in these premises is the educational opportunity offered by the aroused attention of the people. But in most cases this is nullified by a clever concealment of the actual issues at stake; a politician is worth nothing if he cannot invent some interesting and unimportant issues to divert the eyes of the populace from the problems actually involved. So in the Canadian election of 1917 the real issue of conscription vs. volunteering was subtly covered over by pointing out that the defeat of the conscription proposal would mean the domination of Canada by the French element in the population. The English inhabitants rose *en masse* and voted for English domination, and conscription. A good show-window will sell any kind of political shoddy. Elections become a contest in fraud and noise; and as sound arguments make the least sound, truth is lost in the confusion. Add to this the gerrymandering of city dis-

[1] Crozier, J. B., *Sociology Applied to Practical Politics,* p. 48.
[2] *Chartism,* p. 74.
[3] *The Spirit of Laws,* Introduction, p. xxi.

tricts to keep the power with conservative rural communities; the vast floating population which is disfranchised by its mobility; a degree of dishonesty and violence at the polls—and you get democracy. Under such conditions "a vote becomes as valuable as a railway ticket when there is a permanent block on the line." [1] Is it any wonder that the proportion of actual to legal voters decreased from 80% in 1885 to 50% in 1924?—or that intelligent men refuse to stand in line an hour for the privilege of registering, and then again an hour for the privilege of voting—that is to say, the privilege of choosing between A and B, who both belong to X? [2]

Nevertheless, suppose that we have voted. The election is over, stocks rise, and the elected senators and representatives go down to Washington (some months later) to form our Congress, our Parliament or Talk-Shop, our National Palaver. Nothing could be more disconcerting than the surprises which meet these elected ladies and gentlemen. It is not merely that when men come together in assemblies their ears instantly grow longer. [3] They have been chosen for political ability in the American sense—i. e., the ability to get themselves nominated, advertised, applauded, and elected; they possess that sort of ability in a highly developed and specialized form. Normally they are subservient people, amenable to discipline, elastic of conscience, and free from dangerous originality or genius; nothing would so readily disqualify them for office (or for the devious approaches to office) as genius of any kind—above all, genius in statesmanship. It should be apparent by this time that a man has a better chance of arriving at high office if he achieves a reputation for mediocrity.

Now suddenly our representative finds himself assailed by problems all the world away from the kind he has solved on the road to power. Those were problems of politics: of patient loyalty to the ward and district and county leaders; of underground influences and secret understandings; of speeches and charges and denials and manipulated publicity; of contributions inconspicuously solicited, and spent with one eye on the law; of favors done to the powerful, and promises made to the rest. But these problems that fall upon him in Washington, and overwhelm him in a thousand bills, are problems of economics: they have to do with land-ownership, raw materials, coal mines, oil wells, water power, production, competition, transportation, navigation, aviation, arbitration, distribution, marketing, and finance; they involve esoteric details intelligible only to a specialist, and painful beyond bearing to a man whose specialty is wire-pulling.—Our representative takes refuge in his newspaper, and votes as he is told.

As government becomes more complex, elected officials become less and

[1] Chesterton, G. K., *Short History of England*, p. 266.

[2] The proportion of actual to eligible voters increased significantly when, in 1928, they had an opportunity to vote for a qualified man.

[3] Voltaire in Morley, J., *Diderot and the Encyclopedists*, vol. ii, p. 232.

less important, selected experts more and more. The executive "encroaches upon the legislative" power because the executive is armed and buttressed with expert committees—Federal Reserve Boards, Federal Trade Commissions, Labor Boards, Interstate Commerce Commissions, debt commissions. . . . During President Harding's administration the members of Congress were shocked to find themselves placed, in a parade, behind the members of certain of the aforesaid commissions. The Senate protested with ten Whereases and two Therefores, and Mr. Harding answered with that kindly suavity which had sufficed to make him President. But the straw had shown the wind. "Representative government" had broken down; democracy had found no way of electing brains to office; and the brains had been placed in power while democracy was making speeches, or reading newspapers.

Was this the reason why we so insistently recommended democracy to our enemies? Nietzsche speaks of the "disposition which supports the democratic form of government in a neighboring state—*le désordre organisé*, as Mérimée says—for the sole reason that it assumes that this form of government makes the other nation weaker, more distracted, less fit for war." [1] Perhaps this democratic enthronement of mediocrity and incompetence, chicanery and corruption had something to do with the Platonic transition from parliamentary government to "tyranny" or dictatorship in Italy and Spain and Greece and Russia and Poland and Portugal, and the threat of similar developments in France. As for ourselves, see what has happened: the forces of political reform have been beaten most of the time; and where they have won a stray victory it has been through the adoption of the methods used by the "machine,"—so that the triumph of "reform" in certain states has had something of the character of the conversion of the world to Christianity, in which it was not quite clear which of the two parties had been converted to the other. "Politics is now as completely dominated by the machines as it was during the 80's. . . . The professional politicians are more than ever our masters. After fifty years of struggle they have finally defeated their enemy, the reformer." [2] Mediocracy has won. Everywhere intelligence has fled from the hustings of democracy as from an engulfing torrent. Fools are in the saddle and ride mankind.

Yes, this is a partial view, a plaintiff's brief, rather than a complete analysis. The half-redeeming virtues of democracy have been lauded too long to need any litany here. It is true that the oppression of minorities by majorities is (numerically) preferable to the oppression of majorities by minorities; that the democratic disfranchisement of the educated man is no worse than the aristocratic subjection of new talent by ancient pedigree; that democracy has raised the spirit and pride of the common man as much

[1] *Human All Too Human*, vol. i. § 453.
[2] *The New Republic*, Dec. 1925.

as it has broken the spirit and sterilized the genius of the exceptional individual; that the omnipotent voter has now a sense of liberated personality which makes in some degree for courage and character; that there are no (conscious) serfs among us any more, and every man may know that he is a potential president. It may be, as the patient Bryce laboriously concluded, that there are some forms of government worse than democracy.

But the more we examine it the more we are disturbed by its incompetence and its insincerity. Since political power is unreal except as it represents military or economic mastery, universal suffrage is a costly show. Dictatorship may claim one superiority—it is more honest; "absolute power," said Napoleon, "has no need to lie; it acts and says nothing." [1] Democracy without education means hypocrisy without limitation; it means the degradation of statesmanship into politics; it means the expensive maintenance, in addition to the real ruling class, of a large parasitic class of politicians whose function it is to serve the rulers and deceive the ruled.

The last stage of the matter is gangmen rule. Criminals flourish happily in our larger cities, because they are guaranteed the full protection and cooperation of the law. If they belong to the Organization, or have friends in it, they have every assurance that if they commit a crime they will not be arrested, that if arrested they will not be convicted, that if convicted they will not be sent to jail, that if jailed they will be pardoned, that if unpardoned they will be permitted to escape. If, in the practice of their profession, they should be killed, they will be buried with the grandeur and ceremony due to a member of the ruling class, and memorial tablets will be erected in their honor. This is the *dénouement* of municipal democracy.

We are rank cowards if we any longer blink this evil awakening from our wishful dreams. If we cannot find some amendment to democracy that shall cleanse it of its villainy and rid it of its ignorance, we may as well present our Constitution to some stripling nation, and import a king.

IV. NOSTRUM

What shall we do?

Well, even the irate reformer must understand that very little can be done, and nothing rapidly. The most desirable plan would be so lavish an expenditure of our national and private wealth on education, invention, and scientific research as would improve our brains, decrease our numbers, make muscle costlier than mechanical power, dissolve the proletariat, and liberate mankind for the tasks of the Great Society. In the long run there is no solution except in education; until men become intelligent, cities will not cease from ill. But if the world has not done all this for Plato, there is no likelihood that it will do it for us. And we have seen what devilish tricks the

[1] Bertaut, J., *Napoleon in His Own Words*, p. 64.

birth-rate plays with education.—The second expedient would be the con-
vocation of the best-informed and most capable men of the land, chosen
from each profession by the members of that profession, meeting to consider the rejuvenation of our Constitution, recommending new amendments
to Congress and the States, and supporting these recommendations with
the prestige of their professions and perhaps with the money of our millionaires, which every reformer is prepared to spend.—The third best plan
is as follows.

The evil of modern democracy is in the politician and at the point of
nomination. Let us eliminate the politician, and the nomination.

Originally, no doubt, every man was his own physician, and every household prescribed its own drugs. But as medical knowledge accumulated, and
the *corpus prescriptionum* grew, it became impossible for the average individual, even for solicitous spinsters, to keep pace with the *pharmacopœia.*
A special class of persons arose, who gave all their serious hours to the
study of *materia medica,* and became professional physicians. To protect
the people from untrained practitioners, and from those sedulous neighbors
who have an interne's passion for experiment, a distinguishing title and a
reassuring degree were given to those who had completed this preparation.
The process has now reached the point where it is illegal to prescribe medi-
cines unless one has received such training, and such a degree, from a recognized institution. We no longer permit unprepared individuals to deal with
our individual ills, or to risk our individual lives. We demand a life-time's
devotion as a preliminary to the prescription of pills, or the extraction of
teeth.

But to those who deal with our incorporated ills, and risk our hundred
million lives in peace and war, and have at their beck and call all our possessions and all our liberties, no specific preparation is required; it is sufficient if they are friends of the Chief, loyal to the Organization, handsome
or suave, hand-shakers, shoulder-slappers, or baby-kissers, taking orders
quietly, and as rich in promises as a weather bureau. For the rest they may
have been butchers or barbers, rural lawyers or editors, pork-packers or
saloon-keepers; it makes no difference. If they have had the good sense to
be born in log-cabins, it is conceded that they have a divine right to be
president.

Let us imagine a pleasanter picture. Let us suppose that our great universities, which contain the seed of a redeemed America, have added to their
faculties a School of Political Administration. A School not of theory so
much as of practice and concrete detail; not a school for the discussion of
political history, or of the "philosophy of the state," or of monarchy vs.
aristocracy vs. democracy vs. socialism vs. single-tax vs. anarchism; but
a School that will go down with its students into the actual field of municipal

administration; a school that will look upon the problems of a city not as a street-corner statesman might, nor as a loyal elephant or donkey might, but as a scientist would, or an executive whose training and ability have made him see administration as an art. If such a course were as thorough and as conscientious as the curriculum of a good medical school, it would attract only serious and scientifically-minded men; it would admirably frighten away the gentlemen who now rise to power through self-salesmanship and perorations. There would be few candidates for such instruction at the outset, since they would have no guarantee of finding political place upon completing their preparations. But the spread of the city-manager plan would offer openings; the Schools would grow as medical schools once grew; and successful city-managers would be invited to head the teaching staff.

All this is within the realm of possibility; even now our larger universities offer courses that could form the basis of these Administration Schools. But the next step in our hypothetical amendment to democracy calls for more imagination. Let us suppose that while these Schools were preparing men to rule us, other agencies had, through the written and spoken word, prepared the people for the novel and unpatriotic notion of requiring education in their masters, and providing salaries commensurate with the ability demanded in modern government. It is conceivable that a body of opinion might be formed which would make it unwise for a political party to nominate to municipal office any man unarmed with his specific preparation. It is barely conceivable that the time might come when nominations would be dispensed with altogether, as they are in the Constitution, and prepared administrators would offer themselves directly as candidates for election. The choice of the people would be restricted to these, and unrestricted among these; it would be a far wider choice than now; and whatever choice might be made would be a sane one. It would be a fool-proof democracy; and if Heraclitus was right about majorities, this is the only kind of a democracy that can survive in this realistic world.

Would such an amendment destroy the essence of democracy? No. It is essential to democracy that every adult should equally share in the selection of major officials; it is not essential that every adult should be equally eligible for office. Restrictions of birth and age and residence already exist; to add the requirement of preparation is only a corollary of the growing complexity of government. The plan would widen democracy more in increasing the number of candidates than it would narrow democracy in restricting their character. It is rather our present structure that is undemocratic: it limits the voter's choice to two nominees, and it makes but poor provision for the most fundamental democracy of all—equality of educational and economic opportunity. If every graduate who reached a given standard of excellence were assured that municipal and state scholarships would send him on from school to college and from college to university when his own family's funds proved inadequate, then the road to the highest office, and to most of the goods of life, would be open to all on equal terms, and even the restrictions here proposed would be respectably democratic Equality of opportunity is the core of democracy; we have contented our·selves with the husk and meekly surrendered the core. Let us open all the roads to talent wherever born, and for the rest we need not disturb ourselves about forms of government.

Certainly our little nostrum has its flaws, which are to be compared not with Utopia but with the *status quo*. In substituting our universities for our saloons and hotels as the medium of nomination, we do not forget that even universities can be corrupted, and university graduates bought. But it is a question of degree; presumably a man with scientific training, or a man earnest and brave enough to select a career involving a long and arduous preparation, would have something of. the pride of craft that makes a man jealous of his honor and solicitous of his work. There is a slightly higher standard of morals among scientists than among politicians. And though there are thieves and charlatans in the ranks of medicine, it is one of the few professions in which "ethics" is allowed to interfere with income.

As for the universities it is not a question of teaching radicalism or conservatism; the science of administration has very little to do with these majestic and useless divisions. Undoubtedly power would rule under the the new dispensation as effectively as now; but it would rule more efficiently, without the wastage and indecency of stupidity, insolence and knavery. We are not offering here a solution of the "social problem," a plan whereby the weak can be enabled to rule the strong. Presumably a clever minority will continue to use a less clever majority; we have no secret whereby democracy can escape this immoral ordinance of nature. Our purpose here is not to make "brooks run wine and winds whisper music," but to make whatever government there is as capable and honest as human character can bear. That is the problem of politics, and it is the only problem with which we are here concerned.

Our tendency, in these days, is to take corruption and ignorance as the natural privileges of elected persons; and we smile at any proposal to alter this patriotic tradition. But government has not always been incompetent and venal; the English still have some reputation for training in their statesmen and honor in their judges; and the German professional *Bürgermeister* made their cities the best-ruled places in the world. Nothing is impossible but thinking makes it so.

What we have suggested is a very old idea, the dream of Socrates and Plato, of Bacon and Carlyle, of Voltaire and Renan. Perhaps it is nothing more than a dream; and perhaps again it may be a reality when all of us are dreams. For a long time, doubtless, it can be nothing more than a dream;

many decades of instruction would be needed to produce the necessary changes in the public mind. But unless we make some honest effort to bring ability into office, and to break down the democratic hostility to knowledge —unless we can capture for the public good those talents and powers of mind that now are lost in private enterprise and gain—unless we can put into our city halls and our state capitols, and into the halls of Congress, men who have prepared themselves for public administration at least as thoroughly as men prepare for far less vital tasks—then assuredly democracy is a failure, and it might be better for the world if America had never lured and deceived the hopes of men.

CHAPTER XIX

Aristocracy

I. SALVAGING ARISTOCRACY

ARISTOCRACY IS A SUBJECT upon which, in the common judgment, the final words were said in 1776 and 1789. When George III lost his wits, and Louis XVI his head, aristocracy lost its case; and not all the wigs and gowns and heraldry of England can make men reverence it again. The world has gone in for democracy.

Therefore, it is a strange time to suggest reconsideration of aristocracy; without doubt such a proposal will be overwhelmed by the current of the age. However, one does not speak on these subjects with any expectation of affecting events; it is enough if, in the International of the Mind, one is permitted to exchange secrets with unseen friends. And then again, America knows so much more about democracy than the rest of the world can know! Perhaps in this native habitat of popular sovereignty one may make, without too much peril of his life, certain assumptions that will clear the field and open the way to objective thought.

The assumptions can be reduced to this: that in America, at least, democracy has broken down.[1] That is to say, it has visibly failed to give us either a government by the people, or a government by the best. If any gentle reader of this volume believes that the people actually govern in America—that they determine, for example, war and peace, or economic policy, or tariff rates, or nominations to office—it would be better for him to leave at least these pages unread. Likewise, if there are readers who believe that democracy has given us government by the wisest or the ablest men, they too would do well to pass on.

But to say that democracy has failed is not to turn up our noses at it as utterly worthless and beyond repair; it is apparent that there are many

---

[1] This essay was written in 1928. In the quarter-century that has since elapsed democracy in America has undergone an encouraging reinvigoration, and hardly deserves the supercilious cynicism of the text.

virtues in it, and many fine potentialities; and certainly the sovereignty of numbers has done less harm than the forms of government which it replaced. After all, it is better to be ruled by mediocrities than to be shot by kings. Perhaps the great failure was not inevitable, and was due less to the essence than to the form; perhaps if democracy had retained certain features of the old aristocratic system it might have succeeded in creating a political order far superior to that in which we live and move and suffer fools so gladly.

It is a possibility which one would like to explore. What was this aristocracy which prepared statesmen and nurtured art and developed men who valued honor more than life? Had it any qualities which wisdom would care to cherish? Could its virtues be married to those of democracy in a manner that would sterilize the vices of both and bring forth good fruit? Could the election of all major officials by universal suffrage be reconciled with the attraction to office of the finest and cleanest men?

II. FORMS OF GOVERNMENT

It must be admitted that aristocracy has been popular among philosophers even in the days of its defeat. Socrates, Plato, Aristotle, Cicero, Montesquieu, Voltaire, De Tocqueville, Taine, Renan, Anatole France, Goethe, Nietzsche, Burke, Macaulay, Carlyle, Emerson, Santayana: they knew democracy in Athens or in Rome, in Paris or in Washington; and yet with what remarkable unanimity (only Spinoza significantly dissenting) they lifted their voices to Heaven and prayed for government by the best! What is it that these men admired in aristocracy?

"Among nations and in revolutions," said that most realistic of philosophers, Bonaparte, "aristocracy always exists. If you attempt to get rid of it by destroying the nobility, it immediately reëstablishes itself among the rich and powerful families of the third estate (the middle class). Destroy it there, and it survives and takes refuge among the leaders of the workers and the people." [1] "Legislate how you will," said Fitzjames Stephen, "establish universal suffrage, if you think proper, as a law which can never be broken—you are still as far as ever from equality. Political power has changed its shape but not its nature. The result of cutting it up into little bits is simply that the man who can sweep the greatest number of them into one heap will govern the rest. The strongest man, in some form or other, will always rule. If the government is a military one, the qualities which make a man a great soldier will make him a ruler. If the government is a monarchy, the qualities which kings value in councillors, in generals, in administrators will give power. In pure democracy the ruling men will

[1] Bertaut, *op. cit.*, p. 46.

be the wire-pullers and their friends." [1] It is a summary analysis, and rides roughshod over the nuances; but for a preliminary statement of the matter it will serve.

In general there are but two forms of government: rule by one man, and rule by a few. Rule by the majority is an occasional interlude, and for the rest a consoling delusion, which stimulates individuality and lubricates the wheels of government. Minorities can organize, majorities cannot; thereby hangs our tale. Government is oligarchy, or it is monarchy; there is nothing else.

Theoretically, much might be said in defense of monarchy; for given a supreme executive genius like Napoleon, everything (except freedom) prospers under his centered and homogeneous sway. But actual monarchy is rare in modern history. In Ivan the Terrible, in Peter and Frederick, in Louis XIV and Bonaparte it was real; but how often are bedecked kings and queens mere window-dressings for secret oligarchies glad to hide their hands behind royal glamour and prestige! What were the later Tzars but tools for the Tchinovniks, or the late Kaiser but flag-waver and speech-maker in chief for the Junkers? Is there anything in the world more ridiculous (next to an American election) than the stiff-necked guards that pace so terrifyingly up and down before the palace in which the English incarcerate their "king"? How could we bear with England if it had had no Gilbert and Sullivan?

We cannot be put off here by the usual pretense that these vestigial monarchies serve a real function in holding far-flung empires together through the symbolism of a common head. It is true that the people love their kings; but what binds colonies to a mother-state is not the sentiment of the simple, but the need for protection and trade. Only tradition, the fierce delight of keeping to accustomed ways, maintains European monarchs on their thrones. "In all European countries except two," said Francis Thompson (when there were still two), "monarchies are a mere survival, the obsolete buttons on the coat-tails of rule, which serve no purpose but to be continually coming off." [2]

We may take it then as a general principle, illuminated even by its exceptions, that behind every government is an oligarchy; and that the first rule of political analysis should be: *Cherchez les forts*—find the strong. The oligarchy may be military, commercial, or aristocratic: that is to say, the ruling minority may be soldiers, placing a succession of generals upon the throne; or rich business men, ruling through presidents and kings; or members of old families originally empowered by the ownership of land, and traditionally possessed of leadership and prestige. Hence

[1] In Willoughby, W. W., *Social Justice*, p. 57.
[2] *Shelley*, p. 39.

the great argument of the aristocrat is that aristocracy is the sole alternative to rule by crude wealth or brutal force. The break-up of the Roman aristocracy opened the way for barbaric soldier-kings; the break-up of the French and English aristocracy cleared the road for the enthronement of pounds sterling, dollars, and francs. Democracy can forestall a military oligarchy; but no system of elections has yet been made that could keep riches from seizing power. The one preventive of plutocracy is the retriction of government to families with the traditions and qualities of rule. Rule by pedigree is the only alternative to rule by pocketbooks; and only an aristocracy can prevent an oligarchy of the *nouveaux riches* from subjecting the moral and cultural life of a nation to the ideals and standards of the stock exchange, the marketplace, and the factory.[1]

III. STATESMANSHIP

This is all questionable, not to say distasteful; nothing could so weaken the case for aristocracy as to reveal it, at the outset, as a form of hereditary rule. But let us hear the aristocrat for a while without interruption or query, privately discounting his prejudice, and learning from him even while we disagree.

He accepts the inheritance of eligibility to office as a prerequisite of proper government; no man rises to full statesmanship unless it has been carried down into the atmosphere he breathes, by generations of responsibility and place; he needs, in Nietzsche's phrase, "not only intellect but blood." This is what, in the end, Napoleon lacked, despite his comment on D'Enghien ("Neither is my blood ditch-water"); he was the son of a provincial general, and try as he would, he could not reach the poise and judgment of inborn aristocracy.

Leadership, to follow Nietzsche further, requires "great aristocratic families with long traditions of administration and rule; old ancestral lines that guarantee for many generations the duration of the necessary will and the necessary instincts." [2] Therefore the aristocrat protests against speaking of the "accident of birth"; birth is not an accident but a corollary, the conclusion of centuries of development, the promise of ability and intelligence. Today we attach great importance to the pedigree of animals; we inquire carefully not only into their immediate but into their remote and intermediate ancestry. The aristocrat attaches a similar importance to the pedigree of men; he exalts the influence of heredity as obstinately as the democrat emphasizes opportunity, or the socialist, environment. Hence his unwillingness to marry outside his rank, his repugnance for another

---

[1] Cf. Cicero: "There is no uglier form of government than that in which the richest are thought the best." *De Rep.* I, 34, in Bluntschli, J. K., *Theory of the State*, p. 453.

[2] *Will to Power*, § 957.

class as for another species; he understands, with the intelligence of instinct or group tradition, that the crossing of type weakens and for a time destabilizes character, however desirable it may be for the slow generation of a new and complex race.[1]

But again, the inheritance of eligibility to higher office is necessary for the production of competent governors. Some people have to be set aside from their birth to give them the time required for a complete and healthy development of mind and character; life is too brief for the acquisition of both culture and wealth; one or the other must be given at the outset, and one of them cannot. It is for humanity's sake that a few should be liberated from the corroding necessities of individual economic strife; "the greater or the lesser possibility of subsisting without labor is the necessary boundary of intellectual improvement." [2] Aristocracies, then, are the most precious of nurseries, as Taine called them; for through them a nation recruits and prepares its statesmen.[3]

What the democrat does not understand is that it takes more time to make a statesman than to make a bootblack. Until its recent democratization, England's leaders were trained for public place from their boyhood; first at home, then at Eton or Harrow, then at Oxford or Cambridge, and then by appointment to arduous minor offices. The finest aspect of English civilization, after its passion for liberty, was this dedication of its universities not to the arts of finance and trade, not to schools of business and commerce, but to the task of preparing the rulers of the Empire. They were ruthless rulers, and it is not clear that their ruthlessness was indispensable to their rule; but it was these men who lifted little England to the top of the world, from which its present manufacturing statesmen will pull it down.

In a democracy it is useless for men to prepare themselves for statesmanship; they have no guarantee, even of the frailest sort, that they will be able to pass the tests of convention, hustings, and polling booth. Rather, their training will make them gentlemen and thinkers, men who would find the rough-and-tumble of an election forbiddingly painful. Sainte-Beuve foresaw that democracy would drive ability into seclusion; Renan predicted that the sovereignty (i.e., the manipulation) of numbers would put knaves and quacks upon the throne, and give the state over to unscrupulous mediocrity. Even in 1830 De Tocqueville, on his second tour of America, wrote despondently, "At the present day the most able men in the United States are rarely placed at the head of affairs; and it must be acknowledged that such has been the result in proportion as democracy has overstepped all its former limits. The race of American statesmen has

[1] Cf. Ludovici, A. M., *A Defence of Aristocracy,* pp. 340–50.
[2] Tocqueville, A. de, *Democracy in America,* vol. i, p. 209.
[3] Taine, H., *The Modern Régime,* vol. i, p. 149.

evidently dwindled most remarkably in the course of the last fifty years." [1]
Thank God that De Tocqueville is dead, and cannot see us now.

IV. CONSERVATISM

To the aristocrat, order is the beginning of wisdom, and change is a circle of folly. Liberty is precious, but without order how could liberty be? And though aristocracies limit political freedom, who shall say that this is worse than the democratic stifling of individuality and thought by the fanatic pressure of dull majorities? With order it becomes possible for a nation to have a consistent policy and development. Through aristocracy statesmanship is freed from the lottery of elections, and may devote itself to tasks requiring generations. An aristocratic governing body like the Roman Senate, or the English Parliament of Elizabethan days, has a collective continuity, almost a collective immortality; its purposes are not disrupted, they are hardly disturbed, by the death of individuals, or by the chaos and hypocrisy of campaigns. "Almost all the nations which have ever exercised a powerful influence upon the destinies of the world by conceiving, following up, and executing vast designs," says De Tocqueville, "have been governed by aristocratic institutions." [2]

Such a government, it is true, presents an obstinate barrier to experiment or change; but nothing could be more wholesome. Even a liberal, if he has any acquaintance with the past, knows that of ten new ideas at least nine will turn out to be mischievously wrong; the bitterest humor in history is the fact that most of the ideas for which men have died have proved ridiculous. Resistance to change is a clumsy thing, like the brakes on a car; but it is as indispensable.

We are deceived here by the analogy with science and literature; because experiment is the very life of these, we leap to the conclusion that the best government is that which offers the fullest opening to change. But society is not a laboratory, and men do not submit to vivisection, except in war. Even in science the readiness to experiment is confined to realms of research where helpless animals or lifeless things can be used as the material of our trial and error; when it comes to applying the findings of science to matters of human life and death, we are as cautious as Republicans. If there is any field in which we resist change it is not politics, but diet and medicine. To play with ideas is not quite the same as to experiment with lives.

But where a hundred million destinies are involved, four-wheel brakes may be advisable, even when going uphill. Large bodies must move slowly; it is easier to disarrange them than to restore them to health and order.

[1] *Op. cit.*, vol. i, p. 209.
[2] *Ibid.*, p. 247.

In politics, as in medicine, the correction of one ill very often induces another as an unforeseen by-product. The structure of society is even more complex than the structure of our bodies and our minds, for it includes them in their myriad and incalculable interrelations. These mutual relations find a workable adjustment if left alone; but when the selected wisdom, or assembled mediocrity, of a nation attempts to reduce these vital processes to the artificial regularity of law, the result is like trying to walk while analyzing the geometry and mechanics of our legs.

It would be different if society were a logical structure, like mathematics, or engineering, or anything else that does not deal with life; but society, like our own selves, is a growth and not a formula or a syllogism. As Taine put it, "Society was not organized by a legislative philosopher according to sound principle, but it is the work of one generation after another, according to manifold and changing necessities. It is a product not of logic but of history; and the new-fledged thinker shrugs his shoulders as he looks up and sees what the ancient tenement is, the foundations of which are arbitrary, its architecture confused, and its many repairs plainly visible." [1] Every schoolboy knows Burke's answer to Rousseau: society is not a contract between contemporaries, it is an unconscious and gradual formation; and if there is a contract involved it is one between the past, the present, and the future.[2] To break sharply with the past is to court the discontinuity that brings madness, the social amnesia that comes from the shock of sudden blows or mutilations. The sanity of the individual lies in the continuity of his memory; the sanity of a group lies in the continuity of its traditions; in either case a break in the chain involves a neurotic reaction, and a disturbance dangerous to life. So Peter found when he tried to make Russia western in a generation; so Lenin found when he tried to make it socialist. The past will out.

V. GOVERNMENT AND CULTURE

Consider morals and culture. Democracy has bred in the modern soul a fear of the populace which is called conscience; but has it developed that emulation of the highest, that desire for the approval not of masses but of the finest few, which made the sense of honor in the aristocrat? Could an aristocrat be a Puritan or a fanatic, or dictate what other people should drink? Could an aristocracy produce "jazz" or cabarets? Could an aristocrat be a hypocrite, or stoop to conquer by flattering the mob? Is there not a certain vulgarity, in the tone and manners of democratic communities, that could not thrive under the guidance and example of an aristocracy?

[1] Taine, H., *The French Revolution*, vol. ii, p. 7.
[2] *Reflections on the French Revolution*, p. 91.

"Among Americans," says Professor Ross, "business ideals are not held in check by the influence of a landed aristocracy. In most of the Old World the leading social class despises the trader's point of view, and prides itself on appreciating things from the enjoyer's point of view. . . . Since this aristocratic emphasis on living rather than on money-making leaks down through the general community, commercialism is in Europe more confined to the business class." [1] Perhaps the comparison should no longer be so unfavorable to America; Europe too is in the throes of democracy, and tends to take its manners from below, while in America the heads of old-established businesses rich in long traditions, tend to develop that quiet honor and *noblesse oblige* which are the fairest flower of aristocracy.

Even the democrat has in his heart an envious admiration for what is vaguely called aristocracy of soul, a vigor and yet ease of carriage, a sureness of touch in judgment and taste, a readiness of wit and phrase with reserve and moderation of speech, an unassuming dignity and an unfailing generosity; above all, and always, the courtesy of the gentle-man. No wonder that "every Englishman loves a lord," and that, in the words of Anatole France, "there is nothing that a democrat esteems more highly than noble birth." [2] The surest road to social success in a democracy is to behave like an aristocrat; the surest road to success as a speaker in America is to talk like an Englishman. [3]

It is forgivable and natural; for we know, whatever we may say, that it takes many generations to make a gentleman. Seldom can a man begin poor, doomed to pass through the clinging dirt of the economic war, and yet acquire that cleanliness and grace of body and mind, that quiet confidence and security, that modest pride and classic calm, which mark the man who from the beginning has been trained by precept, example, and atmosphere to the amenities and niceties of life. [4] The world must make the hard choice between inheritance and scramble, between refinement that passes from top to bottom by prestige imitation, and a vulgarity that by the compulsion of competition mounts from the bottom to the top.

The difference between the two spirits is visible in the literature which flourishes under the rival modes of life and government. Allowing for the exceptions that disturb every generalization about living things, the literature written for an aristocracy tends to a classic, the literature of a democracy to a romantic, form. For a while the influence of science and socialism gave us an age of "realism," in which literature aped the objectivity of

---

[1] Ross, E. A., *Changing America*, p. 88.

[2] *Penguin Isle*, p. 210.

[3] This last with apologies to Mr. John Cowper Powys, a magnificent orator and a profound novelist.

[4] Keyserling speaks of "the gyroscope which is in the blood of every real aristocrat."— *Europe*, p. 194. A splendid book.

physics, and rebelliously selected for portrayal the evils and injustices of life. But essentially the rivalry in literature lies between classic intellect and romantic imagination, as the rivalry in politics lies between transmitted and acquired wealth. A democratic age tries to redeem the prose of its industrial and mercantile existence with the fancies of romantic *belles-lettres;* it loves to lift itself out of its shops and stores by reading of careless leisure and passionate love. But the aristocrat is ashamed to let his passions run loose, or his speech run wild; his imagination is always under the control of his intelligence; restraint is the essence of him, in literature and in life; he will understate, but not exaggerate; he will "speak quietly to make himself better heard" (as Flaubert says of some one in *Salammbo*); he produces Montaigne's *Essays* or *L'esprit des lois,* but never *Émile* or *Les Misérables.* Doubtless it takes all sorts of books and men to make a literature or a world.

Generally, aristocracies have been more favorable to the arts and sciences, and have patronized more lavishly and discriminatingly the exceptional individual. Tarde has argued that aristocracies are the first to accept new ideas; that innovations, though they may originate anywhere, find their earliest shelter among the educated few, from whom they spread by contagion and suggestion to the ranks below. "Civilization," says Santayana, "has hitherto consisted in the diffusion and dilution of habits arising in privileged centers." [1] "All civilization," said Renan, "is the work of aristocracies"; [2] science, he feared, would decay under democracy, as soon as the mob came to suspect its meaning.[3] "It is the classes who produce variations," says Sumner; "it is the masses who carry forward the traditional mores." [4] "History demonstrates," says Le Bon, "that it is to this small élite that we owe all the progress so far accomplished. The inventors of genius hasten the march of civilization. The fanatics and the deluded create history." [5] It is so.

VI. DEMOCRACY AND CHAOS

Finally, the people themselves prefer an aristocracy. They are conservative in politics as well as in ideas, and they like a government that moves slowly to imperial aims. They make revolutions when they are pressed too hard; but they seem incurably enamored of unelected power. The Italians thrilled with pride at the name of their dictator, especially if they did not live under him; the fact that he rode to leadership over all the

---

[1] *Reason in Society,* p. 125.
[2] In Maine, *op. cit.,* p. 42.
[3] *History of the People of Israel,* vol. iv, p. 179.
[4] *Folkways,* p. 47.
[5] In Todd, p. 382.

forms and fetiches of democracy did not irritate them. The papers read by the common man in England are heavy with news of the aristocracy; and every second store has the royal emblem on its doors, or boasts that it purveys merchandise to His Majesty the King. With one fine exception, the individual most popular in the American press of 1927 was an English Prince; and the most popular woman was a Balkan Queen.

It may be that people are a little happier today than before; invention has multiplied their comforts and their powers, and wealth has given them a new range of travel and interest. But with this variety and vivacity of life has come a nervous discontent of soul; everyone seems to feel that existence is a ruthless competition, a warfare of wills *à l'outrance,* an endless push and pull for dress and car and place. "The new form of society," said Anatole France, "in authorizing all sorts of hopes, excites all the energies. The struggle for life is more desperate than ever, the victory more overwhelming, and defeat more pitiless." [1]

Peace and calm have gone from our hearts along with the ordered structure of aristocratic society. Before the French Revolution (to adopt an analogy of Taine's) society was an edifice of separate stories, between which there were no stairs; the peasantry tilled the fields and seldom thought of climbing, and the aristocracy flourished in the style of Watteau and Fragonard, undisturbed by clamors for their place. "Those who have not lived before 1789," said Talleyrand, "have not known the full sweetness of life." [2] But today every man and every woman burns with the fever; it makes our wealth and it makes our illnesses. Liberty means for us that each of us is fit to be president; and its result is the most restless and persistent strife that history has known. Peace is between unequals; the pretense of equality brings a perennial tug of war. Hence democracy breeds endless conflict in politics, in economics, and in the soul; worry and strain are written on every face, and embitter every home. When society recognizes the natural inequality of men in intellect and will, and eliminates the hypocrisy of egalitarian institutions, men may come to know peace again. Then society will graduate from competition to courtesy, from quantity to quality, from imagination to intelligence, and from wealth to art.

VII. THE FAULTS OF ARISTOCRACY

That is the argument for aristocracy, expressed without trimming to catch any democratic wind. Let us first set aside the items that leave us unconvinced, and then endeavor to absorb the rest into our philosophy.

The aristocrat, of course, has drawn a very partial brief, and left many

[1] *On Life and Letters,* 3rd series, p. 9.
[2] Spengler, *Decline of the West,* vol. i, p. 207.

points obscure. Let us suppose that aristocracy produces subtler statesmen, men with longer vision and larger plans; what guarantee have we in human nature or in history that this superior skill will be devoted to the public good? Aristocracies seldom form with the people such an organic whole of mutual service as binds the brain with the body (to use an old aristocratic comparison); they spend too much of their time unseating rival dynasties, or keeping themselves in power, to permit that watchful devotion of part to whole which characterizes the leadership of the brain.

Recall the addiction of aristocracies to war: it was sport with them, like hunting; the enemy was the prey, and the people who fought were merely their hunting dogs. It is true that they sacrificed themselves liberally in these wars; no one can doubt their courage. And sometimes they were less brutal and pugnacious than the empowered bourgeoisie of Armageddon; Lloyd George talked of hanging the Kaiser to a lamp-post while Lansdowne counselled moderation; and French democrats insisted on sending their last striplings to the sacrifice while Emperor Charles sued humbly for an early peace. But we remember, too, the barbarous Wars of the Roses, and the marauding campaigns of Louis XIV, and the ruthless greed of Frederick, and the bandit-like partitions of Poland, and the relentless Coalitions that fought for twenty years to restore the Bourbons to the throne of France.

Power corrupts in the measure of its irresponsibility and degree. Aristocracies are often cruel, as the Spartans were to their helots, or the Roman patricians to their debtors, or the English landlords to the Irish peasantry. What glory is there in an aristocratic culture that can descend to the brutality of the Romans with the followers of Spartacus, or that of Clive and Hastings in India? It may not yet be true, but it is still a principle worth working up to, that "no man is good enough to govern another without his consent." Here the democratic ideal, though it is only an ideal, has finer possibilities; it encourages every man to be responsible for himself; it stiffens the backbone, and raises the look of the eye. Better a country of chaotic individuals on the road to order, than a nation of slaves whose only refuge is revolution.

Yes, culture has been a minority luxury, and will remain so for as long a time as can concern us now. But no man who knows would associate the arts and sciences with aristocracy. Progress is due to the few, but hardly to the hereditary few. The development of modern science is unmistakably allied with the growth of transport and industry, which are matters whereon the aristocrat would not soil his hands. Occasionally men of rank like Count Rumford have played at science; but if we remove from the list those whose titles came after their work was done, we find that science has been almost entirely the work of the middle class.

And it is the same with art. Aristocracies do not produce art, though they support it. The great epochs in the history of art are not those marked by a settled aristocracy; they are not the age of Agamemnon, nor the Feudal Age in Egypt or in Europe; they are periods distinguished by the rise of a new middle class; and their glory is not on the villa but in the free cities and the trading towns. Almost literally, the Greek drama was the nursling of Greek business men: everybody knows that the great trilogies of Æschylus, Sophocles and Euripides were prepared and staged by opulent gentlemen who took this way of honoring their state and fumigating their fortunes. No delicate princes, but worldly financiers supported Lucretius, Horace and Virgil. No landed barons made the Gothic cathedrals, but the merchant guilds and the wealth of proudly independent cities. English aristocrats helped Shakespeare until he was able to lift himself to riches (like the good business man he was, this riotous butcher's son); but it was the banking house of the Medici that paid the bills of the Renaissance. Aristocrats refused to help Johnson or Burns or Chatterton, and cast out their own Byron and Shelley; but the wealth of growing commerce and industry nourished the vigorous literature of nineteenth-century England and France. Only in Germany, with Frederick the Great, and Duke Karl August of Weimar, and King Ludwig of Bavaria, can the aristocrat build the semblance of a reasonable case.

In truth the aristocrat looks upon artists as manual workers, as the Egyptian aristocracy considered them; he prefers the art of life to the life of art, and would never think of reducing himself to the consuming toil which is the price of genius. He does not often produce literature, for he knows that all writing for publication is exhibitionism. No aristocrat would have frolicked so freely in print as Rabelais, or revealed his political secrets like Machiavelli, or fought so passionately as Rousseau, or made such violent tragedies and metaphors as Shakespeare, or even written the aristocratic essays and stories of Anatole France. For the charm of Anatole (who was a bookseller's son) is in his tender disillusionment; and the aristocrat does not pass through such disillusionment; he has been brought up to take the other world only half seriously, since he already possesses this one.

The result is, in modern aristocracies, a careless and dilettante hedonism, a reckless riot in which the privileges of place are enjoyed to the full, and the responsibilities glossed over or ignored. Given a narrow conception of heredity and a snobbish limitation of marriage alliances to chosen and gilded circles, degeneracy ensues; the type becomes physically delicate and morally lax, and slips within a century from genius to mediocrity. Only a few generations intervened between Peter the Great and Nicholas I, between William of Orange and George III, between *l'état c'est moi* and *après moi le déluge*. The Stuarts degenerated, the Bourbons degenerated, the Hapsburgs degenerated, the Hohenzollerns degenerated, the Romanoffs degenerated; no further instances are needed to beat the conclusion into our philosophy.

The conclusion is that heredity has its Wilhelms as well as its Fredericks, and that in the long run it takes back in small change more than it gives us in gold. Genius has an impish way of appearing in any rank, though it has a better chance of developing where it can get enough to eat; and often it so exhausts a man in its service as to leave his seed powerless to duplicate him. Hereditary aristocracies have had considerable permanence, thanks to the patience and timidity of men; but what is the duration even of the Hapsburgs beside the endless chain of the Papacy? The greatest rulers in Europe have been popes, and the greatest ruling body has been the Church. But in the Church heredity had no place, and any man might work his way from the plough to the Vatican. The strongest government in history was an aristocratic democracy. Perhaps some day that is the sort of government which we shall be wise enough to have.

VIII. NOSTRUM AGAIN

If there is anything clear to us in this confused problem of human rule, it is that the principle of political inheritance is a principle of disintegration; that it protects and transmits incompetence, clogs every channel of administration with pedigreed imbecility, frustrates the ripening of untitled talent, and violates the first necessity of a strong and permanent state—that every talent born within it, of whatever rank, shall be developed to maturity, and welcomed to its service. This is the vital truth beneath the forms and catchwords of democracy: that though men cannot be equal, opportunity can; and that the rights of man are not rights to office and power, but rights to enter every avenue that may test and nourish his fitness for office and power. That is the essence of the matter.

Aristocracy is rule by the best, not necessarily rule by birth. We want aristocracy, we fester and rot for lack of it; but this does not mean that we hunger to be ruled by counts and earls and dukes; it means that we wish to be governed by our ablest men. In every walk of life we meet with men and women trained and equipped for achievement; but in politics they find the road barred beyond passing. Democracy must open the road.

Solutions are difficult, for our decay has engendered cynicism, and our first response to every suggestion is a disillusioned smile. By a kind of olfactory adaptation we have come to believe that the world has always been this way, and will always be; we seem quite reconciled, now that we are so intelligent, to being ruled by wolves and geese. And perhaps Voltaire was right, and the wise man will be resigned to leaving the world substantially as he found it. But the lure of Utopia is in our blood and will not let us rest until we cease to grow. There is some good in aristocracy;

we must find it and weave it into unity with the truth that lies beneath our democratic sham.

Picture a mayoralty election in the America of 1959. It is still a democratic election; every man and woman votes and chooses those who are to govern. Indeed, it is immeasurably more democratic an election than any that we have known. For today our choice is limited to two or three persons, selected privately by small groups over which we have no control; our vaunted sovereignty is restricted to determining what dress our masters' Sergeant-at-Arms shall wear. But here, in this fancied election, choice ranges freely among a hundred candidates, and our sovereignty frolics in its freedom.

How did they ever win a nomination, these hundred candidates? Had they found a hundred "bosses," and a hundred "machines"? By what wire-pulling, and faithful service to the Organization, and unflinching readiness to vote under orders, did they arrive at this door to power? By none of these, and yet by no other means; for they have not been nominated at all. They have merely announced their candidacy and their purposes, and nothing more.

An election without nominations? *Exeunt* controlled conventions, picked delegates, packed primaries, and Blackstone Hotels? But then is any person free to offer himself as prospective mayor, governor, or president? No; nor is any other person, nor any quantity of persons, free to offer him; only his credentials present him, and only preparation nominates him. However wide the popular choice here is, it cannot choose an incompetent man.

For each of these candidates has devoted his life to making himself fit for the office which he seeks; he has passed through college with honors, and then through four years of hard and practical training in a School of Political Administration; government has been with him an art and science to be learned, as medicine is, or engineering, or law; it has not been merely an office to be won. He has emerged at last clarified with knowledge and purified with toil; every knave and shirker has fallen on the way. And now he is free, and many others like him are free, to enter the polls for the mayoralty of any minor city in the land. If he has served such a town for two terms he may present himself as candidate for the mayoralty of a second-class city. If he has served such a city for two terms he may offer himself for election to the leadership of the largest municipalities. If he has served two terms in one of these he may offer himself for governor. If he has twice been governor of the same state he may aspire to be president. Preparation nominates him; and our universities, the finest product of American life, become the nurse and center of our statesmanship. Bureaucracy remains, as it always will; oligarchy remains, as it always will; but it is a trained and responsible bureaucracy, a highly constitutional and limited oligarchy. Democracy remains—in elections— aristocracy is joined with it—through the restriction of office to the best; but it is a democracy without incompetence or corruption, and an aristocracy without heredity or privilege.

It is impracticable, idealistic, visionary? What has not been? Consider a poor scribe prophesying, in Elizabeth's days, a Washington or a Mirabeau; or in Washington's days, the enfranchisement of women; or in Grant's days, the exile of alcohol. Everything is impossible until it is done. Oxford and Cambridge educated statesmen; must our universities be forbidden to equal them? China for centuries limited office to men whose education and preparation had been tested at every step in their advancement; when, in 1911, democratic ideas entered China, this system, of course, was abolished, though it gave almost equal opportunity to all. Germany for a century had cities whose orderliness and cleanliness and quaint beauty were unsurpassed; men ruled them who had been chosen for their specific training in municipal affairs.[1]

But let us not despair. Already there are Schools of Government in our larger universities, or courses capable of forming the nucleus of such Schools; already the hostility to experts begins to break down, and cities like Cincinnati have dared to be ruled by specially trained men. Already every educated person in America knows that our elections are indecent farces; and the masters of the silly game are disturbed by the resolute withdrawal of half the voters from the polls. It is time to call the mess what it is; to say openly that we will not waste our time on the business of voting until it becomes possible to ballot for statesmen. It is our own cowardice that leaves public opinion uninformed, that lets half the nation remain inarticulate in its mute conviction that democracy has broken down. Let us speak out.

That is all that a scribe can do; but consider what "royal works" might be accomplished by men of influence and means. See a hundred periodicals supplied with material, a hundred speakers teaching the nation that the time has come to enfranchise education; see the opinion of the informed, frankly uttered, passing down rank by rank among the people; eyes opening, prejudices cooling; at last, here and there, a willingness to try, a resolve to limit office—or nomination, if nomination there must be—to men honorably equipped and trained. See one city enviously imitating another, until they are all clean and safe, and thieves and venal souls are driven from its offices as well as from its streets.

We older ones cannot hope any more; our hearts have been so blasted

[1] "Our quarrel with Germany must not blind us to the fact that before the War that country was the best governed in Europe." Dean Inge, *Outspoken Essays,* Second Series, p. 94.

and withered with disillusionment that we smile at every enthusiasm and laugh at every ideal. But in our colleges another generation grows, less romantic than we were, and yet braver and more informed. When there are a million of them they will be strong enough to come out into the open and smash the infamy that stifles our public life.

Écrasez l'infâme!

CHAPTER XX

How We Made Utopia

I. ON THE USES OF UTOPIAS

"A MAP OF THE WORLD that does not include Utopia," said Oscar Wilde, "is not worth even glancing at, for it leaves out the one country at which humanity is always landing. And when humanity lands there, it looks out, and seeing a better country, sets sail. Progress is the realization of Utopias." [1]

Is this true? Have Utopias regularly been realized? The grown-up mind has in our days a contrary opinion; it is unfashionable to believe in human betterment any more. "History is circular," says the sceptic; "everything that goes up must come down, especially civilizations; our progress is but the surface turbulence of a sea which in its depths is changeless and still. Utopias are the ethereal poems with which our sensitive souls anesthetize themselves against the caustic operations which life and death perform upon us. But a strong man will take his wounds without anodyne; or if he needs forgetfulness, he will immerse himself in the present and its routine details, taking no thought of humanity's tomorrows. What is has been, and will be. Only fashions change."

We are ungrateful beasts, and now that the Aladdin's lamp of invention has lavished luxuries upon us we sit like a romantic girl amid our riches, and long for some different and distant treasure, infinitely admirable because so far away. Once philosophers dreamed of universal schools; we have them, and pine for universal universities. Once men were naked; now they are clothed, but they suffer agonies because others are clothed more expensively than they. Once men were hungry; now they die by hundreds of thousands every year, in all civilized countries, from diseases of over-eating; but no thanksgiving rises from the earth for the abundance and luxury from which we have the honor to die. Even in Will Shakespeare's day great cities were dark at night, and every street unsafe; today (though every street is still unsafe) the night has lost its terror, and beneficent

[1] *The Soul of Man under Socialism.*

319

light sheds its gayety everywhere; nevertheless men look back disconsolately over their shoulders, and mourn for the days that are no more. Once children of six years, and mothers of large families, slaved fourteen hours a day in filthy factories, and slept at night on the floor beside their machines; now children are kept at school till they are ready to rule the world, and millions of women are preserved in a delicate idleness that would have seemed sinfully Utopian to their grandmas; but oh, how much happier they would be if they could only have just one thing more —a trip to Europe, or a cottage by the sea! Wage-workers, through organization and courage, have won higher remuneration, finer respect, and greater security against the vicissitudes of life; but alas, they have not yet achieved a dictatorship! Once our generals looked forward to the days of universal war; they have seen them, and stand wistful now before the inaccessible stars, longing to send armaments to Jupiter. Writers flourish as nothing in history ever flourished before; invention, transportation and advertisement have made possible such sales as even Byron and Macaulay never knew; an Anatole France becomes a millionaire by writing perfect prose;—but what sadness lies upon the hearts of these successful geniuses!

"If you could read in my soul," says Anatole, "you would be terrified. There is not in all the world a creature more unhappy than I." O enviable Master of beautiful speech!—who surrounded yourself with treasures of art from a hundred ages and lands, who held the hearts of statesmen and revolutionists in the bondage of affectionate admiration, who even in your lifetime were hailed as brother of Rabelais, Montaigne, Voltaire, and the other kings of France; you who had wealth and leisure, and yet never exploited a single soul: if *you* never knew happiness, where shall it be found, and how shall we lesser ones ever possess it?

Why is it that our wealth has issued in pessimism, and our conquest of nature has left us, like Salammbo, miserable in victory?

The Utopias have come true, but only in the external world; imagine our plight if, as some learned philosophers tell us, the external world does not exist! The internal world—ourselves—has changed, but with what geological leisureliness! It has been a simpler thing for us to remake the face of the earth, to bind continents invisibly by land and sea and air, to transmute coal and iron into a million luxuries, than to root out of our souls the instincts of greed, pugnacity and cruelty ingrained in our future by generations of struggle and brutalizing poverty. We are what we had to be; and we remain so even when the necessity has disappeared.

We are right then to be discontent, though wrong to be ungrateful for that half of Utopia which science has given us, and wrong not to understand that this half is the promise and basis of the rest. We know in our hearts that we are animals in Eden, unworthy of the beauty that comes to our eyes, and ready to ruin it with hideous industries; wherever we make our living it becomes impossible to live. And as we squander beauty, so we misuse knowledge; we have multiplied our powers a hundred-fold, and added many cubits to our stature; but our designs are almost as mean and narrow as when we dwelt in ignorance and squalor; we are spiritual pigmies in gigantic frames. Utopia has come everywhere except in the soul of man.

Therefore this modest Utopia that we shall now build with indulgent dreaming will think not of remaking nature any more, nor of "extending the empire of man" (for that Baconian paradise has been achieved); but of remaking ourselves, of building minds and wills that shall be fit to inhabit a better world, that shall be as clear as our knowledge and as strong as our power. Since it is "human nature" and human ignorance that have ruined every Utopia, we shall seek first to cleanse our own hearts and minds, and perhaps all things else will be added unto us.

And so let us sit here under this shady tree; and while the children frolic on the lawn, let us surrender to our imaginations.

II. THE MAYOR RISES

The Mayor was awakened prematurely by the rising sun alighting on his nose. Slowly he came to consciousness; the White House faded, and the growing day persuaded him to clarity. He tried to sleep again, but he could not; and for lack of something better to do, he began to think.

"Good Lord!" he said, "I'm Mayor! How did I ever come to it? What luck! and what accidents! Now if I had never known Tommy Burke. . . . That was mighty fine of him to give me the nomination. But why didn't I know ten years ago that I was going to rule a big city? I might have prepared myself. What a job it is!—worse than running a railway system, or raising a family. And I had no training at all; I'd hardly read a book in my life. And here I am, boss of a million men and women; what I do makes or breaks thousands, and will affect children whose grandfathers aren't born yet. And their problems—already I'm crazy with them. Transit, graft, finance, graft, marketing, graft, zoning, graft, building, graft, street-cleaning, graft, health, graft, education, graft—oh, the job's too big for me! It's a job for a hundred men. I can't do it alone."

The sun, rising higher, beamed hilariously upon the municipal nose. The Mayor yawned, sat up in bed, and fondled his feet. Suddenly his face brightened.

"I know what I'll do. Oh, it'll startle the politicians out of their shoes. It's never been done before. I'll call the biggest scientists from their universities, the biggest money-lenders from their banks, the biggest educators from their schools, the leading ladies from their clubs, the biggest inventors from their laboratories, the biggest executives from their golf, the biggest labor leaders from their excursions,—I'll call them down to the City Hall and beg them to help me.

"O God! I'm so tired of the politicians. They don't want to do things, they want to get things; they don't want the jobs, they want the salaries. And there's ten of them for every job I have to give; and hardly one of them knows anything about the work he thinks he wants to do. I'm tired of them."

The Mayor freed himself from all habiliments, stood bravely before the sun, and apostrophized the spirits of the air.

"After all, there *are* great men in the city. Up there on the hill are some scientists who, they tell me, are known all over the world. And some of the largest firms in the world have their directors here. There's one man in the City who's a statesman; why shouldn't we make use of his brains? I couldn't persuade them to run for office, the best of them; I couldn't even persuade them to let me appoint them to office, the salaries are so low. But if I say to them, 'Gentlemen, I need your help; won't you come and form yourselves into a great committee to advise me?'—I think they'd be willing to give the City some of their time. I have the power to appoint them as a sort of Committee on Municipal Reconstruction. . . ."

The Mayor knelt and prayed.

"O God! give me the nerve!"

III. THE GREAT COMMITTEE

The news of the Great Committee which had been called by the Mayor ran through the City like a baseball score. The office-holders trembled, and wondered how long they could hold their places now; but everybody else was pleased. Even the political machine was publicly enthusiastic; privately it let His Honor know that it did not mind this plan to remake the people, so long as the Organization was left uninjured, intact, and in control of patronage.

The committee met in a quiet assembly hall placed at their disposal by the University. The press was abundantly represented, but the public was courteously asked to stay away; where there are audiences there will be speeches. The Committee numbered only some fifty members, and were a motley crowd, ethnically and sartorially; but every man and woman among them was distinguished for some achievement. There was Professor Gorman, the great biologist, and J. Stonebridge Gorman, the despotic financier; there was Felix Straus, the philanthropist, and Arthur Tompkins, city-manager of a Western town; there was Henry Hubert, engineer, and Edward Hewes, lawyer, both of them known for their record as cabinet officers; there was Theussen the economist, Tawson the psychologist, and Wilbert the architect; there was Dr. Moay the physician, and

Colonel George, another engineer; there was Matthew Green, the labor leader, and Egbert Gray, the manufacturer; there was the great negro leader, Budosi, and the renowned sculptor, Lumborg; the rich Mrs. Laird Crookes sat beside Fanny Cowan, the simple woman who had organized adult education in the needle trades; young John Stoneman, heir to a limitless fortune, rubbed elbows with Morse Hillyer, the Socialist leader; Rabbi Stephen and Marshall Lewis mingled congenially with Monsignor Avella and Dr. Emerson; and Bishop Boyling, the conservative Episcopalian, shook hands, for the first time in his life, with the great Unitarian, James Henry House. There were no salesmen present, no realtors, no politicians, no literary men, and no philosophers.

Then the Mayor, suddenly ennobled with modesty, addressed them:

"Ladies and gentlemen, you have been called together because our city has become too great to be ruled wisely by one man. It has grown too great to be managed by any number of men chosen for their political skill rather than for their economic knowledge and their administrative ability. The time has come when our vast communities must avail themselves of the highest intelligence and character to be found within their borders.

"We need your guidance. Study our problems carefully, scrutinize your recommendations carefully, keep them within the capacity of our human nature and within the City's financial powers; and for my part I promise to support, to the very limit of my influence, every recommendation which comes to me unopposed by any considerable minority either of your Committee or of the people. But I do not think that you will face any great hostility. These problems of civic reconstruction are not political matters, nor are they, as I presume, matters for class legislation. We stand together in chaos, and we must move together towards sanity. Now the City is yours; remake it."

At this juncture the press contributed effectively to the work of the Great Committee. It would have been facile and pleasant to ridicule the enterprise,—to caricature the timid and careless scientists, to predict that no good could come out of so heterogeneous a gathering, and to represent the members as self-conscious saints bent upon forcing their moral astringency upon a people that preferred a loose and lackadaisical existence. But the Mayor had named every important newspaper owner or editor in the City to membership in the Committee; it was a stroke of genius that showed the value of a political training. Encouraged by this recognition, the press rose to its opportunity; it saw that here it might at last become, as men had so long dreamed it might be, the greatest educational medium in the world. It sent its finest writers to report the deliberations, and it gave all possible editorial support to the great enterprise.

Meanwhile the politicians muttered, the contractors revised their specifications and expectations, and the Communists drew derogatory cartoons of Morse Hillyer. Even the public was not quite sure that it cared about this high-brow Committee; and the first recommendations, issued after a week of deliberation, considerably disturbed the popular mind. The biological division of the Committee had reported in favor of the restriction of parentage: only the mentally and physically sound were fit to reproduce. A wave of protest slowly gathered throughout the City. Who were these men and women, these "experts" and capitalists and socialists and intellectuals, to come and tell a sovereign people that parentage was a privilege rather than a birth-right? If the press had not carried Recommendation I in full, great mischief might have been done. But the proposal simply read:

"The first conclusion of the Committee is that reconstruction must begin with the maintenance and improvement of the physical quality of the race. We cannot progress as we might unless we use every possible means to encourage the healthy to have children, and to dissuade the defective from perpetuating their heritable defects.

"But there is no need of prohibitory legislation even in this basic matter. We wish merely to suggest a course to all intelligent men and women; and we would rather rely on their spontaneous good will than attempt to constrain them by law. We propose to apply constraint only to ourselves.

"Therefore we, the members of this Committee on Reconstruction, hereby pledge ourselves, and (with their consent) we pledge our children of marriageable age, to refrain from parentage except upon the approval of physicians appointed for this purpose by the American Medical Association. We invite groups and individuals to make public announcement of their acceptance of this rule. We are confident that the most intelligent sections of the community will be the first to coöperate with this suggestion; and we look to the prestige of their example to influence all.

"We recommend that those possessed of heritable defects shall be left free to marry, but that they shall be encouraged to seek contraceptive advice from authorized physicians.

"We recommend, further, that the acceptance of this rule shall be promoted by offering, to all who bind themselves to its observance, insurance at cost against accident, sickness, unemployment, old age, and death; and by providing a substantial maternity endowment to all women who become mothers under the rule. We trust to the encouragement of the good, rather than to the prohibition of the bad.

"Finally, and above all, we call upon the press, and all our schools and universities, to spread information on this subject: to make plain to every reader that the progress of the race depends upon the improved quality of each generation in health and mind; and to appeal to the patriotism of

the community to exercise this moderate self-restraint as the first step in the re-making of our City."

There followed, in impressive order, the signatures of all members of the Committee except one.

This first pronouncement aroused the wit of the more sceptical critics. Some smiled at the naïve hopefulness of men who thought they could remake a city by spreading knowledge. One critic quoted the comment of Frederick the Great to his Minister of Education, who had proposed to reform mankind through universal schools: "Ah, my dear Zöllner, you don't know the damned race as I do." But many more were pleased with this new conception of government as education, this abstention from regimentation and compulsion, this optimistic plan for furthering human development not so much by denouncing evils as by encouraging all healthy beginnings.

And then pledges of acceptance came in. The physicians of the City called a special meeting and pledged themselves unanimously. The City members of the American Association of University Professors followed; and soon after, the Teachers' Federation. The newspaper profession joined in, and the industrial chemists, and the organized musicians. . . . Great congregations voted their adherence. Finally a voluntary eugenic pledge was suggested for all students receiving diplomas from schools and colleges; and when this met with general approval, the pledge, still voluntary, but backed by the power of public opinion, was made a part of every declaration of citizenship. The first battle was won.

IV. GOVERNMENT BY EDUCATION

A week later Recommendation II, sponsored by the Educational Division of the Committee, was submitted to the Mayor, and printed in the press.

"We recommend," it read, "that the maintenance of public health, and the fullest possible education of children and adults, shall be regarded as the primary tasks of government. We suggest the establishment of municipal hospitals where every illness will be treated competently and at cost. We recommend that the care of the body shall receive as much attention and encouragement in our schools as the development of the mind; we believe that the health of nations is more important than the wealth of nations, and that in health lies the chief secret of happiness. We look for the fostering of every wholesome sport, and insistent instruction in all the arts of cleanliness. We recommend that the passive witnessing of games should be discouraged, and every facility provided for the active participation of all.

"We recommend that the pride of our city should be in its lavish expendi-

ture for education. We urge the gradual increase of the rate of remuneration for all teachers, so that the profession of educator shall again rank with the highest and draw the best. We recommend municipal scholarships for the advancement of all students too poor to go on to higher instruction, so that the City may avail itself of all the talent potential in its citizens. We advise the further endowment of scientific research, with a view to developing inventions that shall make mechanical power cheaper than human muscle, and so put an end to human slavery.

"We recommend that all laudatory references to war shall be eliminated from our schools, and that our people shall be encouraged in their natural inclination to peace, and be relied upon to support all necessary measures for defense.

"We recommend the encouragement of private schools, and experiments in education. We advise full freedom of speech, press, assembly, and worship, as the prerequisites of a strong national character. The extension of the part played by the City in our lives should be balanced by the utmost possible freedom of the mind.

"We recommend that the school be made the intellectual home of the community, open at all hours of day and evening, and offering every facility for physical and mental development.

"We believe that our schools should assume responsibility for the formation of moral character, to balance the decay of other moral forces and institutions; and that no education should be thought complete which does not train the student to see the social bearings and results of individual desire, and develop in him a disposition to limit his conduct within the good of the whole community.

"We urge the owners and editors of our newspapers to develop the press as a great medium for public education. We call upon our philanthropists to subsidize, if necessary, the impartial and readable presentation, through the press, of a thorough education in science, history, literature and art.

"Finally, we recommend that adult education in every branch shall be offered at cost to all who wish it; that the graduates of schools and colleges shall be made to view each commencement as merely a mile-stone in self-development; and that education should be conceived not as a task and a preparation merely, but as a delightful and ennobling intimacy with the cultural heritage of mankind."

The recommendations were signed by all the members of the Committee but two.

Everyone was pleased with these proposals except the tax-payers. The physicians were pleased at the stress which the Committee laid upon health, and the public sighed with relief at the news that hospitals were no longer to be laboratories for the vivisection of the poor. The teachers were willing to receive higher remuneration, and every professor's family began to spend the prospective addition to his income. The innumerable young geniuses who considered poverty as the sole obstacle to their recognition, hailed the suggestion for municipal scholarships. The press appreciated the dignity of the role conferred upon it; and the boys and girls frolicked by anticipation in Utopia's swimming pools.

But Tudor Black, president of the Association of Real Estate Owners, issued a protest that met with the approval of every holder of property.

It is evident [he wrote] that the Mayor's Committee on Reconstruction, after going out of its way, in its first report, to reconstruct not merely the City but the whole human race, has now fallen victim to the naïve idealists, and presumably the more eloquent orators, among its membership. We had hoped that the Committee would keep its proposals within the limits of reason and practicability; we see now that after all these flourishes we are merely to have another Utopia.

This scheme to make Ph.D.'s of all our proletariat is worthy of a sophomore. Every mature mind understands that there is a very limited number of positions, in our economic world, where higher education can be used; already our colleges are turning out more graduates than our professions can place. This flooding of the country with bachelors of arts simply means that a large number of such graduates, finding no opening for their Latin and Greek, will be maladjusted to their situations in industry, and will generalize their personal discontent into revolutionary agitation. No thoughtful man would recommend an addition to this flood; and every experienced educator is already considering ways and means of reducing it.

The recommendations of the Committee are in the line of our current policy of coddling the young. Everyone feels called upon to praise the sins of modern youth—to make light of its egotism, its radicalism, its extravagance, and its immorality. Every parent narrows his own life to leave a fortune to sons and daughters who will squander it in a loose living. These colleges to which we send our children at such a sacrifice are merely athletic clubs and nurseries of unbelief. To provide our young atheists not only with free higher education, but with swimming pools and libraries is to pass from the impossible to the ridiculous.

Will some one explain who is to pay for all this? Already our vast municipal expenditure on schools and colleges entails a monstrous tax on realty. What would the tax be if these wild-cat recommendations should go through? Let every citizen who has a stake in the land calculate the cost of these extravaganzas, and then consider how much will be left him when the national government has sliced away his income, and the city has mulcted him to pay the cost of raising a bumper crop of Bolshevists.

We call upon the Mayor to put a stop to this farce, and to return these recommendations to the Committee with the request that they themselves shall raise the funds required for their schemes.

Yours truly,

Tudor Black

V. SOCIALISM BY MILLIONAIRES

This letter opened a division of opinion in the City which grew sharper and deeper every day. When the Committee, without making any reply to its critics, filed its third report, the adverse comments mounted very nearly to a majority. The rumor went forth that the report had almost split the Committee; and it was at once noted that seven of the fifty members had refused to sign it. It ran as follows:

"We recommend that the City shall perfect its supervision over all food entering its borders: that with the coöperation of the press it shall give wide publicity each week to a fair-price list; and that it shall take steps to prevent a wasteful duplication in the retail distribution of the necessaries of life.

"We recommend that the City shall acquire and operate all public utilities; that it shall build its own hydro-electric plants, or coöperate in the use of plants built by the State; and that it shall sell current at cost to all who care to use it, so that the City may be free from smoke, and all industry may be made healthful and clean.

"We recommend the municipal ownership and operation of all City transit lines; the increase or reduction of the fare to meet the actual cost of maintenance; and the development of these facilities to avoid the present indecent crowding, and to spread our population comfortably out into the countryside.

"We recommend the encouragement of corporations, whose methods shall be supervised and whose dividends shall be both limited and guaranteed by the City, to build apartments and, wherever possible, individual homes, at modest rentals, so that the pleasures of home and parentage may be renewed, and the family may be restored to something of its former position as the nurse of morals and the source of social order.

"We offer our gratitude to those philanthropists who have made possible our great museums and orchestras, and trust that these benefactions will be extended to all sections and classes of the community. We urge the development of the work now being done to promote the understanding and enjoyment of the arts, with a view to nourishing in all of us the taste that will call forth genius, and that sense of beauty which is the best guarantee of the greatness of our City."

Recommendation III was met with apathy, or damned with faint praise, or attacked with scorn. As its proposals were calculated to benefit the community as a whole, rather than any organized and vocal minority, few were found to express approval. The attention which the unusual recommendations of the first report had aroused seemed beyond recapture; people could not be stirred to enthusiasm by considerations of transit and gas supply. And just as the burning of a house draws larger crowds than the building of it, so, as the Committee proceeded to the details of reconstruction, popular interest waned. And whereas there was a general agreement as to the evils from which the City suffered, there were hundreds of plans for their solution, and no single proposal could expect to please more than a small fraction of those who wanted change.

The great provision merchants who sold to the retailers of the City such food as they did not surrender to the sea as a delicate means of maintaining prices for what remained, brought pressure to bear upon the leaders of both parties to disown and discredit the Committee. The great gas and electric companies, having less to be ashamed of, made less complaint, and let it be known that they would not object to municipal purchase if they were permitted to name the price. Certain transit lines quoted the Committee's recommendation, as they called it, for "an increase in fares"; and thousands of people, reading this quotation, became bitterly hostile to the Committee. Investors (some of whom had profited by the Esch-Cummins act, by which the dividends of the railroads had been both limited and guaranteed by the National Government) protested against a municipal guarantee or limitation of building dividends. Bachelors smiled at the proposals for making babies fashionable again. And through all the discussion one insistent query ran: How can these Utopian fantasies be financed?

VI. FINANCING UTOPIA

One month from the date of its assembling the Great Committee submitted its fourth and final report, and adjourned. To the astonishment of the City it was signed, like the first report, by every member of the Committee but one. It read:

"We recommend the extension and limitation of democracy, so that it shall mean the equal opportunity of all to make themselves fit for the highest office, and the restriction of office to those who have made themselves fit. We urge the establishment of Schools of Political Administration in our universities, access to these to be free to all who, whether college graduates or not, pass the entrance tests; and the instruction to be as thorough and as practical as that now required for the practice of medicine. We suggest that our political parties should more and more look, for their candidates

for minor offices, to the graduates of such administration schools; and that they should ultimately restrict all nominations for higher office to men and women who, having graduated from these schools, have served two terms in some office of the next lower rank. We solicit aid for the Bureau of Municipal Research, so that its activities may be extended to cover the study of modern methods of municipal government everywhere, and the continuous scrutiny of the acts of every official in the service of the city.

"To finance the recommendations of this and the preceding Reports, we suggest: first, a tax on unused land, on luxuries, on all private gifts and bequests above a certain value, and on all public amusements which do not contribute to the physical or mental development of the community; and secondly, the issuance of long-term municipal bonds, so that the generations which shall profit by these improvements may bear their share of the cost.

"Recognizing that these sources of revenue will be inadequate, we suggest that those who can afford it shall contribute to a Reconstruction Fund, to be administered by a non-political board chosen by the donors and this Committee. We solicit the aid of the press in raising this fund to a figure accordant with our wealth. And we appeal to the far vision and love of country which must actuate men of great ability and good fortune; without them reconstruction will come, but slowly; with them it would come in a generation, and make our City rival the greatest glory of Athens, Florence, and Rome.

"To express our own earnestness in this matter, we, the members of this Committee, pledge to this fund, for the next five years, one fifth of our total income."

VII. BUT IN REALITY

Who could resist that final paragraph? At one stroke the Committee recaptured the public attention and support which it had lost. As there was precious little unused land in the City, even Tudor Black relaxed into a smile. "One-fifth of our total income!" This was an enormous gift, for the Committee included some of the richest men in the country, and even its socialist members were wealthy. Surely Utopia had already begun!

Under these encouraging circumstances those who had defended the Committee from the beginning were now braver in their praise. They pointed out the moderation of the proposals, and the fact that, with a few exceptions, these recommendations had been approved by conservatives and progressives of all varieties, nationalities and traditions. The press republished the four Reports together, so that readers were enabled to visualize as a whole the bright and healthy community which the authors had had it in view to create. It became plain that what was attempted here was no mechanical Utopia, no paradise of walking sidewalks and commuting airplanes, but, far more basically, the elevation of the physical, mental and moral fibre of the population. Such a race as might come from these measures would produce a Utopia for itself, and be capable of using machinery without becoming its slave.

And, again with the aid of the press, the Reconstruction Fund grew rapidly. Many individuals and families pledged a fifth of their income for a year, conditional on the passage of the Recommendations. One member of the Committee quietly turned over $50,000,000 which he had been collecting for a general education fund. Women sent in jewelry, dying men left bequests, and organizations raised large sums from the small contributions of their members. Within two months after the Committee had adjourned, the fund had reached one hundred millions.

All eyes turned now to the Board of Aldermen. On the day when the Mayor was to present the Recommendations every seat on the floor and in the galleries was taken; and all the faces of the spectators glowed with pleasure, as if they felt that they were witnessing the first dramatic event in the transition from the Age of Gold to the Golden Age. The Mayor read all the Reports, explained that each proposal would be submitted as a separate measure, and made an eloquent appeal for the passage of them all. It was his hope that this Administration would be a cherished memory in all the future of the City if these bills should pass, and the work of realizing them should begin before the end of his term.

When he had finished, an old alderman arose, and spoke against the Recommendations.

"Your Honor," he said, "I condemn these measures as an abject surrender to socialism. What has come over the great industrial leaders who sat on this Committee, that they have yielded on every point to the childish plans of communist dreamers? Behind these bills I see the red hand of Moscow, the secret influence of the Third International; and though some of them are good I shall vote against them all because I love my country and will never consent to its domination by a foreign power."

The gallery laughed, but the aldermen listened gravely. One of them rose and gently ridiculed the notion that the bills were communistic. But the third speaker brought the discussion to the plane of oratory. He was a grayhaired, terrier-visaged bricklayer, who had gravitated through various union offices into the municipal senate. He thundered passionately:

"Gentlemen, these bills are not only a surrender to Russia, they are a surrender to the big interests that have so long sought to control us. What is this so-called 'Great Committee' but a rich man's club? What is their offer of a small part of their income but a bait to get the whole City into their hands? What is their great Fund but a vast sum to be spent by them, not by us, to make the City just as they would like it? What is their talk of buying the transit lines except a hypocritical argument for a higher fare, or for the purchase of these lines at the lines' own price?

"And notice, gentlemen, the unpatriotic attack on war. Was there ever anything so impertinent presented to us as this suggestion that we should no longer have a good word to say for the brave lads and great generals that won our independence, preserved the Union, and made the world safe for democracy?

"And in all these Recommendations not one word about religion. Think of it, gentlemen, not one word about religion! On the contrary the impious suggestion that it is losing its moral influence. And these young ladies in the schools are going to replace it with ethics. Huh! Ethics! Can you beat it?—ethics! What is ethics anyhow? I know what it is; it is a scheme to destroy religion. Half the men on that Committee were atheists; or Unitarians, which is the same thing; or Jews, which is worse. I knew from the beginning that there were too many Jews on that Committee. Too many Jews, I say.

"And Your Honor, how they fooled you! You, brought up in the streets like the rest of us, rising to these sublime heights of Mayor of a great city; they tell you to your face that all Mayors now must be educated in those great universities. Huh! These schoolmasters are going to tell us how to run the City, eh? They want to destroy the democ-r-acy which our fathers fought for, and our brothers preserved on the fields of France! They want to take from honest workers the right to office. Shame on them! Shame on us all as a pack of fools if we vote for a single one of these bills, these treacherous bills that would destroy our government and dishonor our fair City!"

The argument on the bills continued for several days. The Mayor fought patiently for each measure, and many of the Aldermen supported him; while the crowded gallery applauded wildly every affirmative speech or vote. At the end of a week the great issue had been decided, every bill had been voted on, and the crowd went home. Not one of the measures had carried.

Even so, the shade of this tree is sweet; and how pleasant it is to hear the laughter of those children!

PART EIGHT

RELIGION: A DIALOGUE

PERSONS OF THE DIALOGUE

ANDREW, *an Atheist*
ARIEL, *Hostess*
CLARENCE, *an Agnostic*
ESTHER, *a Jewess*
SIR JAMES, *an Anthropologist*
KUNG, *a Chinese*

MATTHEW, *a Catholic*
PAUL, *a Protestant*
PHILIP, *an Historian*
SIDDHA, *a Hindu*
THEODORE, *a Greek*
WILLIAM, *a Psychologist*

The Dialogue is divided into three sessions: On the Lawn, Around the Table, and In the Library.

CHAPTER XXI

On the Lawn

The Making of Religion

I. ANIMISM

ARIEL. Let's range ourselves in a circle about this bed of tulips; we'll be Knights of the Round Garden, sworn to defend—or attack—the Faith. Come, Matthew, you follower of the Grail, and Andrew, you infidel, help me with these benches. Those of you who like sunsets can sit here facing the great god. There! Shall we begin?

PAUL. Just what do you want us to do, Ariel?

ARIEL. I asked you to come and talk about religion. I'm so interested, and so bewildered; and perhaps some others are too. You must explain how

333

religion began, the meaning and value of its various forms, how it stands today, and what is going to happen to it in America. Also you must tell me whether I have an immortal soul, and whether there is a God. That's all!

CLARENCE. It might be done very briefly—if we could agree.

ARIEL. But I'll be most interested where you don't agree. I've lured you out here because I knew you were all different. I love to see you get along so well together, though each of you is sure that the others are badly mistaken. How shall we commence?

ANDREW. By defining our terms. What do you mean by religion?

ARIEL. Oh, definitions are so tiresome!

PHILIP. I once collected definitions of religion; perhaps I can remember a few. Schleiermacher called it a feeling of absolute dependence. Havelock Ellis calls it "an intuition of union with the world." [1] Gilbert Murray says it "is that which brings us into relation with the great world-forces." [2] Spengler describes it as *"lived and experienced* metaphysic—that is, the unthinkable as a certainty, the supernatural as a fact, life as existence in a world that is non-actual, but true." [3] Professor Shotwell thinks it is "nothing but the submission to mystery." [4] Everett Dean Martin defines it "as the symbolic appreciation of the mystery of existence in terms of the interests of man as an ego." [5] Reinach defines it as "a sum of scruples which impede the free exercise of our faculties." [6]

MATTHEW. That's the most spiteful and ridiculous definition I've ever heard.

WILLIAM. They are all models of obscurity.

PHILIP. Tylor's definition should please you better. He calls religion simply "a belief in spiritual beings."

SIR JAMES. But some gods are conceived as material. And belief isn't enough; you must add worship.

PHILIP. How would you define religion yourself, Sir James?

SIR JAMES. As a propitiation or conciliation of powers superior to man, which are believed to direct or control the course of nature and of human life. [7]

ARIEL. You mean it's the worship of supernatural beings?

SIR JAMES. Thank you for that lesson in brevity.

ARIEL. Well, then, how did religion begin?

ANDREW. No one has ever answered that better than Lucretius: "It was fear that first made gods in the world." Primitive life was beset with a

---

[1] Goldberg, I., *Havelock Ellis,* p. 138.
[2] Murray, G., *Four Stages in Greek Religion,* p. 95.
[3] *Decline of the West,* vol. ii, p. 217.
[4] Shotwell, J. T., *The Religious Revolution of Today,* p. 153.
[5] Martin, E. D., *The Mystery of Religion,* p. 378.
[6] Reinach, S., *Orpheus, a History of Religion,* p. 3.
[7] Frazer, Sir J., *The Golden Bough,* p. 50.

thousand dangers, and seldom ended with natural decay; violence or disease came to carry people off long before they could reach old age. Now when a savage can't understand phenomena, he personifies their cause, and supposes, from the analogy of his own body, that a spirit dwells in every natural object, and is responsible for what the object does. Did you ever see the wonder and fear in the eyes of a dog who sees a paper blown across his path by the wind? He can't see the wind; and I'll wager he imagines there's a spirit in the paper, making it move. He's a religious dog, a primitive animist. That's how religion began.

ARIEL. Shall we believe him, Sir James?

SIR JAMES. If you wish. What Andrew calls the first stage was probably a secondary stage, in which the great ocean of wonder-working energy, which the Melanesian Islanders worshipped as *mana,* and the American Indians as *manitou,* was conceived as divided into separate spirits inhabiting individual things.

SIDDHA. That early belief was very profound. It is not very different from the latest belief of modern science, that all matter is energy.

SIR JAMES. The old belief is still with us in many ways. Once mountains, rivers, rocks, trees, stars, and the sky were supposed to be the external forms of spirits; and to this day we like to personify these natural objects. The Greeks thought the sky was the body of the god Uranos; the moon, of the goddess Silene; the earth, of the goddess Gæa; the sea, of the god Poseidon.

THEODORE. It was only poetry, Sir, to the educated Greek.

SIR JAMES. To the average Greek it was literal truth, was it not? But all peoples are the same in this particular. To the early Germans and Scandinavians the woods seemed densely populated with genii, elves, trolls, giants, dwarfs, harpies, fairies, gnomes—see them in *Rheingold* and *Peer Gynt.* The simpler peasants of Ireland still believe in fairies, and fear their influence. Take the fairies out of the Irish literary revival, and only prose remains. The American Indians sometimes attribute their decadence to the fact that the White Man cut down the trees, whose spirits had protected the Red Man. In the Molucca Islands blossoming trees are treated with the same ceremony as a woman with child; no noise or other disturbance is permitted near them lest, like a frightened woman *enceinte,* they should drop their fruit before time. In Amoyna, when the rice fields are in bloom, all loud sounds are prohibited in their neighborhood, lest they should miscarry and abort into straw.[1] In Gaul there were sacred forests, full of specially worshipped trees. In England the Druids gathered with religious ritual the mistletoe of the oak.

ARIEL. There's a certain ritual still attached to the mistletoe, isn't there? But tell us more, Sir James.

SIR JAMES. Well, the same animism was applied to the stars: every one of

[1] Frazer, pp. 112, 115.

them housed a guiding spirit. The Babylonians distinguished seven planets as divine, and gave their names to the days of the week; on Sunday, Monday and Saturday we still do them unwitting reverence. On Tuesday, Wednesday, Thursday and Friday we honor the gods of Scandinavia—Tives, Wodin, Thor and Friga. On those same days the French prefer the gods of Rome—Mars, Mercury, Jove and Venus. Astrology came out of Babylon, from the notion that these stellar spirits governed human fate. To this day our news-stands offer astrologic guides for every month, and we use astrologic language when we speak of *lunatics,* or of *martial* and *jovial* temperaments. Among many tribes a horrible noise is made during lunar eclipses, to drive away the demons that are attacking the moon.[1] Anaxagoras was exiled by the Athenians because he said that the sun was a ball of fire, and not a god. Under Christianity these spirits became angels; Kepler seems to have believed that every planet had one to guide it on its course. The halo around the head of saints is probably a relic of sun-worship.[2] The Mikado is still regarded as the sun-god. I think we can safely say, then, that animism is the primary stuff of religion; and by animism we would mean the belief that spirits dwell in everything.

PHILIP. One form of that early animism is phallic worship, isn't it?

SIR JAMES. Yes. The savage knows nothing of the internal agencies of reproduction, revealed to us by modern cytology; he sees only the external structures, and deifies them because he cannot understand; they too have creative spirits in them, and must be worshipped.

SIDDHA. It seems to me a very reasonable religion. In these structures, more than anywhere else, the miracle of fertility and growth appears; they are the most direct embodiments of the creative power. The symbols of reproduction—the *lingam* and the *yoni*—are still worshipped in my country, and carried as protective charms.[3]

PHILIP. The earliest records of the Egyptians refer to phallic worship as their oldest institution.[4] The Romans also wore phallic ikons as amulets, to bring fertility; and they celebrated the divine mystery of reproduction at the Liberalia, the Bacchanalia, and other feasts. Lucian speaks of the great pillars, almost two hundred feet high, that stood before the temple of Aphrodite at Hierapolis, as phalli.[5]

ANDREW. I believe that all worship, at least in women, is bound up with the ecstasy of love. The visions of St. Theresa were apparently associated with erotic sensations and hallucinations. The same seems to be true of many other holy persons, if we may believe Krafft-Ebing and Havelock Ellis. As

[1] Reinach, pp. 39, 94.
[2] Jung, C. G., *Psychology of the Unconscious,* p. 173.
[3] Sumner, *Folkways,* p. 546.
[4] Howard, C., *Sex-Worship,* p. 63.
[5] *Encyclopaedia Britannica,* 11th ed., vol. xxi, p. 345.

my experience is confined to only one of these associated emotions I can't speak at first hand on the subject.[1]

SIR JAMES. Probably the role of sex in religious feeling, and of phallic worship in primitive religion, has been exaggerated. The explanation of tree-worship, obelisks, May-poles, and circumcision rites as phallic is questionable.[2]

THEODORE. We ought to remember that these ancient ceremonies celebrating reproduction were religious rather than sexual. License grew up around them, as around Mardi Gras in Christian times; but originally the reproductive power was conceived as holy and worthy of all reverence, which is better than conceiving it as unclean.

ANDREW. And is equally unnecessary.

ARIEL. Let us pass on, Sir James. Animism is the first element in the making of religion; what is the second?

II. MAGIC

SIR JAMES. Magic. Having filled the world with spirits, and being unable to control them, as science tries to do, primitive man undertook to propitiate them, and to enlist them in his aid. Magic, as Reinach says, is "the strategy of animism." Usually it is sympathetic magic, and relies upon suggestion. To make rain fall the primitive worshipper, or his hired magician, pours water upon the ground, preferably from a tree. To this day, in the Balkans and parts of Germany, when rain has been long withheld, a young girl is stripped and water is poured over her ceremonially, to the accompaniment of magic formulas.[3] When drought threatened the Kaffirs they asked the missionary to raise his umbrella and walk through the fields.[4] In Sumatra a barren woman makes a wooden image of a child and holds it up in her lap, thinking that this will cure her sterility. In the Babar Archipelago the barren woman makes a doll of red cotton, pretends to suckle it, and repeats a magic formula; then the word is sent out through the village that she is with child, and her friends come to congratulate her. Among the Dyaks of Borneo when a woman is in labor a magician is called in who tries to ease her pains, and to get the child born quickly, by himself going through the contortions of delivery. After some minutes of histrionic suffering he lets a stone drop from his waist, and utters a formula designed to induce the fœtus to imitate the stone. Many of the most famous and trusted cures in history were magical; your own scholar, Dr. James J. Walsh, has recorded

[1] Krafft-Ebing, *Psychopathia Sexualis*, ch. i; Ellis, H., *Studies in the Psychology of Sex*, vol. i., p. 315.

[2] Smith, W. R., *The Religion of the Semites*, vol. i., p. 437; Frazer, p. 120.

[3] Reinach, p. 86.

[4] Hoernlé, R. F. A., *Studies in Contemporary Metaphysics*, p. 181.

them in a fascinating book. If you are troubled with acne, watch for a falling star; as it falls, wipe your face; all eruptions will come away. If they don't it's because you weren't quick enough. Perhaps the arrows transfixing the animals in the pictures found on the walls of the caves at Altamira and elsewhere were intended as suggestive magic. People in the Middle Ages tried to cast a "spell" upon an enemy by piercing his waxen image with pins. Even today we burn people in effigy. When the Peruvians did this they called it "burning the soul." [1]

ANDREW. I believe it is one of your favorite theories, Sir James, that magic is the father of science?

SIR JAMES. Animism is the father of poetry, magic is the father of drama through make-believe, and of science through the desire to control the spirits. When a magic rite failed, the magician sometimes suffered, though the people remembered one magical success more vividly than a dozen failures. It was to the advantage of the magician to study causes and effects, and find natural means of accomplishing the desired end; by using these means, while continuing to employ the magic rite, he could attribute his success to the magic, and improve his reputation as a manipulator of the gods. So out of the primitive magician, wonder-worker, or priest, came the medicine-man and the physician, the astrologer and the astronomer, the alchemist and the chemist; our scientists in every field of research are the direct descendants of those ancient magicians. From that one fount came both religion and science, metaphysics and medicine, the two diverse strains that run like counterpoint through the history of mankind.[2]

In some places the skill of the magician, or the repute of the magic formula, became so great that failure to win the god was attributed not to the imperfection of the rites, but to the obstinacy of the god. In Greece the young men sometimes whipped the statue of Pan if he had not given them a good hunting.[3] Italian fishermen will as likely as not throw overboard the image of the Virgin if a poor catch comes in despite their prayers.[4] The Chinese, when their orisons have failed, may drag a god's image ignominiously through the streets and belabor it with reproaches. "You dog of a spirit," they say to it, "we gave you a magnificent temple to live in, we gilded you prettily, we fed you well, we offered you sacrifice; and yet you are ungrateful." [5] In such queer practices primitive men came close to that conception of *Moira*—or Fate—as above both gods and men, which distinguishes Greek religion, and leads on the one hand to monotheism, and on the other hand to science.

---

[1] Frazer, p. 13; Reinach, p. 111.
[2] Frazer, p. 62; Reinach, p. 22.
[3] Hobhouse, L. T., *Morals in Evolution*, p. 379.
[4] Todd, *op. cit.*, p. 414.
[5] Nietzsche, F., *Human All Too Human*, vol. i, p. 120.

ARIEL. I don't know where it's all driving to, but I suppose it's all necessary.

SIR JAMES. You mustn't look for conclusions so soon, Madame. In studying any field of science or history it's wise to begin by soaking yourself in the facts. If you arrive at your conclusion too soon it will select certain facts for you, and keep you from seeing the rest.

ARIEL. You are right, and I accept your rebuke. Go on, tell us more.

SIR JAMES. Well, magic not only led to science and drama, but it led to religious ritual, sacrifice, and prayer. Many prayers are still of the nature of magic formulas, mumbled over and over again with an advertiser's faith in repetition. Talismans, maledictions, benedictions are developments of magic. But the most instructive and most widespread form into which religious magic grew was the vegetation rite. Primitive men personified the powers of growth as male and female; the word *matter* seems to come from *mater*, mother.[1] The personal way of seeing or thinking of things naturally precedes the impersonal or abstract, just as animism precedes metaphysics. The God of a praying child is a thousand times more definite, you might say more material, than that of the God-intoxicated Spinoza. This is one of the drawbacks of philosophy, that it replaces concrete particulars with generalized abstractions, taking from us the intimate and anthropomorphic deity of our youth and giving us instead an Absolute that it would be ridiculous to picture in human form.

The great problem of every generation, in every year, is how to secure a good crop. Primitive man never thought of working out the problem in terms of renitrogenation, or in any other scientific terms; he approached it on the lines of magic—he would suggest to Mother Earth that she should deliver herself of a great litter of food. So he arranged phallic festivals at sowing time, and achieved the double purpose of fertilizing the earth by suggestion, and giving himself a moral holiday. In some countries the people chose a King and a Queen of the May, or a Whitsun bridegroom and bride, and performed marriage rites over them, as charms to lure the soil into fertility. Often the rite included the full consummation of the marriage, so that Nature (that is, *she who gives birth*) might have no excuse for misunderstanding what was expected of her.

You are again wondering what this has to do with religion. Be patient; when you study comparative religion you will see your own faith in the perspective that corrects delusions. Now primitive man depended on good crops much more completely than we do; he had such meagre provision for famine and drought that he would stop at nothing to ensure an abundant harvest. The notion came to him, as in almost all religions, to sacrifice a living being—at first a man, then, in more genial ages, an animal—to the spirit of the earth; the blood, sinking into the ground, would appease the god and

[1] Jung, *op. cit.*, p. 173.

fertilize the soil. The Indians of Ecuador sacrificed human blood and hearts when they sowed their fields; so did the Pawnee Indians; and among the Bengal tribes the rites were indescribably horrible.[1] Sometimes a criminal was sacrificed. The Athenians kept a number of outcasts ready for any emergency that might require the immediate propitiation of the gods; and when plague or famine came they sacrificed two criminals—one as a substitute for the men of the tribe, the other as a substitute for the women. This is the origin of the theory of vicarious atonement.

ARIEL. What did you say? Do you mean that the most fundamental element in Christian theology goes back to those bloody rites?

SIR JAMES. It would seem so; though I should not call it a fundamental element in Christian theology. I have been very much surprised to find that in America those who put most store by the secondary and inessential elements in religion—the things that differentiate one sect from another—are called Fundamentalists. I should call them, if you will permit a visitor to speak so familiarly, Superficialists. But shall I go on with my story?

ARIEL. Wherever it leads.

SIR JAMES. That's the spirit. Every year, at the festival of the Thargelia, in Athens, two scape-goats, as they were called, were stoned to death as a sacrifice to the gods in atonement for the sins of the people.[2] Often the victim was chosen a year in advance, and was worshipped and petted for twelve months as a king and a god. In the springtime he was killed—in many cases after scourging; no doubt the sadistic impulses of the people found an outlet in this pious and irreproachable way. In later forms of the primitive ritual the victim chosen for the next annual sacrifice was worshipped as the resurrection of the slain victim, on the analogy of spring as the revival of the earth-goddess after her apparent demise in the fall. Myths of the death and resurrection of the god in human form became a part of nearly all the religions of western Asia and northeastern Africa.[3]

From killing the god to eating him was a natural improvement, for the savage believes that he acquires the powers of what he eats. At first the people ate and drank the flesh and blood of the victim; but when they became a little more refined they substituted for the living victim images made of flour, and ate those instead. In ancient Mexico an image of the god was made of grain, seeds, and vegetables, kneaded with the blood of boys sacrificed for the purpose, and consumed by the people, after fasting, as a religious ceremony of "eating the god." The priests uttered magic formulas over the images, and turned them from dough into deities.[4]

[1] Frazer, p. 432.
[2] Allen, G., *Evolution of the Idea of God,* p. 353.
[3] *Ibid.,* p. 246; Frazer, p. 337.
[4] Sumner, p. 336; Frazer, p. 489.

MATTHEW. Surely you would not conclude that the doctrines of the Atonement and the Eucharist are false merely because you find something analogous to them among primitive peoples.

SIR JAMES. No, not at all; it is still quite conceivable that these doctrines are true; I shall not be dogmatic on that point. These rites became more and more civilized with time. The earlier forms reflected a cannibalistic society, and went on the principle that the gods had the same tastes as the chieftain. When cannibalism passed away, animals replaced men in the sacrifice; perhaps the transition is symbolized in the story of Abraham, Isaac, and the ram. But the primitive priest liked flesh as much as the gods; he soon found ways of keeping the most edible parts of the sacrificed animal for himself, leaving for the god only the entrails or the bones, deceptively covered with fat.[1]

ANDREW. The god was not yet conceived as omniscient.

III. TOTEM AND TABOO

SIR JAMES. Meanwhile the dependence of men on animals, and their fear of the larger beasts, brought a third element into religion—totemism. *Totem* is an Indian word signifying mark or sign; it was an image used by the North American Indians to represent an animal or a plant in which the protective spirit of the tribe was believed to dwell.[2] Totemism, the worship of sacred animals and plants, was mostly associated with the hunting stage; but much of it survived into agricultural days. So the sacred dove, fish and lamb passed down into Judaism and Christianity.

CLARENCE. We are all totemists. Some of us are Elks, some of us are Moose; some of us vote for the elephant, and some others of us vote for the perfect democratic symbol, the donkey. Some of us go to war for the Lion, others go to war for the Eagle. We need animals to express all our sublime devotions.

PHILIP. In 1927 the Japanese government had to order the destruction of thousands of small shrines dedicated to the worship of foxes, snakes, and other gods.[3]

WILLIAM. Perhaps the ferocity of Jehovah and contemporary gods was a relic of the worship of wild beasts? During a transition stage the god was figured as having the face of a man and the body of an animal, or *vice versa*. The Sphinx is an example. As the war of man with man replaced the war of man with the beasts, the god came to be thought of as a war-chieftain, a god of hosts, rather than as an animal; but he remained as ferocious as ever.

---

[1] Sumner, p. 340.
[2] Reinach, p. 15.
[3] New York *Times*, July 25, 1927.

Tarde points out that the most despotic gods are also the most revered—very much like husbands.[1]

ARIEL. It's terrible how much you men know. How can we women, between nursery and beauty-parlor, find time to catch up with you? Now, Sir James, you've listed three elements in the origins of religion: animism, magic, and totemism. Are there any more?

SIR JAMES. Two more: taboo and ancestor-worship. *Taboo* is a Polynesian word, meaning prohibited. The Ark of the Covenant was taboo—not to be touched except by members of a privileged priestly family. When David wanted to take it to Jerusalem he had it placed on a cart; the oxen stumbled, and the Ark was about to fall to the ground, when a certain Uzzah sprang forward and held it up; whereupon the Lord struck him dead for violating a taboo.[2] Most taboos were moral customs considered so vital to the tribe that they needed a religious sanction, a divine origin, to buttress them with fear and reverence; the Ten Commandments are an instance. So the Persians tell how one day, as Zoroaster prayed on a high mountain, God appeared to him in thunder and lightning, and delivered to him "The Book of the Law." In Cretan legend King Minos received laws from God on Mt. Dicta; in Greek legend Dionysus was called the Law-Giver, and was represented as holding up two tables of stone on which laws had been engraved. It was an admirable disguise for the chieftain's club. Perhaps we may trace to it the divine right of kings.

CLARENCE. It's a workable plan, and not quite obsolete. I am informed, on the authority of the original legislators themselves, that God was the author of the Eighteenth Amendment.

IV. ANCESTOR-WORSHIP

ARIEL. But Sir James, it seems strange to me that you should have gone so far in the history of religion without arriving at God.

SIR JAMES. That is our last point. You want to know, like the child, "Who made God?"—how did this ocean of deity, these spirits of the field, the forest and the sky, become the human god of later faith? You may remember the ancient legends of the metamorphoses of gods into animals or men. Well, the truth was just the opposite; the corn god and the animal god became the semi-human god. When we hear of Zeus becoming a swan, or read of "owl-eyed Athene" and "heifer-eyed Hera," we suspect that the Greek tribes were mingling with their new-style deities concepts taken from animals they had worshipped in the totemic stage. William has referred to the Sphinx as an example of the transition gods, who were half animals and half men or women. He need not have gone so far; your own splendid mu-

[1] Tarde, *Laws of Imitation*, pp. 270, 273, 275.
[2] Reinach, p. 4.

seum is full of once holy statues half human and half beast. Minotaurs, centaurs, sirens, satyrs, mermaids, fauns, are part of the passage from animal to anthropomorphic gods.[1] Ancestor-worship completed the change.

The worship of ancestors seems to have begun with the appearance of the dead in dreams. It was a slight step from the fright caused by such apparitions, to the worship of the dead. Those who had been powerful during their lives were feared after their death; indeed, this fear of the dead became the most influential force in primitive religion.[2] Animism had made magic; ancestor-worship made what we should call religion. Among some primitive people the word for god actually means "a dead man." "Jehovah" means "the strong one"; apparently he had been a powerful chieftain. In Egypt, Rome, Mexico and Peru the king was worshipped as a god even before he died. Alexander had himself deified because the peoples whom he conquered were accustomed to divine kings: without this transfiguration they would not have accepted him as their ruler. Now the ghosts of such tremendous men had to be propitiated; the funeral rites given them became the first form of religious ceremonies in his memory, honor, and service. All the forms of currying favor with the god were taken from the ritual of servility to earthly chiefs: clasped hands, obeisances, genuflections, adulation, and so forth. To this day no Catholic altar is complete without the remains of departed saints—i. e., heroic ancestors. In this sense ancestor-worship, instead of being confined to China and Japan, is spread throughout the world.

The Greeks and most ancient peoples invoked their dead as Christians invoke the saints.[3] So real is the society of the dead that in many regions messages are sent to them, at great cost: a chief summons a slave, delivers the message to him verbally, and then cuts off his head. If the chief forgets something he sends another decapitated slave after the first, as a postscript.[4] The ghost of the dead man is believed to take on some of that supernatural power or *mana* which was the protoplasm of all later gods. Hence the care with which he was propitiated. *Religio* comes not from *religare,* to bind together, but from *relegere,* to take care of, to tend—the opposite of *neglegere,* to neglect.[5] It is bound up with filial emotions, in which the fear of the dead is gradually transformed into love of the dead. Even a ferocious fellow can be loved when he is dead.

The next step was the conception of the god, or dead chieftain, as father. In modern religion the idea of the fatherhood of God is a thin, spiritual relationship—we do not think of God physically begetting men. But among

---

[1] Reinach, p. 81; Murray, *op. cit.,* p. 37.
[2] Frazer, p. vii.
[3] Reinach, p. 80.
[4] Allen, p. 30.
[5] Reinach, p. 2.

the Greeks and many other early peoples, the idea was physical and direct: the races of men had been procreated by various gods; and at the end of every genealogy stood a deity. The notion, found among the Greeks and Jews, that the gods had fashioned men out of clay, was of later origin.[1]

And so at last humanity conceived a human god. It took a long time; before him, for many centuries, there was the sea of spirits, then the spirits in rocks and trees and stars, then the procreative spirits in reproduction and the soil, then the animal deities, and finally—through the deification of ancestors and kings—the human god. Spencer, as you know, thought that all religion could be reduced to ancestor-worship—a theory as old as Euhemerus, who lived 300 B. C. Ancestor-worship, however, is a late-stage, not the first; before it lay long ages in which there were no man-like gods at all. But when ancestor-worship came it brought a great change in religion: it humanized it, so to speak, and allowed it to conceive deity in terms first of the strongest, then of the finest, men. It prepared the way for the great anthropomorphic faiths of Judea, Greece, and Rome. Now let some one else take up the tale.

V. PAGANISM

ARIEL. Sir James, you've informed and disturbed me tremendously. I notice how patiently Paul and Matthew have listened to you; I hope they'll tell us soon where they can't follow you. But don't you all think we ought first to ask Theodore to explain to us the religion of the Greeks? It must have been so interesting to be a pagan!

THEODORE. Madame, I am not worthy to be called a Greek. The Greeks of today are Slavs; they are not an old people inheriting an old culture, like the Chinese; they are a new people trying to build a new civilization, like the Americans. But I have loved and studied the ancient faith of my country, and I will gladly speak to you. Indeed, I thought you might ask me, and so I brought with me a little quotation from Sir Gilbert Murray.

SIR JAMES. I know him well. He is a kindly gentleman, in times of peace.

THEODORE. He writes very well about my country. In religion as in everything else, Sir Gilbert says, "ancient Greece has the triumphant if tragic distinction of beginning at the very bottom and struggling, however precariously, to the very summits. There is hardly any horror of primitive superstition of which we cannot find some distant traces in our Greek record. There is hardly any height of spiritual thought attained in the world that has not its archetype or its echo in the stretch of Greek literature that lies between Thales and St. Paul."[2] Perhaps I shall be able to show you that wonderful development, and at the same time illustrate, by

[1] Smith, W. R., *op. cit.*, p. 42.
[2] Murray, p. 15.

the example of Greece, the splendid analysis which Sir James has given of the evolution of religion.

At the beginning, like other peoples, the Greeks worshipped the spirits in trees, stars, animals and plants. Probably the first object of worship was the sky. *Zeus*, like the Latin *Deus* and the Sanskrit *Di*, meant sky; even in America you say, "Heaven protect us!" and "I pray to heaven," as if God and sky were one; and all simple persons believe that God is just over the clouds. As late as the third century before Christ the Stoic philosopher Chrysippus named the gods as "The Sun, the Moon, the Stars, the Law, and men who have turned into gods." [1]

The earliest rites that we know of were vegetation rites for the fertilization of the soil. Do you know the story of the princess Danaë, who was locked up in a tower, and was visited by Zeus in the form of a golden rain? The scholars believe that this myth grew out of the old ceremonies by which the earth (personified in Danaë) was made fertile through gold-bringing rain from the spirit or god of the sky. Of course you know the myth of Demeter and Persephone; and you have seen, perhaps, the wonderful Demeter in the British Museum—a more beautiful statue than any by Pheidias or Praxiteles. Demeter was the goddess of the corn; the Romans called her Ceres, and the Americans call her Cereal. Her daughter, Persephone, was snatched away to Hades; but Demeter mourned so much that Persephone was permitted to return to the earth at every harvest-time, provided she would spend the winter in Hades.

ANDREW. If we must go to Hell, it's better to spend our winters there than our summers.

THEODORE. The story was a little drama to symbolize the annual flowering and bounty of the soil. The myths are nearly all made up to explain and, as you say, humanize, the animistic vegetation rites.[2] The beautiful Aphrodite, whom the Greeks took over from the Babylonian goddess Ishtar, came down from the corn spirits of early days; and her festival celebrated the awakening of spring. Of course you know that Easter was originally the feast of spring-time, and of Ishtar.

MATTHEW. The Church, with her divine wisdom, took over the pagan feasts, and adapted the customs of the people to the religion of Christ.

THEODORE. Aphrodite was the lovely symbol of the reproductive energy in nature and man. The ancients did not value chastity as much as the moderns do . . .

CLARENCE. You do not seem to be well acquainted with the moderns, Theodore.

THEODORE. I shall say, then, as much as medieval Christians did, or the Puritans. Rather they admired plentiful maternity; and they worshipped

[1] *Ibid.*, p. 117.
[2] Allen, p. 38; Smith, W. R., p. 18.

love, even honest physical love, with what you might call a reckless indecency. They acknowledged the power, the glory and the rights of Aphrodite, or Ishtar, or Venus, as you will see in the great *Hippolytus* of our
profound master, Euripides. They thought that a man would surely be unfortunate if he lived without paying to the goddess the tribute of the divine
madness of love. In many parts of Asia Minor it was the solemn religious
duty of every lady to stand at the temple gates, and give herself to any
stranger who asked, and then to deposit on the altar of the goddess the
earnings of her holy prostitution. Was it not so, Sir James?

SIR JAMES. Certainly. The sacred precinct was often crowded with women
waiting to be accosted. Some of them had to wait for years.[1]

THEODORE. Adonis was also taken from Babylon. The Semites called him
Tammuz, and sometimes Adon, meaning Lord. The Greeks thought this
title was a name, and gave it to their stolen god. The legends of Babylon
and Greece describe Adonis as killed by a wild boar; perhaps he was a humanized form of the sacred animal worshipped by the early Semites. Once a
year a boar was sacrified, and eaten at a communion feast, while the pious
people mourned the death of Adonis. A few days later they celebrated his
resurrection.[2]

SIR JAMES. Very probably the legend of his death and resurrection goes
back to vegetation rites symbolizing the death and resurrection of the
soil.[3] Everywhere in the development of religion an impersonal force is
turned into a person, and generates a myth.

THEODORE. It is just so with the legend of Dionysus. He represented
the vine, as Demeter represented the corn; and like other vegetation gods he
died and returned to life, like the earth in autumn and spring. His feast too
was commemorated by playing the drama of his death and resurrection.[4]
Out of that ceremony came the theatre of Dionysus, and all the glories
of Æschylus, Sophocles and Euripides; these plays were part of the worship of Dionysus, and had to deal with a religious subject. And yet comedy
came out of the same festival rites: phallic emblems were carried at the
head of the Dionysian processions; and from this phallic feast, called Comus,
together with the sexual humor and song (*oidos*) that went with it, came
com-edy. You will forgive, then, the indecency of Aristophanes; no respectable lady was present at his plays.

SIR JAMES. It was a stag drama, in honor of the goat god.

THEODORE. You are right, Sir James; Dionysus had taken the place of
a sacred goat as human gods had replaced animal gods; and people could
not forget what he had been. A goat was sacrificed to him, and he was

[1] Frazer, p. 330; Ellis, *Studies,* vol. vi, pp. 229 f.
[2] Reinach, p. 40.
[3] Frazer, pp. 335- 7.
[4] *Ibid.,* p. 388.

often pictured in the form of a goat; one of his names was "The Kid." Those who led his procession dressed themselves in goat-masks, which gave us the name for tragedy—*trag-oidos,* the goat song. Sacred animals were mixed up with all the gods, as a relic of totemism; in the Homeric poems ancestor-worship can still be seen in the long process of humanizing the gods. To the Greeks there was no unbridgeable gap between a man and a god; a great man could become a god, or a god could become a great man; the gods mated with human beings, and were like men in almost everything (even vice and virtue), except that they did not die.

When various ancestor-worshipping groups were united in city-states or empires, the gods of these groups were collected into a general pantheon, in which the nature gods of pious days were brought into one family with the heroic ancestors of later faith. Finally the imagination of poets and troubadours ennobled the ancient legends, and the gods of Olympus were born.

ANDREW. Have you ever noticed, Theodore, how closely the Olympian deities modeled their world government on the Cabinet of the President of the United States? Pallas Athene, or Minerva, was Secretary of State; Poseidon, or Neptune, was Secretary of the Navy; Demeter, or Ceres, was Secretary of Agriculture; Hermes, or Mercury, was Director of the Post Office; Ares, or Mars, was Secretary of the Army; and Hera, or Juno, was Secretary of the Interior—her main task being to control the polygamous propensities of the President, Zeus or Jupiter.

THEODORE. Of course there were many more gods than these. The Greeks personified everything, even chance, which became the goddess Tychê. All the ancient peoples liked to have a god for every aspect of life. The Romans, when they took over the Greek pantheon, doubled it. Their very air was alive with deities and demons. There was Abeona who protected children when they left the house, Domiduca who led them back, Interduca who took care of them in between, Cuba who guarded them as they lay asleep, Educa who taught them to eat, Fabulinus who taught them to speak, Statanus who taught them to stand, and hundreds more.[1] Hannibal, after his victory at Cannæ, was marching upon Rome when, at the very gates, he had a dream in which a voice told him to go back. He obeyed the voice, and the grateful Romans built on that spot an altar to a new god whom they named Ridiculus—i. e., the god who makes a man go back.[2] Every field had its Lares, every home had its Penates, every cross-road had its shrine.

ANDREW. Wasn't the worship of guardian angels and local saints a Christian inheritance from this overflowing pantheon?

THEODORE. I think so.

ANDREW. It must have been an awful bore to appease all these gods at

[1] Shotwell, p. 30; Allen, p. 37.
[2] Shotwell, p. 34.

every hour—like living all your life in evening clothes. Anatole France said to Brousson that he disliked the first commandment—"One God alone thou shalt adore"; he wanted to adore "all gods, all temples, and all goddesses." He liked them all because he never had to pray to them. But the Greeks and the Romans had to pray.

THEODORE. Yes, you are right, and Sir James was right: the simple Greek took his gods seriously, feared them, and spent much time in propitiating them; paganism was not all joy. And yet there was great beauty in that religion, and much reason; it was good that the forces and forms of nature should be personified and reverenced; and many gods express better than one god the many conflicts and cross-currents in the world. From that faith came many forms of art: out of burial, sculpture and architecture; out of the religious procession, drama; and out of the hymns that were sung then, music and poetry. In turn art refined religion, and ennobled the ancient gods. Homer and Hesiod gave body and character to the Olympian deities; Pheidias gave them sublimity and majesty; you might say that the gods of Homer died when those of Pheidias were born. The common man had made ferocious and lecherous deities; the artists poured into them the finest human aspirations, and made them reflect the development of civilization and culture among the Greeks. What a difference between the murderous Zeus of Hesiod's fables, and the splendid father of the world formed by the masculine imagination of Æschylus and clothed with the serene wisdom of Sophocles! I have often read of the debt which art owes to religion; no one seems conscious of the debt which religion owes to art.

Nevertheless it was very bad for Greek orthodoxy that drama had come out of the ceremonies of Dionysus. For the drama became literature, and literature became philosophy, and philosophy melts all orthodoxies. It was only a little step from the calm monotheism of Sophocles to the scepticism of Euripides, and the famous utterance of his friend Protagoras—"Whether there are gods or not we cannot know." You see that you were not the first agnostic, my dear Clarence.

CLARENCE. I suspected it.

THEODORE. Indeed, the drama developed an idea that at last destroyed the old gods—the omnipotence of Destiny, a Fate that ruled over gods as well as men. And again from this it was but a step to the conception of universal natural law. This step was taken by the philosophers. The growth of knowledge led men to seek natural explanations, first of ordinary events, then of supposedly supernatural events, and finally of the universe as a whole. The great pre-Socratic philosophers replaced the deities of heaven with water, air, and fire; the Sophists taught men the art of doubt, and took naturalism for granted; soon every up-to-date boy was an atheist. By the time of Plato the original religion of Greece was bankrupt.[1] In the *Laws*

[1] Murray, p. 107.

Plato says: "Since many men have ceased to believe in God, and oaths are out of date, let there be simple affirmation and denial in court." [1]

CLARENCE. We are just about reaching that point in the United States. And still some simpletons talk of progress.

PAUL. You have omitted to say, Theodore, that St. Socrates, as Erasmus called him, proposed a monotheistic religion, and proclaimed, at least in the *Apology*, his firm belief in God.

THEODORE. Yes, and there was a deep religious element in Plato. But the God of Socrates was only a negative "demon"; the God of Aristotle was a cold-blooded perfection lost in self-admiration . . .

CLARENCE. An abstraction fixating its navel.

THEODORE. And the gods of Epicurus were do-nothing kings, without interest in the affairs of men.

ARIEL. They were a lawn-party lasting forever.

THEODORE. How delicately you suggest to me, Ariel, that I must end. Will you give me a minute more? By the time of Pyrrho and the Sceptics, the gods were dead in Greece except for the lower classes. The Hellenistic culture was agnostic; it gave up the pursuit of truth, taught itself resignation, studied the pleasures of art and the arts of pleasure, and consoled itself with the autumn beauty of a dying world. In a sense it was the ripest age of Greece; it was as if all the educated classes had shared the ripeness of men like Thomas Hardy, George Meredith, Georges Clemenceau, and Anatole France.

PAUL. The philosophers triumphed; but in their victory they forgot one thing—they neglected to consider whether a moral code robbed of its supernatural sanctions could teach a nation the self-control necessary for stability and power. The picture ends as perhaps our own picture in this western world will end—with literal de-moralization, individualistic chaos, corruption, crime, suicide.

THEODORE. And yet among the people religion was being born anew. The old oracles at Delphi and Delos, the secret rites at Eleusis, and the rush of Oriental faiths into Greece in the wake of Alexander's returning army, brought to the poorer classes of a defeated nation just the consolation they hungered for. The Orphic cults flourished by transforming the old doctrine of Hades; the dark shades would not swallow all; the good would go to happy Elysian Fields, and even the bad might be saved if their descendants filled the open hands of the priests. "Mendicant prophets," says Plato, "go to rich men's doors and persuade them that they have a power committed to them of making an atonement for their sins, or those of their fathers, by sacrifices or charms, with rejoicings and games. . . . And they produce a host of books written by Musæus and Orpheus . . . according to which they perform their ritual, and persuade not only individuals, but

[1] *Laws,* xii, 948.

whole cities, that expiations and atonements for sin . . . are equally at the service of the living and the dead; the latter they call mysteries, and they redeem us from the pains of hell; but if we neglect them no one knows what awaits us." [1]

Human suffering, the Orphic religion taught, was due to the ancient crime of the Titans, who had rebelled against God; in atonement for this original sin the soul was enclosed in the body as in a jail, and only ascetic virtue and patient ritual could get it out. Men without hope for the good things of this world listened with longing to this new creed. The religion of the *polis,* the old devotion to the city-state, died away, and men talked of individual salvation beyond, and resignation to the evils of the earth. The realm of shades became more real than this earthly scene of defeat and departed glory. It was into this world of piety and hope that Christianity came. The spirit of Greece was conquered by the spirit of the Orient.

ARIEL. Thank you, Theodore. Sir James showed us the birth of religion, and you have shown us its death and resurrection. Come, let us have dinner; and while we feast we shall consider the destiny of the gods.

[1] *Republic,* 365.

CHAPTER XXII

Around the Table

From Confucius to Christ

KUNG. My dear friend Theodore, your conclusion was a reproach to my country. Will you forgive my presumption if I say that your western conception of the Orient is very—very external. You do not realize even the size of Asia; you do not see Europe as merely a pseudopodium, if I may speak so, of the great continent that is the source not only of your religions, but of your languages and your races. If you will remember how vast Asia is, you will understand how great a risk you run in generalizing about it. You cannot indict a continent.

ARIEL. That's splendid, Kung. Tell us more.

KUNG. You see, there are four Asias. There is the militaristic Asia of the Near East—Mohammedan Asia, the land of the religion that came to bring not peace but the sword. Yet even in the Near East what complexity of race and character!—Ottoman Turks, Semitic Arabs and Jews (and even these brothers so different), Persians and Afghans, Caucasians and Armenians. Then there is mystic Asia, the great peninsula of India, of which I trust that Siddha will speak to us. There is Siberia—Mongol and Russian, Korean and Japanese; again a complex mass defying ready formulas. And there is China, the oldest and the youngest nation in the world. How can we take America seriously, with its two centuries of civilization, while that of China is 5,000 years old? The trite contrast between the progressivism of the West and the stagnation of the East amuses me. I wonder how many times the question of progress has agitated China in her succession of civilizations and "middle" ages? China has tried all ideas, and is a little weary of them; it is like Protagoras, who observed the conventions of his time because, after trying all heresies, and finding them all imperfect and conventional, he had concluded that there was too little

351

real difference between one idea and another, or between one religion and another, to warrant any disturbance about them. Until you intoxicated us with the lust for industry, democracy and wealth, we Chinese were content with custom and the prose of peace. If progress is merely superficial change, as some philosophers believe, then China is right: the customs that exist are as good as any, and the life of tillage, with all its toil, is as good as the life of worried industry and business; the simple peasant who tends his fields and piously cares for the graves of his ancestors has found as much happiness as comes to any race on this man-infested earth.

ARIEL. Tell us about Chinese religion, Kung.

KUNG. But, madame, there is no Chinese religion—there are only Chinese religions. There is Chinese Buddhism and Chinese Mohammedanism; there is, among the people, a fetichistic religion of spirits and images, and a totemism of sacred animals. I will not speak of that, for superstition is common to peasants everywhere. There is, among all but the young Nationalists, a stringent ancestor-worship, through which the dead rule the living in almost every act of life. There is the religion of Lao-tse, the Tao or Way, almost absorbed now by Buddhism, but still producing saints of self-denial and meditation. And finally there is Confucianism, the religion of the educated classes in China for hundreds of years. I do not know what adjective could be justly applied to all of these religions together, except that they are Chinese. It would be difficult even to describe them as Oriental, unless you wish to describe Christ and Socrates as Orientals. For the religion of Lao-tse is almost the same, in essence, with that of Christ; and the so-called religion of Confucius (for it is much better described as a philosophy) is strangely like the thought of the great Greek. Shall I recite to you some of the sayings of Lao-tse?

> Requite injury with kindness. To the good I would be good; to the evil I would also be good, in order to make them good. With the faithful I would keep faith; with the unfaithful I would also keep faith, in order that they may become faithful. He who has no faith in others will find no faith in them. Keep behind, and you shall be put in front; he that humbles himself shall be preserved; he that bends shall be made straight. He who is great makes humility his base. He who, conscious of being strong, is content to be weak,— he shall be the paragon of mankind. To know, but to be as one not knowing, is the height of wisdom. The Sage knows what is in him but makes no display; he respects himself, but seeks no honor for himself. All things in nature work silently; they come into being and possess nothing; they fulfil their function and make no claim. All things alike do their work, and then we see them subside. When they have reached their bloom each returns to its origin. Returning to their origin means rest, or fulfilment of destiny. This reversion is an eternal

law. To know that law is wisdom. Do nothing by self-will, but rather conform
to the infinite Will, and everything will be done for you.[1]

MATTHEW. Beautiful, but there's very little religion in it.
KUNG. There is even less in Confucius. He used no supernatural terms,
and had no interest in another life. When a pupil asked him what were
man's duties to spirits, Confucius answered: "Before we are able to do our
duty by the living, how can we do it by the spirits of the dead?"[2] And
when the pupil, persisting, asked about death, the Master said: "Before
we know what life is, how can we know what death is? To give one's self
earnestly to the duties due to men, and while earnestly respecting spiritual
beings to keep away from them, that may be called wisdom."[3] What
religion Confucius had was a lofty pantheism best described to western
minds by comparing it with the system of Spinoza. Consider these sentences,
and see if they do not sound like extracts from the *Ethics* of the great Jew:

> Truth is the law of God. . . . Truth means the realization of our being;
> and moral law means the law of our being. Truth is that by which things
> outside of us have existence. . . . This absolute truth is indestructible. Being
> indestructible it is eternal. Being eternal it is self-existent. Being self-existent
> it is infinite. . . . It is transcendental and intelligent, without being con-
> scious. . . . Because it is infinite and eternal it fills all existence.[1]

What Confucius gave the world is not a theology, not a creed, but a
lofty and aristocratic moral code—"The Way of the Superior Man." In
only a few sentences does he resemble Christ: "What you do not wish others
to do unto you," he says (five centuries before Christ), "do not unto
them." But he resembles far more Socrates, Aristotle and Goethe; he
identifies morality with intelligence, and preaches not humility and gentleness, but the full development of personality. When I studied in China I
had to memorize his precepts; I could recite them to you for many hours.

> What constitutes the higher man? The cultivation of himself with rever-
> ential care. The higher man is catholic, not partisan; the ordinary man is
> partisan, not catholic. The higher man wishes to be slow in his words; for
> men are easily ruined by the mouth. He acts before he speaks, and then speaks
> in accord with his actions. He does not dispute. He conforms to the path of

[1] Brown, B., *The Wisdom of the Chinese*, pp. 85–120.
[2] *Ibid.*, p. 31.
[3] Thorndike, L., *Short History of Civilization*, p. 254.
[4] Brown, pp. 39–41.

the mean. . . . Now there is no end of things by which man is affected; and when his likes and dislikes are not subject to rule, he is changed into the nature of things as they come before him. The higher man seeks all that he wants in himself; the lower man seeks all that he wants from others. The higher man is anxious lest he should not get the truth; he is not anxious lest poverty should come upon him. He is distressed by his want of ability, not by other men's not knowing him. The thing wherein the higher man cannot be excelled is simply this: his work, which other men cannot see.[1]

II. MYSTICISM

SIDDHA. But, my dear Kung, that is not religion! That is only morality; and worse still, it is morality only for the *élite,* for those natural gentlemen who hardly need morality at all. No, religion is something more than morality; and without that something more, morality is a fire too distant to give warmth. Nor is religion a creed, or any other intellectual thing; it is a feeling, the sudden and overwhelming possession of the soul by such a sense of the whole as melts selfishness into devotion, and separateness into loyalty. I wonder if the people of the west ever get such a feeling?

PHILIP. Jakob Böhme had it, St. Francis had it.

ANDREW. Paul Blood said you could get it by taking ether—transcendental anesthetic.

SIDDHA. These are exceptions; their rarity indicates how little hold religion has upon the people of Europe and America. In India this mystical unity of the part with the whole is held to be the very essence of religion; no one would be called religious merely because he believed a creed or attended rites. Our priests, the Brahmins, take their name from their word for God—*Brahma.* But this world does not imply anything so narrow and separate as a personality; it is a neuter noun, and means all Reality; again we are reminded of Spinoza. In the doctrine of the Brahmins only Brahma, the Infinite Reality, exists; all else, all individual separation of persons or things, is Maya, illusion. When you can feel your little personality melting away, and you swim contentedly dissolved in the ocean of being, and everything else but this union seems trivial to you, then you know what religion is, you know what God is, you become a part of God yourself, you are lost in the Divine Infinity.

ARIEL. I remember a sentence of Thoreau's: "Drifting on a sultry day on the sluggish waters of the pond, I almost cease to live, and begin to be." And he spoke of himself as part of "one great creature" with the birds he heard.

SIDDHA. I remember the passages, Madame; they are so beautiful. Do

[1] Williams, E. T., *China Yesterday and Today,* p. 241; Anon., *The Wisdom of Confucius,* p. 132; Thorndike, p. 255; Brown, p. 24.

you know that he read and loved the Hindu philosophers? He says: "It was fit that I should live on rice mainly, who loved so well the philosophy of India."

CLARENCE. But this sense of the whole, even with its emotional background and base, is not necessarily religious. Once on a prosaic local train I saw through the window amber clouds against a sky of white-ribbed blue. I caught my breath as the full beauty of the great vault engulfed me; I felt absorbed into it as a meaningless fragment in a sublime whole. But I assure you that I'm not religious.

ANDREW. This ecstasy of union is not the only thing in Hindu religion. There's sex worship, and a trinity; I understand that Krishna, the second person of the Hindu trinity, became man and redeemed the world. And there's polytheism—loads and loads of gods; Reinach says the Hindu pantheon resembles a tropical forest.[1] What the people love is not a sense of the whole, but a good incredible story; and this mystic rapture of Siddha's is much less to their taste than the legend of how one god drank up the ocean, or another held nuptials with 10,000 virgins in a single night.[2] Next to that they like the delicious satisfaction of ritual—washing their hands in the Ganges (as if the Ganges could ever make anything clean), uttering spells and prayers, and trusting to the divine power of phallic amulets. Now to tell the truth, Siddha, isn't that so?

SIDDHA. No. You have taken again the vulgar shell of religion for the soul of it, just as your philosophers today think that the shell or machine of a man is his essence. Even the simple people whose pious ceremonies you describe will often fast to the point of starvation. I do not think there is a delicious satisfaction in starving, unless it be that it wipes away the sense of self, and merges the passing individual with the world and the eternal. I have seen mystics who had kept their fists tightly closed for so long a time that their nails had grown through the backs of their hands. They had forgotten themselves completely. Or consider Buddha. Like Christ he tried to cast out priestly abuses from the inherited religion, and to bring it back to its ancient purity. He refused to kill the fleas that pestered him, and had a kind word even for the tigers that used to eat so many of us in India. He did not, like the Christians, aim at a heaven of satisfied desires, but at the absolute ending of desire, the utter disappearance of all barriers between the individual personality and the world-spirit. Nirvana means just that: you cleanse yourself of all thought of self, and your whole being is taken up into the eternal reality.

ANDREW. I suspect that we shall all achieve Nirvana. What interests me in Buddha is his atheism: I believe he made a very powerful religion without God, didn't he?

[1] Reinach, p. 60.
[2] Keyserling, Count H., *Travel Diary of a Philosopher,* vol. i, p. 100.

SIDDHA. If by God you mean a supreme Person, yes; but if by God you mean the spirit of the whole, no.

ANDREW. I understand that Buddha, in the legends of the East, is represented as having been born of a Virgin. Every god, it seems, must by his birth cast aspersions upon natural motherhood—which was once the symbol and fountain of all deity.

SIDDHA. You must not take legends literally; in that way you lose the great wisdom which they have clothed in metaphorical form. And again I beg you to remember that these things are not religion.

ANDREW. You mean that they are the fleas on the body of religion.

SIDDHA. If you prefer. Perhaps in another decade or two you of the west will learn what religion is. You cannot know now because you are buried in machines, and your thoughts are always of gold. But industry will destroy itself with war, and suffering will drench all Europe and America; then the pride of personality and individual wealth will pass away; and in the fever of suffering, men will again become conscious of God—that nameless Spirit and Life which the Hindu sage described as the Nothing that remained of the tree when all its parts had been taken away. Even now the Orient comes back to you as you tire of physical things and the flesh; Christian Science grows among you faster than Christianity ever grew; and theosophy is capturing millions upon millions of men and women who know how vain the separate life must be. Some day you will understand India, and religion.

THEODORE. It is possible. The history of religion is an eternal battle between the spirit of the Orient and the spirit of Greece.

III. JUDAISM

ESTHER. I feel, like Siddha, that we have left out some of the most vital elements in religion. We use the phrase "For God's sake"; it is with us only a phrase; but religion takes the words literally; religion means doing things for God's sake, denying one's self unsocial pleasure, or accepting great suffering, for the sake of that final and total plan which is God. I think it is this profound thing in religion, this vision without which morality is mere calculation, that stands out in the religion of the Jews.

ARIEL. Yes; I'm shocked that we've talked so much about religion without mentioning the most religious nation in history. Tell us about Judaism, Esther.

ESTHER. It is not all a lovely story; for this profoundest of all religions began in just such animism and superstition as Sir James has described. The earliest Jews that we know of worshipped rocks, cattle, sheep, and the spirits of caves and wells.[1] They reverenced fetiches like the Teraphim—

[1] Shotwell, p. 30.

portable idols like the Lares of the Romans—and they practised a primitive magic; even the shaking of dice from a box was used to find out the will of the gods.[1]

ANDREW. We still play that game to find out the will of the gods.

ESTHER. Phallic worship had its share too; the serpent and the bull were phallic symbols, and the god Baal was conceived as the male principle that fertilized the female earth.[2] Almost all the Jewish festivals derive from vegetation rites: Mazzoth, Shabuoth (Pentecost) and Sukkoth (Tabernacles) originally celebrated the beginning of the barley-harvest, the end of the wheat-harvest fifty days later, and the vintage time.[3] Pesach (Passover) was the feast of the first fruits of the flocks: a lamb or a kid was sacrificed and eaten, and its blood was sprinkled on the door as a consoling portion for the hungry god. Later this custom was explained as meaning that God had slain the first-born of the Egyptians, and had spared those of the Israelites whose doors were marked with the blood of the lamb; but this was a priestly invention. The Passover feast, like the others, was taken from the conquered Canaanites, among whom it was simply the offering of a kid to the local god. The lamb was originally the totem of a Canaanite tribe; it passed down into Christianity, and became, as *Agnus Dei,* the symbol of Christ. Other totemic relics were the frequent representation of Jehovah as a bull, and the prohibition of pork, which was apparently due to the fact that the wild boar had been a totem of the primitive Jews.

ANDREW. What's that? I thought it was a case of hygiene, not of totemism. All through the Near East the pig is taboo, through fear of trichinosis.

ESTHER. Robertson Smith and Salomon Reinach, who do not agree when they can help it, agree in rejecting the traditional view. In general, throughout the Bible, there is no instance of a disease interpreted as due to the eating of unclean beasts; illness was attributed to the wrath of spirits; and the proper cure was exorcism. Hygiene is a Greek idea. You will be interested, Andrew, to find that Reinach considers the hygienic explanation as a "mark of ignorance." [4]

ANDREW. Well, I read it in Renan.

ESTHER. Reinach laughs at Renan.

ANDREW. Some day the anthropologists will laugh at Reinach. I am not frightened by your barrage of authorities; there are so many hygienic elements in the mosaic code that there is nothing unreasonable in considering the prohibition of pork a matter of hygiene. But go on, Esther; there is always a slight possibility that I am wrong.

ESTHER. A much nobler element than this supposed hygiene, in the so-

---

[1] Reinach, p. 177.
[2] Smith, W. R., p. 101.
[3] Reinach, p. 184.
[4] Reinach, p. 18.

called Mosaic code, was the Ten Commandments. And yet these too were primitive and limited; they were a code for the tribe, not yet for humanity; that had to wait for the prophets. "Thou shalt not kill" was not meant to prohibit war; for time and again Jehovah ordered or approved of wholesale slaughter.

CLARENCE. "And they warred against the Midianites as the Lord had commanded Moses, and they slew all the males. . . . And Moses said unto them, 'Have ye saved all the women alive? . . . Now therefore kill every male among the little ones, and kill every woman that hath known man." [1]

ESTHER. Yes, out of that savagery came at last the highest ethical ideals ever expressed by man; and the "Mosaic" code was a powerful lever in that progress. It formed the strong character of the Jews, enabling them by regularity of life and sternness of philosophy to survive all the evils which this Christian world has put upon them. It was the first code to place cleanliness next to godliness, and to consider the human body as a temple to be cared for with the same religious solicitude as the soul. It is often described as not much better than the code of Hammurabi; but it was the first system of law to establish leniency for slaves, and there was an almost socialistic touch in its institution of the Jubilee Year. "The land shall not be sold forever, for the land is mine. . . . And ye shall hallow the fiftieth year, and proclaim liberty throughout all the land unto all the inhabitants thereof; it shall be a jubilee unto you; and ye shall return every man unto his possession, and ye shall return every man unto his family." [2] It was an ideal rather than a practice, but other nations did not have even the ideal.

As for the murderous "lord" Jehovah whom you mention, Clarence, he was a war-god, only one of the tribal deities of the early Jews. Jeremiah said, "according to the number of thy cities are thy gods, O Judah"; and when Naomi said to Ruth, "Thy sister is gone back unto her people and unto her gods," Ruth answered, "Thy people shall be my people, and thy god my god"; the change of tribe carried with it the change of god.[3] This polytheism continued into the days when the Pentateuch was written; for the story of creation is told first as due to Jehovah, and then as due to Elohim, a plural noun for gods. This legend of creation and Eden was common to the peoples of Asia Minor long before the priests of the Temple set it down in the Bible in the seventh century, B. C. It is found among the Persians, the Phœnicians, the Chaldeans, the Babylonians, etc. Hesiod, writing 800 B. C., tells of the Greek form of the myth,—the Islands of the Blessed, where grew a tree bearing golden apples that gave men immortality.

SIDDHA. Our people had a similar legend. The Vedas tell how the god

[1] Numbers, xxxi, 7, 15, 17.
[2] Leviticus, xxv.
[3] Allen, p. 181; Smith, W. R., p. 37.

Siva dropped a fig tree from heaven, and instigated woman to tempt man with it as conferring immortality. Man ate, and was thereupon cursed by Siva and doomed to misery and toil.[1]

KUNG. In one of the sacred books of the ancient Chinese, the Chi-King, there is the following passage: "All things were at first subject to man, but a woman threw us into slavery by an ambitious desire of knowledge. Our misery comes not from heaven but from woman. She lost the human race. Ah, unhappy Poo See! Thou kindled the fire that consumes us, and which is every day increasing." [2]

PHILIP. Behind all these legends is the feeling that sex and knowledge are the roots of all evil, the twin murderers of a happy innocence. It's a note that goes right through the Bible—down to Ecclesiastes' satire of woman, and his terrible sentence, "He that increaseth knowledge increaseth sorrow." Even Christ disdained sexual love, and exalted the wisdom of children.

CLARENCE. Well, there's a good deal in it. Are we as happy as when we were ignorant? Why do we like the guileless faces of young children? Perhaps it is because we envy them their freedom from sex and from knowledge. But don't let us interrupt your story, Esther.

ESTHER. There are just two things more. The Jews gave the world monotheism, and they gave it the first gospel of social justice. The tribal character of the early deities was due partly to the economic separateness and independence of the group, and partly to each jealous god being the deified ancestor of a particular tribe. The development of trade, and the consequent growth of economic interdependence, brought the coalescence of tribes and the merger of gods; at last it was possible to think in terms of all humanity, and one god. Isaiah was the first to express the larger god, a god almost worthy of Copernicus. "Behold the Lord God, who hath measured the waters in the hollow of his hand, and meted out heaven with the span, and comprehended the dust of the earth in a measure, and weighed the mountains in scales and the hills in a balance. . . . Behold, the nations are as a drop of a bucket; . . . behold, he taketh up the isles as a very little thing." [3] The next development was Job's conception of God as the order of the universe; here the religion of the Jews, after beginning in magic and superstition, rises to the heights of Spinoza, and paves the way for modern science. But greater even than this idea of the unity of God was its natural corollary, the idea of the unity of mankind, the end of war, and the coming of social justice.

CLARENCE. The outlawry of war. We are still considering whether we shall consider that.

[1] Doane, T. W., *Bible Myths,* p. 12.
[2] *Ibid.,* p. 14.
[3] Isaiah, xl.

ESTHER. Amos came up to Jerusalem, "stood in the gate" (on the street-corner, as we should say), and announced the new religion of man. "Forasmuch therefore as your treading is upon the poor, and ye take from him burdens of wheat, ye" (the rich) "have built houses of hewn stone, but ye shall not dwell in them; ye have planted pleasant vineyards but ye shall not drink wine of them. . . . Woe to them that are at ease in Zion; . . . that lie upon beds of ivory, and stretch themselves upon their couches." It will not help them to offer sacrifices on the altars; God will say to them: "I despise your feast-days, and though . . . ye offer me burnt offerings and your meat offerings, I will not accept them. . . . Take thou away from me the noise of thy songs; for I will not hear the melody of thy viols. But let judgment run down as water; and righteousness as a mighty stream." [1] Or hear Isaiah:

> The Lord will enter into judgment with the ancients of his people, and the princes thereof; for ye have eaten up the vineyard; the spoil of the poor is in your houses. What mean ye that ye beat my people to pieces, and grind the faces of the poor? . . . Woe unto them that join house with house, that lay field to field, . . . that they may be placed alone in the midst of the earth! . . . And what will ye do in the day of visitation, and in the desolation which shall come from afar? To whom will ye flee for help, and where will ye leave your glory? . . . To what purpose is the multitude of your sacrifices unto me, saith the Lord; I am full of the burnt offerings of rams, and the fat of fed beasts. . . . Your appointed feasts my soul hateth; they are a trouble unto me; I am weary to bear them. And when ye spread forth your hands, I will hide mine eyes from you; yea, when ye make many prayers I will not hear; your hands are full of blood. Wash ye, make ye clean; put away the evil of your doings from before mine eyes; cease to do evil; learn to do well; seek judgment, relieve the oppressed, judge the fatherless, plead for the widow. [2]

ANDREW. Magnificent! What language, and what power!

ESTHER. There's nothing in the history of religion, and nothing in the history of literature, finer than that. The Greeks, as Renan said, gave the mind liberty, but the Jews gave men brotherhood. Greece had culture, but she had no heart; even her philosophers defended slavery. The Greeks produced art and science, but it remained for the Jews to give the world the conception of social justice and the rights of man. Through this faith little Israel, lost among ancient empires and harassed among modern nations, will win to victory in the end. And today the peoples who conquered or oppress

[1] Amos, **v**, 11, 21 f; vi, 1–4.
[2] Isaiah, i, 11 f.; iii, 14; v, 8; x, 1 f.

her bow to her in spirit, and aspire to the ideals which she gave to the world.

ANDREW. From Isaiah to Trotzky!

ESTHER. Yes. Socialism will be the religion of the world when Christianity is dead.

IV. CHRISTIANITY

ARIEL. You are wonderful, Esther; you make me proud of my people. And now who will tell us about Christianity? Not you, merry Andrew, for you'd do nothing but find fault with it; nor you, Matthew, for you love it too much. Perhaps Philip, who can be impartial when he tries, should give us some historical background, and then we can have a pitched battle. Is it agreed?

MATTHEW. I have listened patiently so far, and I can listen longer. I conclude that comparative religion is an altar on which every religion is sacrificed. As to Philip, he is always wrong, but he is always forgivable.

PHILIP. You speak like a Christian, Matthew, but you will regret your kindness soon. I am glad to see that Ariel recognizes the importance of getting Christianity into proper perspective. As some one here likes to say, perspective is everything. Christianity arose out of two great complexes of historical conditions: first the growth of a helpless and hopeless proletariat, and of industrial and commercial exploitation, in Jerusalem, Alexandria, Antioch, Athens and Rome; and second, the contact and mingling of the moral ideas of the Jews, so well described by Esther, with the philosophical and theological ideas of the Greeks.

From before the days of Solomon the position of Jerusalem at the crossroads of the great trading routes that connected Phœnicia with the Persian Gulf, and the Mediterranean nations with Assyria, Babylonia and Persia, had led to the development of mercantile establishments and pursuits among the Jews, and had widened the gap between the rich and the poor. The Jews who returned from Babylon were destitute. The conquering Greeks and Romans made barbaric slave-raids upon this helpless population, taking young men by the thousands. In the boyhood of Jesus whole towns near Nazareth were sold into slavery by the Romans. Everywhere in the larger ports of the Mediterranean a propertyless class was growing; and a religious outlook was forming among them that was hostile and contrary to that of their masters. The rich, though privately agnostic, supported the old orthodox ritual and faith; the poor developed a moral code that made virtues of their weakness, misfortune and poverty, and a theology that culminated in a heaven for Lazarus the pauper and a hell for Dives the millionaire. Hence Nietzsche's denunciation of Christianity as the victory of a poorer over a more masterful type of man. The proletarian world was ready for a religion that would take the side of the under-dog, preach the virtues of the meek and humble of heart, and offer the hope of a heaven in which all the slings and arrows of a prejudiced fortune would receive compensation in eternal happiness. The greatest tactical problem of modern Christianity is to reconcile its dependence upon the rich with its natural devotion to the poor.

It is against this background of injustice and poverty that I see the communism and ethics of Jesus. For of course he was a communist, believing that all necessary things belong to all, and that the rich should share everything with the poor; today, as Nietzsche said, he would be sent to Siberia. But everybody, rich or poor, who reads his simple story as the earlier gospels give it, is irresistibly drawn to him; he is without comparison the most appealing figure in history. It is a pity, though I suppose it was a necessity, that he came to be associated with a theology and a church; for when that church and that theology pass away, mankind may negligently forget its greatest teacher.

His moral doctrine represents, in a purified and demilitarized form, the ethical conceptions of the noblest Jews. Klausner has shown how thoroughly he was part of his time, and how he inherited the heroic tradition of the prophets and moralists of Israel.[1] Hillel, grandfather of the Gamaliel who taught St. Paul, speaks occasionally with the very words of Christ, a generation before Christ. "Judge not thy neighbor until thou hast been in his place." "My humility is my exaltation, and my exaltation is my humility." "Do not do unto others what thou wouldst not they should do unto thee; this is the whole of the Law—the rest is only commentary."[2] "Jesus was not a Christian," said Wellhausen, "he was a Jew." "Christianity," said Renan, "is the masterpiece of Judaism." It is, in Heine's phrase, a Jewish heresy.[3]

Nevertheless it added to Judaism a doctrine which, along with the personality and legend of Jesus, goes far to explain its victory. At the outset of his preaching Christ did not speak much of another world; he phrased the Kingdom of Heaven in terms of an earthly millennium, or as a selfless purity of soul. The idea of immortality had not been a part of the historical Jewish faith; the Jews had, in the days of their strength, made it almost unnecessary by teaching the individual to merge himself with the community, and labor less for his own salvation than for that of the state. Job was the first of his race to consider personal immortality, because he could not retain his belief in a good God without supposing that in another life God would repay the just man who had suffered on earth. When the Jews had abandoned all hope of victory in this world, the idea of a compensatory

[1] Klausner, J., *Jesus of Nazareth*, Book viii and *passim*.
[2] Reinach, p. 204.
[3] Klausner, p. 363; Renan, E., *History of the People of Israel*, vol. v, p. 355.

heaven found form in the Books of Wisdom, Enoch and Daniel. It was not otherwise with Christ; when he despaired of establishing the Kingdom of Heaven on earth he placed it in Paradise, and spoke of a cruel Last Judgment that would condemn half of the human race, including most of the beautiful women of all time, to an everlasting hell in which the fire would never be extinguished, and the worm would never die.

MATTHEW. I do not recognize in your picture the gentle Son of God.

PHILIP. Perhaps both my picture and yours are wrong, Matthew; who can tell? This is the beauty of philosophy, that nothing in it is certain; therefore philosophers do not kill one another, nor plunge the people into war. If I perceive a strange bitterness in the later Christ it is because I see him against the background of his own ethical doctrine, and judge him by the almost impossible perfection which he preached. That moral idealism is, for me, the essence of Christianity, and surely the greatest of all contributions ever made to the civilizing of mankind. I never get over my wonder that out of the ape and the jungle should have come at last a man able to conceive all humanity as one, able to love it, and suffer for it, without stint.

MATTHEW. Don't you see, Philip, that only a divine will could have borne such suffering, or known such love?

PHILIP. And yet even here we must differ. This moral doctrine of Christ is not to be taken absolutely; there are questionable elements in it, supreme though it is. Few of us have the courage to say what in our hearts most of us believe—that the code of Christ, taken completely, is impracticable. It is impossible to "take no thought for your life, what ye shall eat, or what ye shall drink"; we can't live like the birds of the air, much less like the lilies of the field. It is difficult to love our neighbors as ourselves, and it is impossible to love our enemies. Non-resistance, in a world of men formed by natural selection and the struggle for existence, is an invitation to aggression and enslavement; a people that loved its enemies would be wiped off the face of the earth.

KUNG. Lao-tse also taught, "Love thine enemies." But Confucius said, "With what, then, will you recompense kindness? Return good for good, and for evil, justice."

PAUL. You must remember that even if Christ's doctrine seems too perfect for men, it was just the thing a barbarized world required. The essential function of Christianity has been to moderate, by the inculcation of this extreme gentleness, the natural savagery of our race. And two thousand years of preaching has had some good effect. I believe that we are kinder today, more generous, more peaceable, than the Greeks or the Romans were: that we have alleviated exploitation, softened brutality, and ennobled human character.

PHILIP. I sometimes think that when Christ preached these perfect ways he had in mind his own apostles and disciples, and thought to give them a monastic discipline that would steel them against the temptations of the world. So Plato thought to protect his philosopher-kings by an almost ascetic communism. Christ tells his followers not to marry, and not to possess goods; he is thinking of them as Franciscan monks; he knew as well as we that the majority of men would persist in their absurd addiction to property and marriage. It is the misconception of his doctrine as intended for all, that has plunged Christianity into a pleasant hypocrisy, practically without effect upon the world.

ANDREW. What I dislike in this noble teacher is his hostility to the flesh, his indifference to the simple joys of our human instincts. I think he is a Jewish Puritan.

MATTHEW. You wrong him; he did not disdain to change water into wine at Cana; he was reproached by the foolish of his day for his lenience to feasting publicans and sinning Magdalens; he understood the sins of the flesh as tenderly as a mother. You have forgotten the story of the woman taken in adultery.

PHILIP. The passage is of doubtful authenticity, Matthew; but that it should have been written at all indicates that a certain gentleness towards woman was part of the picture of Christ. That this passionate scorner of the rich, and incorruptible lover of the poor, should have been within a century or two transformed into the hero of a theological legend proves the everlasting hunger of humanity for fables, and the powerful influence which ancient myths exercised in forming the Christian creed. The idea of a Son of God, a Savior born of a virgin, dying in atonement for the sins of men, and rising again from the grave, is found in a great many religions before Christianity, or independent of Christianity: in India, for example, Krishna; in Egypt, Horus; in Mexico, Quetsalcoatl.[1]

THEODORE. Among the simpler Greeks, Orpheus was conceived as a god who died a violent death, descended into hell, and rose to life again. The same story was told of Prometheus, Adonis, and Heracles.[2]

SIR JAMES. Gods who become men are common in early religions. A register of all incarnate gods in the Chinese Empire used to be kept in the Colonial Office at Pekin; the number of gods who had taken out a license to live on the earth was 160. The idea of a Messiah goes back to the scapegoat selected by the people to die for their sins and appease the deities of soil and sky, so that the wheat might grow again. It recurs in every people.[3]

ESTHER. As late as the seventeenth century Zabbatai Zevi claimed to be the Messiah, sent by God to redeem the Jews.

SIR JAMES. We have a later case than that. About 1830 a man appeared

---

[1] Doane, *op. cit.*, pp. 111 f.
[2] *Ibid.*
[3] Frazer, pp. 93, 103, 580 f.

in Kentucky who professed to be the son of God, and the savior of mankind. Thousands believed him, and his gospel flourished until a follower besought him to announce his message in German to the Teutons of the region; they could not understand English, and it was a pity that they should go to Hell merely on that account. The new Savior, however, confessed that he could not speak German. "What!" exclaimed his follower, "you the son of God and you don't even know German?" That was the end of the Kentucky Messiah.[1]

PHILIP. Having made Christ a god, the early Christians were driven to certain theological subtleties in order to meet two demands: one for the logical symmetry of the holy number three; the other for a monotheistic creed. The Jewish tradition led up naturally to monotheism; but the Jewish god was a god of war and power, and the submerged tenth to whom Christianity appealed wanted a god of forgiveness, pity and love. So Jehovah died, and God the Father was born. To reconcile his universality with the existence of evil it was necessary to invent, after the manner of the Persians, a god of evil—Satan, or Lucifer. At the same time the new creed had to fall in with the custom, among the Mediterranean peoples, of worshipping a triad of gods. The Hindus, the Egyptians, the Phœnicians, the Assyrians, and the Romans had worshipped three gods as three gods; but the drive to unity, particularly among the Jews, required a synthesis of the three Christian gods into a trinity; and the philosophers of Alexandria effected this on the lines of Greek philosophy and legend. So the scholars among the Christians interpreted the new religion as monotheistic, while the people saw in it a lovely variation on their familiar polytheistic themes. Mary took the place of Venus, Aphrodite, Ishtar, Isis, and the "Great Mother" of the Phrygian cult; Mars became the archangel Michael, and Mercury became Raphael and Gabriel. Later the saints were installed as heirs of the minor pagan gods; every nation, every town and every guild had its patron saint, like the local deities of old; the natural polytheism of mankind was restored.

Similarly, the old festivals were kept, and feasts like those of All Souls, St. George, and St. John the Baptist were wisely placed on pre-Christian holy days. Easter combined the Jewish Passover, the Babylonian rites of Ishtar, and the Greek celebration of the resurrection of Adonis. Christmas was originally the Egyptian feast of the Birth of the Sun—i. e., the winter solstice, when the holy orb "moved" north, and the days began to lengthen. The Egyptians represented the new-born sun by the image of an infant, which the priests brought out and exhibited to the worshippers.[2] At the same time, old ceremonies were adapted. Baptism was a primitive rite that had marked the initiation of youth into adult life and privileges; it took

[1] *Ibid.*, p. 102.
[2] Frazer, pp. 345–60.

the form of total immersion and a pretended rescue from drowning, which signified a new birth.

THEODORE. In the cult of Dionysus the initiate was called "twice-born." [1]

PHILIP. The Eucharist, as Sir James has shown, developed out of the custom of eating the god. The Mass, aside from the Consecration, was taken over from the old synagogue rites, along with the vestments and chants of the Jews; the first churches were synagogues. Generation by generation these ceremonies became more complex, and the creeds more incredible; the priestly class grew stronger, as necessary specialists in theology and rites, skilled intermediaries between sinful men and a god that could be appeased only in certain sacred ways. The eighteenth century thought that priests had created religion: "Who was it that invented the art of divination?" Voltaire asked; and answered, "The first rogue who met the first fool." [2] But it was not the priests that made religion, but religion that made priests; the ineradicable hope and faith of man made and will always make religion. But it was the priests who made the Church. They organized themselves into a powerful hierarchy, financed from the bottom and ruled from the top. They converted Constantine, imagined the famous "Donation," accepted rich legacies, and at last made the Church of the poor fishermen the wealthiest and strongest organization that the world has ever seen. By the time of the Reformation the Church owned one-third of the arable soil of Europe, and her coffers were full. No wonder she lost the spirit of her Founder, and fell into every manner of worldliness and simony. Europe had converted Christianity; the Oriental severity of the earlier cult was lost in the genial paganism of the Renaissance. Religions are born among the poor, and die among the rich.

The Reformation tried to recapture that primitive asceticism and simplicity. It succeeded, and brought with it a stimulating individualism, and at the same time a stern code of self-discipline that built up independence and strength of character as no other code before; the great men of modern political and economic history are nearly all Protestants. But it did these great things at heavy cost. It put an infallible book in the place of an infallible church; and then, for lack of such a church, it was driven to permit individual interpretation of the Scripture. The result was that every heretic founded a new sect, and Protestantism split up into a thousand pieces. And in trying to renew primitive Christianity it restored the spirit of Judaism, and brought into morals a rigorous and warlike Puritanism that almost destroyed art for two hundred years. Catholicism gave us beauty without truth, and Protestantism tried to give us truth without beauty. I suspect that in the end beauty will win.

[1] Kallen, Horace, *Why Religion,* p. 242.
[2] *Essai sur les mœurs,* in Reinach, p. 9.

V. CATHOLICISM AND PROTESTANTISM

MATTHEW. "Beauty and truth." Have you ever reflected, Philip, that the one is no more objective than the other? We can no more agree about God than about—

ANDREW. Goddesses.

MATTHEW. Very well, you irreverent soul. You cannot feel religion, Andrew, because you cannot feel the beauty that is separated from desire, the overwhelming beauty that the earth sometimes puts on in autumn, or on some fresh morning in winter when every tree is jeweled with sparkling ice, and all the roofs are bright with snow. Truth seems so poor a thing beside such beauty. And how do you know, you unhappy sceptics, that you have the truth? Your science changes every day; it knows far less about matter now than it thought it knew fifty years ago. Your biology passes from one certainty to its opposite every thirty years; in one generation it is all for environment, in the next it is all for heredity, in the next it is all for environment; in one generation it is for fortuitous variations, in the next it is for mutations; in one generation it is for pangenesis, in the next it is for chromosomes and genes; in one generation the ape is our grandfather, in the next he is our cousin, in the next he is no relation to us at all. Your psychology does not know whether consciousness exists, and your mathematics does not know whether a straight line is the shortest distance between two points. And you want me to abandon all the beauty revealed by the Christian view of the world for the sake of these dying "truths." Don't you see that we are vain atoms to think that we can ever understand this universe, or subject all its mysteries and complexities to one fragment of it called human reason? What is your reason but faith in your senses and in logic—senses that distort everything they report, and logic that can make any prejudice seem rational?

As for me, I perceive that there is very little to choose among theories of the world on the score of their truth; and I am content to abide by that doctrine which inspires me with beauty and strengthens me with hope. When all your isms have passed away, the faith which I hold will still kindle the hearts of many hundred millions of men; perhaps your own grandchildren will come to it out of the cold agnosticism which you bequeath to them. Day by day the western world recovers from that terrible mistake, the Reformation; many Protestant sects, tired of dividing and quarreling, will come back into the fold; and the rest will disintegrate through modernism and birth-control. The cancer of individualism is eating away the churches that revolted from Rome. When every man feels himself an authority on philosophy and theology, you get in religion what you get in democracy—disruption and chaos. When the individual replaces the family, and promiscuity replaces monogamy and motherhood, the race decays. Thank God that among Catholics men and women are still loyal to each other till the end, and children are still permitted to bless the home with their divine growth and their happy play.

PAUL. There is a great deal in what you say, Matthew. We Protestants do seem to be weeding ourselves out with sectarianism and contraception. Already your Church numbers two of every five Christian communicants in America; your birth rate dooms us; by the year 2000, if present tendencies continue, this will be your country. In many ways it will be a good thing: I grant you that your religion is happier than mine, and more beautiful; I grant you that there is much wisdom in the Catholic theory of marriage, much nobility in your hierarchy, a fine charity and gentleness in your clergy and your saintly nuns. I was deeply impressed by the hold which your Church evidently had upon its members, when I saw the engineers and firemen coming down from their great engines at the Pennsylvania Station, and kneeling humbly on the platforms to ask the blessing of Cardinal Mercier. And I can't forget Dostoievski's figure of the Grand Inquisitor; perhaps life, with its sickness, bereavements and disillusionments would be unbearable without the poetry which the older faith shed over the economic prose of our existence.

ANDREW. *Populus vult decipi; decipiatur.*

PAUL. But frankly, Matthew, I fear your religion. I can never forget that once your Church supported the Inquisition; that it exiled Copernicus, silenced Galileo, and burned Bruno at the stake. Time and again it has stood in the way of the advancement of knowledge and the emancipation of the human mind. I am uncomfortable when I think that unless great changes come in the birth rate, your Church seems destined, within this century, to become the dominant factor in American life. Already it is the most powerful organized minority. Boston, home of the Puritans, is a Catholic city; Philadelphia, home of the Quakers, is a Catholic city; New York, home of the Dutch and the English Protestants, is a Catholic city.

MATTHEW. Don't you think it's time we had our innings?—that after patiently bearing persecution and ignominy from your Know-Nothings and your Klans we should be rewarded with respect and power? And it isn't true that the Church has opposed the growth of knowledge; it has only opposed—and these in the heyday of their popularity—erroneous ideas which were or are merely the intellectual fashions of a day. It has refused to allow its members to fall into that chaos of mind and theory which prevails in the camps of the advanced intellectuals of our time. It is true that the authority of the Church has sometimes been on the side of an old error; but what do you demand of human beings? Has the political party which you supported in the last election never erred? All in all the Church has been the greatest moral, artistic and intellectual force in the history of the last two thousand years. The Inquisition was a result of the Reformation; it was a temporary panic of fear and self-protection. Who was it that first established freedom of worship in America? Not the Pilgrims of New England, who voted to cure Quakers with red-hot pokers; but the Catholics of Maryland. Which of us is more guilty of obscurantism and hostility to science today—the Catholic Church, whose dominance in Austria, Bavaria and France has offered no obstacle to freedom of thought there, or the Fundamentalists of Protestant America, who allowed rural legislators, or simple peasants, to determine what shall be held true or false in modern biology? Are infallible assemblies, or infallible farmers, better than an infallible Church?

PAUL. It's a palpable hit, Matthew. I have no apologies for those people; they are the last trench in the defense of ignorance, and our schools and universities will get the better of them soon. My own Protestantism is the only refuge from such a reversion to superstition. If we flaunt atheism in the face of a people in whose harassed lives God has been the supreme reality, and immortality an indispensable consolation, we invite a self-protective intolerance, and drive timid souls to compensatory extremes. In this atmosphere of mutual hatred and fear the modernist faith which I profess has little chance to grow; reason is unpopular in times of danger. Nevertheless we shall win. The enlargement of the middle class, and the spread of education, favor us; and perhaps the imminent triumph of Catholicism will lead liberals of all shades to unite in a moderate Christianity that will ask nothing of its adherents except faith in God and the ethics of Christ.

CLARENCE. Paul, your Protestantism is doomed. Look at its decay; it has broken into ten thousand fragments, little obstinate groups, each hugging its heresy till it becomes an immovable orthodoxy, each hating and despising 9,999 other varieties of Protestant. Here is a clipping from the New York *Sun* for November 1, 1928; it speaks of Protestantism in the United States:

> Apparently there are five groups of Adventists, eighteen groups of Baptists, five groups of Brethren and German Baptists, six groups of Plymouth Brethren, three groups of River Brethren, three groups of United Brethren, six groups of the Eastern Orthodox Church, eleven evangelistic associations, four groups of Friends, twenty-three groups of Lutherans, seventeen groups of Mennonites, nineteen groups of Methodists, nine groups of Presbyterians, four groups of the Reformed Church, and various other classifications of from one to three groups each. . . . There are, e. g., General Six Principle Baptists, Free Will Baptists, Regular Baptists, Primitive Baptists, Two-Seed-in-the-Spirit Predestinarian Baptists, and Seventh Day Baptists. There

are Conservative Amish Mennonites, Defenseless Mennonites, and Unaffiliated Mennonite Churches. There are Primitive Methodists, Congregational Methodists, Holiness Methodists, and reformed Methodists. There are—

PAUL. Enough, Clarence; I am convinced that Protestantism divides. It is our way to leave the individual, in his conscience and his community, free to be as different and unbound as he pleases. Better that than the suppression of variation by a rigid and uncontrollable centralized authority.

MATTHEW. Authority is the alternative to chaos.

CLARENCE. Protestantism will be destroyed by lack of mooring and center. It is a half-way house between romanticism and education. What Voltaire said of the people is true of a religion: when it begins to reason, all is lost. Protestantism has been in process of decay ever since the Reformation. Its greatest enemy is the spread of that knowledge which Paul imagines to be its ally. The advance of science leaves Catholicism untouched, because Catholicism does not pretend to reason; it builds on faith, and appeals to the senses and the imagination rather than to the intellect. When sense and hope are satisfied, the mind remains at rest; that is the secret of Catholicism. But Protestantism never appealed to the senses, except with hymns; it feared and condemned the senses; it closed the theatre and put an end to art; it replaced the drama of the Mass with the dreary logic of the sermon; it tried to base religion on argument—which was the greatest error that it could make. Its churches will dwindle, while Catholicism will remain for centuries as strong as now, and will probably grow stronger for many years to come. Protestantism will be crushed between the imaginative and the intelligent. The future in America will be like France today: a highly sceptical minority, and a highly pious majority. The emancipated will live over a volcano of superstition. Not only will Catholicism win the masses, but if poverty comes, as the result of bitter economic competition, or the loss of a great war, the old myths will reappear. The peasants of every land still love the ancient legends; the simpler people everywhere still believe in spirits, taboos, and supernatural signs. Alexander Berkman says that he read on the walls of the old Duma in St. Petersburg—

ANDREW. Petrograd.

ESTHER. Leningrad.

CLARENCE—this legend carved into the stone: RELIGION IS OPIUM FOR THE PEOPLE. But in the chapel nearby, he adds, services were being held, and the place was crowded.[1] The engraver had forgotten that opium is popular in the East. And in the West. We are no better; while free thought grows among the few, new cults arise like weeds in the decaying soil of the older faith. It is an admirable time to found a new religion. Christian Science spreads like a patent medicine because people are unwilling to accept

[1] *The Bolshevik Myth*, p. 56.

either Christianity or science. Theosophy turns unsuccessful clerks and salesmen into Hindu fakirs. Out of 153 religious announcements in a recent paper I found 53 that were of these occult faiths. One man announced a lecture on "Is the Devil a Personal Being, and Will He Be Bound, Shut Up and Sealed in the Bottomless Pit for One Thousand Years?" in the Gaiety Theatre, free, questions answered. There is an old Norse myth that after the Twilight of the Gods—i. e., their destruction by the giants—a new universe emerged, and the gods came to life again; this is almost the history of the world. The gods always come back, and always from the Orient; we are being swamped with new cults from the East, as Greece and Rome were in the last three centuries before Christ, or as Africa and Spain were swamped by the followers of Mohammed. The truth is that people will always demand a religion phrased in imagery and haloed with the supernatural. They don't want science, they are in mortal terror of it; for the one sermon of science is that all life eats other life, and that all life will die. The masses will never accept science until it gives them an earthly paradise. As long as there is poverty there will be gods.

CHAPTER XXIII

In the Library

God and Immortality

I. IMMORTALITY

ARIEL. Here in this library we shall have comfort and quiet. If you are bored with the discussion you may distract and solace yourselves with the books. But I hope you will not go until you have told me the future of man after death, and whether we may still believe in God.

PAUL. It is evident that Clarence takes it for granted that there is no such thing as an immortal soul, and that we all die like dogs.

CLARENCE. Yes. Why shouldn't my dog be as immortal as I? I am as brutal to him as Jehovah himself could be; I am selfish, and give him only what I don't want; I desert him when I like, but he is more faithful to me than Héloïse to Abélard. Of the two of us I think he is the better Christian.

SIR JAMES. Your "soul," Paul, goes back to the spirits that primitive man encountered in his dreams. As he saw the ghosts of the dead apparently divorced from their bodies, he concluded that he too had a separable ghost or soul. We still say that "he gave up the ghost"; and the word *spirit*, like the German word *Geist*, means both soul and ghost. Early man interpreted echoes and shadows as belonging to, or being, one's ghost or double or soul. The Basuto refuses to walk near a stream, lest a crocodile should seize his shadow and eat it. The fact that in sleep the savage saw himself hunting, walking and running about, while later he was assured that his body had not stirred, convinced him that he had a separable soul.[1] Similarly trances, illness and fainting seemed to him to be temporary abstractions of the spirit from the body. West African Negroes believe that a headache is caused by the soul getting lost; they send a medicine-man to search for it in the woods; he comes back with the captured soul in a box, and blows it out of the box into the patient's ear, whereupon the headache is cured.

[1] Spencer, H., *Principles of Sociology*, vol. i, p. 286.

CLARENCE. In a story of Anatole France's a Polynesian says: "The soul is a puff of wind; and when I saw myself on the point of expiring I pinched my nose to keep my soul inside my body. But I did not squeeze hard enough. And I am dead." [1]

SIR JAMES. In Celebes they fasten fish-hooks to a sick man's nose, navel and feet, so that if his soul tries to get out it will be caught by the hook. Sneezing is dangerous, for it may be so strong as to expel the soul; hence when a man sneezed his companions invoked God's blessing upon him, as particularly needed in so vital an emergency. The Hindus snap their thumbs when any one yawns before them, hoping that this will keep his soul from falling out. Many primitive people refuse to be photographed, lest the picture should take their souls with it,—in which case the photographer might come and devour them at his leisure. [2]

ESTHER. Here in New York, recently, in a play called *The Dybbuk,* we had a dramatic study of the separable soul.

SIR JAMES. The belief in immortality grew naturally out of this idea. The Tuscarora Indians say that all good Indians, when they die (as if they are not all good when they are dead), go to a spirit world far off among the stars, where they find handsome women who never grow old or fat, and happy hunting grounds where there is always plenty of deer, no matter how many are shot; the bad Injun, however, will go to a place where the food is scarce, and snakes are the staple of diet. Among the Egyptians the belief in immortality was so strong that the houses built for the body's shelter on earth were mere huts compared to the elaborate "houses of eternity" built for the soul. In India the ineradicable hope took the form of transmigration; as far west as Italy we find Pythagoras saying, "Do not beat that dog, for I recognize in it the voice of my dead friend." In our own time Nietzsche's doctrine of eternal recurrence was merely a variation on the transmigration theme, and indicates how tenaciously the idea holds on, even in a "medicynical" philosophy. The idea of Hell is found almost everywhere, but its form varies according to the particular brand of suffering borne by the people who conceive it as a receptacle for their enemies. Our own notion of Hell came down to us from the Jews, who suffered from the heat of the desert; but the Eskimos think that Hell is a place of eternal cold.

PAUL. You seem to believe that by showing how old the idea of immortality is, you disprove its validity. And yet I accept the idea for almost the same reasons as those which moved the savage. I look within me and find something that simply refuses to be interpreted in material terms. The death of my body will merely liberate that essential self.

WILLIAM. The self may not be material, Paul, but it is temporal; it is

[1] *The Garden of Epicurus,* p. 197.
[2] Allen, p. 49; Frazer, pp. 178 f, 193.

as subject to time and change and death as the body. Obviously what we call "mind" is bound up with body, brain and nerves; they grow and decay together, and bear alike the effects of injury and disease. William James tried to explain this correlation by speaking of the "permissive" function of the brain; but that was a Yankee dodge, unworthy of a man trained in French clarity. Endocrinology, despite its bizarre excesses in amateur hands, has shown that the relation of body to mind is not permissive but regulative. Whole regions have been cleared of idiocy by thyroid extract.

My self or personality is the product partly of inherited action-tendencies, bound up with neural reflexes, and partly of my body's experiences, coming through my physical senses, and recorded in my physical brain as habits and memories. I am not saying that mind or memory is the brain; I am saying that they are bound up with the nervous system, depend upon it, and therefore cannot survive it. My memories can be temporarily or permanently destroyed by ether or other chemicals. Old age eliminates certain areas of memory, and reduces the self, by disintegrating parts of the brain—presumably the association-fibres of the cortex. When my nerves rot in the grave, my peculiar ego disappears with them; for my self, as distinct from yours, is the result of different heredity and experience; and these are written in my perishable flesh. Even the unity of the self, which immortality must presuppose, is doubtful. My personality is a flux; in every decade of my life I have been a different man; and I see as quite another than my present self the boy I was at the age of ten. Which of my many transient selves is or was "myself"? Again, personality can be double or multiple; the self is only a focus or cluster of associations, and there is no guarantee that the cluster I call *me* will not be broken up into two clusters, or alternating personalities, by illness or shock. Which was immortal, Jekyll or Hyde? And even if the soul should survive the body, of what use would it be? Can you really imagine a bodiless existence, or look forward to it with any satisfaction? How could you experience any pleasure, or know any thrill of love, without a body?

MATTHEW. You see, Paul, that if you are going to believe in immortality you must go all the way, and accept the resurrection of the body.

PAUL. No; it's too much to suppose that after my body has been eaten by worms, and nothing remains of it but a rag, a bone and a hank of hair, it will be restored, at the Last Judgment or before, to the original structure and relation of its billion particles. If we can't imagine or picture a soul without a body, it is only a defect in ourselves, not a limitation to possibility; even in physics there are hundreds of things, like electricity, that seem to me incredible, though I am assured they are real. That the spirit can actually survive the body has been proved over and over again by psychical research; the evidence, gathered with the greatest care, by investigators of unquestioned integrity, is so conclusive that men originally hostile or sceptical, like Hyslop, Lombroso and Alfred Russel Wallace, have accepted it. Even the editor of the *Scientific American* concedes that Margery Crandon produced real psychic phenomena, and established communication with a brother long since dead.

WILLIAM. The test of Mrs. Crandon by the *Scientific American* resulted in a divided report: Bird and Carrington for, Houdini and McDougal against. Later tests by Harvard professors brought negative results.[1] Houdini claimed he could duplicate all established psychical phenomena from his bag of tricks. He went from city to city, read from the stage the names and addresses of hundreds of mediums, accused them by name of deliberate fraud, and challenged them to sue him for libel. No one took up the challenge. He offered $10,000 reward for proof of psychical phenomena under scientific conditions; nobody cared to claim it. Mrs. Piper pretended to have communicated with a dead Dr. Phinuit: she was examined by William James, Sir Oliver Lodge, and Mrs. Sidgwick,—all sympathetic to psychical research; and the report was against her. You know the story of Dunglas Home: Browning has given him, so to speak, a temporary immortality. Eusapia Palladino traveled about Europe making great claims of psychic powers. She was tested by Bergson, M. and Mme. Curie, and others appointed by the General Psychological Institute of Paris; a flashlight of the séance (conducted, of course, in the indispensable dark) showed a table raised in the air, with no more visible means of support than Micawber. The learned examiners reported that they had been unable to detect fraud, and could not explain the lady's feat; but they concluded that there was nothing in the performance that might not have been executed by legerdemain, or legerdepied. When Mme. Palladino came to America in 1909 she was examined by Münsterberg at Harvard; as she moved her foot to perform the act of levitation it was caught by the hand of a student—showing that students are much more alert than professors. At Columbia University she was tested by Professor Lord, and again the students exposed her; they took a flashlight for which she was unprepared, and this picture showed the lady lifting the table with her hands. Eusapia returned to Italy in 1910, completely deflated.[2]

PAUL. Yes, there are many frauds. If one medium in a hundred, or in a hundred thousand, is honest, and has achieved real communication with the dead, these stories of fraud become worthless, and immortality is proved. Surely you would not claim that a man like Sir Oliver Lodge is a fraud. Read the literature; the accumulated evidence is so astonishing that in refusing to accept it you place yourself in the position of a timid conservative, like the opponents of Darwin. I should think that the spirit of science would move

[1] Cf. article by Prof. Boring, *Atlantic Monthly*, Jan., 1926.
[2] Leuba, J. H., *Belief in God and Immortality*, p. 160; New York *Times*, May 12, 1910.

you to feel that anything is possible in this world of wonders, that there is no telling what incredible things may come to pass. Remember, our knowledge of the mind is just beginning.

ANDREW. We know too much for comfort. We see that mind—the ability to think—is a part of evolution, like the ability to move, digest, or feel. Too evidently our minds are as natural a product as our bodies; the development is repeated for us in every individual, from the ridiculous embryo to the height of mental maturity. Now at what point in this evolutionary process did the immortal element enter? If man is immortal, so is the ape; if the ape is, so is the flea in his tail; and the worm is as deathless as the bird that eats it. It's an uncomfortable thought, that all the bugs that pester us in vacation time will join us in Paradise. And consider this: all the classes and races we dislike will be there to make the celestial zephyrs heavy with their smells; good Klansmen will meet men from Killarney, and 100% Americans will find Heaven as polyglot as New York. It will be a crowded place. If we of this generation are immortal, so have all the generations been. A billion souls pass to the Beyond every thirty years or so. Since men have existed for several hundred thousand years, Heaven must look like Broadway at noon.

WILLIAM. No doubt our discussion is useless, for the belief in immortality is rooted in instincts that are outside the reach of argument. It is part of the impulse of self-preservation. Life is short, and the ego is sweet; how could it be that we should pass away so soon? The idea of immortality arose in tropical climates, where life ripens and rots so quickly that a belief in a life beyond death is almost indispensable for bearing this one. In Ceylon the women are married at ten, old at twenty-eight, extinct at forty; there, more clearly than elsewhere, the individual is seen to be transitory, an atom of that molecule called the species, which is itself a wave in the ocean of life. And we too, though our lives last twice as long, are discontent with the years allotted to us; we rebel against the inevitableness of death; we long for another youth and another love. Once religion was based on fear; now it rests on hope.

ANDREW. It is still based on fear. We long for immortality not because we love life, but because we fear death. Often we're tired of life, of its eternal worries, illnesses, disillusionments and cares; and we feel like Cæsar, that we have lived long enough. Animals don't fear death because, except for the passing moments in which they see it strike some other animal, they do not know it till it is upon them; and then it is too late to theorize. When animals became men, developed memory, and projected it into anticipation, they discovered death; and for the peace of their minds they invented immortality. To be born, as Victor Hugo said, is to be condemned to death, with a sort of indefinite reprieve. The fear of death is the beginning of religion.

PHILIP. Personally, I get my sense of immortality from being a part of life. We are fragments of a whole, and our immortality lies in what we contribute to that whole. Plato's immortality is not in Heaven, but in the grateful memory of men, and in the books that every hour teach a thousand times more pupils now than when their author taught in the flesh. We live in our children and in our works; ·these are the resurrection of the body and the soul. This kind of immortality is worthless to the individual after his death, but it is invaluable to society; for civilization rests upon the preservation of the accomplishments of the dead. It might be well for us to think of immortality again, as the Greeks and the earlier Jews thought of it, not in terms of our separate selves, but in terms of our community and our race.

CLARENCE. Isn't it strange that we should be arguing a question which Lucretius settled two thousand years ago? Look what I have found here—Mallock's Omaric paraphrase of Lucretius' paraphrase of Epicurus. Listen:

> What! Shall the dateless world in dust be blown
> Back to the unremembered and unknown,
>   And this frail Thou—this flame of yesterday—
> Burn on forlorn, immortal and alone?
>
> Did Nature, in the nurseries of the night,
> Tend it for this—Nature whose heedless might
>   Like some poor shipwrecked sailor takes the babe
> And casts it bleating on the shores of light?
>
> What is it there? A cry is all it is.
> It knows not if its limbs be yours or his.
>   Less than that cry the babe was yesterday;
> The man tomorrow shall be less than this.
>
> Tissue by tissue to a soul he grows,
> As leaf by leaf the rose becomes a rose.
>   Tissue from tissue rots; and as the sun
> Goes from the bubbles when they burst, he goes.
>
> Flakes on the water, on the water cease!
> Soul of the body, melt and sleep like these.
>   Atoms to atoms, weariness to rest—
> Ashes to ashes—hopes and fears to peace.[1]

MATTHEW. It took a good Catholic to make that excellent paraphrase. Surely now you see how old your arguments are, how threadbare and worn?

[1] Mallock, W. H., *Lucretius on Life and Death*, pp. 19 f.

CLARENCE. But I thought that Paul protested that the age of a belief is nothing against it? For my part I think that all truth is old, and only poets, liars and fools can be original. I remember a sentence from Anatole France, who is the last pupil of Epicurus: "Our sun is bearing us with all his following to the constellation Hercules, where we shall arrive in a few milliards of centuries. He will die on the journey, and the earth with him." [1] And we with the earth, if our kind has survived till then. Doesn't it seem ridiculous, Paul, that the precarious product of a transitory planet should claim immortality? And yet why should we deprive you of your fine faith? I know that ours is a sad conclusion, and that the hungry soul will not give thanks for so negative a philosophy.

PAUL. Don't fear; you haven't disturbed me much. One moment of introspection refutes all that your external arguments seem to prove. I see mind within me; and I see that it is something set over against, and superior to, my body; my body is the temporary instrument of mind. I know nothing about the other world—in that I am as much an agnostic as you; I merely take the more encouraging of two equally possible beliefs. I have faith that what I perceive and feel, though I cannot understand it, and cannot make material or geometrical pictures of it for your "constitutionally material-istic" intellects, is none the less as true as what I perceive much less directly through external sense. Let some one whom you love dearly be stricken down, and a new philosophy will come to you; at the side of the grave it will seem to you incredible, unbelievably brutal, of the World-Spirit, that you should never see your friend, or your child, again. I believe that I shall see them; and that belief brings into my life a gladness, and a patience with misfortune, which your empty hearts can never know. When bereavement comes, I pity you.

SIDDHA. I think you are right, Paul.

MATTHEW. I know you are right, Paul.

CLARENCE. I hope you are right, Paul.

II. THE DEAD GOD

ESTHER. It's all very gloomy. I hope you will find something more cheer-ful to say about God.

SIR JAMES. You must not be shocked, Madame, if we cannot give you the God to whom you addressed your childhood prayers. Mankind's con-ception of God is always changing; indeed, the history of humanity might be written in terms of the avatars of God—the repeated death of an old god to make way for a deity that may represent the higher morals and ideals of a developing race. You would be impressed by a list of the various

[1] *On Life and Letters*, 3rd Series, p. 210.

gods that man has at one time or another worshipped as eternal; [1] the supreme deities run into the hundreds, the minor deities into millions. If past generations could return to the earth they would be scandalized to learn that even the omnipotent gods they prayed to are today known only to anthropologists. Every people in every epoch has reinterpreted God after its own fashion, and has been willing to die, or at least to kill, in defense of that passing conception. The historian is not deceived by this slaughter or this martyrdom; he knows that there is no idea so foolish but that some one has died for it; and he is prepared to see the notion of God change in the present and the future as it has in the past. Consequently he is not disturbed by new definitions of deity; he welcomes the attempt to reformulate this eternal idea in harmony with our growing knowledge. Men will always believe in God, because the idea of power united with perfection satisfies and stimulates the soul; it is pleasant to be friends with omnipotence.

The God of our fathers was the last phase in the life of Yahveh or Jehovah. I sometimes wonder (though philology does not give me much support) whether *Yahveh*, like *Iovis*, does not go back to the *Dyaus-pitar*, or Sky-Father, of the Hindus. *Zeus pater*, dean of Olympus, is a translation of *Dyaus pitar*; so is *Jupiter*—i. e., *Iovis pater*. The Freudians have exaggerated the role of the father-image in the making of gods; [2] doubtless the adolescent mind likes to conceive the world as a home, presided over by a father; but the origin of the father-idea lies rather in ancestor-worship, in the notion that the tribes of men are descended from gods. This personification of the deity in terms in the male is the last insult which woman will have to avenge.

The anthropomorphic conception of God, as made in the image and likeness of man, is probably due to the worship of ancestors; God was like a man, only much larger and stronger. As Xenophanes said, 600 years before Christ: "Men imagine gods to be born, and to have raiment and voice and body, like themselves. . . . Even so the gods of the Ethiopians are swarthy and flat-nosed, and the gods of the Thracians are fair-haired and blue-eyed. . . . Even so Homer and Hesiod attributed to the gods all that is a shame and reproach among men—theft, adultery, deceit and other lawless acts. . . . Even so oxen, lions and horses, if they had hands wherewith to grave images, would fashion gods after their own shapes, and make them bodies like to their own."

This complaint about the immortality of the Olympian family reveals the process whereby gods die: they are left behind in the moral develop-

---

[1] Mr. H. L. Mencken made an imposing array of them in one of his most interesting *Prejudices*.

[2] Cf. Freud, S., *Leonardo da Vinci*, p. 104; Jung, C. G., *Analytical Psychology*, p. 172; Jones, E., *Papers on Psychoanalysis*, p. 383.

ment of humanity; they perish through their divine unchangeability. The adulterous, thieving, and lying gods of the early Greeks were formed by men to whom such behavior seemed legitimate; it was an age of piracy, rape and war; and the gods were conceived as ideal experts in these ancient accomplishments. It was the progress of moral refinement that made these villainous deities repulsive to the spirit of Xenophanes and Plato. So with all the gods; the picture formed of them in early ages repels the finer feelings of later minds. It is the misfortune of every civilization that it inherits barbaric gods.

In the case of our own inherited deity, Jehovah, we have to bear in mind, if we are to understand his decease, that he was above all a war-chief, a god of hosts, just such a god as every nation conscripted for its armies in 1914. As the idea of hell reflected the cruelty of primitive men and savage chieftains, so the idea of god reflected the insecurity of tribal life in a world unorganized, and harassed with hostility and danger at every turn. When social order grew, and life became safer, war less frequent, and man in consequence less cruel, the old notions of a warrior-god, condemning millions to hell, became offensive to mature minds. Social organization demanded and developed in men the habits and ideals of a coöperative morality; gradually the conception of what a perfect man would be diverged more and more from the conception of the old god. John Stuart Mill, you will remember, announced with some bravado that if such a barbarous deity as medieval theology had pictured really existed, he was not a god but a devil; and "if such a being can sentence me to hell for not calling him 'good,' to hell I will go." The moral development of man had outrun his conception of God.

This refinement of human nature had been brought about partly by the increased security of economic provision and political order, partly by nineteen hundred years of the ethics of Christ. It was Christ who killed Jehovah; it was Christianity that killed the supposedly Christian god. I do not believe, despite our militarism and our political corruption, that these two thousand years of moral training have been without effect on the character of man. And therefore what we are witnessing in these days is not by any means the death of Christianity, but rather the death of that old "grim beard of a god," as Nietzsche called him, who by some queer crossing came down into Christianity along with a system of morality, an exaltation of gentleness and peace, totally inconsistent with Jehovah, and at last strong enough to destroy him. So now men's minds are left free to make for themselves a better god.

ANDREW. No doubt the greatest glory of a religion would be to be destroyed by the perfection of its own morality. But both the causes and the results are wider than you describe them. From the moment when Copernicus announced that the earth was only a speck of dust in an infinity of worlds, the old faith was doomed. There was no center, no up or down, any more. The earth lost all its dignity, and it became impossible to believe that the organizing power behind this immeasurably enlarged universe had come down to this planet and taken the form of man to suffer and die for the negligible sins of a negligible race. No wonder Anatole France considered this astronomic revolution "the greatest event in the whole history of thought." [1] The world did not see at once the implications of this replacement of Heaven by empty space, this reduction of the globe and of man to the level of moments in the history of the stars. Bruno was burned alive for seeing and announcing the implications; but the Reformation went on as if Copernicus and Galileo had never lived.

Darwin completed the destruction. As the astronomer had lost the earth in the infinity of space, so the biologist lost man in the infinity of time, in the long procession of transitory species. One could still believe in design after Copernicus; but after Darwin it was impossible. Providence gave way to natural selection; eternal love gave way to eternal strife; war became again "the father of all things." In the days of Paley every organ seemed intelligently constructed for the purpose it served; and every animal, before vegetarianism, had obviously been created for the needs of man. But not only did Darwin explain all this design away; he revealed, almost without wishing it, the planless absurdity of cosmic and human life. Could anything be more ridiculous than the way in which man reproduces his kind? God is refuted by both birth and death; no doctor and no general believes in him. Could an intelligent creator have made a world whose law, for living things, is a ruthless and restless struggle for existence, in which only the brutal, the cunning, and the unscrupulous survive? Struggle everywhere: of man with man, of tribe with tribe, of empire with empire, of species with species—some day, if we progress sufficiently, of planet with planet; even now the stars seem driven against one another by some Satanic spirit that revels in destruction.

As for ourselves, on this footstool of God, this home of his beloved son, every invention of our growing minds adds to our misery, and every machine extends our slavery; we have learned to fly in order that in the next war we may kill non-combatants by the million. Beethoven, needing ears more than any other man, goes deaf; Nietzsche, needing eyes, goes blind; Dr. Johnson, great only as a talker, loses the power of speech; Reynolds, the painter, loses the use of his arm. The other day I saw a paralytic woman: once, twenty years ago, when she was young and beautiful, she swam too soon after a tennis game; she was pulled from the water crippled for life. Some subtle poison has crept from joint to joint of her body, so that now she lies unable to move any limb; her face swollen with disease, everything in her broken and rotting but her mind, which is left clear and keen

[1] *On Life and Letters,* 3rd Series, p. 212.

to her so that she may suffer more. The world is what Henry Adams called it—"a picture of suffering, sorrow, and death; plague, pestilence and famine; inundations, droughts and frosts; catastrophes world-wide, and accidents in corners; cruelty, perversity, stupidity, uncertainty, insanity; virtue begetting vice, vice working for good; happiness without sense, selfishness without gain, misery without cause, and horrors undefined,"— with death as the impartial reward of all. To speak of Providence is an insult to the suffering of men.[1]

MATTHEW. You speak so feelingly of evil, Andrew, that I have hopes that you will some day win back your religious belief. The Church has always recognized the bitter reality of evil; Pope Innocent II wrote a treatise *On the Misery of the Human Lot;* and every dogma in our faith presumes that this is a world of suffering. Don't you see that is why we must believe? How could we bear to live if we knew that this suffering will never be atoned for with heavenly happiness? You haven't learned yet even Voltaire's lesson, that if there were no God we would have to invent him.

ANDREW. Matthew, you are a good man; and when you bear so patiently with our heresies I could almost yield to everything you say. There is no pride in my opposing you; these are the heresies of one who hopes with all his heart that his opponents are in the right. But your whole theology is based on the "Fall" of man, and his redemption by Christ; and evolution has made these doctrines incredible. Your theology collapsed when Adam disappeared from history. In truth, history has been almost as disastrous to you as biology; it is impossible to consider the rise and fall of nations, the ruin of art by war, the perpetual triumph of thieves, fanatics and murderers, without concluding, with Anatole France, that "the world is a tragedy, by an excellent poet"—or perhaps a comedy by "the Aristophanes of Heaven."

CLARENCE. I am interested in Matthew's reaction to your tirade, Andrew. Evil makes for belief as well as unbelief. Every soldier is religious until he is promoted to the rear; all generals are atheists. Suffering, which to you disproves God, proves him to the soul that must be comforted. As long as there is poverty or death there will be gods. The growth of wealth is a more fundamental cause of the decadence of religion than any that you have mentioned. Wealth kills asceticism, and floods our cities with luxury and immortality; and when religion denounces luxury and immortality every one turns against religion except those who cannot afford to be wicked.

PAUL. Even more fundamental than wealth, as a cause of irreligion, is the machine. The Industrial Revolution has done wonders with mechanism, and the modern mind cannot resist the conclusion that mechanism is everything. The Middle Ages saw in nature the glory of God, and so they worshipped it, and strove to equal its beauty with great art; modernity sees

[1] Adams, H., *Mont St. Michel and Chartres,* p. 370.

in nature only so much raw material for useful articles: it tears down trees to make newspapers, and poisons the air and the streams with chemicals; it turns a quiet village into the inferno of a mining town; it forges new tools, and hurries to "control" the earth. The decay of belief is due, in great part, to the increasing egotism of man, dressed in a little brief omnipotence: he can do everything with his levers, and so he has no more use for God. When men tilled the soil they were more modest, and perhaps more profound; they saw the mystery of life in everything that grew out of the earth, and they never thought of calling their children machines.

CLARENCE. Spencer half agreed with you; he thought that supernaturalism is strongest in pre-industrial military societies, where obedience must be firmly inculcated; and that it was weakened by industry, which develops and depends upon intelligence. I suppose also that industry disturbs religion because it brings men together into cities, where different creeds rub elbows so long that at last they die by attrition. And industry makes democracy; the old autocratic god who reflected irresponsible monarchy yields to the deistic deity of constitutional government, and then to the "religion of humanity" which comes with the worship of numbers. You're right, Paul, there's a good deal of swagger in our unbelief.

ANDREW. While you are listing the causes of our infidelity you must not forget education. The college student today is flung into physical and chemical laboratories where he sees the world dissolved and reconstructed under his eyes, without so much as a mention of God. He takes courses in biology, and unless he has the ill or good fortune to belong to a state where they settle scientific questions by plebiscite or legislation, he learns that "design" is only a "favorable variation," and that the human eye is such a botch that, as Helmholtz suggested, no decent oculist would be guilty of it. He studies anthropology and comparative religion, reads Sir James's volumes, and sees his own faith and ritual in a vast perspective that melts his superstitions into the vestigial remnants of ancient ignorance. No wonder the antediluvians charge our colleges with being hotbeds of atheism; they are. They can't help it.

WILLIAM. You have all forgotten the War. Among the poor it helped religion; but among the prosperous it generated scepticism; it was hard to believe that a world committing suicide was the creation of a supreme and benevolent intelligence.

PHILIP. Whatever the causes may be, it is clear that religion has lost its hold on the western world, and that a great wave of secularization is sweeping along one after another of those phases of life which once belonged to religion. These colleges that you mention were until recently sectarian institutions, presided over by clergymen. But industry found that under such leadership the colleges were turning out philosophers, poets, orators and theologians, instead of engineers, accountants, metallurgists and bookkeepers. Industry complained; and when the colleges learned that the plaintiff had money, they acknowledged the justice of his complaint, dismissed the clergymen, installed financiers as presidents, scrapped their sectarian constitutions to let their professors come under the terms of the Carnegie pension fund, replaced literature and philosophy with physics and chemistry, and flooded the country with bachelors of science. Science has captured the universities from religion.

That is the source of our secularization. From this origin the stream has broadened to include nearly all of human life. Holydays give way to holidays; the saints that once brightened and saddened our calendars are neglected and forgotten. Agriculture used to be a matter of prayer and ritual; now it is a matter of tractors and chemistry. Law, which was formerly the decree of God, is now the inspiration of congressmen and aldermen. The State, which once identified itself with religion, and its head with God, separates itself more and more even from the empty formulas of political piety; it will not even condescend to hire religion as an agent of police.[1] Our Government is Christian on Thanksgiving Day, but makes up for it during the rest of the year. The Turkish Republic renounces the religion of Mohammed, and only half the Turkish press considers the matter important enough for mention.[2]

It is true that in many communities, and in unsuspected cellars of even emancipated minds, absurd superstitions and irrational beliefs survive; but beside the bloody rites and bizarre beliefs of the past they are reasonable and tame. Compare Western Europe with the Orient, and you catch the extent of our secularity. Gibbon says the early Christians "felt, or they fancied, that on every side they were incessantly assaulted by demons, comforted by visions, instructed by prophecy, and surprisingly delivered from danger, sickness, and from death itself, by the supplications of the Church"[3]; how much of that is left today? The history of civilization itself is the history of secularization.[4] The sermons we hear no longer tell us of visions, demons, prophecies; hell, purgatory, even miracles are left out; everything is being rationalized, and theology, losing its old fervor, becomes a polite mixture of philosophy and morals. But morals, which were once the special property of the Church, are today loosened from both Church and State; the old supernatural sanctions melt away, and the sense of sin utterly decays; the moral ideal of our youth is not virtue any more, but caution.

ANDREW. I have some statistics here that are pretty pertinent. First, a report by Charles Booth, that 75% of the people of London never see the inside of a church.—Second, Taine says that even as far back as 1890, in

[1] Adams, B., *The Laws of Civilization and Decay,* p. 293.
[2] New York *Times,* Apr. 12, 1928.
[3] *Decline and Fall of the Roman Empire,* vol. i, p. 461.
[4] Shotwell, p. 9.

the city of Paris, with a population of 2,000,000 supposed Catholics, only 100,000 performed their Easter duty, which is the most sacred obligation of the religious year; and that out of 32,000,000 Catholics in France, only 2,000,000 went to confession.[1] Religion, in Latin countries, is a secondary sexual character of the female. The cathedrals of France are maintained not for worship, but for tourists; it is the tourists, not the worshippers, that support them.—Third: a questionnaire sent to the readers of the London *Daily News* revealed that 30 per cent of the rather average people reached by that paper were atheists; 45 per cent denied the divinity of Christ, 60 per cent rejected the historicity of Genesis. The same questionnaire sent to the readers of the London *Nation* and the *Athenæum* showed 50 per cent of these intellectuals to be atheists; and out of 10,088 who replied, only 88 accepted the veracity of the Pentateuch.[2]—Fourth: a census taken by the New York *World* showed 7,500 theists, and 2,924 atheists; 6,292 believers in immortality, and 3,954 disbelievers in immortality; 6,327 believers in prayer, 4,063 disbelievers in it; 5,556 believers in the special inspiration of the Bible, 4,614 disbelievers; 4,951 attendants at religious services of some kind, 5,388 non-attendants; 2,684 with family worship in their homes, 7,320 with none.[3] These figures are for New York City; of course the ratio of believers to non-believers would have been much higher if the census had been national, or if it had been answered by illiterate as well as literate people.

CLARENCE. Your last few words are the most damning of all. And for Christianity the situation is worse even than these figures indicate. For many of the affirmative answers came from sects and cults not usually accounted Christian, like the theosophists. There are in America some forty millions who go to church; the rest stay in bed till noon one day per week. All the signs are that Christianity is undergoing the same rapid decay that fell upon the old Greek religion after the coming of the Sophists and the "Greek Enlightenment." Voltaire was Protagoras. Diderot was Democritus, Kant was Plato, Spencer was Aristotle, Anatole France was Epicurus. We live in the Twilight of the Gods.

III. THE FUNCTION OF RELIGION

PAUL. There is a note of sadness in your voice, Clarence; you are as religious as any of us, but that disruptive intellect of yours, which you trust too much, forbids you to believe. Are you sure that your logic is sounder than your heart? Is all this astronomy, this physics, this biology,

[1] *The Modern Régime,* vol. ii, pp. 132–3.
[2] New York *Sun,* Sept. 13, 1926.
[3] New York *World,* Dec. 16, 1926.

so certain that you are wise in letting them destroy the hopes which have sustained so many lives?

CLARENCE. I know what a consolation faith can be. I have an old uncle in the mountains who is nearing ninety. He worked on his farm till his legs wouldn't carry him any more; now he sits by the kitchen stove all day, quiet and cheerful, waiting for death. "I ain't been such a bad fellow," he says, "but I done a mean thing or two in my time. Just the same, God'll forgive me; he's good." By his side his old wife reads her Bible in the evening, drinking in with mumbling happiness every word of Christ, and every promise of bliss to come. I would not think of casting doubts upon such hopes; why shouldn't they be consoled? Down in the village is the little church they go to—clean, white, and neighborly; its modest spire has lifted up, I suppose, a hundred thousand souls. Behind the church is the cemetery; some graceful angel, or the trusted cross, rock of ages, is on every tomb; and all the epitaphs welcome the dead into the arms of Christ. How they hope, the people! I grant you, Paul, the world would be more lovable if these simple folk were right.

ANDREW. You're too sentimental, Clarence. You let Matthew tell you how much happiness the hope of Heaven has brought to men; but you don't remind him of the terror which the Church brought into millions of lives by preaching eternal punishment in the fires of Hell as the destiny (for so the Scriptures seem to assure us) of the great majority of men. You don't remind him of the bitterness which religion brought into human life: the families broken apart by hard dogmatism and petty differences; the nations prodded into war to determine the victory of creeds, the men and women killed in *autos-da-fé* for fear some little private heresy would upset an inspired Book and a rock-founded infallible church. You remind me of a sentence in Spengler: Atheism, he says, is entirely compatible with a wistful desire for real religiousness—therein resembling Romanticism, which likewise would recall that which has irrevocably gone.[1] The first decades of our century were full of religious atheists, like Anatole France, George Moore, George Santayana—romantic mourners for their dead faith. They were a transition: their children do not feel as they did; and their grandchildren will not know this wistfulness at all. If we could accustom mankind to forget the idea of immortality for two or three generations, this poetic sadness would pass away.

WILLIAM. I don't think so, Andrew. Belief is natural. It comes directly out of instinctive and emotional needs—out of the hunger for self-preservation, for reward, for companionship, for security, even for submission. Sometimes gratitude for good fortune overwhelms us, and we wish that the World-Spirit had ears to hear our thanksgiving; Nietzsche

[1] *Decline of the West*, vol. i, p. 408.

says that the way misfortunes had of turning into good luck tempted him to believe in God.[1] Suppress all religion for a century, then take off the lid, and religion would grow again within a year. Belief is more natural than doubt, and therefore easier. Doubt inhibits and contracts; faith expands, improves the appetite and the circulation; every sceptic has a bad stomach. Hence optimism, which is a form of faith, is more widespread and spontaneous than pessimism, which is a form of doubt; and most beloved writers are, in Napoleon's phrase, "dealers in hope." Doubt is work, and man is lazy. Mentally, the masses are parasites, and the few do most of the work. Only the strong can afford to doubt: nothing is so exhausting.

MATTHEW. There is another source of religion which you have forgotten; and that is the poetic spirit in man. Religion has not only taken the sting out of death, it has beautified life with ceremony, with architecture, sculpture, painting, drama and music. It has lifted the routine events of human existence, from birth through marriage to death, to the level of sacraments, making these common things holy experiences, deepening them with feeling and transfiguring them with art; it has changed the sordid tragedy of life into a poetic pilgrimage to an ennobled end. Without it, life is dull and mean, like a body without a soul. I sometimes wonder how the atheist feels on Sunday evening when the church-bells ring—doesn't a great loneliness come over him? The Sabbath is like any other day to you, Andrew and Clarence; not all your concerts and theatres can take the place of St. Patrick's or St. Thomas's on a Sunday morning.

ANDREW. Come now, Matthew, tell the truth; you're bored to death by going to church.

MATTHEW. Perhaps, occasionally; but in my clear moments I know that that hour in church helps me all week, and gives a buoyant radiance to my life. On the other hand, how empty Christmas must be for you. I remember how, on the night before Christmas, our whole family would kneel before the hard chairs in our little dining-room, and recite the Rosary together; I can still hear my father saying the *Our Father* and the *Hail Mary* lovingly and without haste. Then, the next morning, Holy Communion, and High Mass; everybody bright and merry; clean white snow, and tinkling sleigh-bells, and Christmas trees gleaming; the young happy in receiving gifts, the old happier in giving them. And on New Year's Day we all knelt down before my father, children and grandchildren alike, and asked his blessing. There were families in those days! No wonder the family decays, and crime riots free, now that reverence is dead.

CLARENCE. A dear friend of mine says that there are four stages of development in the understanding of religion. The first he calls emotional belief; the second, metaphysical belief; the third, absolute disillusionment;

[1] *Joyful Wisdom*, § 277.

the fourth, esthetic understanding.[1] I should like to be at that fourth stage with you, Matthew. But the trouble is, you take it all literally.

MATTHEW. We must, else it would all seem a tragic farce. How could it be beautiful if it were untrue?

PAUL. You have shown only one side of the vital function of religion, Matthew. You have spoken of its value to the individual; but its value to society is just as great. The religious solemnization of marriage not only glorified the event for the parties concerned, it welded them into wedlock by the emotional intensity and the reverential awe that religion cast over what otherwise would have been merely a license to cohabit; and in this way it made for the stability of the family, and therefore of the state. At every turn, in human affairs, we find the individualistic instincts stronger than the social instincts; the reproductive instinct, the strongest of all, is not necessarily social, and it may lead to disruption and chaos, as it does today. The great function of religion is, by sacraments, by moral instruction, and by the promise of heaven—

ANDREW. I must remind you again to add the fear of Hell.

PAUL. —to buttress the altruistic impulses, or, better, the impulses to aid and coöperate, as against those ancient selfish impulses, bred by a million years of the struggle for existence, to fight and seize and eat and rule. I do not believe in Hell, but I am sure that the thought of it has kept many a man out of mischief; and I see that when a lad discovers that there is no Hell he is likely to go to the devil. The function of morality is to represent the whole against the part, and the future against the present,—which is just what religion tries to do; religion is, as Höffding says, the conservation of values. Without religious sanctions, morality becomes mere calculation; the sense of duty disappears, and every youngster devotes his whole intelligence and education to outwitting the commandments.

PHILIP. There is no doubt that religion was the great debrutalizing force in history before schools came. Benjamin Kidd thought that all civilization rested on the supernatural sanctions which religion gave to morals. Tarde believed that the noble lives of certain atheists had been due to the persisting influence of their religious training—what Carlyle called the *Nachschein* or afterglow of Christianity. This again is what Renan referred to when he wrote his famous lines: "We are living on the shadow of a shadow; what are people going to live on after us?"—how are they going to control their appetites, their impulses to lie and rob and kill, when even this afterglow of a dying creed is gone? "Religion," Renan concluded, "is an indispensable illusion." [2] Dostoievski wrote the greatest novels in the world just to show how man became "possessed" with demons when they abandon God. No wonder that until the French and American Revolutions the State always

---

[1] Powys, J. C., *The Religion of a Sceptic.*
[2] *History of the People of Israel*, vol. v, p. 92.

allied itself with some religion, and gave it financial and military aid in return for moral support. The modern enmity between Church and State is due to the fact that Christianity became an international, instead of a national, religion; the Church became master instead of servant in her relation with governments; and every modern state, in establishing its sovereignty, was compelled to fight the power of the Church. This alienation of the male from the female principle in government is a rare phenomenon, and may be of very brief duration.

Plutarch says somewhere that "a city might be more easily founded without territory, than a state without belief in God." [1] Bayle held that an atheistic state was entirely practicable, but Voltaire was of the opinion that if Bayle had been appointed to rule over six hundred peasants, he would at once have preached divine retribution to them.[2] Napoleon thought that the greatest miracle in Christianity was that it kept the poor from murdering the rich. "If the Pope had not existed," he said, "I should have had to invent him." [3] Certainly a common religion gives to a people a unity and fervor that make them admirable warriors; consider the Moslems and the Japanese.

ANDREW. There's a great deal of nonsense in this supposed necessity of religion to government or morals. Dean Swift, who ought to have known religion well, said that we have just about enough of it to make us hate, but not enough to make us love, one another. Religion makes for division as well as for unity; just recall the election of 1928. An Irishman, presumably without episcopal *Imprimatur,* remarked recently: "The trouble with us is our religion. Some of us are Protestants, and some of us are Catholics. If we were all atheists we could live together like Christians." [4] As for what you call unity, I call it stagnation. The unity which a religion gives to a people is the unity of tradition, of unquestioning obedience; its ideal form is the ancestor-worship of the East. As to religion debrutalizing man and making for morality, how do you explain human sacrifice in ancient faiths, and the defense of slavery and the *status quo* by the modern Church? Hume long since refuted this notion of religion being the mother or the basis of morals. Religion came much later than morality; and if there is any relation between the two it is that morality, improving through education and security, exercises a refining influence on religion. Sumner put it bravely: "The Church," he says, "never was on the level of the better mores of any time. Every investigation which we make leads us not to the Church as the inspirer and leader, but to the dissenting apostles of righteousness, to the great fluctuations in the mores." [5]

[1] In Bluntschli, *Theory of the State,* p. 287.
[2] Lange, *History of Materialism,* vol. ii, p. 17.
[3] Todd, *op. cit.,* p. 434.
[4] *The Arbitrator,* May, 1922.
[5] *Todd,* p. 428.

MATTHEW. But isn't it obvious to everyone that the decay of religious belief has brought a serious break-up of morality? Behold our riot, our sexual promiscuity, our pornographic literature, our exhibitionistic drama; do you find them among loyal sons and daughters of the Church, or among "emancipated" souls? Darwinism has led to fatalism, pessimism, and a gloomy epicureanism. Thomas Hardy speaks of "the chronic melancholy which is taking hold of the civilized races with the decline of belief in a beneficent power" [1]—what better authority could you ask? It is a sad generation; its gayety is an attempt to forget in the fulness of its mouth the emptiness of its heart. You know the old saying: religion is at the cradle of every nation, and philosophy is at its grave.

PHILIP. Napoleon said that "a good philosopher makes a bad citizen."

MATTHEW. A bad citizen cannot be a good philosopher. No man who loves his country can rest content while a superficial and transitory science destroys the religion which built our civilization and our morality. How long do you suppose a religionless Europe, disintegrating into selfish fragments—petty states, class interests, and individualistic gourmands—can hold its own before an East strengthened by industry or inspired by religious belief? How can you prevent misery and despair from filling every heart if you deny, in your teaching, the dearest hopes that men have ever had? Listen: here is a book almost a century old—*The Confessions of a Child of the Century;* and yet at the very outset of it De Musset flings at you a question which you can never answer.

The antagonists of Christ therefore said to the poor, "You wait patiently for the day of justice: there is no justice; you wait for the life eternal to achieve your vengeance: there is no life eternal; you gather up your tears and those of your family, the cries of the children and the sobs of the women, to place them at the feet of God at the hour of death: there is no God."

Then it is certain that the poor man dried his tears, and he told his wife to check her sobs, his children to come with him, and that he stood on the earth with the power of a bull. He said to the rich: "Thou who oppressest me, thou art only man"; and to the priest: "Thou who hast consoled me, thou hast lied." That was just what the antagonists of Christ desired. Perhaps they thought this was the way to achieve man's happiness, sending him out to the conquest of liberty.

But if the poor man, once satisfied that the priests deceive him, that the rich rob him, that all men have rights, that all good is of this world, and that misery is impiety; if the poor man, believing in himself and his two arms, says to himself some fine day: "War on the rich! for me, happiness here in this life, since there is no other! for me, the earth, since heaven is

[1] Hardy, T., *Tess of the d'Urbervilles*, p. 133.

empty! for me and for all, since all are equal." Oh, reasoners sublime who have led him to this, what will you say to him *if he is conquered?* [1]

Don't you see that one of the profound functions of the Church has been to comfort the weak in their inevitable subjection to the strong? You preach, to the weak, rebellion; you do not realize that in conflict with the rich, the clever, the powerful, and the unscrupulous, the weak are doomed to be defeated; you take God from them, and offer them liberty; but how can liberty come without knowledge and power? What will you say to these men when they are conquered, when revolution has spilt their blood in the streets, and the struggle for existence, the survival of the strongest, and the will to power, has given them new tyrants for old?

PHILIP. It is quite possible that our society will be broken up by the decay of the supernatural sanctions with which its moral system was allied. Perhaps science will be unable to replace what it has so lustily destroyed. I know of no solution but to trust in the spread of knowledge.

MATTHEW. But a little knowledge is a dangerous thing; and that is all that the people have time to acquire. The education you trust in is only a machine for turning men and women into calculating villains.

PHILIP. Yes, we are in the stage of little knowledge now; but we shall go further. Some day knowledge will widen into wisdom, at least in the leaders of our people; and then Socrates will be right—the only permanent morality, the only morality secure from the inevitable death of theologies and creeds—will be the morality of wisdom and intelligence. If we can't trust education we can't truth anything.

MATTHEW. A few of you will rise to the pagan virtue of the Stoics; most of you will eat, drink, and get divorced. Perhaps after a generation or two mankind will see where unbelief leads it, and the churches—even your churches, Paul, which are now shooting Niagara—will be filled again. We forget that only a small minority has been touched by atheism: around us everywhere are simple people who still worship God. When you are all gone, gentlemen, the Church will still carry on, stronger and more beneficent than ever, teaching its children kindness and loyalty, lifting up their hearts with examples of holiness, and comforting them against the evils of life and the dark certainty of death. The world will forget you as it forgot Democritus and Lucretius; and it will return to Christ.

CLARENCE. Very probably.

IV. THE NEW GOD

PAUL. When I listen to you, Matthew, I could almost become a convert to your Church. But I do not think the future is with you. As education

[1] Musset, A. de, *Confessions of a Child of the Century*, p. 21.

raises the mental level of the race, men will come to distinguish more resolutely between beauty and truth. If Christianity is not to become merely the comfort of the uninformed, it will have to build its temples within the world revealed by Copernicus and Darwin. Perhaps these years of misfortune for religion are a great boon to it; now our faith must remake itself in wider terms than before; we must conceive a deity worthy of the new universe we have found. *"Élargissez Dieu!"* said atheist Diderot.[1] He was right; we must enlarge God.

"The next great task of science," said Lord Morley, "is to create a new religion for humanity." Religion will not disappear; we shall go on looking for something greater than ourselves, that we may worship. Men will continue to seek a consistent interpretation of the world,—which is philosophy; and they will continue to vitalize that interpretation with feeling,—which is religion. They will continue to long for union and coöperation with the whole of which they are separately insignificant parts. That total perspective which, when merely intellectual, is philosophy and truth, becomes, when touched with devotion to the whole, the essence and secret of religion. Through some such formulation we may again bring science and religion together in the same soul, as they were brought together in Leonardo, and Spinoza, and Goethe.

ARIEL. Tell us how, Paul.

PAUL. The God I believe in is the oldest of the gods—the *mana* or *manitou* of primitive men, that ocean of life or spirit from which all living things derive their being. God is Life. God is the creative vitality of the world; in St. Thomas's phrase he is *Actus Purus*—pure activity. Wherever I probe deeply enough I come upon this seething, germinating force,— "always and always the procreant urge of the world." Every profound mind from Heraclitus to Havelock Ellis has sensed an inward life even in the stillest of inert things. "It is a world," says Ellis, "full of infinite life. What has revealed this to us? Science. Science, that we thought was taking from us all that was good and beautiful—science has shown us *this.*" [2]

Yes, it is physics and biology that will give us the new God. Physics that finds abounding vitality in every atom; biology that shows us the everlasting miracle of growth. Religion was right after all: the highest reality in the world is the creative power, that Life without which, in the words of Spinoza, nothing is or can be conceived. Spinoza was right: "All things in some degree are alive." Schopenhauer and Nietzsche were right: behind "matter" is Will. Hegel was right: God is that process of development whereby each phase bursts into an internal contradiction—a mitotic division—that makes for further growth. Aristotle was right: in all things there is this strange impulse to development and perfection, to the realiza-

[1] Morley, J., *Diderot and the French Encyclopedists*, vol. i, p. 128.
[2] Goldberg, I., *Havelock Ellis*, p. 71.

tion of every inherent possibility. Bergson was right: in life and choice the inner secret of reality is revealed. But Bergson was wrong: there is no enmity between matter and life; matter is not the foe but the form of life, the external shape and feature of that inward power. Life is the *Natura naturans* of the Scholastics and Spinoza, nature creative; it is the *entelechy* of Aristotle, by which each thing struggles to attain its natural completeness; it is the Desire which in the biological philosophy of Lamarck creates organ after organ, and slowly moulds the body in the image of the will.

It is science that makes my religion, for it is evolution that proves my God. How could a mechanism have evolved? That would be a hundred times more incredible than the legends in the Bible, nor would it be redeemed by the symbolic significance and poetic beauty that make those legends almost truer than the truth. Think of evolution not as Darwin did (for what biologist now thinks of it as Darwin did?), but as Lamarck and Schopenhauer and Nietzsche saw it; not as a forming of organisms by the environment, but as the transformation of environments by organisms, whose very essence, to quote Spinoza again, is insatiable desire. Can you think of that long upward struggle of life from the *Amœba* to Einstein and Edison and Anatole France, without seeing the world once more as the garment of God? What marvelous beasts we are! We come and go like ripples on a stream; we fight and bleed and die on the economic battlefields of the world; we lie and steal and exploit and tyrannize and kill; but sometimes we make Parthenons and Sistine Chapels, sometimes we write a *Choral Symphony* or *Leaves of Grass*, sometimes we give our lives for our children and our race. And our climb is only begun; we are in the youth and puberty of our development; everything is budding around and within us; the things we have done are but a halting promise of what we shall do. No formula has yet exhausted or described us. You may call it poetry and sentiment, but I can't look at a green shoot sprouting up through the soil, without saying, This is God. I can't look at a child growing and singing without saying, This is God. Every Madonna with her babe moves me, not as the image of one mother or one faith, but as the highest symbol of that creative force which hides behind mechanism, and moves, as Dante said, the earth and the other stars.

ANDREW. I was wondering a little about the gender of your God. To reduce God to identity with Life is to rob him of personality and make him neuter. But then you see him—or shall I say her, or it—above all in motherhood. Perhaps you are going to accept Shaw's challenge, and construe your deity as of the female sex?

PAUL. Sex is a late and superficial thing; and personality is later and more superficial still; God is beyond and around them. To attribute personality to God in the sense in which we use the word of ourselves is childishly anthropomorphic and egotistic; we should have to read Xenoph-

anes again. Personality is separateness, a special form of will and character. God could not be such a separate and partial self; he is the sum and
source of this universal vitality or spirit of which our little egos and personalities are abstracted fragments and experimental proliferations. Personality is too narrow a mould for God since Copernicus and Darwin
wrote. You may speak of my God as neuter if you wish, though that would
be an unworthily negative description; for my part I shall continue to
speak of him symbolically through the masculine pronoun, as we speak
of man through the masculine, by a sort of patriarchal license. If we
may speak of the sun with masculine pronouns, all the more should this
be reasonable (provided we remember its limitations) when we have in
mind the super-personal source of all personality.

And yet there is much to be said for Shaw's view. The male is an incident
and an instrument; the female is the carrier and continuity of the race,
the direct embodiment of physical creation. Her sole equal, as the clearest
incarnation of deity, is the genius—the vehicle of spiritual creation, the
maker of new knowledge and new values. In motherhood and in genius:
there above all is God. Humanity is not God, as Comte thought; no one
who is familiar with humanity will care to worship it. Most of us are raw
material, mere bricks and mortar in an edifice whose design we can not
understand. Only in our rare moments of painful upward choice, and in the
creative suffering of genius, do we discover the presence of something that
touches God; this is again the Incarnation and the Crucifixion. Nietzsche,
that pious atheist, said that when he walked with Wagner he knew what
God was, he felt the breath of divinity blowing upon him. Free will and
genius are delusions if God is external and omnipotent, or if the world
is a machine (mechanism is merely Calvinism dressed up by the Industrial
Revolution); some minimum of free will becomes evident, and some efficacy
in genius becomes possible, if God is within us, in the persistent Life that
lifts itself from the energy of the atom to the art of Pheidias and the
vision of Christ. To see life through all its material disguises; to sense
deity, as the earliest men did, in every tree, in every animal, in all love and
birth, in all greatness of mind and soul, even in inevitable decay and
death; to judge all things in terms of their good for the totality of life; to
"join a whole" and willingly coöperate with growth: this is religion.
Reverence for genius, reverence for mothers and children and all growing
things, loyalty to life—this is the worship of God.

ANDREW. It is all very poetical, Paul, but it won't hold water. Don't
deceive yourself: every scientist will smile at the deification of a life
which, as Santayana said, can be ended in a moment by a stray bullet, or
a rise or fall of temperature, or a decrease of oxygen in the air. And every
pious soul will laugh bitterly at a religion which takes God out of the
skies and puts him into roses and thorns, dogs and fleas, fat mothers, in-

fants wetting their diapers, and Richard Wagner, the greatest charlatan in the history of music.

PAUL. Forget Wagner, and remember Christ. My religion would have in it these two elements—the Living God and the human Christ; for Christ, as the old theology symbolically understood, was the highest incarnation of God. The greatest creation of life is not thought, but love; and the greatest triumph of human genius is not the plays of Shakespeare, nor the marbles of the Parthenon, but the ethics of Christ; next to parental care, this is the finest force for good that ever came into the world. I know, Philip, that you consider Christ's moral doctrine as impracticable. But I have heard you quote with approval the last line of Spinoza's *Ethics*— that "all excellent things are as difficult as they are rare." To say that something is difficult is no objection to it; it is the function of an ethical ideal to lift us, against all the weight of instincts made rapacious by the struggle for existence, to levels of consideration and courtesy where civilization and the coöperative life become possible. So long as the counsels of Christ are within the limits of our ideal strength, it is good that they should hold up to us the perfection towards which we should grow, and which we may keep perpetually in mind. What is the doctrine of Christ but the Golden Rule—and is the Golden Rule quite impracticable? On the contrary it is the essence of wisdom in our relations with men. I have found that where I fought back I multiplied resistance and raised new obstacles against myself; where I did kindnesses they came back to me a hundred-fold; where I loved I won. If I could have my way I would define an atheist as one who is disloyal to life or irreverent to growth; and I would define a Christian as a man who accepts, and sincerely tries to practise, the ethics of Christ.

PHILIP. Splendid, Paul. I will join your church at once, if you won't insist on personal immortality.

PAUL. Why should we not differ on some things and work together where we can? After all, we differ only in phrases: the older generation meant what we mean—reverence for all life, and loyalty to the largest whole; they merely used other symbols and other words. Now that the battle is over we see how close we were, how we are all members of one another still. In my ideal church all would be welcome who accepted the Golden Rule; there would be no other test. You would all be eligible—even Philip, who thinks Christ unpractical, and Andrew, who considers himself a machine, and Clarence, who doubts everything but loves all. I vision a Church as all-embracing as Christ's affection, accepting all and rejecting none. It would honor truth and beauty as well as goodness, this Church of mine; it would nourish every art, and make its every chapel and cathedral a citadel of adult education, bringing science and history, literature and philosophy, music and art to those too old for school, and yet young enough to learn. But it would hold knowledge barren without brotherhood; it would allow every division, and every doubt, except that in the end love is the highest wisdom.

ARIEL. Let us end there. Here among these books, coming to us from the genius of a hundred lands, we may admit that we are brothers, that religion and brotherhood ought to be one, that Confucius and Buddha, Isaiah and Christ, Spinoza and Whitman, are prophets of one faith. If we can agree on what these men held in common, it is enough.

SIR JAMES. Madame, I know your religion well; for here in your copy of Whitman I find a poem marked that might be the guide and motto of us all. It is called "To Him That Was Crucified."

ARIEL. Read it to us; perhaps it will cool our nerves after this argument. (*Sir James reads.*)

ARIEL. It is very beautiful.

MATTHEW. It is beautiful, but conceited and impious.

PHILIP. If that is Christianity, I'm a Christian.

PAUL. No one ever caught better the essence of Christianity.

WILLIAM. It satisfies me.

KUNG. I understand your Christ much better now.

SIDDHA. I accept him gladly as a great Buddhist.

ESTHER. I accept him as a great Jew.

CLARENCE. And a thorough-going anti-clerical.[1]

THEODORE. I will accept him if you will make *Leaves of Grass* a part of the Scriptures.

SIR JAMES. He is the most lovable of the gods.

ANDREW. I trust that he existed. Let us go to bed.

[1] Bernard Shaw.

CHAPTER XXIV

On Life and Death

CAN WE COMPRESS into one summarizing chapter a perspective of human life? It is impossible; for life is in its basis a mystery, a river flowing from an unseen source; and in its development an infinite subtlety too complex for thought, much less for utterance. And yet the thirst for unity draws us on. To chart this wilderness of experience and history, to force into focus on the future the unsteady light of the past, to bring into significance and purpose the chaos of sensation and desire, to discover the direction of life's stream and thereby in some measure to control its flow: this insatiable metaphysical lust is one of the nobler aspects of our questionable race. And so we shall try, however vainly, to see human existence as a whole, from the moment when we are flung unasked into the world, until the wheel on which we are bound comes full circle in death.

I. CHILDHOOD

"After the argument," says Walt, "a group of little children, with their ways and chatter, flow in, like welcome rippling water on my heated nerves and flesh."

We like children, first of all, because they are ours, prolongations of our luscious and unprecedented selves; but we like them, too, because they are what we would but cannot be—coördinated animals, whose simplicity and unity of action are spontaneous, whereas in the philosopher they come only after struggle and control. We like them because of what in us is called selfishness—the naturalness and undisguised directness of their instincts. We like their unhypocritical candor; they do not smile to us when they

long for our annihilation. *Kinder und Narren sprechen die Wahrheit*—
"Children and fools speak the truth"; and somehow they find happiness
in their sincerity.

See him, the new-born, dirty but marvelous, ridiculous in actuality, infinite in possibility, capable of that ultimate mystery—growth. Can you
conceive it—that this queer bundle of sound and pain will come to know
love, anxiety, prayer, suffering, creation, metaphysics, death? He cries;
he has been so long asleep in the quiet warm womb of his mother; now
suddenly he is compelled to breathe, and it hurts; compelled to see light,
and it pierces him; compelled to hear noise, and it terrifies him. Cold strikes
his skin, and he seems to be all pain. But it is not so; nature protects him
against this initial onslaught of the world by covering him with a general
insensitivity. He sees the light only dimly, he hears the sounds as muffled
and coming from afar. For the most part he sleeps.

His mother calls him a little monkey, and she is right; until he walks
he will be like an ape, and even less of a biped, the womb-life having given
his funny little legs the angularity of a frog's. Not till he talks will he
leave the ape behind, and begin to climb perilously to the stature of man.
Watch him, and see how, bit by bit, he learns the nature of things by
random movements of exploration. The world is a Chinese puzzle for him;
and these haphazard responses of grasping, biting and throwing are the
pseudopodia which he puts out to a questionable and dangerous experience.
Curiosity consumes and develops him; he would touch and taste everything
from his rattle to the moon.

This child might be the beginning and end of our philosophy. In his
insistent curiosity and growth lies the secret of all metaphysics; looking
upon him in his cradle, or creeping across the floor, we see life not as an
abstraction, but as a flowing reality that breaks through all our mechanical
categories, all our physical formulas. Here in this expansive urgency, this
patient effort and construction, this resolute rise from helplessness to
power, from infancy to maturity, from wonder to wisdom—here is the
Unknowable of Spencer, the Noumenon of Kant, the *Ens Realissimum* of
the Scholastics, the Prime Mover of Aristotle, the *To ontos on,* or Thing
That Really Is, of Plato; here we are nearer to the basis of things than in
the weight and solidity of matter, or in the wheels and levers of a machine.
Life is that which is discontent, which struggles and seeks, which fights to
the very end. No mechanistic scheme can do it justice, or understand the
silent growth and majesty of a tree, or compass the longing and tenderness
of children.

II. YOUTH

Childhood may be defined as the age of play; therefore some children
are never young, and some adults are never old. Youth is the transition from

play to work, from dependence on the family to dependence on one's self. It is a little anarchic and egotistic, because in the family its every whim or want was favored by unstinting parental love. Passing into the world, youth, petted for years and now for the first time free, drinks in the deep delight of liberty, utters its wild barbaric yawp, and advances to conquer and remould the world.

Good oratory, said Demosthenes, is characterized by three points: action, action, and action. He might have said it just as well of youth. Youth is as confident and improvident as a god. It loves excitement and adventure more than food. It loves the superlative, the exaggerated, the limitless, because it has abounding energy and frets to liberate its strength. It loves new and dangerous things; a man is as young as the risks he takes.

Youth bears law and order grudgingly. It is asked to be quiet when noise is its vital medium; it is asked to be passive, when it longs for action; it is asked to be sober and judicious, when its very blood makes youth "a continuous intoxication." [1] It is the age of abandon, and its motto, undelphianly, is *Panta agan*—"Nothing succeeds like excess." It is never tired; it lives in the present, regrets no yesterdays, and dreads no morrow; it climbs buoyantly a hill whose summit conceals the other side. It is the age of sharp sensation and unchilled desire; experience is not soured yet with repetition and disillusionment; to have sensations at all is then a glorious thing. Every moment is loved for itself, and the world is accepted as an esthetic spectacle, something to be absorbed and enjoyed, something of which one may write verses, and for which one may thank the stars.

Happiness is the free play of the instincts, and so is youth. For the majority of us it is the only period of life in which we live; most men of forty are but a reminiscence, the burnt-out ashes of what was once a flame. The tragedy of life is that it gives us wisdom only when it has stolen youth. *Si jeunesse savait et vieillesse pouvait*—"If youth had wisdom, and old age had strength!"

Health lies in action, and so it graces youth. To be busy is the secret of grace, and half the secret of content. Let us ask the gods not for possessions, but for things to do. In Utopia, said Thoreau, each would build his own home; and then song would come back to the hearts of men, as it comes to the bird when it builds its nest. If we cannot build our homes we can at least walk and throw and run; and we should never be so old as merely to watch games instead of playing them. *Let us play* is as good as *Let us pray*, and the results are more assured.

Hence youth is wise in preferring the athletic field to the classroom, and in rating baseball above philosophy. When a bespectacled Chinese student described American universities as "athletic associations in which certain opportunities for study are provided for the feeble-bodied," his remark was not so destructive as he supposed, and it described himself as much

[1] La Rochefoucauld, *Reflections*, no. 271.

as the universities. Every philosopher, like Plato, should be an athlete; if he is not, let us suspect his philosophy. "The first requisite of a gentleman," said Nietzsche, "is to be a perfect animal." On that foundation education should rise and build; instruction in the care of the body should equal the lore of the mind.

Meanwhile youth is learning to read, which is all that one learns in school; and learning where and how to find what he may later need to know—which is the best of the arts that he acquires in college. Nothing learned from a book is worth anything unless it is used and verified in life; and only then does it begin to affect behavior and desire. It is life that educates; and perhaps love more than anything else in life.

For meanwhile puberty has come. Suddenly the boy loses the readiness and unity of indeliberate action, and the pale cast of thought overshadows him. The girl begins to bedeck herself more carefully, to dishevel her hair more artfully; ten hours a day she thinks of dress, and a hundred times a day she draws her skirt down over her knees with a charming futility. The boy begins to wash his neck and shine his shoes; half his income goes to the girl, the other half to the tailor. The girl learns the technique of blushing, and the young man, in the presence of beauty, walks "as if he had stolen his legs."

Intellectual development comes step by step with the growing consciousness of sex. Instinct gives way to thought, action slips into quiet brooding. Youth examines itself and the world: it stretches out numberless tentacles of questioning and theory to grasp the meaning of things; it asks inescapably about evil, and origins, and evolution, and destiny, and soul, and God. The mind bubbles forth with inexhaustible effervescence; every word or thought suggests a hundred more; youth passes into the age of boyish puns and girlish laughter. The full heart flowers into song and dance; the esthetic sense is nourished with the overflow of desire; music and art are born.

Discovering the world, youth discovers evil, and is horrified to learn the nature of man. The principle of the family was mutual aid, the help of the weak by the strong, and the sharing of the spoils; but the principle of society, youth finds, is competition, the struggle for existence, the elimination of the weak and the survival of the strong. Youth, shocked, rebels, and calls upon the world to make itself a family, and give to youth the welcome and protection and comradeship of the family; this is how socialism comes. And then slowly youth is drawn into the gamble of this individualistic life; the zest of the game creeps into the blood; acquisitiveness is aroused and stretches out both hands for gold and power. The rebellion ends, and the game goes on.

Finally, youth discovers love. It has known "calf-love," that ethereal prelude to the coming symphonies of flesh and soul; and it has known the lonely struggles of premature and uninformed desire. But these were only harmless preliminaries that would deepen the spirit and make it ready for the self-abandonment of devotion. See them in love, this boy and this girl; is there any evil this side of mortality that can balance the splendor of this good? The girl suddenly made quiet and thoughtful as the stream of life rises to conscious creation in her; the youth eager and restless, and yet all courtesy and gentleness, knowing all the luxuries of courtship, aflame with something based in the hunger of the blood and yet rising to tenderness and loyalty. Here is a fulfilment of long centuries of civilization and culture; here, in romantic love, more than in the triumphs of thought or the victories of power, is the topmost reach of man.

Youth, if it were wise, would cherish love beyond all things else, keeping body and soul clean for its coming, lengthening its days with months of betrothal, sanctioning it with a marriage of solemn ritual, making all things subordinate to it resolutely. Wisdom, if it were young, would cherish love, nursing it with devotion, deepening it with sacrifice, vitalizing it with parentage, making all things subordinate to it till the end. Even though it consumes us in its service and overwhelms us with tragedy, even though it breaks us down with its passing and weighs us down with separations, let it be first.

III. MIDDLE AGE

And so youth marries, and youth ends.

A married man is already five years older the next day, and a married woman too. Biologically, middle age begins with marriage; for then work and responsibility replace care-free play, passion surrenders to the limitations of social order, and poetry yields to prose. It is a change that varies with customs and climes: marriage comes late now in our modern cities, and adolescence lengthens; but among the peoples of the south and east marriage comes at the height of youth, and age on the heels of parentage. "Young Orientals who exercise marital functions at thirteen," says Stanley Hall, "are worn out at thirty, and have recourse to aphrodisiacs. . . . Women in hot climates are often old at thirty. In the main it is possible that those who mature late age late." Perhaps if we could delay our sexual maturity till our economic maturity has come we should, by lengthening adolescence and education, rise to a higher plane of civilization than the past has ever known.

Each age of life has its virtues and its defects, its tasks and its delights. As Aristotle found excellence and wisdom in the golden mean, so the qualities of youth, maturity and old age may be arranged to give a fair face to the central division of human life. For example:

Youth	Middle Age	Old Age
Instinct	Induction	Deduction
Innovation	Habit	Custom
Invention	Execution	Obstruction
Play	Work	Rest
Art	Science	Religion
Imagination	Intellect	Memory
Theory	Knowledge	Wisdom
Optimism	Meliorism	Pessimism
Radicalism	Liberalism	Conservatism
Absorption in future	Absorption in present	Absorption in past
Courage	Prudence	Timidity
Freedom	Discipline	Authority
Vacillation	Stability	Stagnation

Such a list could be continued indefinitely, piling platitudes like Pelion on Ossa. Out of it at least this consolation emerges for middle age, that it is the epoch of achievement and establishment. For the exhilaration and enthusiasm of youth life gives then the calm and pride of security and power, the sense of things not merely hoped for but accomplished. At thirty-five a man is at the height of his curve,[1] retaining enough of the passion of younger years, and tempering it with the perspective of widened experience and maturer understanding. Perhaps there is some synchronism here with the cycle of sex, which reaches its zenith about thirty-two, midway between puberty and the age of virtue; Ellis has shown that most British men and women of genius were born when their parents were between thirty and thirty-four.[2]

As we find a place in the economic world the rebellion of youth subsides; we disapprove of earthquakes when our feet are on the earth. We forget our radicalism then in a gentle liberalism—which is radicalism softened with the consciousness of a bank-account. The more adjusted we become to our environment the more we fear the pain of readjustment that would be required by any fundamental change. After forty we prefer that the world should stand still, that the moving picture of life should freeze into a tableau.

Partly the increased conservatism of middle age is the result of intelligence, which perceives the complexity of institutions and the imperfections of desire; but partly it is the result of lowered energy, and corresponds

[1] This truism, together with the first words of § IV below, was transformed by a journalistic genius into "Men should die at thirty-five," and was sent for adjudication to every American philosopher from Mr. Dempsey to Mr. Coolidge.

[2] Ellis, H., *A Study in British Genius.*

to the immaculate morality of exhausted men. We perceive, at first incredulously and then with despair, that the reservoir of strength no longer fills itself after we draw upon it; that in Schopenhauer's phrase we are living on our capital and not on our income any more. The discovery darkens life for some years; we begin to mourn the brevity of the human span, and the impossibility of wisdom or fulfilment within so limited a circle; we stand at the top of the hill, and without straining our eyes we can see, at its bottom, death. We had not admitted its existence before; it was an abstract and academic notion which no strong man would ponder. But suddenly it is there, relentlessly before us; and try as we will we slip down the hill within its reach. We work all the harder to forget that it is waiting for us; we turn our eyes back in memory to the days that were not darkened with its presence; we revel in the company of the young because they cast over us, transiently and incompletely, their divine carelessness of mortality.

Hence it is in work and parentage that middle age finds its fulfilment and its happiness. As youth's ambitious hopefulness modulates into the quiet industry and patience of the central years, the zest of things done replaces the dream of conquered worlds; and maturity, like Sancho Panza, prefers an island in the Mediterranean to a continent in Utopia.

It is the function of youth to be keenly sensitive to new ideas, as possible means to the further conquest of the environment; it is the function of old age to oppose the new in a ruthless battle that tries the strength of the idea before society subjects itself to the experiment; it is the function of middle age to moderate the idea within the limits of practicality, and to find ways for its modest realization. Youth proposes, age opposes, middle age disposes. Youth dominates in periods of revolution, old age in periods of custom, middle age in periods of reconstruction. "It is with men," said Nietzsche, "as with the charcoal fires of a forest. It is only when young men have cooled down and have gotten charred, like these piles, that they become useful. As long as they fume and smoke they are perhaps more interesting, but they are too often uncomfortable and useless." [1]

Youth is romantic, and rightly so, imagination and feeling dominating it; old age is classic in its tastes, loving order and restraint more than passion and liberty; middle age hovers between the two, and weaves their values patiently into the pattern of achievement. The middle years give us at last a disciplined will, and the clarity of mind that illuminates and coördinates desire. The rule of knowledge, said Descartes, is to think clearly; only that which is clearly understood is true. And the rule of conduct, in large measure, is to desire clearly; only so do desires fuse into character and will.

The great quality of middle age, then, is moderation; and its great peril

---

[1] *Human All Too Human*, vol. i, § 585.

is mediocrity. How easy it is to relapse from effort into routine, from the vertical to the horizontal life! That danger is always present, and most of us succumb to it; the afternoon nap is its symbol and beginning. But moderation need not be mediocrity; it may be strength and depth of mind, not readily ruffled by contrary circumstance, and as resolute in action as it is modest in desire and speech. Even the immoderate Nietzsche wrote: "Of two quite lofty things, measure and moderation, it is best never to speak. A few know their force and significance." [1]

Barring such philosophic types, the commuter is the picture of middle age. He breakfasts between headlines, and kisses his wife and children a hurried good-bye; he rushes to the station, exchanges meteorological platitudes with his duplicates along the platform, reads his repetitious paper and smokes his manly pipe in the train, walks precariously through south Manhattan's fruit and filth, and clings like a drowning man to a subterranean strap while he is whirled with seismic discomfort to his toil. Arrived, his importance subsides; instead of great decisions to be made he finds, for the most part, a soporific routine of trivial details, in which he is a superfluous encumbrance to his stenographer. He plods through this business loyally, looks longingly at the clock that keeps him from his home, and thinks how pleasant it will be to spend the evening with his family. At five he rides again in suspended animation to his train, exchanges alcoholic bravados with his duplicates, and smokes again in philosophic dignity as he contemplates the daily tragedies of the national game. At six he is home, and at eight he wonders why he hurried so.

For by this time he has explored the depths of love, and has found the war that lurks in its gentle guise. Familiarity and fatigue have cooled the fever in his flesh; and then, again, it is so hard to love a woman in the morning! His wife does not dress for him, but only when he has gone away and is no longer in her mind; he sees her in disheveled negligée, while all through the day he meets women powdered and primped and curled, whose round knees and inviting frocks and encouraging smiles and aphrodisiac perfumes leave him hovering hourly over the abysses of disloyalty. But he tries hard to love his wife, and kisses her regularly and promptly twice a day. He has an escapade or two, discovers the dulness in adultery, thanks God that he has not been detected, and reconciles himself to prose.

For the rest he mows his lawn, plays bridge and golf, and dabbles amateurishly in local politics. The last recreation soon sours on him: he finds that the machinery of politics is so arranged as to frighten off all honest men, and penalize all efforts at statesmanship and competence; and either he adapts himself with accommodating conscience to the rules of the silly game, or he returns to his home a quieter and a profounder

[1] *Ibid.*, vol. ii, § 230.

man. In the end he concludes that the wisest words of tongue or pen were those of the much-traveled Scarmentado: "As I had now seen all that was rare or beautiful on earth, I resolved for the future to see nothing but my own home; I took a wife, and soon suspected that she deceived me; but notwithstanding this doubt, I still found that of all conditions of life this was much the happiest." [1]

In the interim his wife had learned something of life too. In the romantic years she had been a divinity; now she is a housekeeper. The discovery is discouraging. Why should she maintain the laborious allurements of dress and rouge for a man who looks upon her as an economical substitute for a maid? Or she does not cook, and does not clean; these things, and many more, are done for her, and she is left free, respectable, and functionless all the livelong day. She spends her mornings making her toilette, and her afternoons reforming the proletariat; she reads on hygiene and maternity, and tells poor mothers how to bring up babies, when the harassed women merely wish to learn how to stop their coming. She enters politics, circulates petitions, and votes for one villain in indignant protest against another. She attends extension classes, organizes clubs, and listens with romantic patience to peripatetic novelists, philosophers, and Englishmen.

And then suddenly, somehow, she is a mother. She is pleased and terrified. Perhaps it will kill her to bear a child; not for a long time has she had the chance to do the wholesome work that would have fitted her physically for this supreme adventure. But she is proud too, and feels a new maturity; she is a woman now, and not an idle girl, not an ornament or a sexual utility any more. She goes through her ordeal bravely, praying for a son; when she sees it is a girl she weeps for a moment and then marvels at the unprecedented beauty of her child. Fondly she toils for it, through busy days and fragmentary nights, never having time to look for "happiness," and yet showing in her eyes a new radiance and content. How pretty the baby looks perambulating under the winter sun! And what is this new tenderness in her husband's eyes?—So Nature solaces our slavery, and attaches to our greatest sacrifice our greatest happiness.

IV. DEATH

"Men ought to die at their zenith," says a merciless friend. But they do not; and therefore youth and death meet one another as they walk the streets.

What is old age? Fundamentally, no doubt, it is a condition of the flesh, of protoplasm that finds inevitably the limit of its life. It is a physiological and psychological involution. It is a hardening of the arteries and categories,

---

[1] Voltaire, *The Travels of Searmentado.*

a retardation of thought and blood; a man is as old as his arteries and as young as his ideas.

The ability to learn decreases with each decade of our lives, as if the association fibres of the brain were accumulated and overlaid in inflexible patterns. New material seems no longer to find room, and recent impressions fade as rapidly as a politician's promises, or the public's memory. As decay proceeds, threads and unities are lost, and coördination wavers; the old man falls into a digressive circumstantiality that compels reference to Juliet's ebullient nurse; and De Quincey's "anecdotage" comes.

Then, just as the child grew more rapidly the younger it was, so the old man ages more quickly with every day. And just as the child was protected by insensitivity on its entry into the world, so old age is eased by an apathy of sense and will, and nature slowly administers a general anesthesia before she permits time's scythe to complete the most major of operations. As sensations diminish in intensity, the sense of vitality fades; the desire for life gives way to indifference and patient waiting; the fear of death is strangely mingled with the longing for repose. Perhaps then, if one has lived well, if one has known the full term of love and all the juice and ripeness of experience, one can die with some measure of content, clearing the stage for a better play.

But what if the play is never better, always revolving about suffering and death, telling endlessly the same idiotic tale? There's the rub, and there's the doubt that gnaws at the heart of wisdom, and poisons age. Here is the auto-stage that last year took us from Cleveland to Elyria; how strange that it should run when we have no need for it! Soon it will break down, and be replaced; soon the riders will die and be replaced; always new seekers, new vehicles, and the same end. Here is shameless adultery and brutal calculating murder; well, they have always been, and apparently they will always be. Here is a flood, sweeping before it a thousand lives and the labor of generations. Here are bereavements and broken hearts, and always the bitter brevity of love. Here still are the insolence of office and the law's delay; corruption in the judgment seat, and incompetence on the throne. Here is slavery, stupefying toil that makes great muscles and little souls. Here and everywhere is the struggle for existence, life inextricably enmeshed with war. Here is history, seemingly a futile circle of infinite repetition: these youths with eager eyes will make the same errors as we, they will be misled by the same dreams; they will suffer, and wonder, and surrender, and grow old.

This can be the great tragedy of old age, that looking back with inverted romantic eye, it may see only the suffering of mankind. It is hard to praise life when life abandons us; and if we speak well of it even then it is because we hope we shall find it again, of fairer form, in some realm of disembodied and deathless souls.

These steeples, everywhere pointing upward, ignoring despair and lifting hope, these lofty city spires, or simple chapels in the hills,—they rise at every step from the earth to the sky; in every village of every nation on the globe they challenge doubt and invite weary hearts to consolation. Is it all a vain delusion?—is there nothing beyond life but death, and nothing beyond death but decay? We cannot know. But as long as men suffer these steeples will remain.

And yet what if it is for life's sake that we must die? In truth we are not individuals; and it is because we think ourselves such that death seems unforgivable. We are temporary organs of the race, cells in the body of life; we die and drop away that life may remain young and strong. If we were to live forever, growth would be stifled and youth would find no room on the earth. Death, like style, is the removal of rubbish, the excision of the superfluous. Through love we pass our vitality on to a new form of us before the old form dies; through parentage we bridge the chasm of the generations, and elude the enmity of death. Here, even in the river's flood, children are born; here, solitary in a tree, and surrounded by raging waters, a mother nurses her babe. In the midst of death life renews itself immortally.

So wisdom may come as the gift of age, and seeing things in place, and every part in its relation to the whole, may reach that perspective in which understanding pardons all. If it is one test of philosophy to give life a meaning that shall frustrate death, wisdom will show that corruption comes only to the part, that life itself is deathless while we die.

Three thousand years ago a man thought that man might fly; and so he built himself wings, and Icarus his son, trusting them and trying to fly, fell into the sea. Undaunted, life carried on the dream. Thirty generations passed, and Leonardo da Vinci, spirit made flesh, scratched across his drawings (drawings so beautiful that one catches one's breath with pain in seeing them) plans and calculations for a flying machine; and left in his notes a little phrase that, once heard, rings like a bell in the memory— "There shall be wings." Leonardo failed and died; but life carried on the dream. Generations passed, and men said man would never fly, for it was not the will of God. And then man flew. Life is that which can hold a purpose for three thousand years and never yield. The individual fails, but life succeeds. The individual dies, but life, tireless and undiscourageable, goes on, wondering, longing, planning, trying, mounting, attaining, longing.

Here is an old man on the bed of death, harassed with helpless friends and wailing relatives. What a terrible sight it is—this thin frame with loosened and cracking flesh, this toothless mouth in a bloodless face, this tongue that cannot speak, these eyes that cannot see! To this pass youth has come, after all its hopes and trials; to this pass middle age, after all its torment and its toil. To this pass health and strength and joyous rivalry; this arm once struck great blows and fought for victory in virile games. To this pass knowledge, science, wisdom: for seventy years this man with pain and effort gathered knowledge; his brain became the storehouse of a varied experience, the center of a thousand subtleties of thought and deed; his heart through suffering learned gentleness as his mind learned understanding; seventy years he grew from an animal into a man capable of seeking truth and creating beauty. But death is upon him, poisoning him, choking him, congealing his blood, gripping his heart, bursting his brain, rattling in his throat. Death wins.

Outside on the green boughs birds twitter, and Chantecler sings his hymn to the sun. Light streams across the fields; buds open and stalks confidently lift their heads; the sap mounts in the trees. Here are children: what is it that makes them so joyous, running madly over the dew-wet grass, laughing, calling, pursuing, eluding, panting for breath, inexhaustible? What energy, what spirit and happiness! What do they care about death? They will learn and grow and love and struggle and create, and lift life up one little notch, perhaps, before they die. And when they pass they will cheat death with children, with parental care that will make their offspring finer than themselves. There in the garden's twilight lovers pass, thinking themselves unseen; their quiet words mingle with the murmur of insects calling to their mates; the ancient hunger speaks through eager and through lowered eyes, and a noble madness courses through clasped hands and touching lips. Life wins.

Bibliographical Guide to Editions Used

*Books marked with a * are recommended to the reader.*

Adams, Brooks. *The Law of Civilization and Decay.* London, 1895.
* Adams, Henry. *The Education of Henry Adams.* Boston, 1919.
—— *Mont St. Michel and Chartres.* Boston, 1926.
Adler, Alfred. *The Neurotic Constitution.* New York, 1917.
Allen, Grant. *Evolution of the Idea of God.* New York, 1897.
Angell, A. R. *Psychology.* New York, 1908.
Anon. *The Wisdom of Confucius.* Harper & Bros., no date.

Babbitt, Irving. *Democracy and Leadership.* Boston, 1922.
Bacon, Francis. *Philosophical Works,* ed. J. M. Robertson. London, 1905.
Barnes, H. E. *The New History and the Social Sciences.* New York, 1925.
Beard, Charles. *The Economic Basis of Politics.* New York, 1923.
* —— ed. *Whither Mankind?* New York, 1928.
Bergson, Henri. *Matter and Memory.* London, 1911.
Berkman, A. *The Bolshevik Myth.* New York, 1925.
* Bertaut, J. *Napoleon in His Own Words.* Chicago, 1916.
Bluntschli, J. K. *Theory of the State.* Oxford, 1911.
Bölsche, W. *Love-Life in Nature.* 2 vol. New York, 1926.
Bosanquet, B. *History of Æsthetic.* London, 1904.
Bradley, F. H. *Appearance and Reality.* London, 1920.
—— *Principles of Logic.* London, 1883.
* Brandes, Georg. *Main Currents in Nineteenth Century Literature.* 6 vol. New York, 1905.
Brousson, J. J. *Anatole France en Pantoufles.* Paris, 1924.
* —— *Anatole France Himself.* New York, 1926. (Translation of preceding.)
Brown, Brian. *The Wisdom of the Chinese.* New York, 1921.

Buckle, H. T. *Introduction to the History of Civilization.* 4 vol. New York, 1913.
Burke, Edmund. *Reflections on the French Revolution.* Everyman Library.
Bury, J. B. *The Idea of Progress.* London, 1920.

Carlyle, Thomas. *Chartism.* New York, 1901.
—— *Heroes and Hero-Worship.* New York, 1901.
Carpenter, E. *Towards Democracy.* London, 1911.
Cassirer, E. *Substance and Function.* Chicago, 1923.
Chamberlain, H. S. *The Foundations of the Nineteenth Century.* 2 vol. New York, 1912.
Chesterton, G. K. *Short History of England.* New York, 1917.
Clemens, S. L. ("Mark Twain"). *What Is Man?* New York, 1917.
Condorcet, M. J. A., Marquis de. *A Sketch of a Tableau of the Progress of the Human Spirit.* New York, 1796.
Croce, Benedetto. *History: Its Theory and Practice.* New York, 1921.
Crozier, J. B. *Sociology Applied to Practical Politics.* London, 1911.

* Darwin, Charles. *The Descent of Man.* A. L. Burt, New York, no date.
Dewey, John. *Experience and Nature.* Chicago, 1925.
Disraeli, Benjamin. *Tancred.* London, 1924.
Doane, T. W. *Bible Myths and Their Parallels in Other Religions.* New York, 1882.
Drever, J. *Instinct in Man.* Cambridge University Press, 1917.
Driesch, Hans. *Science and Philosophy of the Organism.* University of Edinburgh Press, 1908.
Durant, Will. *Philosophy and the Social Problem.* New York, 1917.

* Eckermann, J. *Conversations with Goethe.* New York, 1852.
Eddington, A. S. *The Nature of the Physical World.* New York, 1929.
Ellis, Havelock. *The Dance of Life.* Boston, 1923.
* —— *Studies in the Psychology of Sex.* 6 vol. Philadelphia, 1910–11.
—— *A Study in British Genius.* London, 1904.
Eltzbacher, Paul. *Anarchism.* New York, 1908.
Emerson, R. W. *Representative Men.* Philadelphia (McKay), no date.
Encyclopaedia Britannica. 11th ed.

Fisher, I. *National Vitality.* Government Printing Office, Washington, 1908.
* Flaubert, Gustave. *Works,* 4th ed. New York (W. J. Black), 1928.
* France, Anatole. *The Garden of Epicurus.* New York, 1908.
* —— *M. Bergeret in Paris.* New York, 1921.
* —— *On Life and Letters.* Four series. New York, 1914–24.

* —— *Penguin Isle*. London, 1924.
* —— *Thaïs*. London, 1909.
* Frazer, Sir James. *The Golden Bough*. 4th ed. New York, 1925.
Freud, Sigmund. *Interpretation of Dreams*. New York, 1913.
—— *Leonardo da Vinci*. New York, 1916.
—— *Three Contributions to the Theory of Sex*. New York, 1918.
Fuller, Sir B. *Man as He Is*. London, 1916.

Gallichan, W. M. *The Great Unmarried*. London, no date.
* Gibbon, Edward. *Decline and Fall of the Roman Empire*. 6 vol. Everyman Library.
Gobineau, Count A. de. *The Inequality of Human Races*. New York, 1915.
Godwin, W. *Political Justice*. London, 1890.
* Goethe, J. W. von. *Faust*. Tr. Martin. New York, 1902.
* —— *Truth and Fiction*. New York, 1902.
Goldberg, I. *Havelock Ellis*. New York, 1926.
Gomperz, T. *Greek Thinkers*. 4 vol. New York, 1901.
Gorki, Maxim. *Reminiscences of Tolstoi*. New York, 1920.
Gourmont, Remy de. *The Natural Philosophy of Love*. New York, 1922.
Grant, Madison. *The Passing of the Great Race*. New York, 1916.
Grote, G. *History of Greece*. 12 vol. Everyman Library.

Haldane, J. B. S. *Possible Worlds*. New York, 1928.
Haldane, J. S. *Mechanism, Life and Personality*. London, 1921.
Hall, G. S. *Adolescence*. 2 vol. New York, 1905.
Hammond, J. L., and B. *The Town Labourer, 1760–1832*. London, 1917.
* Hardy, Thomas. *Tess of the d'Urbervilles*. New York, 1892.
—— *Jude the Obscure*. New York, Harper & Bros.
Headlam, J. W. *Bismarck*. New York, 1899.
Hegel, G. W. F. *Philosophy of History*. New York, 1910.
Heine, Heinrich. *Memoirs*. 2 vol. London, 1910.
Herder, J. G. von. *Outlines of a Philosophy of the History of Man*. London, 1800.
Hobhouse, L. T. *Morals in Evolution*. London, 1915.
Hoernlé, R. F. A. *Studies in Contemporary Metaphysics*. New York, 1920.
Holmes, S. J. *Studies in Evolution and Genetics*. New York, 1923.
Holt, E. *The Concept of Consciousness*. London, 1912.
Howard, C. *Sex Worship*. Chicago, 1909.
Huxley, H. T. *Evolution and Ethics*. New York, 1886.

* Inge, Dean R. W. *Outspoken Essays*. Second Series. New York, Longmans, no date.

James, William. *The Meaning of Truth*. New York, 1909.
Jennings, H. S. *Behavior of the Lower Organisms*. New York, 1923.
Johnson, R. M. *The Corsican*. Boston, 1910.
Jones, Sir E. *Papers on Psychoanalysis*. London, 1913.
—— *Analytical Psychology*. New York, 1916.
Jung, C. G. *Psychology of the Unconscious*. New York, 1916.

Kallen, H. *Why Religion*. New York, 1927.
* Kellogg, *J. H. The New Dietetics*. Battle Creek, 1927.
* Keyserling, Count Hermann. *Europe*. New York, 1928.
* —— *Travel Diary of a Philosopher*. New York, 1925.
—— *The World in the Making*. New York, 1927.
Kisch, E. H. *The Sexual Life of Woman*. New York, 1910.
Klausner, J. *Jesus of Nazareth*. New York, 1926.
Köhler, W. *The Mentality of Apes*. New York, 1925.
Krafft-Ebing, R. F. von. *Psychopathia Sexualis*. New York, 1906.
Kropotkin, P. *Mutual Aid as a Factor in Evolution*. New York, 1902.

Langdon-Davies, J. *The New Age of Faith*. New York, 1925.
Lange, F. *History of Materialism*. New York, 1925.
* La Rochefoucauld, François de. *Reflections*. London, 1871.
Lea, H. C. *History of the Inquisition of Spain*. 4 vol. New York, 1922.
Le Bon, G. *The Evolution of Forces*. New York, 1914.
—— *The Evolution of Matter*. New York, 1914.
Leuba, J. H. *Belief in God and Immortality*. New York, 1916.
Loeb, J. *Comparative Physiology of the Brain*. New York, 1900.
—— *The Organism as a Whole*. New York, 1916.
Lubbock, Sir J. (Lord Avebury). *The Origins of Civilization*. London, 1870.
* Lucretius. *On the Nature of Things*. Tr. Munro.
Ludovici, A. M. *A Defense of Aristocracy*. London, 1915.

Maine, Sir Henry. *Popular Government*. London, 1886.
* Mallock, W. H. *Lucretius on Life and Death*. New York, 1900.
Marshall, H. R. *Instinct and Reason*. New York, 1898.
* Martin, E. D. *The Meaning of a Liberal Education*. New York, 1926.
—— *The Mystery of Religion*. New York, 1924.
Marx, Karl. *Critique of Political Economy*. New York, 1904.
McCabe, J. *The Evolution of Mind*. London, 1910.
* McCollum, E. V. *The Newer Knowledge of Nutrition*. New York, 1918.
McDougall, W. *Social Psychology*. 13th ed.
Mencken, H. L. *Prejudices*. Four Series. New York, 1919–24.

Meredith, George. *Ordeal of Richard Feverel*. Boston, 1888.
Mill, J. S. *The Subjection of Women*. London, 1911.
Moll, A. *The Sexual Education of the Child*. New York, 1913.
* Montesquieu, C. de. *Spirit of Laws*, 2 vol. New York, 1900.
* Morley, J. *Diderot and the Encyclopedists*. 2 vol. London, 1923.
* —— *Voltaire*. London, 1878.
Muirhead, J. H. *Contemporary British Philosophy*. London, 1924.
Murray, Gilbert. *Four Stages of Greek Religion*. New York, 1912.
Musset, Alfred de. *Confessions of a Child of the Century*. New York, 1905.

Nietzsche, Friedrich. *Antichrist*. New York, 1915.
—— *Beyond Good and Evil*. New York, 1914.
—— *Dawn of Day*. London, 1911.
—— *Human All Too Human*. 2 vol. London, 1911–15.
—— *The Joyful Wisdom*. London, 1910.
* —— *Thus Spake Zarathustra*. New York, 1906.
—— *The Will to Power*. 2 vol. London, 1913–14.
Nordau, Max. *The Interpretation of History*. London, 1910.

Paine, Thomas. *The Rights of Man*.
Pellissier, G. *Voltaire Philosophe*. Paris, 1908.
Petrie, Flinders. *The Revolutions of Civilization*. London, no date.
Pirandello, Luigi. *Three Plays*. New York, 1922.
* Plato. *Works*. Tr. Jowett. 4 vol. Jefferson Press, New York, no date.
* Plutarch. *Lives*. New York (Hurst), no date.
Powys, J. C. *The Religion of a Sceptic*. New York, 1925.
Pringle, H. F. *Alfred E. Smith*. New York, 1928.

Reinach, S. *Orpheus, a History of Religions*. New York, 1909.
Renan, E. *History of the People of Israel*. 5 vol. Boston, 1886–96.
Ribot, T. *Psychology of the Emotions*. London, 1906.
Ripley, W. Z. *The Races of Europe*. London (Kegan Paul), no date.
Rivers, W. H. *Psychology of Politics*. London, 1923.
Rockow, L. *Contemporary Political Thought*. London, 1925.
Ross, E. A. *Changing America*. New York, 1912.
Rousseau, J. J. *Social Contract; Discourses*. Everyman Library.
Royden, A. M. *Woman and the Sovereign State*. London, 1917.
Russell, Bertrand. *Analysis of Matter*. London, 1927.
* —— *Education and the Good Life*. New York, 1926.
—— *Philosophy*. New York, 1927.
—— *Sceptical Essays*. New York, 1928.
—— *What I Believe*. New York, 1925.

414 *Bibliographical Guide to Editions Used*

* Salter, W. *Nietzsche the Thinker*. New York, 1917.
* Santayana, George. *Reason in Society*. New York, 1905.
—— *The Sense of Beauty*. New York, 1896.
Schopenhauer, Arthur. *The World as Will and Idea*. 3 vol. London, 1883.
Sellars, R. *The Next Step in Democracy*. New York, 1916.
Semple, E. C. *Influence of Geographic Environment*. New York, 1911.
Shotwell, J. T. *The Religious Revolution of Today*. Boston, 1913.
⃰ Siegfried, A. *America Comes of Age*. New York, 1927.
Simkhovitch, V. *Toward the Understanding of Jesus*. New York, 1921.
Sinclair, May. *The New Idealism*. New York, 1922.
Smith, Adam. *The Wealth of Nations*. 3 vol. Everyman Library.
Smith, W. R. *The Religion of the Semites*. 2 vol. New York, 1889.
Spencer, Herbert. *Principles of Biology*. 2 vol. New York, 1910.
—— *Principles of Psychology*. 2 vol. New York, 1910.
—— *Principles of Sociology*. 3 vol. New York, 1910.
* Spengler, Oswald. *Decline of the West*. 2 vol. New York, 1926–8.
* Spinoza, Benedict. *Ethics*. Everyman Library.
Stirner, Max (Caspar Schmidt). *The Ego and His Own*. Modern Library.
* Sumner, W. G. *Folkways*. New York, 1906.
Sutherland, A. *Origin and Growth of the Moral Instincts*. 2 vol. London, 1898.
* Symonds, J. A. *The Renaissance in Italy*. 7 vol. New York, 1900.

* Taine, Hippolyte. *The French Revolution*. 3 vol. New York, 1878–85.
* —— *History of English Literature*. New York (Hurst), no date.
* —— *The Modern Régime*. 2 vol. New York, 1890.
Tarde, G. *The Laws of Imitation*. New York, 1903.
Thomas, W. I. *Sex and Society*. Chicago, 1907.
Thompson, F. *Shelley*. Girard, Kan. Little Blue Book Series.
Thompson, H. B. *Mental Traits of Sex*. Chicago, 1903.
Thorndike, E. L. *Individuality*. Boston, 1911.
—— *The Original Nature of Man*. New York, 1913.
Thorndike, L. *A Short History of Civilization*. New York, 1926.
Todd, A. J. *Theories of Social Progress*. New York, 1922.
Tocqueville, Alexis de. *Democracy in America*. 2 vol. New York, 1912.

Vico, G. B. *Principi di Scienza Nuova*. Milano, 1831.
* Voltaire, F. M. A. de. *General History* (Essay on the Morals and Character of the Nations). St. Hubert Guild ed. 22 vol. New York, 1901.

Walsh, J. J. *Cures*. New York, 1923.
* Watson, J. B. *Behavior*. New York, 1914.
Weininger, O. *Sex and Character*. New York (Putnam), no date.

Westermarck, E. *History of Human Marriage*. London, 1894.
Weyl, W. *The End of the War*. New York, 1918.
Whitehead, A. N. *Science and the Modern World*. New York, 1926.
Wilde, O. *The Soul of Man under Socialism*, in Works, 1909.
Williams, E. T. *China Yesterday and Today*. New York, 1927.
Williams, H. S. *The Science of Happiness*. New York, 1909.
Willoughby, W. W. *Social Justice*. New York, 1900.

Xenophon. *Memorabilia*. Everyman Library.

Zimmern, A. *The Greek Commonwealth*. Oxford, 1915.

Index

A Note About the Author

WILL DURANT was born in North Adams, Massachusetts, in 1885. He was educated in the Catholic parochial schools there and in Kearny, New Jersey, and thereafter in St. Peter's (Jesuit) College, Jersey City, New Jersey, and Columbia University, New York. For a summer he served as a cub reporter on the New York *Journal*, in 1907, but finding the work too strenuous for his temperament, he settled down at Seton Hall College, South Orange, New Jersey, to teach Latin, French, English, and geometry (1907–11). He entered the seminary at Seton Hall in 1909, but withdrew in 1911 for reasons which he has described in his book *Transition*. He passed from this quiet seminary to the most radical circles in New York, and became (1911–13) the teacher of the Ferrer Modern School, an experiment in libertarian education. In 1912 he toured Europe at the invitation and expense of Alden Freeman, who had befriended him and now undertook to broaden his borders.

Returning to the Ferrer School, he fell in love with one of his pupils, resigned his position, and married her (1913). For four years he took graduate work at Columbia University, specializing in biology under Morgan and Calkins and in philosophy under Woodbridge and Dewey. He received the doctorate in philosophy in 1917, and taught philosophy at Columbia University for one year. In 1914, in a Presbyterian church in New York, he began those lectures on history, literature, and philosophy which, continuing twice weekly for thirteen years, provided the initial material for his later works.

The unexpected success of *The Story of Philosophy* (1926) enabled him to retire from teaching in 1927. Thenceforth, except for some incidental essays, Mr. and Mrs. Durant gave nearly all their working hours (eight to fourteen daily) to *The Story of Civilization*. To better prepare themselves they toured Europe in 1927, went around the world in 1930 to study Egypt, the Near East, India, China, and Japan, and toured the globe again in 1932 to visit Japan, Manchuria, Siberia, Russia, and Poland. These travels provided the background for *Our Oriental Heritage* (1935) as the first volume in *The Story of Civilization*. Several further visits to Europe prepared for Volume II, *The Life of Greece* (1939) and Volume III, *Caesar and Christ* (1944). In 1948, six months in Turkey, Iraq, Iran, Egypt, and Europe provided perspective for Volume IV, *The Age of Faith* (1950). In 1951 Mr. and Mrs. Durant returned to Italy to add to a lifetime of gleanings for Volume V, *The Renaissance* (1953); and in 1954 further studies in Italy, Switzerland, Germany, France, and England opened new vistas for Volume VI, *The Reformation* (1957).

Mrs. Durant's share in the preparation of these volumes became more and more substantial with each year, until in the case of Volume VII, *The Age of*

Reason Begins (1961), it was so pervasive that justice required the union of both names on the title page. In 1968, their joint labor was crowned with a Pulitzer Prize, awarded for the tenth and final volume of *The Story of Civilization, Rousseau and Revolution.*